Diagnostic Clinical Neuropsychology

Diagnostic Clinical Neuropsychology

REVISED EDITION

by ERIN D. BIGLER

UNIVERSITY OF TEXAS PRESS, AUSTIN

This book is dedicated to
those individuals most important to me:
my wife, Janet, my children, Alicia and Daniel,
and my parents, Natalie and Boley

Printed in the United States of America

Revised Edition, 1988

Library of Congress Cataloging-in-Publication Data
Bigler, Erin D., 1949–
Diagnostic clinical neuropsychology.

Includes bibliographies and indexes.
1. Neuropsychological tests. 2. Brain—Diseases—Diagnosis. I. Title. [DNLM: 1. Nervous System Diseases—diagnosis. 2. Neuropsychology. WL 141 B593d]
RC3866.N48B53 1988 616.8′0475 87-5834
ISBN 0-292-71537-4

Contents

Acknowledgments

I would like to acknowledge the efforts of numerous individuals who have assisted in the development of this book. Foremost, I am grateful for the support of the Austin Neurological Clinic and Doctors Douglas Hudson, Peter Werner, Albert Horn, David Steinman, Dilip Karnik, Michal Douglas, and Michael Hummer. I am likewise grateful for the assistance given me by my students and colleagues at the University of Texas at Austin and the University of Texas Neuropathy Museum; in particular, I am grateful for the assistance of Doctors Munro Cullum, Nancy Nussbaum, and Stuart Hall. The secretarial assistance of Jeannette Butler and Trudy Turner is particularly appreciated. Last, the staff of the University of Texas Press is gratefully acknowledged.

Key to Case Study Abbreviations

Motor Examination

FOD, Finger Oscillation Test—Dominant
FOND, Finger Oscillation Test—Nondominant
SOGD, Strength of Grip Test—Dominant
SOGND, Strength of Grip Test—Nondominant
TPTD, Tactual Performance Test—Dominant
TPTND, Tactual Performance Test—Nondominant
TPTBoth, Tactual Performance Test—Both
L, Left
R, Right

Language Examination

SSPT, Speech Sounds Perception Test
SRT, Seashore Rhythm Test

Memory Examination

WMS, Wechsler Memory Scale
MQ, Memory Quotient
LM, Logical Memory
Digits, Digit Span
VM, Visual Memory
AL, Associate Learning
TPT-M, Tactual Performance Test—Memory
TPT-L, Tactual Performance Test—Localization

Intellectual/Cognitive Examination

CT, Category Test
TM, Trail-Making Test (*A* and *B*)
WAIS, Wechsler Adult Intelligence Scale
WISC-R, Wechsler Intelligence Scale for Children—Revised
VIQ, Verbal IQ
PIQ, Performance IQ
FSIQ, Full-Scale IQ

WAIS-R Results

I, Information
C, Comprehension
S, Similarities
A, Arithmetic
D, Digit Span
V, Vocabulary
DS, Digit Symbol
PC, Picture Completion
BD, Block Design
PA, Picture Arrangement
OA, Object Assembly

Minnesota Multiphasic Personality Inventory (MMPI) Results

L, L_K Scale
F, Frequency Scale
K, K Scale
Hs, Hypochondriasis
D, Depression
Hy, Hysteria
Pd, Psychopathic Deviate Scale
MF, Masculinity-Femininity Scale
Pa, Paranoia Scale
Pt, Psychasthenia Scale
Sc, Schizophrenia Scale
Ma, Hypomania Scale
Si, Social Introversion Scale

Other Notation

DC, Discontinued
WNL, Within Normal Limits
NA, Not Administered

Diagnostic Clinical Neuropsychology

1. Overview of Functional Neuroanatomy

The human nervous system, which comprises several billion cells, is by far the most complex system of the body. This complexity is demonstrated by the existence of over 100,000 miles of neural fibers within the nervous system (Angevine and Cotman, 1981). Another example of this complexity is the approximately 300,000 motor neurons innervating skeletal muscles and some one and a half to three million sensory neurons supplying information to the brain (Kandel, 1981). If there were not order to this exquisite complexity, studying the nervous system and its control over behavior would be virtually an impossible task. Fortunately, there is consistent structure as well as systematically organized function within the nervous system.

This chapter is devoted to a brief overview of basic neuroanatomy and functional neural systems. For more detailed treatment of anatomy, see the excellent texts of Angevine and Cotman (1981); Brodal (1981); Crosby, Humphrey, and Lauer (1962); Schadé and Ford (1973); or Sidman and Sidman (1965). Neuronal anatomy and physiology will not be discussed in this text, but are fully covered in the Angevine and Cotman (1981) and Brodal (1981) texts as well as in the work by Cooper, Bloom, and Roth (1978).

Many structures within the brain are labeled or referenced by their relationship to one another or their relationship to an imaginary central point within the brain. There are basically six anatomical directions that may be used to indicate position: *superior* (top), *lateral* (side), *medial* (middle), *ventral* (bottom; also sometimes referred to as *inferior*), *anterior* (front), and *posterior* or *dorsal* (back). Although not synonymous with any of these terms, *rostral* may be used to identify structures anterior to an imaginary central point in a nose-to-tail plane. *Caudal* is thereby the term used to identify location in the posterior-ventral aspect of this plane. Figure 1.1 depicts these various positions and planes. *Ipsilateral* means on the same side; *contralateral* means on the opposite side. *Proximal* means close to and *distal* refers to structures farther apart. *Efferent* refers to motor output; *afferent*, sensory input.

Neural communication occurs by neuronal-neuronal electrochemical interaction. The functional congregation of similarly projecting axons forms fiber tracts. When describing these fiber tracts, like the spinothalamic tract, one merely refers to the origin (spine) and termination (thalamus) of the synaptic connections. Thus, with the dentatorubrothalamic tract, the origin is within the dentate nucleus of the cerebellum, passing to the nucleus ruber of the midbrain where it synapses, continuing on to a termination point in the thalamus.

There are five major bones of the skull—the frontal, parietal, occipital, temporal, and sphenoid (see figs. 1.2 and 1.3). In the infant, these bones are separated by sutures that in association with fontanels (soft spots) permit hinge-like action of the cranial bones so that minor distortion of the skull can take place during the birthing process. During maturation the bones permanently fuse along the suture lines. The skull provides maintenance of brain position and structural integrity and is assisted in this function by the falx cerebri and tentorium cerebelli, folds of the dura mater (see fig. 1.4).

Major Central Nervous System Divisions

The mammalian central nervous system (CNS) is divided into two major structures—the brain and the spinal cord. The spinal cord is phylogenetically the oldest part of the central nervous system, and there are close similarities between the spinal cord of humans and that found in lower vertebrate animals. The spinal cord ends at the emergence of the medulla, the oldest region of the brain and the first structure found just past the spinal entrance to the skull. The brain develops according to distinct embryologically determined patterns, the first being an undifferentiated neural tube. Rapidly, as the embryo develops, the neural tube divides into three main segments—the forebrain, midbrain, and hindbrain (see fig. 1.5)—from which all brain structures develop. As with the spinal cord, the more primitive structures of the human brain, namely the medulla, pons, cerebellum, and midbrain, have considerable similarity in structure and function with lower vertebrate animals.

Spinal Cord

The spinal cord is housed by the spinal column, which is divided (see fig. 1.6) into thirty-one segments: eight cervical, twelve thoracic, five lumbar, five sacral, and one coccygeal. Both motor (efferent) and sensory (afferent) pathways course through the spinal cord according to specifically differentiated systems (see fig. 1.7). Likewise, the spinal cord and its efferent system innervate specific muscle groups according to well-determined pathways. Similarly, afferent innervation of peripheral sensory areas follows a well-defined system, labeled a dermatomal system (see fig. 1.8). Thus, spinal cord damage will affect sensory and motor function in a rather precise manner according to the level involved. Similarly, if a peripheral nerve is damaged, the loss of function will also correspond to a specific pattern.

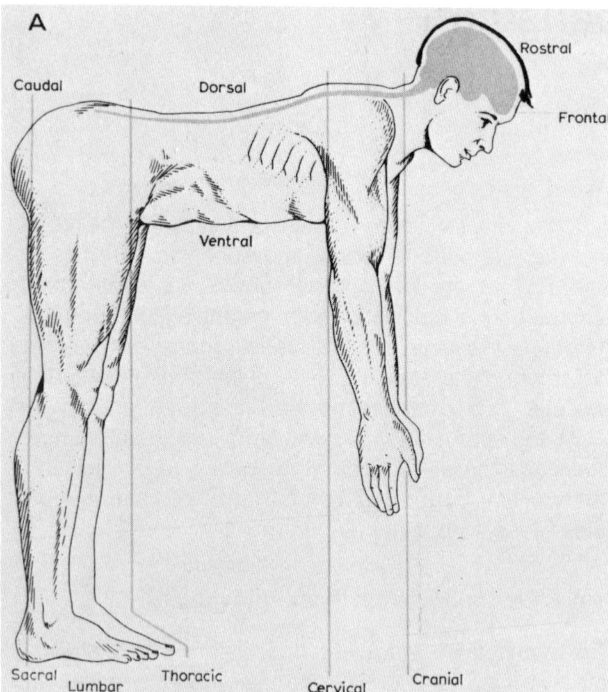

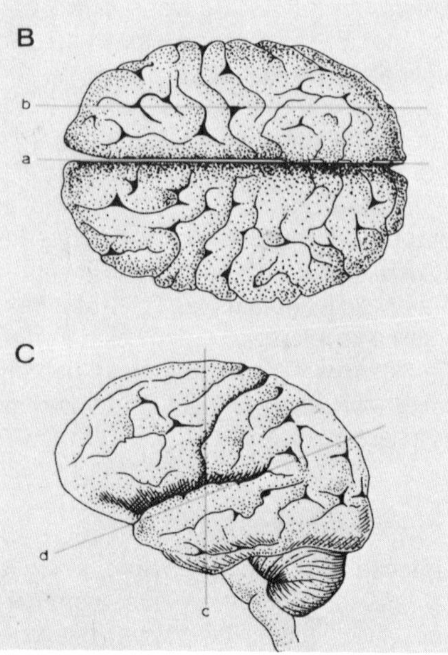

Fig. 1.1. *A*, sketch of the human primate in an anatomic position consistent with that of quadrupeds. This positioning orients the brain and nerve roots in such a way that the anterior and posterior, and rostral and caudal components may be compared with related structures of lower species. *B* and *C*, the common planes for sectioning the brain for anatomical or pathological study: *a*, midsagittal; *b*, parasagittal; *c*, coronal; *d*, 15°–20° from horizontal plane. From Schadé and Ford (1973).

Hindbrain (Rhombencephalon)

Medulla (Myelencephalon). The ventral aspect of the medulla is basically continuous with the spinal cord, but is given its origin by being housed within the skull proper, at the spinal cord's entrance at the foramen magnum. The medulla is formed around the central canal, which is continuous with the central canal that extends down the center of the spinal cord. Its upward extension forms the floor of the fourth ventricle. Surrounding the central canal is the central gray area of the medulla, which is a complex intercalated neuronal system. Lateral to this central gray region is a complex network of cells and fiber tracts that makes up the reticular formation, which then extends rostrally through the pons to the midbrain with functional extension into the diencephalon. The descending pyramidal tracts decussate (cross) on the ventral surface of the medulla just prior to passing into the spinal cord. Figures 1.9–1.14 depict dorsal, lateral, and ventral views of the medulla.

Pons (Metencephalon). The pons is situated just ventral to the cerebral peduncles (the compacted descending pyramidal and ascending sensory fibers), but just above the pyramids of the medulla. On the outer surface of the ventral side a slight furrow splits the pons into two lobes with the furrow corresponding to the position of the basilar artery. There are three (superior, middle, and inferior) major fiber tracts (peduncles) that arise at the level of the pons making connection with the cerebellum. These pathways house critical connections for proprioceptive input, along with both afferent and efferent connections with cerebral cortex. Figures 1.11–1.14 depict lateral and ventral views of the pons.

Cerebellum. The cerebellum has been characterized as the first structure of the brain to specialize for specific sensory-motor coordination. The cerebellum sits beneath the posterior aspect of the cerebral hemispheres, being separated by the tentorium cerebelli (see fig. 1.4). This region that houses the cerebellum is also described as the posterior cranial fossa. The cerebellum is composed of two symmetric hemispheres of three lobes each (see fig. 1.15), and each lobe is phylogenetically differentiated. The flocculonodular lobe is the oldest (archicerebellum); the anterior lobe (paleocerebellum), intermediate; and the posterior lobe (neocerebellum), the most recently developed and in humans being the most expanded directly corresponding to cerebral specialization. As such, the neocerebellum possesses a complex interactive system with the cortex, particularly in terms of complex and integrative motor control. As for the less-developed lobes, the archicerebellum is the cerebellar basis of the vestibular system, and the paleocerebellum, particularly the vermis, functions in proprioception.

Midbrain (Mesencephalon)

The midbrain sits between the upper margin of the pons and ventral aspect of the diencephalon-telencephalon.

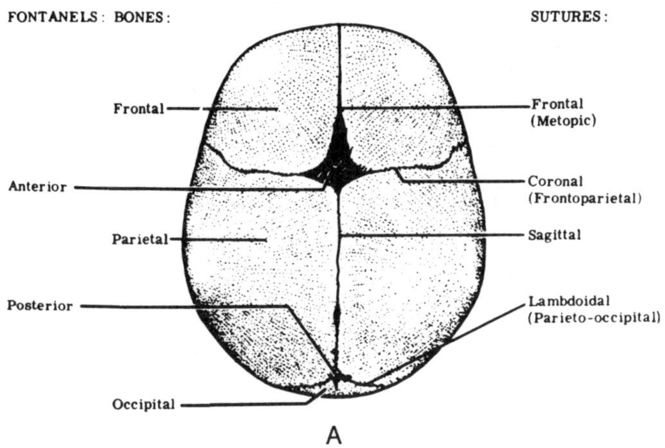

Fig. 1.2. Fontanels, bones, and sutures of the infant cranium in *A*, dorsal and *B*, lateral views. From DeMyer (1974). Used with permission.

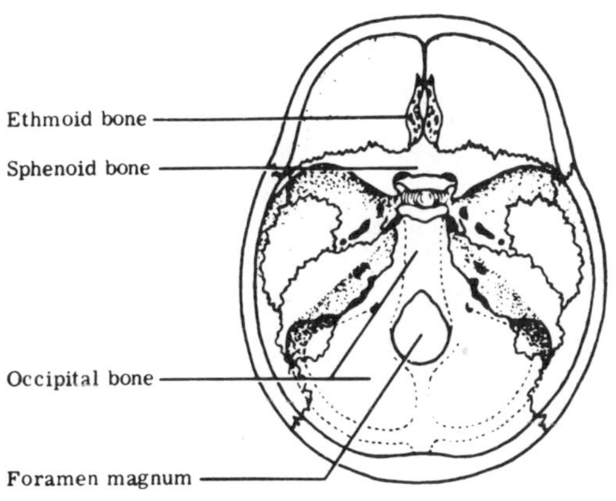

Fig. 1.3. The bones of the ventral surface of the skull. From DeMyer (1974). Used with permission.

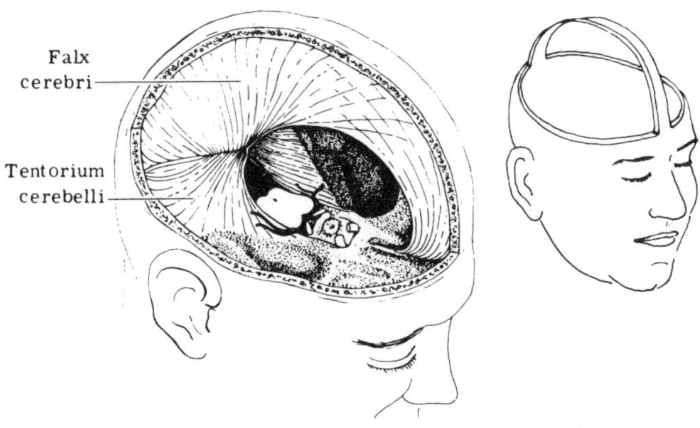

Fig. 1.4. Basket-handle dissection of the head, with removal of the cerebral hemispheres. Notice the partitioning of the intracranial space by the falx cerebri and tentorium cerebelli, folds of the dura mater. Notice how the brain stem has been sectioned at the mesencephalon and left in situ. From DeMyer (1974). Used with permission.

The midbrain is divided into dorsal (tectum) and ventral (tegmentum) sections separated by the aqueduct of Sylvius. The tectum is distinguished by four protuberances on the dorsal surface—the corpora quadrigemina. The corpora quadrigemina are further divided into the superior and inferior colliculi. The tegmentum functionally houses the cerebral peduncles. Two important nuclear groups are found within the tegmentum—the nucleus ruber (red nucleus) and the substantia nigra. The midbrain may be seen in figures 1.9 and 1.10. Aspects of the undifferentiated reticular activating system are housed within the midbrain with projection to the cortex. This system plays a regulatory role in arousal.

Forebrain (Prosencephalon)

Diencephalon. The diencephalon is made up of the thalamus and the hypothalamus. The thalamus is centrally situated in the brain with well-defined boundaries (see figs. 1.22–1.25). The medial aspect of the thalamus surrounds the third ventricle, and the internal capsule bounds the lateral margins of the thalamus. The thalamus plays a crucial role in the projection (relay) of sensory information to cortex. The three main (direct) relay nuclei are the lateral and medial geniculate nuclei and the ventral posterior nucleus. The lateral geniculate nuclei represent the synaptic termination of the optic nerve by the optic tract and subsequent projection to the visual cortex. The medial geniculate nuclei receive auditory input from the eighth cranial nerve by the inferior colliculus and project that input to the auditory cortex in the temporal lobe. The ventral posterior nucleus is the major somatosensory nucleus of the thalamus with sensory input from various body regions and facial nerves, with projection to somatosensory regions of parietal cortex. The thalamus is also composed of several association nuclei that interconnect with cortical areas, but do not necessarily act as relay stations of direct afferent input. The more important

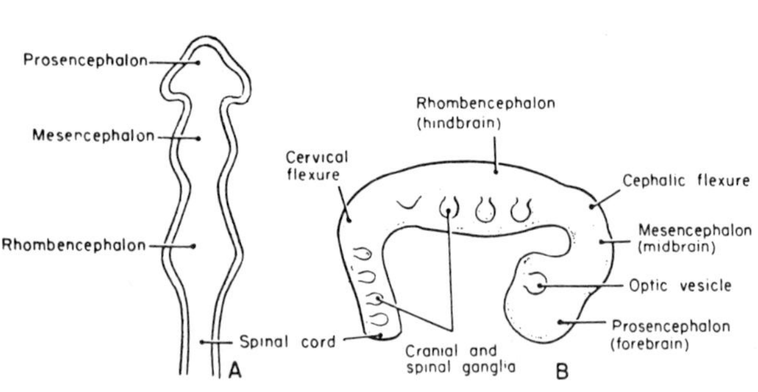

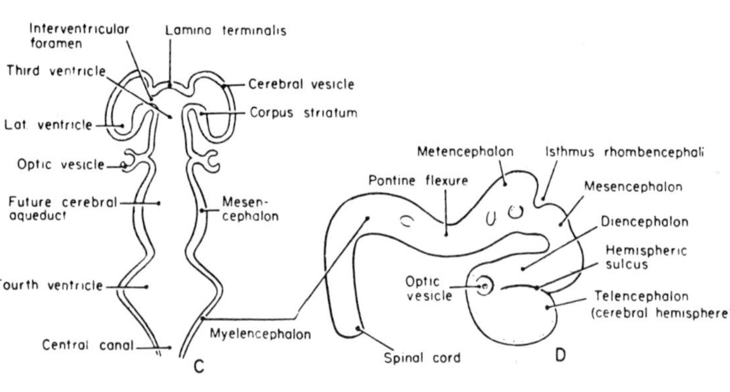

Fig. 1.5. Diagrams of the developing brain vesicles and ventricular system. *A* and *B* represent the three-brain vesicle stage of a 4-week-old embryo. *C* and *D* represent the three-brain vesicle stage of a 6-week-old embryo, a stage that begins to represent the eventual form of the fetal brain. From Truex and Carpenter (1969).

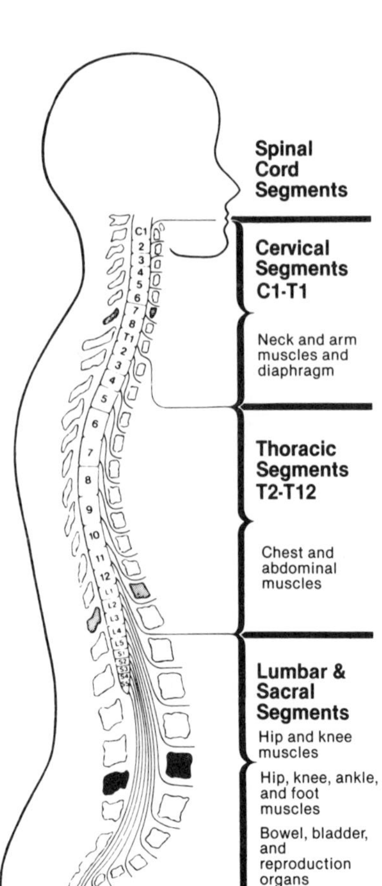

Fig. 1.6. Lateral representation of spinal column and cord and the various subdivisions.

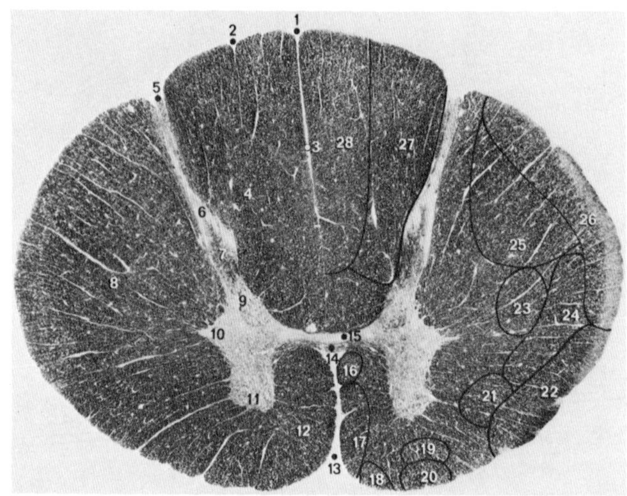

Fig. 1.7. Spinal cord system: (1) dorsal (posterior) median sulcus, (2) dorsal (posterior) intermediate sulcus, (3) posterior median septum, (4) posterior funiculus, (5) posterior lateral sulcus, (6) substantia gelatinosa, (7) dorsal (posterior) gray column, nucleus proprius, (8) lateral funiculus, (9) thoracic nucleus, (10) intermediolateral gray column, (11) ventral (anterior) gray column, (12) ventral funiculus, (13) anterior median fissure, (14) ventral white commissure, (15) intermediate gray substance, (16) medial longitudinal fascicle, (17) anterior corticospinal tract, (18) anterior tectospinal tract, (19) reticulospinal tract, (20) vestibulospinal tract, (21) spinotectal tract, (22) anterior spinocerebellar tract, (23) rubrospinal tract, (24) lateral spinothalamic tract, (25) lateral corticospinal tract, (26) posterior spinocerebellar tract, (27) cuneate fascicle, and (28) gracile fascicle. From Gluhbegovic and Williams (1980).

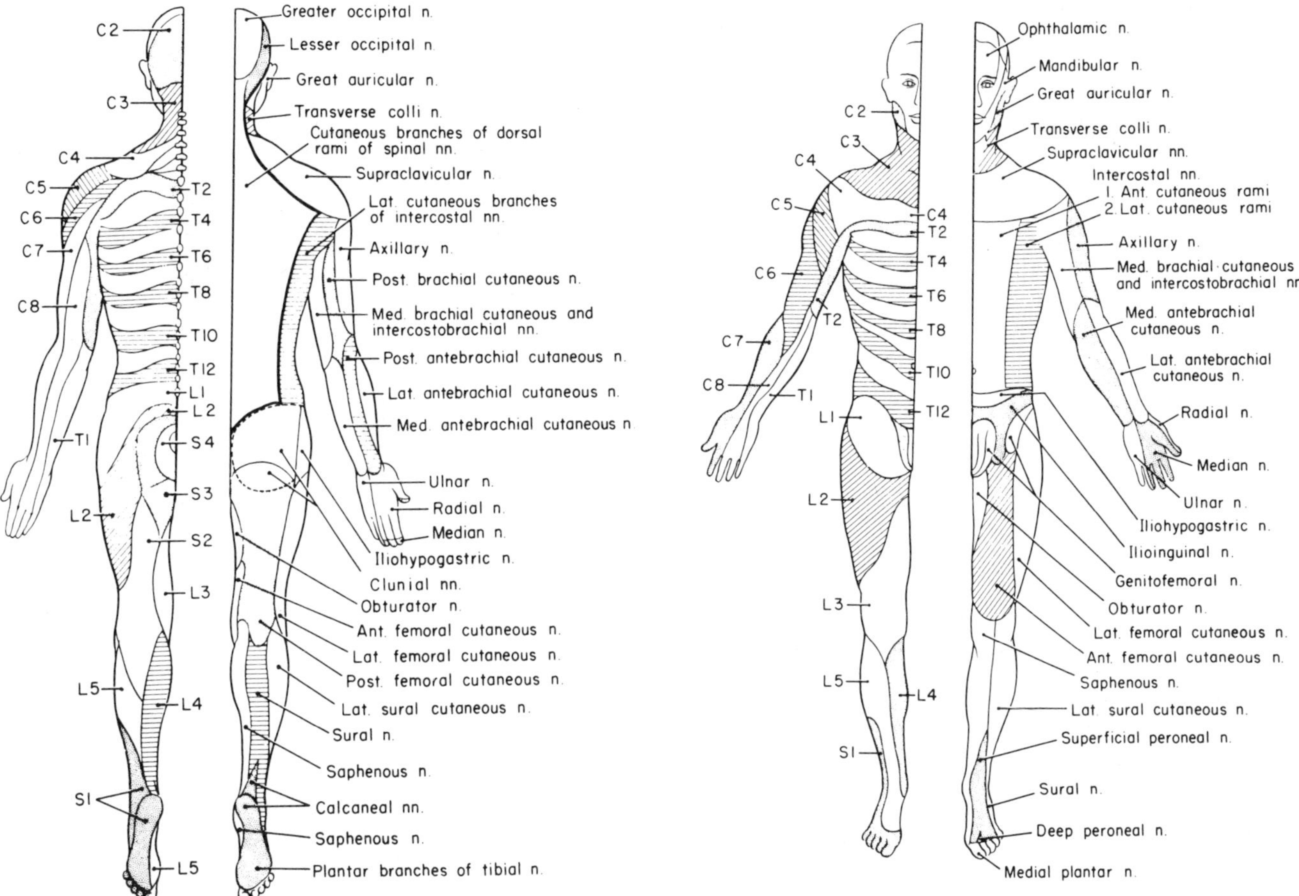

Fig. 1.8. Posterior (*left*) and anterior (*right*) views of dermatomes and cutaneous areas supplied by individual peripheral nerves. From Truex and Carpenter (1969).

association nuclei include the pulvinar with its important role in visual perception; the lateral nucleus, which functions in an associative manner with parietal cortical areas; the dorsal medial nucleus, which has a reciprocal innervative relationship with frontal cortical association areas; and the anterior nucleus with its projection to cortex by the cingulate gyrus and its receipt of input from mamillary bodies (and thereby from the limbic system) via the mamillothalamic tract. Within the thalamus, the centrum median possesses various intrathalamic connections.

The hypothalamus is located just ventral to the thalamus with only a small area, the subthalamus, separating the thalamus from the hypothalamus (see figs. 1.17, 1.22–1.25). The hypothalamus is continuous with the infundibulum (stalk of the pituitary) and posteriorly adjacent to the optic chiasm. Despite its small size, the hypothalamus houses extremely complex neural systems that play key roles in various regulatory functions. Some of these important nuclei are the supraoptic, paraventricular, and preoptic nuclei, which are involved in homeostatic fluid regulation; the lateral nucleus, which is a food stimulatory center; and the ventramedial nucleus, which is a food satiation center. The medial forebrain bundle constitutes a system of afferent connections with the olfactory regions of the brain (rhinencephalon) and efferent connections with the midbrain reticular formation (see figs. 1.16 and 1.17). Another important pathway is the corticomamillary tract (fornix), which arises in the hippocampus and terminates in the mamillary bodies. The hypothalamus also possesses direct regulatory control over the autonomic nervous system. Stimulation of the rostral aspect results in excitation of parasympathetic activity, producing sweating, vasodilation, and reduced cardiac contractions. Reversed symptoms occur when this area is damaged. Oppositely, stimulation of the caudal aspect causes excitation of the sympathetic system, resulting in vasoconstriction, accelerated cardiac output, pupillary dilation, and inhibited peristalsis.

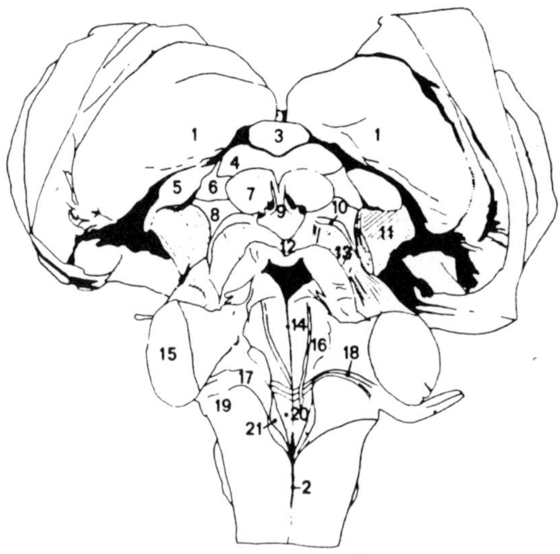

Fig. 1.9. Dorsal view of the brain stem: (1) pulvinar of thalamus, (2) posterior median sulcus, (3) pineal body, (4) superior colliculus, (5) medial geniculate body, (6) brachium of inferior colliculus, (7) inferior colliculus, (8) lemniscal trigone, (9) frenulum of superior medullary velum, (10) trochlear nerve, (11) basis pedunculi, (12) superior medullary velum, (13) superior cerebellar peduncle, (14) median sulcus of rhomboid fossa, (15) middle cerebellar peduncle, (16) facial colliculus, (17) vestibular area, (18) striae medullares of fourth ventricle, (19) inferior cerebellar peduncle, (20) hypoglossal trigone, and (21) vagal trigone. From Gluhbegovic and Williams (1980).

Fig. 1.10. Photograph of dorsal view of the brain stem. From Gluhbegovic and Williams (1980).

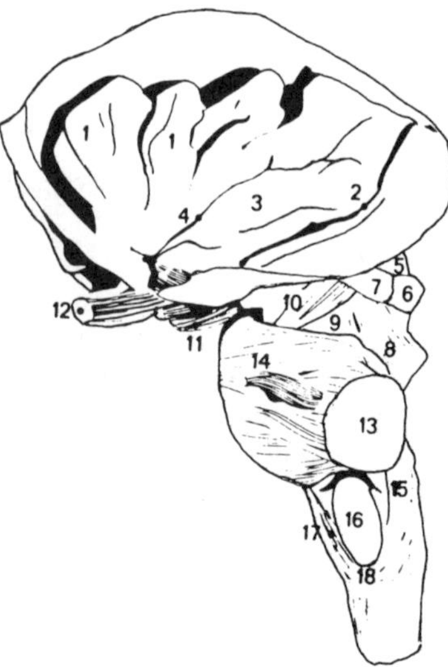

Fig. 1.11. Lateral view of the brain stem: (1) short gyri of insula, (2) circular sulcus of insula, (3) long gyrus of insula, (4) central sulcus of insula, (5) superior colliculus, (6) inferior colliculus, (7) brachium of inferior colliculus, (8) superior cerebellar peduncle, (9) lemniscal trigone, (10) basis pedunculi, (11) oculomotor nerve, (12) optic nerve, (13) middle cerebellar peduncle, (14) trigeminal nerve, (15) inferior cerebellar peduncle, (16) olive, (17) pyramid of medulla oblongata, (18) circumolivary bundle. From Gluhbegovic and Williams (1980).

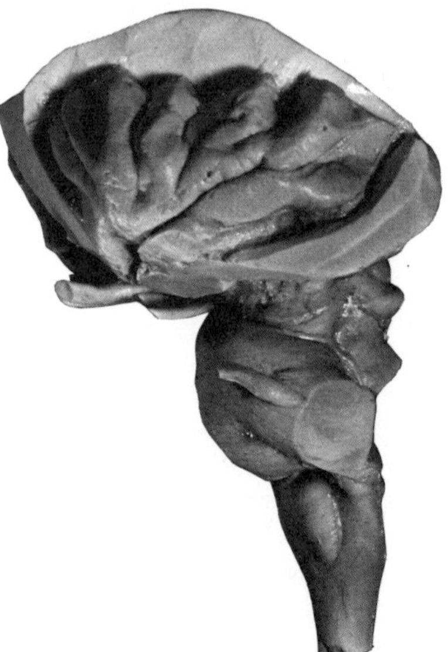

Fig. 1.12. Photograph of lateral view of the brain stem. From Gluhbegovic and Williams (1980).

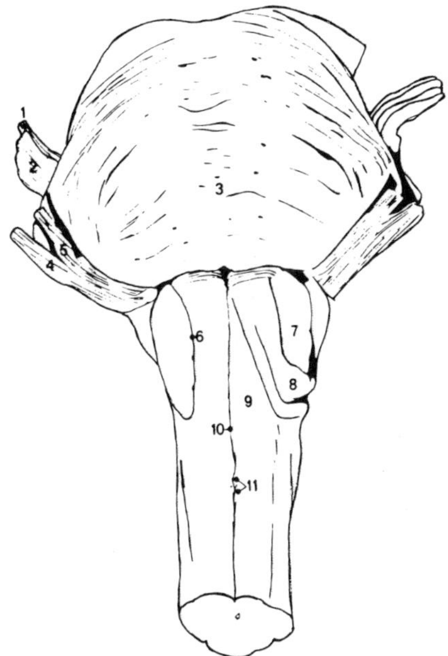

Fig. 1.13. Ventral view of the brain stem: (1) motor (minor) root of trigeminal nerve, (2) sensory (major) root of trigeminal nerve, (3) basilar sulcus of pons, (4) vestibulocochlear nerve, (5) facial nerve, (6) ventrolateral sulcus of medulla oblongata, (7) olive, (8) circumolivary bundle, (9) pyramid of medulla oblongata, (10) ventral (anterior) median fissure, (11) pyramidal decussation. From Gluhbegovic and Williams (1980).

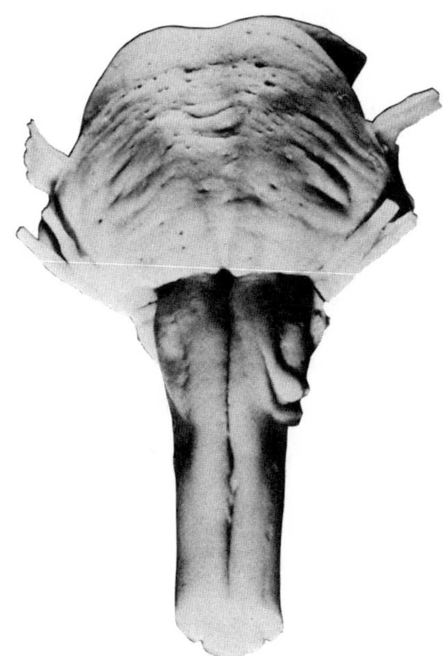

Fig. 1.14. Photograph of ventral view of the brain stem. From Gluhbegovic and Williams (1980).

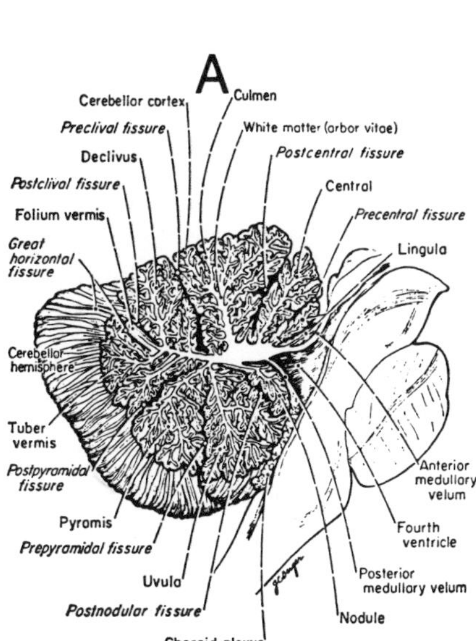

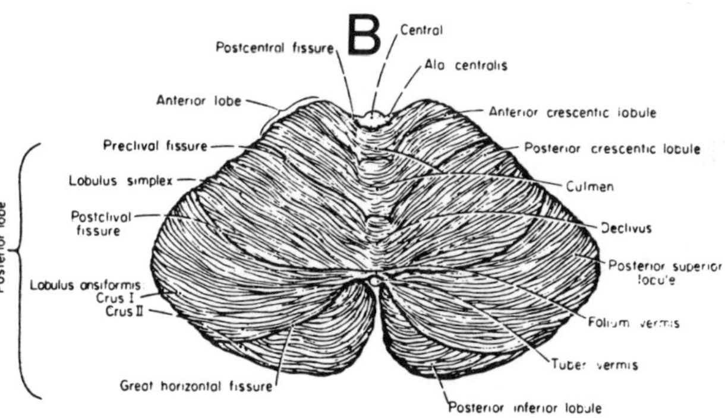

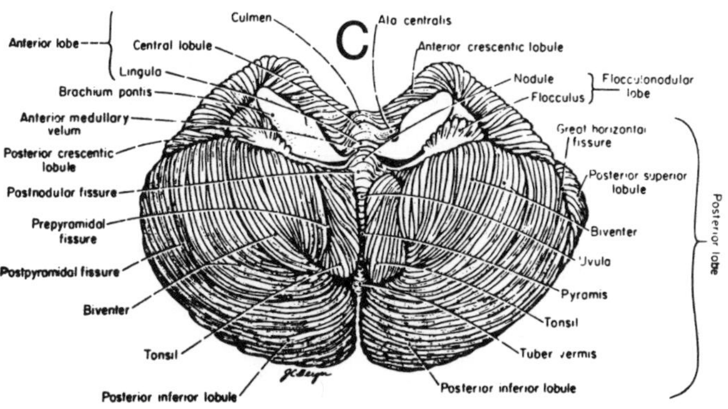

Fig. 1.15. A, sagittal, B, dorsal, and C, ventral views of the cerebellum. From Crosby, Humphrey, and Lauer (1962).

Telencephalon. The telencephalon is divided into two symmetric hemispheres (right and left) with each being connected with the other by the corpus callosum (see figs. 1.18–1.20). Each hemisphere is likewise divided into four major lobes: frontal, parietal, temporal, and occipital. Figures 1.18–1.20 display these four lobes and the landmarks that differentiate. The frontal and parietal lobes are easily demarcated by the central sulcus—the frontal lobe is anterior and the parietal lobe, posterior. The sylvian or lateral fissure bisects the frontal and temporal lobes, and similarly the anterior aspect of the parietal lobe from the temporal. The brain sulci (the linear clefts on the surface) and gyri (the ridges between sulci) are also systematically organized, and their relationship to one another forms various landmarks as outlined in figures 1.18–1.20. Figures 1.25 and 1.44 present coronal, sagittal, and horizontal views of the brain, depicting the major telencephalic structures and their locations. Much of the concern and investigation in clinical neuropsychology deals primarily with telencephalic structures and functions because these areas control the higher cognitive functions. As such, further anatomic and neurophysiologic function will be provided when appropriate in the following chapters. Careful study of figures 121–125 is essential.

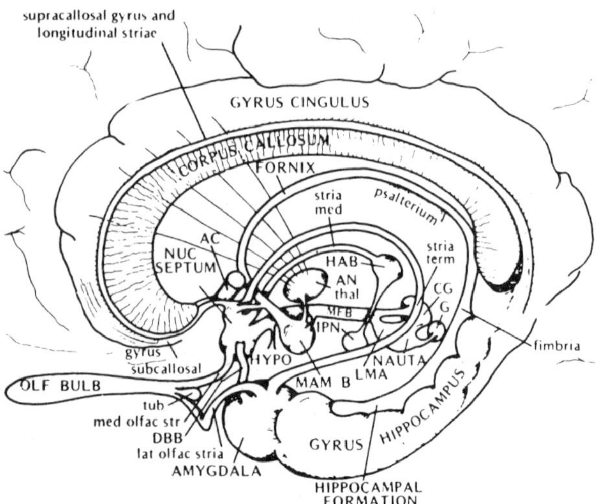

Fig. 1.17. Schematic drawing depicting limbic system pathways. Abbreviations are as follows: NUC SEPTUM, septal nucleus; AC, anterior commissure; AN thal, anterior nucleus of the thalamus; CG, central gray matter of the midbrain; DBB, diagonal band of Broca; G, Gudden's deep tegmental nucleus; HAB, habenula; HYPO, hypothalamus; IPN, interpeduncular nucleus; LMA NAUTA, lateral midbrain area of Nauta; lat olfac stria, lateral olfactory stria; med olfac str, medial olfactory stria; MFB, medium forebrain bundle; MAM B, mamillary bodies; stria med, stria medullaris; and stria term, stria terminalis. From Heilman and Valenstein (1979).

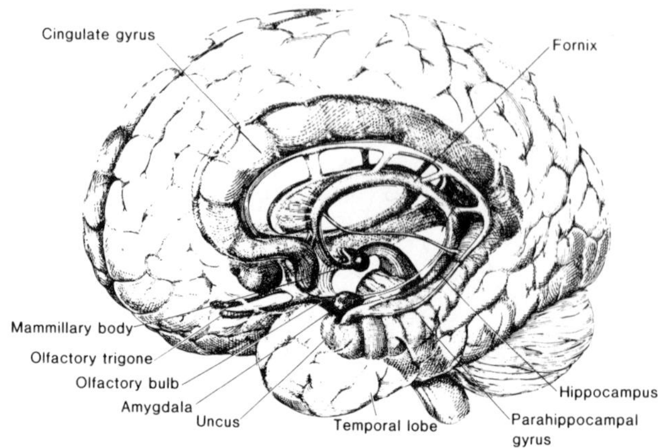

Fig. 1.16. The limbic system. From Synder (1977).

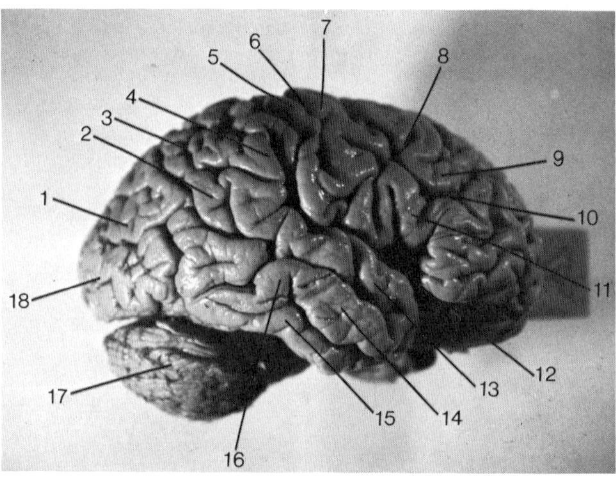

Fig. 1.18. Lateral view of the telencephalon (first of three views): (1) lateral occipital gyrus, (2) parietal lobe, (3) angular gyrus, (4) supramarginal gyrus, (5) postcentral gyrus, (6) central sulcus, (7) precentral gyrus, (8) frontal lobe, (9) middle frontal gyrus, (10) inferior frontal sulcus, (11) inferior frontal gyrus, (12) sylvian fissure, (13) superior temporal gyrus, (14) middle temporal gyrus, (15) inferior temporal gyrus, (16) temporal lobe, (17) cerebellum, and (18) occipital lobe.

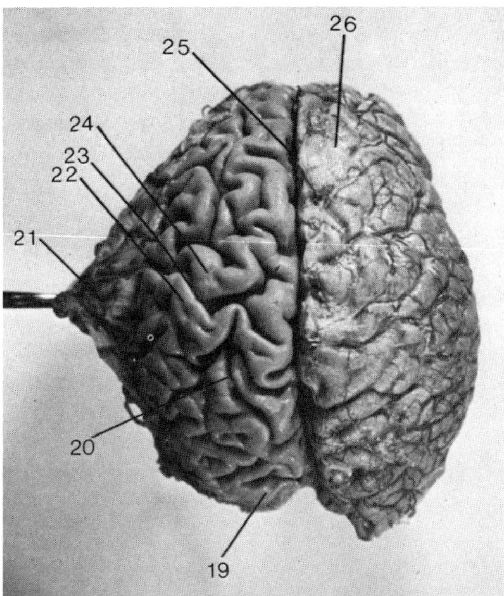

Fig. 1.19. Dorsal view of the telencephalon (second of three views): (19) occipital lobe, (20) parietal lobe, (21) pia mater, (22) postcentral gyrus, (23) central sulcus, (24) precentral gyrus, (25) interhemispheric fissure, and (26) frontal lobe.

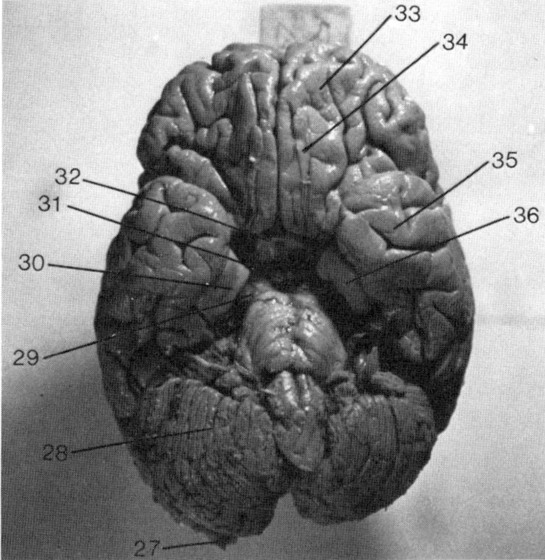

Fig. 1.20. Ventral view of the telencephalon (last of three views): (27) occipital lobe, (28) cerebellum, (29) cerebral peduncle, (30) uncus, (31) mamillary bodies, (32) optic chiasm, (33) frontal lobe, (34) olfactory bulb, (35) temporal lobe, and (36) uncus.

Vascular System

Blood supply to the brain can be functionally separated into the anterior and posterior circulation divisions (Raichle, Devivo, and Hanaway, 1978). The anterior circulation depends on the internal carotid artery (ICA), which originates from the common carotid artery when it bifurcates into the internal and external divisions (see figs. 1.26 and 1.27). The ICA then branches into the middle and anterior cerebral arteries. The posterior circulation of the brain is supplied by the vertebral-basilar system, which originates from the symmetric vertebral arteries that fuse at the level of the pons to become the basilar artery. The basilar artery in turn extends up to the midbrain where it bifurcates, forming the superior and posterior cerebellar arteries. Three cerebral arteries—the anterior (ACA), middle (MCA), and posterior (PCA)—supply all of the blood to the telencephalon (see fig. 1.28). The ACA supplies the medial surface of the brain from anterior frontal to the parietal-occipital fissure with branches feeding the anterior limb of the internal capsule, putamen, and the head of the caudate nucleus. The MCA, which is the largest cerebral artery, supplies most of the lateral surface of the brain affecting all lobes. Branches of the MCA penetrate the brain supplying the remaining portions of the basal ganglia and posterior limb of the internal capsule. The PCA supplies the medial and ventral surface of the temporal lobe including the hippocampal complex along with the visual cortex of the occipital lobe. Like the ACA and MCA, branches of the PCA penetrate the brain to supply the subthalamic and certain thalamic (ventral basal sensory complex) nuclei. Figure 1.29 depicts the venous blood system of the brain. As with the anatomic figures of the previous section, the figures representing the vascular system should be carefully studied because vascular disorders represent the most common of neurological disorders.

Ventricular System and Cerebrospinal Fluid

The internal cavitations of the brain form the ventricular system in which the cerebrospinal fluid (CSF) is produced (in the choroid plexus) and circulated (see fig. 1.30). The major role of the CSF is to mechanically preserve the general shape of the brain along with some apparent homeostatic functions. Overproduction of CSF or obstruction of one of the ventricular pathways may enlarge the entire ventricular system and produce hydrocephalus.

Functional Systems and Clinical Signs

Motor System

The direct corticospinal (pyramidal) tract originates in the precentral gyrus, which courses downward first passing through the internal capsule and the cerebral peduncle; then about 90 percent of the fibers cross to the opposite

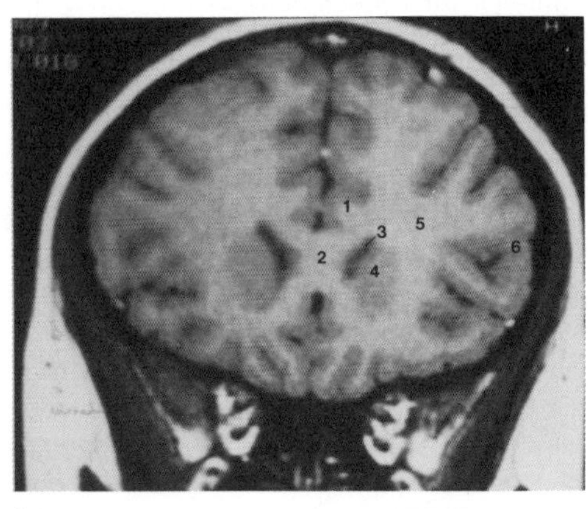

1

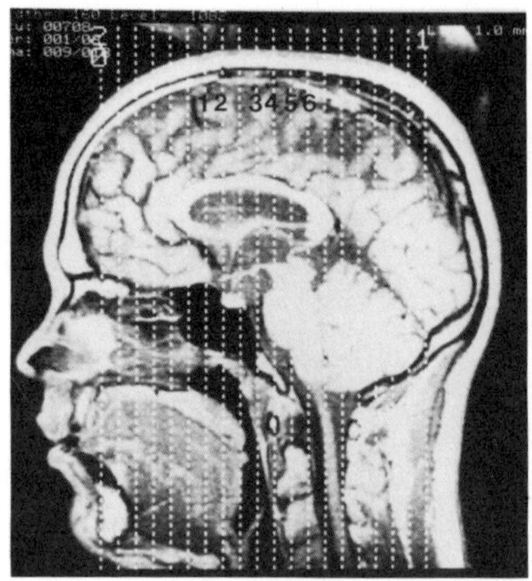

Fig. 1.21. Sagittal MRI view depicting approximate coronal placement of sections in fig. 1.22.

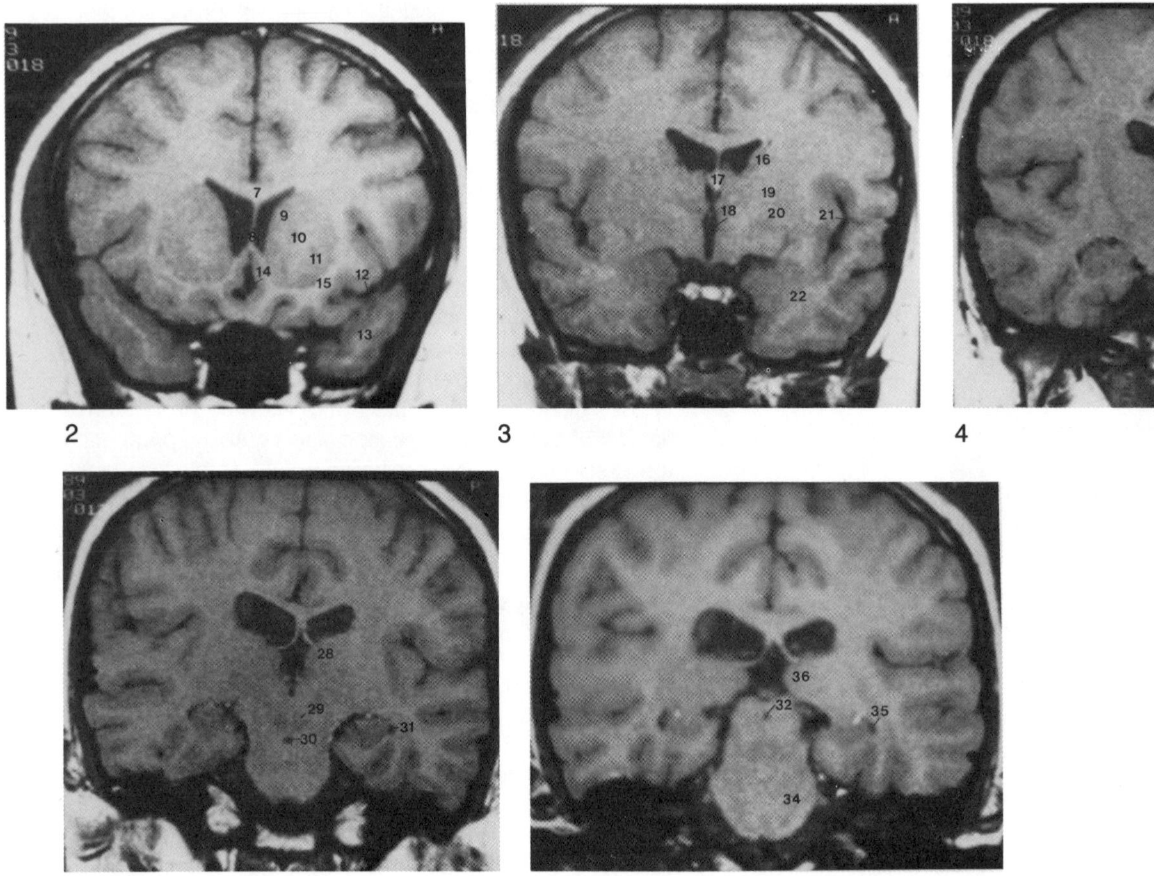

2 3 4

5 6

Fig. 1.22. Coronal sections of the cerebrum corresponding to the MRI view in fig. 1.21: (1) cingulate gyrus, (2) corpus callosum, (3) anterior horn of lateral ventricle, (4) caudate nucleus, (5) white matter, (6) gray matter of outer cortex, (7) corpus callosum, (8) septum pellucidum, (9) caudate nucleus, (10) internal capsule, (11) putamen, (12) Sylvian fissure, (13) anterior tip of temporal lobe, (14) interhemispheric fissure/optic recess, (15) external capsule, (16) body of caudate nucleus, (17) fornix, (18) third ventricle, (19) internal capsule, (20) Putamen/Globus pallidus complex, (21) sylvian fissure, (22) temporal lobe, (23) fornix, (24) thalamus, (25) anterior horn of lateral ventricle, (26) internal capsule, (27) hippocampus, (28) posterior thalamus, (29) red nucleus, (30) aqueduct of sylvius, (31) temporal horn of lateral ventricle, (32) Aqueduct of Sylvius, (33) cistern, (34) pons, (35) posterior horn of lateral ventricle, and (36) posterior thalamus.

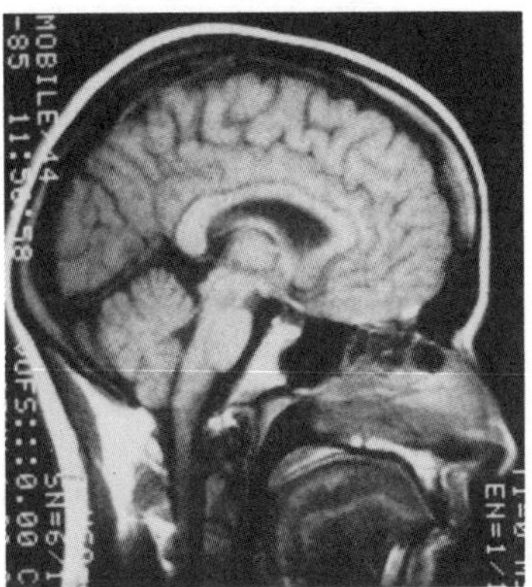

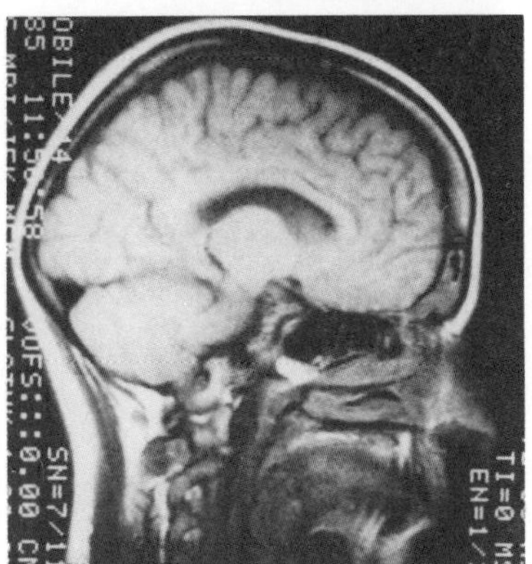

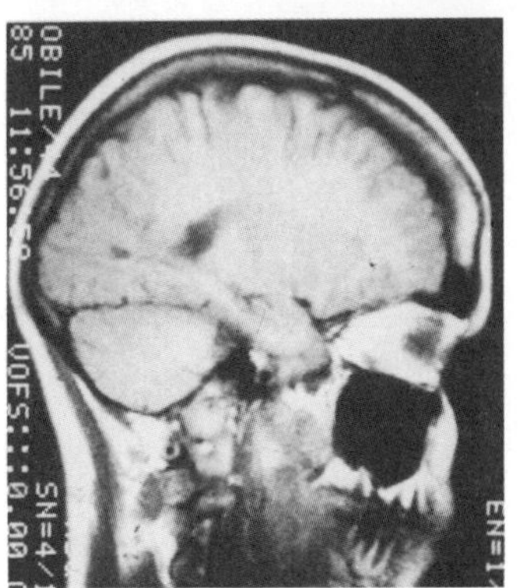

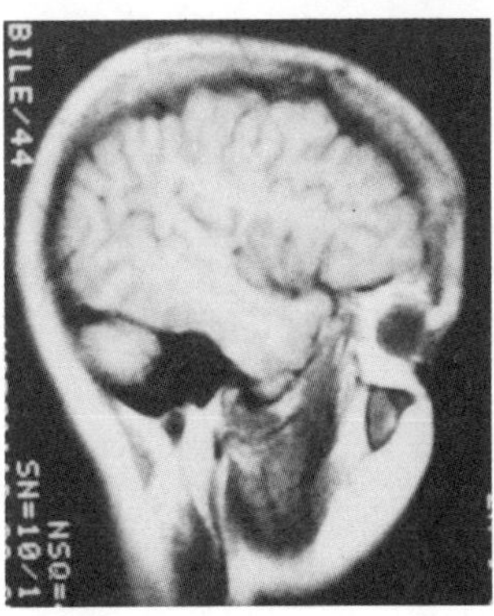

Fig. 1.23. Sagittal sections utilizing MRI scanning demonstrating normal anatomy.

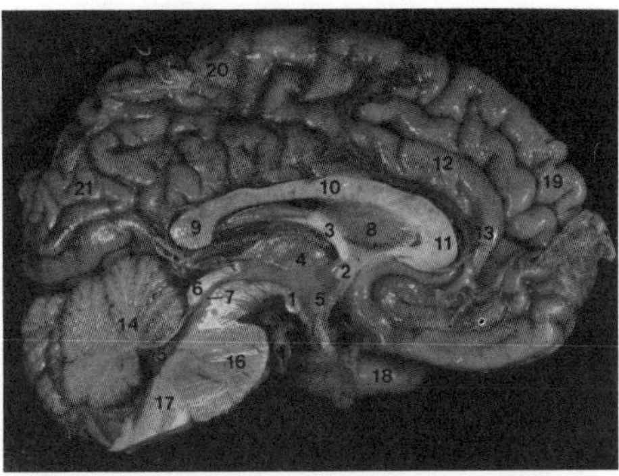

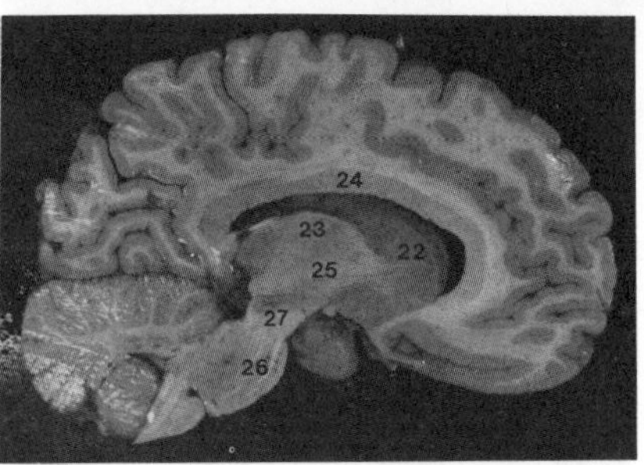

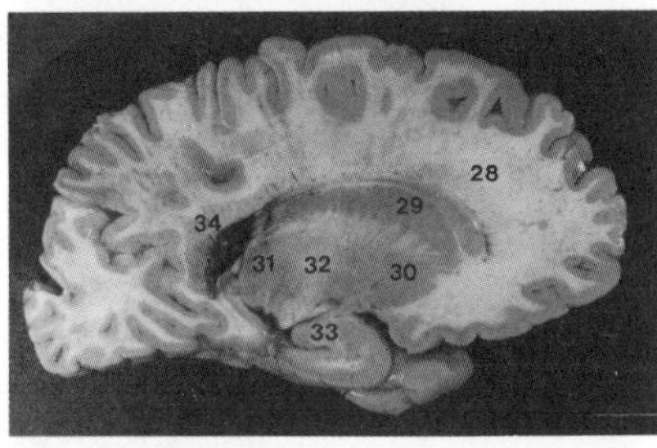

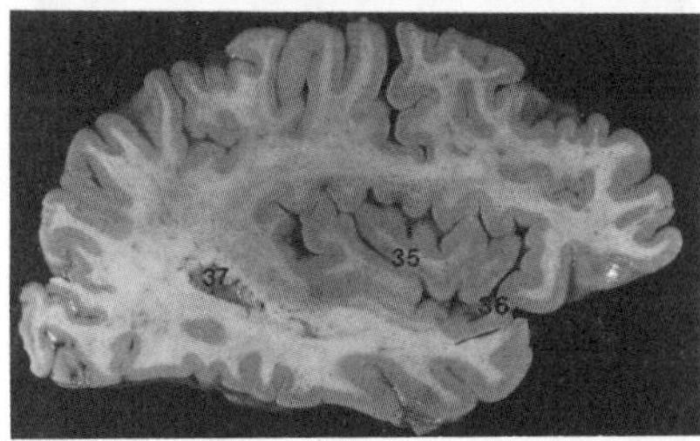

Fig. 1.24. Actual anatomic sagittal sections of the cerebrum corresponding to fig. 1.23: (1) mamillary body, (2) anterior commissure, (3) fornix, (4) thalamus, (5) hypothalamus, (6) corpora quadrigemini (superior and inferior colliculi), (7) Aqueduct of Sylvius, (8) septum pellucidum, (9) splenium of corpus callosum, (10) body of corpus callosum, (11) genu of corpus callosum, (12) cingulate gyrus, (13) anterior cerebral artery, (14) cerebellum, (15) fourth ventricle, (16) pons, (17) medulla, (18) temporal lobe, (19) frontal lobe, (20) parietal lobe, (21) occipital lobe, (22) caudate nucleus (head), (23) thalamus, (24) corpus callosum, (25) internal capsule, (26) pons, (27) midbrain, (28) white matter of frontal lobe, (29) caudate nucleus, (30) globus pallidus putamen complex, (31) thalamus, (32) internal capsule, (33) temporal lobe, (34) posterior horn of lateral ventricle, (35) sylvian fissure (insular cortex), (36) sylvian fissure, and (37) posterior horn of lateral ventricle.

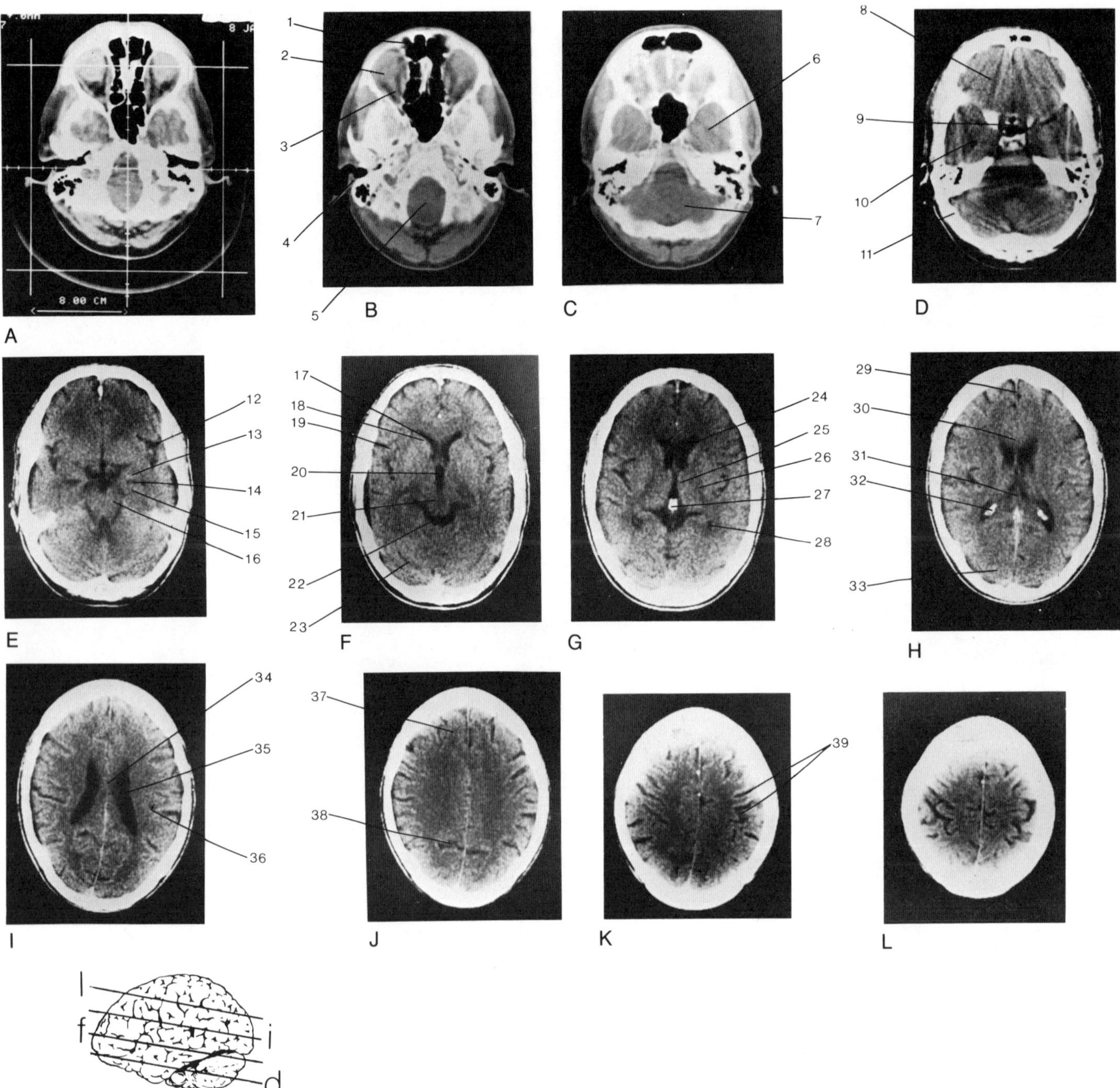

Fig. 1.25. Horizontal sections through the cerebrum as depicted by computerized axial tomography (CAT): (1) sinus cavity, (2) eye, (3) optic nerve, (4) ear, (5) foramen magnum, (6) temporal lobe, (7) cerebellum, (8) frontal lobe, (9) pituitary, (10) temporal lobe, (11) skull, (12) sylvian fissure, (13) uncus, (14) inferior (temporal) horn of lateral ventricle, (15) hippocampus, (16) midbrain, (17) anterior horn of lateral ventricle, (18) caudate nucleus, (19) sylvian fissure, (20) third ventricle, (21) midbrain, (22) posterior cistern (quadrigeminal plate cistern), (23) cerebellum, (24) septum pellucidum, (25) thalamus, (26) internal capsule, (27) pineal gland, (28) posterior (occipital) horn of lateral ventricle, (29) interhemispheric fissure, (30) genu of corpus callosum, (31) splenium of corpus callosum, (32) choroid plexus, (33) occipital lobe, (34) corpus callosum, (35) body of lateral ventricle, (36) corona radiata, (37) frontal lobe (superior frontal gyrus), (38) parieto-occipital sulcus, and (39) cortical gyri. Schematic drawing depicts levels of CAT scan imaging. Letters correspond to CAT scan sections.

Notice the general symmetry of the brain. Irregularities from this normal symmetry may have pathologic implications; however, there are certain subtle asymmetries that are normal. The posterior aspect of the left cerebral hemisphere is larger than its contralateral counterpart, with the reverse being true of the right frontal region (Koff et al., 1986; Yeo et al., 1987). Also, it needs to be emphasized that CAT abnormalities reflect only structural and not functional defects (see Knopman and Rubens, 1986).

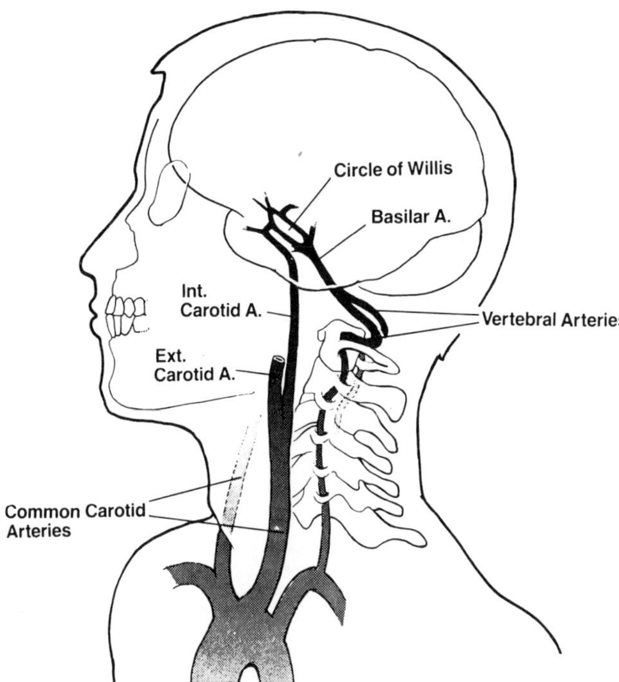

Fig. 1.26. Cerebral vascular supply in lateral view. From the *Harvard Medical School Health Letter* (illustration by Harriet R. Greenfield).

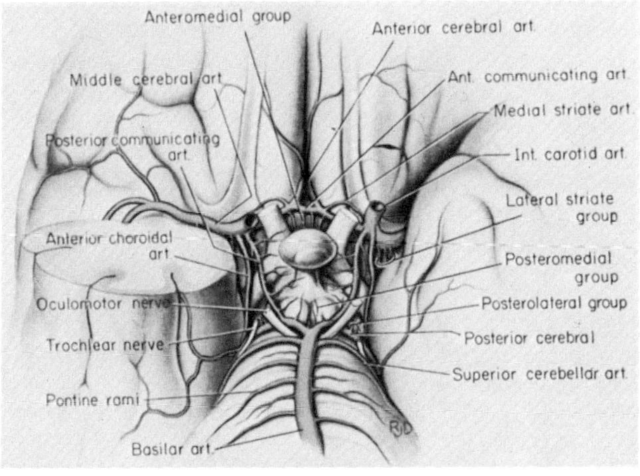

Fig. 1.27. Ventral view of major cerebral arteries. From Truex and Carpenter (1969).

side at the level of the medulla and finally terminate in the spinal cord (see figs. 1.31–1.33). Lesions in the motor cortex, or the upper motor neuron, produce contralateral hemiparesis, hypertonic musculature in the affected side, hyperactive tendon reflexes, minimal atrophy, absence of muscle fasciculations, and presence of pathologic reflexes (i.e., Babinski reflex). Lesions that are postsynaptic, thus being lower motor neuron lesions, produce muscle flaccidity, absent or hypoactive tendon reflexes, muscle atrophy, and fasciculations.

The corticospinal tract is but one of numerous interconnected motor systems, inasmuch as the nearly infinite positions of movement require more than a direct descending pathway. The important nuclei for the remainder of the motor system, imprecisely termed the *extrapyramidal motor system* (see figs. 1.31–1.33), are the caudate nucleus, globus pallidus, putamen, subthalamic nucleus (corpus Luysii), substantia nigra, red nucleus, reticular formation of the brain stem, and various cerebellar nuclei (see figs 1.34 and 1.35 for location of these structures). The caudate nucleus and the lentiform nucleus (putamen and globus pallidus) are referred to as the *basal ganglia*. The caudate and putamen form the striatum (sometimes also referred to as the *neostriatum*), and this striatal complex forms an important interconnection with the dopamine-rich centers of the substantia nigra, thereby forming the nigrostriatal system. This system, depicted in figures 1.31–1.33, controls background movement, including various postural adjustments that accompany precise motor movements controlled by the corticospinal (pyramidal) tract (see also figs. 1.34 and 1.35).

Disorders of motor control and movement depend upon which aspect and level of the motor system are involved. Although these disorders will be discussed in further detail in subsequent chapters, a brief introductory overview is in order. Parkinson's disease is one of the most common disorders of movement. Its two most salient features are background tremor and difficulty in initiating movements (hypokinesia). The nigral-striatal system contains high concentrations of acetylcholine (Ach) and dopamine, Ach being excitatory to striatal neurons and dopamine playing an inhibitory role, thereby providing for a dynamic excitatory-inhibitory interactive system. In Parkinson's disease, dopamine concentrations are substantially reduced, and this alteration in the dopaminergic system creates the motor disturbance observed. Chorea is likewise a common movement disorder, but distinctly different from parkinsonism in that gross involuntary movements are involved that are irregular, random, and jerky. The most common disorder with chorea is Huntington's disease, which is known to be a result of degeneration of the striatum, particularly the caudate, along with changes in cortex. Other disorders of movement may include ballism (gross, uncontrolled flinging of extremities, usually associated with a lesion at the subthalamus), athetosis (twisting distortions of purposeful body and limb movements, usually associated with a lesion of the striatum), and dystonia

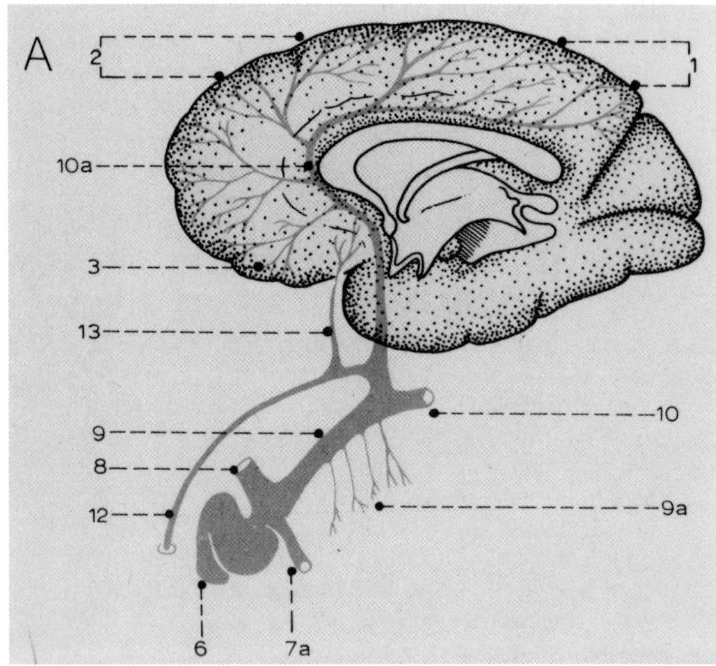
A
2
1
10a
3
13
9
10
8
12
9a
6
7a

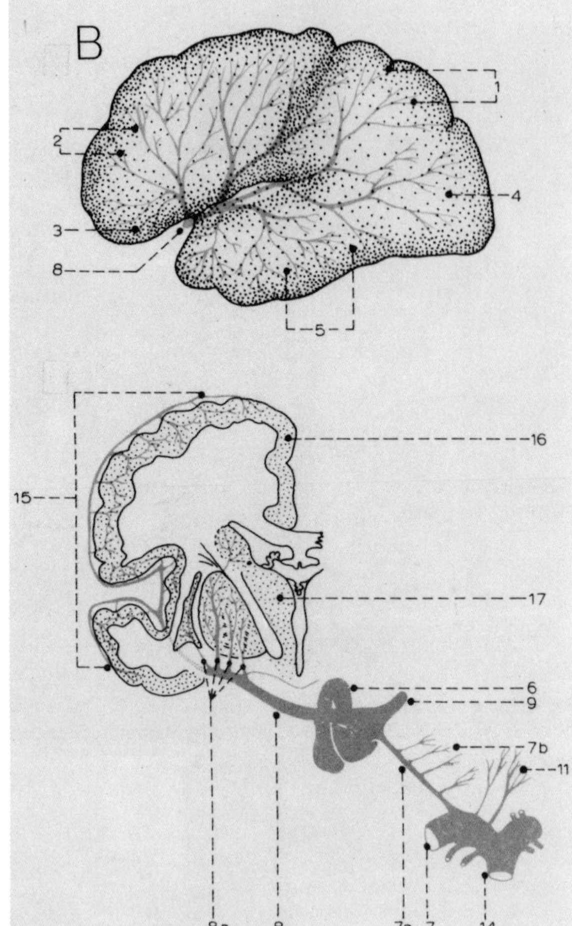
B
1
2
4
3
8
5
16
15
17
6
9
7b
11
8a
8
7a
7
14

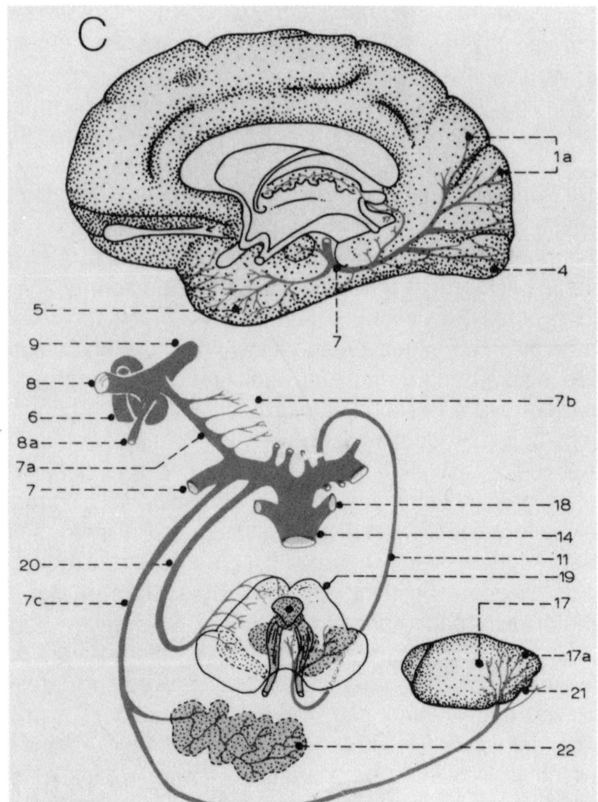
C
1a
4
5
7
9
8
7b
6
8a
7a
7
18
14
11
20
19
7c
17
17a
21
22

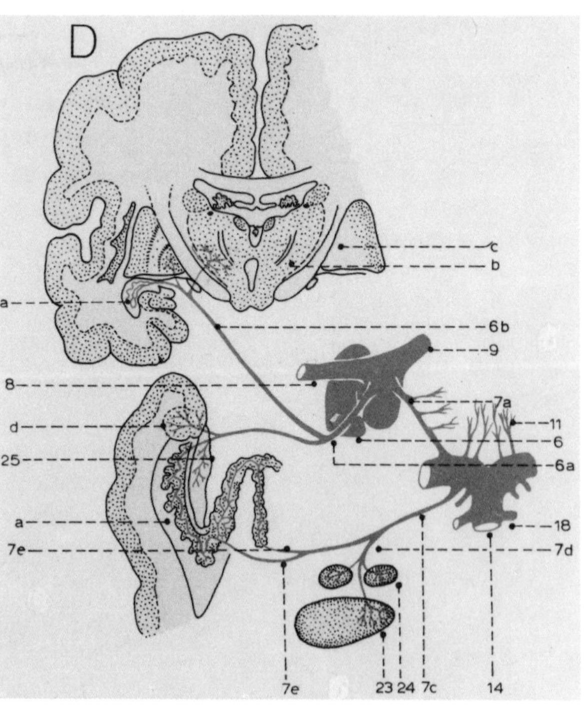
D
c
b
a
6b
9
8
7a
11
d
6
25
6a
a
18
7e
7d
7e
23
24
7c
14

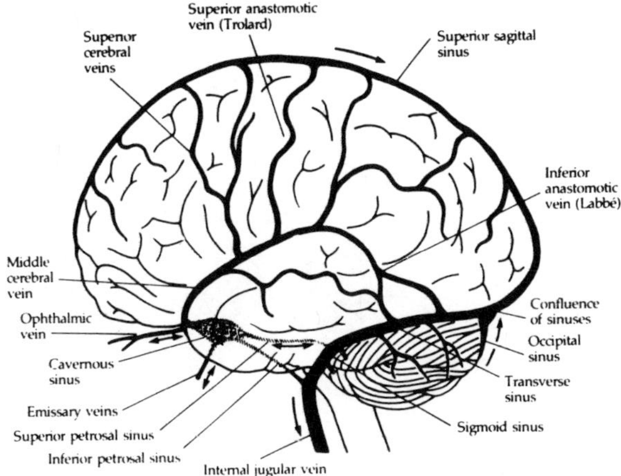

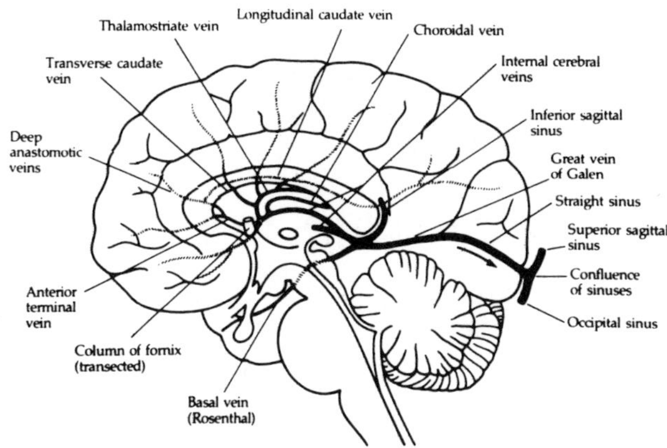

Fig. 1.29. Venous drainage of the brain. Adapted from Truex and Carpenter (1969).

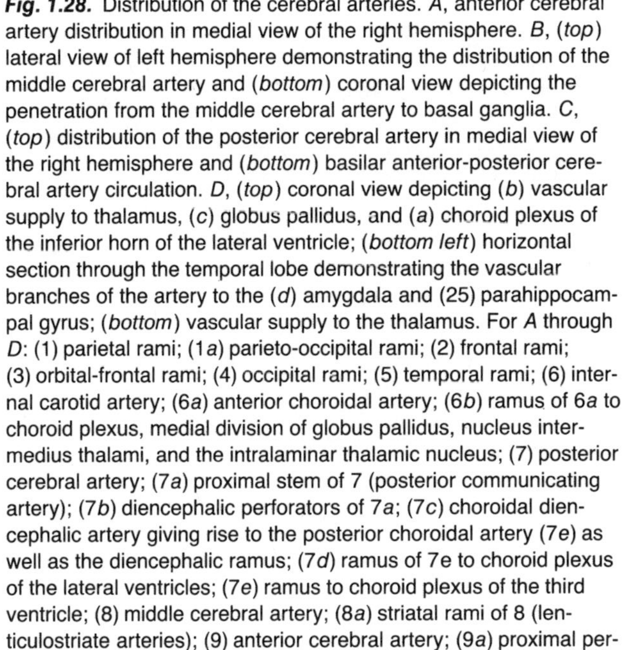

Fig. 1.28. Distribution of the cerebral arteries. *A*, anterior cerebral artery distribution in medial view of the right hemisphere. *B*, (*top*) lateral view of left hemisphere demonstrating the distribution of the middle cerebral artery and (*bottom*) coronal view depicting the penetration from the middle cerebral artery to basal ganglia. *C*, (*top*) distribution of the posterior cerebral artery in medial view of the right hemisphere and (*bottom*) basilar anterior-posterior cerebral artery circulation. *D*, (*top*) coronal view depicting (*b*) vascular supply to thalamus, (*c*) globus pallidus, and (*a*) choroid plexus of the inferior horn of the lateral ventricle; (*bottom left*) horizontal section through the temporal lobe demonstrating the vascular branches of the artery to the (*d*) amygdala and (25) parahippocampal gyrus; (*bottom*) vascular supply to the thalamus. For *A* through *D*: (1) parietal rami; (1*a*) parieto-occipital rami; (2) frontal rami; (3) orbital-frontal rami; (4) occipital rami; (5) temporal rami; (6) internal carotid artery; (6*a*) anterior choroidal artery; (6*b*) ramus of 6*a* to choroid plexus, medial division of globus pallidus, nucleus intermedius thalami, and the intralaminar thalamic nucleus; (7) posterior cerebral artery; (7*a*) proximal stem of 7 (posterior communicating artery); (7*b*) diencephalic perforators of 7*a*; (7*c*) choroidal diencephalic artery giving rise to the posterior choroidal artery (7*e*) as well as the diencephalic ramus; (7*d*) ramus of 7*e* to choroid plexus of the lateral ventricles; (7*e*) ramus to choroid plexus of the third ventricle; (8) middle cerebral artery; (8*a*) striatal rami of 8 (lenticulostriate arteries); (9) anterior cerebral artery; (9*a*) proximal perforators of 9 to preoptic area; (10) anterior communicating artery; (10*a*) pericallosal stem of 10; (11) posteromedial perforators to tegmental mesencephalon; (12) ramus centralis of 9 (striata medialis artery of Heubner); (13) ramus of 12 to septal area; (14) basilar artery; (15) cortical rami; (16) cerebral cortex; (17) diencephalon; (17*a*) pulvinar; (18) superior cerebellar artery; (19) mesencephalon; (20) tectal artery; (21) geniculate bodies; (22) choroid plexus (choroidal diencephalic artery); (23) thalamic nuclei; and (24) thalamic nuclei. Adapted from Schadé and Ford (1973).

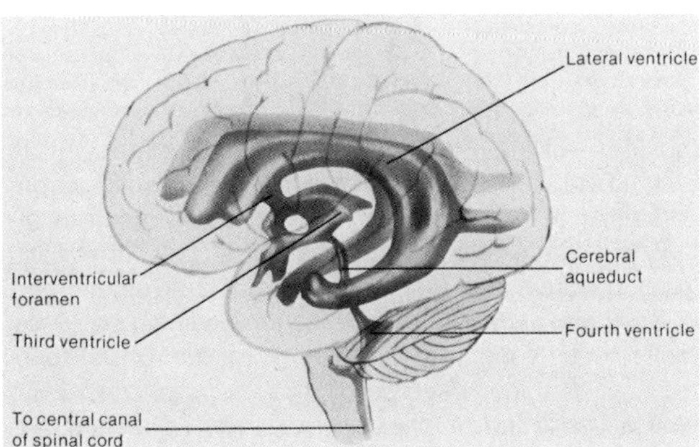

Fig. 1.30. Lateral view of the ventricles of the brain. From Hole (1981). Artwork by Diane Nelson and Associates.

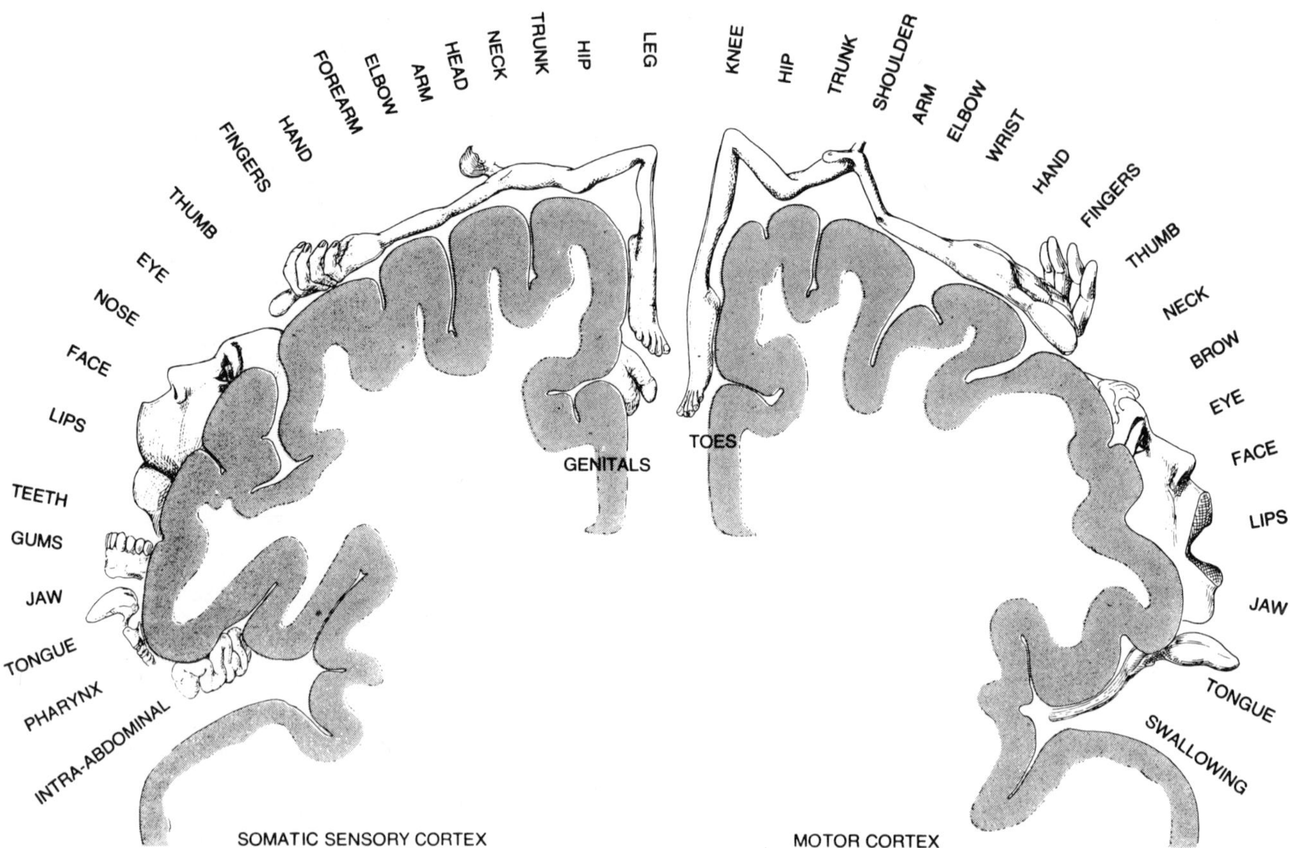

Fig. 1.31. Somatic sensory and motor regions of the cerebral cortex. These regions are specialized in the sense that every site in these regions can be associated with some part of the body. In other words, most of the body can be mapped onto the cortex, yielding two distorted homunculi. The distortions come about because the area of the cortex dedicated to a part of the body is proportional not to that part's actual size but to the precision with which it must be controlled. In humans the motor and somatic sensory regions given over to the face and to the hands are greatly exaggerated. Only half of each cortical region is shown: the left somatic sensory area (which receives sensations primarily from the right side of the body) and the right motor cortex (which exercises control over movement in the left half of the body). From Geschwind (1979).

(rigidity involving peculiar disturbance of posture, usually tonic in nature). Disorders of movement resulting from cerebellar damage typically take the form of some combination of the following abnormalities: loss of muscle tone; incoordination (ataxia) of volitional movement, particularly as a deficit in initiating or ending purposeful movement, along with errors in direction of volitional movement; minor degrees of muscle weakness, along with fatigability and impairment of associated movements; and disorders of equilibrium (impaired postural reflexes) and gait.

Sensory Function

Somatosensory. The various pathways involved in somesthesis are presented in figure 1.36. Typically, there are three main systems—(1) proprioception-stereognosis, (2) pain and temperature, and (3) touch. (See fig. 1.8 for a depiction of dermatomal segments that relate to pe-

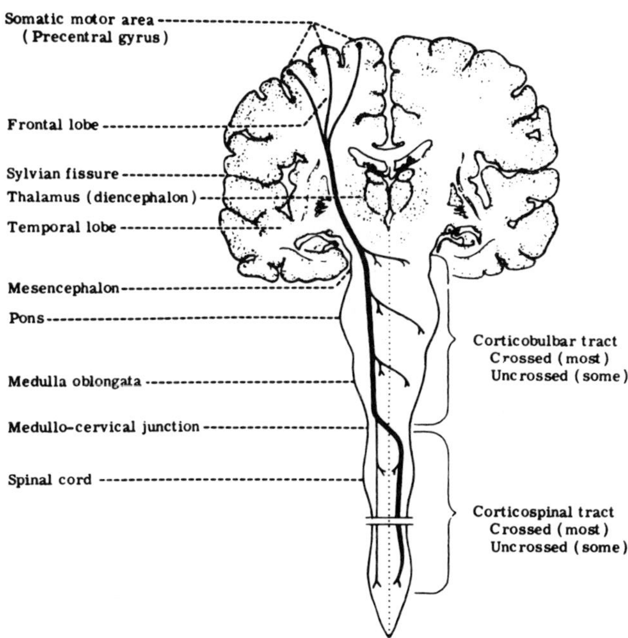

Fig. 1.32. Diagrammatic representation of the direct corticospinal (pyramidal) tract. From DeMyer (1974). Used with permission.

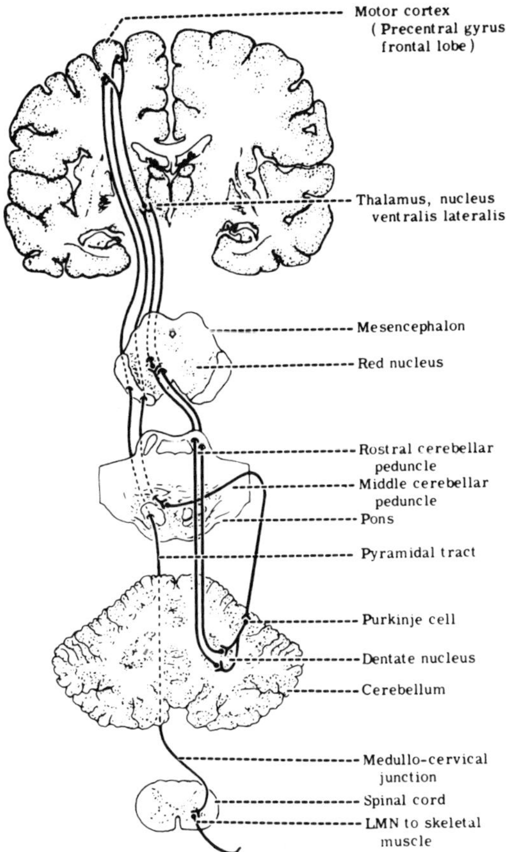

Fig. 1.33. Diagrammatic representation of some of the pathways and interconnections of the extrapyramidal motor system. From DeMyer (1974). Used with permission.

ripheral nerve innervation and sensory distribution over the body.)

In proprioception-stereognosis, input from muscles, tendons, joints, and attached ligaments provides critical kinesthetic feedback (position of limb and movement). Lesions at various levels may produce these deficits including the gracile and cuneate nuclei, medial lemniscus, thalamus, and postcentral gyrus. If the lesion is at or above the level of the thalamus, the common deficit is in stereognosis (form perception) with impairment or loss of ability to discriminate between various forms, finger localization, and graphesthesia (palm writing). Differentially, lesions below the level of the thalamus tend to affect more the ability to recognize limb position and to result in loss or diminution in two-point discrimination, loss of vibratory sense, and positive Romberg test findings. Skilled motor movement may also be affected because of impaired sensory feedback.

Figure 1.36 depicts the pain and temperature pathways. Deficits in temperature associated with alterations in pain thresholds in the absence of other sensory deficits are usually related to peripheral nerve dysfunction. Thus, while definitive cortical areas are involved in pain and temperature, it is more common for these to be affected by peripheral nerve involvement. Pain limited to one or more dermatomal areas is known as radicular pain. Dorsal root irritation may produce paresthesias or spontaneous sensations of prickling, tingling, numbness, or hyperesthesia (responsiveness to tactile stimulation being grossly exaggerated). If there is loss of peripheral nerve function, then hypesthesia (diminished sensitivity) may develop, which may progress to complete anesthesia.

Touch is represented by the direct spinothalamic tract (see fig. 1.36). Clinically this is determined by simple touch (pressure or absence by the use of a wisp of cotton or Von Frey hairs).

Audition

The auditory system is depicted in figure 1.37. Although there are fibers that remain ipsilateral to the side of input, functionally the auditory system develops in a contralateral fashion. Thus the left hemisphere maintains processing control and efficiency over the right ear and vice versa. Figure 1.38 shows a CAT scan of a patient with an acoustic neuroma. Recent electrophysiological advances have demonstrated that the brain stem auditory-evoked response (BAER) is an effective means of evaluating auditory system (brain stem–midbrain) integrity. This is depicted in figure 1.39.

Vision

The visual system is similar to the somatosensory and motor systems in that there is contralateral hemispheric control (see figs. 1.40–1.42). The pathways of the visual system (see Bigler, 1977) actually course the entire brain in an anterior-posterior plane (see figs. 1.40, 1.41, and 1.42). Similarly, lesions at various levels correspond to

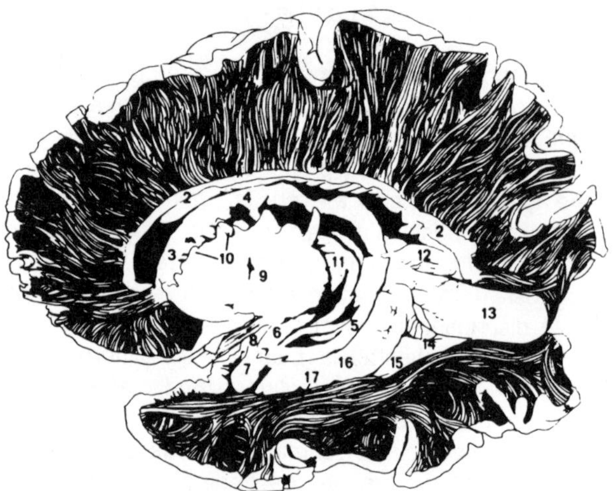

Fig. 1.34. Lateral view depicting the position of the major nuclei that form the basal ganglia. The parts include (1) corona radiata, (2) corpus callosum, (3) head of caudate nucleus, (4) body of caudate nucleus, (5) tail of caudate nucleus, (6) "foot" of lentiform nucleus, (7) amygdaloid nuclear complex, (8) optic tract, (9) putamen, (10) gray connections between putamen and caudate nucleus, (11) pulvinar of thalamus, (12) bulb of occipital horn of lateral ventricle, (13) calcar avis, (14) collateral trigone, (15) collateral eminence, (16) hippocampus, (17) inferior longitudinal fasciculus, and (18) short arcuate fibers. From Gluhbegovic and Williams (1980).

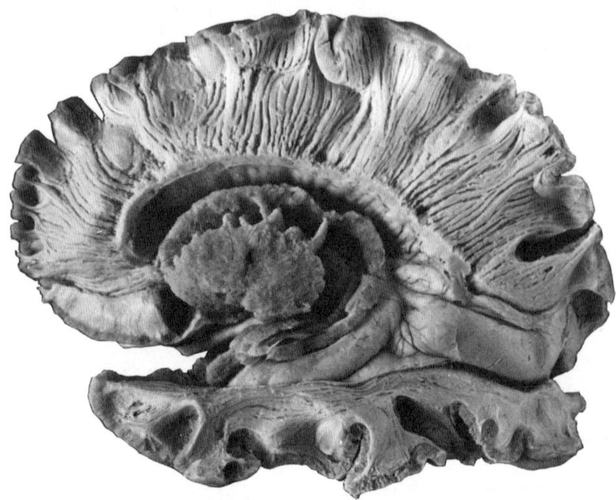

Fig. 1.35. Photograph of lateral view depicting the position of the major nuclei that form the basal ganglia and corresponding to fig. 1.34. From Gluhbegovic and Williams (1980).

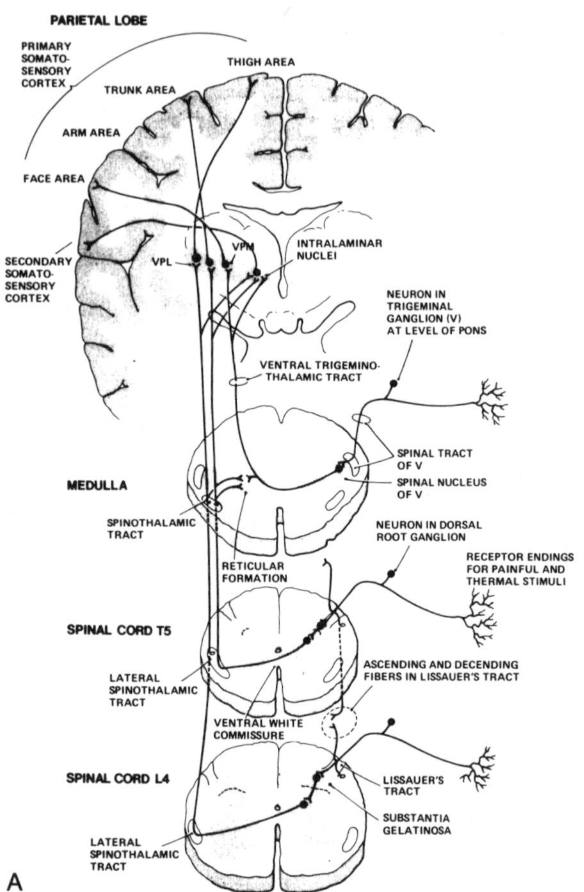

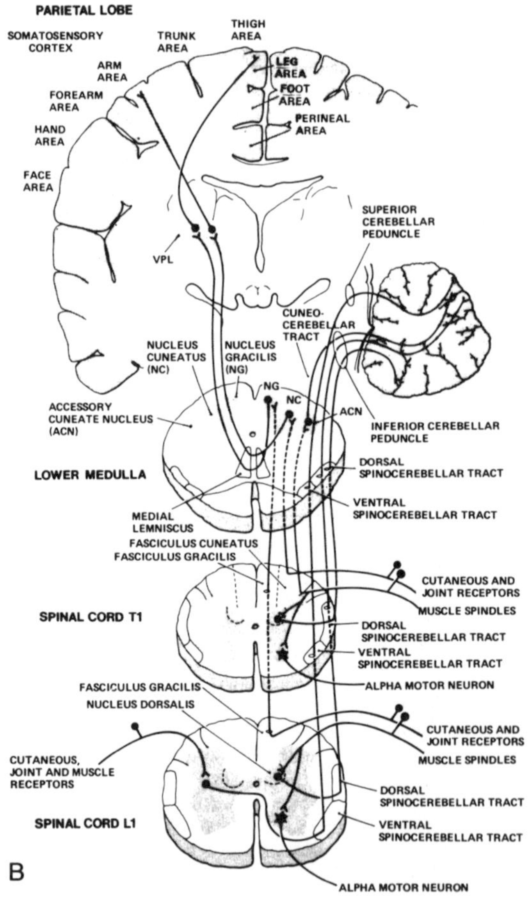

Fig. 1.36. Somatosensory system. *A*, somatosensory pathways involved in touch, pain, and temperature; *B*, somatosensory pathways involved in proprioception and stereognosis. From Gilman and Winans (1982).

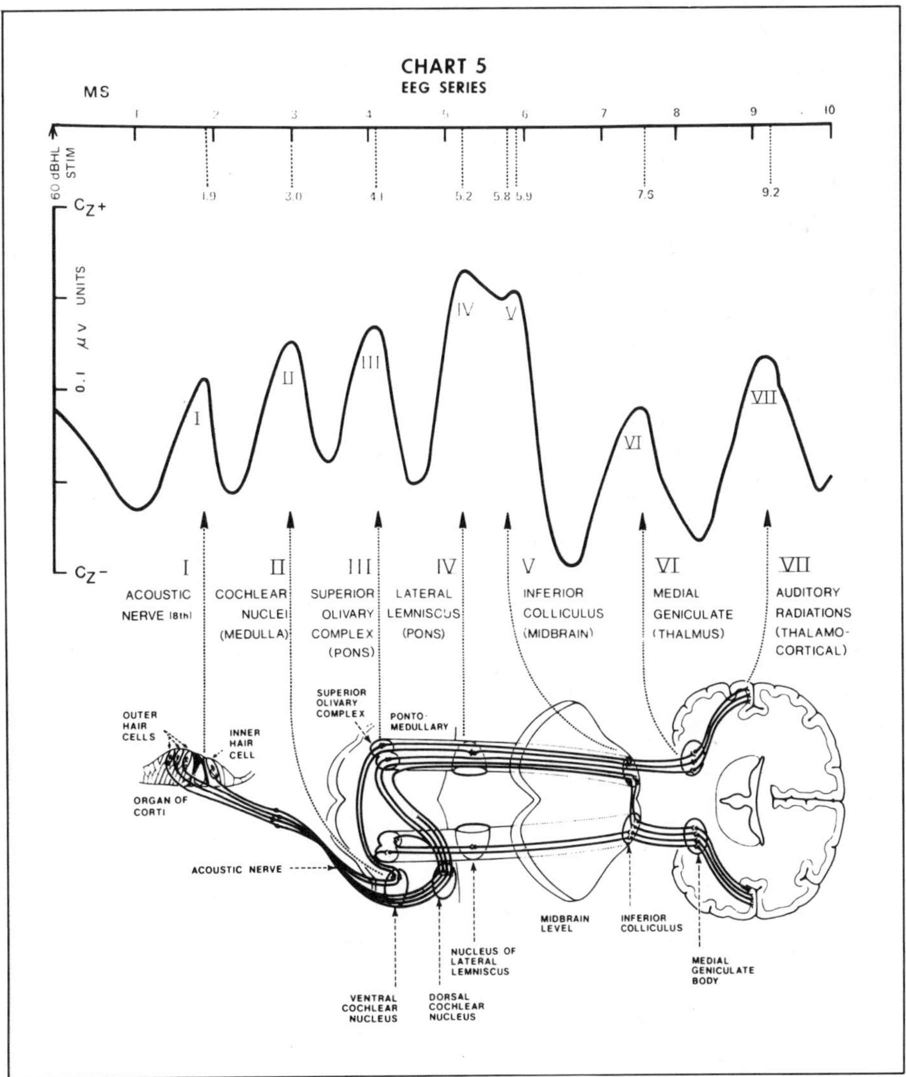

Fig. 1.37. Diagrammatic representation of the auditory projection system. Reprinted with permission from Grass Instruments.

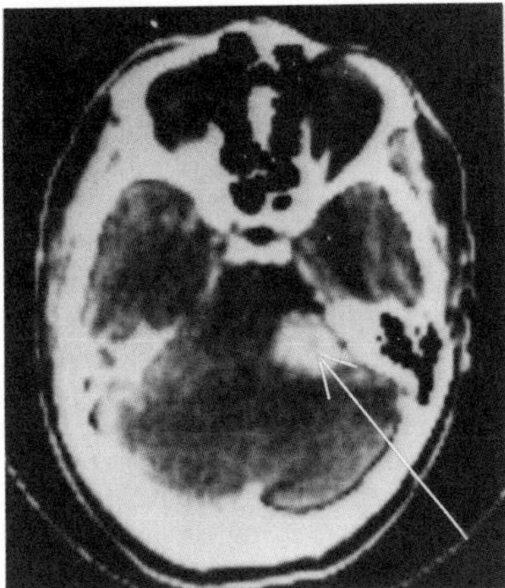

Fig. 1.38. CAT scan of a patient with an acoustic neuroma (*arrow*) in the cerebellopontine region.

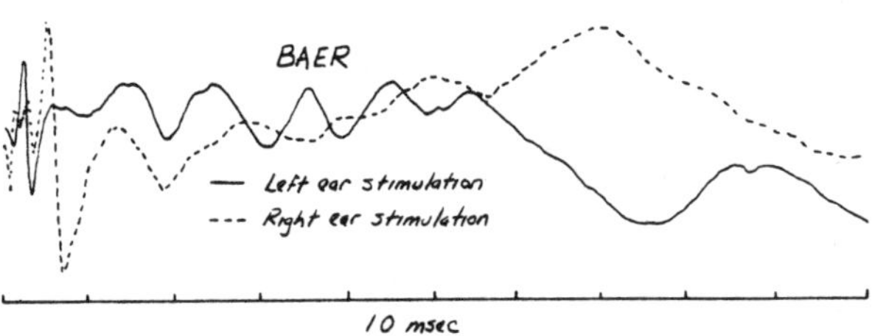

Fig. 1.39. Corresponding brain stem auditory-evoked response (BAER) test results of patient whose CAT scan is in fig. 1.38. Note the generally normal results until wave IV–V complex with left ear stimulation and the markedly abnormal BAER after wave I with right ear stimulation. Such findings specify the locus of pathology to be on the right side of the brain stem.

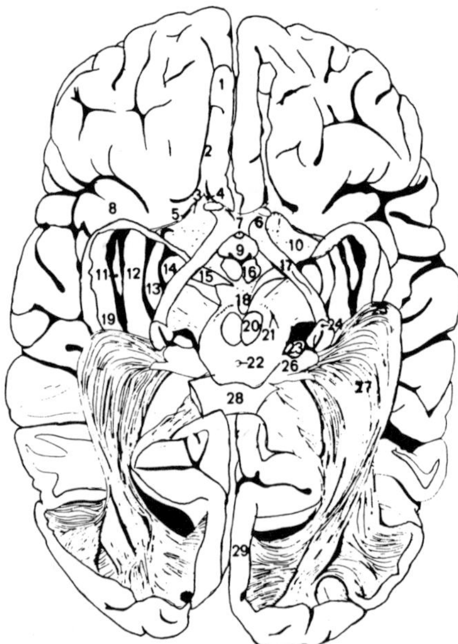

Fig. 1.40. Ventral view of the visual projection system with the temporal lobe dissected away. The parts labeled by numbers are (1) olfactory bulb, (2) olfactory tract, (3) olfactory trigone, (4) medial olfactory stria, (5) lateral olfactory stria, (6) optic nerve, (7) optic chiasma, (8) limen insulae, (9) tuber cinereum with infundibulum, (10) anterior (rostral) perforated substance, (11) claustrum, (12) putamen, (13) lateral part of globus pallidus, (14) medial part of globus pallidus, (15) basis pedunculi, (16) mamillary body, (17) optic tract, (18) posterior (interpeduncular) perforated substance, (19) cortex of insula, (20) superior cerebellar peduncle, (21) substantia nigra, (22) mesencephali (cerebral) aqueduct, (23) medial geniculate nucleus, (24) lateral geniculate nucleus, (25) temporal genu of optic radiation, (26) pulvinar of thalamus, (27) sagittal striatum, (28) splenium of corpus callosum, and (29) upper lip of calcarine sulcus. From Gluhbegovic and Williams (1980).

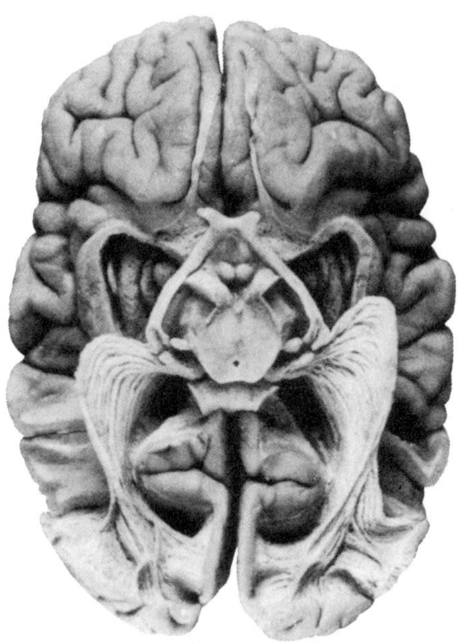

Fig. 1.41. Photograph of ventral view of the visual projection system with the temporal lobe dissected away. Compare with fig. 1.40. From Gluhbegovic and Williams (1980).

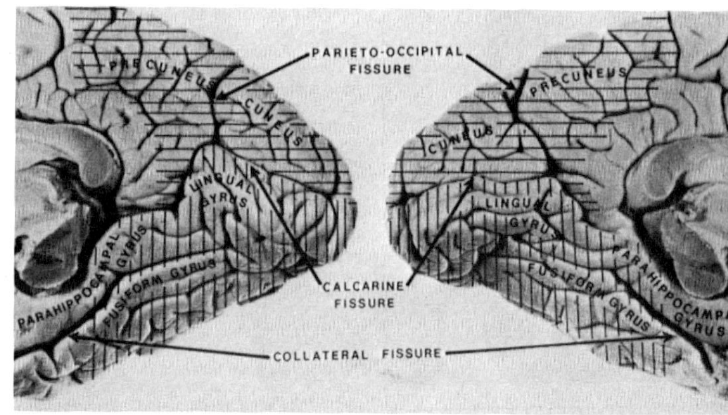

Fig. 1.43. Primary and association areas of the visual system that, when damaged, result in various neurobehavioral syndromes. The sections depicted are representative of a partial mesial view of both hemispheres of a human brain, showing major sulci and gyri. Cases of prosopagnosia and visual agnosia involve bilateral structures of the occipitotemporal region (*vertical hatching*) composed of lingual, fusiform, and parahippocampal gyri. Most cases of visual disorientation have bilateral lesions in the occipitoparietal region (*horizontal hatching*), which is composed of the cuneus and precuneus. Unilateral lesions of either occipitotemporal region can produce visual field defects (contralaterally) and hemiachromatopsia (also contralaterally). Unilateral lesions of the left occipitotemporal region often produce the syndrome of pure alexia (in patients with left cerebral dominance for language, provided that connections of the corpus callosum are also damaged). The asymmetry of cortical structures (note the calcarine fissures and lingual gyri) is striking, underscoring the unlikelihood of even hypothetically symmetric lesions producing entirely comparable field defects. From Damasio, Damasio, and Van Hoesen (1982).

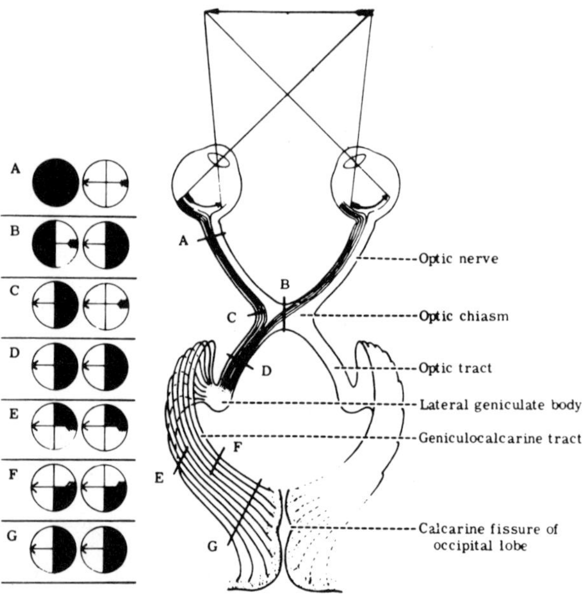

Fig. 1.42. Visual field defects and their relationship to visual system pathology. From DeMyer (1974). Used with permission.

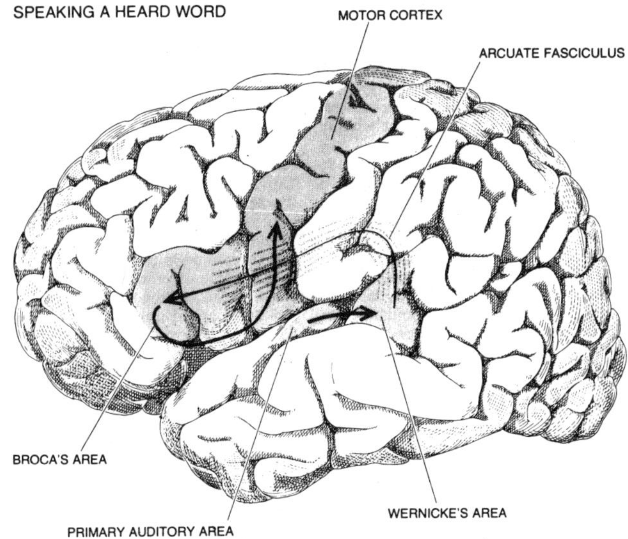

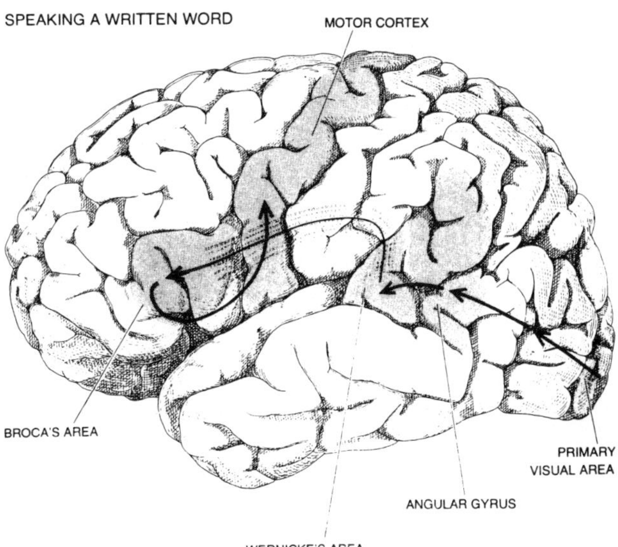

Fig. 1.44. Linguistic competence requires the cooperation of several areas of the cortex. When a word is heard (*upper diagram*), the sensation from the ears is received by the primary auditory cortex, but the word cannot be understood until the signal has been processed in Wernicke's area nearby. If the word is to be spoken, some representation of it is thought to be transmitted from Wernicke's area to Broca's area through a bundle of nerve fibers called the arcuate fasciculus. In Broca's area the word evokes a detailed program for articulation, which is supplied to the face area of the motor cortex. The motor cortex in turn drives the muscles of the lips, the tongue, the larynx, and so on. When a written word is read (*lower diagram*), the sensation is first registered by the primary visual cortex. It is then thought to be relayed to the angular gyrus, which associates the visual form of the word with the corresponding auditory pattern in Wernicke's area. Speaking the word then draws on the same systems of neurons as before. From Geschwind (1979).

specific visual field abnormalities, which in turn specify the locus of damage (see fig. 1.42). Since visual radiations from lateral geniculate pass through both parietal and temporal lobes on their way to termination in the visual cortex, the examination for visual field deficit is critical in determining cerebral pathology.

The complexity of visual experience and behavioral response to visual stimuli is dependent on the visual association areas of the cerebrum (see figs. 1.40–1.44). Benton (1979) has outlined (see below) three major associative processes and the related disorders that may accompany pathology in these areas.

I. Visuoperceptual
   A. Defective visual analysis and synthesis
   B. Visual object agnosia
   C. Impairment in facial recognition
      1. Facial agnosia (prosopagnosia)
      2. Defective discrimination of unfamiliar faces
   D. Impairment in color recognition
II. Visuospatial
   A. Defective localization of points in space
   B. Defective judgment of direction and distance
   C. Defective topographical orientation
   D. Unilateral visual neglect
III. Visuoconstructive
   A. Defective assembling performance
   B. Defective graphomotor performance

Basic visuoperceptual functioning is dependent upon the integrity of the direct visual projection system, and lesions within the projection system will produce the visual field defects outlined in figure 1.42. Incomplete involvement of the cortical visual projection areas may alter visual discrimination, there being some tendency for greater visual discrimination deficits with right hemisphere pathology. Deficits in color discrimination may also occur as well as deficits in color naming (color anomia) with lesions in the visual cortical projection system. Color anomia, however, may be more akin to a dysphasic disorder than visual discriminative dysfunction. Prosopagnosia (loss of ability to recognize familiar faces) has been frequently associated with visual discriminative deficits, and while some research has indicated greater right hemisphere occipital involvement, recent findings suggest the role of bilateral occipital pathology in the genesis of this syndrome (Damasio, Damasio, and Van Hoesen, 1982; see also fig. 1.43).

Visuospatial functioning typically is subsumed as involving integrative processes of temporal-parietal-occipital visual associative areas. Deficits in such functions as impaired perception or judgment of direction and distance, impaired geographic and topographic discrimination, deficits in defining points in space, and unilateral neglect of the contralateral body side may accompany damage in these regions. In general, the nondominant right hemisphere plays more of a role in the integration of these functions, and this occurs as a rather nonspecific process (see Kertesz and Dobrowolski, 1981). When visuospatial deficits do occur as a result of right cerebral infarction, the degree of impairment is, in part, related to the size of the lesion and, in older individuals, the degree of preexisting cerebral atrophy (Levine et al., 1986).

Visuoconstructive functioning is related to visuospatial functioning, with similar cerebral areas subserving both these functions. Visuoconstructive deficits are typically seen in terms of impaired figure copying or drawing or deficits in manipulative assembly of objects. Visuospatial deficits are typically manifested in terms of impaired spatial awareness or environmental or directional disorientation. While there is greater tendency for these deficits to be expressed with right hemisphere pathology, visuopraxic and visuoconstructive deficits may be seen in association with left hemisphere involvement, which is typically associated with aphasia (Basso et al., 1981).

Ojemann and his colleagues (see Fried et al., 1982) have demonstrated that in terms of visuospatial functions these functions are somewhat specifically localized in the right hemisphere in a manner somewhat analogous to language function in the left hemisphere. From their studies of direct cortical stimulation they have shown that the superior temporal gyrus region is critical for short-term processing of visuospatial functions. Perceptual processing of visuospatial information was also found to be dependent upon the parieto-occipital junctional area. The inferior frontal region in the right hemisphere, the homologue of Broca's area in the left, was found to be critical for the verbal expression of spatial information and thereby represents a visuospatial-verbal link.

Olfaction

The olfactory nerve passes through the olfactory bulb to the amygdala, terminating in the piriform lobe (the anterior aspect of the parahippocampal gyrus and the uncus of the temporal lobe) (see figs. 1.16 and 1.17). Some olfactory nerve projections course initially to the contralateral olfactory nerve. Thus there are both ipsilateral and contralateral olfactory impulses impinging on olfactory cortex. From the piriform cortex there are projections to the medial dorsal nucleus of the thalamus and also to the hypothalamus. Much of the olfactory system constitutes critical structures of the limbic system (see figs. 1.16 and 1.17) and thus has a role in emotional integration. Intactness of the olfactory nerve can be tested by common nonirritating olfactory stimuli such as vanilla extract, peppermint oil, coffee, lemon, or other similar stimuli. Recently, "scratch and sniff" tests of olfactory function have been developed, yielding a more objective assessment of smell (Doty, Shaman, and Dann, 1984). While the most common cause for the loss of smell (anosmia) is sinus infection, damage to the floor of the anterior skull or compression of the nerve by a space-occupying lesion may cause anosmia.

Gustation

The anterior two-thirds of the tongue is innervated by the lingual division of the fifth cranial nerve, the posterior one-third being supplied by the seventh. There are four primary qualities of taste: sweet, salt, sour, and bitter. All taste is a combination of these qualities. The anterior aspect of the tongue is most sensitive to sweet; the back, bitter; and side, sour. Salt taste sensation of the tongue is rather ubiquitous. Taste is usually examined by using salt or sugar crystals applied to the tongue, but ageusia (loss of taste) is a rare neurologic entity and of little value in neuropsychologic assessment.

Language Function

The cerebral hemispheres, while possessing considerable anatomic similarity, functionally are quite different (Geschwind and Galaburda, 1985 *a, b, c*). The left hemisphere, even in most left-handed individuals, is the controlling or dominant hemisphere for language. The right hemisphere thus functions primarily in terms of nonverbal, more spatial-performance–oriented functions. Because language represents one of the highest levels of cerebral organization, the examination of language disorders has always been of critical importance in neuropsychological examination. Damage to various brain regions may produce aphasia, the loss or impairment of language caused by damage or dysfunction to certain brain regions. The various syndromes of aphasia are displayed in table 1.1, and figure 1.45 depicts critical brain regions involved in different linguistic processes. Apraxia, or the loss of ability to carry out purposive, skilled acts even though sensory and motor systems remain intact, is frequently associated with damage to brain regions that also produce aphasia, although apraxic disturbance may result in the absence of language impairments (DeRenzi, Faglioni, and Sorgato, 1982). Because of the proximity of Broca's area to the primary motor cortex, a right hemiparesis or hemiplegia is commonly associated with an expressive aphasia, although it need not always be present (Henderson, 1985). The inability to learn to comprehend written or printed words is termed alexia. Alexia or dyslexia (partial deficit) may be a feature of various aphasic disorders, but likewise the primary deficit may be in reading itself without severe deficit in other language functions.

The complexity of language can be appreciated by reviewing figure 1.44, which depicts the rudimentary connections required for naming a seen word. First, the visual image is processed by visual cortex. Visual cortical processing along with input from visual association areas (see figs. 1.46 and 1.47) is then transferred to the angular gyrus, which possesses memory functions to appropriately retrieve auditory pattern recognition in Wernicke's area. This information is, in turn, transmitted through the arcuate fasciculus to the motor association (Broca's) area. At this point, motor centers involved in the expression of language are stimulated, and the stimulation is trans-

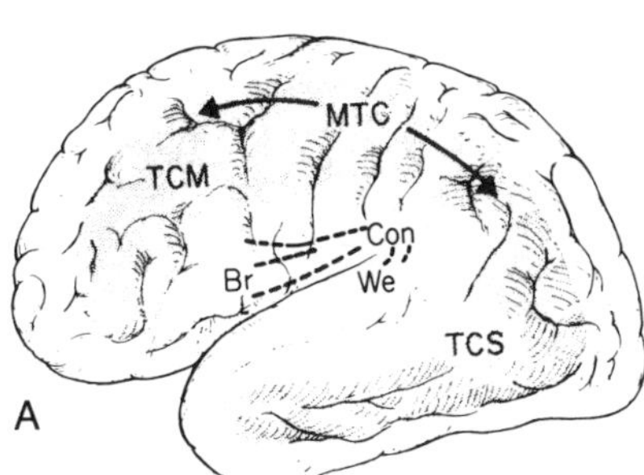

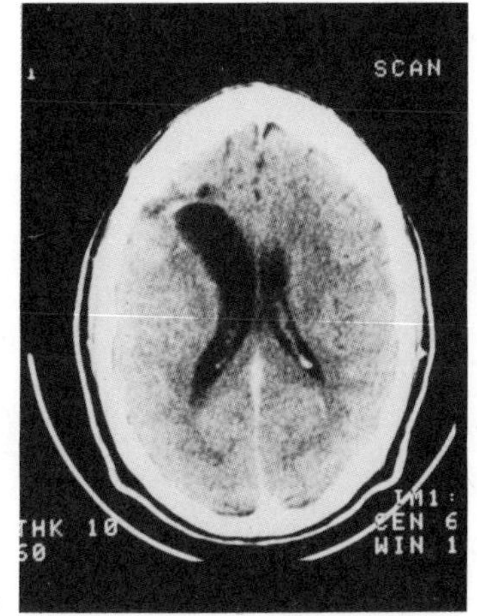

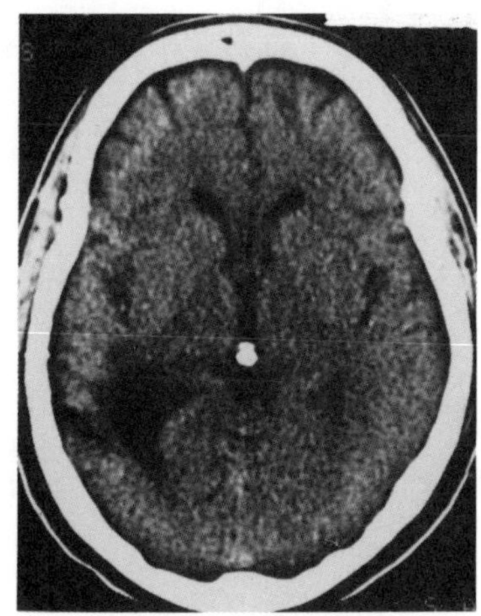

Fig. 1.45. *A*, lateral surface of left cerebral hemisphere indicating areas in which damage most often produces specific aphasia syndromes. The entire area enclosed by stippling is in the distribution of the left middle cerebral artery and represents the language area. The outer stippled area can be considered border zone and the inner white is the perisylvian area. Abbreviations: BR, Broca; Con, conduction; We, Wernicke; TCM, transcortical motor; TCS, transcortical sensory; MTC, mixed transcortical. From Benson (1979). *B*, the CAT scan on the left is from a patient with a chronic Broca's aphasia. The patient suffered a spontaneous intracerebral hemorrhage as a result of a rupture involving the anterior distribution of the left middle cerebral artery. The scan to the right is from a patient with a chronic Wernicke's aphasia. This patient suffered a spontaneous intracerebral hemorrhage involving the posterior distribution of the left middle cerebral artery. In the patient with Broca's aphasia, notice the abnormal enlargement of the anterior segment of the lateral ventricle extending into the frontal region and with some encephalomalacia (brain wasting) surrounding the anterior extension. In the patient with Wernicke's aphasia, notice the dilation of the posterior horn and surrounding encephalomalacic changes. Note also that in this patient there is no change or malconfiguration of the anterior ventricular structures or anterior cerebral regions.

Table 1.1. ***Aphasia Syndromes***

	Perisylvian Aphasia Syndromes			Borderline Aphasia Syndromes Transcortical Aphasia			Nonlocalizing Aphasia Syndromes	
Test Function	Broca's	Wernicke's	Conduction	Motor	Sensory	Mixed	Anomic	Global
Conversational speech	Nonfluent	Fluent but paraphrasic	Fluent, paraphrasic	Nonfluent	Fluent, paraphrasic, echolalic	Nonfluent with echolalia	Fluent but empty	Severely disturbed
Comprehension of spoken language	Relatively normal	Abnormal	Good to normal	Relatively normal	Severely defective	Severely defective	Normal to mildly defective	Severely disturbed
Repetition of spoken language	Abnormal	Abnormal	Abnormal	Good to normal	Good to excellent	Good	Good	Severely disturbed
Confrontation-naming	Abnormal	Abnormal	Usually normal	Defective	Defective	Severely defective	Defective	Severely disturbed
Reading Aloud	Abnormal	Abnormal	Abnormal	Defective	Defective	Defective	Good or defective	Severely disturbed
Comprehension	Normal or abnormal	Abnormal	Good to normal	Often good	Defective	Defective	Good or defective	Severely disturbed
Writing	Abnormal	Abnormal	Abnormal	Defective	Defective	Defective	Good or defective	Severely disturbed

Source: Adapted from Benson (1979).

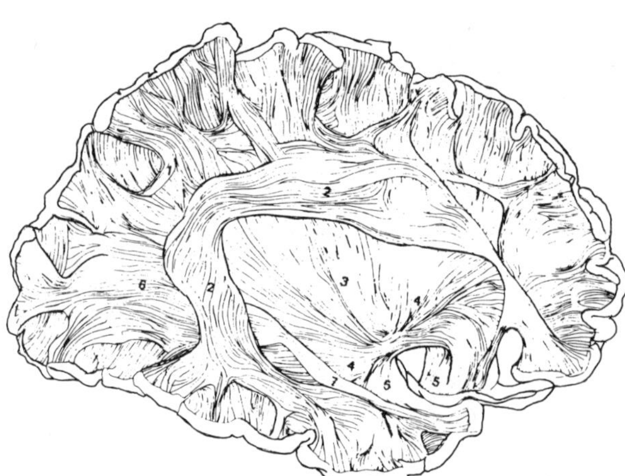

Fig. 1.46. Association fiber tracts: (1) short arcuate fibers, (2) superior longitudinal fascicle, (3) external capsule, (4) inferior occipitofrontal fascicle, (5) uncinate fascicle, (6) sagittal stratum, and (7) inferior longitudinal fasciculus. From Gluhbegovic and Williams (1980).

Fig. 1.47. Photograph of association fiber tracts. Compare with fig. 1.46. From Gluhbegovic and Williams (1980).

ferred to specific facial motor areas in the precentral gyrus. If left side movement is required, then transfer across the corpus callosum must occur.

The neurogenic disorders of language can be delineated along several different characteristics of language including fluency, repetition of language, comprehension, naming, and reading. These five areas will be discussed fully in later chapters. The following section summarizes the comprehensive works of Benson (1979), Geschwind (1972), and Albert et al. (1981).

Fluency. Nonfluent aphasic output is usually accomplished only with great effort and paucity of output, with word output usually less than ten words per minute (normal is 100–150 words per minute). Accompanying the struggle to speak, there may be facial grimacing, hand or body gesturing, along with severe articulation (dysarthric) disturbance. The speech is frequently "telegraphic," usually being single words uttered with impaired melody and rhythm. Although word output is severely affected, the words expressed may convey appropriate meaning. As depicted in figure 1.45, frontal lobe damage, particularly in the inferior, posterior region, produces these symptoms. Ludlow et al. (1986) have demonstrated that, in addition to damage to this area, patients with nonfluent aphasia associated with penetrating injury who do not recover fluency have lesions that extend into basal ganglia and posterior language areas, as well.

Quite oppositely, the patient with fluent aphasia displays distinctly nondysarthric speech that is flowing and effortless, but with notably empty content and meaning. Word output is in the normal range or even elevated. Phrase length will be normal (five to eight words) with normal melodic tone. Meaningful words are absent with frequent circumlocution. Paraphasic speech is commonplace. Paraphasic disturbance may take the form of a literal or phonemic substitution (substitution of one syllable for another), a verbal or semantic substitution (substitution of one word for another), or neologistic speech (substitution of a meaningless nonsense word). Speech may be pressured and this coupled with the meaningless content results in the fluent aphasic's speech appearing "empty." Figure 1.45 outlines the areas of cerebral damage, most typically in posterior regions, that produce this type of language disturbance.

Below is an example of paraphasic speech in a fluent aphasic patient. The patient was a 27-year-old, high school–educated male who sustained diffuse cerebral injury as a result of a motor vehicle accident. The following passage was a spontaneous response and is characteristic of fluent paraphasia: "I love off thime that thinp when thinp that I lofe as coffe out."

Paraphasic speech can occur in the patient with nonfluent aphasia, but it is typically in the form of a phonemic substitution with background articulatory disturbance. In fact, the phonemic substitution may be directly related to incorrect articulatory expression and thus not represent true paraphasia. Also, the patient with nonfluent aphasia may be aware that what is being said is incorrect, whereas patients with fluent aphasia may be oblivious to their failure in communication.

Repetition. Disease in the perisylvian region may result in abnormal repetition of spoken words (Selnes et al., 1985). Aphasia with normal repetition is typically associated with pathology outside this central region. Thus, within the perisylvian region, there are three types of major aphasic syndromes in which repetition may be affected—Broca's aphasia, Wernicke's aphasia, and conduction aphasia. As previously reviewed, Broca's aphasia is most commonly associated with pathologic changes in the posterior-inferior frontal lobe. Wernicke's aphasia most commonly occurs secondary to pathologic changes in the posterior-superior temporal region. Conduction aphasia, as its name implies, is a mixture of Broca's and Wernicke's aphasic disturbances because the changes that produce this syndrome typically occur within the arcuate fasciculus (the pathway between Wernicke's area and Broca's area) (see figs. 1.44–1.46).

Comprehension. Benson (1979) delimits four main types of comprehension deficits in aphasia: receptive, perceptive, semantic, and syntactic/sequential. In receptive comprehension deficits, a severe defect in simple comprehension and repetition of language is present (so-called pure word deafness), but reading comprehension is intact. Pathology in this type of comprehension deficit typically involves the Heschl's gyral region of the dominant temporal lobe or its afferent input. In perceptive comprehension disorders, the disability is more extensive and involves comprehension, repetition, *and* reading (frequently marked), with the underlying pathology usually of temporal-parietal origin. Semantic comprehension deficits are seen in the form of comprehension and reading impairments but with preserved repetition. Additionally, there may be intact the ability to comprehend general information or concepts, but an impaired ability to comprehend single words. Pathology is usually in parietal-temporal border zone regions, the angular gyrus, and its connections to posterior-inferior temporal cortex. Syntactic/sequential comprehension deficits, as their name implies, are typically manifested in the form of deficits in phrase or sentence comprehension, with single-word comprehension being relatively spared. In its "pure" form this comprehension deficit usually involves the dominant frontal lobe. Regardless of the type of comprehension deficit, there may be varying degrees of deficits present, and in clinical practice isolated comprehension disorders are relatively uncommon. Thus, the clinical picture that more typically is seen is one of partial deficit or a mixture of syndromes.

Naming. Naming difficulties are commonplace in the aphasic disorders. Benson (1979) outlines five potential clinical subgroups of naming disability—word production, word selection, semantic, category-specific, and modality-specific. In *word production anomia* there is an inability to produce the correct word even though the patient may appear to know what the word is. Prompting may facilitate naming. In these cases the difficulty is in expressing the word, and thus the underlying pathology is usually frontal or involves projective pathways to Broca's region. *Word selection anomia* refers to deficits in saying the appropriate word, although the patient may be able to correctly select the word when given several choices. This has also been termed *word dictionary anomia* with the pathology typically involving posterior temporal regions. *Semantic anomia* is similar to word selection anomia, but the patient is even unable to correctly select or identify the correct word when given choices. In this syndrome, the dominant angular gyrus is usually involved. With *category-specific anomia* names from one category are misnamed or substituted for others from another category with different meaning. *Modality-specific anomia* occurs within a single modality of sensory input: for example, being unable to name in visual confrontation but able to do so in the tactile modality. In category- and modality-specific anomic disorders, either a posterior association language area or its afferent input is involved. Recently, Lüders et al. (1986) demonstrated severe anomia following direct electrical stimulation of the left basal temporal gyrus in a patient being operated on for intractable epilepsy.

Reading. In a general sense, three variates of alexia can be distinguished based on underlying pathologic locus: frontal, parietal-temporal, and occipital. With frontal pathology there is usually a Broca's aphasia, the reading deficit is usually partial or incomplete, and the most substantial deficit is grammatical comprehension of word context within a sentence. Temporal-parietal involvement may result in an alexia with agraphia syndrome in which the patient is unable to read or write. In alexia without agraphia (usually in association with a right homonymous hemianopsia) the patient has a striking dichotomy of symptoms: the patient cannot read but can write and spell, frequently being able to correctly write a sentence (either spontaneously or on command) but unable to read what she has just written (see case 5 in chapter 3). Pathology in this syndrome usually resides within the medial-occipital region of the dominant hemisphere and the splenium of the corpus callosum.

Damasio and Damasio (1983) have reviewed several cases of pure alexia. The underlying pathology crucial for the expression of pure alexia appears to reside in the paraventricular white matter of the left occipital lobe, with the lesion disrupting both inter- and intrahemispheric visual pathways (see also Henderson, 1985; Henderson et al., 1985). Damasio and Damasio also demonstrated that color anomia was related to damage in the mesial occipital temporal junction of the left hemisphere. Regard, Landis, and Hess (1985) presented an interesting case of pure alexia in a patient who premorbidly was an expert stenographer who suffered cerebral metastases involving the left occipital region. He could still read stenographic print, indicating intact visual-spatial processing of the right hemisphere in "alternative" reading. Such cases indicate that the deficit in pure alexia may be specific to the processing of lexical symbols.

Subcortical Lesions and Aphasia

As stated previously, a variety of subcortical lesions may produce aphasia. Damage to, in, or around the internal capsule, basal ganglia, or thalamus may produce aphasic symptoms (Tanridag and Kirshner, 1985). This is particularly true when the lesions involve these subcortical structures within the dominant hemisphere.

Aphasia in Left Handers. Many left-handed patients maintain ipsilateral language functions within the left cerebral hemisphere (Geschwind and Galaburda, 1985). However, Naeser and Borod (1986) have shown various combinations of mixed language dominance in left-handed individuals who developed aphasia after a stroke. Some patients even had Broca's area localized to the right frontal, but Wernicke's remained in the left cerebral hemisphere. For the clinician examining the left-handed patient, one needs to keep these particular relationships in mind and to remember that even patients with familial history of left-handedness may not have complete right hemisphere dominance for language.

Cranial Nerves

Emerging, in general, at the level of the brain stem are the cranial nerves, which occur in pairs. Several of the cranial nerves have already been discussed (i.e., optic, olfactory, and acoustic); table 1.2 summarizes cranial nerve function and figure 1.48 depicts position of various cranial nerves.

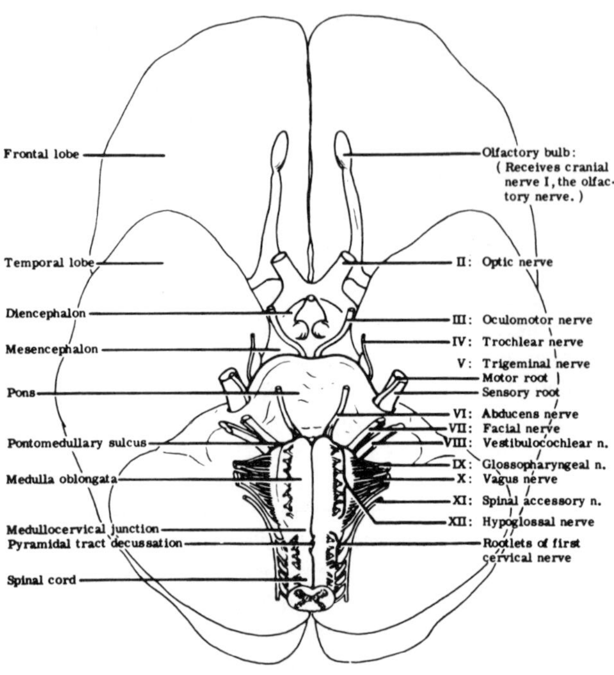

Fig. 1.48. Diagram indicating the relative position of the twelve cranial nerves. From DeMyer (1974). Used with permission.

Table 1.2. ***Cranial Nerves and Function***

Number and Name of Nerve			Main Function	Tests	Signs of Dysfunction
I	Olfactory	S	Olfaction (smell)	Detection of odor	Anosmia
II	Optic	S	Vision	Visual acuity, visual field	Anopsia
III	Oculomotor	M	Eye movement	Lateral eye movements, lid retraction, pupillary responses	Outward deviation, ptosis, pupillary dilation
IV	Trochlear	M	Eye movement	Vertical eye movements	Outward and downward deviation impaired
V	Trigeminal	S, M	Muscles of mastication, sensory to jaw	Facial touch, temperature discrimination, jaw reflex, corneal reflex	Facial numbness and paralysis, brief attacks of severe pain (trigeminal neuralgia—tic douloureux)
VI	Abducens	M	Eye movement	Lateral eye movements	Medial deviation
VII	Facial	M	Facial movement	Facial movement	Asymmetric facial movement, facial paralysis
VIII	Auditory-vestibular	S	Hearing, body position	Hearing tests, BAER,[a] vestibular-equilibrium tests	Deafness, disequilibrium
IX	Glossopharyngeal	S, M	Movement of tongue and pharynx	Taste and gag reflex	Loss of taste, upper pharynx anesthesia
X	Vagus	S, M	Innervation of internal viscera and movement of larynx and pharynx	Palatal reflexes, gag reflex	Hoarseness, lower pharynx anesthesia, visceral disturbance
XI	Spinal accessory	M	Neck muscles and efferent viscera	Movement and tonic control of neck and shoulder muscles	Wasting of neck and shoulder muscles, inability to shrug
XII	Hypoglossal	M	Tongue movements	Tongue movement	Tongue atrophy or deviation

Note: S, sensory; M, motor.
[a]BAER, brain stem auditory-evoked response test.

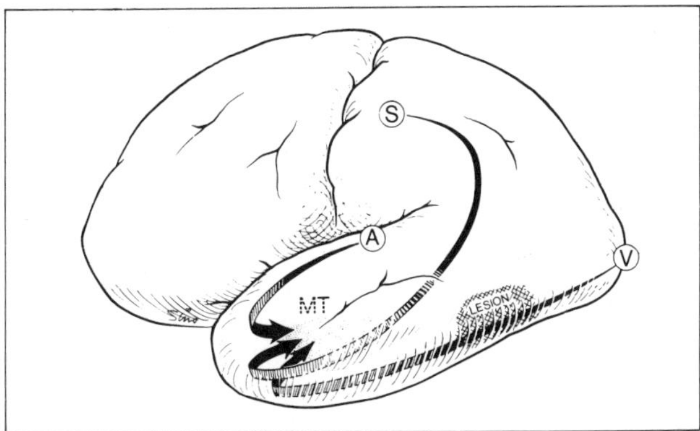

Fig. 1.49. Schematic drawing demonstrating separate but converging anatomical routes from the primary sensory cortices to the medial-temporal lobe. If a lesion bilaterally disrupts the visual, somatosensory, or auditory cortices from accessing the medial-temporal lobe, then a sensory-specific disorder of recent memory will result. From Ross (1982).

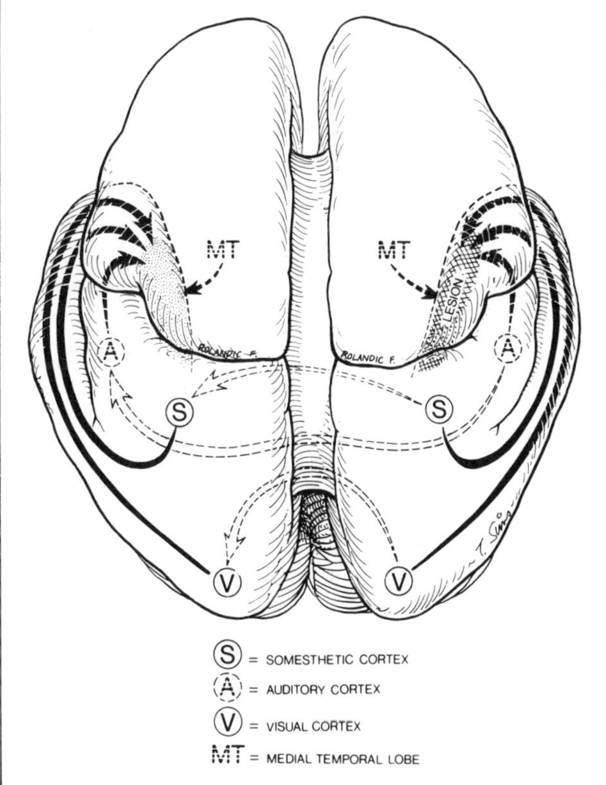

Fig. 1.50. Schematic drawing demonstrating callosal pathways between sensory areas (*opened dashed arrows*) and the converging pathways to medial-temporal lobe (*solid arrows*). If a unilateral lesion occurs in medial-temporal lobe, then a fractional disturbance of recent memory results. Recovery may take place if connections from sensory areas in lesioned hemisphere (*opened dashed arrows*) can be strengthened to contralateral medial-temporal lobe. From Ross (1982).

Corpus Callosum (Callosal Syndromes)

As previously outlined, the two cerebral hemispheres are interconnected by the myelinated, and thereby white, fiber tracts that constitute the corpus callosum. Interhemispheric communication is dependent upon the corpus callosum. Thus, when the corpus callosum is damaged, there may be disconnection between the right and left hemispheres (Kinsbourne and Smith, 1974). Bogen's review (1979) of the callosal syndromes provides further detail of the role of the corpus callosum in transferring and integrating information (see also Gazzaniga et al., 1985).

When the corpus callosum is damaged, interesting behavioral syndromes may develop. For example, words or objects presented to the right visual field will be readily read or identified. However, similar information presented to the left visual field cannot be verbally identified, although the object can be touched and matched with similar objects with the left hand. This dichotomy demonstrates the disconnection of left hemisphere language areas from the right hemisphere. Similarly, if a dichotic listening task is utilized, only words presented to the right ear (therefore requiring left temporal lobe processing) will be recognized. In motor faculties, a left-hand dyspraxia may be present, resulting from isolation of frontal motor regions of the nondominant right hemisphere from the verbal command analyzers of the left hemisphere. Likewise, objects touched by the right hand can be verbally identified and also matched to other objects by touch or function. However, identical objects presented to the left hand can only be tactilely or functionally matched and not verbally identified. Again, this condition results from disconnection of dominant verbal language areas.

Other features of the callosum syndrome may be as follows: *intermanual conflict* in which one hand performs one task while the other performs a counterproductive or opposing task (e.g., one hand buttoning a shirt, the other unbuttoning). The nondominant hand may be perceived by the patient as an "alien" hand in that it will not follow appropriate commands. *Unilateral (left) agraphia* will be present with the nondominant hand only. *Unilateral (right) constructional apraxia* will be present with the dominant hand because of left hemisphere disconnection from right hemisphere visuospatial centers.

Memory Systems

Anatomic substrates of memory have not been clearly delimited because of the divergent complexity of higher cognitive processes involved in memory (Tulving, 1985). Thus, unlike motor and sensory systems, there is not an underlying and anatomically distinct "memory" system, although it is well established that damage to the medial aspect of the temporal lobe or midline diencephalon produces impaired memory function (Squire, 1986). There is abundant information, however, that limbic-temporal structures are critical for certain aspects of memory processing and retrieval (Russell, 1981; Squire, 1982; see fig. 1.16). It is also apparent that intact memory abilities are also dependent upon whole-brain integrity and that there are also hemispheric differences, left hemisphere deficits affecting verbal memory and right hemisphere dysfunction affecting visual-spatial-perceptual aspects of memory (see figs. 1.49 and 1.50, and 1.16 and 1.17).

The memory process can be divided into several different stages, and accordingly memory can be disrupted at any stage or level. The first stage is, of course, at the sensation or perception level. This initial information, called a memory trace, is immediately held in a brief sensory register. The information is rapidly processed for its significance, and if significant then an immediate interface between this sensory memory process and short-term memory (STM) occurs. Short-term memory comprises an immediate memory component, which initially stores the memory trace, and a retrieval system. If the information is not utilized, the memory trace may decay. If, however, it continues to possess significance, then a long-term memory (LTM) process ensues. Consolidation of the memory trace is thus an intermediate phase involving aspects of both STM and LTM. The final process if memory is to be retained is an effective retrieval system.

Considerable speculation about underlying anatomic loci of memory processes comes from the work done with patients having Wernicke-Korsakoff syndrome. The initial aspects of this syndrome begin with the triad of symptoms of ophthalmoplegia, ataxia, and mental confusion. The pathologic substrates have been well documented and include symmetrical lesions in the paraventricular regions of the thalamus and hypothalamus; mamillary bodies; the periaqueductal region of the midbrain; and the floor of the fourth ventricle, particularly in the regions of dorsal motor nuclei of the vagus and vestibular nuclei of the superior vermis. These lesions are usually associated with thiamine (vitamin B) deficiency, but may result from such other disorders as neoplasia, vascular conditions, or infectious diseases. The ensuing Korsakoff's psychosis is manifested by both anterograde and retrograde amnesia, frequently in the absence of other marked cognitive deficits. The anterograde amnesia is by far the most marked deficit, with the patient being essentially unable to process any short-term information. These clinical studies, as well as others (see Butters, 1979), make it apparent that the hippocampus, mamillary bodies, and mesial thalamus are critical to short-term memory processing, and pathology either within this system or in other specific structures may disrupt memory function. Thus, a patient with specific short-term memory deficits in the relative absence of other cognitive deficits may have pathology at this level. It should also be noted that the relationship between memory disturbance and emotional disturbance is due to the similar role of limbic structures in both disorders.

The hippocampus (see fig. 1.51) is rich in acetylcholine (Mesulam et al., 1986). Integrity of such cholinergic pathways is essential to normal memory functioning and, oppositely, is the basis of many memory disorders. Squire (1986) presents data on a case of severe anterograde amnesia secondary to ischemic damage to the hippocampus in a patient who was otherwise cognitively intact. During the five years that he lived post stroke, this patient was followed and tested repeatedly. There was no change or improvement in his short term memory functioning. At his death, histological examination revealed circumscribed bilateral lesions of the hippocampus in a position (i.e., CA 1 field) so as to disrupt hippocampal output. Squire argues that this lesion site significantly disrupted the interaction between the hippocampus and memory storage sites, thereby disrupting the consolidation and storage of new information. Cummings et al. (1984) demonstrated similar results in a patient with anoxic brain damage that was restricted to the hippocampus, bilaterally.

The role of the fornix has been demonstrated to be a critical structure in memory functioning as well. Grafman et al. (1985) demonstrated both incoding and recall deficits in a patient with traumatic penetrating injury that severed the columns of the fornix but produced no temporal lobe damage (although there was some minimal thalamic damage). Thus, damage restricted to the fornix may also produce impaired memory functioning.

Damage to the basal forebrain region, including the septal nuclei, nucleus accumbens, and substantia innominata, also disrupts memory functioning (Damasio, Graff-Radford, et al., 1985; Salazar et al., 1986). When the damage extends beyond the basal forebrain, to include bilateral temporal lobe damage, marked retrograde as well as anterograde amnesia may develop (Damasio, Eslinger, et al., 1985). Risse, Rubens, and Jordan (1984) have also demonstrated that the inferior frontal lobe and basal ganglia may be critical in the initiation of the retrieval

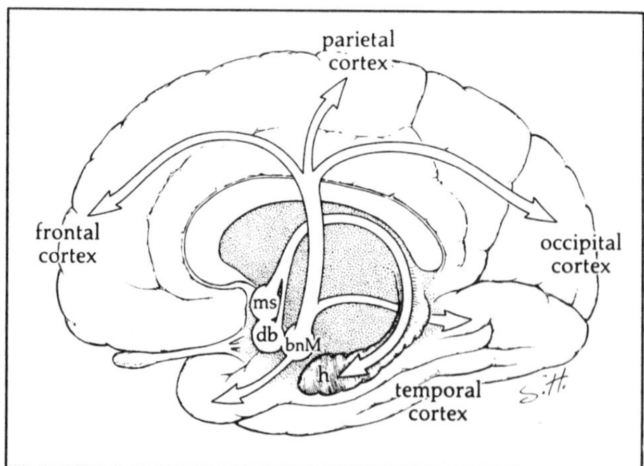

Fig. 1.51. Cholinergic innervation of cerebral cortex and hippocampus (h) from basal forebrain nuclei: medial septal nucleus (ms), diagonal band of Broca (db), and basal nucleus of Meynert (bnM). From Schwartz (1985).

process of memory. Salazar et al. (1986) present evidence that the basal forebrain is functionally related to the reticular formation and to the limbic-hippocampal memory system and that it is the disruption of this system that produces the specific memory disorder when damage is restricted to the basal forebrain. This also explains why such patients may demonstrate a rather marked memory disorder but show no specific deficit in terms of intellectual impairment.

References

Albert, M. L., H. Goodglass, N. A. Helm, A. B. Rubens, and M. P. Alexander. 1981. *Clinical aspects of dysphasia*. Disorders of Human Communication, vol. 2. New York: Springer-Verlag, 1981.

Angevine, J. B., and C. W. Cotman. 1981. *Principles of neuroanatomy*. New York: Oxford University Press.

Basso, A., E. Capitani, C. Luzzatti, and H. Spinnler. 1981. Intelligence and left hemisphere disease: The role of aphasia, apraxia, and size of lesion. *Brain* 104:721–734.

Benson, D. F. 1979. *Aphasia, alexia, and agraphia*. New York: Churchill Livingstone.

Benton, A. 1979. Visuoperceptive, visuospatial, and visuoconstructive disorders. In *Clinical neuropsychology*, ed. K. M. Heilman and E. Valenstein. New York: Oxford University Press.

Bigler, E. D. 1977. Neurophysiology, neuropharmacology, and behavioral relationships of visual system evoked afterdischarges: A review. *Biobehavioral Reviews* 1:95–112.

Bogen, J. E. 1979. The callosal syndrome. In *Clinical neuropsychology*, ed. by K. M. Heilman and E. Valenstein. New York: Oxford University Press.

Bottomley, P. A. 1984. NMR in medicine. *Computerized Radiology* 8:57–77.

Brodal, A. 1981. *Neurological anatomy in relation to clinical medicine.* New York: Oxford University Press.

Butters, N. 1979. Amnesic disorders. In *Clinical neuropsychology*, ed. by K. M. Heilman and E. Valenstein. New York: Oxford University Press.

Cooper, J. R., F. E. Bloom, and R. H. Roth. 1978. *The biochemical basis of neuropharmacology*. 3d ed. New York: Oxford University Press.

Crosby, E. C., T. Humphrey, and E. W. Lauer. 1962. *Correlative anatomy of the nervous system*. New York: Macmillan.

Cummings, J. L., U. Tomiyasu, S. Read, and D. F. Benson. 1984. Amnesia with hippocampal lesions after cardiopulmonary arrest. *Neurology* 34:679–681.

Damasio, A. R., and H. Damasio. 1983. The anatomic basis of pure alexia. *Neurology* 33:1573–1583.

Damasio, A. R., H. Damasio, and G. W. Van Hoesen. 1982. Prosopagnosia: Anatomic basis and behavioral mechanisms. *Neurology* 32:331–341.

Damasio, A. R., P. J. Eslinger, H. Damasio, G. W. Van Hoesen, and S. Cornell. 1985. Multimodal amnesic syndrome following bilateral temporal and basal forebrain damage. *Archives of Neurology* 42:252–259.

Damasio, A. R., N. R. Graff-Radford, P. J. Eslinger, H. Damasio, and N. Kassell. 1985. Amnesia following basal forebrain lesions. *Archives of Neurology* 42:263–271.

DeMyer, W. 1974. *Technique of the neurologic examination*. New York: McGraw-Hill.

DeRenzi, E., P. Faglioni, and P. Sorgato. 1982. Modality-specific and supramodal mechanisms of apraxia. *Brain* 105:301–312.

Doty, R., P. Shaman, and M. Dann. 1984. Development of the University of Pennsylvania Smell Identification Test: A standardized microencapsulated test of olfactory function. *Physiology & Behavior* 32:489–502.

Farde, L., H. Hall, E. Ehrin, and G. Sedvall. 1986. Quantitative analysis of D2 dopamine receptor binding in the living human brain by PET. *Science* 231:258–261.

Fried, I., C. Mateer, G. Ojemann, R. Wohns, and P. Fedio. 1982. Organization of visuospatial functions in human cortex. *Brain* 105:349–371.

Gazzaniga, M. S., J. D. Holtzman, M. D. F. Deck, and B. C. P. Lee. 1985. MRI assessment of human callosal surgery with neuropsychological correlates. *Neurology* 35:1763–1766.

Geschwind, N. 1972. Language and the brain. *Scientific American* 226:76–89.

———. 1979. Specializations of the human brain. *Scientific American* 241:180–199.

Geschwind, N., and A. M. Galaburda. 1985*a*. Cerebral lateralization. Biological mechanisms, associations, and pathology. I, A hypothesis and a program for research. *Archives of Neurology* 42:428–459.

———. 1985*b*. Cerebral lateralization. Biological mechanisms, associations, and pathology. II, A hypothesis and a program for research. *Archives of Neurology* 42:521–552.

———. 1985*c*. Cerebral lateralization. Biological mechanisms, associations, and pathology. III, A hypothesis and a program for research. *Archives of Neurology* 42:634–654.

Gilman, S., and S. S. Winans. 1982. *Mantor and Gatz's essentials of clinical neuroanatomy and neurophysiology*. Philadelphia: F. A. Davis.

Gluhbegovic, N., and T. H. Williams. 1980. *The human brain*. Hagerstown, MD.: Harper & Row.

Grafman, J., A. M. Salazar, H. Weingartner, S. C. Vance, and C. Ludlow. 1985. Isolated impairment of memory following a penetrating lesion of the fornix cerebri. *Archives of Neurology* 42:1162–1168.

Heilman, K. M., and E. Valenstein, eds. 1979. *Clinical neuropsychology*. New York: Oxford University Press.

Henderson, V. W. 1985. Lesion localization in Broca's aphasia. *Archives of Neurology* 42:1210–1212.

Henderson, V. W., R. B. Friedman, E. L. Teng, and J. M. Weiner. 1985. Left hemisphere pathways in reading: Inferences from pure alexia without hemianopia. *Neurology* 35:962–968.

Hole, J. W. 1981. *Human anatomy and physiology*. 2d ed. Dubuque, IA: William C. Brown.

Kandel, E. R. 1981. Brain and behavior. In *Principles of neural science*, ed. E. R. Kandel and J. H. Schwartz. New York: Elsevier/North-Holland.

Kertesz, A., and S. Dobrowolski. 1981. Right-hemisphere deficits, lesion size, and location. *Journal of Clinical Neuropsychology* 3:283–299.

Kinsbourne, M., and W. L. Smith. 1974. *Hemispheric disconnection and cerebral function*. Springfield, IL: C. C. Thomas.

Knopman, D. S., and A. B. Rubens. 1986. The validity of computed tomographic scan findings for the localization of cerebral functions. *Archives of Neurology* 43:328–332.

Koff, E., M. A. Naeser, J. M. Pieniadz, A. L. Foundas, and H. L. Levine. 1986. Computed tomographic scan hemispheric asymmetries in right- and left-handed male and female subjects. *Archives of Neurology* 43:487–491.

Levine, D. N., J. D. Warach, L. Benowitz, and R. Calvanio. 1986. Left spatial neglect: Effects of lesion size and premorbid brain atrophy on severity and recovery following right cerebral infarction. *Neurology* 36:362–366.

Lüders, H., R. P. Lesser, J. Hahn, D. S. Dinner, H. Morris, S. Resor, and M. Harrison. 1986. Basal temporal language area demonstrated by electrical stimulation. *Neurology* 36: 505–510.

Ludlow, C. L., J. Rosenberg, C. Fair, D. Buck, S. Schesselman, and A. Salazar. 1986. Brain lesions associated with nonfluent aphasia fifteen years following penetrating head injury. *Brain* 109:55–80.

Mesulam, M-M., L. Volicer, J. K. Marquis, E. J. Mufson, and R. C. Green. 1986. Systematic regional differences in the cholinergic innervation of the primate cerebral cortex: Distribution of enzyme activities and some behavioral implications. *Annals of Neurology* 19:144–151.

Naeser, M. A., and J. C. Borod. 1986. Aphasia in left-handers: Lesion site, lesion side, and hemispheric asymmetries on CT. *Neurology* 36:471–488.

Rafal, R. D., M. J. Posner, J. A. Walker, and F. J. Friedrich. 1984. Cognition and the basal ganglia. *Brain* 107:1083–1094.

Raichle, M. E., D. C. Devivo, and J. Hanaway. 1978. Disorders of cerebral circulation. In *Neurological pathophysiology*, ed. S. G. Eliasson, A. L. Prensky, and W. B. Hardin. 2d ed. New York: Oxford University Press.

Regard, M., T. Landis, and K. Hess. 1985. Preserved stenography reading in a patient with pure alexia. *Archives of Neurology* 42:400–402.

Risse, G. L., A. B. Rubens, and L. S. Jordan. 1984. Disturbances of long-term memory in aphasic patients. *Brain* 107: 605–617.

Roberts, M., and J. Hanaway. 1970. *Atlas of the human brain in section*. Philadelphia: Lea & Febiger.

Ross, E. D. 1982. Disorders of recent memory in humans. *Trends in Neurosciences* 5:170–173.

Russell, E. W. 1981. The pathology and clinical examination of memory. In *Handbook of clinical neuropsychology*, ed. S. B. Filskov and T. J. Boll. New York: John Wiley & Sons.

Salazar, A. M., J. Grafman, S. Schlesselman, S. C. Vance, J. P. Mohr, M. Carpenter, P. Pevsner, C. Ludlow, and H. Weingartner. 1986. Penetrating war injuries of the basal forebrain: Neurology and cognition. *Neurology* 36:459–465.

Salazar, A. M., J. H. Grafman, S. C. Vance, H. Weingartner, J. D. Dillon, and C. Ludlow. 1986. Consciousness and amnesia after penetrating head injury: Neurology and anatomy. *Neurology* 36:178–187.

Schadé, P., and D. H. Ford. 1973. *Basic neurology*. 2d ed. Amsterdam: Elsevier.

Schwartz, A. S. 1985. Research in Alzheimer's disease: Some recent developments. *BNI Quarterly* 1:2–9.

Selnes, O. A., D. S. Knopman, N. Niccum, and A. B. Rubens. 1985. The critical role of Wernicke's area in sentence repetition. *Annals of Neurology* 17:549–557.

Sidman, R. L., and M. Sidman. 1965. *Neuroanatomy: A programmed text*. Boston: Little, Brown.

Squire, L. R. 1982. The neuropsychology of human memory. *Annual Review of Neuroscience* 5:241–273.

———. 1986. Mechanisms of memory. *Science* 232:1612–1619.

Synder, S. H. 1977. Opiate receptors and internal opiates. *Scientific American* 239:44–56.

Tanridag, O., and H. S. Kirshner. 1985. Aphasia and agraphia in lesions of the posterior internal capsule and putamen. *Neurology* 35:1797–1801.

Truex, R. C., and M. B. Carpenter. 1969. *Human neuroanatomy*. Baltimore: Williams & Wilkins.

Tulving, E. 1985. How many memory systems are there? *American Psychologist* 40:385–398.

Woods, D. L., and R. T. Knight. 1986. Electrophysiologic evidence of increased distractibility after dorsolateral prefrontal lesions. *Neurology* 36:212–216.

Yeo, R. A., E. N. Turkheimer, N. Raz, and E. D. Bigler. 1987. Volumetric parameters of the human brain: Intellectual correlates. *Brain and Cognition* 6:15–23.

2. Neuropsychological Assessment

Neuropsychologic Technique

Numerous specific tests of brain function exist (see Lezak, 1983; Smith, 1975), but to establish a truly definitive diagnosis the examiner should take a systematic approach to evaluating brain function. As such, this chapter is devoted to establishing a comprehensive outline of assessment technique that can be used in evaluating human brain function. Although the length of such an exam can be prohibitive, as the clinician becomes more experienced certain aspects of the exam can be abbreviated or eliminated altogether.

Mental Status

The mental status exam represents the initial clinical interview and recording of medical history (Taylor, 1981). Because many disorders of cerebral function will affect various aspects of mentation, it is important to document cerebral function by examining the patient's mental status. Information obtained in the mental status exam can also help the examiner determine the direction of the formal neuropsychologic exam. The mental status exam also helps differentiate between the patient with organic brain disease and one with functional disorder. The mental status exam is typically broken down into the following areas.

Orientation. Is the patient oriented to time, place, and person? (What is today's date? What is the day? month? year? Where are you? What is the name of the city? the hospital? What is your name? What do you do?) These questions should always be asked directly. Never assume that because someone looks oriented they are. Disorientation is common with disorders that diffusely affect cerebral function.

Appearance and Behavior. The examiner should note how the patient is dressed and groomed. Frequently the patient with organic disease tends to neglect certain aspects of personal hygiene. The examiner should also note whether the patient is behaving appropriately for his age, his education, and his vocational status.

Language. The examiner should take note of whether conversational speech appears normal or whether there appears to be a paucity of content or loquaciousness. Are straightforward aphasic deficits present? Is there perseveration of topics in speech? Disorders of language frequently accompany diffuse cerebral disorders as well as disorders more focally affecting the dominant hemisphere.

Affect and Mood. Is there evidence of depression, mania, euphoria, agitation, or rage? If the patient is depressed, is there a cause? Does the patient have a history of psychologic disorder? Are the patient's speech and mannerisms congruent with the affect displayed? Frequently, careful examination in this domain can readily assist in differentiating the patient with organic disease from one with a functional disorder (see table 5.5 in chapter 5).

Thought Content. Does the patient display loose tangential thinking that skips from topic to topic? (This thinking is typically seen in schizophrenia and also seen in affective disorders.) Are there obsessions, compulsions, phobias, or rituals present? During the prodromal phase (the early warning stage) of many organic disorders there may be initial disturbance in thought content. An examiner should be cautious about ruling out organic disease simply because the patient developed a peculiar delusion, which appears to be a functional disorder.

Memory. Memory should be briefly evaluated in terms of immediate recall (i.e., simple digit span; memorization of four words—pen, table, house, dictionary—and their immediate recall as well as recall after five minutes), recent memory (current events in news; how did the patient get to the office or hospital), and remote memory (date of birth; names of past presidents; names of parents, spouse, or children; historical events). Typically, of the types of memory, recent memory is the type most affected in organic disease, and the examiner should be cautious to clarify that memory is not disturbed secondary to generalized confusion or functional state (i.e., severe depression).

General Information, Insight, and Judgment. The patient's fund of general information is akin to remote memory and can be tested in a similar fashion. Reasoning should also be assessed by asking the patient what is the difference between a baby and a midget or how a paintbrush and a pencil are alike. Interpretations or proverbs are also helpful in determining if the patient is making concrete (literal) or more abstract insights. Concrete interpretations are commonly associated with lower intellectual levels as well as signs of cognitive deterioration in those with previously normal intellectual levels. Such proverbs as "A stitch in time saves nine," "One should not change horses in the middle of the stream," and more difficult ones such as "A drowning man will grasp at a straw" or "People who live in glass houses should not throw stones" are examples of proverbs that are clinically used to test intellectual level.

Gait and Station

From the moment the patient enters the examining room, careful attention should be directed to gait and station. Formal exam of these faculties should include having the patient walk in a normal fashion for a distance of fifteen to twenty feet, first moving away from the examiner and then back. Careful scrutiny should be directed toward ascertaining the presence (normal) or absence (abnormal) of motor symmetry, the presence of ataxia or spasticity, and any evidence of weakness. If weakness, spasticity, or ataxia are present, further delineation may be obtained by having the patient walk on tiptoes or heels. Disturbance of cerebellar or vestibular function can frequently be observed by testing tandem gait—walking heel-to-toe as if on a railroad track. The posture and position of the head, arms, and trunk should always be evaluated with the patient in the normal standing position as well as in various walking circumstances. Posture may be affected by extrapyramidal or cerebellar disorders. Ability to initiate movement may be disturbed (i.e., gait dyspraxia) as seen in various diseases of the frontal lobes or in generalized disorders. Conversely, motor perseveration may be seen in which the patient does not have trouble with initiation, but with cessation. Motor impersistence may also occur, which is characterized by the patient's inability to sustain a simple motor act (i.e., keeping eyes closed or arms outstretched) even though no focal weakness is present. The Romberg test requires the patient to stand erect with feet together. Swaying, losing posture, or falling with eyes open suggests the presence of cerebellar lesion, whereas if station is normal with eyes open but abnormal when eyes are closed a disturbance in postural sense is suspected rather than a cerebellar lesion.

Head and Spine

In the patient who has sustained cerebral trauma, undergone neurosurgical intervention, or both, the head should be examined to determine the presence and localization of skull defects and to locate surgical scars. Such findings may provide important insights about the regions of cerebral damage. In pediatric patients, the head should be examined for symmetry and measured in terms of circumference, inasmuch as abnormally small or large heads or cranial malformations may be associated with various neurologic abnormalities (see chapter 9). The examiner checking head circumference should consider the size and body type of the child (normative data on head circumference, body weight, and height are given in a table in fig. 2.12). Scoliosis is especially common in muscular dystrophy as well as in certain chronic cerebellar diseases, but is, of course, not diagnostic of either.

Cranial Nerves

In chapter 1, figure 1.48 depicted the anatomic location of the twelve cranial nerves and table 1.2 reviewed cranial nerve function. That which follows deals primarily with the clinical assessment of cranial nerve function.

The cranial nerve exam is an integral part of the medical neurologic exam performed by a physician, and not in the direct purview of the psychologist. Understanding cranial nerve function and pathology is, however, critical to understanding integrated neural systems. Additionally, cranial nerve dysfunction may alter performance on various neuropsychologic measures (e.g., pupillary dilation and ocular paralysis unrelated to cerebral factors will affect visual perception and thereby affect visuopraxic and visual discrimination abilities). Accordingly, not understanding cranial nerve function or defect may lead to misunderstanding neuropsychologic test performance. There are certain cranial nerve tests (i.e., corneal reflex, gag reflex) that are clearly left to the physician because of potential complications and risk in testing. Frequently, by the time the patient comes to the psychologist the cranial nerve exam will have already been conducted by the referring physician and, thus, the result simply may be recorded from the chart.

First Cranial Nerve. In testing for olfaction, the main concern is for the appreciation of smell and not necessarily for the precise discrimination between odors. Aromatic but nonirritating odors such as coffee, peppermint, or cloves should be used. Each nostril should be tested separately. The patient should also be asked if there is any change in the appreciation of taste. Any patient who is suspected of having frontal lobe disease should be tested as should all patients suffering trauma, because the olfactory nerve is highly vulnerable in traumatic injury.

Second Cranial Nerve. Each eye should be tested for visual acuity typically using a Snellen eye chart. Visual fields are tested by having the patient fix his gaze on the examiner's nose, and then identify a small object when it enters the visual field periphery. Each quadrant should be tested separately. Simultaneous visual stimulation is tested by having the patient fix his gaze on the examiner's nose; the examiner raises his arms into the lateral extent of either the superior or inferior quadrant; he then discretely moves one hand (finger) or both simultaneously. If the patient perceives stimulation in either quadrant with singular stimulation, but does not perceive stimulation in one quadrant or entire visual field with simultaneous stimulation, this pattern is typically pathognomonic for contralateral dysfunction in the visual system as outlined in figure 1.42 in chapter 1. The lack of perception in one aspect of the visual field (or on one body side) with simultaneous stimulation has been given several terms, including extinction, simultaneous imperception, unilateral inattention, and simultagnosia.

Third Cranial Nerve. Commonly, unilateral pupillary dilation is accompanied by deficits in third nerve functioning and is common with traumatic injury to the brain. The pupillary light reflex involves a direct pathway to the midbrain from the optic tract. Shining a light in one eye normally leads to constriction of both pupils (the consensual reflex). Pupillary constriction is also a part of accommodation and convergence necessary for focusing. The Argyll Robertson pupil constricts during accommodation, which is normal, but does not constrict to light. It is presumed that this is related to pathology at the pretectal level. Horner's syndrome occurs when there is unilateral pupillary constriction, slight ptosis, and decreased sweating that results from a lesion or interruption of the sympathetic pathways to the eye. This syndrome may occur as a result of a lesion in the medulla, cervical spine, or cervical sympathetic chain.

Third, Fourth, and Sixth Cranial Nerves. Extraocular movements are mediated by the action of the third, fourth, and sixth cranial nerves. The sixth cranial nerve innervates the lateral rectus muscle, which functions solely to abduct (laterally turn) the eye. As such, lateral movement will be affected when the sixth cranial nerve is damaged. Such damage may cause diplopia (double vision) because of the eyes' inability to position for binocular focusing. Diplopia may occur with third or fourth nerve paresis, also. The fourth cranial nerve innervates the superior oblique muscle, and the remaining ocular muscles are innervated by the third cranial nerve. Third and fourth cranial nerve function can be assessed by having the patient follow a target up (third nerve) and down (third and fourth nerves). The ocular motility exam should also include determination of amblyopia (wandering eye), nystagmus (vibratory movements of the eye), and efficiency of conjugate gaze (ability to move the eyes together), all of which may affect visual discriminative abilities.

Fifth Cranial Nerve. The trigeminal nerve is divided into sensory and motor sections. The motor division innervates the muscles of mastication and is tested by palpating the masseter and temporal muscles simultaneously while the jaw is clenched. The examiner should also test for any deviation in movement of the mouth on opening. The sensory division is divided into three distinct branches: (1) ophthalmic—sensation to forehead and anterior to include two to three inches of the scalp; (2) maxillary (upper jaw)—sensation to maxillary region; and (3) mandibular (lower jaw)—sensation to the mandibular region. Each of these should be tested separately, the ability to sense being ascertained by the patient's perception of light touch or touch by a wisp of cotton.

Seventh Cranial Nerve. The seventh cranial nerve innervates the muscles of the face not innervated by the fifth cranial nerve. Examination of the seventh cranial nerve is straightforward and should include inspection for any asymmetry in facial musculature at rest, as well as spontaneous movement and movement on command (wrinkle forehead, frown, grimace, smile).

Eighth Cranial Nerve. Hearing can be screened by determining if the patient can hear a wristwatch ticking, a common word being whispered, or by light whisping or snapping of the fingers. To test for auditory extinction, the examiner should simultaneously stimulate each ear by lightly rubbing the fingers together very quickly and sharply. Although inattention (extinction) to one side (when normal hearing has been proved to exist in that ear) implies contralateral temporal dysfunction, and *not* eighth nerve impairment, this procedure is discussed here because the appropriate time to examine for extinction is when testing for eighth nerve function. Examination of vestibular function has already been discussed and deficits in such functioning are reflected in gait, station, and nystagmus.

Ninth, Tenth, and Twelfth Cranial Nerves. Because of its appearance (i.e., a bulb), the medulla has been termed the bulbar region of the brain stem. The ninth, tenth, and twelfth cranial nerves all originate at this level. The ninth and tenth form a nuclear complex, and their functions are tested together. Symmetric deviation of the palate, symmetric gag reflex, normal quality of speech, and normal swallowing all connote intact ninth and tenth cranial nerve function. Hoarseness, the onset of whispering, or the inability to enunciate the letter *e* may indicate unilateral vocal cord paralysis. The twelfth cranial nerve innervates the tongue and is tested by examining the tongue for any asymmetry, wasting, or fasciculations. If tongue paresis is present, the tongue will protrude to the side of weakness when the patient sticks out his tongue.

Eleventh Cranial Nerve. The spinal accessory nerve innervates the sternocleidomastoid muscle and the upper one-third of the trapezuis muscle. The nerve is tested by having the patient shrug his shoulders, turn his head to each side, and bow his head.

Primitive Reflexes

In a variety of diffuse disorders, particularly those related to aging, rudimentary or primitive reflexes may be elicited (Paulson, 1977). Although these reflexes may also be elicited in the normal individual (Jacobs and Gossman, 1980), their presence in association with other neurologic findings usually connotes a pathologic relationship (however, see Tweedy et al., 1982). The following primitive reflexes are recommended for examination:

Grasp Reflex. A positive grasp reflex is present when stimulation of the palm results in flexion (bending) of the fingers, frequently imposing a forced grasp (see fig. 2.1). This is best elicited by diagonally stroking the length of the patient's open palm.

Snout Reflex. Stroking or stimulating the oral region may elicit either the snout (puckering) reflex, rooting (puckering response as well as head movement and orientation toward the stimulus) reflex, or sucking movements. Figure 2.2 depicts this response.

Palmomental Reflex. This is a palm-chin reflex. It consists of unilateral contraction of the mentalis muscle (corner of the mouth) when the ipsilateral hand (typically the thenar eminence of the palm) is briskly stimulated. This is illustrated in figure 2.3.

Blink or Glabellar Tap Reflex. The presence of the blink or glabellar tap reflex is actually related to the absence of inhibition of the blink reflex with repeated nonmeaningful tapping between the eyes (see fig. 2.4).

Table 2.1 provides a guide for recording the presence or absence of a primitive reflex. Caution needs to be used to prevent overinterpretation regarding the significance of these reflexes. For example, Jacobs and Gossman (1980) have demonstrated that with the palmomental reflex, in the third decade of life, this is found in some

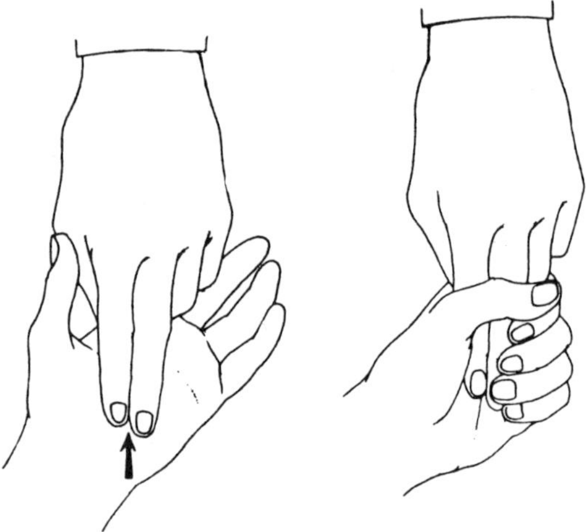

Fig. 2.1. Grasp reflex: *left*, palmar stimulation; *right*, grasp response. From Wells (1977).

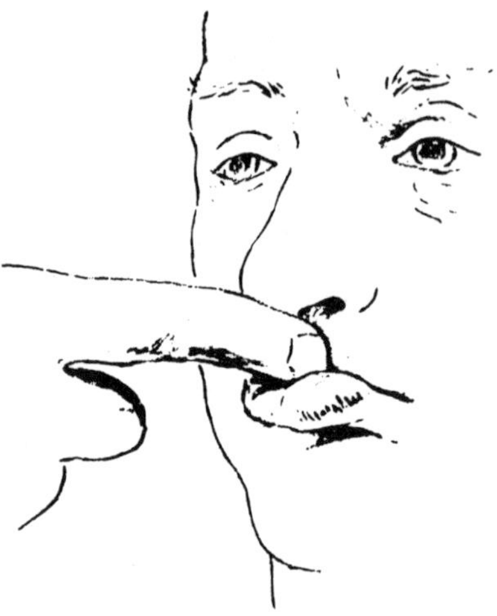

Fig. 2.2. Snout reflex: puckering, protrusion, and elevation of the lower lip and depression of the corners of the mouth when the examiner's finger is pushed backward against the upper lip. From Jacobs and Gossman (1980).

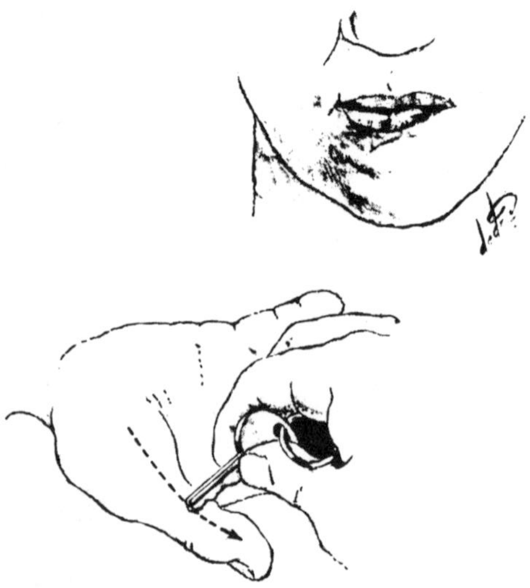

Fig. 2.3. Palmomental reflex: elevation-protrusion of the lower lip and wrinkling of the skin of the chin when the ipsilateral thenar eminence is briskly stroked by a key. From Jacobs and Gossman (1980).

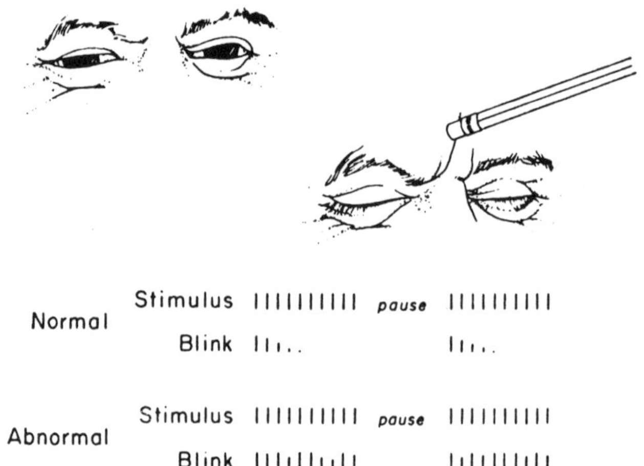

Fig. 2.4. Blink or glabella tap reflex: *top*, eyes at rest; *bottom*, response to stimulus. From Wells (1977).

Table 2.1. *Primitive Reflexes Scoring Chart*

Reflex	Present		Incomplete or Equivocal		Absent	
Grasp	Right	Left	Right	Left	Right	Left
Snout (puckering, sucking, rooting)						
Palmomental	Right	Left	Right	Left	Right	Left
Blink or glabella tap reflex						

25 percent of "normal" individuals, whereas by the ninth decade of life it is present in approximately 60 percent of normal patients. Nonetheless, the presence of a rudimentary or primitive reflex may be of significance, and because this is a relatively easy test to administer, it may be instructive to utilize this exam regularly with all patients the physician suspects of having underlying organic disorders of a diffuse degree.

Lateral Dominance

The Reitan-Kløve (see Reitan and Davison, 1974) lateral dominance examination has been found to be a rapidly administered and effective measure of hand, foot, and eye dominance. (This exam is summarized later in fig. 2.12.) Briefly explained, this test requires the patient to perform various tasks with either the hands, eyes, or feet. Consistent use of one extremity or eye for various tasks implies dominance for that side. When, for example, the right hand is used for handwriting, but the left hand is used for opening a door or waving, then such a patient would be classified as right side preferred but with some degree of mixed dominance. The presence of mixed body side dominance has some implications for diminished laterality of cerebral functions, although the exact relationship between mixed body side dominance and cerebral lateralization is not clearly understood (Springer and Deutsch, 1981).

Motor Function

Individual muscles and extremities should be examined for symmetry as well as the presence or absence of hypertrophy, atrophy, and adventitious movements. Muscular atrophy may result from disuse, but typically such atrophy connotes lower motor neuron disease. *Fasciculations* (abnormal muscle twitching) occur usually as a result of peripheral (lower motor neuron) disease. *Spasm* is typified by brief episodes of extensor rigidity, usually associated with upper motor neuron disease of the spinal cord. *Myoclonus* (clonic muscle spasm) is characterized by jerking of a limb or muscle group and is usually associated with serious progressive diseases of the central nervous system (CNS), the most common ones being myoclonic epilepsy, subacute sclerosing panencephalitis (measles encephalopathy), and Jakob-Creutzfeldt disease. *Tremor* may develop at rest as seen in Parkinson's disease or with intention as commonly seen with cerebellar disease. *Choreatic* movements are defined as quick, inappropriate movements that consist of arm flailing and random thrusting along with similar purposeless movements of the head and lower extremities. Choreiform movements are most commonly associated with Sydenham's chorea in childhood and Huntington's chorea in adulthood. *Athetosis* is a writhing, nondeforming movement of the extremities typically associated with cerebral palsy. *Dystonia* is closely allied to athetosis, differing in that its duration of position abnormality is longer. Frequently, dystonic posturing takes the form of an extended hand held in an overflexed position or a pulling to one side or retracting of the head with arching and twisting of the back. Disorders of the basal ganglia are frequently implicated in dystonia. *Buccal-lingual dyskinesias* (dystonic movements of the face and mouth) may develop after administering a variety of medications, in particular the phenothiazines and L-dopa. Chronic phenothiazine treatment is considered to be at the basis of tardive dyskinesias. *Spasmodic torticollis* is a type of dystonia in which the patient's head and neck are twisted and fixed in a spasmodic fashion to one side or bent backwards. *Hemiballismus* is a movement disorder characterized by unilateral throwing movements of the arm or leg (or both) with the presence of such abnormal movements being associated with destruction of the subthalamic nucleus of Luysii. *Habit spasms* or *tics* are typically seen in children and are usually of psychogenic origin, although Gilles de la Tourette's syndrome may be associated with brain stem–level dysfunction. *Astasia-abasia* is an inability to stand or walk, although the patient retains normal lower limb use and tone while in a reclining position. The presence of such disturbance in movement is typically associated with functional disorder if all other organic causes can be ruled out.

Strength and Fatigability. The hand dynamometer is commonly used to measure strength of grip in each hand. Typically, the examiner gives two or three trials for each hand and records an average grip strength. The dominant hand tends to be somewhat stronger than the nondominant, usually by 8–12 percent. In testing for fatigability, repeated hand squeezes with a dynamometer may reveal rapid fatigue. When examining at the bedside, a hand dynamometer may not be available. In such cases having the patient squeeze the examiner's index and middle fingers with each hand simultaneously may also reveal weakness. Such hand squeezing may also aid in differentiating functional patients. They may hardly register a grip, despite dramatic demonstrations of attempts to squeeze with all their effort. Position maintenance testing may also assist in detecting weakness. In this test, the patient holds arms out in front with fingers and thumb extended, palms upward, and eyes closed. Inability to maintain position on one side may be due to weakness and should be explored further. Smorto and Basmajian (1980) give further details.

Accuracy and Coordination. The finger oscillation test is a simple test of fine motor control and speed. The patient places the index finger with palm down on a lever that will register a count each time depressed. The patient is instructed to depress the lever as fast as possible over a ten-second period. A normal score is typically considered to be 45 or higher, with the dominant hand performing the task somewhat more efficiently with tapping speeds of 8–12 percent greater with the dominant hand. Accuracy and coordination can also be tested by having the patient touch his finger to his nose, alternating fingers to thumb and other rapid alternating movements (diadokokinesis).

One hand should be judged against the other; the exam should also be directed toward judging how integrated, coordinated, and smooth the responses are performed. Finger oscillation speed deficits imply possible contralateral frontal lobe dysfunction, if subcortical, spinal, and peripheral factors can be ruled out. Dysdiadokokinesia generally implies a nonspecific type of disturbance of the motor system and is seen frequently with different disorders of the frontal lobes.

Learned Acts (Praxis)

Praxis refers to skilled, learned, and purposeful movements that require considerable integrative control, normal strength, and intact dexterity. Examples of this are abilities to copy (draw) figures, use simple tools, put on clothes, use some type of utensil, or perform other simple but meaningful movements. Disorders of learned motor acts, in their pure form, occur in the absence of focal motor deficit (i.e., hemiparesis). Thus, the deficit is not related to weakness or fatigability, but rather to a deficit in motor planning and execution. There are several types of apraxic or dyspraxic disorders and these are reviewed below.

Ideomotor Apraxia. Ideomotor apraxia represents the most common form of apraxia. The patient is simply unable to carry out a previously learned motor act. The apraxia may be limited to the facial musculature (buccofacial apraxia) or extremity (limb apraxia) or the whole body (whole-body apraxia). In assessing for apraxia deficit, the examiner should give the patient commands by verbal instruction only. If failure occurs, the examiner should display or pantomime the act, and have the patient imitate it. When giving limb commands (e.g., asking the patient to throw a ball), the examiner should test each limb separately. If failure occurs at this level, test should end. Various sample commands used to test for apraxia include the following:

Tests for buccofacial movement
1. "Show me how to blow out a match."
2. "Drink through a straw."
3. "Cough."

Tests for limb movement
1. "Flip a coin."
2. "Comb your hair."
3. "Throw a ball."
4. "Kick a ball."
5. "Use a screwdriver."
6. "Hammer a nail."
7. "Salute."
8. "Cut paper."
9. "Squash a bug."

Tests for bilateral limb movement
1. "Play a piano."
2. "File fingernails."

Tests for whole-body movement
1. "Stand like a boxer, golfer, batter, or diver."
2. "Shovel dirt."
3. "Take a bow."

Because the patient must first comprehend the spoken command, auditory comprehension (Wernicke's area) must be intact. If the patient has receptive aphasic deficits, then it may be difficult to differentiate between true apraxia and praxic deficit secondary to impaired comprehension. Inasmuch as a dominant hemisphere lesion may produce both aphasia and apraxia, careful aphasia examination is always necessary in evaluating the patient with praxic disorder.

A variety of lesion sites may produce ideomotor apraxia. This is so because a considerable amount of cortex is necessary to process a command (receptive areas of the dominant hemisphere), retrieve memories for motor movement (likely a frontotemporoparietal interaction), and initiate motor movement (frontal lobe), which likewise depends on kinesthetic and proprioceptive (parietal lobe) feedback to be executed efficiently. Thus a lesion anywhere in this system may produce apraxia. However, Heilman, Rothi, and Valenstein (1982) have suggested that posterior cerebral lesions that produce a fluent aphasic disturbance may be accompanied by the severest forms of ideomotor apraxia. Kertesz and Ferro (1984) have demonstrated that the parietal cortex may not play the primary role in ideomotor apraxia, but rather their research indicated lesions of the deep parieto- and occipitofrontal and anterior callosal fibers were the areas, when damaged, to be associated with ideomotor apraxia. Patients with lesions in the anterior corpus callosum or in the left frontal region (typically Broca's aphasia with right hemiplegia) may also display a specific apraxia of the left hand (see Watson, Heilman, and Bowers, 1985). Lesions of the right hemisphere, particularly the parietal region, may also produce apraxia. Also, it should be noted that buccofacial and limb apraxia may occur in the absence of whole-body apraxia, since there appears to be a relationship between extent of brain dysfunction and expression of whole-body praxic deficits. Buccofacial and limb movements are dependent on more discrete neural systems than are whole-body movements.

Ideational Apraxia. Ideational praxic functions are considered to require a higher level of cortical organization than ideomotor functions. Ideational apraxia occurs when there is a deficit in following a verbal command to perform a motor task that requires linkage of various skilled movements, such as folding a letter and placing it in an envelope, sealing it, and placing a stamp on it. Other examples of commands that may reveal ideational apraxia are "Take a cigarette from a pack, light, and smoke it"; "Pour coffee into a cup, add sugar, stir, and drink"; "Take a toothbrush, squeeze toothpaste onto the brush from a tube, and brush your teeth." Ideational apraxia is commonly found in patients with more generalized or diffuse brain disorders and, accordingly, is seen frequently in degenerative disease.

Motor Impersistence. Motor impersistence (Benton et al.,

1983) is the term used to classify or describe a patient's inability to sustain simple motor acts, such as keeping the mouth open, conjugate gaze, protruding the tongue, eye fixation, keeping eyelids shut, holding of the breath, or exerting steady pressure such as during hand grip. Kertesz et al. (1985) demonstrated that these features tend to be present more frequently with right frontal lesions, although they do occur with a variety of lesion sites, including left frontal and nonspecific involvement.

Sensory Function

The Reitan-Kløve Sensory-Perceptual Examination (SPE) is a comprehensive series of tests that examine visual, auditory, and somesthetic functioning (see Reitan and Davison, 1974). The testing of visual fields along with simultaneous visual (see section on second cranial nerve) and auditory (see section on eighth cranial nerve) stimulation have already been given. The remainder of the exam is described below.

Tactile Double Simultaneous Stimulation (DSS). This procedure is similar to that described for visual and auditory DSS. Initially each hand is tested to ensure that there is no specific sensory loss or unilateral anesthesia. Either may be determined by simple touch or through use of an anesthesiometer. Once it is established that there is no serious unilateral sensory loss, the patient is instructed to close his eyes. The examiner will touch one hand, and the patient is to indicate whether the right or left hand was touched. (If patient is aphasic or has right-left confusion, then the patient may simply lift the hand touched.) Touch should be brief and light. The hands are then unilaterally stimulated in a random fashion initially, and then the stimulation is interspersed with bilateral stimulation. Extinction or inattention occurs when touch to one side is not perceived when DSS is applied. Such unilateral inattention suggests pathology in the contralateral cerebral hemisphere, usually in the parietal lobe. This approach to testing can also be enhanced by using materials of different textures, thus requiring discrimination not only of simple touch but also of stimulus quality (see Bigler and Tucker, 1979).

Tactile Finger Recognition. Tactile finger recognition tests the ability of the patient to identify individual fingers when they are touched. First the fingers are numbered in serial fashion with the thumb being number one and so on (if for some reason numbers are a problem, the actual names may be substituted—thumb and index, middle, ring, and little finger). The patient then closes his eyes. Each finger is randomly touched, and the patient's responses are recorded. The examiner should make sure that the fingers are not moved because proprioceptive cues may provide adventitious feedback that obscures results. A deficit in finger recognition is referred to as finger agnosia. Unilateral finger agnosia implies dysfunction in the contralateral hemisphere, again typically the parietal region. Benton et al. (1983) have outlined an even more detailed examination of finger localization.

Graphesthesia. Graphesthesia is the ability to discriminate between numbers or letters written on the palm or finger of the hand. In the Reitan-Kløve SPE, finger-tip number (3, 4, 5, and 6) writing is employed. Each number is written on the tip of the finger, and the patient is instructed to verbally identify the number written. As with other tactile tests, deficits on one side implicate the opposite hemisphere, and more specifically the parietal region.

Stereognosis. Stereognosis refers to the ability to distinguish form with the tactile sense. In the Reitan-Kløve SPE, stereognosis is evaluated by tests of tactile coin recognition (penny, nickel, dime) and tactile form recognition (plastic shapes of circle, cross, triangle, and square). Other common items such as a paper clip, hair pin, or safety pin, may be used. Deficits in form perception likewise indicate a dysfunctional state whose cause lies in the contralateral hemisphere, usually the parietal region. Benton et al. (1983) have outlined even more detailed assessment of tactile form perception in their test battery.

Visual Agnosia. Visual agnosia implies that the patient cannot visually recognize or identify objects, given that visual acuity is normal and that the deficit cannot be ascribed to purely aphasic disorder or blindness. Although the patient may not be able to visually identify the object, the object may be readily identified with other sensory or kinesthetic cues. Thus the patient may be able to hold the object and easily identify it. Prosopagnosia (the inability to recognize common faces, even members of the patient's immediate family) and color agnosia are also common forms of visual agnosia. Visual agnosias are typically found in association with posterior parietotemporal lesions, occipital lesions, or both.

Neglect. Patients with posterior cerebral lesions, particularly involving the right cerebral hemisphere, may develop inattention to or neglect of the contralateral visual space (see fig. 2.5). With right hemisphere lesions, this may be quite severe to the point where the patient may not recognize the left side of the body, may not dress or shave on the left side, and may only visually scan to midline. The following demonstrates this degree of neglect as outlined by Joseph (1985):

Examiner: Give me your right hand! (Correct hand presented.) Now give me your left hand! (The patient presented the right hand again. The right hand was held.) Give me your left! (The patient looked puzzled and did not move.) Is there anything wrong with your left hand?
Patient: No, doctor.
Examiner: Why don't you move it, then? (The left hand was held before her eyes.)
Patient: I don't know.
Examiner: Is this your hand?
Patient: Not mine, doctor.
Examiner: Whose hand is it, then?
Patient: I suppose it is yours, doctor.

Examiner: No, it is not. Look at it carefully.
Patient: It is not mine, doctor.
Examiner: Yes, it is, look at that ring; whose is it?
Patient: That is my ring; you've got my ring, doctor.
Examiner: Look at it, it is your hand.
Patient: Oh, no doctor.

Gerstmann's Syndrome. This syndrome deserves mention here, although it should be immediately pointed out that there is considerable disagreement over whether it is truly a syndrome with pathognomonic significance (see Strub and Black, 1981). Gerstmann's syndrome is said to be present when finger agnosia, right-left disorientation, dysgraphia, and dyscalculia are found. In its pure form, it is considered to be associated with dominant parietal lobe dysfunction (Roeltgen, Sevush, Heilman, 1983). It is common to find Gerstmann's syndrome in patients with degenerative disease, but this finding does not reflect focal deficit, but rather the diffuseness of the damage.

Language Skills

Comprehensive language evaluation may be accomplished using a variety of assessment batteries (see Lezak, 1976, 1983; Smith, 1975; Blumstein, 1981). In terms of comprehensive neuropsychologic assessment, the aphasia screening test modified by Reitan (Reitan and Davison, 1974) or the aphasia exam proposed by Strub and Black (1981) is adequate. The Reitan-Indiana Aphasia Screening Test is presented in figure 2.6. The legend to figure 2.6 describes the administration of this test. It should be readily realized by the clinician that much of the aphasia exam can actually be developed during the course of the initial clinical exam of the patient—that is, the alexic patient is going to have alexia regardless of assessment technique utilized. As discussed in chapter 1, fluency, comprehension, repetition, naming, and reading should always be carefully evaluated.

Construction or Graphomotor Skills

The ability to copy or reproduce by drawing is a nonverbal, complex, higher cerebral function (Hecaen and Albert, 1978). Deficits in reproductional or constructional abilities are typically suggestive of parietal lobe dysfunction, and there is a somewhat higher incidence of right hemisphere pathology, particularly right parietal, responsible for the deficit. It should also be mentioned that there is a tendency for there to be errors of fragmentation—that is, lines separating or breaking the configurational segments into fragments—with dominant hemisphere damage, whereas the constructional deficit tends to be more pervasive with nondominant hemispheric involvement (Binder, 1982). The items that require copying on the Reitan-Indiana exam test for constructional praxis. Drawing a tobacco pipe, flower pot, house, bicycle, and necker cube also has been used in testing. The Bender visual-motor gestalt test (Bender, 1938) is also a test designed specifically to examine constructional praxis; however,

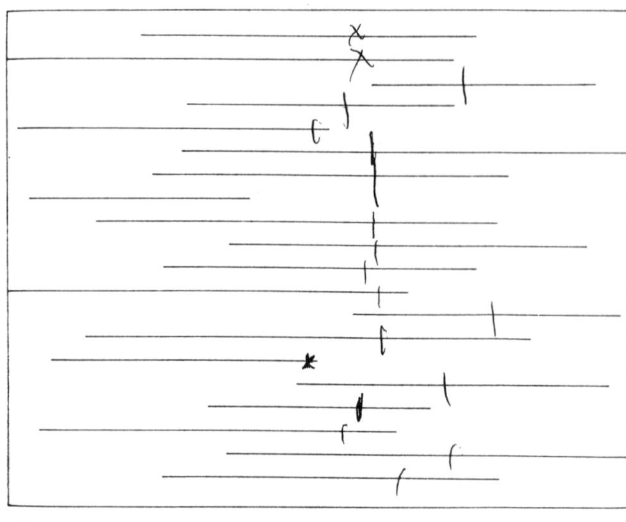

Fig. 2.5. *A*, the Line Bisection Test (Schenkenberg, Bradford, and Ajax, 1980). This patient had extensive right hemisphere damage. Note the complete neglect of the left visual space. CAT scan results are presented in figure 2.7 along with this patient's performance on the Rey-Osterrieth Figure Test, which also demonstrates neglect. *B*, the CAT scans on the left demonstrate locus of lesion in the left cerebral hemisphere and the corresponding effects on the patient's ability to copy the Greek cross and skeleton key. The CAT scans on the right present similar information for right hemisphere damaged patients. Note that even though the left hemisphere damaged patients have similarly large lesions, their constructional praxic abilities are relatively preserved, whereas the right hemisphere damaged patients demonstrate severe constructional apraxia and features of left-side neglect.

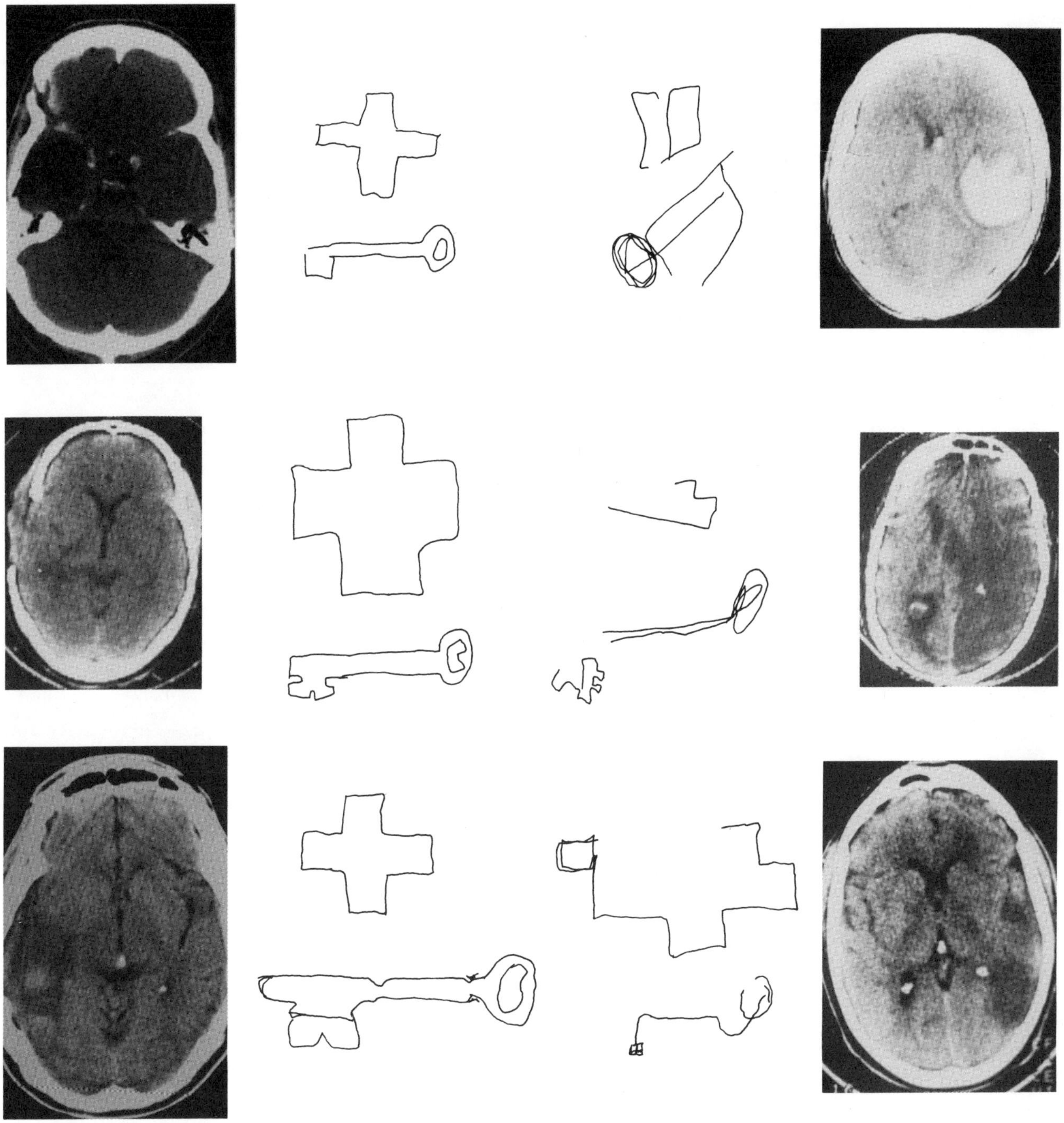

B

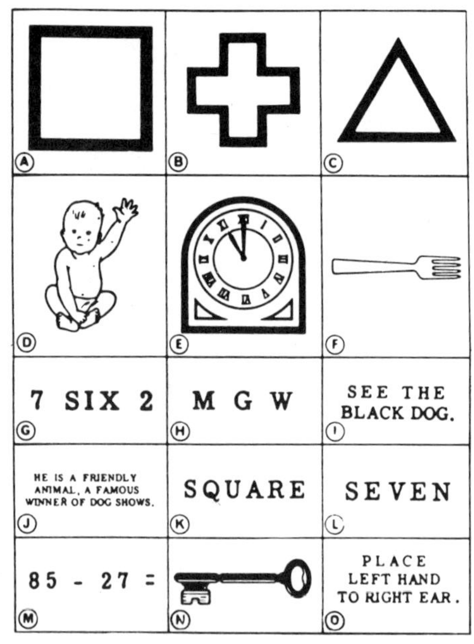

1. Copy *square* (*A*) — *First, draw this on your paper.* (Point to square, item *A*.) *I want you to do it without lifting your pencil from the paper. Make it about this same size.* (Point to square.) Elaborate on the requirement for a continuous line if necessary. If the patient is concerned about making a heavy or double line, point out that only a reproduction of the shape is required. If the patient has obvious difficulty in drawing any of the figures, encourage him to proceed until it is clear that he can make no further progress. If he does not accomplish the task reasonably well on his first try, ask him to try again, and instruct him to be particularly careful to do it as well as he can.
2. Name *square.* — *What is that shape called?*
3. Spell *square.* — *Would you spell that word for me?*
4. Copy *cross* (*B*). — *Draw this on your paper.* (Point to cross.) *Go around the outside like this until you get back to where you started.* (Examiner draws finger line around the edge of the stimulus figure.) *Make it about this same size.* (Point to cross.) Additional instructions, if necessary, should be similar to those used with the square.
5. Name *cross.* — *What is that shape called?*
6. Spell *cross.* — *Would you spell that word for me?*
7. Copy *triangle* (*C*). — Similar to 1 and 4 above.
8. Name *triangle.* — *What is that shape called?*
9. Spell *triangle.* — *Would you spell that word for me?*
10. Name *baby* (*D*). — *What is this?* (Show baby, item *D*.)
11. Write *clock* (*E*). — *Now I am going to show you another picture, but do not tell me the name of it. I don't want you to say anything out loud, just write the name of the picture on your paper.* (Show clock, item *E*.)
12. Name *fork* (*F*). — *What is this?* (Show fork, item *F*.)
13. Read *7 six 2* (*G*). — *I want you to read this.* (Show item *G*.) If the subject has difficulty, attempt to determine whether he can read any part of the stimulus figure.
14. Read *M G W* (*H*). — *Read this.* (Show item *H*.)
15. Reading I (*I*). — *Now I want you to read this.* (Show item *I*.)
16. Reading II (*J*). — *Can you read this?* (Show item *J*.)
17. Repeat *triangle.* — *Now I am going to say some words. I want you to listen carefully and say them after me as carefully as you can. Say this word: triangle.*
18. Repeat *Massachusetts.* — *The next one is a little harder, but do your best. Say this word: Massachusetts.*
19. Repeat *Methodist Episcopal.* — *Now repeat this one: Methodist Episcopal.*
20. Write *square* (*K*). — *Don't say this word out loud.* (Point to stimulus word *square*, item *K*.) *Just write it on your paper.* If the patient prints the word, ask him to write it.
21. Read *seven* (*L*). — *Can you read this word out loud?* (Show item *L*.)
22. Repeat *seven.* — *Now, I want you to say this after me: seven.*
23. Repeat-explain, *He shouted the warning.* — *I am going to say something that I want you to say after me, so listen carefully: He shouted the warning. Now you say it. Would you explain what that means?* Sometimes it is necessary to amplify by asking the kind of situation to which the sentence would refer. The patient's understanding is adequately demonstrated when he brings the concept of impending danger into his explanation.
24. Write: *He shouted the warning.* — *Now I want you to write that sentence on the paper.* Sometimes it is necessary to repeat the sentence so that the patient understands clearly what he is to write.
25. Compute 85 − 27 = (*M*). — *Here is an arithmetic problem. Copy it down on your paper any way you like and try to work it out.* (Show item *M*.)
26. Compute 17 × 3. — *Now do this one in your head:* 17 × 3.
27. *What is this?* (key).
28. (Still presenting the picture of the key) — *If you had one of these in your hand, show me how you would use it.* (Show item *N*.)
29. Draw *key* (*N*). — *Now I want you to draw a picture that looks just like this. Try to make your key look enough like this one so that I would know it was the same key from your drawing.* (Point to key, item *N*.)
30. Read (*O*). — *Would you read this?* (Show item *O*.)
31. Place *left hand to right ear.* — *Now, would you do what it said?*
32. Place *left hand to left elbow.* — *Now I want you to put your left hand to your left elbow.* The patient should quickly realize that it is impossible.

A

Fig. 2.6. *A*, stimulus figures for the Reitan-Indiana Aphasia Screening Test. Instructions to administer the test follow (patient's task, *on left*; examiner's instructions, *right*). With permission from Ralph Reitan. *B*, descriptive example of the test results on the Reitan-Indiana Aphasia Screening Test in a fluent aphasic patient who was a 66-year-old retired female pharmacist. The patient was found to have arteriosclerotic disease with up to 33 percent stenosis at the bifurcation of the left internal carotid artery from the common carotid. Interestingly, the patient's CT evaluations revealed no focal abnormalities, even several weeks poststroke. Her EEG, however, demonstrated a left midtemporal slow wave focus. As demonstrated in the Reitan-Indiana Aphasia Screening results, the patient has a fluent aphasia with anomia, alexia, acalculia, dyspraxia, impaired comprehension, and spelling. She could repeat words correctly, but her performance in repeating sentences was inconsistent. Speech was fluent with appropriate prosody but vacant content. She was perseverative at times as indicated by her repeated attempts at copying the square. There was no paralysis present, and the patient wrote/copied with her dominant right hand.

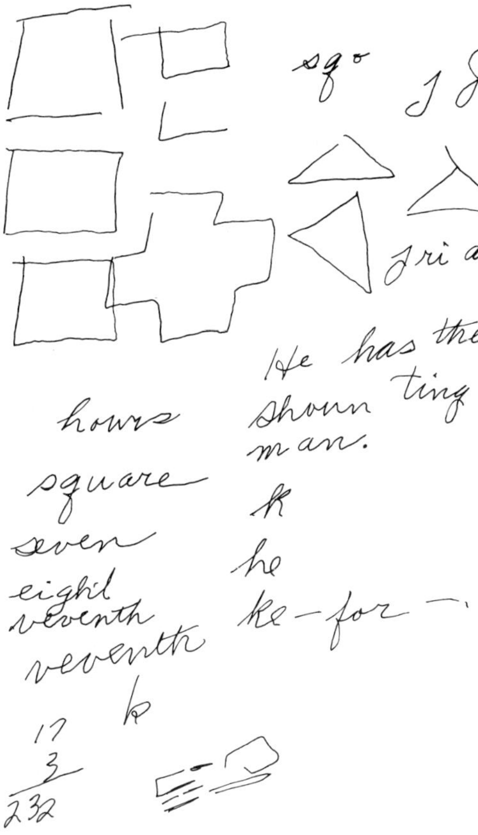

sq°
J Jri an dular
jri
Jri an dular
He has the shoun ting of the man.
hours
square
seven
eight
veventh
veventh
k
he
ke—for—
k
17
3
232

REITAN-INDIANA APHASIA SCREENING TEST

Form for Adults and Older Children

Name: ______ Age: 66 Date: 8-20-84 Examiner: EDB

Copy SQUARE: was able to copy	Repeat TRIANGLE: could correctly repeat with intact articulation
Name SQUARE: Kept drawing square instead of naming. Kept asking "Is this what you mean?"	Repeat MASSACHUSETTS: could correctly repeat with intact articulation
Spell SQUARE: could not comprehend the question	Repeat METHODIST EPISCOPAL: could correctly repeat with intact articulation
Copy CROSS: was able to copy	Write SQUARE: wrote in cursive
Name CROSS: responded with "Millet" followed by "Calip"	Read SEVEN: could not understand instructions, ended up copying the word
Spell CROSS: could not comprehend	Repeat SEVEN: could repeat correctly
Copy TRIANGLE: was able to copy	Repeat/Explain HE SHOUTED THE WARNING. Repeated "He heard the meeting of the" Could not explain the meaning
Name TRIANGLE: responded with "delta" "equa equalantern"	Write HE SHOUTED THE WARNING. attempted with numerous disjointed written words (see center of page)
Spell TRIANGLE: could orally spell correctly, but when attempted to write, she wrote "J Jri an dular"	Compute 85 − 27 = : tried to write out the problem unsuccessfully
Name BABY: responded with "I presume its an elephant, ... a child, a infant. Taking a bathe, swimming."	Compute 17 X 3 = : gave an answer of 232
Write CLOCK: responded with "hours" and then wrote "Veventh" "veventh"	Name KEY: was able to name correctly
Name FORK: responded with "dinner"	Demonstrate use of KEY: Tried to write the word Key
Read 7 SIX 2: responded with "S-I-X S-E-V-E-N" Then wrote seven and eight.	Draw KEY: aproxic drawing
Read MGW: responded with "M x W" "I don't know what this means"	Read PLACE LEFT HAND TO RIGHT EAR. unable to read
Reading I: responded with "See dog. Black. Black dog."	Place LEFT HAND TO RIGHT EAR Could not comprehend instructions
Reading II: responded with "Sandrayshil, animal, famous dog, winner, dog, show"	Place LEFT HAND TO LEFT ELBOW. Could not comprehend instructions

B

there are significant limitations with the sole use of this instrument (see Bigler and Ehrfurth, 1980, 1981). With these limitations in mind, though, the Bender is an appropriate test to examine for ability to copy geometric form. Attention should also be directed to the Block Design subtest on the Wechsler Adult Intelligence Scale (WAIS), because it correlates highly with the presence of constructional dyspraxia (see Strub and Black, 1981). The Benton Visual Retention Test (BVRT) (Benton, 1974) and the Rey-Osterrieth Complex Figure Test (Osterrieth, 1944) may also be used in the graphomotor examination, as well as visual memory tests (see below). The complex figure test is presented in figure 2.7.

Frontal Lobe Syndrome (FLS). Many patients with frontal lobe damage develop an alteration in personality, socially appropriate behavior, goal-directed behavior, and affect (Mesulam, 1986). Orbital frontal lesions may produce shallow affect, substantial irritability, and distractibility. Such patients may become angry and aggressive with little provocation. Lhermitte and colleagues (see Lhermitte, 1986; Lhermitte, Pillon, and Serdaru, 1986) have demonstrated that patients with FLS tend to develop stimulus-bound interaction with their environment with automatic imitation of many behaviors. There are no specific assessment techniques for this condition other than behavioral observation. Such patients do, however, typically function poorly on such measures as the Category Test and the Wisconsin Card Sorting Test.

Memory

The Wechsler Memory Scale (WMS) is probably the most thoroughly studied psychometric test of memory (Russell, 1981). However, before administering the WMS the examiner should ensure that the patient has adequate attention. As recommended by Strub and Black (1981), attention can be evaluated by having the patient tap with a pencil every time the letter *A* is given in the following sequence:

A C Q F A A X M D I R E A Z B G E L H J A A A N A.

Patients with adequate attentive abilities should have little difficulty with this measure. Information obtained during a mental status examination should also permit the clinician to ascertain whether appropriate attention is present.

Wechsler Memory Scale. The WMS was first introduced by Wechsler in 1945. It consists of seven subtests: (1) information, (2) orientation, (3) mental control, (4) memory passages, (5) digits, (6) visual reproductions, and (7) associate learning.

The first two subtests are more a test of orientation, although some remote memories are tapped. Factor analytic studies (see Russell, 1981) suggest four types of memory assessed by WMS: short-term memory—digit span; associative verbal memory—paired associate; meaningful verbal memory—paragraph recall; and figural memory—visual reproductions. It is also recommended that the visual reproductions and logical memory tests be repeated following a thirty-minute interval (Brinkman et al., 1983). With this procedure the number of words and figures can be calculated as well as percentage retained in terms of a long-term memory function.

The WMS correlates highly (0.8) with the Wechsler-Bellvue test, forerunner of the WAIS and WAIS-revised (WAIS-R) (cited in Russell, 1981). Thus, an impaired memory quotient ($\geq$ 12 points below) in relation to WAIS or WAIS-R scores is suggestive of possible memory disturbance (Prifitera and Barley, 1985; Solomon et al., 1985). If verbal memory tests show impairment but that visual reproductions are intact, left hemispheric dysfunction is suggested. Opposite results are more suggestive of right hemispheric involvement, particularly of the right temporal area (Jones-Gotman, 1986). An example of the results obtained from the WAIS is presented in figure 2.10. WMS data are in the legend.

Additional Tests of Memory. During the mental status examination, if formal testing with the WMS is not to be undertaken, then a good measure of short- and long-term memory (see Strub and Black, 1981) is to ask the patient to memorize four words (brown, honesty, tulip, and eyedropper) and test the patient's immediate recall, recall after five minutes, and recall at the end of the examination. Likewise, visual memory may be assessed by selecting four items in the exam room (door, desk, table, book) and similarly having the patient recall immediately, after five minutes, and at the end of the examination. (Note that the words for the object are not given, the objects are pointed to only.) Likewise, four objects (pen, pencil, paper clip, coin) can be hidden about the room, again having the patient recall them at the various times.

Inasmuch as the WMS relies on verbal tasks (Russell, 1981), it is frequently appropriate to examine visual memory in further detail. The BVRT is well suited for this purpose. Additionally, the BVRT may provide lateralization information. The Rey-Osterrieth test is also a good measure of visual recall, with the figure typically being drawn from memory after a three-minute interference period (see fig. 2.7). Lezak (1983) provides scoring data on this measure. The Graham-Kendall Memory-for-Designs Test (Graham and Kendall, 1960) is also a visual memory test that assesses immediate visual recall.

In certain disorders, such as degenerative disease or posttraumatic head injuries in which detailed psychometric evaluation of memory is necessary, the Rey Auditory-Verbal Learning Test (Rey, 1964) should be administered. In this test a list of fifteen words is read to the patient, and the examiner then uses five trials to test recall. The test is outlined in figure 2.8.

After completing the Rey Auditory-Verbal Learning Test (RAVLT), a recognition trial may be useful. The following paragraph (from Lezak, 1976) is given to the patient with instructions to circle the words in italics that were in the memorized list: "The *teacher* swallowed his *coffee* quickly and hurried down the *road* toward the *river*. He crossed the *bridge* and tipped his *hat* to the *farmer* clean-

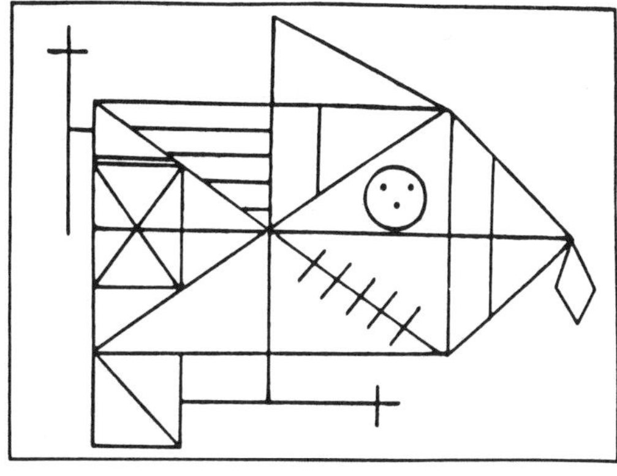

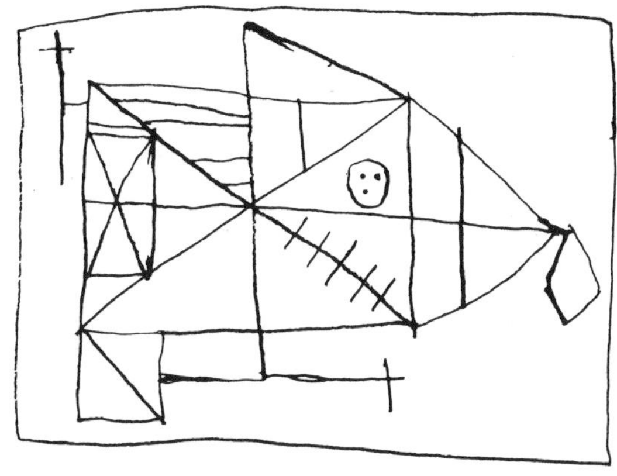

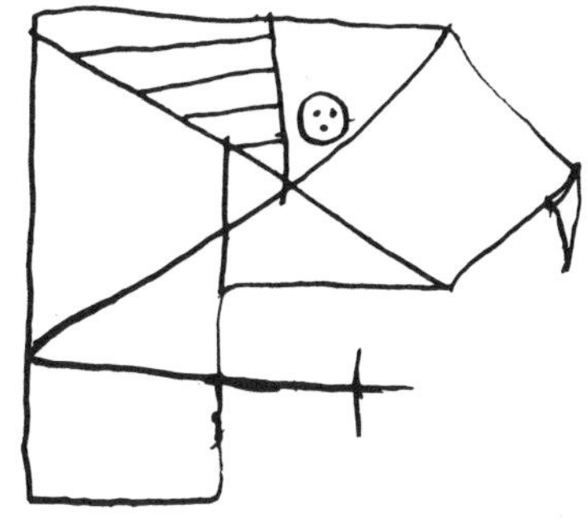

A

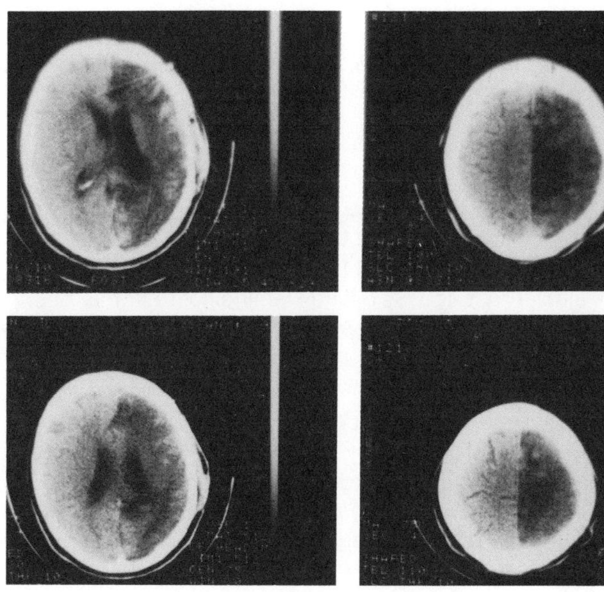

B

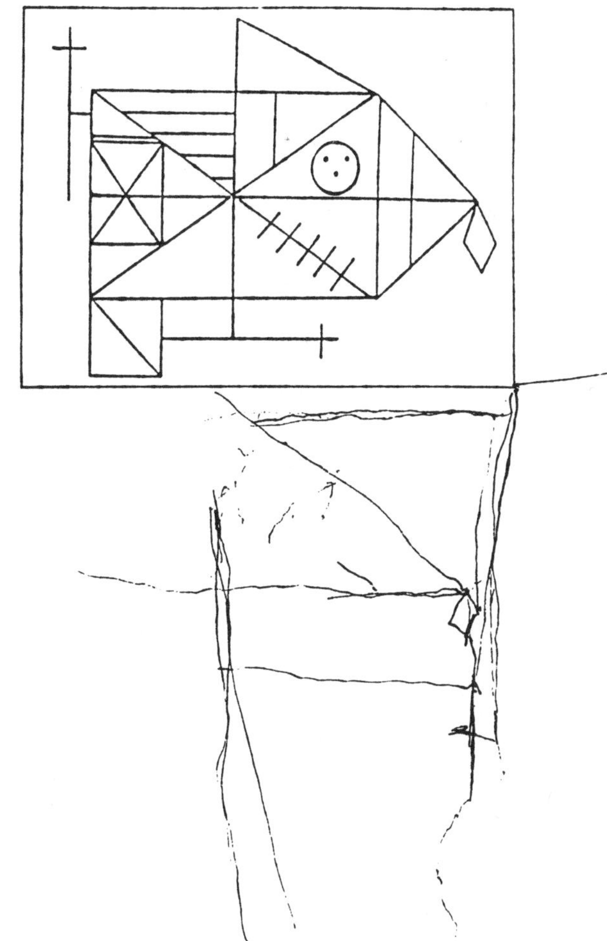

Fig. 2.7. *A*, Rey-Osterrieth Complex Figure Test (*above*). Top right drawing represents patient's copying. Bottom right drawing represents the patient's recall. This patient had right temporal lobectomy for intractable epilepsy. Patients with right temporal lobe involvement typically display visual memory deficits on the Rey-Osterrieth figure recall, as does this patient. *B*, Rey-Osterrieth drawing by a patient with diffuse right hemisphere damage. Note the severe constructional apraxia and the left side neglect. The CAT scans on the left depict complete infarction of the right hemisphere.

List A	Trial					List B (interference)	Recall	Recognition	Alternate List C
	I	II	III	IV	V				
Drum						Desk			Book
Curtain						Ranger			Flower
Bell						Bird			Train
Coffee						Shoe			Rug
School						Stove			Meadow
Parent						Mountain			Harp
Moon						Glasses			Salt
Garden						Towel			Finger
Hat						Cloud			Apple
Farmer						Boat			Chimney
Nose						Lamb			Button
Turkey						Gun			Key
Color						Pencil			Dog
House						Church			Glass
River						Fish			Rattle
Number Recalled									

Fig. 2.8. Rey Auditory-Verbal Learning Test. The fifteen words in list *A* are read, in order, to the patient. The patient is instructed to listen carefully and to try to remember as many words as possible, irrespective of order. After the patient has recalled as many words from the list as possible, the list is repeated with a similar recall trial. This is done until five trials have been completed. At this point, list *B* is read to the patient as an interference procedure. Following this the patient is asked to recall as many words as possible from list *A*. The following scoring notation has been recommended: *R*, repeated correctly; *RC*, repeated after a spontaneous correction; *RQ*, the word has already been recalled, but the patient questions whether the word has been said or not; *E*, error.

ing his *turkey pen*. Every *minute* or so, he wiped his *forehead* and *nose* with his *kerchief*. He arrived at the *school house* just as the last *bell* rang. His *moon face* was the *color* of a *garden beet*. Through the *classroom curtain* he saw a *parent* pace the *floor* while the *children* played *soldier* with a *broomstick gun* and a *drum*." In individuals who do not have brain damage, the recognition level is generally equal to trial 5 recall. Norms indicate that approximately thirteen to fourteen out of the fifteen words should be recalled by trial 5. However, for patients with various kinds of brain damage the average recall after five trials has been reported to be 9.85 (Lezak, 1976). Following the interference procedure, a decrease of three or more words from that recalled in trial 5 is abnormal, according to Lezak (1976), reflecting either a retention or a retrieval problem. Normative data for the RAVLT by age are presented in Table 2.2.

Bigler et al. (in preparation) have examined RAVLT performance in patients with dementia and cerebral trauma. In this study, mean recall on trial 1 was 2.9 for the dementia group and 4.9 for the trauma group. By trial 5, the dementia group had only improved to a mean recall of 5.2 with the mean recall for the trauma group being 9.3. Following interference, the dementia group's recall dropped off to 2.1 with the trauma group being 7.5. Recognition trial performance demonstrated a mean recall of 7.2 for the dementia group and 11.9 for the trauma group.

A similar test, the Selective Reminding Test, has been adapted by Levin and co-workers (1981). It yields similar information and is particularly useful when assessment time is limited (see fig. 2.9). In this test, a list of ten words is initially read to the patient at a rate of one word every two seconds. The patient then tries to recall all of the words in the list in any order (free recall). The patient is then *selectively reminded* of only those words that were not recalled on that trial. The patient is then asked to recall as many words from the list as can be remembered. This procedure of selectively reminding the patient of only the words omitted from the previous trial is continued until the patient correctly recalls all ten words on three consecutive trials or until twelve trials have been presented. This permits the patient to demonstrate learning from items recalled, by spontaneously retrieving them from trial to trial. This is one way to measure long-term retrieval (LTR). Normal patients usually recall all ten words by the third trial. If the word is "lost" and not retained in the next trial (remember, only the words not recalled from trial to trial are presented on subsequent trials), this response can be used as a measure of short-term recall (STR). A measure of long-term storage (LTS) would be the number of items recalled from trial to trial without reminding. Gass and Russell (1986) have recently examined the effects of depression on memory performance. Significant memory impairments were found only with patients who were brain damaged. Thus, clinical differentiation could be achieved.

The following provides an excellent example of the type of memory disturbance seen with bilateral temporal lobe damage: R. A. was a 64-year-old retired nurse when, during cardiovascular surgery for the implantation of a pacemaker, she suffered a basilar artery vessel spasm that in turn produced bilateral ischemic damage to the inferior and mesial temporal lobes. When evaluated three months later, she was found to be intellectually intact (VIQ = 93, PIQ = 97, FSIQ = 93), and she displayed no deficits in language, motor, or sensory-perceptual function. No visual field defects were present. However, she had profound memory disturbance, being essentially amnestic to anything 90 to 100 seconds after initial processing. For example, she could repeat seven digits in the forward direction and six digits in the reverse and had a Wechsler Memory Scale Memory Quotient of 85. However, she had no recall of any of the Wechsler Memory Scale items after 15 minutes and had no recall of the Rey-Osterrieth Figure after 3 minutes. On the Rey Auditory-Verbal Learning Test, she demonstrated only recency and primacy effects, recalling only the first and last three words on each trial, never recalling any of the words presented in the middle. This yielded a "flat" learning/memory curve. The Benton Visual Retention Test was also performed in the impaired range (9 errors: 5 in the left visual field, 4 in the right visual field). Her category test performance was impaired (67 errors), with this being due to her inability to transfer new information from trial to trial,

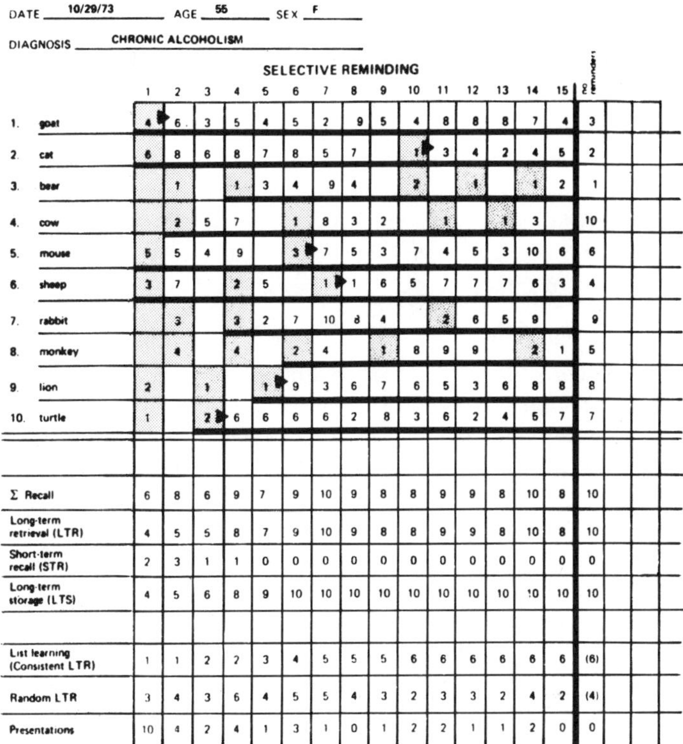
DATE 10/29/73 AGE 55 SEX F

DIAGNOSIS CHRONIC ALCOHOLISM

SELECTIVE REMINDING

	1	2	3	4	5	6	7	8	9	10	11	12	13	14	15	
1. goat	4	6	3	5	4	5	2	9	5	4	8	8	8	7	4	3
2. cat	6	8	6	8	7	8	5	7		1	3	4	2	4	5	2
3. bear		1		1	3	4	9	4		2		1		1	2	1
4. cow		2	5	7		1	8	3	2		1		1	3		10
5. mouse	5	5	4	9		3	7	5	3	7	4	5	3	10	6	6
6. sheep	3	7		2	5		1	1	6	5	7	7	7	6	3	4
7. rabbit		3		3	2	7	10	8	4		2	6	5	9		9
8. monkey		4		4		2	4		1	8	9	9		2	1	5
9. lion	2		1		1	9	3	6	7	6	5	3	6	8	8	8
10. turtle	1		2	6	6	6	6	2	8	3	6	2	4	5	7	7
Σ Recall	6	8	6	9	7	9	10	9	8	8	9	9	8	10	8	10
Long-term retrieval (LTR)	4	5	5	8	7	9	10	9	8	8	9	9	8	10	8	10
Short-term recall (STR)	2	3	1	1	0	0	0	0	0	0	0	0	0	0	0	0
Long-term storage (LTS)	4	5	6	8	9	10	10	10	10	10	10	10	10	10	10	10
List learning (Consistent LTR)	1	1	2	2	3	4	5	5	5	6	6	6	6	6	6	(6)
Random LTR	3	4	3	6	4	5	5	4	3	2	3	3	2	4	2	(4)
Presentations	10	4	2	4	1	3	1	0	1	2	2	1	1	2	0	0

Fig. 2.9. The selective reminding test. Introduced by Buschke and Fuld (1974), this test provides a brief but excellent test of verbal memory that measures initial storage, retention, and retrieval from long-term memory storage. The stippled cells show which items were presented on each trial; numbers show recall order on each trial. Underlining shows retention in long-term storage. Arrows show onset of consistent retrieval without any further presentation. This patient suffered from an alcoholic encephalopathy with particular disturbance of memory. An alternative test form is included in figure 2.12. From Buschke and Fuld (1974).

Table 2.2. *Normative Data by Age for the Rey AVLT*

Age	*N*	Trial I $\bar{X}$	Trial I *SD*	Trial V $\bar{X}$	Trial V *SD*	Recall $\bar{X}$	Recall *SD*	Recognition $\bar{X}$	Recognition *SD*	I–V Diff.
15–24	54	6.15	1.46	11.50	0.63	9.80	1.66	12.81	2.26	5.35
25–29	88	5.98	1.43	11.27	1.87	9.91	2.36	12.16	2.51	5.29
30–34	109	5.68	1.17	10.71	4.19	9.08	2.94	13.03	1.57	5.03
35–39	54	5.49	1.77	11.80	1.94	9.55	2.05	13.45	1.12	6.31
40–44	50	5.51	1.44	11.14	1.59	9.37	2.60	12.86	2.25	5.63
45–49	52	5.10	1.27	10.43	1.92	8.18	2.91	12.23	1.70	5.33
50–54	83	5.01	1.62	9.38	2.66	7.12	3.40	11.48	2.67	4.37
55–59	81	4.53	2.50	8.80	5.04	5.96	4.28	10.75	6.41	4.27
60–64	57	4.09	1.61	7.54	2.57	5.81	2.64	9.96	2.62	3.45
65–69	26	4.12	1.26	7.29	6.12	5.21	2.58	9.50	3.33	3.17
70+	23	3.14	1.50	5.86	2.04	3.45	2.92	8.91	3.64	2.72

Source: From Query and Megran (1983).

and an excessive number of errors during the last trial, which is the memory retention trial. Her Raven's Test was borderline normal (28/36) for her age. Patients with memory deficits typically can function adequately on the Raven's Test because it does not require any new learning, learning from trial to trial, or short-term memory retention. This represents the typical neuropsychological profile seen in patients with damage restricted to the temporal lobes with the remainder of the cerebrum being essentially intact.

Intelligence

Several tests of intellectual functioning exist with the most common, in terms of its utility in neuropsychologic assessment, being the Wechsler scales of intelligence—the Wechsler Adult Intelligence Scale, the Wechsler Intelligence Scale for Children-Revised, and the Wechsler Pre-School and Primary Scale of Intelligence (WPPSI). The WAIS has just recently been revised. Initial studies (Kelly et al., 1984) suggest that WAIS-R scores tend to be lower than those obtained with the WAIS, but pattern interpretation of the WAIS-R is similar to that of the WAIS.

Wechsler Adult Intelligence Scale. The WAIS comprises eleven subtests, six that make up the verbal part and five that constitute the performance part (see Wechsler, 1958). Each subtest is scaled so that the raw score is transformed to a scaled score with a range from 0 to 19. A scaled score of 10 is considered an average score; the standard deviation is 3. The six scaled scores for the verbal part are added together to calculate the verbal IQ (VIQ), which has a mean of 100 and a standard deviation of 15. Similarly, the five performance subtests are added together to yield the performance IQ (PIQ), which also has a mean of 100 and a standard deviation of 15. The VIQ and PIQ scaled scores are then added together. The resulting score yields the full-scale IQ (FSIQ). The individual subtests follow:

Verbal Subtests

1. *Information.* This is a measure of general information. It tends to remain relatively stable in various neurologic disorders, but when severely affected it is suggestive of significant brain disease. When not affected, this subtest may be a measure to estimate the patient's premorbid level of intellectual functioning.

2. *Comprehension.* This test assesses the patient's ability to use simple judgment and his comprehension. In terms of diagnosing neurologic disorders, it is similar to *Information.*

3. *Similarities.* In this subtest the patient is asked the common link between objects or functions (e.g., how are a pencil and chalk alike). This subtest's results are commonly affected in patients with neurologic disorders, particularly if the lesion site is dominant temporal or parietal.

4. *Arithmetic.* This test assesses the patient's ability to perform mental arithmetic. Patients may make low arithmetic scores if they suffer some neurologic disorder, but scores are also affected by anxiety, poor attention span (of either organic or nonorganic etiology), and other psychologic states.

5. *Digit Span.* The patient is presented orally with random numbers that increase in length every other trial, and the patient is first required to recite the numbers in the forward direction and then in the reverse direction. It is common to find this subtest score affected when the patient has an organic disorder. Implications of digit span deficits have been previously discussed in the section on memory.

6. *Vocabulary.* This test requires the patient to define individual words orally. This task tends to be an overlearned task, and when brain damage or dysfunction does not involve the speech-language areas of the dominant hemisphere or diffuse cerebral dysfunction, the Vocabulary test score may be average or above. Again, this score may be an estimate of premorbid intellectual functioning.

Performance Subtests

1. *Digit Symbol.* This subtest is the most sensitive singular test for indicating the presence of organic brain dysfunction. The test's task requires the patient to transpose into randomly numbered squares a symbol associated with numbers one to nine. The reason that this task is so sensitive to brain dysfunction is that it requires considerable cerebral involvement in its execution. Thus, visuomotor coordination, visual and visual-verbal associative memory (verbal in that numbers are used and several of the symbols are similar to verbal symbols, for example, an upside down *T* or backwards *C*), and motor speed. An alternative form of the Digit Symbol subtest has been developed by Smith (1975) to be used singularly (Symbol-Digits Modality Test).

2. *Picture Completion.* The task in this subtest is to identify the missing aspect in a picture. Subtest scores of patients who have sustained cerebral injury may be affected little, unless visuospatial deficits are present.

3. *Block Design.* This test requires patients to position blocks in a manner that copies a stimulus figure. Originally, test givers believed this task was dependent on nondominant parietal lobe function, but now they believe it may be affected by either right or left parietal involvement. It can sometimes be utilized as a measure of praxis.

4. *Picture Arrangement.* This task requires the patient to reposition a series of cartoon pictures in such an order as to make sense. When scores on this task are singularly affected but other PIQ tasks show relatively average performance, the results suggest right temporal lobe damage or dysfunction.

5. *Object Assembly.* This task is essentially putting various jigsaw puzzles together. This task is somewhat related to praxis and visual-perceptive functioning, as is the Block Design.

Interpretation of WAIS. The WAIS should only be interpreted in the context of additional neuropsychologic measures (Goldstein and Shelly, 1984). Originally, it was thought that lowered VIQ was indicative of left brain injury, and lowered PIQ was related to right brain injury (see McFie, 1975); however, this has not entirely proven to be the case (see Bigler, 1982; Bigler, Steinman, and Newton, 1981*a*, 1981*b*; Leli and Filskov, 1981; Russell, 1979). These studies have demonstrated no strong relationship between VIQ differences and PIQ differences and lateralization of dysfunction. For example, in Russell's work, he found that 40 percent of patients with left brain damage had higher VIQs than PIQs. Such findings underscore the necessity of not relying solely on WAIS findings for neuropsychological interpretation. Previous research had indicated the sensitivity of the Arithmetic and Digit Span subtests in detecting organic brain damage. This, however, has not been proved to be the case. The single most predictive subtest for the presence of organic dysfunction, irrespective of location or type, is the Digit Symbol subtest. Further mention should be made in terms of "hold" or "crystallized" and "don't hold" or "fluid" aspects of intelligence. Russell's work clearly shows the verbal subtests of Information, Comprehension, and Vocabulary to be well-established, overlearned, "crystallized" tests. Conversely, Digit Symbol, Block Design, Picture Arrangement, and Object Assembly subtests depend upon new learning, adaptive, "fluid" aspects of intelligence. Thus, when brain injury occurs, regardless of locus (with the exception of lesions that produce a frank aphasia), the fluid aspects of intelligence will be more greatly affected than the crystallized. Thus, the admonition should be stated again that VIQ-PIQ differences and subtest pattern analyses should only be undertaken in relation to other aspects of the neuropsychological test battery. An example of WAIS results of a patient with degenerative disease is presented in figure 2.10.

In a large retrospective study of 656 patients with lateralized cerebral lesions, Warrington, James, and Maciejewski (1986) found that the VIQ measure was impaired in all left hemisphere damaged subgroups, but the converse was not true. The PIQ measure was only significantly impaired in patients with the lesion locus in the right parietal region. In this group of right parietal damaged patients, the Block Design and Picture Arrangement subtests were the most affected. They found no sex differences associated with lateralized WAIS findings (see also Bornstein and Matarazzo, 1984; Yeo, Turkheimer, and Bigler, 1984).

Premorbid IQ. In assessing the intellectual deficit of a patient with cerebral dysfunction, it is important to establish some type of comparison with an estimate of premorbid level of function. Lezak (1983) (see also Klesges, 1982) has reviewed in some detail the shortcomings in estimating premorbid IQ. Although Wilson et al. (1978) have developed a formula to predict premorbid IQ based on educational level, occupation, and socioeconomic status, it is usually adequate to estimate a general range of IQ based on the clinical data described above. Additionally, but for

TABLE OF SCALED SCORE EQUIVALENTS

	RAW SCORE											
Scaled Score	Information	Comprehension	Arithmetic	Similarities	Digit Span	Vocabulary	Digit Symbol	Picture Completion	Block Design	Picture Arrangement	Object Assembly	Scaled Score
19	29	27-28		26	17	78-80	87-90					19
18	28	26		25		76-77	83-86	21		36	44	18
17	27	25	18	24		74-75	79-82		48	35	43	17
16	26	24	17	23	16	71-73	76-78	20	47	34	42	16
15	25	23	16	22	15	67-70	72-75		46	33	41	15
14	23-24	22	15	21	14	63-66	69-71	19	44-45	32	40	14
13	21-22	21	14	19-20		59-62	66-68	18	42-43	30-31	38-39	13
12	19-20	20	13	17-18	13	54-58	62-65	17	39-41	28-29	36-37	12
11	17-18	19	12	15-16	12	47-53	58-61	15-16	35-38	26-27	34-35	11
10	15-16	17-18	11	13-14	11	40-46	52-57	14	31-34	23-25	31-33	10
9	13-14	15-16	10	11-12	10	32-39	47-51	12-13	28-30	20-22	28-30	9
8	11-12	14	9	9-10		26-31	41-46	10-11	25-27	18-19	25-27	8
7	9-10	12-13	7-8	7-8	9	22-25	35-40	8-9	21-24	15-17	22-24	7
6	7-8	10-11	6	5-6	8	18-21	29-34	6-7	17-20	12-14	19-21	6
5	5-6	8-9	5	4		14-17	23-28	5	13-16	9-11	15-18	5
4	4	6-7	4	3	7	11-13	18-22	4	10-12	8	11-14	4
3	3	5	3	2		10	15-17	3	6-9	7	8-10	3
2	2	4	2	1	6	9	13-14	2	3-5	6	5-7	2
1	1	3	1		4-5	8	12	1	2	5	3-4	1
0	0	0-2	0	0	0-3	0-7	0-11	0	0-1	0-4	0-2	0

Fig. 2.10. An example of a WAIS profile of a patient with Alzheimer's disease. This 57-year-old man (Case 1, p. 79) had a college education (B.S. in engineering) and worked as a highway engineer. At the time of this examination, he had had a three-year decline in mental functioning. His WAIS scores were as follows: verbal IQ = 75, performance IQ = 67, full-scale IQ = 70. The pattern of results illustrates well how vocabulary is least affected, but digit symbol, digit span, and picture arrangement are markedly impaired. These last tests are more "fluid" measures. Also note the more substantial effect on performance subtests than on verbal tests, but without much difference between actual VIQ and PIQ values. This is because of the larger correction factor for increasing age on PIQ measures. This patient also displayed rather dramatic memory disturbance of generalized proportions as evidenced by the Wechsler Memory Scale results. On the WMS the patient obtained a memory quotient of 54, which is substantially below what would even be predicted by his IQ, thus reflecting the severity of the memory disorder. The WMS subtest scores were as follows: (1) Information, *0;* (2) orientation, *0;* (3) mental control, *0;* (4) memory passages, 0; (5) digits, 3; (6) visual reproduction, 2; and (7) associate learning, 6. This patient's Halstead-Reitan Neuropsychological Test Battery profile is presented in Case 1, which further depicts the diffuse nature of the cerebral dysfunction present in this patient.

only nonaphasic patients, taking the average score of the three highest scores of the Wechsler subtests and using this average to prorate an IQ score may give an estimate of premorbid IQ level.

Wechsler Intelligence Scale for Children-Revised (WISC-R). The WISC-R is to a certain extent a downward extension of the WAIS (Kaufman, Long, and O'Neal, 1986). Many of the same inferences that have been made with the WAIS can be made with the WISC-R. However, much of the neuropsychological research with children has suggested that the factor structure of the WISC-R indicates three grouping areas that may have clinical significance. The three factors that have been described are as follows:

1. *Verbal Comprehension.* All verbal subtests except arithmetic and digit span.
2. *Perceptual Organization.* All performance subtests except coding.
3. *Freedom from Distractibility.* Includes the arithmetic, digit span, and coding subtests.

The term used to label Factor 3—Freedom from Distractibility—however, has been questioned by Ownby and Matthews (1985), who demonstrated that Factor 3 included visual spatial organization, rapid shifting mental operations based on symbolic material, and sustained attention during complex cognitive processing. They suggest that instead of naming these various factors clinicians should just use the number label (i.e., Factors 1, 2, or 3). It appears that from the neuropsychology standpoint this approach to conceptualizing the WISC-R has clinical merit.

Raven's (Coloured) Progressive Matrices Test. The Raven's Progressive Matrices and the Coloured Progressive Matrices provide an index of nonverbal visual-spatial reasoning and problem solving. The task has no motor requirements, and this is frequently useful in patients with dominant side paralysis and aphasia or other restrictions in motor control. Norms have been published in the accompanying handbook by Raven (1960, 1965). In a study by Bigler et al. (in preparation) the mean number correct out of 36 trials was 19 for dementia patients and 27 for cerebral trauma patients. Normal controls have little difficulty with this test and typically score above 32.

Personality Measures

The Minnesota Multiphasic Personality Inventory (MMPI) continues to be the test most often used in evaluating personality features in neurologic patients. However, several lines of research (Cullum and Bigler, 1987; Gass and Russell, 1985) have suggested that there is no specific "organic" pattern on the MMPI associated with brain damage. Patients with brain damage, irrespective of the locus or lateralization of the lesion, tend to show mild dysphoria, dissatisfaction, withdrawal, decreased initiative, and mild somatic preoccupations. As presented in figure 2.11, the MMPI configurations from the Cullum and Bigler (1987) study demonstrate little difference in the overall mean configuration from patients with restricted left, right, or diffuse cerebral damage. From the clinical standpoint, the MMPI should be utilized as an objective measure of the patient's self-reported symptomatology, and it cannot be used as an inferential method for lesion lateralization or localization or even for the presence of brain damage.

Sex Differences in Neuropsychological Performance

Several lines of research have implicated that males may be more lateralized than females and that, accordingly, when lateralized lesions occur males will demonstrate more striking deficits in terms of lateralized functioning (Lawson and Inglis, 1983; Lawson, Inglis, and Stroud, 1983; Yeo et al., 1984). However, this speculation is far from being resolved at this time, and much research is needed to address this question in terms of its clinical implications. Recent work by Bornstein (1984), Bornstein and Matarazzo (1984), Snow and Sheese (1985), Sundet (1986), and Warrington, James, and Maciejewski (1986) has failed to fully support such differences.

Other Neuropsychological Tests

Benton and his colleagues (see Benton et al., 1983) have made seminal contributions to the development of clinical neuropsychology and have summarized their work in this 1983 text. In this collection of tests, a variety of assessment guidelines are provided for the following tests: Temporal Orientation, Right-Left Orientation, Serial Digit Learning, Facial Recognition, Judgment-of-Line Orientation, Visual Form Discrimination, Pantomime Recognition, Tactile Form Perception, Finger Localization, Phoneme Discrimination, Three-Dimensional Block Construction, and Motor Impersistence. This is an excellent collection of tests designed to be used on an individual basis to provide greater clinical insight into specific neuropsychological problems.

Neuropsychologic Test Batteries

The two most common neuropsychologic test batteries are the Halstead-Reitan Neuropsychological Test Battery (HRNTB) (see Reitan and Davison, 1974) and the Luria-Nebraska Neuropsychological Battery (LNNB) (see Golden, Hammeke, and Purisch, 1978). Other test batteries have been developed, primarily from various individual tests as reviewed by Lezak (1983), but the HRNTB and the LNNB remain the tests most commonly utilized. Both will be briefly reviewed.

Luria-Nebraska Neuropsychological Battery

Luria was an eminent Russian neuropsychologist (see Luria, 1966, 1973; Luria and Majovski, 1977) who was not only an adroit clinician but also an important theorist. He considered standardization inappropriate—that clinical diagnosis was best made by careful clinical delineation of the problem and not based on whether the patient made or surpassed some type of "cutoff" score indicative of brain pathology. Thus, none of Luria's procedures were standardized. Keeping in this tradition, Christensen (1979) published a book that reviewed Luria's technique but did not provide scoring or standardization. Golden and his associates (Golden, Hammeke, and Purisch, 1978) took the Christensen analysis of the Luria technique along with their own tests and developed the LNNB. It is divided into eleven clinical scales as follows (name of each scale implies function tested): motor functions, rhythm and pitch, tactile and kinesthetic functions, visual functions, receptive language, expressive language, writing scale, reading scale, arithmetic scale, memory scale, and intelligence scale. Additionally, there is a pathognomonic scale that is sensitive to the severity and acuteness of neurologic dysfunction as well as a left and right hemisphere scale that aids in lateralization. Golden (1981) provides further reading. Several limitations of this battery have also been demonstrated (see Adams, 1980, 1984; Delis and Kaplan, 1983; Mittenberg, Kasprisin, and Farage, 1985; Spiers, 1981, 1982), and it continues to be revised. Its utilization should probably be limited until all of the appropriate standardization and revision studies have been completed.

Halstead-Reitan Neuropsychological Test Battery

The HRNTB is undoubtedly the most commonly used neuropsychological battery at this time (Boll, 1981; Swiercinsky, 1978). The nuclear tests of the battery were originally developed by Halstead (1947) with Reitan (see Reitan and Davison, 1974) standardizing the measures with a clinical population as well as adding and deleting several tests. The HRNTB is basically composed of the following tests: Category, Tactual Performance, Seashore Rhythm, Speech Sounds Perception, Finger Oscillation, Lateral Dominance, Strength-of-Grip, Trail-Making, and Reitan-Indiana Aphasia Screening (Reitan-Indiana AST), and the Reitan-Kløve Sensory-Perceptual Examination. The Finger Oscillation, Strength-of-Grip, and Lateral Dominance tests, Reitan-Indiana AST, and Reitan-Kløve SPE have been previously discussed. Because the diagnostic outline of this text relies on several of the Halstead-Reitan measures, the remainder of the tests are described.

The Category Test (CT) is a test of nonverbal abstract reasoning, problem solving, and concept formation. A total of 218 visual stimuli are separately presented in seven different subtests. The patient has immediate feedback on whether a response is correct or incorrect. The CT is a nonlocalizing test, because it indicates impairment secondary to brain damage/dysfunction in a variety of areas and systems (50 or more errors are in the impaired range). There is some tendency for the patient with serious frontal or generalized cerebral dysfunction to make more than 100 errors. Since performance on the CT correlates highly with IQ, resultant IQ and CT error comparisons can be clinically useful (see table 2.3). The CT is related somewhat to the Wisconsin Card Sorting Test, although the two are not interchangeable (Bond and

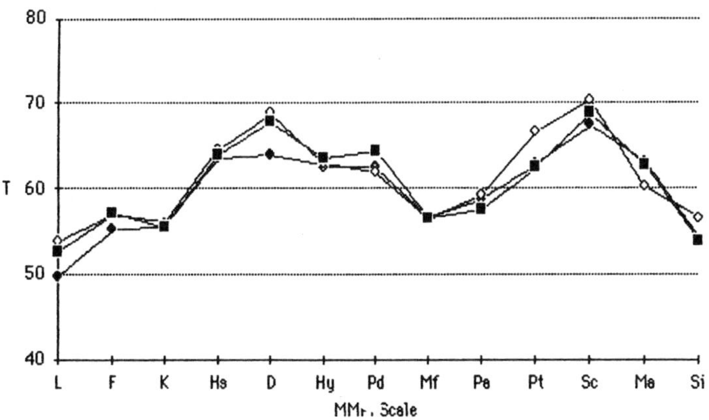

Fig. 2.11. MMPI results in patients with left (*open diamond*; *N* = 47), right (*dark diamond*; *N* = 47), and diffuse (*dark square*; *N* = 59) cerebral damage. Note that there is little difference across the groups. The configuration of the MMPI in the various groupings indicates tendency toward mild elevations on the depression, psychasthenia, and schizophrenia subscales. From Cullum and Bigler (1987).

Table 2.3. *Predicted Category Test Error Scores from Observed Performance IQ Scores*

Normal Controls (*N* = 69)		Brain Damaged (*N* = 92)	
Observed Performance IQ	Predicted Category Test Errors	Observed Performance IQ	Predicted Category Test Errors
140	22	140	27
130	24	130	37
120	26	120	47
110	28	110	58
100	30	100	68
90	32	90	79

Note: This table provides an index for assessing the degree of cognitive deficit as measured by the Category Test in relation to Performance IQ. A preliminary study (Cullum, Steinman, and Bigler, 1984) determined that Performance IQ was most predictive of the observed Category Test error score. Thus, if a patient had a brain injury that resulted in a Performance IQ of 90, the expected Category Test error score would be 79. However, if the actual Category Test error score obtained was higher than 79, the score would suggest a greater degree of cognitive deficit than would have been predicted given the Performance IQ level. These types of comparisons may be particularly useful in assessing the degree of cognitive impairment.

Buchtel, 1984). The Tactual Performance Test (TPT) is actually a modification of the Sequin-Goddard formboard (Thompson and Parsons, 1985). The adult form has ten blocks that are to be separately placed into only one position on the formboard. This is done first with the dominant hand, then the nondominant, and then both. The patient is blindfolded to make the test strictly a sensory (somesthesis-kinesthesis)–motor performance test. Since it is first performed with one hand and then the other, right-left comparisons can be made with lateralizing implications. Thus, if the task is performed poorly with the nondominant hand in comparison to the performance by the dominant hand, then this may be correlated with a nondominant hemispheric lesion. Associated with the TPT is a memory and spatial localization component. Since the memory is for the number of block shapes as well as their position, this tends to tap more nondominant hemispheric functions of a spatial or tactile memory nature. Russell (1985) has presented evidence demonstrating that the six-hole formboard can be substituted for the ten-hole TPT board. This is particularly appropriate for the patient with substantial neurologic impairment, the difficult to test patient, or the aged patient.

The Speech Sounds Perception Test (SSPT) is a test of visual-verbal discrimination in which the patient attempts to discriminate and match a nonsense word auditorily presented with that visually presented in a list of four words. This test tends to be sensitive to receptive language functions of the posterior temporal and parietal regions of the dominant hemisphere. In this test there are sixty nonsense syllables arranged into six series of ten each. Although there was an attempt in its original construction to counterbalance the difficulty of the visual-verbal discrimination, the majority of errors tend to occur over the first three subtests (Bornstein, Weizel, and Grant, 1984).

The Seashore Rhythm Test (SRT) is a measure of ability to discriminate whether two rhythms (beat patterns) that are presented sequentially are the same or different. The test requires sustained attention as well as auditory sequential discrimination. Test results are usually impaired in patients with lesions of the dominant hemisphere, particularly in auditory and language association areas. SSPT scores will usually also be affected. For patients with lesions in the nondominant hemisphere, performance on this test may be affected owing to deficits in sequential processing of the stimuli as well as their musical relationships, factors that tend to be based in the nondominant hemisphere. In such cases SSPT results are usually not affected.

The Trail-Making Test (TM) comprises two subtests, *A* and *B*. In *A*, the numbers from 1 to 25 are randomly presented (but in a standardized form), and the patient is required to sequentially connect the numbers. In *B*, thirteen numbers (1–13) and twelve letters (*A* through *L*) are randomly presented, but on a standardized form, and the patient is again required to sequentially connect first the first number with the first letter, then the second number with the second letter, and so on (i.e., 1-A, 2-B, 3-C, . . . , L-13). Table 2.4 presents the cutoff values indicative of impairment, table 2.5 outlines the correlation between certain HRNTB measures and locus of cerebral dysfunction, and table 2.6 provides normative data.

Reitan (1985) proposes that an impairment index (II) be used to identify the presence of brain damage. The subtests that are used to calculate the II are Finger Oscillation–dominant hand, Tactual Performance total time, Localization, Memory, Speech Sounds Perception, Seashore Rhythm, and Category. The total number of impaired tests are divided by the total number of tests administered (typically 7). The impairment index will range from 0.1 (no impairment) to 1.0 (maximum impairment across all tests). Reitan (1985) suggests that when measured IQ is 100 or above the impairment index cutoff 0.4 or greater be used to identify brain damage, but when IQ is below 100 the cutoff score should be 0.5 or greater. A case study provides HRNTB results and interpretation concerning a patient with degenerative brain disorder.

Brief Screening Methods

Some mention should be made concerning neuropsychological screening tests. While brief screening measures appear to perform adequately in terms of the clinical differentiation of advanced dementia and delirium, they display too many false-negatives as well as false-positives for most of the other neurologic disorders. Nelson, Fogel, and Faust (1986) demonstrated that this was particularly true with patients with right hemisphere pathology. Accordingly, screening tests cannot be substituted for the more complete, thorough, and elaborate neuropsychological workup of the patient with neurologic disorder.

Table 2.4. *Halstead-Reitan Neuropsychological Test Battery Cutoff Values Indicative of Impairment*

Test	Score Impaired Range
Category Test	> 51
Tactual Performance Test	
Dominant	> 6–7 minutes
Nondominant	> 4–5 minutes
Both	> 3–4 minutes
Total time	≥ 15.7 minutes
Memory	≤ 5 blocks
Localization	≤ 4 blocks
Seashore Rhythm Test	> 5 errors
Speech Sounds Perception Test	> 7 errors
Trail Making-A	> 39 seconds
Trail Making-B	> 91 seconds
Finger Oscillation Test	
Dominant	< 50
Nondominant	< 45

Table 2.5. ***Association between Impaired Test Performance and Cerebral Deficit***

Halstead-Reitan Neuropsychological Test Battery Measures	Localized Cerebral Deficit
Right Finger Oscillation speeds diminished, elevated right-side Tactual Performance Test score, absence of sensory or aphasic deficits (other than dysarthria or expressive deficit), and possibly significantly elevated Category Test score.	Left frontal
Left Finger Oscillation speeds diminished, elevated left-side Tactual Performance Test time, absence of sensory deficit or significantly impaired deficits in constructional praxis. Possibly significantly elevated Category Test score.	Right frontal
Right Finger Oscillation speeds within normal limits, but right-side somesthetic sensory errors present, elevated Tactual Performance Test times in absence of significant motor deficit. Possibly dysphasic signs of receptive nature.	Left parietal
Left Finger Oscillation speeds within normal limits, but left-side somesthetic sensory errors present, elevated Tactual Performance Test times in absence of significant motor deficit. Significant constructional dyspraxia may be present.	Right parietal
Absence of motor signs but presence of receptive dysphasic deficits along with impairment on Speech Sounds Performance Test and Seashore Rhythm Test. Right-side auditory extinction.	Left temporal
Absence of motor signs but presence of left ear auditory extinction. Possibly impaired Seashore Rhythm Test performance in the absence of deficits on Speech Sounds Performance Test.	Right temporal
Right homonymous hemianopsia and potentially some receptive dysphasic deficits, in particular alexia without agraphia.	Left occipital
Left homonymous hemianopsia in the absence of constructional apraxia.	Right occipital

Table 2.6. ***Normative Data for the Halstead-Reitan Neuropsychological Tests***

Speech Sounds Perception Test (total errors)

Age	*N*	*M*	*SD*	Range
15–17	32	4.6	2.4	1–13
18–23	76	4.2	2.0	1–10
24–32	57	4.1	2.2	1–10
33–40	18	3.6	2.0	1–8
41–64	10	4.4	1.8	1–7

Seashore Rhythm Test (total errors)

Age	*N*	*M*	*SD*	Range
15–17	32	2.1	1.4	0–5
18–23	75	2.5	2.1	0–9
24–32	57	2.4	1.9	0–9
33–40	18	2.3	2.1	0–8
41–64	10	3.9	2.1	1–6

Category Test (total errors)

Age	*N*	*M*	*SD*	Range
15–17	32	35.8	16.2	16–68
18–23	71	35.9	21.2	9–106
24–32	55	30.5	13.6	10–68
33–40	18	36.3	14.3	11–67
41–64	10	53.0	21.0	29–96

Trail-Making Test (seconds)

		Part A			Part B		
Age	*N*	*M*	*SD*	Range	*M*	*SD*	Range
15–17	32	23.4	5.9	15.2–39.0	47.7	10.4	25.4– 81.0
18–23	76	26.7	9.4	12.0–60.1	51.3	14.6	23.3–101.0
24–32	57	24.3	7.6	11.8–46.0	53.2	15.6	29.1– 98.0
33–40	18	27.5	8.3	16.0–52.7	62.1	17.5	39.0–111.0
41–64	10	29.7	8.4	16.5–42.0	73.6	19.4	41.9–102.0

Finger Localization Test (total errors per hand)

		Preferred Hand			Nonpreferred Hand		
Age	*N*	*M*	*SD*	Range	*M*	*SD*	Range
15–17	32	2.8	2.3	0–9	3.1	2.2	0–8
18–23	76	2.8	2.7	0–12	3.0	3.3	0–20
24–32	54	2.3	2.4	0–10	2.8	2.4	0–9
33–40	18	2.4	2.6	0–9	2.5	3.2	0–14
41–64	10	2.9	1.8	0–7	3.7	2.6	0–8

Source: From Fromm-Auch and Yeudall (1983).

Table 2.6. *(continued)*

Tactual Performance Test (minutes)							
		Preferred Hand			Nonpreferred Hand		
Age	*N*	*M*	*SD*	Range	*M*	*SD*	Range
15–17	32	4.6	1.2	2.6– 6.8	3.3	1.2	1.1– 6.4
18–23	74	5.1	2.2	1.9–13.5	3.5	1.6	1.1–10.8
24–32	56	4.5	1.8	1.7– 9.5	3.1	1.1	1.5– 7.1
33–40	18	4.9	1.7	1.9– 9.0	3.7	1.0	2.2– 5.9
41–64	10	5.6	1.5	4.0– 9.0	4.2	1.6	2.4– 8.1
		Both Hands			Total Time		
15–17	32	1.7	0.5	0.8–3.3	9.5	2.1	4.7–14.1
18–23	74	2.1	1.3	0.4–9.3	10.6	4.5	4.2–29.1
24–32	56	1.8	0.8	0.5–4.6	9.4	3.0	3.8–18.8
33–40	18	2.3	0.8	1.4–4.4	10.9	2.9	5.9–19.4
41–64	10	2.5	1.2	1.4–5.5	12.2	3.6	8.3–20.6

Tactual Performance Test (total correct blocks)							
		Localization			Memory		
Age	*N*	*M*	*SD*	Range	*M*	*SD*	Range
15–17	32	6.8	2.5	1–10	8.9	1.0	6–10
18–23	74	5.7	2.1	1–10	8.2	1.3	4–10
24–32	57	5.5	1.8	2–9	8.3	1.1	6–10
33–40	18	5.6	2.2	1–9	8.6	1.1	6–10
41–64	10	4.9	1.8	2–7	7.7	1.3	6–9

Tactile Form Recognition Test (total errors)							
Errors							
		Preferred Hand			Nonpreferred Hand		
Age	*N*	*M*	*SD*	Range	*M*	*SD*	Range
15–17	32	0.06	0.24	0–1	0.03	0.18	0–1
18–23	54	0.02	0.14	0–1	0.19	0.14	0–1
24–32	47	0.02	0.15	0–1	0.02	0.15	0–1
33–40	18	0	0	0	0	0	0
41–64	10	0	0	0	0	0	0

Finger-Tip Number Writing Test (total errors)							
		Preferred Hand			Nonpreferred Hand		
Age	*N*	*M*	*SD*	Range	*M*	*SD*	Range
15–17	32	1.3	1.7	0–7	1.2	1.1	0–4
18–23	69	2.3	2.4	0–10	1.9	2.1	0–9
24–32	54	1.3	1.8	0–7	0.94	1.3	0–5
33–40	18	2.4	2.3	0–10	1.3	1.0	0–3
41–64	8	2.5	2.5	0–7	1.1	1.6	0–4

Table 2.6. *(continued)*

Finger Tapping Test[a]							
		Preferred Hand			Nonpreferred Hand		
Age	*N*	*M*	*SD*	Range	*M*	*SD*	Range
Males							
15–17	17	47.6	5.8	38.0–55.6	43.6	4.9	33.4–51.8
18–23	44	49.5	6.9	26.6–64.6	45.4	6.9	26.8–58.6
24–32	31	50.6	6.6	38.2–66.2	46.0	6.1	28.8–55.0
33–40	12	53.4	5.9	39.0–61.0	49.8	4.7	41.0–57.8
41–64	4	44.4	5.8	35.8–48.2	41.4	3.5	36.6–44.4
Females							
15–17	15	42.7	7.9	30.2–54.0	41.1	6.2	31.6–51.0
18–23	30	43.6	7.5	30.6–65.6	41.2	6.5	32.8–61.8
24–32	25	45.2	6.7	31.0–60.0	40.9	5.7	28.6–53.6
33–40	6	45.8	5.5	40.6–55.6	44.3	4.6	40.6–53.2
41–64	6	40.4	4.8	34.2–48.4	38.6	4.8	32.0–46.6

[a] Average number of taps over five trials.

Dynamometer[a]							
		Preferred Hand			Nonpreferred Hand		
Age	*N*	*M*	*SD*	Range	*M*	*SD*	Range
Males							
15–17	17	38.0	8.4	22.2–51.0	35.8	9.6	21.0–57.5
18–23	43	49.7	9.7	30.0–71.2	46.6	9.9	26.7–73.0
24–32	31	51.8	8.1	37.0–65.5	49.6	7.2	30.5–66.0
33–40	12	52.9	8.3	41.0–67.0	51.2	7.9	36.2–62.5
41–64	4	44.5	10.9	30.5–57.0	47.9	11.9	32.0–58.7
Females							
15–17	15	28.1	5.0	21.0–37.5	26.3	5.2	17.8–33.5
18–23	29	28.8	7.8	8.5–43.8	26.4	6.2	13.5–38.0
24–32	24	34.4	9.2	20.5–64.7	30.2	6.8	20.5–49.5
33–40	6	27.7	3.2	23.0–31.5	28.6	3.1	25.2–33.5
41–64	6	28.0	6.2	18.7–37.5	24.1	6.8	16.7–36.5

[a] Kilogram average of two trials.

Neuropsychological Assessment Outline

The outline of neuropsychological assessment that is subsequently provided (fig. 2.12) is the format for neuropsychological evaluation utilized in this text. The left-hand column is a description of the tests utilized with space therein to record the patient's response. The column on the right-hand side is for highlighting abnormalities so that the information can be rapidly scanned. All of the case studies subsequently provided will be based on this type of neuropsychological format.

Fig. 2.12. Neuropsychologic Evaluation Summary (pp. 53–68).

NEUROPSYCHOLOGIC EVALUATION SUMMARY

NAME: ______________________ DOB: __________ HEIGHT: __________

AGE: __________ DOE: __________ WEIGHT: __________

HANDEDNESS: __________ OCCUPATION: ______________

PRESENTING PROBLEM:

BACKGROUND HISTORY:

Specific Neurologic History:

General Medical History:

Children-Developmental History:

MENTAL STATUS

	ABNORMAL FINDINGS
Level of Consciousness Type — Comment: [] Normal-Alert [] Lethargic [] Stupor [] Coma	Level of Consciousness
Orientation Sphere — Comment: [] Time [] Place [] Person	Orientation
Appearance and Behavior [] Normal [] Abnormal - Comment	Appearance and Behavior
Language Normal / Abnormal-Comment Spontaneous [] ________ Conversational [] ________ Articulation [] ________ Content [] ________	Language

	ABNORMAL FINDINGS
Affect and Mood [] Normal [] (Hypo) Manic [] Depressed [] Agitated [] Blunted [] Euphoric [] Flat [] Other ________	Affect and Mood
Thought Content [] Appropriate to presumed educational, intellectual and vocational level.	Thought Content

[] Inappropriate - Explain __________

____

[] Hallucinations - Type ___________

____

[] Delusions - Type ________________

____

[] Illusions - Type ________________

____

Memory

Immediate Recall-Digits

Forward	Pass	Fail
2 5 9	[]	[]
8 1 6 4	[]	[]
7 3 9 2 5	[]	[]
6 2 9 5 8 4	[]	[]
Reverse		
1 3 9	[]	[]
5 7 1 8	[]	[]
6 4 9 1 5	[]	[]

Four Word Recall
(Pen, Table, House, Dictionary)

Interval	Number Recalled
Immediate	____
5 minutes	____
30 minutes	____

Current Events
Recall 2 major news events

Remote Memory
List past Presidents starting with the most current (Stop after six consecutive correct).
Number Correct ____

When were you born?
Correct [] Incorrect []

Approximate dates of World War II.
Correct [] Incorrect []

New Learning-Verbal Recall
Alica, / a pretty/ 6 year old girl/ sat patiently/ awaiting the start/ of the fireworks display./ However, once the fireworks began/ she became afraid/ covered her ears/ and closed her eyes/ and jumped/ back into her father's arms./

Total memory passages = 12

Number correctly recalled ____

Confabulation? __________________

General Information, Insight & Judgment

Fund of Knowledge
(Based on previous content ascertained from Mental Status Exam)
[] Normal/Adequate
[] Impaired. Describe: ________________

____

Memory

Immediate Recall-Digits

Four Word Recall

Current Events

Remote Memory

ABNORMAL FINDINGS

New Learning-Paragraph Recall

General Information, Insight & Judgment

Similarities

How are a baby and a midget alike?

Incorrect	Correct	Concrete	Abstract
[]	[]	[]	[]

How are a paintbrush and pencil alike?

Incorrect	Correct	Concrete	Abstract
[]	[]	[]	[]

Judgment

What should you do to protect yourself during severe thunderstorm?

Incorrect	Correct	Concrete	Abstract
[]	[]	[]	[]

If you are in a boat and it begins to sink, what should you do?

Incorrect	Correct	Concrete	Abstract
[]	[]	[]	[]

Why should you read instructions before mixing chemicals?

Incorrect	Correct	Concrete	Abstract
[]	[]	[]	[]

ABNORMAL FINDINGS

Proverbs

A stitch in time saves nine.

Incorrect	Correct	Concrete	Abstract
[]	[]	[]	[]

One shouldn't change horses in the middle of the stream.

Incorrect	Correct	Concrete	Abstract
[]	[]	[]	[]

A drowning man will grasp at a straw.

Incorrect	Correct	Concrete	Abstract
[]	[]	[]	[]

LATERAL DOMINANCE EXAM

ABNORMAL FINDINGS

Hand

Preferred Hand

With which hand do you

	Right	Left
Write	[]	[]
Flip a coin	[]	[]
Use a knife	[]	[]
Throw a ball	[]	[]

Total Right _____

Total Left _____

Handedness

Eye

	Right	Left
Look through a telescope.	[]	[]
Aim a pistol.	[]	[]

Eyedness

Foot

	Right	Left
Kick a ball.	[]	[]
Step on a bug.	[]	[]

Footedness

Dominance	Right	Left	Mixed
Hand	[]	[]	[]
Eye	[]	[]	[]
Foot	[]	[]	[]

HEAD AND SPINE

ABNORMAL FINDINGS

Facial Symmetry Present Yes [] No []

Comment: ______________________________

____

General Comment: ______________________________

____

Symmetry

WEIGHT AND HEIGHT PERCENTILE TABLE: GIRLS (2-16)

Weight in lbs. 10%	50%	90%	Age	Height in in. 10%	50%	90%
23.5	27.1	31.7	2 yr	32.3	34.1	35.8
27.6	31.8	37.4	3 yr	35.6	37.7	39.8
31.2	36.2	43.5	4 yr	38.4	40.6	43.1
34.8	40.5	49.2	5 yr	40.5	42.9	45.4
39.6	46.5	54.2	6 yr	43.5	45.6	48.1
44.5	52.2	61.2	7 yr	46.0	48.1	50.7
48.6	58.1	69.9	8 yr	48.1	50.4	53.0
52.6	63.8	79.1	9 yr	50.0	52.3	55.3
57.1	70.3	89.7	10 yr	51.8	54.6	57.5
62.6	78.8	100.4	11 yr	53.9	57.0	60.4
69.5	87.6	111.5	12 yr	56.1	59.8	63.2
79.9	99.1	124.5	13 yr	58.7	61.8	64.9
91.0	108.4	133.3	14 yr	60.2	62.8	65.7
97.4	113.5	138.1	15 yr	61.1	63.4	66.2
100.0	117.0	141.1	16 yr	61.5	63.9	66.5

WEIGHT AND HEIGHT PERCENTILE TABLE: BOYS (2-16)

Weight in lb. 10%	50%	90%	AGE	Height in In. 10%	50%	90%
24.7	27.7	31.9	2 yr.	33.1	34.4	35.9
28.7	32.2	36.8	3 yr	36.3	37.9	39.6
32.1	36.4	41.4	4 yr	39.1	40.7	42.7
35.5	40.5	46.7	5 yr	40.8	42.8	45.2
40.9	48.3	56.4	6 yr	43.8	46.3	48.6
45.8	54.1	64.4	7 yr	46.0	48.9	51.4
51.2	60.1	73.0	8 yr	48.5	51.2	54.0
56.3	66.0	81.0	9 yr	50.5	53.3	56.1
61.1	71.9	89.9	10 yr	52.3	55.2	58.1
66.3	77.6	99.3	11 yr	54.0	56.8	59.8
72.0	84.4	109.6	12 yr	56.1	58.9	62.2
77.1	93.0	123.2	13 yr	57.7	61.0	65.1
87.2	107.6	136.9	14 yr	59.9	64.0	67.9
99.4	120.1	147.8	15 yr	62.1	66.1	69.6
111.0	129.7	157.3	16 yr	64.1	67.8	70.7

AVERAGE HEAD CIRCUMFERENCE
OF AMERICAN CHILDREN

AGE	MEAN IN.	MEAN CM.	STANDARD DEVIATION IN.	STANDARD DEVIATION CM.
Birth	13.8	35.0	0.5	1.2
1 mo	14.9	37.6	0.5	1.2
2 mo	15.5	39.7	0.5	1.2
3 mo	15.9	40.4	0.5	1.2
6 mo	17.0	43.4	0.4	1.1
9 mo	17.8	45.0	0.5	1.2
12 mo	18.3	46.5	0.5	1.2
18 mo	19.0	48.4	0.5	1.2
2 yr	19.2	49.0	0.5	1.2
3 yr	19.6	50.0	0.5	1.2
4 yr	19.8	50.5	0.5	1.2
5 yr	20.0	50.8	0.6	1.4
6 yr	20.2	51.2	0.6	1.4
7 yr	20.5	51.6	0.6	1.4
8 yr	20.6	52.0	0.8	1.8
10 yr	20.9	53.0	0.6	1.4
12 yr	21.0	53.2	0.8	1.8
14 yr	21.5	54.0	0.8	1.8
16 yr	21.9	55.0	0.8	1.8
18 yr	22.1	55.4	0.8	1.8
20 yr	22.2	55.6	0.8	1.8

GAIT AND STATION

ABNORMAL FINDINGS

Motor Symmetry	Present	Absent
	[]	[]

Comment: ______________________

General Coordination	[]	[]

Comment: ______________________

Romberg	+ []	- []

Gait	Normal	Abnormal
Heel-to-toe	[]	[]
Toe walk	[]	[]
Heel walk	[]	[]

Comment: ______________________

____

CRANIAL NERVES

ABNORMAL FINDINGS

Olfaction (I)

I

Peppermint

Right Nostril		Left Nostril	
Detect	Absent	Detect	Absent
[]	[]	[]	[]

Clove

Right Nostril		Left Nostril	
Detect	Absent	Detect	Absent
[]	[]	[]	[]

Optic (II)

II

Visual Acuity OD ________

OS ________

Visual Fields

OD OS
(Patient facing Examiner)

ABNORMAL FINDINGS

Double Simultaneous Stimulation

	OD	OS
Upper Quadrant	/ / / / / /	/ / / / / /
Lower Quadrant	/ / / / / /	/ / / / / /

Visual Complaints: ______________________

____

Pupillary Function

	Yes	No
Constriction		
OD	[]	[]
OS	[]	[]
Consensual Reflex		
OD	[]	[]
OS	[]	[]

Pupillary Asymmetry
Describe: ____________________

Ocular Motility (III, IV, VI)

III Upward Movement Following Target

OD		OS	
Normal	Abnormal	Normal	Abnormal
[]	[]	[]	[]

III & IV Downward Movement Following Target

OD		OS	
Normal	Abnormal	Normal	Abnormal
[]	[]	[]	[]

VI Lateral Eye Movements Following Target

OD		OS	
Normal	Abnormal	Normal	Abnormal
[]	[]	[]	[]

Nystagmus

OD		OS	
Absent	Present	Absent	Present
[]	[]	[]	[]

Type: ____________________

Conjugate Gaze

Normal
[]

Abnormal
[] Describe: ____________

____

Trigeminal (V)
Palpate masseter and temporal muscles.

Normal [] Abnormal [] Describe: ______

____

Deviation of mouth on opening.

None(Normal) [] Right [] Left []

Sensation

	Normal	Impaired
Ophthalmic	[]	[]
Maxillary	[]	[]
Mandibular	[]	[]

Comment: ____________________

____

Facial (VII

	Normal	Impaired		
Facial Symmetry	[]	[]	R[]	L[]
Facial Movements to Command				
Wrinkle Forehead	[]	[]	R[]	L[]
Frown/Grimace	[]	[]	R[]	L[]
Smile	[]	[]	R[]	L[]

Pupillary Function

III, IV, VI

ABNORMAL FINDINGS
V

VII

Bulbar Function (IX, X, XII) | IX, X, XII

IX and X

	Normal	Abnormal
Symmetric Gag Reflex	[]	[]
Speech Quality	[]	[]

Describe: ______________________________

Swallowing	[]	[]

XII

	Normal	Abnormal
Protrude Tongue	[]	[] R[] L[]
Tongue Symmetry	[]	[] R[] L[]
Tongue Apperance		Wasting
	[]	[] R[] L[]
	Absent	Present
Fasciculations	[]	[]

Spinal Accessory (XI) | XI

	Normal Bilateral	Abnormal Right	Left	Both
Shoulder Shrug	[]	[]	[]	[]
Head Turn	[]	[]	[]	[]

PRIMITIVE REFLEXES

ABNORMAL FINDINGS

Grasp Reflex

	Present	Incomplete or Equivocal	Absent
Right	[]	[]	[]
Left	[]	[]	[]

Oral Reflex (Snout, Rooting, Suck)

	Present	Incomplete or Equivocal	Absent
	[]	[]	[]

Palmomental

	Present	Incomplete or Equivocal	Absent
Right	[]	[]	[]
Left	[]	[]	[]

Glabella Tap Reflex

	Present	Incomplete or Equivocal	Absent
	[]	[]	[]

MOTOR FUNCTION

ABNORMAL FINDINGS
Physical Inspection

Physical Inspection

	Present	Absent
Astasia-Abasia	[]	[]
Athetosis	[]	[]
Chorea	[]	[]
Dystonia		
Buccal-lingual dyskinesia	[]	[]
Spasmodic torticollis	[]	[]
Tardive dyskinesia	[]	[]
Fasciculations	[]	[]

Hemiballismus	[]	[]
Myoclonus	[]	[]
Spasm	[]	[]
Tic	[]	[]
Tremor	[]	[]

General Comment: ______________________

____

Strength

Hand Dynamometer
(Dominant Hand - R[] L[])

Right _____ Left _____
_____ _____
_____ _____
_____ _____

$\bar{x}$ = _____ $\bar{x}$ = _____

Position Maintenance (Arms Extended)
Normal [] Drift [] Fatigue []

Accuracy & Coordination
(Dominant Hand - R[] L[])

Finger Oscillation

Trial	Right	Left
1	_____	_____
2	_____	_____
3	_____	_____
4	_____	_____
5	_____	_____
Σ	_____	_____
$\bar{x}$	_____	_____

Finger-to-Nose

Normal	Maladroit	Abnormal
[]	[]	[]

Index Finger-to-Thumb

Normal	Maladroit	Abnormal
[]	[]	[]

Alternating Fingers-to-Thumb

Normal	Maladroit	Abnormal
[]	[]	[]

Diadokokinesis

Alternating Hand-Fist

Normal	Maladroit	Abnormal
[]	[]	[]

Knee Slap

Normal	Maladroit	Abnormal
[]	[]	[]

Strength

Accuracy & Coordination

ABNORMAL FINDINGS

LEARNED ACTS (PRAXIS)

Ideomotor

Buccofacial:

	Pass (Normal)	Fail (Abnormal)
Show me how to blow out a match.	[]	[]
Drink through a straw.	[]	[]
Cough.	[]	[]

ABNORMAL FINDINGS
Ideomotor

Limb: (On selected ones test each hand separately.)

Flip a coin.	[]	[]
Comb your hair.	[]	[]
Throw a ball.	[]	[]
Kick a ball.	[]	[]
Use a screwdriver.	[]	[]
Salute.	[]	[]

Bilateral Limb:

Play a piano.	[]	[]
File fingernails.	[]	[]

	Pass (Normal)	Fail (Abnormal)
Whole Body:		
Stand like a boxer.	[]	[]
Shovel dirt.	[]	[]
Take a bow.	[]	[]

ABNORMAL FINDINGS

Ideational

Fold an envelope, seal it, place a stamp on it.	[]	[]
Pour a drink into a cup, add sugar, stir and drink.	[]	[]
Squeeze toothpaste onto a toothbrush and brush your teeth.	[]	[]

General Comments: ______________________

____

____

Ideational

SENSORY EXAM

Visual

Results from II Cranial Nerve Function Tests: ______________________

____

Visual Form Recognition

Objects:	Normal	Abnormal
Pencil	[]	[]
Paper clip	[]	[]
Faces:		
Family	[]	[]
Familiar	[]	[]

ABNORMAL FINDINGS

Visual

Tactile

Aesthesiometer

	Right	Left
1	____	____
2	____	____
3	____	____
Σ	____	____
$\bar{X}$	____	____

Double Simultaneous Stimulation

	Right	Left
Hand	/ / / / /	/ / / / /
Hand	/ / / / /	/ / / / /
Face	/ / / / /	/ / / / /

Tactile Finger Recognition

Right Hand

1/ / / / 2/ / / / 3/ / / / 4/ / / / 5/ / / /

Left Hand

1/ / / / 2/ / / / 3/ / / / 4/ / / / 5/ / / /

Graphesthesia

Right Hand

/3/6/5/4/ /6/5/4/3/
/ / / / / / / / / /

/3/5/4/6/ /6/3/5/4/ /5/4/6/3/
/ / / / / / / / / / / / / / /

Left Hand

/3/6/5/4/ /6/5/4/3/
/ / / / / / / / / /

/3/5/4/6/ /6/3/5/4/ /5/4/6/3/
/ / / / / / / / / / / / / / /

Stereognosis

Right Hand	/○/□/△/+/	/+/□/△/○/
Errors	/ / / / /	/ / / / /
Left Hand	/+/□/△/○/	/○/□/△/+/
Errors	/ / / / /	/ / / / /

Gerstman's Syndrome

	Present	Absent
Finger agnosia	[]	[]
R-L Disorientation	[]	[]
Dysgraphia	[]	[]
Dyscalculia	[]	[]

Auditory

Results from VIII Cranial Nerve Test For Audition: ____________________

____

Tactile

ABNORMAL FINDINGS

Auditory

LANGUAGE

	ABNORMAL FINDINGS
Reitan-Indiana Aphasia Screening Battery	Summarize Language Disturbance:
Speech Sounds Perception Test	
Errors _____	
Seashore Rhythm Test	
Errors _____ Scaled Score _____	
1. Copy SQUARE. (A)	1. ______
2. Name SQUARE.	2. ______
3. Spell SQUARE.	3. ______
4. Copy CROSS. (B)	4. ______
5. Name CROSS.	5. ______
6. Spell CROSS.	6. ______
7. Copy TRIANGLE. (C)	7. ______
8. Name TRIANGLE.	8. ______
9. Spell TRIANGLE.	9. ______
10. Name BABY. (D)	10. ______
11. Write CLOCK. (E)	11. ______
12. Name FORK. (F)	12. ______
13. Read 7 SIX 2. (G)	13. ______
14. Read M G W. (H)	14. ______
15. Reading I. (I)	15. ______
16. Reading II. (J)	16. ______
17. Repeat TRIANGLE.	17. ______
18. Repeat MASSACHUSETTS.	18. ______
19. Repeat METHODIST EPISCOPAL.	19. ______
20. Write SQUARE. (K)	20. ______
21. Read SEVEN. (L)	21. ______
22. Repeat SEVEN.	22. ______
23. Repeat/Explain HE SHOUTED THE WARNING.	23. ______
24. Write HE SHOUTED THE WARNING.	24. ______
25. Compute 85 - 27 = (M)	25. ______
26. Compute 17 x 3 =	26. ______
27. Name KEY. (N)	27. ______
28. Demonstrate use of KEY.	28. ______
29. Draw KEY.	29. ______
30. Read PLACE LEFT HAND TO RIGHT EAR. (O)	30. ______
31. Place LEFT HAND TO RIGHT EAR.	31. ______
32. Place LEFT HAND TO LEFT ELBOW.	32. ______
Aphasia Summary	
Conversational Speech	
Comprehension	
Repetition of Spoken Language	
Confrontation	

Reading

Aloud
Comprehension

Writing

Calculations

Wechsler Block Design Score _____

Wechsler Object Assembly Score _____

Draw a clock.

Copy the box below.

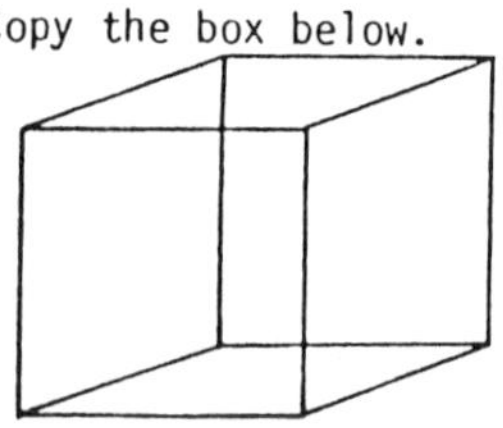

MEMORY

Date: ______________

FORM 2

SELECTIVE REMINDING TEST

Name: ____________________ Age: _____ Education: __________ Sex: ________

Examiner: ____________ UH#: ____________ Diagnosis: ____________________

	1	2	3	4	5	6	7	8	9	10	11	12
shine												
disagree												
fat												
wealthy												
drunk												
pin												
grass												
moon												
prepare												
prize												
duck												
leaf												

shine	
disagree	
fat	
wealthy	
drunk	
pin	
grass	
moon	
prepare	
prize	
duck	
leaf	
TOTALS:	

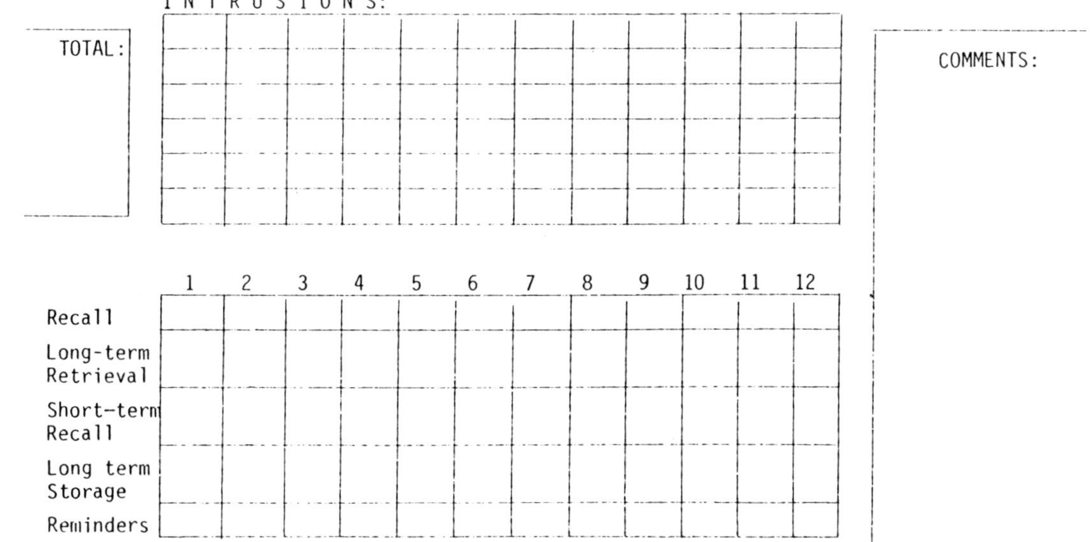

INTRUSIONS:

TOTAL:

COMMENTS:

	1	2	3	4	5	6	7	8	9	10	11	12
Recall												
Long-term Retrieval												
Short-term Recall												
Long term Storage												
Reminders												

REY AUDITORY-VERBAL LEARNING TEST

List A	Trial					List B (interference)	Recall	Recognition	Alternate List C
	I	II	III	IV	V				
Drum						Desk			Book
Curtain						Ranger			Flower
Bell						Bird			Train
Coffee						Shoe			Rug
School						Stove			Meadow
Parent						Mountain			Harp
Moon						Glasses			Salt
Garden						Towel			Finger
Hat						Cloud			Apple
Farmer						Boat			Chimney
Nose						Lamb			Button
Turkey						Gun			Key
Color						Pencil			Dog
House						Church			Glass
River						Fish			Rattle
Number Recalled									

Recognition Trial Paragraph: The teacher swallowed his coffee quickly and hurried down the road toward the river. He crossed the bridge and tipped his hat to the farmer cleaning his turkey pen. Every minute or so, he wiped his forehead and nose with his kerchief. He arrived at the school house just as the last bell rang. His moon face was the color of a garden beet. Through the classroom curtain he saw a parent pace the floor while the children played soldier with a broomstick gun and a drum. (From Lezak, 1976.)

	ABNORMAL FINDINGS
Attention	Attention

Attention

Patient is to tap with pencil each time the letter A is said.

A C Q F A A X M D I R E

A Z B G E L H J A A A N A

Total A's = 8

Errors _____

Wechsler Memory Scale Results

MQ = _____

Subtest Results:	Score
I Information	_____
II Orientation	_____
III Mental Control	_____
IV Logical Memory	_____
V Digit Span	_____
VI Visual Memory	_____
VII Associate Learning	_____

WMS Results

Other Tests

Interval Verbal Recall

Brown, Honesty, Tulip, Eyedropper

Interval	# Recalled
0 min	_____
5 min	_____
30 min	_____

Hidden Objects

Comments: ______________________________

____

Other

INTELLECTUAL

ABNORMAL FINDINGS
Adult IQ Status

Adult

WAIS or WAIS-R

VIQ=_____ PIQ=_____ FSIQ=_____

Verbal Subtests	
Information	_____
Comprehension	_____
Arithmetic	_____
Similarities	_____
Digit Span	_____
Vocabulary	_____

	ABNORMAL FINDINGS
Performance Subtests	
Digit Symbol _____	
Picture Completion _____	
Block Design _____	
Picture Arrangement _____	
Object Assembly _____	
Children	Child & Adolescent IQ Status
WISC-R	
VIQ=_____ PIQ=_____ FSIQ=_____	
Verbal Subtests	
Information _____	
Similarities _____	
Arithmetic _____	
Vocabulary _____	
Comprehension _____	
(Digit Span) (_____)	
Performance Subtests	
Picture Completion _____	
Picture Arrangement _____	
Block Design _____	
Object Assembly _____	
Coding _____	
(Mazes) (_____)	
Young Children	Young Child IQ Status
WPPSI	
VIQ=_____ PIQ=_____ FSIQ=_____	
Verbal Subtests	
Information _____	
Vocabulary _____	
Arithmetic _____	
Similarities _____	
Comprehension _____	
Performance Subtests	
Animal House _____	
Picture Completion _____	
Mazes _____	
Geometric Design _____	
Block Design _____	

ACHIEVEMENT

	ABNORMAL FINDINGS
WRAT Results	
Reading _____ Grade Level	
Spelling _____ Grade Level	
Arithmetic _____ Grade Level	
Other Tests of Achievement	

GENERAL COGNITIVE FUNCTIONING

	ABNORMAL FINDINGS
Category Test	
Errors _____	

Trail-Making Test

Trails A   Time _____ Errors _____

Trails B   Time _____ Errors _____

Other Tests

HALSTEAD-REITAN NEUROPSYCHOLOGIC
SUMMARY SHEET

WAIS RESULTS:

Verbal I.Q. _____
Performance I.Q. _____
Full Scale I.Q. _____
Information _____
Comprehension _____
Arithmetic _____
Similarities _____
Digit Span _____
Vocabulary _____
Digit Symbol _____
Picture Completion _____
Block Design _____
Picture Arrangement _____
Object Assembly _____

WECHSLER MEMORY SCALE RESULTS:

Logical Memory _____
Digits _____
Visual Memory _____
Associate Learning _____

WIDE RANGE ACHIEVEMENT TEST:

Reading: Score_____ Grade Level_____
Spelling: Score_____ Grade Level_____
Arithmetic: Score_____ Grade Level_____

REITAN-KLOVE SENSORY-PERCEPTUAL EXAM:

Tactile: RH___ LH___ Both RH___ LH___
Auditory: RE___ LE___ Both RE___ LE___
Visual: RV___ LV___ Both RV___ LV___
Finger Recognition: RH___ LH___
Finger-Tip Number Writing: RH___ LH___
Coin Recognition: RH___ LH___
Tactile Form Recognition: RH___ LH___

LATERAL DOMINANCE EXAMINATION:

	Eye	Hand	Foot
Right	_____	_____	_____
Left	_____	_____	_____
Mixed	_____	_____	_____

Strength of Grip
Dominant Hand _____ kg
Non-Dominant Hand _____ kg

REITAN-INDIANA APHASIA SCREENING TEST:

Comments:

HALSTEAD NEUROPSYCHOLOGICAL TEST BATTERY:

Category Test _____

Tactual Performance Test
Dominant Hand _____
Non-Dominant Hand _____
Both Hands _____
Total Time _____
Memory _____
Localization _____

Seashore Rhythm Test
Raw Score _____ Scales Score _____

Speech Sounds Perception Test _____

Finger Oscillation Test _____
Dominant Hand (R L) _____
Non-Dominant Hand (R L) _____

Impairment Index _____

Trail-Making Test
Trails A _____sec Errors _____
Trails B _____sec Errors _____

MMPI RESULTS:

Clinical Scale		T Score
L	_____	_____
F	_____	_____
K	_____	_____
Hs	_____	_____
D	_____	_____
Hy	_____	_____
Pd	_____	_____
Mf	_____	_____
Pa	_____	_____
Pt	_____	_____
Sc	_____	_____
Ma	_____	_____
Si	_____	_____

Synopsis of Neuropsychological Assessment by Lobe

Frontal Lobe

Motor Function. Damage to the frontal precentral gyral area or the subcortical white matter projection system (prior to decussation) produces a contralateral spastic hemiplegia. Damage just anterior to the precentral gyrus will produce some paralysis, typically less severe than with direct precentral damage and frequently with less spasticity. Damage to the prefrontal cortex may not produce paralysis, but typically there will be a decrease in coordinated and integrative motor control and possibly some loss in strength. Also, with extensive, typically bilateral frontal damage, primitive reflexes (i.e., suck, grasp, rooting) may be released and elicited.

Hemiplegia is quite obvious on clinical examination and, associated with the paralysis, some degree of spasticity is usually present. When such obvious motor signs are not present, the motor exam should include measurement of grip strength (there should be equal to slightly greater strength in the dominant hand in comparison to the nondominant), finger dexterity (rapid index finger–to–thumb tapping, alternating sequential finger–thumb tapping), and rapid alternating movements (alternating palm-fist, alternating vertical-horizontal hand movements; see Christensen, 1979). Formal assessment of finger oscillation speed can be obtained with the finger oscillation test (Reitan and Davison, 1974), and strength of grip can be assessed with a hand dynamometer. Integrative motor control can best be evaluated by the motor examination outlined by Luria (1966) and formalized by Christensen (1979).

Language. Dominant hemisphere frontal lesions may affect expressive language abilities. Focal lesions in the inferior frontal operculum (Broca's area, see fig. 1.44) may result in impaired expressive language characterized by dysarthric, effortful speech that is telegraphic and typically agrammatical. In association with the expressive language deficits there is typically contralateral paralysis. With severe damage to this area, there may be a complete loss of expressive speech. Despite the marked deficits in expressive language with frontal lesions, comprehension, in comparison, may be relatively preserved. If Broca's area is spared, but surrounding regions are damaged, an interesting clinical picture may emerge. This is the so-called transcortical motor aphasia (Albert et al., 1981; Benson, 1979) in which the patient has absent or deficient spontaneous speech, but repetition is relatively preserved. For example, the patient may be able to repeat, "It is a cold, snowy day outside," but when asked to comment about the weather outside, the self-generated response from the patient may be quite devoid of content (i.e., the patient may respond only with "cold, snow"). Confrontation naming may also be affected with frontal lesions of the dominant hemisphere. Both nondominant or dominant hemisphere frontal lesions may affect speech prosody (Ross and Rush, 1981).

Considerable information concerning language disturbance can be gathered during astute clinical observation and interviewing of the patient. Any language evaluation needs to include a separate assessment of word articulation, word fluency, reading, spelling, writing, and comprehension. However, a quickly administered aphasia survey, sufficient for screening purposes, is the Reitan-Indiana Aphasia Screening Test (Reitan, 1984; Reitan & Davison, 1974). If, through either clinical observation and/or aphasia screening, language disturbance is noted, then more-comprehensive language examination may be needed to fully document the extent of language disturbance. There are several excellent comprehensive language batteries, such as the Western Aphasia Battery (Kertesz, 1982), the Boston Diagnostic Aphasia Examination (Goodglass and Kaplan, 1972), and the Porch Index of Communicative Abilities (Porch, 1967).

Intellectual Functions. Damage to the frontal regions typically affects intellectual functions in some fashion (Damasio, 1985; Stuss and Benson, 1984). Well-learned or overlearned behaviors are frequently quite resistant to frontal lobe damage, whereas new learning and particularly complex reasoning and problem solving are impaired.

The WAIS (see review by or revised edition Wechsler, 1958; Wechsler, 1981) is the most well-established and thoroughly researched assessment tool for measuring current intellectual levels. However, the WAIS is limited because it tends to assess well-learned abilities and not the patient's adaptive intelligence, particularly on tasks that require new learning. Because of this, it is frequently instructive to examine performance on the various subtests rather than actual IQ scores, as several of the WAIS subtests are more sensitive to intellectual deficits than others. Studies (reviewed by Russell, 1979) have shown that the Information and Vocabulary subtests are typically least affected by cerebral dysfunction and most resistant to cerebral injury, whereas the Block Design, Digit Span, and Digit Symbol subtests may be more affected when brain injury occurs. Knowing this relationship, the Information and Vocabulary subtest scores in the nonaphasic brain injured individual may actually provide some general estimate of the patient's premorbid level of intellectual ability and, in comparison, the results on the Digit Symbol and Block Design subtests may be reflective of the degree of the patient's decline.

Patients with brain damage in frontal regions (and in many cases irrespective of the location) tend to give "concrete" responses. This can be assessed by asking the patient to interpret various proverbs. For example, if asked to explain what "You shouldn't change horses in the middle of the stream" means the concrete frontal lobe damaged patient may respond with, "Because you would get wet" or "Because you can't do it," rather than a more abstract response, such as, "You should persist until you accomplish your goal." The patient with frontal lobe damage may not even be able to appreciate the significance or meaning of the more abstract response, even if it is explained. Formal testing for deficits in cognitive shifting, problems with deficits in concept generalization, abstract reasoning, and complex problem solving can be assessed by using some of the following tests: Category Test (Reitan and Davison, 1974), Wisconsin Card Sorting Test (Berg, 1948; see Lezak, 1983, for update and modifications of this procedure), Raven's (Coloured) Progressive Matrices Test (1965), and Stroop Word Color Test (Stroop, 1935; see Lezak, 1983, for review of applications).

Personality. A wide spectrum of behavioral changes may develop following damage to the frontal areas (Blumer and Benson, 1975; Damasio, 1985; Freemon, 1981; Stuss and Benson, 1984). There is, however, no clear correspondence between a frontal lesion site and emotional response and behavioral change. The differences may be subtle to marked. The most common findings are a lack of drive/motivation, lack of initiative, diminished spontaneity, and disregard for social amenities. Inappropriate jocularity and excessive silliness/giddiness as well as emotional lability are commonplace. The frontal areas are frequently the site of damage in head injury and the accompanying behavior change may be associated with such damage. Similar behaviors may be associated with the early behavioral changes seen in a variety of degenerative disorders (i.e., Alzheimer's disease) and are most common in such patients after the fifth decade of life. Frontal neoplastic or vascular disease may also produce such behavioral effects.

There are no formal psychometric tests designed to measure personality change in the brain damaged individual. Thereby, this is best accomplished by careful history taking with consideration of the chronology of the change. In taking such a history, patients with frontal lobe disease are notoriously poor historians and, accordingly, a spouse or a close relative is an invaluable source of information. Lezak (1978) suggested that in head injured individuals there may be five identified areas of personality change. These are listed in table 4.4. While these changes were noted with traumatic disorder associated with frontal damage, similar observations have been made with individuals with frontal lobe involvement secondary to a variety of etiologies (Stuss and Benson, 1984) and this description by Lezak is a most fitting guideline for the clinician in the evaluation of personality change.

The Minnesota Multiphasic Personality Inventory (MMPI) has been frequently studied in various neurological patient populations (see Cullum and Bigler, 1987), but no consistent MMPI profile appears to be associated with cerebral dysfunction. In patients with neurologic disorder, it is common for the depression, psychasthenia, and schizophrenia (as a result of problems with mentation and not psychosis) subscales to be elevated. There is some tendency for left hemisphere damaged patients to have significantly elevated depression scales (Cullum and Bigler, 1987; see fig. 2.11).

Memory. Memory functions are frequently affected with frontal lobe damage, but the relationship between memory processes and frontal lobe functioning is not well understood. Some speculate that the memory difficulties are mainly related to the frontal lobe syndrome effects (i.e., diminished concentration, impaired motivation, lack of attention to detail, etc.) and deficits in new learning and thus is not a true disorder of memory (Damasio, 1985). However, there are a variety of important limbic system and thalamic projections into frontal regions (Brodal, 1981) and such interconnections are thought to perform some regulatory role in memory processing (Squire and Butters, 1984). Accordingly, in patients with damage restricted to the frontal regions who display memory deficits in which motivational and other frontal lobe syndrome features are not considered to be the primary cause, impairment of memory functioning is likely due to disruption of frontal-thalamic-limbic interconnections. Tests for evaluating memory will be outlined in the temporal lobe section.

Temporal Lobe

Motor Function. The temporal lobe is not involved in direct motor control, but with damage to the posterior association areas of the temporal region, particularly the region of the temporal-parietal junction, an apraxia of movement may develop (Heilman, Rothi, and Kertesz, 1983). Ideomotor apraxia is the most common type and involves the failure of carrying out a previously learned motor act to command, and such findings may be observed in buccal-facial, upper and lower extremities, or truncal musculature. The command that is to be carried out is a simple, straightforward motor act (i.e., facial musculature—show me how you drink from a straw, blow out a match; limb musculature—throw a ball, comb your hair, kick a ball, crush out a cigarette) and the deficit in performance is not related to impaired comprehension (i.e., aphasia) or paralysis. It should be pointed out, though, that patients with such apraxia frequently have some degree of dysphasia and, accordingly, it is difficult sometimes to fully rule out that comprehension deficits may not be contributing to the movement disorder. Ideational apraxia represents a higher order disturbance in the execution of the sequence of motor planning (i.e., show me how you would pour a drink into a cup and stir it) and is most typically seen with bilateral disease. Constructional praxic deficits, most directly revealed by paper and pencil drawing of familiar figures may also be found with temporal lesions, but are more commonly seen with temporal-parietal or parietal lesions, particularly with nondominant parietal involvement.

Sensory. The auditory projection system terminates in the upper extension of the superior temporal gyrus. Damage to this area produces a classic Wernecke's aphasia (fluent paraphasic speech associated with impaired comprehension, naming, reading, and writing). Posterior to and surrounding Wernecke's area is the large temporal association cortex and damage in this area also results in disturbed language functioning (see the following language section). While these patients usually do not display an actual deafness (cortical deafness typically is seen most commonly with bilateral superior temporal gyrus involvement), they may display contralateral auditory inattention when auditory stimulation is presented simultaneously to each ear. (The methods for administration of double simultaneous stimulation are reviewed on page 37 and in Lezak, 1983; Kolb and Whishaw, 1985; Reitan and Wolfson, 1985). Vision may also be affected as visual projection fibers course through the posterior aspect of the temporal lobe and damage along this projection tract produces a contralateral quadrantanopia in the superior visual field. The mesial temporal cortex is the terminus for olfactory projections, but other than testing for anosmia (via olfactory stimulation using aromatic compounds) no specific behavioral measures of olfactory cortex functioning have been developed. It should be noted, however, that an olfactory sensation may be produced during seizure ictus, and this may be a clinical finding implicating temporal lobe disturbance.

Language. When examining language deficits, it is frequently best to first distinguish between fluent and nonfluent disorders. As discussed in the frontal lobe section, nonfluent speech disorders are typically associated with frontal damage. Fluent aphasic disorders are associated with damage/dysfunction posterior to the rolandic and sylvian fissures implicating temporal or parietal areas. In fluent aphasia, speech quality, while being fluent, is contaminated with "paraphasic" errors. Paraphasic errors may be either literal or phonemic—transposition of sounds or syllables (i.e., stool for pool)—or lexical or semantic—entire word substitutions (i.e., chair for table). Sometimes the paraphasic word is a nonsense, newly created word (i.e., "My *clak* is broken"). This is termed neologistic paraphasia. The major aphasic disorders associated with temporal lobe damage, typically in the lateral superior association cortex regions, are presented below (outline based on the work of Albert et al. [1981]; Benson [1979]; and Goodglass and Kaplan [1972]):

1. *Wernicke's Aphasia.* Fluent but paraphasic speech associated with impaired comprehension, naming, reading, and writing.
2. *Anomic Aphasia.* Fluent speech, but with impaired naming and word finding difficulty. Comprehension may be relatively intact in comparison to naming deficits. Reading and writing may or may not be affected, but both are typically severely impaired with large posterior temporal-parietal lesions.
3. *Conduction Aphasia.* Phonemic paraphasia, fluent speech associated with frequent blocking (particularly evident during attempts at repetition), dyslexia, and dysgraphia are commonplace. The areas of damage responsible for this syndrome are on the perisylvian region, usually including damage to the arcuate fasciculis.
4. *Transcortical Sensory Aphasia.* Repetition is remarkably preserved in the patient but otherwise grossly paraphasic speech associated with poor comprehension, anomia, alexia, and agraphia. The area responsible for this syndrome is damage surrounding but not including Wernicke's area.

The language disorders outlined above arise from damage to the dominant cerebral hemisphere. Correspondingly, nondominant hemispheric damage typically does not interfere with language functions per se but may affect the receptive awareness of affective quality of speech (i.e., a receptive dysprosodia; see Ross and Rush, 1981). Also, nondominant temporal lobe damage may affect the patient's appreciation of rhythm in musical processing.

With temporal and parietal lobe lesions affecting language areas, there should be an examination based on comprehensive assessment of verbal abilities, as previously outlined in the frontal lobe section. Briefly, clinical examination, sometimes created at bedside, should always assess the patient's articulation, reading, comprehension, writing, repetition, and copying abilities. Several excellent comprehensive language batteries have been developed and were previously discussed in the frontal lobe section.

Memory. Verbal memory, particularly immediate or recent recall, is affected by medial and ventral lesions of the dominant temporal lobe and, correspondingly, visual memory is affected with damage to similar areas of the nondominant temporal lobe. With bilateral hippocampal damage amnestic syndromes may develop in which a rather complete loss of short-term memory is present with remote memory remaining relatively intact. The most notable syndrome with these features is Korsakoff's disease secondary to alcoholism. In Korsakoff syndrome, in addition to hippocampal damage there is involvement of the dorsomedial nucleus of the thalamus and surrounding diencephalic and upper midbrain structures. Memory disturbance is commonplace also with a variety of generalized disorders (i.e., Alzheimer's disease), but it is frequently impossible to determine whether the memory disturbance is due to direct temporal lobe involvement or is secondary to generalized cerebral failure.

Clinical interview of the patient can frequently outline the major aspects of disturbed memory, but for specific documentation of affected memory more detailed assessment is necessary. On direct clinical interview, the examiner should first establish whether the patient is oriented to time, place, and person as disorientation and confusion can mimic memory disturbance. Next, the examiner should ask about current news events. This permits an assessment of recent memory. At the beginning of the interview, the patient should be requested to learn and recite four words—brown, honesty, tulip, and eyedropper (see Strub and Black, 1981). The normal individual should have little difficulty in recalling these words and any patient who requires three or four trials to learn them may have short-term verbal retention deficit or deficit in new learning. Without notifying the patient, approximately five minutes after the first presentation, the patient should be asked to recall the four words again. The intact individual should have little difficulty in recalling all four words at a five-minute interval or at later intervals. This should then be repeated in about thirty minutes. A good technique for interim interview so as not to interfere with or contaminate the word list recall is to discuss current news or sports events. This also permits the assessment of the patient's processing of incidental information. Assessing visual memory is also an excellent measure during this intervening period, because it does not provide interference or contamination for verbal memory/learning. Remote memory (i.e., date of birth, vocational history, family history, and historical facts—name four presidents of the United States since 1900, when was WW II, etc.) should also be assessed. Another rather straightforward clinical interview measure of short-term verbal retention is a short-form associate learning task. Strub and Black (1981) suggest the following list: weather—bad; high—low; house—income; book—page. Note that two of the word pairs are easily related associations and two are not. The normal individual should have little difficulty in learning this list within two trials and should likewise have little difficulty in recalling all word pairs immediately post acquisition or after a ten-to-fifteen-minute interval.

More-detailed studies of memory functioning can be achieved by use of the following tests: Benton Visual Retention Test (Benton, 1974), Rey Auditory Verbal Learning Test (Rey, 1964), Rey-Osterrieth Complex Figure Test (Osterrieth, 1944), Selective Reminding Test (Buschke and Fuld, 1974), Wechsler Memory Scale (Wechsler, 1945), Denman Memory Battery (Denman, 1984), and California Verbal Learning Test (Delis et al., 1986).

Personality. There is no one personality syndrome associated with temporal lobe damage. However, since the temporal lobes house the major nuclei of the limbic system, temporal lobe damage, particularly that which is ventral and mesial, may affect a wide spectrum of emotional behaviors. Depression is more associated with dominant hemisphere lesions whereas nondominant temporal damage may result in indifference. Where temporal lobe involvement also acts as a focus for seizure activity, this may be associated with a variety of symptoms, including impulsiveness, aggressiveness, hypo- or hypersexuality, increased emotionality, anger and irritability, and impulsive behaviors (Strub and Black, 1981). The so-called Kluver-Bucy syndrome is seen with bilateral temporal lobe damage and the patient displays a hypersexuality, hyperorality, visual gnosia, and amnesia (Cummings and Duchen, 1981). As will be discussed in the section on epilepsy, there are a variety of neurobehavioral syndromes associated with temporal lobe epilepsy as well.

Parietal Lobe

Motor. The area around the postcentral gyrus is not a pure tactile sensory area as numerous motor fibers coexist within this primary sensory region. Also, since it is rare to have precisely focal vascular or traumatic damage to the postcentral area exclusively, such damage to the pericentral area typically results in both motor and sensory loss. Thus, even with anterior parietal lesions, there will usually be some motor involvement in addition to disturbance in tactile perception. However, with parietal lobe damage the sensory loss will typically be greater than the motor involvement and noting the relationship between motor and tactile sensory dysfunction enables one to implicate greater frontal or parietal involvement. Parietal lesions may also produce apraxic deficits as have been previously outlined. This further underscores the observation that praxic deficit, while a pathologic sign, is a nonlocalizing sign.

Sensory. The primary function of the postcentral gyral region is for touch perception and direct damage to this gyrus results in loss of touch, which obviously then affects all other kindred aspects of tactile perception. If the postcentral gyrus is spared or minimally involved, then the tactile processing deficits will involve more-complex aspects of tactile functioning. Such lesions may interfere with finger recognition, hand/finger graphesthesic perception, and stereognosis. Also, an imperception may develop contralateral to the lesion site when simultaneous tactile stimulation is applied to both hands or both sides of the face. This is the so-called extinction phenomenon (Bender, 1952) in which the patient does not perceive stimulation on the contralateral hand or face (to the lesion site) when simultaneous stimulation is applied, but can perceive the stimulation following unilateral application. Thus, the presence of tactile extinction on one hand implicates contralateral parietal lobe dysfunction. Because of the overlap between such higher-order tactile functions and language, it is common that patients with fluent dysphasic deficits secondary to parietal lobe involvement frequently have contralateral tactile extinction, finger dysgnosia, dysgraphesthesia, or dysstereognosis. Sensory examination of the patient with parietal lobe involvement also requires visual field studies. One-half of the thalamic visual projections course through the posterior parietal area on their way to visual cortex. Damage in this projection area will produce an inferior contralateral quadrant anopia.

Benton et al. (1983) have developed a variety of sensory-perceptual tests that can be used to examine the major aspects of parietal lobe functioning. Also, the sensory-perceptual examination outlined by Reitan and Kløve (see Reitan, 1984) is an excellent screening battery that covers assessment of stereognosis, graphesthesia, finger gnosis, and tactile extinction.

Language. Damage to the dominant parietal lobe may result in dysphasia. The posterior and inferior regions of the parietal region are involved in a variety of functions critical to reading, writing, calculations, naming, and higher-order language processing. Dominant hemisphere parietal lesions may affect any or all of these functions. The major aphasic syndromes have been reviewed earlier under temporal lobe language function and that outline also applies here. Typically, the patient with aphasia secondary to dominant parietal lobe involvement will have greater tactile-perception deficits and/or motor disturbance than the aphasic patient with just temporal lobe damage, and this enables clinical differentiation. One language-sensory syndrome does need further mention here and is typically associated with dominant parietal lobe damage. The Gerstmann's syndrome (see Strub and Geschwind, 1983) is comprised of the following clinical findings: right-left disorientation, finger agnosia, acalculia, and agraphesthesia. The observation of these findings in relative isolation of any other major neurocognitive deficit implies dominant hemisphere parietal damage.

Memory Functioning. With lesions limited to the parietal lobe, memory functioning may be relatively spared or only mildly affected and there are no specific "parietal" lobe memory syndromes. However, memory functioning may be affected secondary to dysphasic deficits associated with dominant parietal lobe involvement and visual-spatial deficits with nondominant parietal damage. Accordingly, these deficits in memory may not be true memory disorders, but rather deficits in sensory processing and encoding information. The memory tests that were reviewed in the temporal lobe section would also apply here from the assessment standpoint.

Visual-Spatial. This area has not been fully discussed until now, because it is in large part a lateralized, nondominant hemisphere (and relatively specific function) of the parietal lobe. Dominant hemisphere parietal damage may affect visual-spatial and manipulospatial abilities to some degree, typically in the form of diminished attention to detail and oversimplification when copying geometric forms. With nondominant parietal damage the full spectrum of visual-spatial/manipulospatial deficits can be seen. Figure 2.7b depicts severe constructional apraxia in a patient with right parietal lobe lesion who is not aphasic and does not have any type of specific motor involvement, but cannot carry out the visual praxic copying task. With large parietal lesions the patient may develop a contralateral hemispatial neglect. In some cases the severity of the neglect reaches a point where the patient may deny a contralateral paralysis and/or sensory loss. Such patients may only shave one side of the face or comb one side of the head or dress on just the nonaffected side and feel quite confident that they have completed their task.

Probably the most straightforward tests are the pencil and paper tests utilizing simple geometric form copying. These can be made up at bedside (i.e., copy a square, flower, etc.) or more formalized testing can be obtained with the Bender Visual-Motor Gestalt Test (Bender, 1938) or the Beery-Buktenica Visual Motor Integration Test (1982). Also, the Block Design subtest on the WAIS is an excellent measure of constructional praxic abilities that does not require drawing skill. A major contributing factor to the overall performance IQ (PIQ) score on the WAIS is also based, to a large extent, on the patient's manipulospatial abilities, and therefore the PIQ score is somewhat of an index of visual-spatial-motor abilities. A PIQ score that is substantially below VIQ (i.e., greater than one standard deviation—15 scaled score points) may have implications for impaired abilities on nondominant hemispheric functioning.

Personality. With nondominant hemispheric lesions that involve the parietal lobe, the patient may develop a neglect syndrome, as described above, which may be mistaken for a change in personality. These patients typically demonstrate a lack of concern over the deficits present and an apparent unwillingness to accept the loss. However, this is just part of the neglect syndrome and probably relates to impaired complex sensory and spatial processing due to the parietal lobe damage. There is no specific personality change associated with dominant hemispheric lesions that has been documented in the literature, although there has been some indication that dominant temporal-parietal lesions may be associated more with depression and the corresponding nondominant analog with indifference (Ross and Rush, 1981).

Occipital Lobe

Of the four different lobes, the occipital lobe is the only one most dedicated to a single specific function, that being visual-perceptual abilities.

Sensory. Focal damage to visual cortical areas always produces some deficit in visual processing or cortical blindness. Because of the continuity between temporal-occipital and parietal-occipital regions, there is frequently overlap with dysphasic and visual deficits (contralateral hemi- or quadrantanopia) with posterior dominant lesions and visual-spatial deficits with posterior nondominant hemisphere lesions. Dominant hemisphere occipital damage that includes the splenium of the corpus callosum (and may involve posterior temporal and parietal areas) produces a condition of alexia without agraphia and contralateral hemianopia. The corresponding analog with nondominant hemisphere damage of the occipital lobe is a contralateral hemispatial neglect as well as hemianopia. Regardless of whether occipital involvement is in the dominant or nondominant hemisphere, where damage is incomplete and the patient still has some visual perceptual abilities in the affected visual field, there will frequently be inattention to double simultaneous visual stimulation contralateral to the affected occipital lobe. With bilateral occipital damage that is not of sufficient magnitude to produce a complete cortical blindness, the patient's ability to perceive and discriminate objects (i.e., agnosia) and faces (prosopagnosia; see Damasio, Damasio, and Van Hoesen, 1982) may be affected.

Satisfactory visual field assessment can be achieved with standard visual field confrontation techniques. For more-objective visual field studies, formal perimetry techniques are recommended. Visual agnosia can be informally tested by having the patient name objects presented visually, given that the patient is not dysphasic or demented. Formal assessment of facial recognition and visuospatial judgment can be obtained through the use of tests developed by Benton and colleagues (1983). Double simultaneous visual stimulation techniques employ simultaneous movement in both visual fields, usually accomplished by brief finger movements.

Language Functioning. As discussed above, there may be posterior temporal and/or parietal damage in association with occipital damage because of the overlap in vascular supply by the posterior (to ventral temporal and occipital lobe) and middle (to posterior lateral surface of temporal lobe, lateral surface of the parietal, and border zone parietal-occipital region) cerebral arteries as well as the physical proximity. Deep parietal and particularly parietal-temporal lobe lesions may also isolate the occipital area, even producing a visual field defect although the occipital area may not be focally damaged. This in effect "disconnects" the occipital lobe, producing a contralateral hemanopia. Accordingly, involvement of the posterior parietal and/or temporal area of the dominant hemisphere will frequently produce some dysphasia as well as visual field defect, either a homonymous hemianopia or quadrantanopia.

Assessment by Presenting Problem

In the preceding sections brain functioning and its assessment have been outlined by examining functions lobe by lobe. In this last section, an outline is provided that overviews brain pathology by presenting symptom. In this section the presenting problems of motor disturbance, language disorder, memory loss, and sensory, personality, and intellectual change are all reviewed in terms of the area(s) of possible cerebral involvement and tests to determine the presence or absence of cerebral pathology; certain clinical considerations will also be reviewed. The selected tests presented in this section indicate those most commonly used, but by no means is this intended to be an exhaustive overview. For an extensive treatment of the subject of test utilization in neuropsychology, the reader is referred to Lezak (1983).

Motor Disturbance

If a spastic hemiplegia is present, this suggests precentral gyrus or pyramidal tract involvement contralateral to the side of paralysis. If motor exam is normal for power and strength but integrative movements are impaired, this suggests damage anterior to the precentral gyrus. If the patient is apraxic, then this needs to be correlated with language evaluation as apraxic movement disorder may result from frontal, parietal, or temporal lesions. Apraxic disorders also may arise from diffuse nonspecific cerebral dysfunction.

See frontal lobe section for more complete description of tests. Paralysis is obvious on clinical examination; however, more subtle motor deficits may only be elucidated by careful motor examination. Hand grip should be tested bilaterally and should be generally equal, with possibly slightly greater strength noted in the dominant hand. Finger movements should be examined bilaterally, and integrative and alternating hand movements with extensive frontal lobe involvement primitive reflexes may be elicited. Also, with extensive frontal lobe damage in addition to motor involvement, the patient may develop a frontal lobe behavioral syndrome (inability to maintain a series of directed associations or to function efficiently during interference, inability to make conceptual shifts, apathy, or motivational disturbance, impaired judgment, and/or diminished social awareness). The presence of such behavioral findings in association with motor disturbance suggests extensive frontal lobe involvement.

Tests:

Luria-Christensen Motor Exam (Christensen, 1979)
Finger Oscillation Test (Reitan and Davison, 1974; Reitan and Wolfson, 1985)
Strength-of-Grip Test (Reitan and Davison, 1974; Reitan and Wolfson, 1985)

Language Disorder

Fluent Speech without Articulation Disturbance but Impaired Content. Lesions of the dominant hemisphere posterior to the central sulcus usually produce this type of dysphasia. The presence of a visual field defect may specify greater focal involvement of the temporal (superior quadrant anopia) or parietal (inferior quadrant anopia) lobe. If repetition is intact, this suggests sparing of Wernicke's area with damage in the surrounding perisylvian region. The presence of pure word deafness suggests bitemporal lobe involvement.

Comprehensive batteries examining language function were discussed in the frontal, temporal, and parietal lobe sections. Any evaluation of language function needs to examine articulation, naming, reading, spelling, repetition, calculations, handwriting, and comprehension. Praxic abilities should also be examined.

Nonfluent, Dysarthric Speech That Is Agrammatic and Telegraphic. Lesions of the dominant hemisphere anterior to the central sulcus usually produce this type of dysphasia. Additionally, the nonfluent dysphasic (Broca's aphasia) patient is typically hemiparetic/hemiplegic and this permits further delineation to the involvement of the frontal region. If repetition is intact and dysarthria is minimal or absent, then this implies sparing of Broca's region but with surrounding frontal damage.

Speech articulation can be informally evaluated during clinical interview and observations. Formal testing can be accomplished with the language tests previously recommended. Associated with such frontal lesions may be a buccofacial apraxia and, accordingly, praxic movements of the face, lips, and tongue should be examined. Since the nonfluent aphasic patient typically has some motor involvement, the motor tests previously outlined should also be administered and observation should be focused on whether there is indication for any behavioral features of a frontal lobe syndrome. Naming may also be affected with frontal lobe lesions and should be examined.

Tests:

Western Aphasia Battery (Kertesz, 1982)
Boston Diagnostic Aphasia Examination (Goodglass and Kaplan, 1972)
Reitan-Indiana Aphasia Screening Test (Reitan, 1984)
Porch Index of Communicative Ability (Porch, 1967)

Memory Loss

Damage to frontal and/or temporal areas, either unilateral or bilateral, or diffuse cerebral dysfunction may affect memory. The delineation of the locus of damage/dysfunction depends upon the presence of focal (i.e., frontal or temporal) as opposed to bilateral or nonspecific findings. For example, the patient with a specific amnestic syndrome but otherwise normal examination is suspect for focal temporal lobe (hippocampus) involvement, whereas global memory loss associated with a variety of frontal lobe behavior symptoms suggests a more nonspecific process, such as that seen with degenerative disease. In Wernicke-Korsakoff syndrome there is marked short-term memory loss, but relatively preserved long-term memory. Bilateral hippocampal involvement is implicated in this disorder as well as a variety of other subcortical lesion sites. If memory deficits are predominantly affected but verbal retention and visual-spatial memory are unaffected, then this suggests dominant hemisphere temporal lobe involvement. The opposite of this, intact verbal memory but impaired visual-spatial memory, implicates nondominant temporal-parietal involvement.

The various tests of memory function were outlined in the frontal and temporal lobe sections. One should always attempt to assess short- as well as long-term memory for both verbal as well as visual-spatial abilities. Since memory disorder is commonplace following head injury, in such patients one needs to differentiate whether the memory disturbance is due to focal frontal-temporal effects or general disruption of cerebral functioning. Drug and alcohol history needs to be taken into consideration because of the association between substance abuse and memory disorders. Vascular insufficiency in the basilar artery–posterior cerebral arteries may produce global amnesia that is temporary and transient. Likewise, transient ischemic attacks involving the distribution of the middle cerebral artery may produce disrupted memory function that may also be temporary and potentially treatable (i.e., carotid endarterectomy).

Tests:

Wechsler Memory Scale (Wechsler, 1945)
Denman Memory Battery (Denman, 1984)
Selective Reminding Test (Buschke and Fuld, 1974)
Benton Visual Retention Test (Benton, 1974)
Rey Auditory Verbal Learning Test (Rey, 1964)
California Verbal Learning Test (Delis et al., 1986)

Sensory Change

Tactile. The primary cortical processing area for tactile perception is in the parietal lobe. If there is a complete loss of simple touch, provided peripheral and spinal cord function is normal, this implicates damage involving the postcentral gyrus. If simple touch is intact, but finger gnosis, graphesthesia, and stereognosis are impaired, this implicates more posterior parietal involvement, particularly if motor findings are minimal or absent.

Since higher-order tactile perception (i.e., stereognosis) is dependent on the integrity of brain regions in the parietal lobe that also subserve language function, in the absence of motor findings but with the presence of tactile perceptual deficits in association with receptive dysphasic disturbance, dominant hemisphere parietal lobe involvement is implicated. Also, parietal lobe lesions may damage visual projection fibers producing an inferior quadrantanopia. With nondominant parietal lesions, tactile perception may be affected and associated with visual-spatial and/or visuopraxic deficits. Dominant lesions may also produce the so-called Gerstmann's syndrome (R-L confusion, acalculia, finger agnosia, and agraphia).

Tests:

Double Simultaneous Tactile Stimulation (Bender, 1952)
Reitan-Kløve Sensory-Perceptual Examination (Reitan, 1984)
Finger Localization Test (Benton et al., 1983)
Tactile Form Perception Test (Benton et al., 1983)

Hearing (Audition). The superior temporal gyrus houses the cortical terminations of the auditory projection system. Damage to this area, when bilateral, produces pure word deafness. Typically, damage is not just restricted to the superior temporal gyrus and involves much of the perisylvian region of the temporal lobe. This does not necessarily affect "hearing" per se, but does impair auditory perception of language.

Damage to the VIII cranial nerve does produce unilateral hearing loss, but no dysphasia. Invariably when the superior and posterior aspects of the dominant temporal lobe are involved, there is some type of dysphasia. In such cases, the patients do not display a deficit in hearing (i.e., audiogram will be negative) but they will have substantial deficits in perception of language.

Tests:

Double Simultaneous Auditory Stimulation (Bender), 1952)
Reitan-Kløve Sensory-Perceptual Examination (Reitan, 1984)

Vision/Visual-Perception. The visual system projects the entire length of the brain and, accordingly, damage to any lobe may affect visual functioning. Frontal injury or space-occupying lesion may be associated with optic nerve damage, which will produce optic nerve dysfunction or blindness. Occipital or temporoparietal damage may produce a contralateral hemianopia. Focal temporal damage disrupting the visual projection fibers coursing back to visual cortex will produce a superior quadrant anopia. Similarly, focal parietal damage may produce an inferior quadrant anopia. Bilateral visual cortex damage may produce cortical blindness or visual agnosia. Prosopagnosia (facial agnosia) usually implicates bilateral occipital damage.

Careful visual field examination is invaluable in examining for focal cerebral damage since either directly or indirectly the visual system is associated with each lobe. Since quadrant anopias are associated with parietal or temporal involvement, language and spatial-perceptual functions should always be assessed when quadrant anopia is found on examination. Partial unilateral occipital damage may not produce an actual visual field cut, but the patient may display visual inattention to double simultaneous stimulation, and such testing should be a part of every examination.

Tests:

Reitan-Kløve Sensory-Perceptual Examination (Reitan, 1984)
Facial Recognition Test (Benton et al., 1983)
Visual Form Discrimination Test (Benton et al., 1983)

Olfaction. The location of the olfactory nerve and bulb makes them vulnerable to compression with space-occupying lesions and cerebral edema, as well as to contusion effects with trauma. Accordingly, the loss of smell is frequently considered to be an indication of possible ventral frontal lobe damage. The actual termination of the olfactory projection system is in the mesial temporal lobe, and temporal damage at this level may also affect smell, although damage to the olfactory nerve and bulb is considerably more common than anosmia secondary to temporal lobe damage.

Brief testing for anosmia is not formalized and consists of a simple discrimination task (i.e., the patient can or cannot smell the substance presented). Each nostril is tested separately with an aromatic compound (i.e., coffee grounds, peppermint extract) as to whether smell is present or absent. The presence of anosmia in association with other frontal and/or temporal lobe signs aids in lesion localization. More formal assessment in disorders of smell has been developed by the use of microencapsulated odorants (i.e., "scratch and sniff").

Tests:

Smell Identification Test (Doty et al., 1984)

Personality Change

Damage to frontal and/or temporal regions may be associated with change in personality as well as disorders that affect the entire cerebrum. Patients with parietal and/or occipital damage infrequently show significant changes in personality functioning, although nondominant parietal-occipital damage may produce an indifference that is mistaken for a change in personality.

There are no formal psychometric test batteries for personality change associated with an organic brain syndrome. Probably the best approach here is the correlation of cortical function studies with documented history of change in personality as corroborated by spouse, other family members, minister, or employer. In cases of possible dementia, pseudodementia may mimic basic personality change and impaired cognition, but on formal testing neuropsychological studies will usually be negative and such tests as the Minnesota Multiphasic Personality Inventory (MMPI; Hathaway and McKinley, 1951) will frequently demonstrate presence of depression and related psychiatric symptomatology.

Tests:

Minnesota Multiphasic Personality Inventory (MMPI; Hathaway and McKinley, 1951)

Intellectual Change

Changes in intellect typically involve either diffuse cerebral dysfunction or damage/dysfunction in frontal and/or temporal lobes.

In examining for intellectual change, one needs to determine an estimate of probable premorbid level of functioning. Typically, this can be gained by historical facts, such as education, employment, and socioeconomic status as well as family input. The WAIS is the most standardized measure of intelligence but is too dependent on overlearned material and thereby may not necessarily demonstrate reduction in IQ. The comparison of WAIS scores with level of performance on tasks more dependent on new learning (i.e., Raven's, Category Test, Wisconsin Card Sorting) can, however, assist in determining if there is in fact cognitive decline.

Tests:

Wechsler Adult Intelligence Scale-Revised (WAIS-R, Wechsler, 1981)
Raven's (Coloured) Progressive Matrices (Raven, 1960, 1965)
Wisconsin Card Sorting Test (Berg, 1948)
Halstead Category Test (Reitan and Davison, 1974)

Neuropsychological Evaluation

The following actual case is presented as a suggested format for reporting neuropsychological test results.

RE: V. R.
__________ Hospital Medical Center
Our #: __________
Date: __________

Presenting Problem

The patient underwent surgery for a partial right frontal and temporal lobectomy for intractable seizures on September 8, 1983. There was a postoperative complication with spontaneous hemorrhage over the right hemisphere, which required surgical intervention to remove the hematoma as well as coagulate the bleeding vessels. The patient is referred for baseline neuropsychological studies and assistance in rehabilitation programming.

Background History:

The patient's neurologic history dates back to December 1969, when he sustained a gunshot wound (apparently .12 gauge shotgun) to the right frontal region. He was hospitalized at ________________ Hospital and attended to by Dr. ________________, who performed a right frontal craniectomy and debridement of the wound. The patient had an uneventful early recovery but developed a posttraumatic seizure disorder several months following this. The seizures had a focal onset with left-hand jerking being the initial sign, but then would rapidly progress to a major motor seizure with generalized tonic-clonic movement and loss of consciousness. The patient was treated with Dilantin, and with time the seizures came under good control. He was subsequently able to return to work as a ceramic tile layer, and between 1972 and 1980 he was seizure free. Unfortunately, in 1980 he was involved in an altercation and was hit over the head with a liquor bottle and lost consciousness. He did not seek medical attention at that time, but approximately five days later he began having seizures. The seizures increased unrelentlessly and were not responsive to various anticonvulsant regimes, despite anticonvulsant serum levels being in the therapeutic range. From August 1982 to September 1983, he was administered various combinations of anticonvulsant medications to attempt some type of seizure control, and he was still having several major seizures per week. They were incapacitating, and he was unable to work or carry on normal life. Because of this and because of the focal nature of his seizure disorder and original brain injury, he was considered a good candidate for surgery.

CAT scan prior to surgery showed a large area of low density tissue in the right frontotemporal area, which was felt to be posttraumatic infarcted tissue. He subsequently underwent surgery for removal of these infarcted areas and resultant scar tissue in September 1983. Visual inspection of the brain during surgery showed dense scarring and temporal lobectomy was undertaken, starting anterior to the precentral gyrus and removing all the anterior fossa region of the temporal lobe. No complications were encountered at the time of the initial surgical procedures. The patient awakened from the anesthesia with no significant paralysis and no speech or language complications. Unfortunately, several hours later, he began to show obtundation and rapid emergence of a left-side hemiparesis. A STAT CT scan was obtained, which showed a large evolving right hematoma. The patient was immediately operated on a second time for hematoma evacuation and blood vessel coagulation. Subsequent to these complicating factors, he developed a left hemiparesis and left hemianopsia. The patient is now on the Neurology/Rehabilitation Service at ________________ Hospital. He is under the care of Dr. ________________, and Dr. ________________'s history and physical report of October 25, 1983, is present in the chart and details further information. The patient had a CAT scan on admission to the hospital. It showed a very large area of encephalomalacia involving essentially the entire right hemisphere but sparing subcortical structures, including the striata and medial portion of the occipital lobe.

Previous Medical History

Other than the cerebral injuries as noted above, the patient has been in good health. He was a moderate drinker prior to surgery. He was a pack-a-day cigarette smoker.

Family/Personal History

The patient is married. This is his second marriage. His wife is in good health. He has two children, both in good health. Both of his parents are living. There is no known familial neurologic history. There is no prior history of seizure disorder in the family. He has a seventh-grade formal education. It is difficult to know from the history whether he had learning problems or not, but he reports that he dropped out of school to go to work. He is bilingual, and Spanish was his first language. He has worked as a general construction worker and ceramic tile layer.

Medications

Mysoline.

Mental Status Examination

V. R. is a 40-year-old Hispanic male. He has a dense left-side hemiparesis as well as a left homonymous hemianopsia. He constantly drools out of the left side of his mouth and is oblivious to the presence of the drool. His affect is definitely blunted. It is apparent there is a marked prosodic disturbance present. It is noted that he can determine affect changes in the examiner's voice, although he could not mimic the affect. He spontaneously scans from midline to the right but does not scan past midline to the left. He is oriented as to time, place, and person. He can state the current president of the United States as well as past presidents. He is able to recite some current news and is capable of giving some details of the current Lebanon crisis. Behaviorly, he shows features of an anosognosia in that he denies the significance of his paralysis and the visual defect. He states that he is ready to go to work just as soon as he is released from the hospital and has apparently tried to make some contact with former employers. He was cooperative during the examination.

Tests Administered

Clinical Examination
Wechsler Adult Intelligence Scale-Revised
Wechsler Memory Scale
Rey-Osterrieth Complex Figure Test
Benton Visual Retention Test

Line Cancellation Test
Reitan-Indiana Aphasia Screening Test
Reitan-Kløve Sensory-Perceptual Examination
Trail-Making Test
Finger Oscillation Test
Strength-of-Grip Test

Test Results

The patient is right-side dominant. He has a dense left hemiparesis as has been described above. He has no purposeful movement of the left side. This also involves the left facial area. He is nonambulatory and is wheelchair bound for movement. Although he does not show paralytic involvement on the right, he does show diminished finger oscillation speeds and grip strength on the right.

Reitan-Kløve Sensory-Perceptual Examination reveals dense left visual field homonymous hemianopsia. This is also documented in the chart with formal Goldman visual fields. The patient can perceive inconsistently simple touch on the left side but has a complete loss of stereognostic, graphesthesic, and finger gnostic perception. He spontaneously scans to the right and back to midline, but does not scan from midline to the left. Double simultaneous tactile stimulation results in classic visual field neglect. Language evaluation reveals speech to be slightly slurred, which appears to be, in part, related to his left facial paralysis and drooling. Naming is intact, provided the visual information is presented in the right visual field. For example, when showing him the clock (item 10) on the Aphasia Screening Test, which was presented to him at midline, he could not tell what it was. He did not spontaneously move his head or scan the visual stimulus. When the examiner moved the card into his right visual field, he had no difficulty identifying the figure. Another example of his neglect is copying of SQUARE, in which he copied only QUAR. Left visual neglect is also present on the Line Cancellation Test. He displays pronounced constructional apraxia, particularly noted on the Rey-Osterrieth Complex Figure Test as well as his drawings on the Wechsler Memory Scale. He could adequately demonstrate the use of a key but had difficulty with multiple stage commands and, accordingly, displays features of an ideomotor apraxia. He is markedly apraxic on all of the performance intellectual tests. He displays a spelling apraxia (although it should be noted that he has only a seventh-grade formal education, and the wife reports that he was "never a good speller"). Calculations are impaired. He does better with mental calculations than he does calculating on paper. Memory studies indicate generally intact verbal memory (Wechsler Memory Scale Memory Quotient of 80), but distinctly impaired visual memory. The patient was unable to do the Benton Visual Retention Test because of the severe visual neglect and constructional apraxia. Intellectual studies indicated a VIQ score of 73, a PIQ score of less than 54, and a Full Scale IQ score of 62. Accordingly, there are marked deficits on all performance-based tests.

Impression

Neuropsychological studies reflect clearly lateralized right cerebral involvement that appears to affect the entire right hemisphere. The patient's most prominent deficits are as follows: dense left-side hemiparesis, left-side astereognosis, agraphesthesia and finger agnosia, left homonymous hemianopsia, left-side sensory neglect syndrome, marked visual memory defect, and marked constructional apraxia. Accordingly, the patient displays marked deficits on all visuopraxic/manipulospatial tasks.

DSM-III Classification

Axis I: 310.2. Organic brain syndrome secondary to traumatic encephalopathy and postsurgical complications.
Axis II: V71.09. No diagnosis applicable.
Axis III: Left-side hemiparesis; left homonymous hemianopsia; status partial right frontal and temporal lobectomy; generalized right hemisphere encephalomalacia as documented on CT scan; seizure disorder.
Axis IV: Psychosocial stressors: patient was independently functioning prior to 1980; now he is totally dependent with permanent neurologic deficits, although he will undergo extensive rehabilitation training. Severity: 6—extreme.
Axis V: Highest level of adaptive functioning past year: because of poor seizure control, the patient has been unable to work. 5—poor.

Recommendations

1. The patient will be undergoing extensive rehabilitation training. He will receive a specific OT program for left hemiplegia with left-side neglect as well as a comprehensive cognitive rehabilitation program for the various visuopraxic deficits present. I will check with the OT clinician working with V. R. every other week.
2. Followup testing in six months to monitor progress.

Erin D. Bigler, Ph.D.

[CAT scan and Rey-Osterrieth performance presented in fig. 2.7.]

CASE STUDY

Case 1. Interpreting the HRNTB should always be done in a systematic fashion, typically presenting the results by groups of related tests that are tapping similar functions (e.g., motor function). Thus, it is recommended that the test results be summarized in terms of motor function, then sensory function, followed by language, memory, and general measures of cognitive integrity. For this patient motor test results reveal diminished finger oscillation speeds bilaterally with relatively preserved strength of grip. Tactual Performance Test is performed markedly in the impaired range with either hand, suggesting integrative motor dysfunction. Sensory perceptual exam similarly indicates bilateral processing deficits, without lateralizing implications. Such findings also suggest that sensory and kinesthetic deficits may contribute to the impaired Tactual Performance Test performance. Language exam reveals spelling dyspraxia, dysnomia, dyscalculia, and constructional dyspraxia along with an inability to perform either the Seashore Rhythm Test or the Speech Sounds Perception Test. Tactual Performance Test memory tests are markedly in the impaired range, and this is consistent with Wechsler Memory Scale results previously presented. Tests of general cognitive integrity (CT and TM) were also performed in the markedly impaired range, consistent with the level of observed intellectual deficit (full-scale IQ = 70); see fig. 2.10 for details of intellectual test results). Comparing these results with the interpretive indicators (see Table 2.6) it is apparent that there are no clear lateralizing findings and that the deficits are generalized. The conclusions of examination include the findings of generalized cerebrocortical dysfunction with deficits in essentially all higher cortical functions, associated marked dementia, and generalized memory disturbance consistent with what would be expected in Alzheimer's disease.

Halstead-Reitan Neuropsychological Test Battery (HRNTB) Interpretation

```
Age 57   Sex male   Handedness right
Education 18   Vocation engineer

Category Test  131 errors (CT)
Tactual Performance Test (TPT)
   Dominant Hand   10 min DC* 2 placed*
   Non-Dom. Hand   10 min DC  0 placed
   Both            10 min DC  3 placed
   Memory          1
   Localization    0
Speech Sounds Perception Test (SSPT)
                   20+ errors DC
Seashore Rhythm Test  DC      (SRT)
Finger Oscillation Test
   Dominant Hand   41
   Non-Dom. Hand   33
Strength of Grip Test
   Dominant Hand   42
   Non-Dom. Hand   37
Reitan-Klöve Sensory Perceptual Exam
   Double Simultaneous Stimulation
      Tactile      R 3  L 2 errors
      Auditory     R 1  L 2 errors
      Visual       R 2  L 1 errors
   Finger Recognition
                   R 5  L 7 errors
   Finger Tip Number Writing
                   R 7  L 9 errors
   Coin Recognition
                   R 2  L 2 errors
   Tactile Form Recognition
                   R 3  L 4 errors
Trail Making Test (TM)
   Trails A 100 sec DC
   Trails B 100 sec DC
```

References

Adams, K. 1980. In search of Luria's battery: A false start. *Journal of Consulting and Clinical Psychology* 48:511–516.

———. 1984. Luria left in the lurch: Unfulfilled promises are not valid tests. *Journal of Clinical Neuropsychology* 6:455–458.

Albert, M. L., H. Goodglass, N. A. Helm, A. B. Rubens, and M. P. Alexander. 1981. *Disorders of human communication.* Vol. 2, *Clinical aspects of dysphasia.* New York: Springer-Verlag.

Beery, K. E. 1982. *Revised administration, scoring, and teaching manual for the Developmental Test of Visual-Motor Integration.* Cleveland: Modern Curriculum Press.

Bender, L. A. 1938. A visual motor Gestalt test and its clinical use. *American Orthopsychiatric Association Research Monographs,* no. 3.

Bender, M. B. 1952. *Disorders in perception.* Springfield, IL: C. C. Thomas.

Benson, D. F. 1979. *Aphasia, alexia, and agraphia.* New York: Churchill Livingstone.

Benton, A. L. 1974. *The revised visual retention test.* 4th ed. New York: Psychological Corporation.

Benton, A. L., K. de S. Hamsher, N. R. Varney, and O. Spreen. 1983. *Contributions to neuropsychological assessment.* New York: Oxford University Press.

Berg, E. A. 1948. A simple objective test for measuring flexibility in thinking. *Journal of General Psychology* 39:15–22.

Bigler, E. D. 1982. Clinical assessment of cognitive deficit in traumatic and degenerative disorders: Brain scan and neuropsychologic findings. In *Neuropsychology and cognition,* ed. R. N. Malathesa and L. Hartlage. The Hague: Martinus Nijhoff Publishers.

Bigler, E. D., and J. W. Ehrfurth. 1980. Critical limitations of the Bender-Gestalt test in clinical neuropsychology: Response to Lacks. *Clinical Neuropsychology* 2:88–90.

———. 1981. The continued inappropriate singular use of the Bender Visual Motor Gestalt test. *Professional Psychology* 12:562–569.

Bigler, E. D., S. Hall, J. L. Harris, L. J. Rosa, D. F. Schultz, and B. R. Thayer. Performance profiles of dementia and cerebral trauma patients on the Rey AVLT, Raven's CPM, and Rey-Osterrieth CFD. In preparation.

Bigler, E. D., D. R. Steinman, and J. S. Newton. 1981*a.* Clinical assessment of cognitive deficit in neurologic disorder. I, Effects of age and degenerative disease. *Clinical Neuropsychology* 3:5–13.

———. 1981*b.* Clinical assessment of cognitive deficit in neurologic disorder. II, Cerebral trauma. *Clinical Neuropsychology* 3:13–18.

Bigler, E. D., and D. M. Tucker. 1979. The quality extinction test: Results with psychiatric patients. *Clinical Neuropsychology* 1:8–12.

Binder, L. M. 1982. Constructional strategies on complex figure drawings after unilateral brain damage. *Journal of Clinical Neuropsychology* 4:51–58.

Blumer, D., and D. F. Benson. 1975. Personality changes with frontal and temporal lobe lesions. In *Psychiatric aspects of neurologic disease,* ed. D. F. Benson and D. Blumer. New York: Grune and Stratton.

Blumstein, S. E. 1981. Neurolinguistic disorders: Language-brain relationships. In *Handbook of clinical neuropsychology,* ed. S. B. Filskov and T. J. Boll. New York: John Wiley & Sons.

Boll, T. J. 1981. The Halstead-Reitan neuropsychology battery. In *Handbook of clinical neuropsychology,* ed. S. B. Filskov and T. J. Boll. New York: John Wiley & Sons.

Bond, J. A., and H. A. Buchtel. 1984. Comparison of the Wisconsin Card Sorting Test and the Halstead Category Test. *Journal of Clinical Psychology* 40:1251–1254.

Bornstein, R. A. 1984. Unilateral lesions and the Wechsler Adult Intelligence Scale-Revised: No sex differences. *Journal of Consulting and Clinical Psychology* 52:604–608.

Bornstein, R. A., and J. D. Matarazzo. 1984. Relationship of sex and the effects of unilateral lesions on the Wechsler Intelligence Scales. *Journal of Nervous and Mental Disease* 172: 707–710.

Bornstein, R. A., M. Weizel, and C. D. Grant. 1984. Error pattern and item order on Halstead's speech sounds perception test. *Journal of Clinical Psychology* 40:266–270.

Brinkman, S. D., J. W. Largen, Jr., S. Gerganoff, and N. Pomara. 1983. Russell's revised Wechsler Memory Scale in the evaluation of dementia. *Journal of Clinical Psychology* 39:989–994.

Brodal, A.. 1981. *Neurological anatomy in relation to clinical medicine.* New York: Oxford University Press.

Buschke, H., and P. A. Fuld. 1974. Evaluating storage, retention, and retrieval in disordered memory and learning. *Neurology* 24:1019–1925.

Christensen, A. L. 1979. *Luria's neuropsychological investigation.* New York: Spectrum.

Cullum, C. M., and E. D. Bigler. 1987. Short-form MMPI findings in patients with predominantly lateralized cerebral dysfunction: Neuropsychological and CT-derived parameters. Paper presented at the annual conference of the International Neuropsychological Society, Washington, D.C.

Cullum, C. M., D. R. Steinman, and E. D. Bigler. 1984. Relationship between "fluid" and "crystallized" cognitive function using category and WAIS test scores. *Clinical Neuropsychology* 6:172–174.

Cummings, J. L., and L. W. Duchen. 1981. The Klüver-Bucy syndrome in Pick's disease. *Neurology* 31:82–83.

Damasio, A. R. 1985. The frontal lobes. In *Clinical neuropsychology,* ed. K. M. Heilman and E. Valenstein. New York: Oxford University Press.

Damasio, A. R., H. Damasio, and G. W. Van Hoesen. 1982. Prosopagnosia: Anatomic basis and behavioral mechanisms. *Neurology* 32:331–341.

Delis, D. C., and E. Kaplan. 1983. Hazards of a standardized neuropsychological test with low content validity: Comment on the Luria-Nebraska Neuropsychological Battery. *Journal of Consulting and Clinical Psychology* 51:396–398.

Delis, D. C., J. H. Kramer, E. Kaplan, and B. A. Ober. 1986. *The California Verbal Learning Test.* Orlando, FL: Psychological Corporation.

Denman, S. B. 1984. *Denman neuropsychology memory scale.* Charleston, SC: Privately published.

Doty, R. L., P. Shaman, C. P. Kimmelman, and M. S. Dann. 1984. University of Pennsylvania smell identification test: A rapid quantitative olfactory function test. *Laryngoscope* 94: 176–178.

Freemon, F. R. 1981. *Organic mental disorders.* New York: Spectrum Publications.

Fromm-Auch, D., and L. T. Yeudall. 1983. Normative data for the Halstead-Reitan Neuropsychological Tests. *Journal of Clinical Neuropsychology* 5:221–238.

Gass, C. S., and E. W. Russell. 1985. MMPI correlates of verbal-intellectual deficits in patients with left hemisphere lesions. *Journal of Clinical Psychology* 41:664–671.

———. 1986. Differential impact of brain damage and depression on memory test performance. *Journal of Consulting and Clinical Psychology* 54:261–263.

Golden C. J. 1981. A standardized version of Luria's neuropsychological tests: A quantitative and qualitative approach to neuropsychological evaluation. In *Handbook of clinical neuropsychology,* ed. S. B. Filskov and T. J. Boll. New York: John Wiley & Sons.

Golden, C. J., T. Hammeke, and A. Purisch. 1978. Diagnostic validity of the Luria neuropsychological battery. *Journal of Consulting and Clinical Psychology* 46:1258–1265.

Goldstein, G., and C. Shelly. 1984. Discriminative validity of various intelligence and neuropsychological tests. *Journal of Con-*

sulting and Clinical Psychology 52:383–389.

Goodglass, H., and E. Kaplan. 1972. *Assessment of aphasia and related disorders.* Philadelphia: Lea & Febiger.

Graham, F. K., and B. S. Kendall. 1960. Memory-for-designs test: Revised general manual. *Perceptual and Motor Skills,* Monograph Suppl. nos. 2–7, 11:147–188.

Halstead, W. C. 1947. *Brain and intelligence: A quantitative study of the frontal lobes.* Chicago: University of Chicago Press.

Hathaway, S. R., and J. C. McKinley. 1951. *The Minnesota Multiphasic Personality Inventory Manual.* Rev. ed. New York: Psychological Corporation.

Hecaen, H., and M. L. Albert. 1978. *Human neuropsychology.* New York: John Wiley & Sons.

Heilman, K. M., L. J. Rothi, and A. Kertesz. 1983. Localization of apraxia producing lesions. In *Localization in neuropsychology,* ed. A. Kertesz. New York: Academic Press.

Heilman, K. M., L. J. Rothi, and E. Valenstein. 1982. Two forms of ideomotor apraxia. *Neurology* 32:342–346.

Jacobs, L., and M. D. Gossman. 1980. Three primitive reflexes in normal adults. *Neurology* 30:184–188.

Jones-Gotman, M. 1986. Memory for designs: The hippocampal contribution. *Neuropsychologia* 24:193–203.

Joseph, R. 1985. Confabulation and delusional denial: Frontal lobe and lateralized influences. *Journal of Clinical Psychology* 41:573–579.

Kaufman, A. S., S. W. Long, and M. R. O'Neal. 1986. Topical review of the WISC-R for pediatric neuroclinicians. *Journal of Child Neurology* 1:89–98.

Kelly, M. P., M. L. Montgomery, E. S. Felleman, and W. W. Webb. 1984. Wechsler Adult Intelligence Scale and Wechsler Adult Intelligence Scale-Revised in a neurologically impaired population. *Journal of Clinical Psychology* 40:788–791.

Kertesz, A. 1982. *The western aphasia battery.* New York: Grune & Stratton.

Kertesz, A., and J. M. Ferro. 1984. Lesion size and location in ideomotor apraxia. *Brain* 107:921–933.

Kertesz, A., I. Nicholson, A. Cancelliere, K. Kassa, and S. E. Black. 1985. Motor impersistence: A right-hemisphere syndrome. *Neurology* 35:662–666.

Klesges, R. C. 1982. Establishing premorbid levels of intellectual functioning in children: An empirical investigation. *Clinical Neuropsychology* 4:15–17.

Kolb, B., and I. Q. Whishaw. 1985. *Fundamentals of human neuropsychology.* 2d ed. New York: W. H. Freeman.

Lawson, J. S., and J. Inglis. 1983. A laterality index of cognitive impairment after hemispheric damage: A measure derived from a principal-components analysis of the Wechsler Adult Intelligence Scale. *Journal of Consulting and Clinical Psychology* 51:832–840.

Lawson, J. S., J. Inglis, and T. W. F. Stroud. 1983. A laterality index of cognitive impairment derived from a principal-components analysis of the WAIS-R. *Journal of Consulting and Clinical Psychology* 51:841–847.

Leli, D. A., and S. B. Filskov. 1981. Clinical-actuarial detection and description of brain impairment with the W.B. Form 1. *Journal of Clinical Psychology* 37:615–622.

Levin, H. S., C. A. Myers, R. G. Grossman, and M. Sarwar. 1981. Ventricular enlargement after closed head injury. *Archives of Neurology* 38:623–629.

Lezak, M. D. 1976. *Neuropsychological assessment.* New York: Oxford University Press. 2d ed., 1983.

———. 1978. Living with the characterologically altered brain injured patient. *Journal of Clinical Psychiatry* 39:592–598.

Lhermitte, F. 1986. Human autonomy and the frontal lobes. Part II, Patient behavior in complex and social situations: The environmental dependency syndrome. *Annals of Neurology* 19:335–343.

Lhermitte, F., B. Pillon, and M. Serdaru. 1986. Human autonomy and the frontal lobes. Part I, Imitation and utilization behavior: A neuropsychological study of 75 patients. *Annals of Neurology* 19:326–334.

Luria, A. R. 1966. *Higher cortical functions in man.* New York: Macmillan.

———. 1973. *The working brain.* New York: Basic Books.

Luria, A. R., and L. V. Majovski. 1977. Basic approaches used in American and Soviet clinical neuropsychology. *American Psychologist* 32:959–968.

McFie, J. 1975. *Assessment of organic intellectual impairment.* New York: Academic Press.

Mesulam, M.-M. 1986. Frontal cortex and behavior. *Annals of Neurology* 19:319–323.

Mittenberg, W., A. Kasprisin, and C. Farage. 1985. Localization and diagnosis in aphasia with the Luria-Nebraska Neuropsychological Battery. *Journal of Consulting and Clinical Psychology* 53:386–392.

Nelson, A., B. S. Fogel, and D. Faust. 1986. Bedside cognitive screening instruments. *Journal of Nervous and Mental Disease* 174:73–84.

Osterrieth, P. A. 1944. Le test de copie d'une figure complexe. *Archives de psychologie* 30:206–356.

Ownby, R. L., and C. G. Matthews. 1985. On the meaning of the WISC-R third factor: Relations to selected neuropsychological measures. *Journal of Consulting and Clinical Psychology* 53:531–534.

Paulson, G. W. 1977. The neurological examination in dementia. In *Dementia,* ed. C. E. Wells. 2d ed. Philadelphia: F. A. Davis Co.

Porch, B. E. 1967. *Porch index of communicative ability.* Palo Alto, CA: Consulting Psychologists Press.

Prifitera, A., and W. D. Barley. 1985. Cautions in interpretation of comparison between the WAIS-R and the Wechsler Memory Scale. *Journalism of Consulting and Clinical Psychology* 53:564–565.

Query, W. T., and J. Megran. 1983. Age-related norms for AVLT in a male patient population. *Journal of Clinical Psychiatry* 39:136–139.

Raven, J. C. 1960. *Guide to the Progressive Matrices.* London: H. K. Lewis. [Currently published by Psychological Corporation, New York.]

———. 1965. *Guide to using the Coloured Progressive Matrices.* London: H. K. Lewis. [Currently published by Psychological Corporation, New York.]

Reitan, R. M. 1984. *Aphasia and sensory-perceptual deficits in adults.* Tucson, AZ: Neuropsychology Press.

———. 1985. Relationships between measures of brain functions and general intelligence. *Journal of Clinical Psychology* 41:245–253.

Reitan, R. M., and L. A. Davison. 1974. *Clinical neuropsychology: Current status and applications.* Washington: Winston.

Reitan, R. M., and D. Wolfson. 1985. *The Halstead-Reitan neuropsychological test battery: Theory and clinical interpretation.* Tucson, AZ: Neuropsychology Press.

Rey, A. 1964. *L'examen clinique en psychologie.* Paris: Presses Universitaires de France.

Roeltgen, D. P., S. Sevush, and K.M. Heilman. 1983. Pure Gerstmann's syndrome from a focal lesion. *Archives of Neurology* 40:46–47.

Ross, E. D., and A. J. Rush. 1981. Diagnosis and neuroanatomical correlates of depression in brain-damaged patients. *Archives of General Psychiatry* 38:1344–1354.

Russell, E. W. 1979. Three patterns of brain damage on the WAIS. *Journal of Clinical Psychology* 35:611–620.

———. 1981. The pathology and clinical examination of memory. In *Handbook of clinical neuropsychology,* ed. S. B. Filskov and T. J. Boll. New York: John Wiley & Sons.

———. 1985. Comparison of the TPT 10 and 6 hole form board. *Journal of Clinical Psychology* 41:68–81.

Schenkenberg, T., D. C. Bradford and E. T. Ajax. 1980. Line bisection and unilateral visual neglect in patients with neurologic impairment. *Neurology* 30:509–517.

Smith, A. 1975. Neuropsychological testing in neurological disorders. In *Advances in neurology,* ed. W. J. Friedlander. Vol. 7. New York: Raven Press.

Smorto, M. P., and J. V. Basmajian. 1980. *Neuromotor examination of the limbs.* Baltimore: Williams & Wilkins.

Snow, W. G., and S. Sheese. 1985. Lateralized brain damage, intelligence, and memory: A failure to find sex differences. *Journal of Consulting and Clinical Psychology* 53:940–941.

Solomon, G. S., R. L. Greene, S. P. Farr, and M. P. Kelly. 1985. Relationships among Wechsler intelligence and memory scale quotients in adult closed head injured patients. *Journal of Clinical Psychology* 42:318–323.

Spiers, P. A. 1981. Have they come to praise Luria or to bury him? The Luria-Nebraska battery controversy. *Journal of Consulting and Clinical Psychology* 49:331–341.

———. 1982. The Luria-Nebraska battery revisited: A theory in practice or just practicing. *Journal of Consulting and Clinical Psychology* 50:301–306.

Springer, S. P., and G. Deutsch. 1981. *Left brain, right brain.* San Francisco: W. H. Freeman & Co.

Squire, L. R., and N. Butters. 1984. *Neuropsychology of memory.* New York: Guilford Press.

Stroop, J. R. 1935. Studies of interference in serial verbal reactions. *Journal of Experimental Psychology* 18:643–662.

Strub, R. L., and F. W. Black. 1981. 2d ed. *The mental status examination in neurology.* Philadelphia: F. A. Davis.

Strub, R. L. and N. Geschwind. 1983. Localization in Gerstmann syndrome. In *Localization in neuropsychology,* ed. A. Kertesz. New York: Academic Press.

Stuss, D. T., and D. F. Benson. 1984. Neurological studies of the frontal lobe. *Psychological Bulletin* 95:3–28.

Sundet, K. 1986. Sex differences in cognitive impairment following unilateral brain damage. *Journal of Clinical and Experimental Neuropsychology* 8:51–61.

Swiercinsky, D. 1978. *Manual for the adult neuropsychological evaluation.* Springfield, IL: Charles C. Thomas.

Taylor, M. A. 1981. *The neuropsychiatric mental status examination.* New York: Spectrum Publications.

Thompson, L. L., and O. A. Parsons. 1985. Contribution of the TPT to adult neuropsychological assessment: A review. *Journal of Clinical and Experimental Neuropsychology* 7: 430–444.

Tweedy, J., M. Reding, C. Garcia, P. Schulman, G. Deutsch, and S. Antin. 1982. Significance of cortical disinhibition signs. *Neurology* 32:169–173.

Warrington, E. K., M. James, and C. Maciejewski. 1986. The WAIS as a lateralizing and localizing diagnostic instrument: A study of 656 patients with unilateral cerebral lesions. *Neuropsychologia* 24:223–239.

Watson, R. T., K. M. Heilman, and D. Bowers. 1985. Magnetic resonance imaging (MRI, NMR) scan in a case of callosal apraxia and pseudoneglect. *Brain* 108:535–536.

Wechsler, D. 1945. A standardized memory scale for clinical use. *Journal of Psychology* 19:87–93.

———. 1958. *The measurement and appraisal of adult intelligence.* Baltimore: Williams & Wilkins.

———. 1981. *Wechsler Adult Intelligence Scale-Revised (WAIS-R).* New York: Psychological Corporation.

Wells, C. E. 1977. *Dementia.* 2d ed. Contemporary Neurology Series. Philadelphia: F. A. Davis.

Wilson, R. S., G. Rosenbaum, G. Brown, D. Rourke, D. Whitman, and J. Grisell. 1978. An index of premorbid intelligence. *Journal of Consulting and Clinical Psychology* 46:1554–1555.

Yeo, R., E. Turkheimer, and E. D. Bigler. 1984. The influence of sex and age on unilateral cerebral lesion sequelae. *International Journal of Neuroscience* 23:299–301.

3. Vascular Disorders of the Nervous System

Disorders affecting the cerebral vessels are among the most common disorders of the brain (Weinfeld, 1981). It has been estimated by Brust (1981) that there are currently approximately two million people affected by vascular disorder in the United States. Proportionately, there is a large vascular supply to the cerebrum, and therefore many of the vascular disorders bring about cognitive disturbance. The vascular system has been fully reviewed from an anatomic standpoint in chapter 1. Figure 3.3 depicts the cortical distribution of the anterior, middle, and posterior cerebral arteries as identified in horizontal CAT sections.

Basically, three main types of vascular disorder occur: embolic, thrombotic, and hemorrhagic. However, the effects on brain tissue occur as a result of either occlusion (almost always associated with thrombosis or embolism) or hemorrhage. Temporary interruption of blood supply produces ischemia and may result in only a transient neurologic deficit, hence the term *transient ischemic attack*. Severe or prolonged ischemia will produce infarction as a result of neuronal and nonneuronal cellular death (see figs. 3.1, 3.2, and 3.4).

Thrombosis

Thrombosis is defined as vessel occlusion by alteration in the vessel wall that interrupts blood supply sufficiently to produce neurologic disturbance (see figs. 3.5–3.8). Common causes have been listed (Adams and Victor, 1977; Whisnant et al., 1979), including arteriosclerosis; subintimal hemorrhage; inflammatory disorders, such as giant cell arteritis, syphilitic endarteritis, polyarteritis nodosa, or lupus erythematosis; hematologic disorders—polycythemia, leukemia, and sickle cell anemia the most prevalent; and serum lipid abnormalities. Alterations in cerebral circulation secondary to heart failure, myocardial infarction, cardiac arrhythmia, and trauma may also be factors in the thrombotic disease process.

Probably the most common factor in thrombotic disorders is arteriosclerosis associated with plaque accumulation in the inner vessel wall lining. This, in turn, is most common in neurologic cerebrovascular disease at the bifurcation of the common carotid artery (see fig. 3.7). Occlusion at this level will have substantial effects on cerebral function, commonly producing initial unilateral transient effects. Hypertension is likewise a common component in thrombotic disease, some studies suggesting a tenfold increase in the risk of thrombotic occurrence in the hypertensive patient (Scheinberg, 1977). While any of the cerebral vessels may be affected, there is greater likelihood of middle cerebral artery involvement.

Transient ischemic attacks are most commonly associated with thrombotic process and usually related to atherosclerotic thrombosis (Adams and Victor, 1977). These attacks are due to transient focal ischemia, usually affecting distal arterial branches. The symptoms or syndrome may precede a complete thrombotic stroke. Likewise, repetitive attacks may evolve into a permanent neurologic deficit (fig. 3.8).

Embolism

Embolic disorder is also an occlusive disease, but the occlusion of the vessel occurs as a result of globular (foreign) material lodging within the arterial system (Adams and Victor, 1977). The origin of the embolus is either cardiac or noncardiac. With cardiac genesis an embolus is most commonly a result of cardiac arrhythmia, myocardial infarction with mural thrombosis, bacterial endocarditis, or any of a variety of cardiac disorders. Hart et al. (1986) suggest that up to one in six of all ischemic strokes are related to cardiogenic embolism. Noncardiac emboli are most commonly associated with atherosclerosis of the aorta and carotid arteries, from sites of cerebral artery thrombosis, fat emboli, or tumor cells. As with thrombosis, the middle cerebral artery is the most commonly affected cerebral artery. The nature of embolic disorder (the temporal sequence present, i.e., very rapid onset) usually specifies embolism rather than thrombosis, which typically displays a somewhat slower evolving picture.

Hemorrhage

Bleeding in or around the brain most commonly occurs intracerebrally, within the subarachnoid space, intraventricularly, or subdurally. The multifactorial pathogenesis of hemorrhage includes hypertension, ruptured saccular aneurysm, ruptured arteriovenous malformation, trauma, or hematologic disease (e.g., hemophilia or leukemia), or its appearance may be secondary to neoplasm or hemorrhagic infarction, or simply idiopathic (Raichle, DeVivo, and Hanaway, 1978) (see figs. 3.9–3.14). The most common hemorrhage is secondary to hypertension (Brust, 1981). Hemorrhage of a major vessel, if substantial bleeding occurs, may result in compressive distortion of the brain with such mechanical distortion frequently leading to infarction in other regions. The brain tissue supplied by the affected vessel eventually necrotizes, affecting both white and gray matter, with the result being areas of cavitation surrounded by a sclerotic zone of glial tissue. Ac-

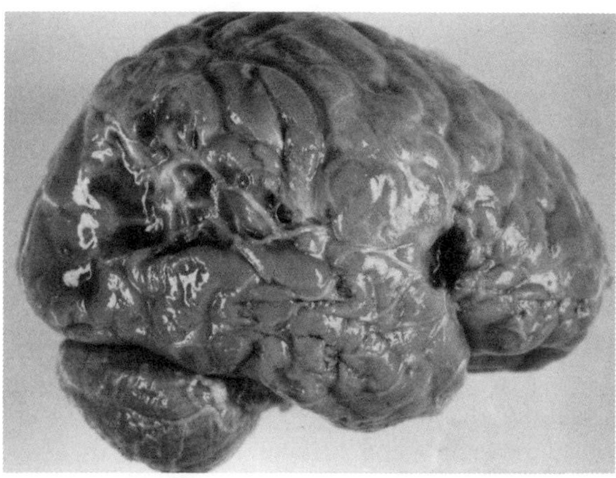

Fig. 3.1. Cerebral infarction involving the posterior cerebral artery. Note the wasting in the posterior parietal-temporal region and all of the occipital region.

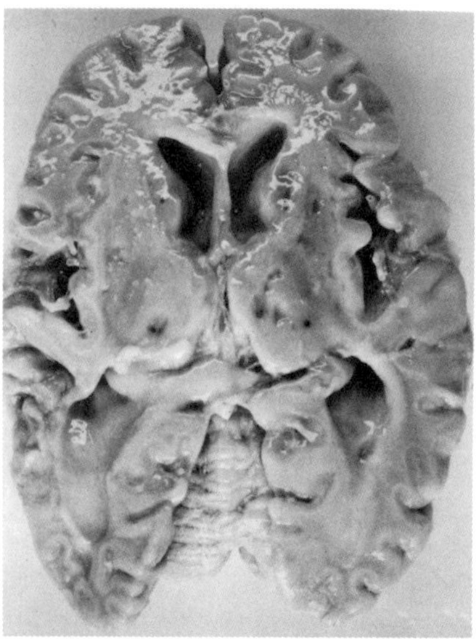

Fig. 3.2. Multi-infarction syndrome. Note the several areas of small infarction.

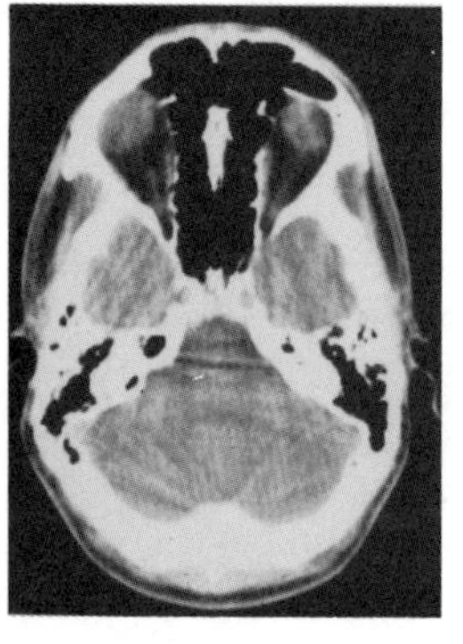

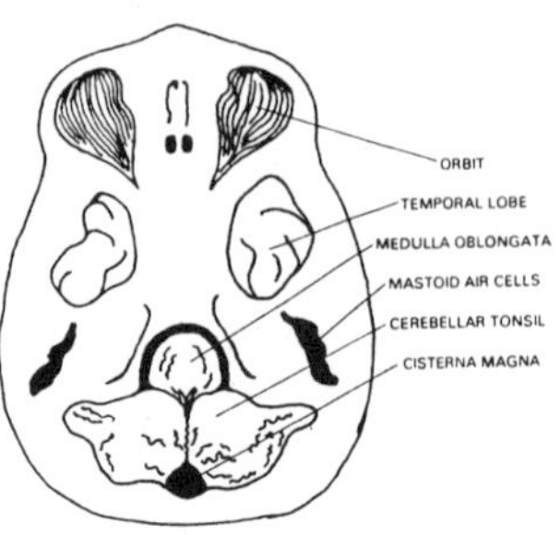

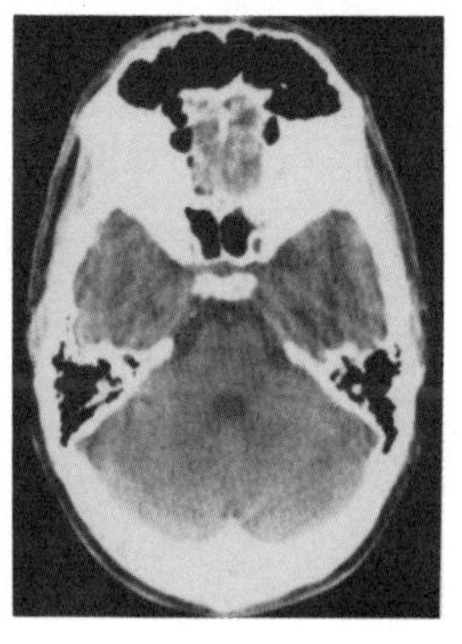

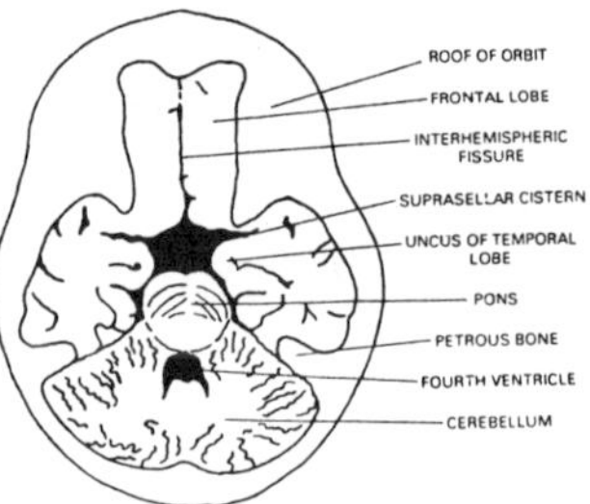

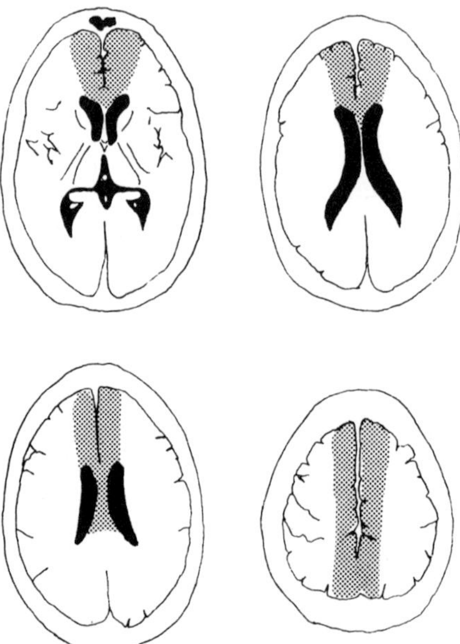

Fig. 3.3. CAT scan depiction of the vascular supply from the three major cerebral arteries. Compare this with Table 3.1.

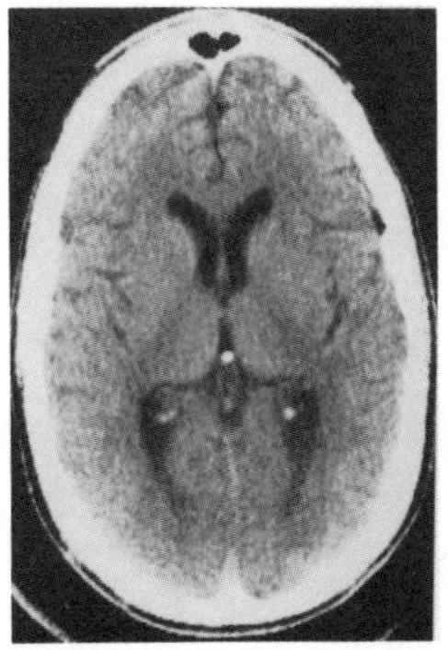

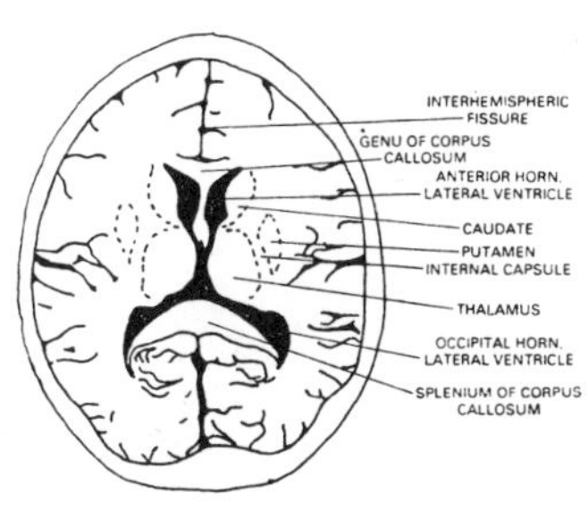

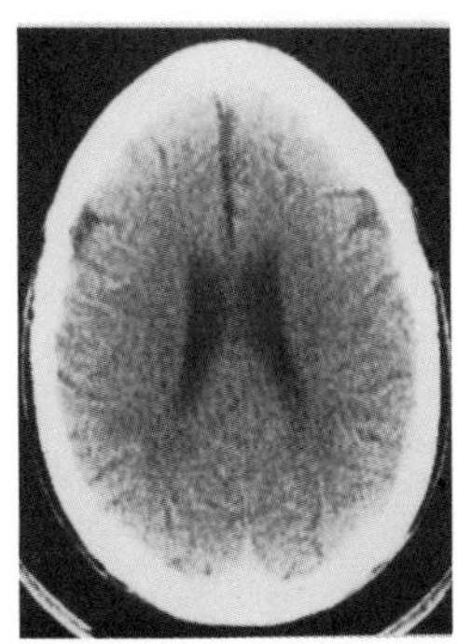

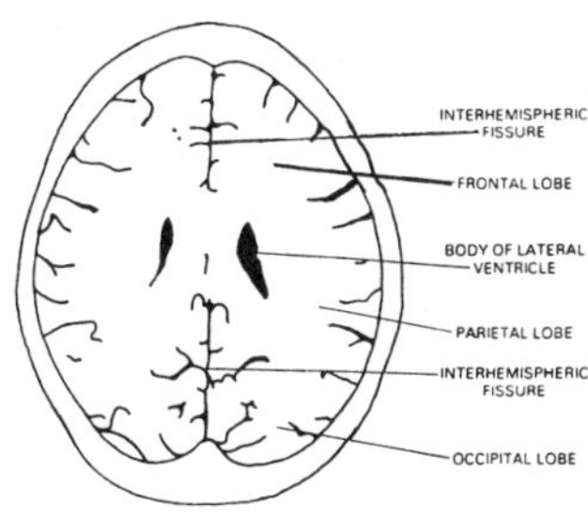

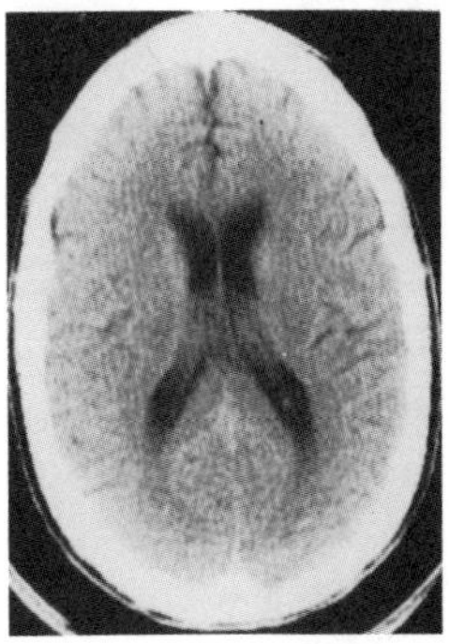

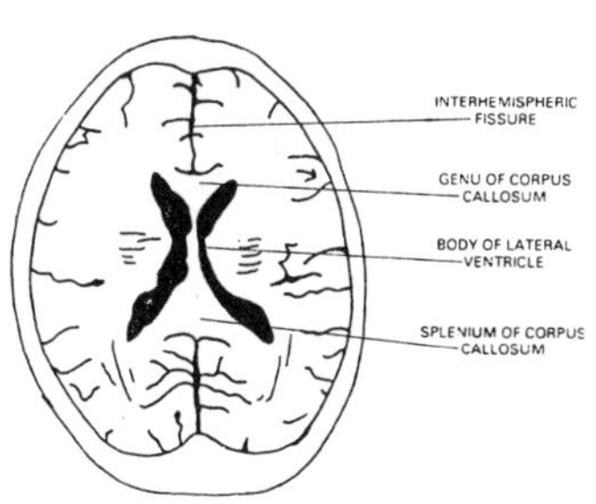

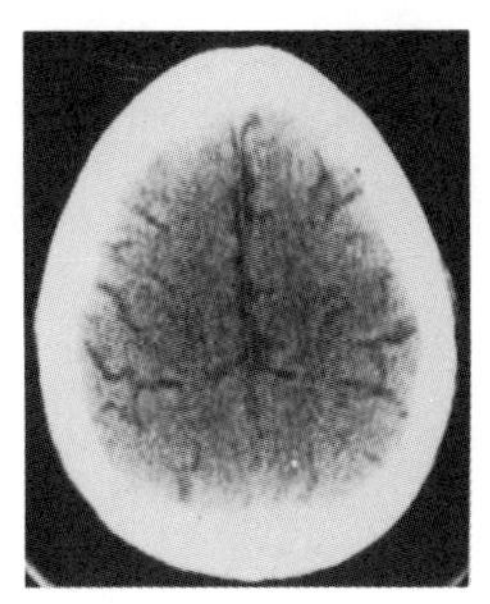

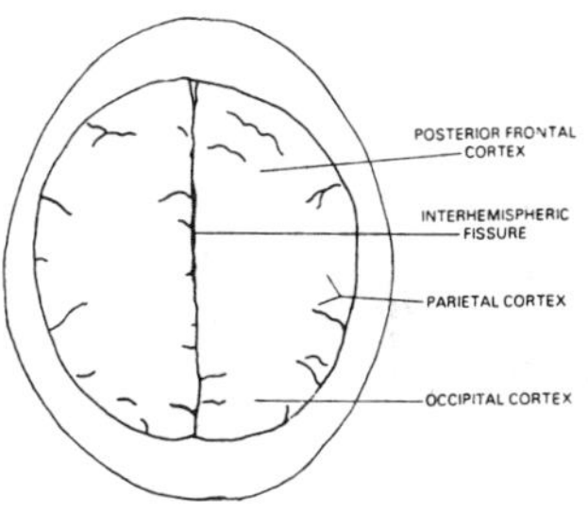

MIDDLE

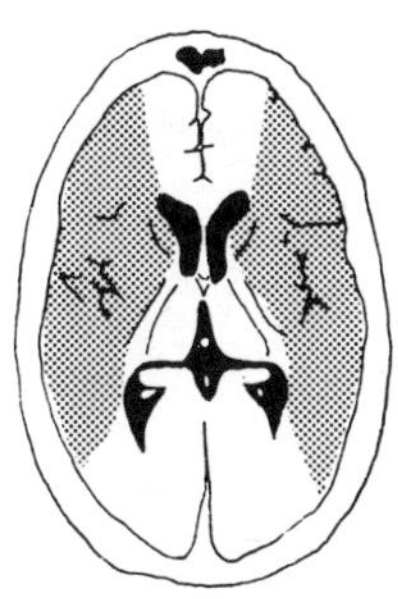

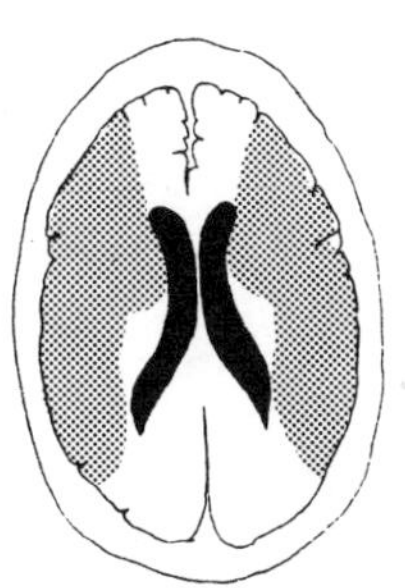

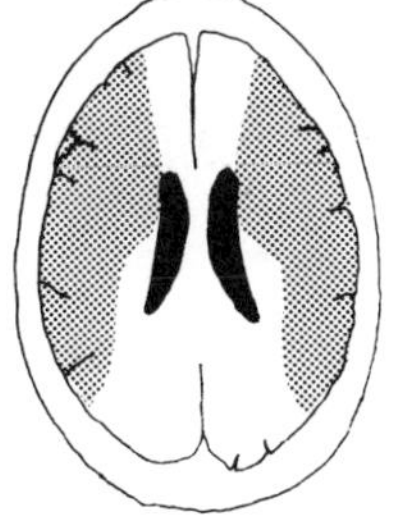

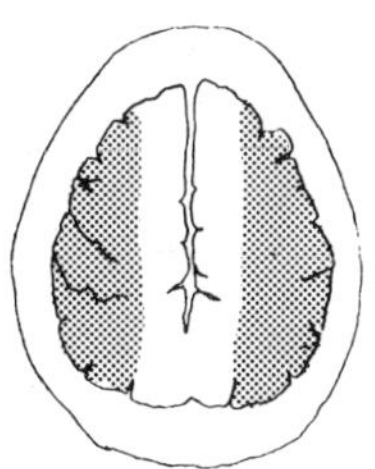

POSTERIOR

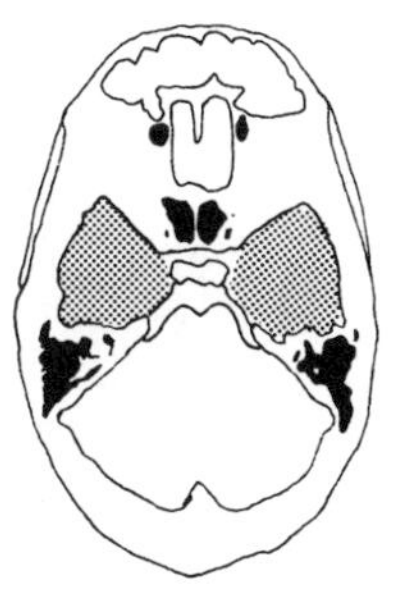

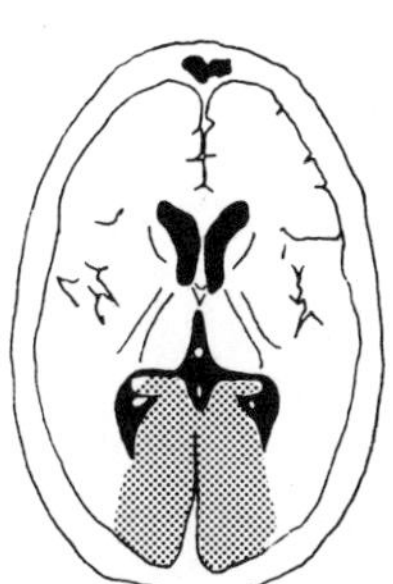

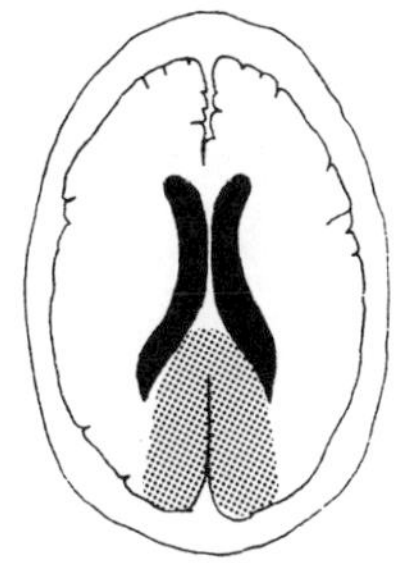

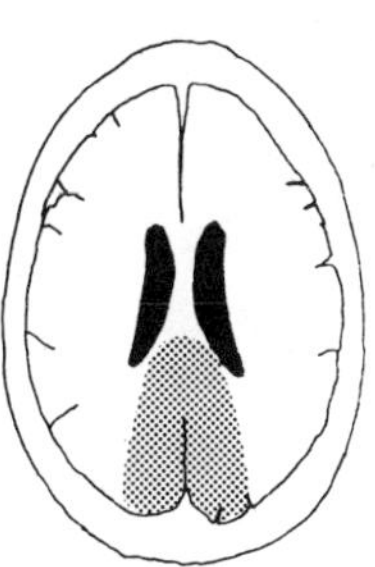

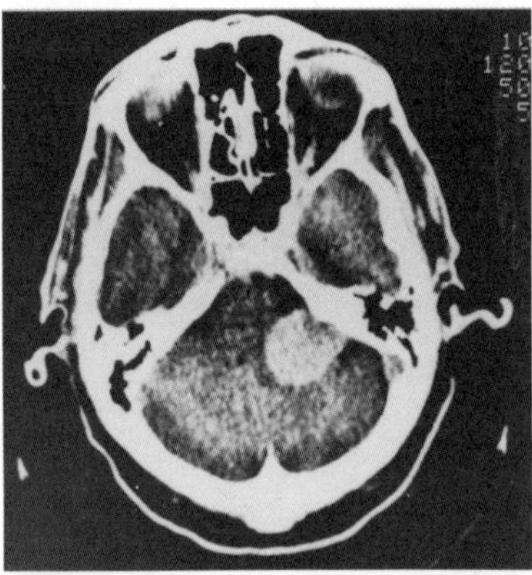

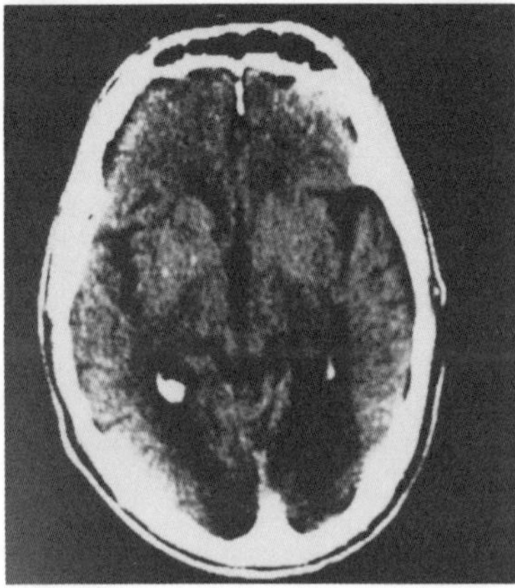

Fig. 3.4. Cortical blindness secondary to bilateral occipital lobe infarction. The infarction resulted from vertebrobasilar artery compression owing to an expanding acoustic neuroma.

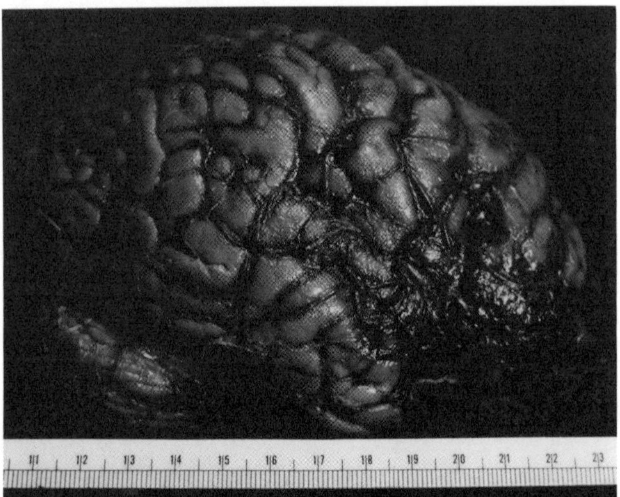

Fig. 3.5. Middle cerebral artery hemorrhage over the posterior frontal and anterior temporal lobe. Note the blood clot formation.

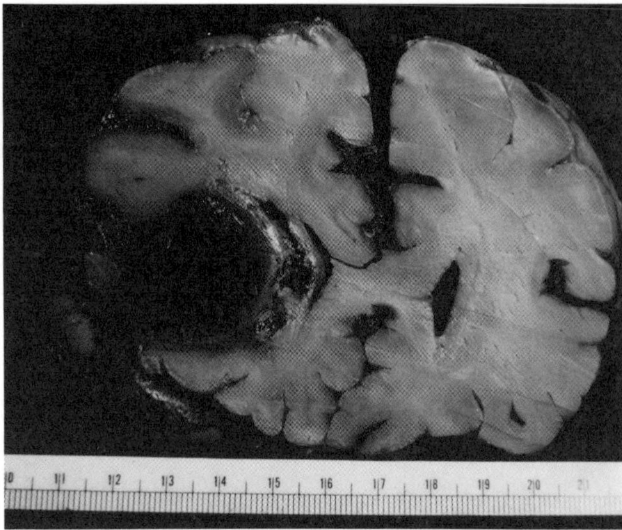

Fig. 3.6. Cerebral thrombosis. Note the large hemorrhagic clot, ventricular and midline displacements.

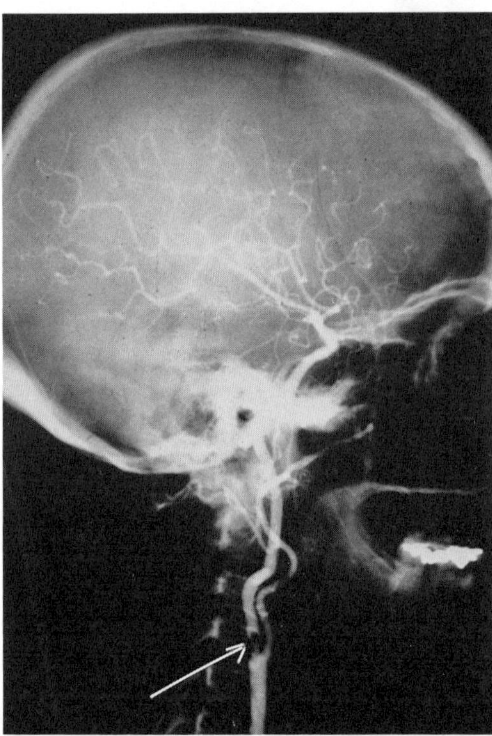

Fig. 3.7. Stenosis. The arteriogram depicts stenosis at the bifurcation of the common carotid into the internal and external divisions. The stenosis is much greater in the internal carotid branch.

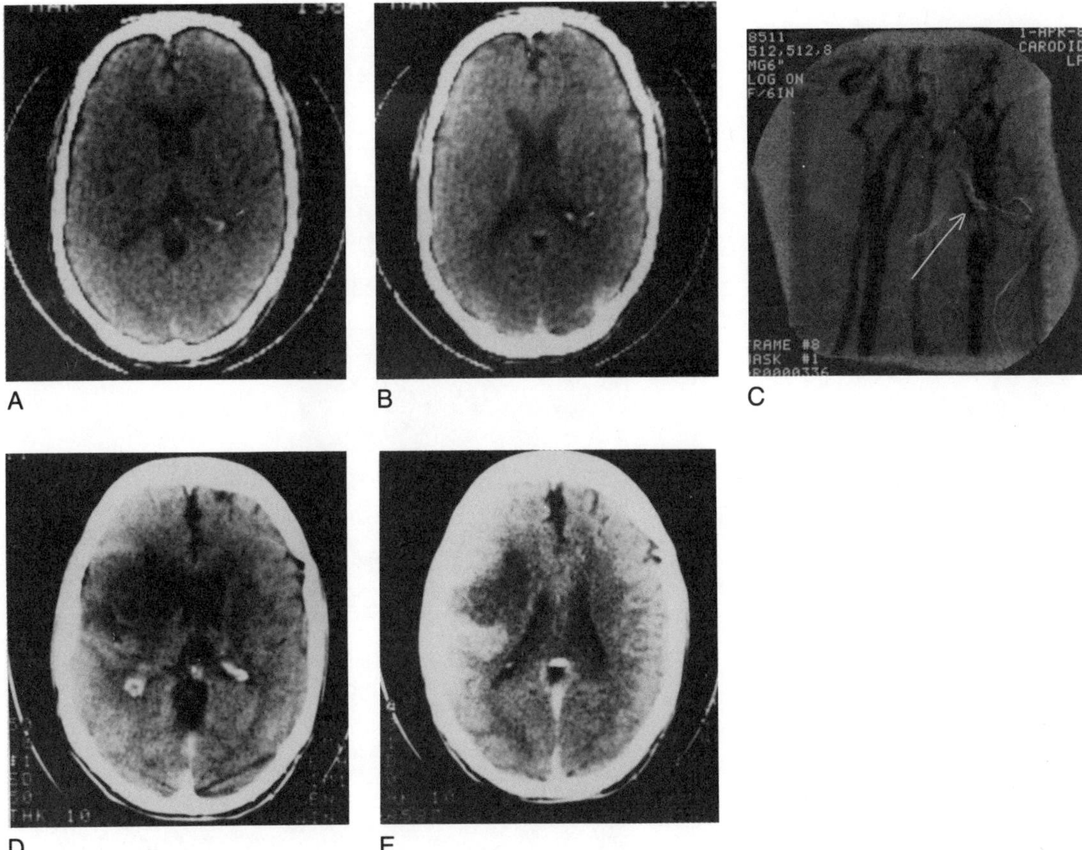

Fig. 3.8. The CAT scans (*A*, *B*) were taken after this 67-year-old patient developed transient weakness in the right arm and leg with associated dysphasia. The digital subtraction radiography images (*C*) depict occlusion of the left internal carotid. The patient declined to submit to operation (endardectomy) and three months later suffered a massive infarction of the mid-anterior left hemisphere resulting in right hemiplegia and dysfluent aphasia. The CAT scans (*D*, *E*) depict the extent of cerebral infarction.

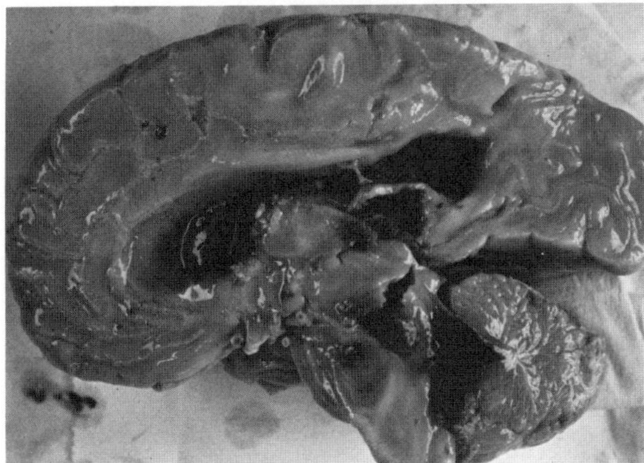

Fig. 3.9. Diffuse intraventricular hemorrhage.

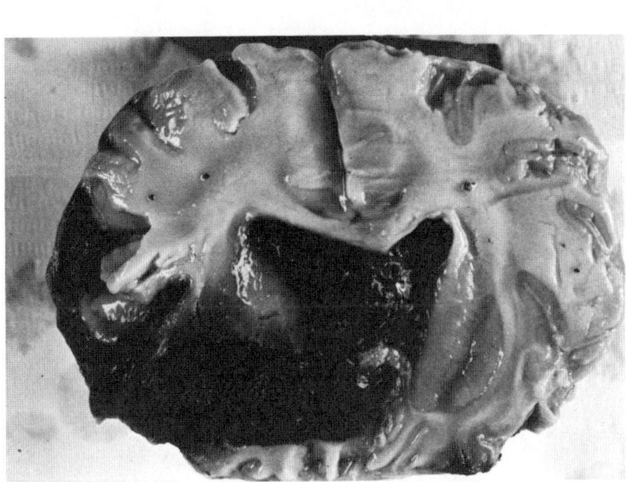

Fig. 3.10. Traumatic injury resulting in intracerebral, intraventricular, and extracerebral hemorrhaging.

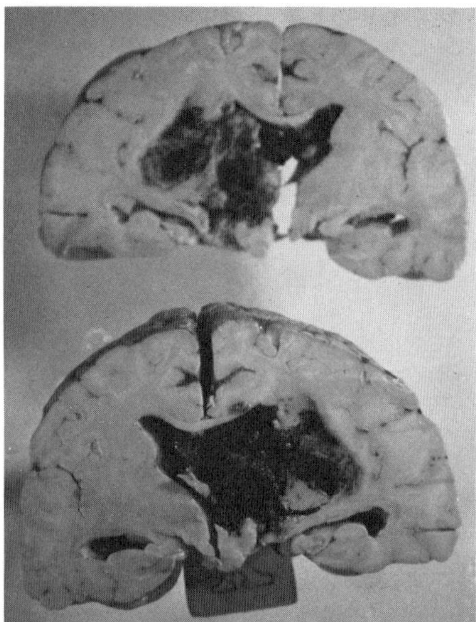

Fig. 3.11. Intraventricular hemorrhage associated with neoplastic enlargement.

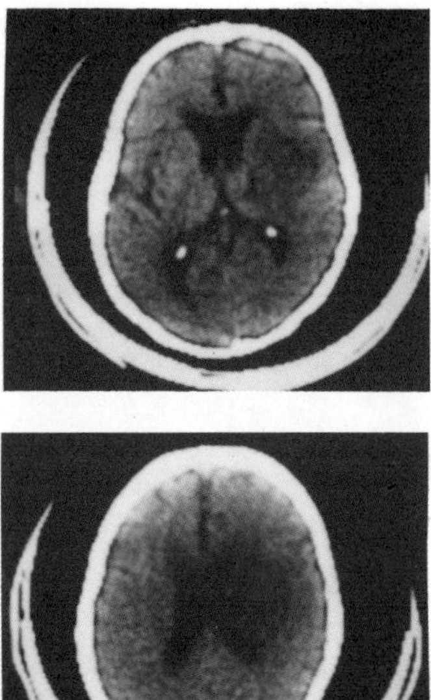

Fig. 3.13. Central infarction in the right hemisphere. A rather massive area at different levels is depicted.

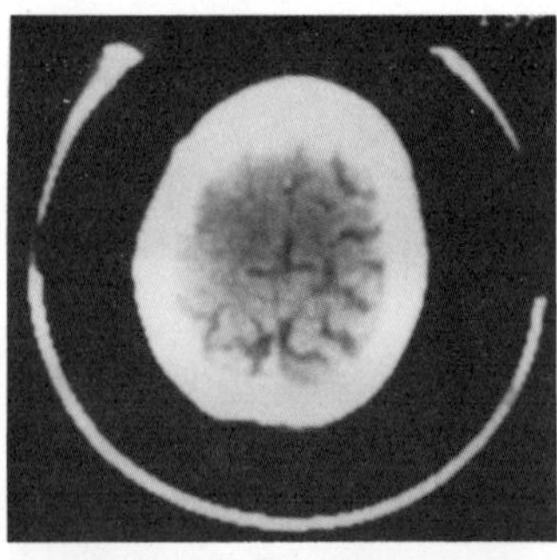

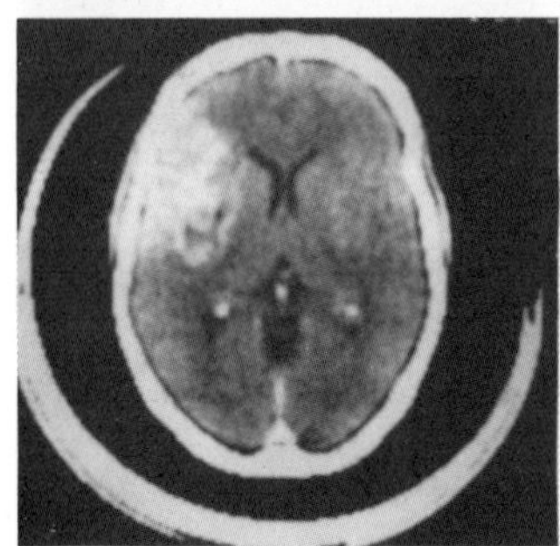

Fig. 3.12. Cerebral hemorrhage in a 71-year-old woman. Note the absence of sulci markings in the left frontal region, suggestive of increased density compatible with subarachnoid hemorrhage. CAT scan the following day reveals large hemorrhagic mass in left frontal region.

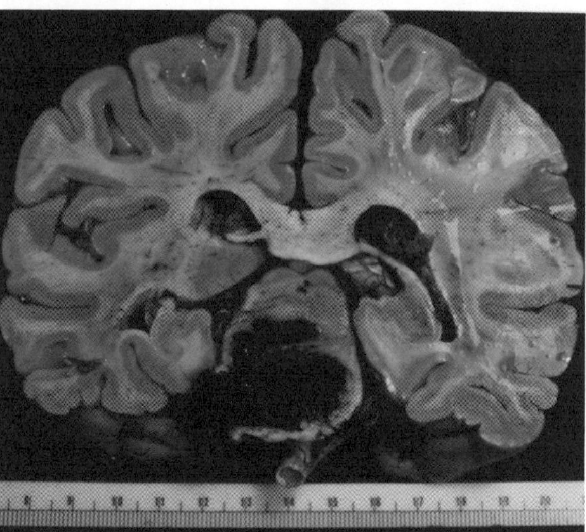

Fig. 3.14. Pontine level hemorrhage. Note the devastating effects of a hemorrhage at this level while the cerebrum is essentially unaffected. Hemorrhage at this level is almost always accompanied by loss of consciousness and ensuing death. Less complete strokes at this level may produce paralysis without cognitive deficit or the "locked-in" syndrome.

cording to Adams and Victor (1977) the most common sites of intracerebral hemorrhaging are the (1) putamen and adjacent internal capsule, (2) central white matter, (3) thalamus, (4) cerebellum, and (5) pons.

Hemorrhage may also result from a ruptured aneurysm (see case 4). An aneurysm develops as a large, space-occupying lesion as the vessel wall weakens and the aneurysmal sac enlarges (see figs. 3.15 and 3.16). Hemorrhage from a ruptured aneurysm may have devastating consequences (see case 4 and fig. 3.17).

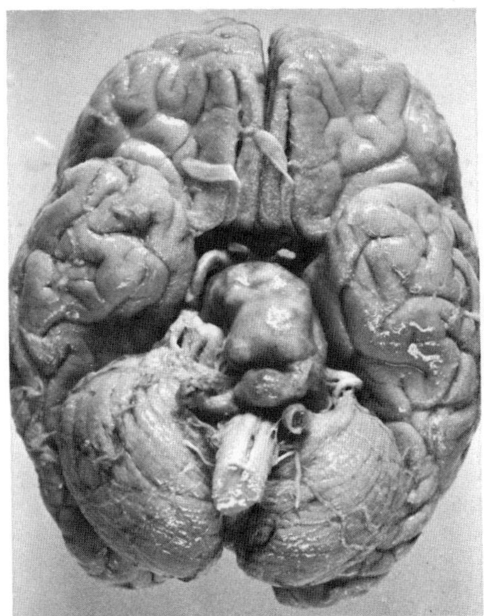

Fig. 3.15. Basilar artery aneurysm.

Other Aspects of Vascular Disorder

Anoxia

Cerebral dysfunction secondary to anoxia is more completely discussed in chapter 4 (see also fig. 3.18). When hemorrhage, thrombosis, or embolism occurs, one of the features of cellular degeneration is oxygen loss.

Infarction

Infarction, a region of neural tissue death, results from obstruction of local circulation (see figs. 3.1, 3.4; also 3.16, 3.19–3.20). The degree and extent of infarction are dependent particularly on the length of hypoxia to the tissue. Hypoxia for sixty seconds or less may produce dramatic clinical signs (e.g., loss of consciousness, convulsion), but the course of dysfunction may be transient with no permanent loss of neural tissue or function. However, one to two minutes of oxygen deprivation may be sufficient to initiate neural necrosis within the cerebral cortex and particularly, within the hippocampus and cerebellum (Raichle, DeVivo, and Hanaway, 1978). Four minutes of hypoxia and circulatory arrest may be sufficient to initiate intracellular swelling, particularly in glial cells. This condition frequently leads to compression of cerebral capillaries. These effects may in turn alter blood flow, even if it is returned, thus complicating the neuropathologic picture. Nedergaard, Astrup, and Klinken (1984) have demonstrated that low blood flow and metabolism surrounding an infarct are due in part to neuronal disconnection and cortical deactivation. This may render adjacent structures dysfunctional, even though they may be intact anatomically. Other common complications are transtentorial herniation with cerebral infarction and tonsillary herniation with cerebellar infarction. As a result of infarction, porencephaly (a condition of the intracerebral cystic area that communicates with the ventricular system and meninges) may develop (see figs. 3.21 and 3.22).

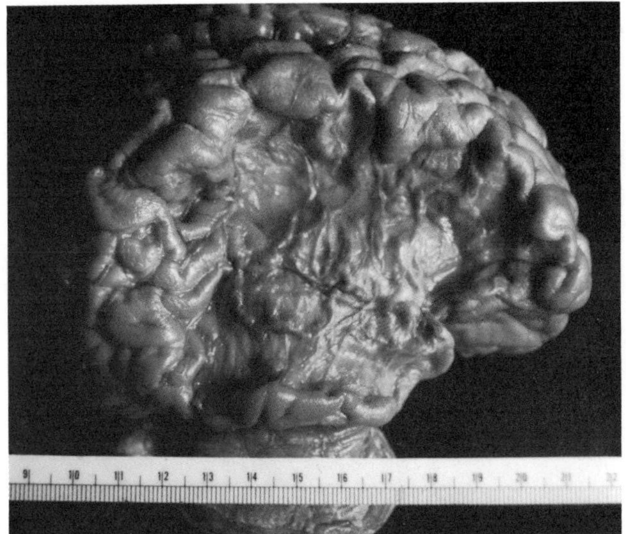

Fig. 3.16. This patient suffered from chronic stenosis of the main branch of the middle cerebral artery. Note the complete infarction along its distribution while those regions supplied by the posterior and anterior cerebral arteries are unaffected.

Transient Ischemic Attacks

A sudden onset of neurologic deficit that is transient (lasting no longer than twenty-four hours followed by complete recovery) is usually related to what has been termed a transient ischemic attack (TIA). Some TIA episodes are extremely brief, lasting only a few seconds. The transient neurologic disturbance, of course, depends on whether

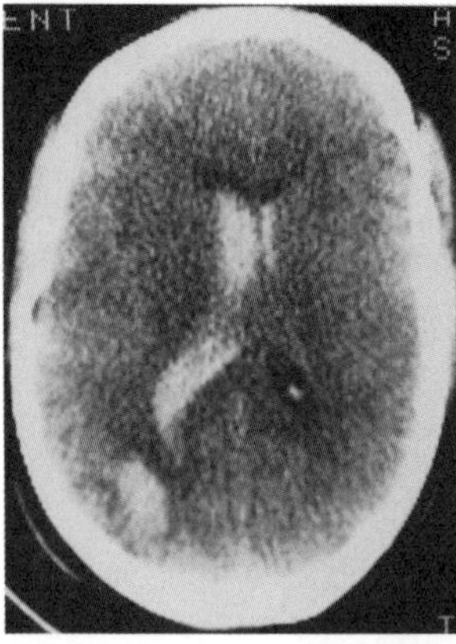

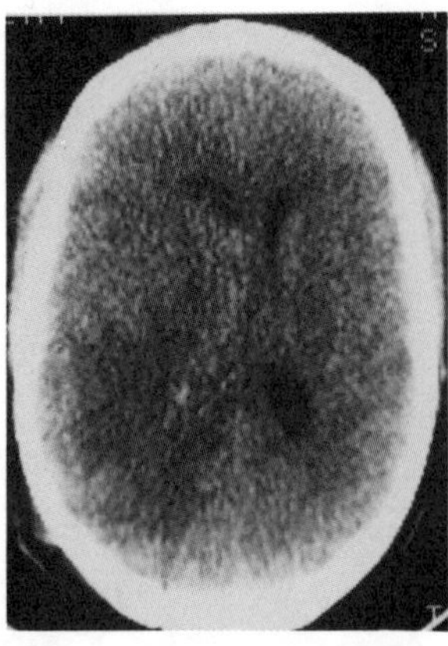

Fig. 3.17. CAT scan of a patient who initially developed pure alexia following a posterior cerebral artery aneurysm that ruptured into the posterior temporal-parietal-occipital region as well as into the left ventricular system (*CAT scan on left*). Follow-up CAT scanning one week later demonstrated dissolution of the hemorrhage, but a rather widespread infarction involving the posterior-temporal-parietal and lateral occipital region. The patient had a right hemianopia. His alexia persists, despite extensive rehabilitation training efforts.

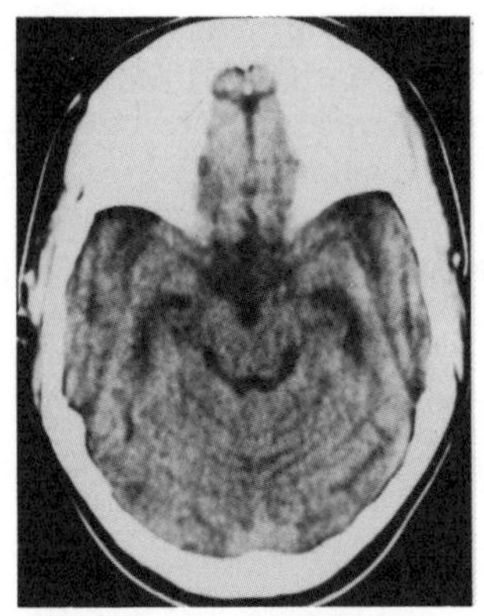

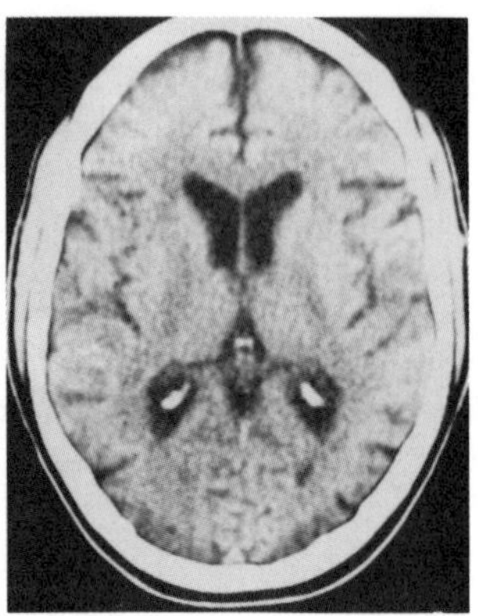

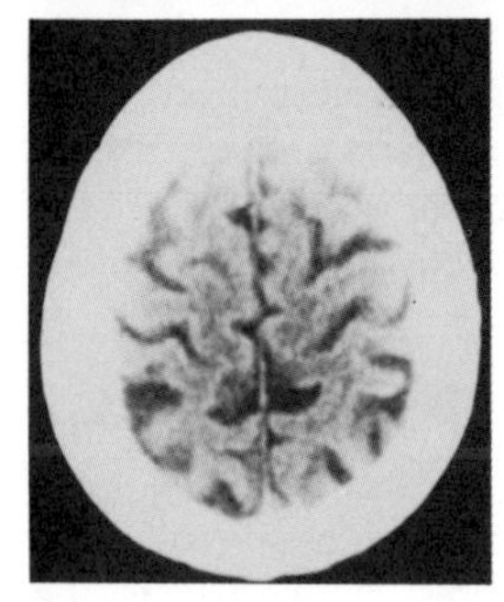

Fig. 3.18. This patient suffered anoxic cerebral damage as a result of a drug-induced cardiac arrest. Note the widespread and diffuse cerebral atrophy. The patient displayed global deficits in intellectual and memory functioning (VIQ = 60, PIQ = 50, FSIQ = 51; Raven's Score = 2/36; MQ = 48).

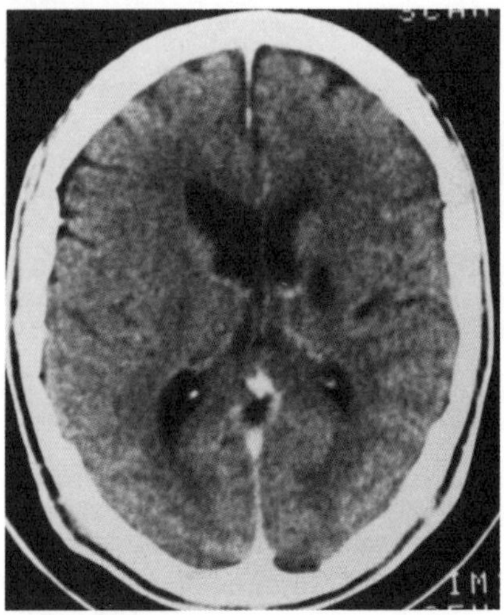

Fig. 3.19. CAT scan of a 64-year-old male patient who suffered a right internal capsule infarct. This produced a dense left hemiplegia and altered left sensory function, but otherwise the patient's neuropsychological studies were entirely within normal limits. There were no specific deficits in terms of visual-spatial functioning, and the patient's intellectual test results (VIQ = 119, PIQ = 111, FSIQ = 119, MQ = 125, Raven's Score = 27/36) were within normal limits. This case demonstrates that certain brain lesions in critical motor or sensory regions may produce dramatic deficits (i.e., hemiplegia) but spare cognitive functioning.

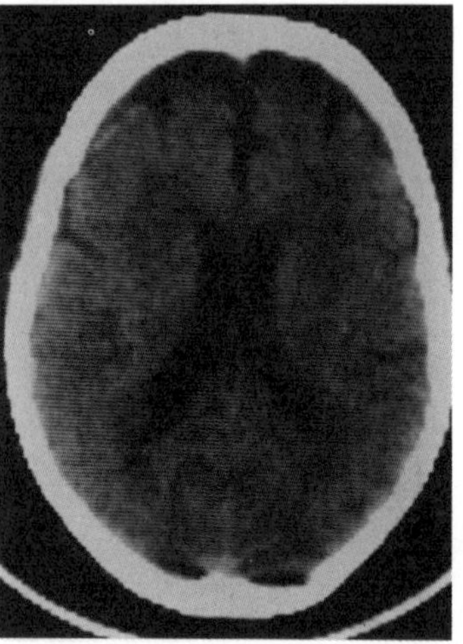

Fig. 3.20. Binswanger's encephalopathy (subcortical arteriosclerotic disease). This patient had a chronic history of hypertension and progressive dementia. Angiography demonstrated 70 percent stenosis of the internal carotid artery on the left and 40 percent stenosis on the right. CAT scan results demonstrate atrophy and significant density decrease (i.e., increased lucency) in central white matter. Intellectual testing indicated a VIQ of 73 and PIQ of 61; MQ was equal to 63.

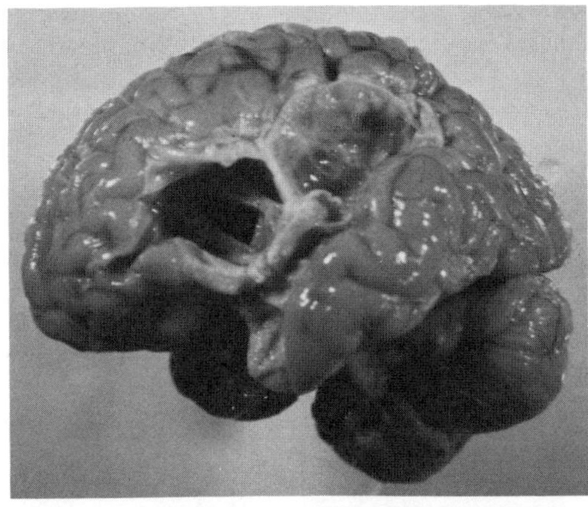

Fig. 3.21. Porencephaly. This postmortem photograph depicts a large porencephalic cyst in left posterior-inferior aspect of frontal lobe. Note also the wasting of the central region.

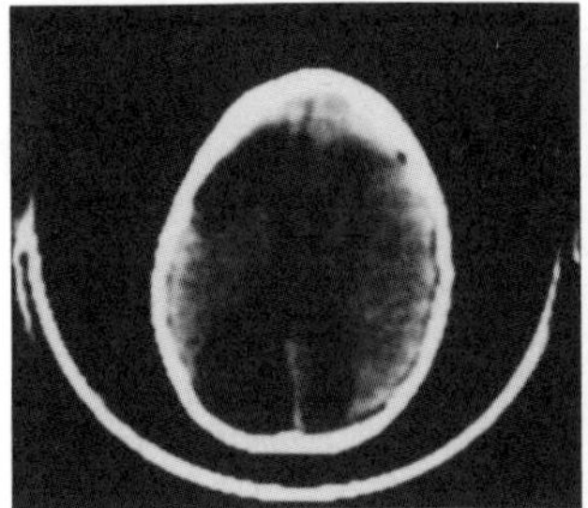

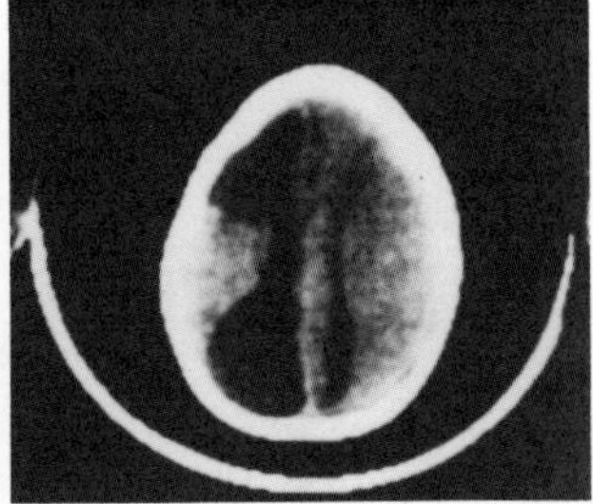

Fig. 3.22. Porencephalic cysts. These CAT scans reveal a large porencephalous cyst in a 7-year-old boy who had respiratory complications at birth. The child had moderate mental retardation, cortical blindness, right hemiplegia, and seizure disorder.

the carotid or the vertebral-basilar system is involved. With carotid origin the most frequent symptoms involve transient hemiparesis or monoparesis, aphasia, and sensory loss. Vertebral-basilar system involvement, however, may be much more variable, and its symptoms include vertigo, diplopia, dysarthria, dysphasia, ataxia, cranial nerve palsy, drop attack, homonymous hemianopsia or cortical blindness, confusion, and transient global amnesia (Scheinberg, 1977). TIA pathogenesis is usually related to minor embolization phenomena. If this is related to carotid arteriosclerotic plaque accumulation, the condition may be treatable with carotid endarterectomy (see case 11). Patients with vertebrobasilar insufficiency may show rather specific deficits in memory functioning but demonstrate preservation of other cortical functions, although both verbal as well as nonverbal memory processes may be impaired (Ponsford, Donnan, and Walsh, 1980). Chronic hypertension may also be associated with frequent TIAs, ending with hypertensive encephalopathy (Healton et al., 1982).

Delaney, Wallace, and Egelko (1980) have suggested, based on their research with patients who have "recovered" from TIAs, that there may be residual deficits in higher cortical functioning (impaired abstract reasoning, diminished complex memory and verbal fluency, along with impaired perceptual-motor functioning) in such patients. Accordingly, the prior history of TIAs may have deleterious effects on long-term cognitive outcome (see also Nielsen et al., 1985). However, in patients who have a singular TIA episode associated with transient global amnesia without other neurologic abnormalities or sequelae, such residual deficits may not develop (Haas and Ross, 1986; Regard and Landis, 1984).

Arteriovenous Anomalies

Arteriovenous malformations (AVMs) are a developmentally related vessel disorder in which the arterial and venous systems intertwine, tangle, and proliferate, forming a distinctly abnormal vascular collection (see case 9). Because the AVM may continue to develop abnormally or to develop saccular aneurysms, the AVM may act like a space-occupying lesion (see fig. 3.23). Although present from birth, the AVM typically does not cause clinical symptoms to appear until the ages of 10–30 years, but symptoms may be delayed until the fifth decade (see fig. 3.24). In many patients the first sign is commonly associated with intracerebral or subarachnoid hemorrhage; others may display seizures, headache, hemiparesis, and mental retardation. In Sturge-Weber syndrome, characteristic AVM is usually present in the hemisphere ipsilateral to the port wine stain.

Lacunar Lesion

The distal branches of the cerebral arteries may become occluded and the resultant infarction may be so extremely small that it does not produce any specific neurologic symptom in and of itself. In addition, the subsequent minor necrotic cavitation may not produce alteration in brain morphology or position. However, as lacunae, as they are termed, accumulate, a variety of neurologic syndromes may evolve, depending on the number, distribution, and position of the lesions. It should be noted that the lacunar state is most commonly associated with the arteriosclerosis-hypertension combination and to a lesser degree with diabetes mellitus (Adams and Victor, 1977; see also Skenazy, 1982). The small lacunar lesions may produce very specific neurologic deficits in the absence of any other cause. Thus, a "pure" hemiparesis may develop because of lacunae in the pyramidal tract area only. Such lesion sites will equally affect upper and lower extremities, but may not affect sensory functioning whatsoever. Most of the lacunar infarcts occur in "nonessential" brain regions, especially the nonpyramidal corona radiata (Brust, 1981). If these areas become numerous and bilateral, however, a syndrome of progressive dementia, shuffling gait, and pseudobulbar palsy may evolve. Ishii, Nishihara, and Imamura (1986) have also demonstrated that where

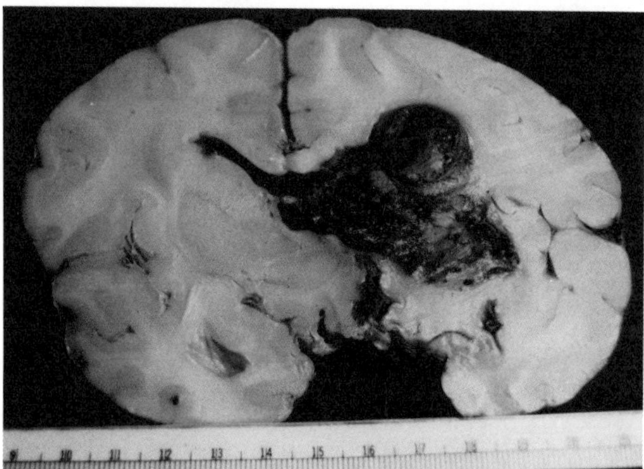

Fig. 3.23. Hemangioma of the cerebrum. Note the extent of the vascular malformation and how it acts as a space-occupying mass.

frontal lobe symptoms predominate (i.e., dementia, abulia, emotional lability, small-stepped gait, dysarthria, urinary incontinence, grasp reflex, pyramidal signs, and akinetic mutism) the lacunar state is likely disseminated throughout the frontal lobes (see fig. 3.20).

Arteritis

Inflammation of the cerebral arteries may occur and, if typical, result in some form of thrombosis. Again, the location and position of the affected artery are the critical features in the development of neurologic symptoms and residual neuropsychological deficit (see case 1).

Subcortical Stroke

Although the lesion size of subcortical strokes tends to be small in comparison with cortical strokes, their neurobehavioral effects may be just as devastating (Fromm et al., 1985). Anterior thalamic strokes tend to affect memory. Left thalamic strokes may produce various dysphasic symptoms, whereas right thalamic strokes may impair visuospatial functioning (see fig. 3.37).

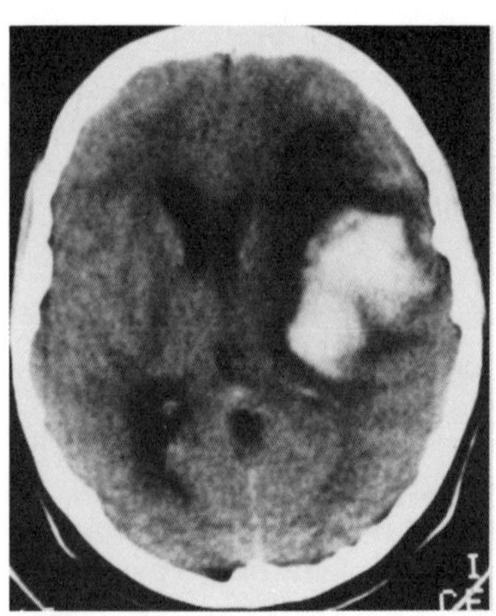

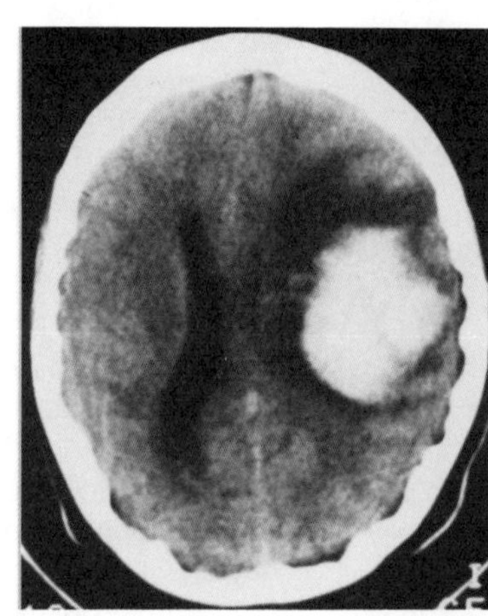

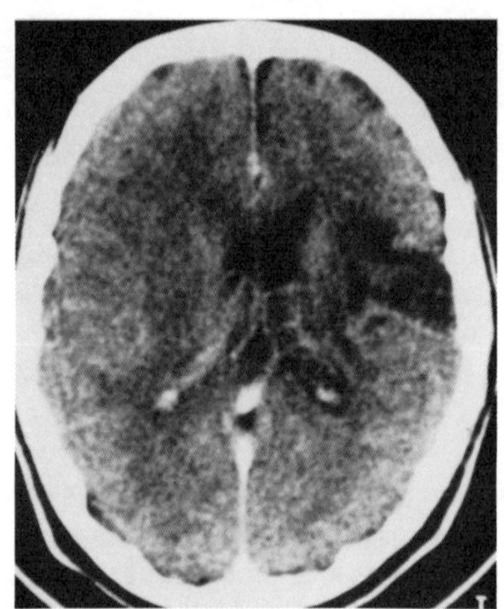

Fig. 3.24. This patient suffered a spontaneous intracerebral hemorrhage that resulted from a ruptured congenital arteriovenous malformation. The malformation was rather substantial, and there was impaired cerebral blood flow to the right temporal region premorbidly. This case demonstrates cerebral plasticity that may occur when the pre-existing lesion was of a congenital nature. Despite the massive hemorrhage as evidenced in the CAT scan above left and the residual poststroke encephalomalacia in the posterior right frontal and anterior and mesial right temporal lobe, the patient's neuropsychological studies were essentially within normal limits except for a residual left hemiparesis. She did not display any specific deficit in memory functioning nor any deficit in visual-spatial functioning (VIQ = 101, PIQ = 100, FSIQ = 102, MQ = 114).

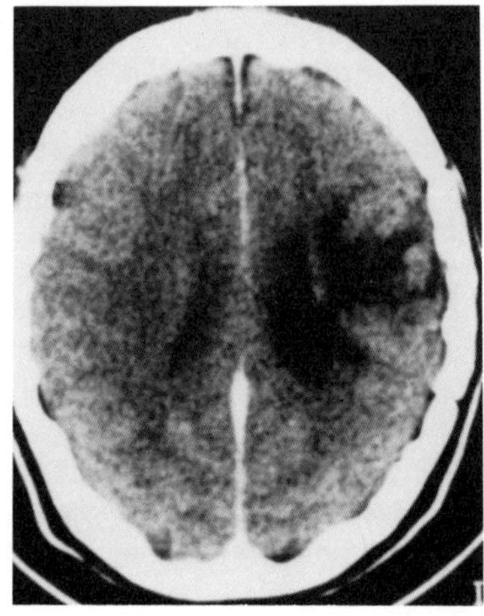

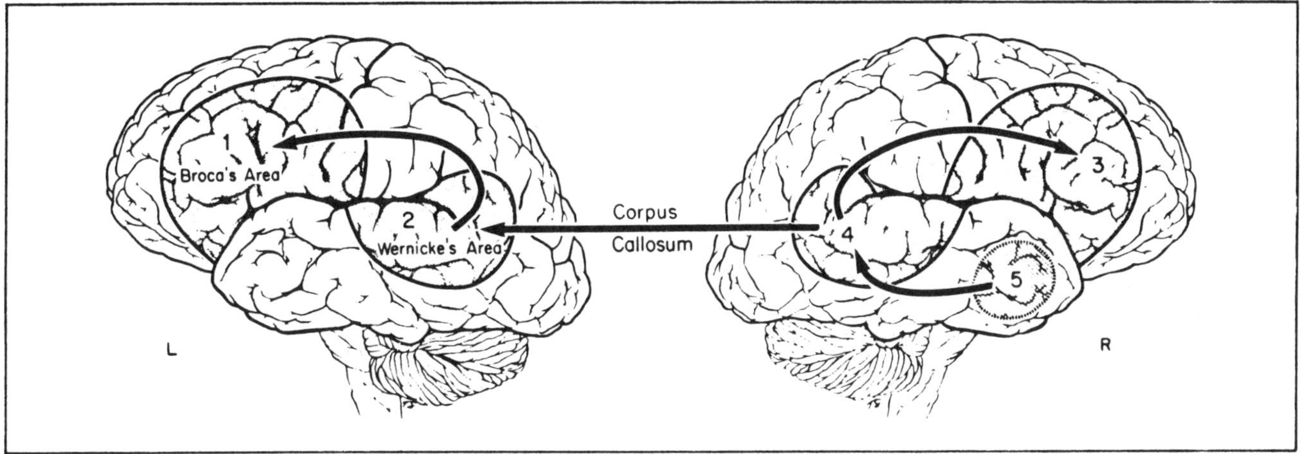

Fig. 3.25. Neuroanatomical model of endogenous depression. From Ross and Rush (1981). Copyright © 1981, American Medical Association.

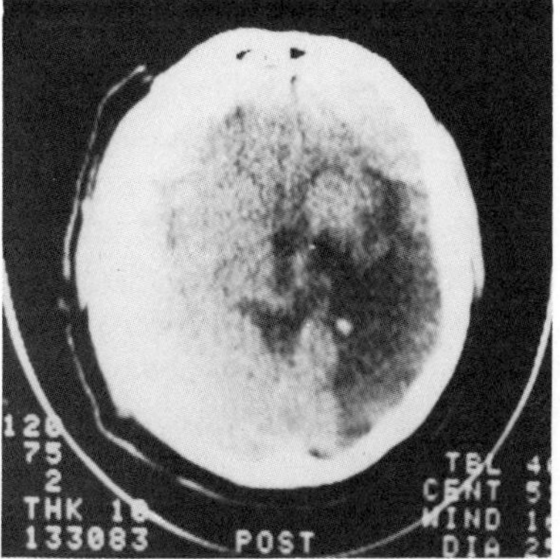

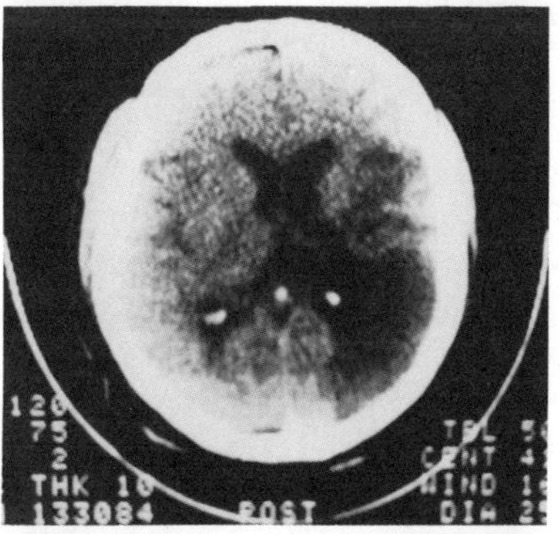

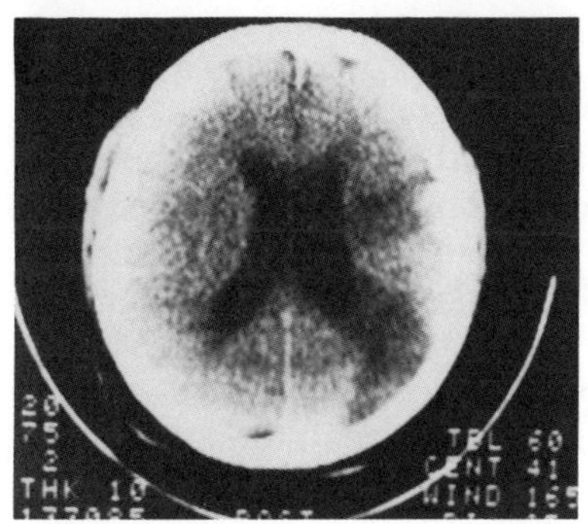

Outcome Following Acute Stroke

Within the first three months following a stroke, considerable spontaneous recovery may occur. Allen (1984) in a study of 148 consecutively admitted patients for stroke found that by four months post stroke there was little change in the level of residual disability for most patients. The combination of hemiplegia and hemianopia in association with higher cerebral dysfunction comprised the combination that predicted the worst outcome and the one least likely to change. Most of this type of research, however, tends to focus more on the physical recovery than on recovery of cognitive functioning (see Wade, Wood, and Hewer, 1985). With the current emphasis on cognitive rehabilitation programs (see Prigatano, 1986), this may change in the future.

MRI versus CAT Imaging in Cerebrovascular Disease

At the time of this writing, MRI has just been recently introduced, and its clinical efficacy is being demonstrated in cerebrovascular disease. Figures 3.27 and 3.28 demonstrate this point. Both these cases demonstrate areas of hemorrhage or infarction that cannot be fully outlined by CAT results but can by MRI findings.

Fig. 3.26. CAT scans of a 65-year-old man who developed a paranoid psychosis six years following a massive infarction of most of the posterior right hemisphere. He thought that his family was stealing his money and, particularly, his cigarettes. He believed they were plotting against him and that his wife was carrying on an affair (all of which were unfounded). He became combative and threatening and was hospitalized. For six years after the infarction he displayed none of these symptoms; in fact, he displayed features of mild to moderate anosognosia. The patient responded well to environmental support and structure along with neuroleptic and anticonvulsant medication.

Neuropsychological Findings in Vascular Disorders

Table 3.1 summarizes the major neuropsychological findings in patients with vascular disorders affecting one of the major cerebral arteries. Neuropsychological examination will invariably take place after the expression of neurologic symptoms and usually after the patient has had a complete neurodiagnostic evaluation. As such, by the time neuropsychological studies are undertaken the extent of structural damage has been fairly well delimited. However, the functional brain changes following cerebrovascular accident or disease require neuropsychological examination for documentation. This is very important, because lesion site and extent may only poorly correlate with deficits in function (Basso et al., 1981; Kertesz and Dobrowolski, 1981). The patient with vascular disorder should always have a comprehensive neuropsychological evaluation, special attention being paid not so much to the obvious focal signs that may be present (i.e., hemiplegia), but rather directed toward evaluating surrounding systems and the general integrity of whole-brain functions. Thus, the patient with a right hemiplegia should not just be evaluated in terms of the unilateral motor deficits, but additionally for whether there are any associated deficits in language function or sensory involvement, any organic affective or behavioral changes, or any similar effects. Since there is a greater incidence of vascular disorder with age, age effects are a separate variable that should be taken into consideration in the evaluation of the older patient with vascular disorders. Serial neuropsychological studies can be very useful in monitoring a patient's recovery as well as outlining cognitive rehabilitation strategies.

Prosody. In the patient who has suffered a cerebral vascular accident there may be changes in affect that may also be of diagnostic significance. This may also be true with other neurologic disorders, but with vascular disorders the effects tend to be more localized and circumscribed. With nonvascular disorders, such as trauma or infection, there may be more widespread damage in addition to whatever focal damage may be present. Thus, the localizing significance is commonly lost in nonvascular disorders, but this is frequently not the case with vascular disorders with focal effects. Ross and Rush (1981) have reviewed the literature on the effects of right hemisphere vascular lesions on the modulation (prosody) of the affective components of language and behavior. These authors make the suggestion, based on their case studies, that the affective disturbance associated with pathology in the right hemisphere may be categorized according to the scheme commonly utilized for description of the aphasic disorders and their anatomic significance. This approach is presented in figure 3.25 and table 3.2. As can be seen from table 3.3, aprosodic disorders may fall into the motor, sensory, global, conduction, or mixed categories, all with different effects on the tone and gestural makeup of speech. Figure 3.25 and these tables provide an anatomic outline for different types of aprosodias.

In the aphasic patient, the resultant affective disturbance may relate to the psychological consequences of the verbal-cognitive deficits and the frustration over the loss of function along with the inability to effectively communicate. Dissimilarly, the patient with right hemisphere lesion may display deficits in emotional output associated with aprosodic voice patterns and dysfunctional gesturing. Accordingly, such patients may appear to have a flattened affect, which in actuality is a disturbance in prosody. Such patients may report symptoms of dysphoric mood in a monotonous tone and uncaring or unconvincing manner (see case 8) or they may show pathologic crying or laughing. Underlying depression in such patients may be masked by their inappropriate presentation. If a lesion can be documented in the right hemisphere, particularly in the right inferior frontal region, then the disturbance in affect can usually be attributed to the underlying organic deficit and not to some functional or nonneurologic origin.

When evaluating for affect changes, one should always be cautious not to confuse the type of "pathologic affect" that may be associated with pseudobulbar palsy and that of right hemisphere origin. The term pseudobulbar palsy refers to upper motor neuron disease typically affecting either the corticospinal tracts, the corticobulbar tracts, or both. This is different from bulbar palsy, which indicates lower motor neuron involvement. Emotional output is affected by pseudobulbar involvement because these systems control the final common path for the motor expression of emotion, whatever the emotion may be. Thus, the patient with bilateral corticospinal or corticobulbar involvement may display inappropriate or "pathological" crying or laughing, because of aberrant efferent output and not emotional disturbance.

Patients with left hemisphere vascular disease may show a catastrophic affect with profound depression without prosodic impairment (Watson and Heilman, 1982). Robinson and colleagues (see Robinson, Lipsey, and Price, 1985; Robinson et al., 1983; Robinson et al., 1985) have demonstrated that patients with left hemisphere strokes, particularly in the left frontal region, may develop clinically significant depression. This is in contrast to patients with right hemisphere strokes, who tend to display an inappropriately cheerful but apathetic state, again particularly with right frontal lesions. Sinyor et al. (1986) have failed to fully replicate these findings, however, and their research suggests that there may be some relationship between right hemisphere damage and depression as well.

Alexander and LoVerme (1980) have demonstrated an interesting phenomenon that needs experimental verification but may provide further ability to neuropsychologically differentiate between a cortical and subcortical locus of damage. In their clinical studies they found that the catastrophic affect that may accompany left hemisphere stroke did not occur with the same regularity when the vascular lesion was subcortical. The left subcortical lesions typically produced a flattened affect, but not of cata-

Table 3.1. ***Neuropsychological Findings in Vascular Disorders***

Function	Anterior Cerebral	Middle Cerebral	Posterior Cerebral
Motor	Contralateral weakness or paralysis, typically most affecting the distal lower extremity. Rapid alternating movements may be impaired or an inability to maintain them.	Contralateral paralysis with face and upper extremity more affected than lower.	Typically motor involvement not present except when proximal arteries are affected; then hemiballismus may result because of subthalamic nucleus lesion, cranial nerve palsy, or hemiparesis owing to involvement of the corticospinal tract as it passes down the brain stem.
Sensory	Absent or mild contralateral tactile loss.	Depending on extent of involvement, there may be contralateral auditory, visual, and tactile sensory disturbance.	If unilateral, then contralateral hemianopsia typically develops. Cortical blindness occurs if bilateral. Proximal occlusion may affect the thalamus, producing sensory disturbance, pain, or both.
Language	Impaired articulation or disturbance in motor inertia may be present.	With left hemisphere involvement may develop a Broca's, Wernicke's, global, or conduction aphasia depending on site and extent of involvement.	If involving the left hemisphere, alexia without agraphia or other aphasic symptoms may occur.
Praxis	If anterior corpus callosum is affected, there may be left arm apraxia.	Apraxia may occur with lesions in either hemisphere. Constructional apraxia (in the absence of aphasia) and dressing apraxia are common with right hemisphere involvement.	Constructional apraxia with right hemisphere involvement may occur.
Spatial-perceptual	Typically not affected.	If right hemisphere is affected, varying degrees of impairment may be present.	If right hemisphere is affected, primarily visuospatial functions will be impaired.
Memory	Some disturbance in new memory may be present.	With left hemisphere involvement greater tendency for disturbance in verbal memory; with right hemisphere greater tendency for visual memory disturbance.	Global amnesia may occur that is either transient or permanent. Permanent short-term memory deficits may also occur.
Gnosis	Infrequently may display features of anosognosia (failure to appreciate loss of function).	With right hemisphere involvement, may have greater tendency to develop topographagnosia (loss of direction) as well as anosognosia.	Typically not affected.
Behavior	Frontal lobe syndrome may develop; with right hemisphere, prosody may be affected.	Impaired prosody if right hemisphere involved.	No particular behavioral syndrome is characteristic.

Table 3.2. ***Neuroanatomical Model for Signs and Symptoms of Endogenous Depression***

Area[a]	Neurological Syndrome and Function	Postulated Function in Endogenous Depression
1 (Broca's area)	Motor (Broca's) aphasia; organizes motor output for propositional language	Expression of depressive verbal-cognitive set through propositional language
2 (Wernicke's area)	Sensory (Wernicke's) aphasia; involved in comprehension of propositional components of language	Internal formulation and ultimate expression of depressive verbal-cognitive set through propositional language.
3	Motor aprosodia; organizes motor output for affective components of language and behavior	Expression of depressive affect through affective components of language and behavior
4	Sensory aprosodia; involved in comprehension of affective components of language and behavior	Internal formulation of "depressive-affective set" that allows, via corpus callosum, Wernicke's area to formulate mood-congruent depressive verbal-cognitive set and area 3 to ultimately express mood-congruent depressive affect
5	Not known	Unknown structure or structures essential for initiating and/or modulating critical features of endogenous depression (e.g., dysphoria, vegetative behavior, hypothalamic dysfunction)

Source: From Ross and Rush (1981); copyright © 1981, American Medical Association.
[a]Areas are shown in fig. 3.20.

Table 3.3. ***The Aphasias and Aprosodias***

	Aphasias				Aprosodias			
	Fluency	Repetition	Comprehension	Reading Comprehension	Spontaneous Prosody and Gesturing	Prosodic Repetition	Prosodic Comprehension	Comprehension of Emotional Gesturing
Motor	Poor	Poor	Good	Good	Poor	Poor	Good	Good
Sensory	Good	Poor	Poor	Poor	Good	Poor	Poor	Poor
Global	Poor	Poor	Poor	Poor	Poor	Poor	Poor	Poor
Conduction	Good	Poor	Good	Good	Good	Poor	Good	Good
Transcortical motor	Poor	Good	Good	Good	Poor	Good	Good	Good
Transcortical sensory	Good	Good	Poor	Poor	Good	Good	Poor	Poor
Mixed transcortical	Poor	Good	Poor	Poor	Poor	Good	Poor	Poor
Anomic (alexia with agraphia)	Good	Good	Good	Poor	Good	Good	Good	Poor

Source: From Ross and Rush (1981).
Note: The existence of the conduction and anomic aprosodias has been hypothesized; the others have been described. Motor, sensory, global, and transcortical sensory aprosodias have good anatomical correlation with lesions in the left hemisphere known to cause homologous aphasias.

strophic proportions. Watson and Heilman's (1982) review of this work suggests that if aphasic disturbance is present in a patient without catastrophic depressive response a subcortical lesion may be present.

Considerable other research has also focused on the role of subcortical structures in language function (Damasio et al., 1982; Eidelberg and Galaburda, 1982; Galaburda and Eidelberg, 1982; Naeser et al., 1982). As of this date, though, consistent neuropsychological findings alone do not permit the distinction between cortical and subcortical etiology. However, the combination of CAT scanning, neuropsychological examination, and detailed aphasiological examination permits quantification of subcortical lesions and form of language defect.

The prosodic examination should be given whenever affective disturbance is present in the neurologic patient. Correlation of neuropsychological findings with prosodic deficits may well determine the locus of pathology. Utilization of the Minnesota Multiphasic Personality Inventory (MMPI) may also be helpful in the examination of affect and behavior change in the brain-damaged patient. Black and Black (1982) have shown that posterior cerebral lesions, regardless of hemisphere, showed greater psychopathology (i.e., higher elevations on the depression, schizophrenic, psychopathic deviancy, and L and K scales) than those with frontal lesions. More will be said about the relationship between the right hemisphere and affect in chapter 10.

Infrequent Neuropsychological Findings in Vascular Disease

Although infrequent, aphasic disturbance has been reported following right hemisphere cerebrovascular accident (CVA) (see Brust et al., 1982). Such results likely occur as a result of the right hemisphere being uniquely dominant for language but not for motor function. Estimates (reviewed by Brust et al., 1982) suggest that only 0.8 percent to 4.0 percent of all right-handed people may have such a crossed dominance. Henderson, Alexander, and Naeser (1982) also have found alexia in combination with a visuospatial deficit in a right-handed man who had a right thalamic infarction.

The patient with mixed body dominance, and many people whose left side is dominant, may have bilateral cerebral language functions (Benson, 1979; Albert et al., 1981). Aphasic deficits in these individuals tend to be less severe than in those who are truly right-body-side/left-hemisphere dominant. These mixed and left-hand dominant individuals also may show better spontaneous recovery.

Palinopsia, the persistence or recurrence of visual images seen after the cessation of the stimulus, may occur with vascular disease, typically when it affects posterior circulation. Usually, the patient has a visual field defect, and it is more commonly the left visual field. Although this phenomenon has been well documented in the literature for many years, the underlying cerebral pathology necessary for its expression as well as the mechanisms of expression remain unknown (see Cummings et al., 1982, for review). Mention should also be made that visual hallucinations may accompany cortical blindness (see fig. 1.43) and such symptoms are more common than palinopsia and easily differentiated.

Capgrass syndrome, or reduplicative paramnesia, may also accompany certain vascular accidents. For example, we evaluated a 43-year-old woman who suffered a spontaneous subarachnoid hemorrhage owing to a ruptured aneurysm located within the middle cerebral artery of the right hemisphere. Although she had lived in Austin, Texas, for a number of years she insisted that she was in Charlotte, North Carolina—that we had tricked her by making the scenery outside her hospital window look like Austin, but it *actually* was Charlotte. This syndrome has been reviewed by Benson, Gardner, and Meadows (1976) and Alexander, Stuss, and Benson (1979). Neuropsychological studies of such patients tend to implicate multiple factors in the expression of this disorder, including visuoperceptual and visuospatial deficits and dysfunctional memory (Morrison and Tarter, 1984; Patterson and Mack, 1985). Levine and Grek (1984) have also demonstrated delusions involving orientation in time and place, events in the recent past, and identities of familiar individuals in patients with infarction of the right cerebral hemisphere. There was no indication that size or location of the lesion was a critical factor, only that the lesion be in the right hemisphere. Presence of cerebral atrophy was a major determinant in the development of delusional behavior in these poststroke patients.

Price and Mesulam (1985) reviewed the cases of five patients who developed acute psychotic disturbances following infarcts in the right hemisphere. These patients presented with agitation, inattention, suspiciousness, paranoid delusions, hallucinations, and lack of appropriate concern. There was no specific locus of infarction that appeared to be necessary or sufficient to produce this acute psychotic disturbance. Price and Mesulam suggest that the possibility of a right hemisphere lesion needs to be entertained in patients who present with atypical psychotic features.

Levine and Finklestein (1982) have also described a syndrome of delayed psychosis after right temporal-parietal infarction. They demonstrated that the psychosis develops rather spontaneously, may have a variety of schizophreniform features, and is associated with the presence of focal electroencephalogram abnormalities in the nondominant temporal-parietal region. The psychosis was not considered to be related to postictal phenomena but was associated with cognitive deficits in affect and awareness. The CAT scans in figure 3.26 are of a 65-year-old man who seven years earlier had a posterior right hemisphere stroke but developed this delayed psychosis syndrome.

One final cautionary note should be mentioned when

evaluating patients with hypertensive cerebrovascular disease. Solomon et al. (1983) have demonstrated that the antihypertensive medications, methyldopa or propanolol, produced a decrement in verbal memory. Visual memory was not affected. Thus, iatrogenic effects of antihypertensive medications on memory must be considered. Also, it should be noted that MRI scanning may be superior to CAT scanning in identifying the extent of hemorrhaging (see figs. 3.27 and 3.28).

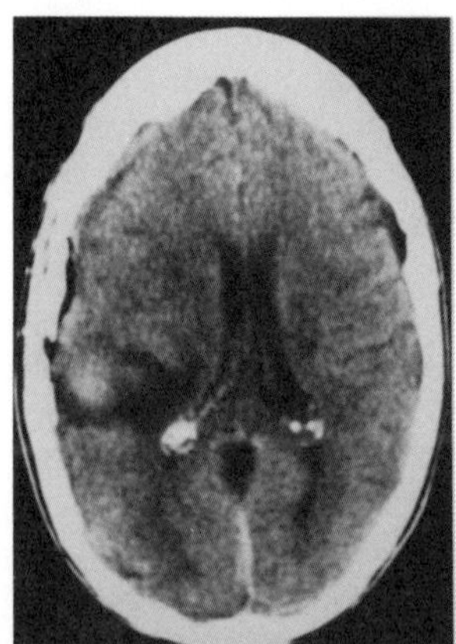

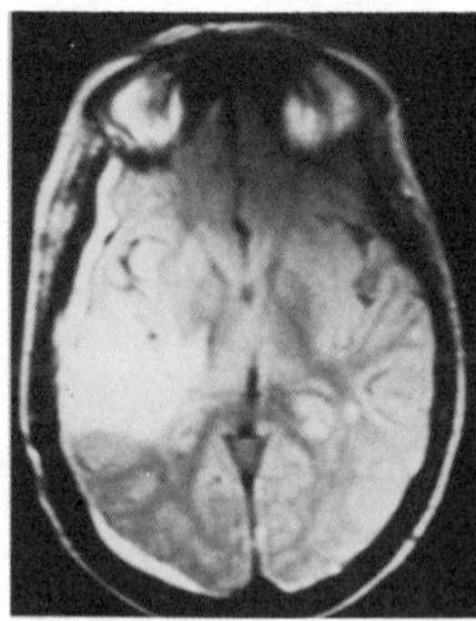

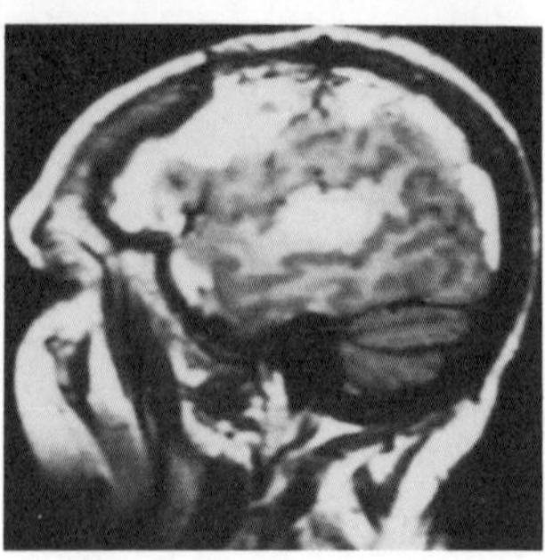

Fig. 3.27. This patient sustained intracerebral hemorrhage that is depicted at upper left in the CAT scan, but the involvement of subarachnoid hemorrhage cannot be clearly defined by CAT. However, in the other two images, the top being in the horizontal plane and the bottom being in the left sagittal plane, the extent of the hemorrhage can be clearly identified as well as its impact on adjacent cortical structures.

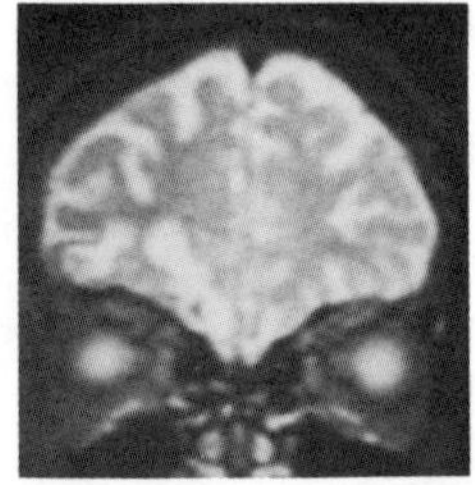

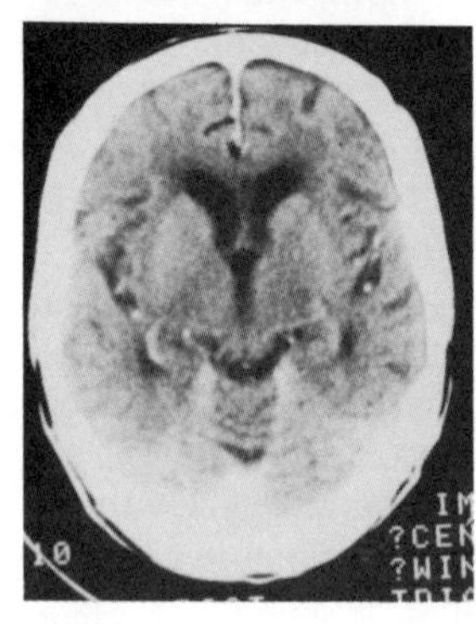

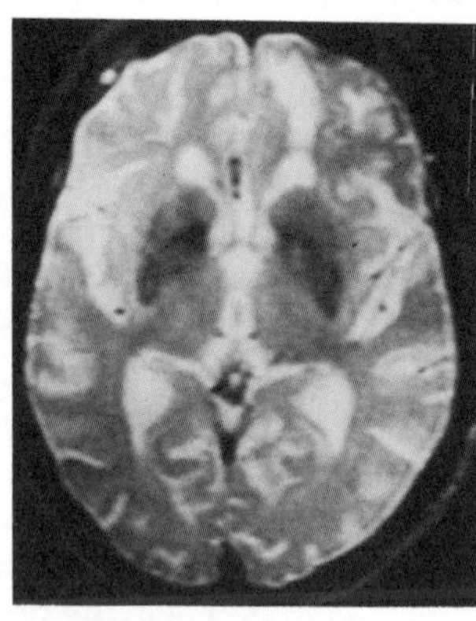

Fig. 3.28. The CAT scan on the lower left shows just a slight indication of a density change in the mesial right frontal region. However, the MRI presented in the coronal plane, just above the CAT scan, and the horizontal plane MRI on the right clearly depict the extent of the infarction. The MRI that is above the CAT scan, presented in the coronal plane, should be viewed as if the reader were looking face-to-face with the patient.

CASE STUDIES

Case 1. This 19-year-old patient sustained infarction of the right middle cerebral artery secondary to inflammation associated with arteritis. Note that verbal abilities are well intact, but integrative motor (see TPT results), left-side motor, sensory function, and visuospatial abilities (see performance IQ results) are all impaired. Aphasia screening examination revealed no dysphasic findings (the patient's drawing and spelling of cross are presented displaying intact drawing, naming, and spelling). The observation that he does not have severe constructional dyspraxia indicates that the extent of right hemisphere involvement does not extend into parietal regions associated with such functioning. The patient does have an impaired Seashore Rhythm Test score, but in the absence of dysphasic deficit, this finding indicates impaired musical pattern discrimination and not impaired auditory processing. CAT scan results reveal focal area of destruction in posterior frontal and anterior parietal areas and some extension along the lateral margin of the parietal lobe (fig. 3.29).

Age 19
Sex M
Education 12

Lateral Dominance Exam

	Eye	Hand	Foot
Right	x	x	x
Left			
Mixed			

Motor Examination
FOD 52 SOGD 68
FOND 11 SOGND 17
Patient unable to perform TPT with right hand even though given 3 trials
Left hemiparesis present

Sensory Examination
Left side extinction (complete) along with left side astereognosis, finger agnosia, and agraphesthesia.

Aphasia Examination
Essentially WNL. Some minor deficits in copying (examples on the left).
SRT 19 scaled score 10
SSPT 17 errors

Memory Examination
WMS MQ=99
LM 11
Digits 14
VM 9
AL 14
TPT-M 5
TPT-L 2

Intellectual/Cognitive Examination
WAIS Results: VIQ=129, PIQ=89, FSIQ=113

I	14	D.S.	9
C	17	P.C.	9
A	14	B.D.	9
S	13	P.A.	7
D	14	O.A.	7
V	15		

Category Test
89 errors

Trail Making Test
A 34
B 87

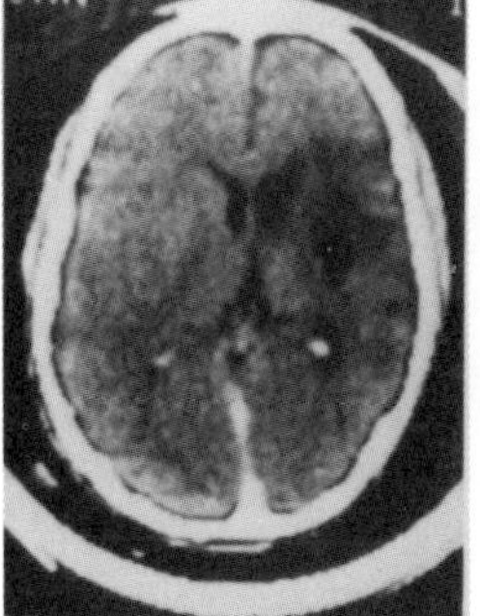

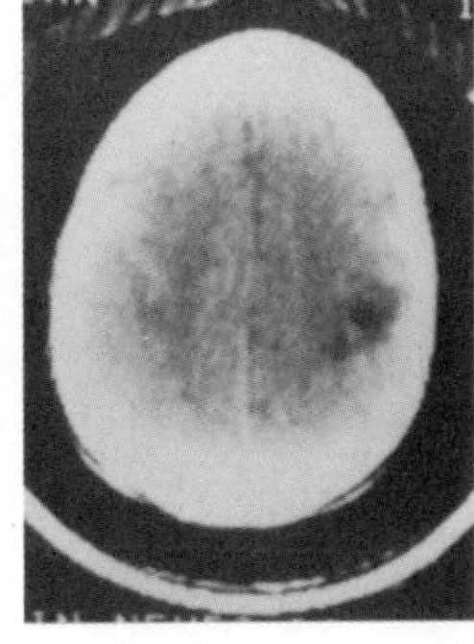

Fig. 3.29. Case 1.

Case 2. This 70-year-old retired schoolteacher was hospitalized with progressive but episodic memory loss and confusion. Neuropsychological studies revealed distinctly diminished memory quotient in relation to IQ along with generalized decline in cognitive functioning (subtest scatter on WAIS, impaired Category Test performance, impaired Trail-Making performance). Note also the presence of tremor on the aphasia screening test as well as the patient's initial difficulty in writing "He shouted the warning." CAT scan results (see fig. 3.30) reveal numerous areas of diminished density likely representing areas of encephalomalacia, presumably related to multiple sites of infarction. Note also the prominence of the sylvian fissures, suggesting frontotemporal atrophy.

Age 70
Sex M
Education 16

Lateral Dominance Exam

	Eye	Hand	Foot
Right	x	x	x
Left			
Mixed			

Motor Examination

FOD	32	SOGD	27	TPTD	9.7
FOND	30	SOGND	28	TPTND	11.3
				TPT Both	8.9

Tremor present. Alternating movements slow.

Sensory Examination
Left ear auditory extinction. Inconsistent errors bilaterally on finger gnosia and graphesthesia exam.

Aphasia Examination
Exam is generally WNL, but note the patient incorrectly started with "He hollered" for "He shouted the warning". Also note the tremor present when copying geometric form and cross.

Memory Examination
WMS
MQ=99 LM 6, Digits 9, VM 8, AL 13

Intellectual/Cognitive Examination
WAIS Results: VIQ=128, PIQ=101, FSIQ=117

I	13	D.S.	5
C	13	P.C.	9
A	14	B.D.	5
S	12	P.A.	6
D.S.	7	O.A.	5
V	17		

Category Test
72 errors

Trail Making
A 75
B 123

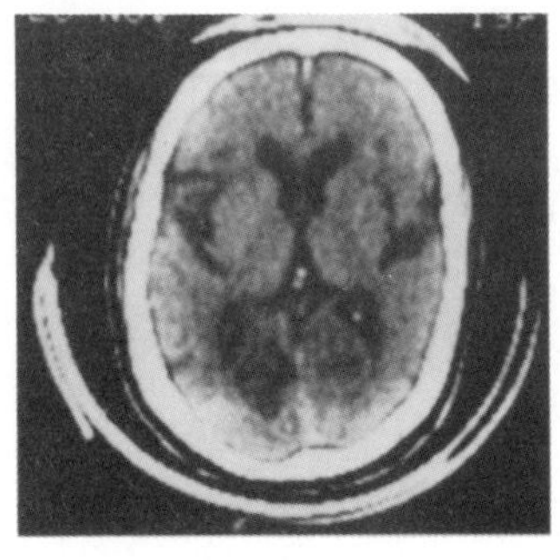
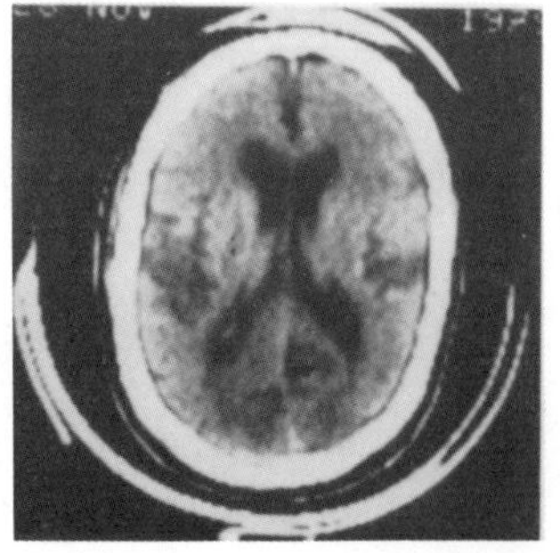
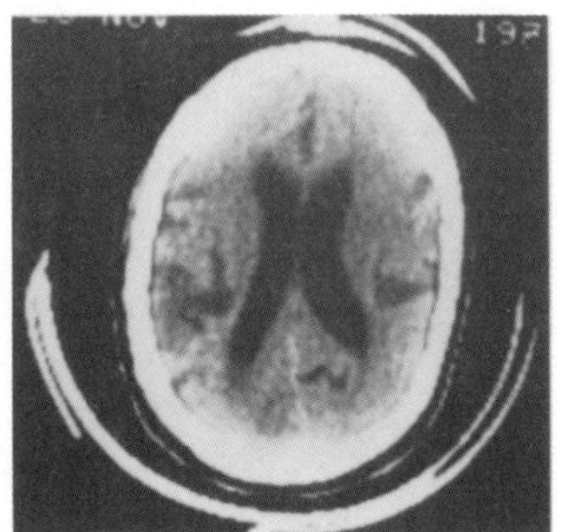

Fig. 3.30. Case 2.

Case 3. This 51-year-old schoolteacher had a long-standing history of hypertension and diabetes mellitus. He suffered a spontaneous vascular accident involving the base of the middle cerebral artery resulting in massive infarction of the mid-left hemisphere, as can be readily visualized by diagrams of the CAT results (see fig. 3.31). Neuropsychological examination revealed rather global aphasia. This is an excellent case demonstrating the devastating effects of massive dominant hemisphere dysfunction on all other cerebral functions. This is the phenomenon of diaschisis (disruption of one neural system interrupting normal functioning in other systems, even though they may not be directly affected). Thus, even though the damage in this patient's case is restricted to the left hemisphere, his functional deficit is widespread. This is always more the case with lesions of the left or dominant hemisphere (contrast the neuropsychological profile in this case with the ones in cases 1 and 8 involving the right hemisphere).

Age 51
Sex M
Education 18

Lateral Dominance Exam

	Eye	Hand	Foot
Right		x	
Left			x
Mixed	x		

Motor Examination
Mild right hemiparesis
FOD 36, FOND 42, SOGD 12, SOGND 32

Sensory Examination
Right tactile and auditory extinction. Right side astereognosis and agraphesthesia.

Aphasia Examination
Conversational speech: Dysarthric, paraphasic
Comprehension: Impaired
Repetition of spoken language: Paraphasic, neologistic
Confrontation - Naming: Markedly impaired
Square - shop, o'poppa
Triangle - tigger
Baby - strawberry, legary, you know

Reading
Aloud: Markedly impaired, dyslexic
Comprehension: Markedly impaired

Writing: Hemiparetic but left handwriting (as seen at left) is impaired.

Calculations: Markedly impaired

SRT 18 errors
SSPT DC

Memory Examination
Exam is contaminated by aphasia, but visual memory was impaired on WMS (score=8).

Intellectual/Cognitive Examination
WAIS Results: VIQ deferred because of aphasia, PIQ=74

D.S.	2
P.C.	NA
B.D.	6
P.A.	4
O.A.	5

Category Test DC at 50 errors
Trail Making Test
A 138
B 180+ DC

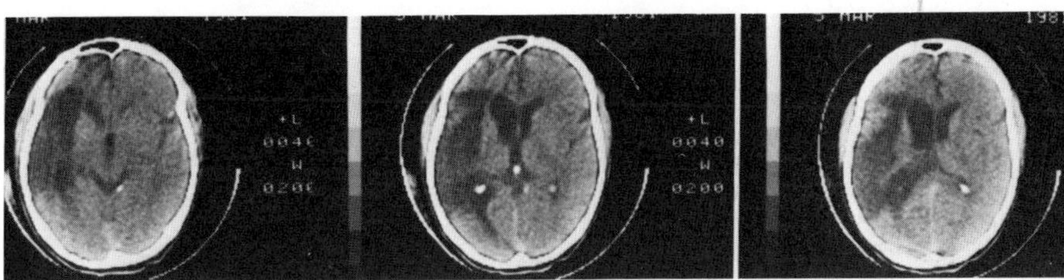

Fig. 3.31. Case 3.

Case 4. Seven patients (see Table 3.4) are presented in which the anterior communicating artery ruptured as a result of an aneurysm (adapted from Steinman and Bigler, 1986). This produces bifrontal mesial infarction as depicted in figures 3.32 and 3.33. The neurobehavioral consequences of such damage typically include pronounced short-term memory deficit, relatively preserved intellectual functioning, but behavioral features of a frontal lobe syndrome (FLS). Table 3.5 depicts the behavioral changes seen in these patients as rated by a family member (typically a spouse). Notice that the majority of patients demonstrated particular changes in capacity for self-control, learned social behavior, and ability to learn. Alexander and Freedman (1984), Damasio et al. (1985), Okawa et al. (1980), and Weisberg (1985) have all demonstrated similar findings in patients with anterior communicating artery rupture. Damage to the basal forebrain structures, which disrupts the hippocampal output to cortex, appears to be the necessary condition for producing the amnestic features of this syndrome.

Table 3.4. *Neuropsychological Findings in Seven Patients Who Suffered Spontaneous Rupture of an Anterior Communicating Artery Aneurysm*

Patient	1	2	3	4	5	6	7
Age	45	32	39	45	41	45	62
Education	15	18	12	16	16	11	16
Vocation	Contractor	Social Worker	Programmer	Teacher	Engineer	Welder	Engineer
Sex	Male	Female	Male	Female	Male	Male	Male
Time since CVA	11 months	13 months	14 months	24 months	9 years	7 years	11 months
Neuropsychological Measures							
WAIS results							
VIQ	88	115	86	112	123	90	[e]
PIQ	72	—[a]	98	101	131	89	70
FSIQ	80	—	90	108	128	89	—
WMS results							
MQ	64	79[b]	112	72	93	78	—
Logical Memory	0	6	11.5	7.5	8.5	5	—
Digits	9	12	10	12	13	10	—
Visual Memory	1	NA[g]	11	8	7	3	0
Associate Learning	7	11	16.5	8.5	8	13.5	—
Halstead-Reitan results							
Category Test (errors)	79	112	70	117	18	88	DC[f]
Tactual Performance Test	DC[f]	NA[g]	—	—	—	DC[f]	NA[g]
Total time	—	—	9.5	15.4	19.4	—	—
Memory	—	—	8	5	6	—	—
Localization	—	—	2	2	6	—	—
Seashore Rhythm Test (errors)	NA[g]	12	3	14	4	0	NA[g]
Speech Sounds Perception Test (errors)	NA[g]	1	11	7	3	8	NA[g]
Finger Oscillation Test							
Right	52[c]	—	54[c]	38	57[c]	36[c]	0[c]
Left	29	—	46	39[c]	51	40	13
Strength-of-Grip Test							
Right	15	—	41	19	39	37	0
Left	12	—	34	20[c]	37	48	21
Aphasia Screening[d]							
Verbal	2	0	1	2	0	2	5
Spatial	2	NA[a]	1	2	0	1	5
Sensory Perceptual Exam Total errors							
Right	1	3	2	15	1	2	NA
Left	3	18	2	12	4	3	NA

Source: Adapted from Steinman and Bigler (1986).
[a]Patient is quadraplegic, no motor testing could be done.
[b]Estimate based on Charter's (1981) formula.
[c]Signifies dominant hand.
[d]Scored according to the Russell, Neuringer, and Goldstein (1971) method.
[e]Patient is aphasic, unable to do verbal tests.
[f]DC—Discontinued due to clearly impaired performance.
[g]NA—Not administered.

Table 3.5. ***Behavioral/Personality Change Following Anterior Communicating Artery Rupture***

Behavioral Category	Patient 1	2	3	4	5	6	7	% Change
Capacity for social perceptiveness								
Self-centered behavior	*	*			*			
Diminution or loss of self-criticism	*	*	*	*	*	*	*	66
Loss of ability to show empathy	*	*			*		*	
Capacity for self control								
Random restlessness	*			*	*		*	
Impatience and impulsivity	*	*	*	*	*	*	*	78
Learned social behavior								
Diminution or loss of initiative	*	*	*	*	*	*	*	
Impaired judgment	*	*	*	*	*	*	*	100
Increased social dependency	*	*	*	*	*	*	*	
Ability to learn								
Mental slowness	*	*		*		*	*	
Rigidity of thought	*	*	*		*	*	*	90
Reduced learning capacity	*	*	*	*	*	*	*	
Emotion								
Irritability		*						
Silliness	*				*			
Lability of mood		*	*	*	*	*	*	54
Apathy	*	*	*	*	*	*	*	
Increased sexual drive	*	*	*		*			
Diminished sexual drive				*		*	*	

*Indicates that the family member rated this as a problem area and a definite change from premorbid level of functioning.
Note: Based on the categories of change outlined by Lezak (1978) and Bond (1983).

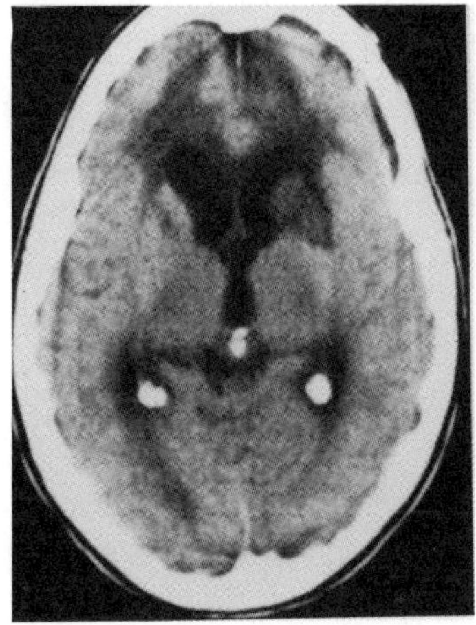

Fig. 3.32. Case 4.

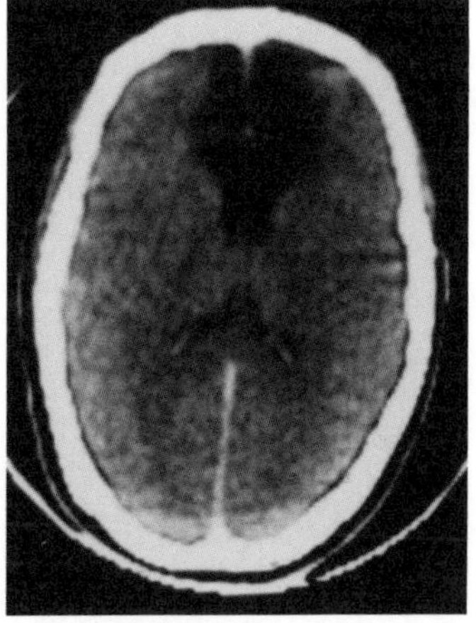

Fig. 3.33. Case 4.

Case 5. This 63-year-old nurse suffered infarction in the posterior left hemisphere, producing the classic syndrome of alexia without agraphia. Note that she cannot read whatsoever, but she can correctly spontaneously write. She can copy figures but cannot copy letters or words without making substantial errors (note her correct spontaneous writing of *square* to verbal command, but her inability to copy *square* visually presented). She could spontaneously write "He shouted the warning," but could not read what she had just written. CAT scan results (see fig. 3.34) reveal the extent of infarction following the superior distribution of the posterior cerebral artery. In terms of correlating the delimited effects of damage with the distribution of the various cerebral arteries, this case clearly displays the extent of the posterior cerebral artery, and cases 3 and 8 display the distribution of the middle and anterior cerebral arteries, respectively.

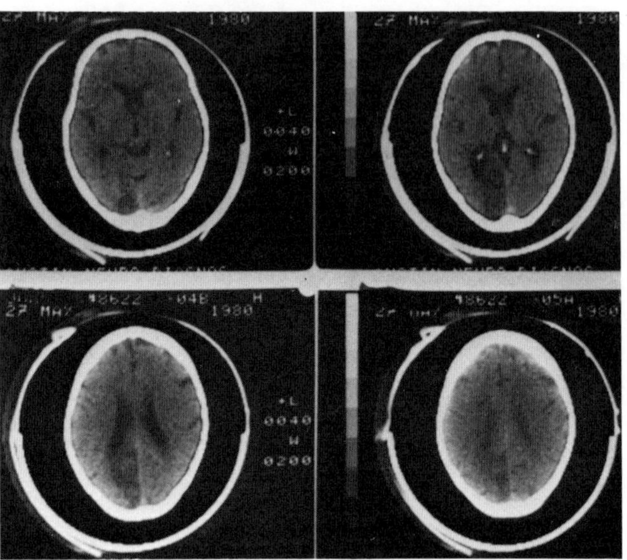

Fig. 3.34. Case 5.

Square
(SPONTANEOUS WRITING)

SQUTHT
(attempt at copying SQUARE)

He shouted the warning

Age 63	Lateral Dominance Exam	Eye	Hand	Foot
Sex F	Right		x	x
Education 18	Left	x		
	Mixed			

Motor Examination
FOD 46, FOND 42, SOGD 24, SOGND 24
Unable to perform TPT with either hand.
Motor exam otherwise WNL.

Sensory Examination
Dense right hemianopsia present, bilateral finger dysgnosia, bilateral finger dysgraphesthesia, bilateral astereognosis

Aphasia Examination
Conversational speech: Fluent, essentially intact
Comprehension: Generally intact
Repetition of spoken language: Intact
Confrontation - Naming: Mildly impaired with some word substitutions
Reading:
Aloud: Alexic
Comprehension: Impaired secondary to alexia
Writing: Can sponataneously write and spell correctly as her cursive writing of square to the left depicts. However, letter/word copying is distinctly impaired. She could spontaneously write "He shouted the warning", also shown at the left, but was unable to then read what she had just written.
Calculations: Impaired.
SRT: 15 errors
SSPT: DC after 10 consecutive errors on Trial A

Memory Examination
WMS MQ=76
LM 4
Digits 7
VM 3
AL 8
TPT-M 0
TPT-L 0

Intellectual/Cognitive Examination
WAIS Results: VIQ=100, PIQ=71, FSIQ=87
I 11, C 10, A 7, S 10, D 7, V 11
D.S. NA, P.C. 2, B.D. 4, P.A. 2, O.A. 4
Category and Trail Making Test were discontinued because of excessive errors.

Case 6. Two years before neuropsychological examination, this 69-year-old businessman suffered a left hemisphere infarction associated with transient right-side hemiplegia and expressive dysphasia. He recovered well enough to return to his business, but over the six months before examination he had been displaying increased erratic behavior and confusion. CAT scan results (fig. 3.35) reflect ventricular dilation, presence of previous area of infarction in the left internal capsular area as well as other sites of likely infarction. Radiographically, then, this patient displays the features of multiple infarction syndrome. Neuropsychological examination is likewise consistent, revealing a generalized picture of dysfunction superimposed upon more focal areas of dysfunction.

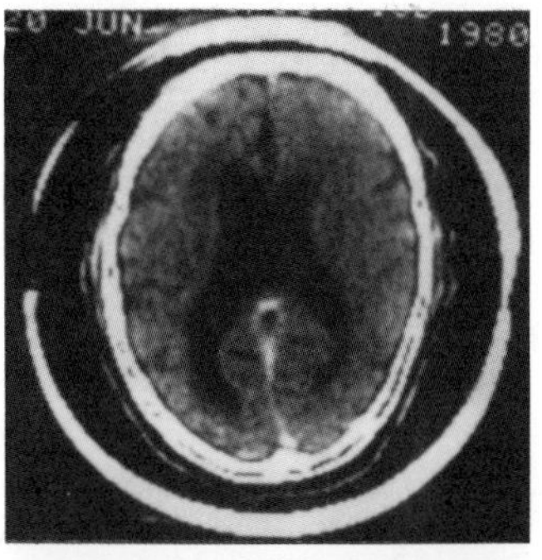

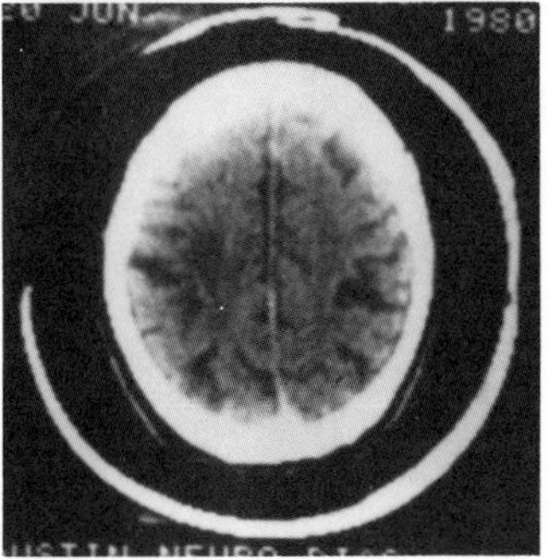

Fig. 3.35. Case 6.

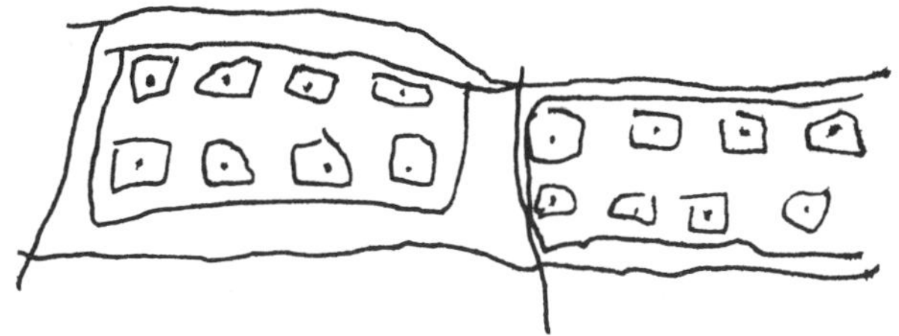

Sensory Examination
Right side tactile extinction bilateral finger dysgnosia and dysgraphesthesia.

Aphasia Examination
Conversation speech: Fluent, essentially intact
Comprehension: Essentially intact, some minor misinterpretations.
Repetition of spoken language: Intact.
Confrontation-Naming: Essentially intact
Reading:
Aloud: Generally intact
Comprehension: Generally intact
Writing: Dysgraphic along with spelling dyspraxia
Copying (see examples on left) reveals constructional dyspraxia.
Calculations: Impaired, dyscalkulia present

Memory Examination
WMS = 76
LM 9 TPT-M 2
Digits 7 TPT-L 0
VM 2
AL 4

Age 69
Sex M
Education 12

Lateral Dominance Exam

	Eye	Hand	Foot
Right	X	X	X
Left			
Mixed			

Intellectual/Cognitive Examiantion
WAIS Results VIQ=85, PIQ=93, FSIQ=88

I 7	D 4	D.S 3	O.A. 7	Category Test
C 7	V 8	D.C. 9		97 errors
A 6		B.D. 2		Trail Making Test
S 8		P.A. 8		A 83
				B 235

Motor Examination

FOD 25	SOGD 23	TPTD 10'DC
FOND 26	SOGND 33	TPTND 10'DC
		TPT Both 9.2

Alternating movements slow, otherwise no additional motor findings.

Case 7. This 70-year-old nurse suffered spontaneous rupture of an aneurysm producing massive hemorrhaging and infarction in the right hemisphere. She displays the classic constructional apraxia associated with right hemisphere etiology. Note that she does not have any verbal language deficits. CAT scan results depict the extent of right hemisphere involvement (see fig. 3.13).

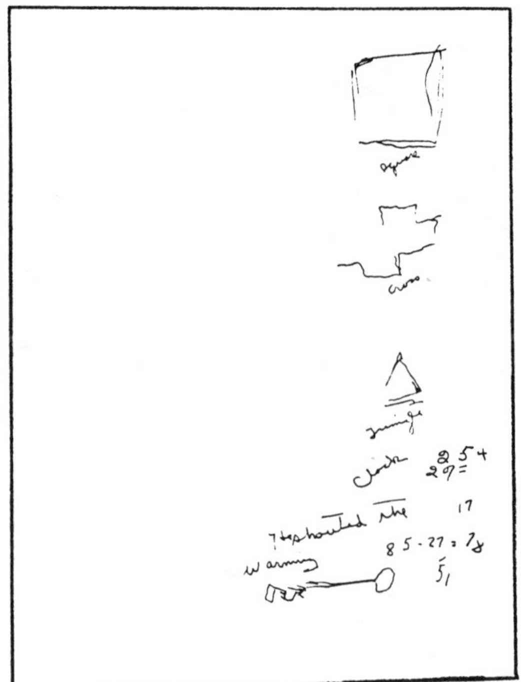

Age 70
Sex F
Education 16

Lateral Dominance

	Eye	Hand	Foot
Right	X	X	X
Left			
Mixed			

Motor Examination
Left side hemiparesis

Sensory Examination
Left side dysstereognosis, dysgraphesthesia and finger dysgnosia, left side neglect.
(Note her neglect of the left side of the page on aphasia drawings)

Language Examination
Verbal language functions intact.
Constructional dyspraxia (note the patient's lack of left side closure on her figure drawings)

Memory Examination
WMS MQ = 103
LM 12, Digits 9, VM 1, AL 13.5

Intellectual/Cognitive Functioning
WAIS Results
VIQ = 113, PIQ = 78, FSIQ = 98
I 13, C 10, A 8, S 10, D 7, V 13
DS 0, PC 4, BD 2, PA 4, OA 0

Case 8. This 33-year-old woman suffered infarction along the distribution of the right anterior cerebral artery. Note the focal nature of the infarction as visualized from CAT scan results (fig. 3.36). Neuropsychological examination reveals right-side motor deficits, greater in the lower extremity than upper, but with absence of marked sensory deficit. This association always implicates frontal involvement. No verbal or aphasic deficits are present. No constructional praxic impairments are present, thereby specifying the more anterior locus of pathology. Note also the distinctly elevated Category test score (in viewing the CAT scan, note that it is in the radiographic right-left position). This patient also displayed a marked aprosodia with inability to simulate expressive tone or emotional gesture. When asked how she felt about her loss of function she began to cry but showed no concomitant facial expression and no change or alteration in her monotonous tone of voice.

Square cross Triangle Clock SQUARE

He shouted the warning!

85 − 27 = 58   17 × 5

Age 33
Sex F
Education 12

Lateral Dominance Exam

	Eye	Hand	Foot
Right	X	X	X
Left			
Mixed			

Motor Examination

FOD 37	SOGD 27	TPTD 6.9
FOND 17	SOGND 16	TPTND 12.0 DC 3 in.
		TPT Both 4.3

Left side hemiparesis, greater in lower extremity

Sensory Examination
WNL

Language Examination
WMS MQ = 86
LM 9, Digits 9, VM 8, AL 8
TPTM 8 TPTL 2

Intellectual/Cognitive Examination
FSIQ = 83

VIQ = 82	PIQ = 88
I 6	DS 8
C 8	PC 7
A 7	BD 9
S 7	PA 7
D 7	OA 10
V 8	

Category Test 116 errors
Trail Making Test A 46, B 102

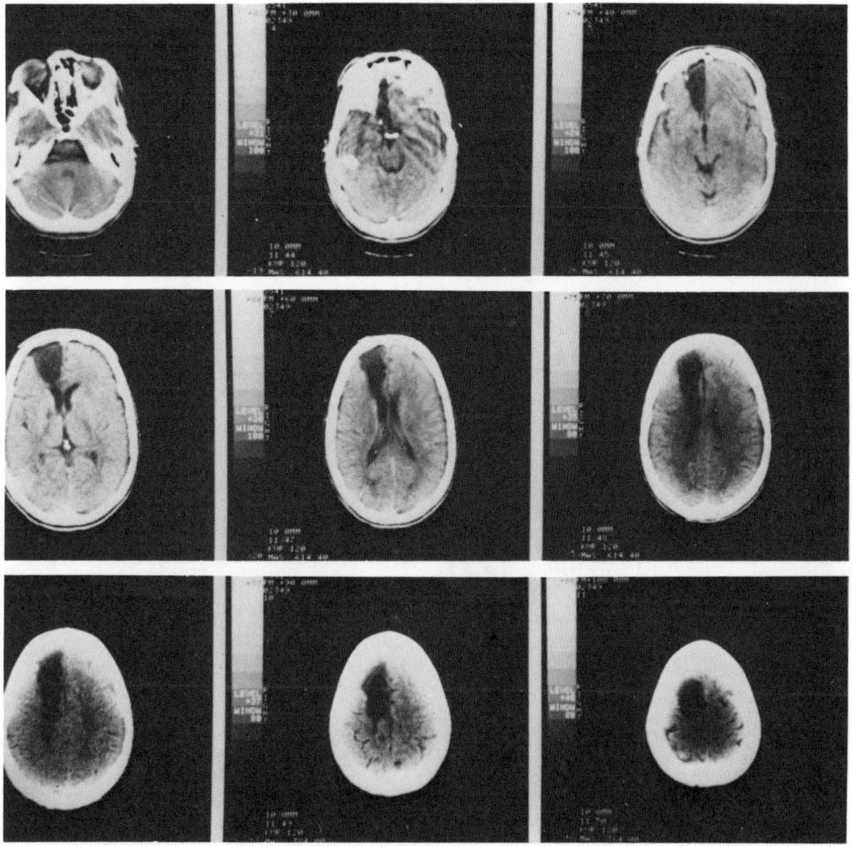

Fig. 3.36. Case 8.

Cases 9 and 10. Both of these cases display large AVMs of the left hemisphere. In case 9 the patient's aphasic deficits are more of a receptive nature, whereas in case 10 the deficits are more in line with a global aphasia (see figs. 3.37 and 3.38).

Age 65
Sex M
Education 12

Lateral Dominance Exam

	Eye	Hand	Foot
Right	X	X	X
Left			
Mixed			

Motor Examination

FOD 36	SOGD 39	TPTD 10.7
FOND 33	SOGND 37	TPTND 9.9
		TPT Both 11.3

Sensory Examination
- Right side tactile extinction
- Bilateral finger agnosia
- Bilateral dysgraphesthesia and dysstereognosis, greater on right side
- Right hemianopsia

Language Examination
- Conversational speech: Mild paraphasia
- Comprehension: Moderately impaired
- Repetition of spoken language: Mild impairment
- Reading:
  - Aloud: Dyslexic
  - Comprehension: Impaired
- Writing: Dysgraphic
- Calculations: Acalculic

Memory Examination:
- WMS MQ = 94
  - LM 5.5, Digits 8, VM 13, AL 7
  - TPT-M 3 TPT-L 0

Intellectual/Cognitive Examination
- FSIQ = 89, VIQ = 93, PIQ = 86
- I 10, C 9, A 6, S 8, D 6, V 8
- DS 1, PC 7, BD 7, PA 5, OA 4
- Category Test: 79 errors
- Trail Making: A 234 B 300 TDC

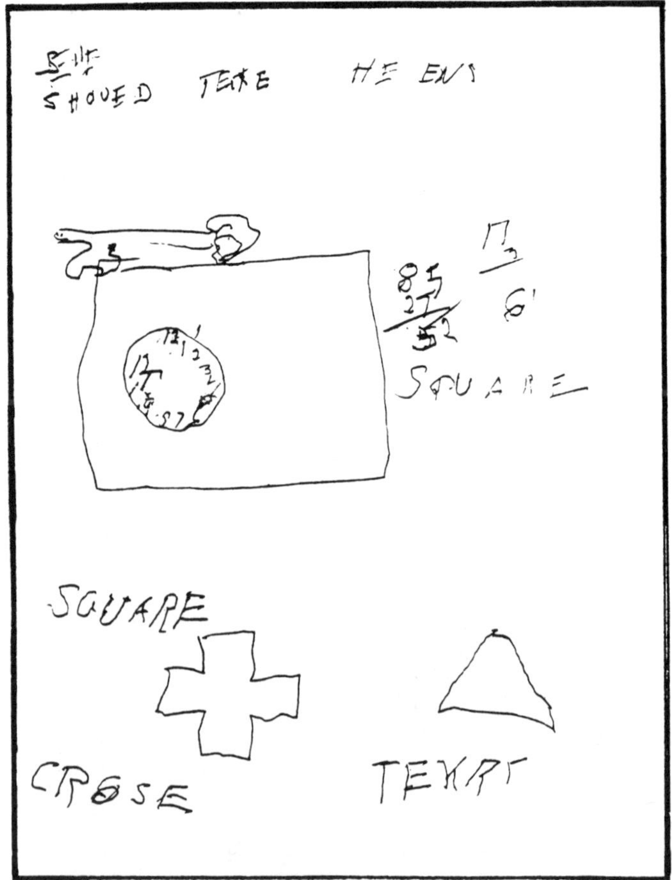

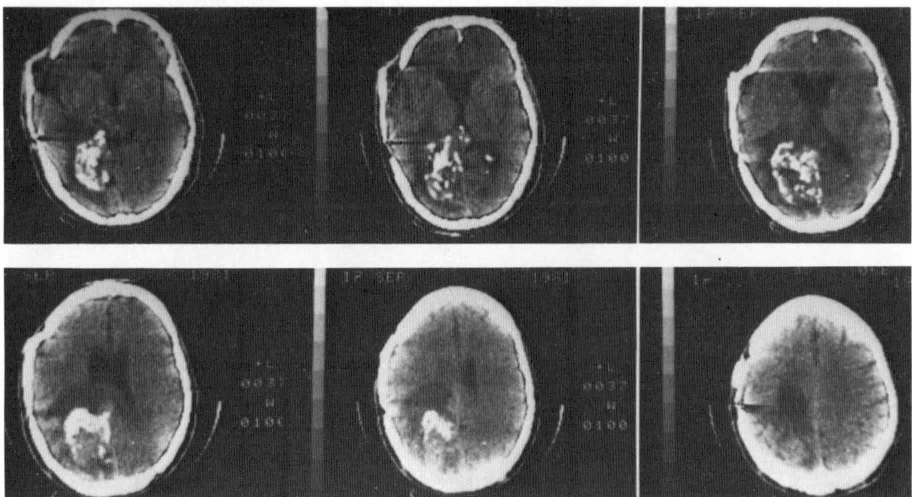

Fig. 3.37. Case 9.

Age 29
Sex F
Education 16

Lateral Dominance Exam

	Eye	Hand	Foot
Right			
Left	X	X	X
Both			

Motor Examination

Dense right hemiplegia

FOD 0 SOGD 0
FOND 29 SOGND 20

Sensory Examination

Right side tactile and visual extinction to USS; right side finger dysgnosia, dysgraphesthesia and asterognosis

Language Examination

Conversational speech: Mild dysarthria, paraphasic, halting
Comprehension: Moderately impaired
Repetition of spoken language: Impaired
Confrontation-Naming: Dysnomic, i.e., name baby "yes but...daddy, pencil"
name key "so...they...key...no"

Reading
Aloud: Dyslexic - can recognize numbers and raise appropriate fingers to indicate number
Comprehension: Impaired

Writing: Right side paralyzed, drawings above are with left hand
Patient cannot spontaneously spell but can copy the written word

Calculations: Impaired

WRAT Reading K,3
Spelling 1,5
Arithmetic 1,4

SRT 11 errors
SSPT 16 errors

Memory Examination

Marked aphasic disturbance interferes with memory examination.

Intellectual/Cognitive Examination

Verbal intellectual scores unobtainable because of aphasia
PIQ = 65

DS 2
PC 2
BD 2
PA 4
OA 7

Category Test
58 errors

Trail Making
A 184 sec.
B 300+ sec. DC

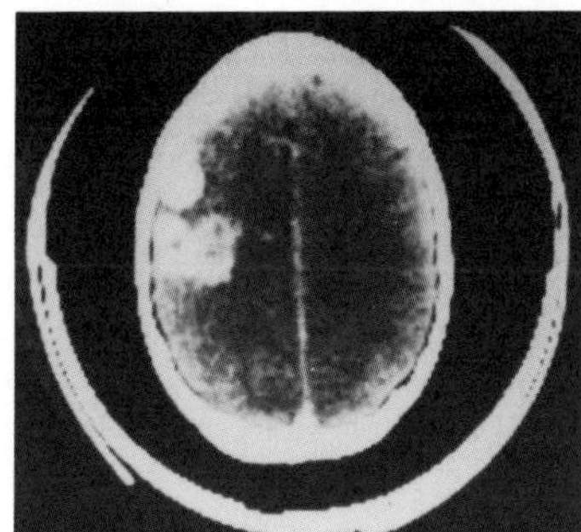

Fig. 3.38. Case 10.

Case 11. This case excellently demonstrates the marked improvement in cerebral status that may accompany endarterectomy for carotid artery stenosis. This patient presented with dysphasia, dystaxia, confusion, and marked memory disturbance. Stenosis of the left carotid artery was determined to be the primary cause. Note the marked deficits in neuropsychological performance from the exam taken prior to the operation. Subsequent to the endarterectomy, there is dramatic improvement in all functions; in particular compare the intellectual, language, and memory studies.

Age 79

Sex M

Education 20

Lateral Dominance Exam

	Eye	Hand	Foot
Right		X	X
Left			
Mixed	X		

PRE ENDARTERECTOMY

Motor Examination:
FOD 25 SOGD 31 Ataxic Gait
FOND 23 SOGND 35 Generalized tremor

Sensory Perceptual Examination:
Right side tactile extinction, bilateral dysgnosia, dysgraphesthesia, dysstereognosis

Aphasia Examination:
Conversational Speech: Paraphasic
Comprehension: Impaired
Repetition of Spoken Language: Impaired
Confrontation-Naming: Dysnomic
Reading:
Aloud: Dyslexic
Comprehension: Impaired
Writing: Dysgraphic, spelling dyspraxia
Constructional dyspraxia.
Calculations: Impaired

Memory Examination:
WMS MQ = 59, LM 2, Digits 5, VM 0, AL 2

Intellectual/Cognitive Examination:
VIQ = 70, PIQ = 81, FSIQ = 73
I 5, C 3, A 3, S 3, O 1, V 3
DS 0, PC 2, BD 0, PA 6, OA 2
Trail Making Test: A 121, B 150+DC

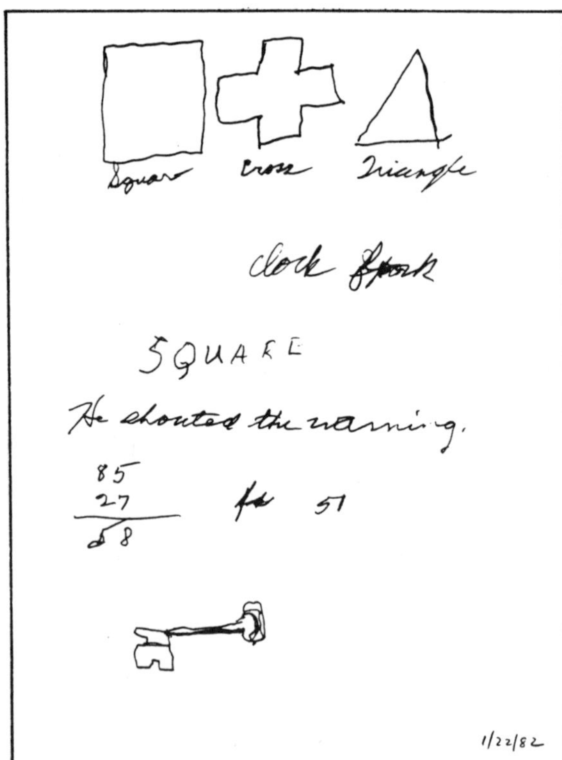

POST ENDARTERECTOMY (5 months)

Motor Examination:
FOD 41 SOGD 38 Mild generalized tremor
FOND 27 SOGND 37 (see aphasia exam)

Sensory Perceptual Exam:
WNL

Aphasia Examination:
WNL - see above
Some constructional dyspraxia-not abnormal for age.

Memory Examination:
WMS MQ = 94
LM 6, Digits 9, VM 0, AL 12

Intellectual/Cognitive Examination:
VIQ = 111, PIQ = 103, FSIQ = 108
I 12, C 11, A 7, S 6, D 7, V 12
DS 4, PC 8, BD 4, PA 7, OA 4

Trail Making Test: A 43 B 11y

Case 12. This 54-year-old truck driver, who had a history of hypertension, developed an acute amnesia. CAT scan demonstrated an area of focal hemorrhage in the anterior left thalamic region (fig. 3.39). Damage to the left anterior thalamic region tends to affect verbal memory more than visual (Kawahara et al., 1986). Oppositely, right thalamic lesions tend to affect visual-spatial memory (Speedie and Heilman, 1983). These amnestic effects occur because the anterior thalamic projections are interrupted, and this disrupts hippocampal output to the basal forebrain. In this particular patient, it is important to note that his motor examination, sensory perceptual examination, and language examination were essentially within normal limits. He did have some mild naming difficulties, though. Memory studies reflected marked memory disturbance, particularly on the Rey Auditory-Verbal Learning Test and the example given of the Rey-Osterrieth Complex Figure Test. Notice his copying of the Rey-Osterrieth Complex Figure is quite good, but even after a three-minute retention, he can only recall the basic outline and then confabulates a house. One important clinical note should be made. The patient's intellectual test results are somewhat low. This is a reflection of the memory problems as well. For example, on several of the WAIS-R results, the patient would forget the question asked of him during his response and then would confabulate the response, which would negate his effort. As can be noted by the comparison of his WAIS results with his Raven's, the patient performed very well on the Raven's Test. The Raven's Test does not put any demands upon short-term memory; hence, amnestic patients typically do very well on the Raven's. This is a test that can aid the clinician in differentiating between intellectual decline that is associated to generalized dysfunction and intellectual deficit associated with short-term memory impairment, as was the case in this patient.

Age 54
Sex M
Education 12

Lateral Dominance Exam

	Eye	Hand	Foot
Right	x	x	x
Left			
Mixed			

Motor Examination
WNL

Sensory Examination
WNL

Language Examination
Conversational speech: WNL
Comprehension: Intact
Repetition of spoken language: Intact
Confrontation naming: Mild dysnomia
Reading: WNL
Calculations: WNL

Memory Examination:
WMS MQ = 76
LM 3 (0), D 7, VM 11 (5), AL 3 (0)

Rey AVLT
I 1, II 5, III 3, IV 2, V 2, interf. 0

Intellectual/Cognitive Examination
WAIS-R Results: VIQ = 80, PIQ = 84, FSIQ = 82
I 6, D 4, V 5, A 10, C 6, S 5, PC 6, PA 4,
BD 6, OA 9, DS 5

Raven's Results: 32/36

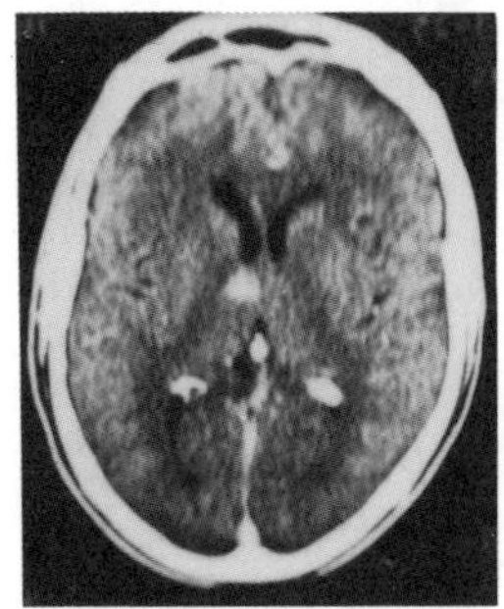

Fig. 3.39. Case 12.

References

Adams, R. D., and M. Victor. 1977. *Principles of neurology.* New York: McGraw-Hill.

Albert, M. L., H. Goodglass, N. A. Helm, A. B. Rubens, and M. P. Alexander. 1981. *Clinical aspects of dysphasia.* Disorders of Human Communication vol. 2. New York: Springer-Verlag.

Alexander, M. P., and M. Freedman. 1984. Amnesia after anterior communicating artery aneurysm rupture. *Neurology* 34: 752–757.

Alexander, M. P., and S. LoVerme. 1980. Aphasia after left hemisphere intracerebral hemorrhage. *Neurology* 30:1193–1202.

Alexander, M. P., D. T. Stuss, and D. F. Benson. 1979. Capgrass syndrome: A reduplicative phenomenon. *Neurology* 29: 334–339.

Allen, C. M. C. 1984. Predicting the outcome of acute stroke: A prognostic score. *Journal of Neurology, Neurosurgery, and Psychiatry* 47:475–480.

Basso, A., E. Capitani, C. Luzzatti, and H. Spinnler. 1981. Intelligence and left hemisphere disease: The role of aphasia, apraxia, and size of lesion. *Brain* 104:721–734.

Benson, D. F. 1979. *Aphasia, alexia, and agraphia.* New York: Churchill Livingstone.

———. 1985. Language in the left hemisphere. In *The dual brain,* ed. D. F. Benson and E. Zaidel. New York: Guilford Press.

Benson, D. F., H. Gardner, and J. C. Meadows. 1976. Reduplicative paramnesia. *Neurology* 26:147.

Black, F. W., and I. Black. 1982. Anterior-posterior locus of lesion and personality: Support for the caudality hypothesis. *Journal of Clinical Psychology* 38:468–477.

Bond, M. R. 1983. Effects of the family system. In *Rehabilitation of the head injured adult,* ed. M. Rosenthal, E. R. Griffith, M. R. Bond, and J. D. Miller. Philadelphia: F. A. Davis.

Brust, J. C. M. 1981. Stroke: Diagnostic, anatomical, and physiological considerations. In *Principles of neural science,* ed. E. R. Kandel and J. H. Schwartz. New York: Elsevier/North Holland.

Brust, J. C. M., C. Plank, A. Burke, M. M. I. Guobadia, and E. B. Healton. 1982. Language disorder in a right-hander after occlusion of the right anterior cerebral artery. *Neurology* 32:492–497.

Charter, R. A. 1981. Prorating the Wechsler Memory Scale. *Journal of Clinical Psychology* 37:183–185.

Cummings, J. L., K. Syndulko, Z. Goldberg, and D. M. Treiman. 1982. Palinopsia reconsidered. *Neurology* 32:444–447.

Damasio, A. R., H. Damasio, M. Rizzo, N. Varney, and F. Gersh. 1982. Aphasia with nonhemorrhagic lesions in the basal ganglia and internal capsule. *Archives of Neurology* 39:15–20.

Damasio, A. R., N. R. Graff-Radford, P. J. Eslinger, H. Damasio, and N. Kassell. 1985. Amnesia following basal forebrain lesions. *Archives of Neurology* 42:263–271.

Delaney, C. R., J. D. Wallace, and S. Egelko. 1980. Transient cerebral ischemic attacks and neuropsychological deficits. *Journal of Clinical Neuropsychology* 2:107–114.

Eidelberg, D., and A. M. Galaburda. 1982. Symmetry and asymmetry in the human posterior thalamus. I, Cytoarchitectonic analysis in normal persons. *Archives of Neurology* 39:325–332.

Fromm, D., A. L. Holland, C. S. Swindell, and O. M. Reinmuth. 1985. Various consequences of subcortical stroke. *Archives of Neurology* 42:943–950.

Galaburda, A. M., and D. Eidelberg. 1982. Symmetry and asymmetry in the human posterior thalamus. II, Thalamic lesions in developmental dyslexia. *Archives of Neurology* 39:333–336.

Haas, D. C., and G. S. Ross. 1986. Transient global amnesia triggered by mild head trauma. *Brain* 109:251–257.

Hart, R. G. 1986. Cardiogenic brain embolism. *Archives of Neurology* 43:71–84.

Healton, B., J. C. Brust, D. A. Feinfeld, and G. E. Thomson. 1982. Hypertensive encephalopathy and the neurologic manifestations of malignant hypertension. *Neurology* 32: 127–132.

Henderson, V. W., M. P. Alexander, and M. A. Naeser. 1982. Right thalamic injury, impaired visuospatial perception, and alexia. *Neurology* 32:235–240.

Ishii, N., Y. Nishihara, and T. Imamura. 1986. Why do frontal lobe symptoms predominate in vascular dementia with lacunes? *Neurology* 36:340–345.

Kawahara, N., K. Sato, M. Muraki, K. Tanaka, M. Kaneko, and K. Uemura. 1986. CT classification of small thalamic hemorrhages and their clinical implications. *Neurology* 36:165–172.

Kertesz, A., and S. Dobrowolski. 1981. Right-hemisphere deficits, lesion size, and location. *Journal of Clinical Neuropsychology* 3:283–299.

Levine, D. N., and S. Finklestein. 1982. Delayed psychosis after right temporal-parietal stroke or trauma: Relation to epilepsy. *Neurology* 32:267–273.

Levine, D. N., and A. Grek. 1984. The anatomic basis of delusions after right cerebral infarction. *Neurology* 34:577–582.

Lezak, M. D. 1978. Living with the characterologically altered brain-injured patient. *Journal of Clinical Psychiatry* 39: 592–600.

Morrison, R. L., and R. E. Tarter. 1984. Neuropsychological findings relating to Capgras syndrome. *Biological Psychiatry* 19:1119–1123.

Naeser, M. A., M. P. Alexander, N. Helm-Estabrooks, H. L. Levine, S. A. Laughlin, and N. Geschwind. 1982. Aphasia with predominantly subcortical lesion sites. *Archives of Neurology* 39:2–14.

Nedergaard, M., J. Astrup, and L. Klinken. 1984. Cell density and cortex thickness in the border zone surrounding old infarcts in the human brain. *Stroke* 15:1033–1039.

Nielsen, H., E. Højer-Pedersen, G. Gulliksen, J. Haase, and E. Enevoldsen. 1985. A neuropsychological study of 12 patients with transient ischemic attacks before and after EC/IC bypass surgery. *Acta Neurologica Scandinavia* 71:317–320.

Okawa, M., S. Maeda, H. Nukui, and J. Kawafuchi. 1980. Psychiatric symptoms in ruptured anterior communicating aneurysms: Social prognosis. *Acta Psychiatrica Scandinavia* 61:306–312.

Patterson, M. B., and J. L. Mack. 1985. Neuropsychological analysis of a case of reduplicative paramnesia. *Journal of Clinical and Experimental Neuropsychology* 7:111–121.

Payne, E. E. 1969. *An atlas of pathology of the brain.* East Hanover, NJ: Sandoz Pharmaceuticals.

Ponsford, J. L., G. A. Donnan, and K. W. Walsh. 1980. Disorders of memory in vertebrobasilar disease. *Journal of Clinical Neuropsychology* 2:267–276.

Price, B. H., and M.-M. Mesulam. 1985. Psychiatric manifestations of right hemisphere infarctions. *Journal of Nervous and Mental Disease* 173:610–618.

Prigatano, G. P. 1986. *Neuropsychological rehabilitation after brain injury.* Baltimore: Johns Hopkins University Press.

Raichle, M. E., D. C. DeVivo, and J. Hanaway. 1978. Disorders of cerebral circulation. In *Neurological pathophysiology,* ed. S. G. Eliasson, A. L. Prensky, and W. B. Hardin. 2d ed. New York: Oxford University Press.

Regard, M., and T. Landis. 1984. Transient global amnesia: Neuropsychological dysfunction during attack and recovery in two "pure" cases. *Journal of Neurology, Neurosurgery, and Psychiatry* 47:668–672.

Robinson, R. G., J. R. Lipsey, and T. R. Price. 1985. Diagnosis and clinical management of post-stroke depression. *Psychosomatics* 26:769–775.

Robinson, R. G., L. B. Starr, K. L. Kubos, and T. R. Price. 1983. A two-year longitudinal study of poststroke mood disorders:

Findings during the initial evaluation. *Stroke* 14:736–741.
Robinson, R. G., L. B. Starr, J. R. Lipsey, K. Rao, and T. R. Price. 1985. A two-year longitudinal study of poststroke mood disorders: In-hospital prognostic factors associated with six-month outcome. *Journal of Nervous and Mental Disease* 173:221–230.
Ross, E. D., and A. J. Rush. 1981. Diagnosis and neuroanatomical correlates of depression in brain-damaged patients. *Archives of General Psychiatry* 38:1344–1354.
Scheinberg, P. 1977. *Modern practical neurology*. New York: Raven Press.
Sinyor, D., P. Jacques, D. G. Kaloupek, R. Becker, M. Goldenberg, and H. Coopersmith. 1986. Poststroke depression and lesion location. *Brain* 109:537–546.
Skenazy, J. A. 1982. Neuropsychological and psychological effects in diabetes mellitus. Doctoral dissertation. University of Texas at Austin.
Solomon, S., E. Hotchkiss, S. M. Saravay, C. Bayer, P. Ramsey, and R. S. Blum. 1983. *Archives of General Psychiatry* 40: 1109:1112.
Speedie, L. J., and K. M. Heilman. 1983. Anterograde memory deficits for visuospatial material after infarction of the right thalamus. *Archives of Neurology* 40:183–186.
Steinman, D. R., and E. D. Bigler. 1986. Neuropsychological sequelae of ruptured anterior communicating artery aneurysm. *International Journal of Clinical Neuropsychology* 8:135–140.
Wade, D. T., V. A. Wood, and R. L. Hewer. 1985. Recovery after stroke: The first 3 months. *Journal of Neurology, Neurosurgery, and Psychiatry* 48:7–13.
Watson, R. T., and K. M. Heilman. 1982. Affect in subcortical aphasia. *Neurology* 32:102–103.
Weinfeld, F. D. 1981. The national survey of stroke. *Stroke* 12:1–91.
Weisberg, L. A. 1985. Ruptured aneurysms of anterior cerebral or anterior communicating arteries: CT patterns. *Neurology* 35:1562–1566.
Whisnant, J. P., R. M. Crowell, R. H. Patterson, S. J. Peerless, J. T. Robertson, A. L. Sahs, and F. M. Yatsu. 1979. Cerebrovascular disease. *Archives of Neurology* 36:734–738.

4. Traumatic Disorders of the Nervous System

Trauma to the head is an all-too-frequent occurrence, with estimates indicating that 200–300 persons per 100,000 population have suffered such an injury (Jennett and Teasdale, 1981; Levin, Benton, and Grossman, 1982). Brain injury secondary to trauma is considered to have occurred when one of the following criteria is met: (1) level of consciousness is altered, if only for a brief period; (2) evidence of neurologic deficit, such as weakness or aphasia, develops, or results of neurodiagnostic tests (i.e., CAT scan) reveal presence of neurologic damage (Becker et al., 1979). The severity that accompanies cerebral injury is highly variable and rather difficult to impose appropriate or strict classificatory guidelines upon. Nonetheless, the following system has been suggested by Jennett and Teasdale (1981), Becker et al. (1979), and Coxe and Grubb (1978). When head trauma occurs there is either closed (skull remains intact) or open (skull is perforated or penetrated) injury. With a closed head injury there is a greater likelihood of more generalized cerebral damage, but there is greater propensity for focal brain damage with open head injury. Regardless of whether open or closed head injury occurs, the following classificatory schema has been suggested:

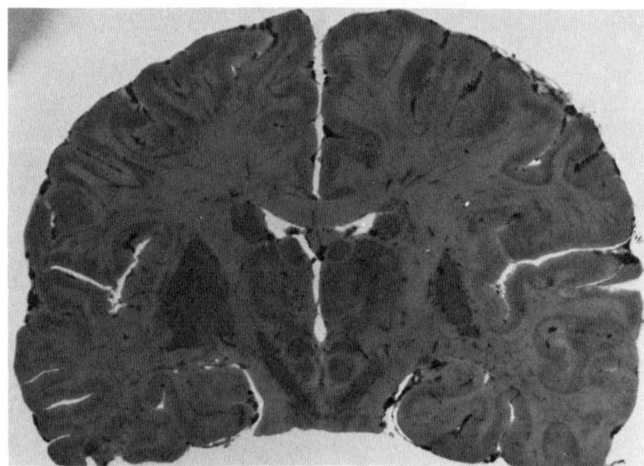

Fig. 4.1. Cerebral concussion. This coronal section depicts marked congestion of the cerebral vessels. These areas of congestion were petechiae scattered throughout the cerebrum. From Payne (1969).

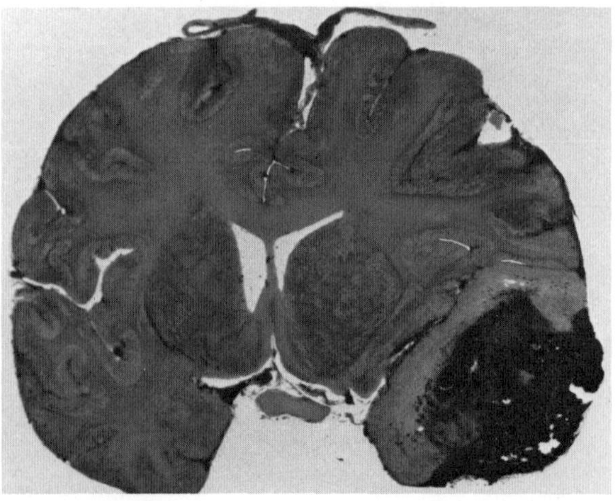

Fig. 4.2. Cerebral contusion. This coronal section shows large area of hemorrhage and encephalomalacia occupying most of the temporal lobe. This contusion lay adjacent to a comminuted fracture of the skull. From Payne (1969).

1. *Mild brain injury.* Transient loss or alteration in consciousness in the absence of definitive lateralizing or focal signs, brief amnestic period of no longer than sixty minutes, and rapid return to previous level of consciousness. This type of injury was thought to typically involve only transient dysfunction; however, data are accumulating that indicate potential permanent damage even with such "mild" head injuries (Ewing et al., 1980). It is relatively common for an onset of symptoms of irritability, fatigability, and lassitude to occur transiently for several weeks following mild injury (Jennett and Teasdale, 1981). This type of mild injury has commonly been referred to as concussion (see fig. 4.1).

2. *Moderate brain injury.* One hour after moderate brain injury impaired consciousness or disorientation persists, but the patient can follow simple commands. Or, the patient may be alert but with focal neurologic deficit. Posttraumatic amnesia of up to twenty-four hours is commonplace. A generally favorable recovery outcome may occur that depends, in part, on the extent of the brain involved and whether critical (i.e., language, motor, etc.) systems were involved. Posttraumatic behavioral syndrome, as described above, is also a common development.

3. *Severe brain injury.* The patient with severe brain injury is immediately incapacitated in terms of following simple commands or may be fully comatose. Motor defi-

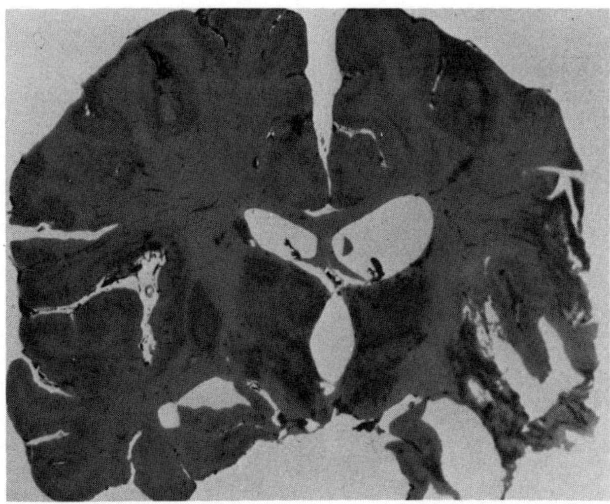

Fig. 4.3. Brain laceration. This coronal section depicts marked laceration injury to the temporal lobe. From Payne (1969).

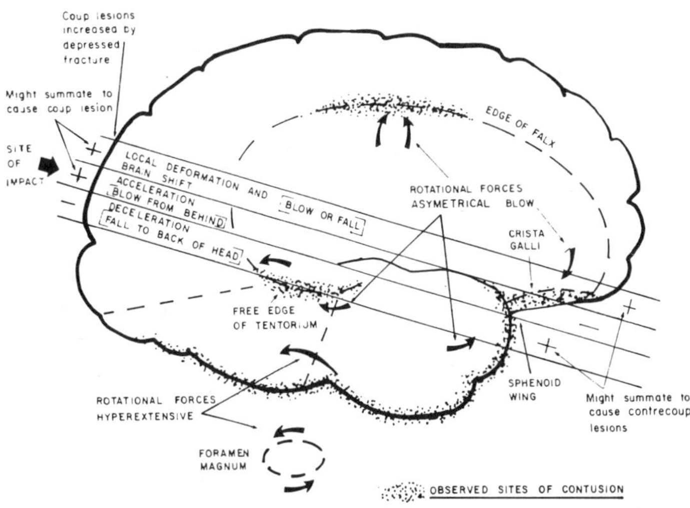

Fig. 4.4. Lateral view of brain (*falx and tentorium indicated by dashed lines*) showing observed common sites of contusion. The three parallel lines indicate possible summation of positive and negative pressures owing to acceleration, deceleration, and whole-brain shift. Arrows indicate theoretical locations of rotational forces in relation to areas of relative fixation. From Lewis (1976).

cits are usually present but varied. Pathologic reflexes are commonplace. Posttraumatic amnesia persists for one to seven days or longer. Brain contusion (bruising) is common along with shearing damage to white matter (see figs. 4.2–4.3). Recovery is typically limited, and some degree of permanent neurologic deficit persists.

4. *Very severe (profound) brain injury.* Immediately or shortly thereafter the patient is rendered unconscious and unresponsive. No communication is present (even inappropriate communication), and the patient follows no commands. Many patients die a few minutes after injury. Those who have persisting coma are thought to have diffuse impact, shearing damage to the white matter, and disconnection between the cerebral structures and brain stem. If the patient does survive, a persistent vegetative state is common. If the patient improves past vegetative state, severe and permanent neurologic deficits are usually present. Posttraumatic amnesia is usually greater than seven days.

Factors Involved in Trauma

Impact of Injury

A skull fracture may occur at the site of impact; however, the locus of fracture may have little or no relationship to the distribution of damage. This is because of the tendency of impact injuries to produce widespread and diffuse effects by shearing, tearing, and contusing (Jennett and Teasdale, 1981; see figs. 4.2–4.4). There is some indication that occipital impact may produce greater damage to the frontal areas (a contrecoup effect), but it is likewise true (see fig. 4.7) that irrespective of the site of impact the areas for maximum contusion are the anterior and ventral surface of the frontal lobes and the anterior poles and ventral surface of the temporal lobes (Adams et al., 1977; see figs. 4.5–4.7). The reason for this localization of damage is related to the position of the frontal and temporal lobes in the cranial vault and the various bony protuberances on the frontal and basal surfaces. It should also be noted that with impact injury that results in brain contusion there are typically multiple sites of contusion that develop that are bilateral but asymmetric (see figs. 4.7–4.9).

Metabolic Alterations

The brain requires and normally maintains a very consistent and stable metabolic state possessing oxygen and glucose requirements that are extremely high (see Siesjo, 1978). Much of this metabolic process is necessary for the maintenance of electrochemical gradients required for synaptic transmission and integrity of intracellular mechanisms. Thus, any significant alteration in basic brain metabolism may have serious and immediate consequences. If energy requirements fail, neuronal dysfunction begins to occur within seconds, and permanent structural damage may develop within minutes (Jennett and Teasdale, 1981). Barclay et al. (1985) have demonstrated reduced cerebral blood flow reflecting decreased cerebral metabolism in patients with chronic head injury syndrome. Such results indicate permanent metabolic alterations in cerebral function in patients with neuropsychological impairment as a result of cerebral trauma.

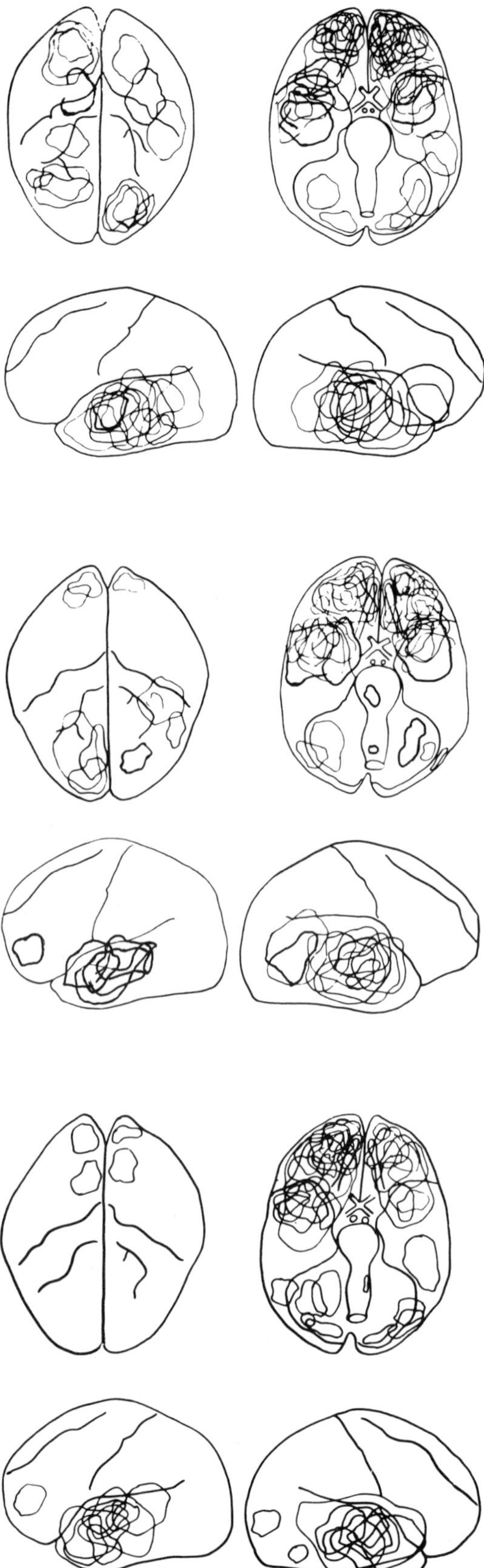

Fig. 4.5. A composite of 191 cerebral contusions in 152 consecutively autopsied patients with craniocerebral trauma. Contusions are most commonly seen in the frontal and temporal lobes. Occipital surface contusions are rare. Posterior fossa contusions are seen in greater numbers than occipital lobe contusions and are due to a downward thrust of the brain mass toward the foramen magnum. From Gurdjian (1975). Courtesy of Charles C Thomas, Publisher, Springfield, Illinois.

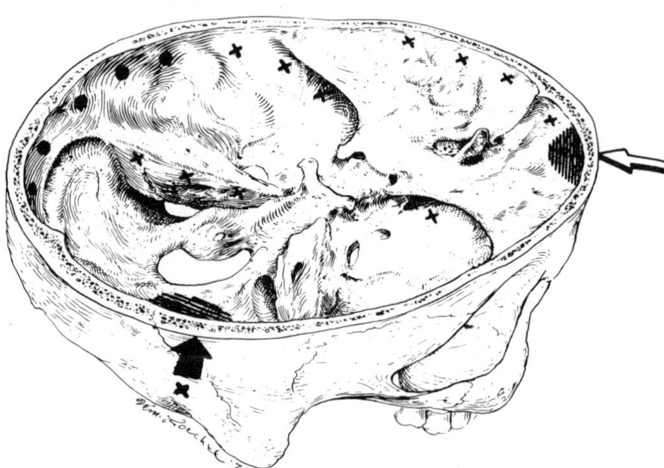

Fig. 4.6. Inertial stress propagation is diagrammed from a midfrontal and right parietomastoid impact. The large dots indicate the inertial propagation at the occipital poles from a midfrontal impact. Movements of the brain in the frontal and temporal base and against the lesser wing of the sphenoid result in contusions of the frontal and temporal lobes with midfrontal and midoccipital impacts. A parietomastoid impact may result in contrecoup contusions of the contralateral frontotemporal brain. From Gurdjian (1975). Courtesy of Charles C Thomas, Publisher, Springfield, Illinois.

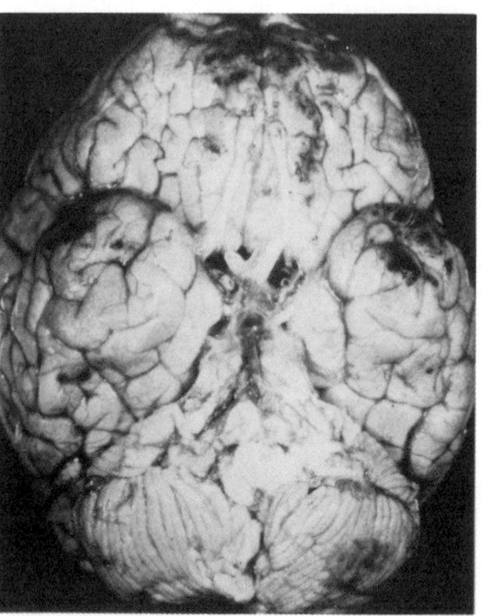

Fig. 4.7. Consequences of cerebral trauma. Contrecoup temporal and frontal contusions (*dark areas*) of a pedestrian struck by a car. The back of the patient's head hit the pavement. No coup lesion is present. From Gurdjian (1975). Courtesy of Charles C Thomas, Publisher, Springfield, Illinois.

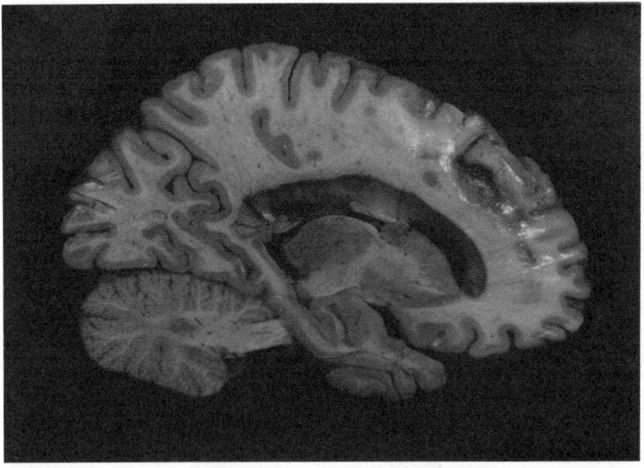

A

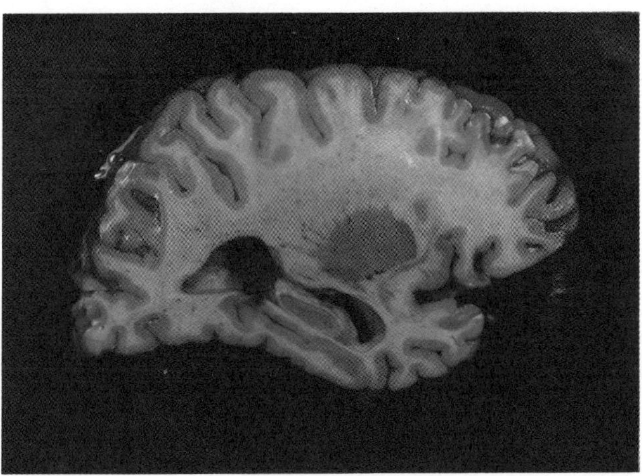

B

Fig. 4.8. Postmortem sagittal sections in a 22-year-old patient who five years previous sustained a severe closed head injury. Note the cavitation in the dorsal frontal region secondary to contusion (*B*). Note ventricular enlargement for a man this age, particularly in the posterior and temporal horns (*A* and *B*).

Ischemia

Ischemia is defined as loss of blood flow to the brain; with interruption of the blood supply to neural tissue infarction of that tissue subserved may develop. The consequence of ischemia is multifactorial. With reduced or absence of blood flow, immediate metabolic interruption may occur, affecting neural tissue as described above. This loss also results in immediate accumulation of metabolic by-products that in turn have toxic consequences on intracellular function. Figure 4.10 shows the progressive consequences of ischemia and subsequent infarction on the brain resulting from brain edema and compression of the anterior cerebral artery. It is significant to note that in the Glasgow study (Jennett and Teasdale, 1981) in 91 percent of all patients succumbing to head injury, ischemic damage was present. Vasospasm or edema may occur secondary to trauma and hence produce ischemia. The length and duration of these ischemic episodes will determine the degree of brain injury.

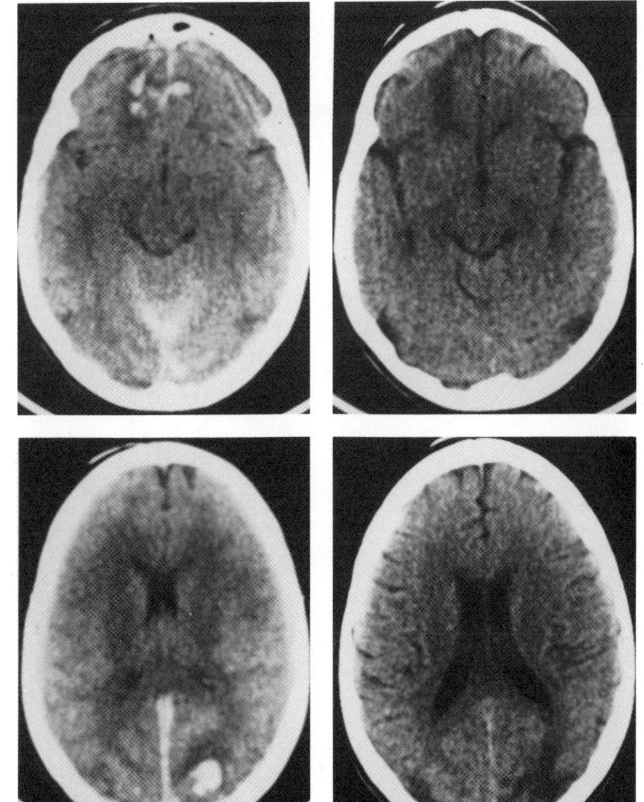

Fig. 4.9. These CAT scans were taken from an 18-year-old female who sustained a left inferior frontal contusion and a subsequent countrecoup contusion over the right occipital area. The scans on the left depict the left frontal contusion (*top*) and the right occipital contusion (*bottom*). The scans on the right were taken approximately three weeks later, depicting density change and the appearance of encephalomalacia secondary to the contusion in the left frontal (*top*) and right occipital parietal region (*bottom*). Note also on the CAT scans on the right that the patient's sylvian fissures have enlarged.

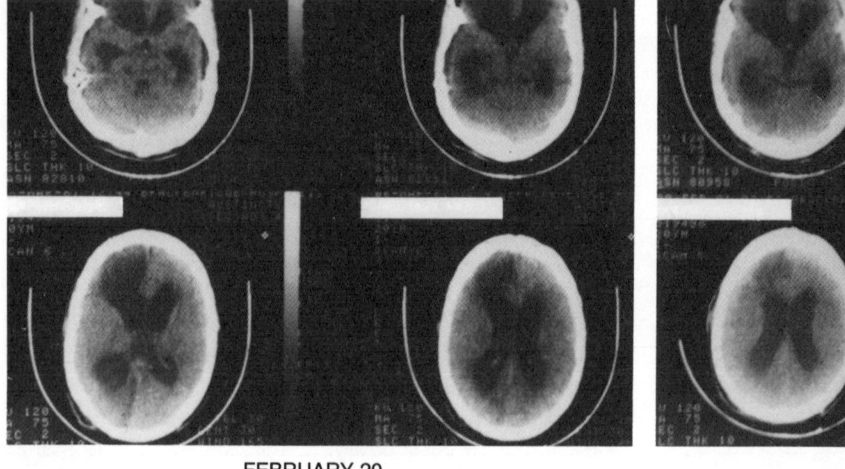

DECEMBER 13

DECEMBER 18

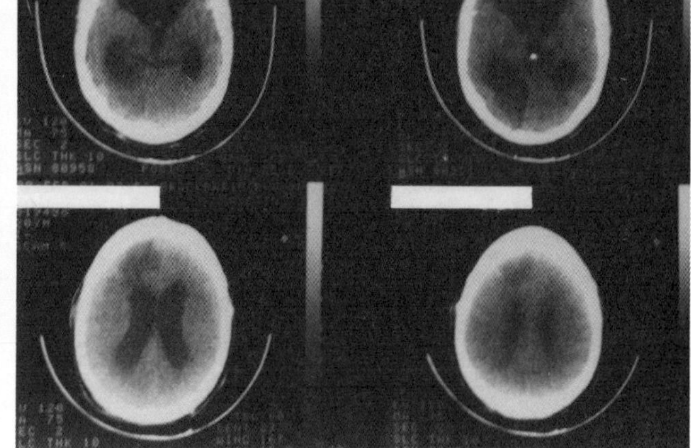

FEBRUARY 20

MARCH 6

Fig. 4.10. Sequential CAT scans of one patient (*from top left*). This patient sustained severe closed head injury on December 13. CAT scan on that day reveals some degree of ventricular compression, indicative of cerebral edema. There is greater compression of the left ventricular system. This continues to be seen on December 18. However, by February 20, marked ventricular dilation of the entire ventricular system has developed as well as infarction in frontal regions (more so on the left). These became chronic, static deficits as seen by the films of March 6.

Structural Distortion

Anatomic distortion may result from hemorrhagic collections, or edema, or both (see figs. 4.11–4.13). Mechanical distortion of the brain as a result may produce marked cerebral deficit.

Anoxia

As previously indicated, oxygen is essential to the metabolic requirements for neuronal functioning. Thus, anoxia—absence or loss of oxygen—may produce devastating and widespread effects on the brain (see fig. 4.14). There is some reversibility in damage, if the anoxia is secondary to ischemia and is less than three to four minutes, provided blood flow is fully restored.

Cerebral Edema

Water content of the brain is considerable, making up 70–80 percent of its mass (Jennett and Teasdale, 1981). Two types of edema occur (Coxe and Grubb, 1978): vasogenic (outflow of fluid from within the vessel into extracellular space) and cytotoxic (intracellular fluid collection). Vasogenic edema is thought to be the more prevalent type of edema with brain trauma. Regardless of the type, cerebral edema is usually found in association with contusions and hematomas, but may also occur in a generalized and diffuse manner (see figs. 4.11, 4.13, 4.15–4.17).

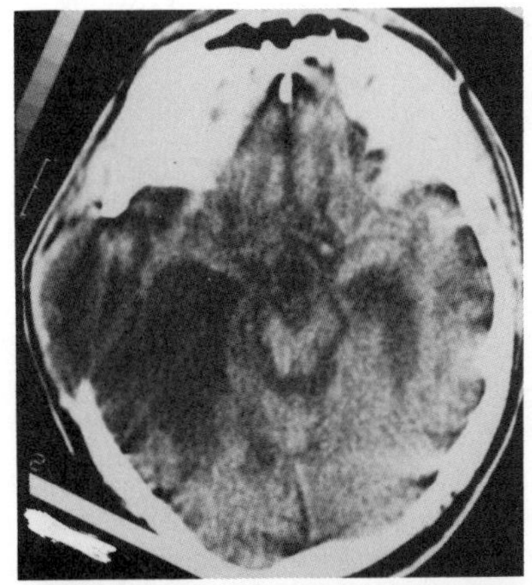

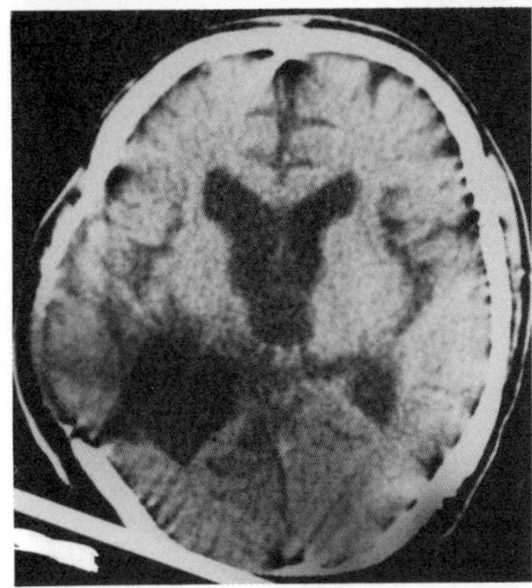

Fig. 4.12. This patient sustained a severe head injury when he fell some eighty feet off the top of an oil derrick. He had a depressed skull fracture over the left temporal region with a massive left temporal subdural hematoma that was surgically evacuated. The CAT scan depicts ventricular dilation; in particular note the dilation of the third ventricle and the temporal horns. A partial left temporal lobectomy was undertaken, and there is considerable encephalomalacic change in the left temporal area as well. There is also diffuse cerebral atrophy present. The patient has remained globally aphasic and quadraplegic.

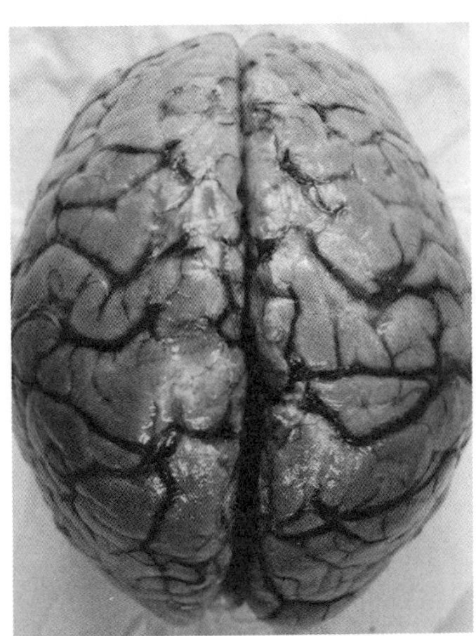

Fig. 4.11. Diffuse cerebral edema. Note the swollen condition of the gyri with diminished or absent sulci space.

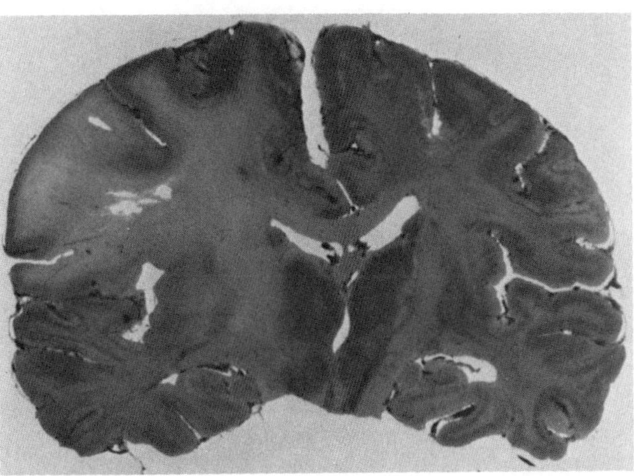

Fig. 4.13. Edema. This coronal section shows an area of marked edema in the left parietal lobe. The white matter in the affected area is swollen and pale, and the sulci are almost obliterated. The ventricular system and upper brain stem are displaced across the midline. From Payne (1969).

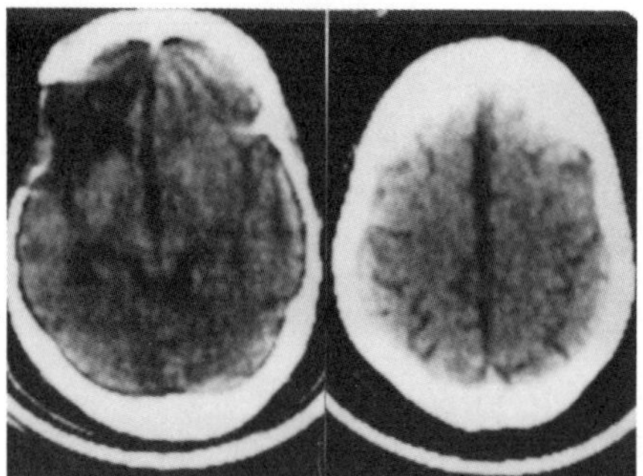

Fig. 4.14. Anoxic damage. This 29-year-old motor vehicle accident victim sustained penetrating injury to the left frontal region and anoxic damage secondary to an obstructed airway. CAT results reveal marked encephalopathy diffusely distributed, but with focal destructive effects in left frontal region. Note the presence of cortical atrophy in the film on the right.

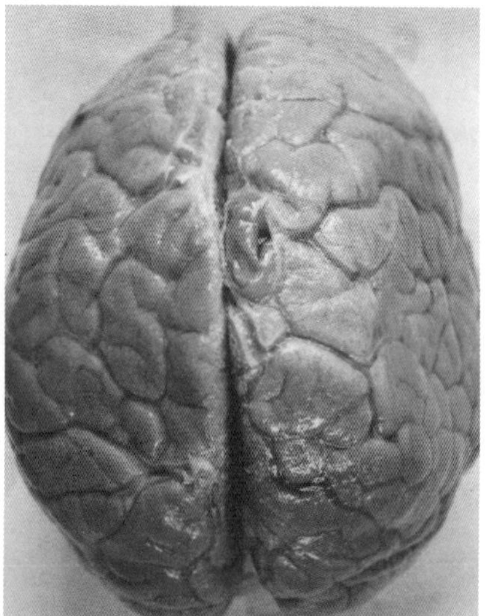

A

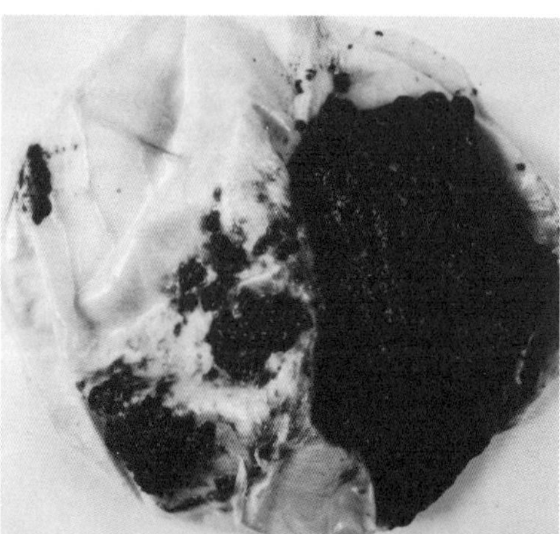

B

Fig. 4.15. *A*, massive extradural hemorrhage. Note the compression over the right hemisphere and posterior aspect of the left hemisphere. Note the edematous appearance of the brain. *B*, blood clot of the dural cap.

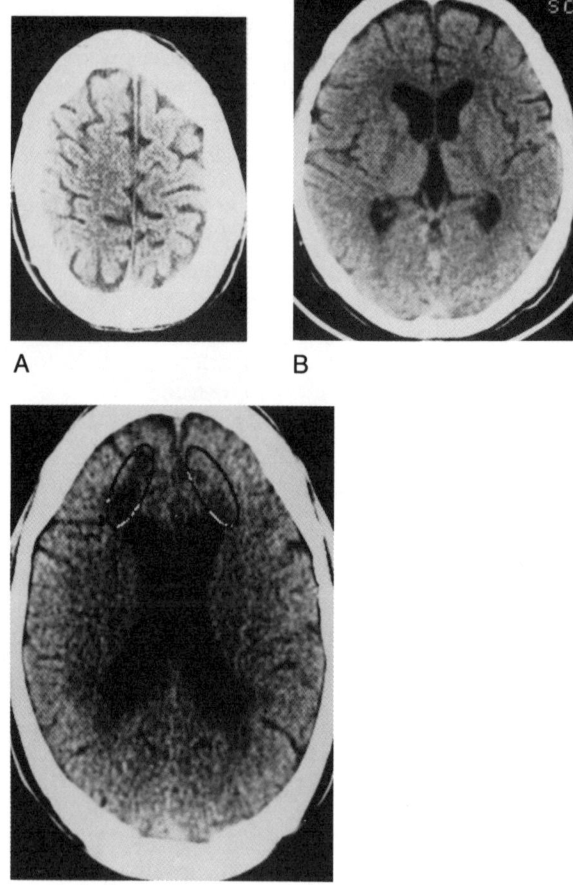

A B

C

Fig. 4.16. The three CAT scans presented above demonstrate the various types of gray and white matter atrophic processes that may occur as a consequence of cerebral injury. *A*, diffuse cortical atrophy in a 20-year-old male patient. This patient sustained a closed head injury. There was no fracture. He was in a coma for approximately three days. Note the marked cortical atrophy present that is distributed in a diffuse manner. *B*, this CAT scan depicts primarily anterior frontal atrophy in a 17-year-old patient who sustained severe closed head injury. There was no skull fracture. The patient was unconscious for approximately thirty-six hours. The patient was to be the valedictorian of his high school class, but as a result of the cerebral injury, marked intellectual and cognitive deficits ensued. Six months postinjury the patient's full scale IQ score was 87. Note that there is some enlargement of the ventricular system with respect to the size of the anterior horns. This is typically felt to represent an ex vacuo state, in which the ventricles enlarge in a compensatory fashion secondary to tissue loss. *C*, this patient sustained a serious closed head injury when he was thrown from a pickup truck that struck an embankment. He struck his head against the embankment, and it was estimated that he was traveling in the range of 35 mph at the time of impact. Note the ventricular dilation for this 25-year-old male patient. Also, the two semi-oval markings on the scan demonstrate white matter contusion areas with associated encephalomalacia. This patient at the time of the accident was one week away from graduating from college, with a 3.5 grade point average. The patient suffered marked intellectual decline as a result of this cerebral injury, and his full scale intellectual score was 83, three years postinjury.

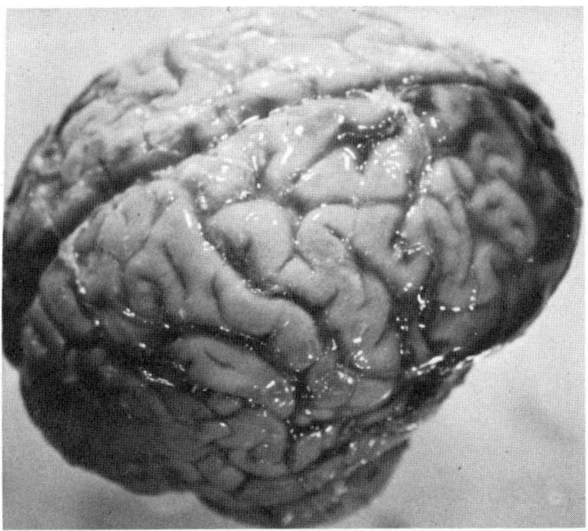

Fig. 4.17. Subarachnoid hemorrhage secondary to trauma. Note location of primary hemorrhage over the frontal region.

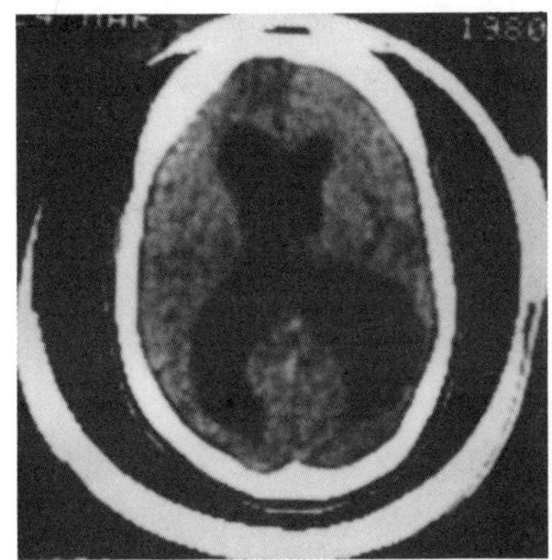

Fig. 4.18. Ventricular enlargement secondary to closed head injury. In this CAT scan of a 19-year-old man five years after head trauma, note the spotty areas of encephalomalacia.

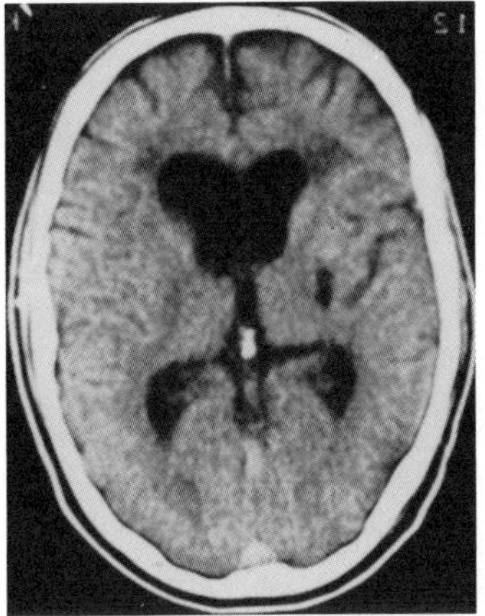

Fig. 4.19. Ventricular enlargement secondary to closed head injury. This CAT scan is that of a 29-year-old male, eighteen months postinjury. Notice the frontal pole atrophy. Notice also the density changes scattered about in the anterior frontal regions. There is also an area of cavitation in the right internal capsule area. This is due to a deep shearing effect/contusion of the white matter. This did result in a left-side hemiplegia. The patient has marked intellectual and cognitive deficit as well as deficits in short-term memory (VIQ = 78, PIQ = 69, FSIQ = 73; MQ = 59).

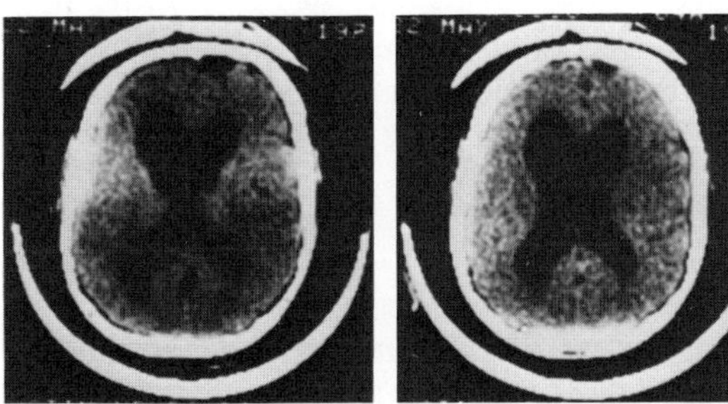

Fig. 4.20. Obstructive hydrocephalus. A 37-year-old man sustained blunt trauma to the back of his head in an altercation.

Subdural Hematoma

Up to 30 percent of patients with closed head injury will develop hematoma (Cullum and Bigler, 1985). In a study examining the effects of prior hematoma on brain morphology and neuropsychological outcome, Cullum and Bigler (1985) found greater cerebral atrophy, particularly in frontal regions, and ventricular dilation in patients with a history of closed head injury. These patients also were more impaired on neuropsychological measures, particularly memory, than were closed head injury patients who did not develop a subdural (see also Cullum and Bigler, 1986).

Hydrocephalus

There are generally three types of hydrocephalus that may develop following brain injury: (1) hydrocephalus ex vacuo, which represents ventricular dilation secondary to wasting of the white matter; (2) impaired flow of cerebrospinal fluid; and (3) normal-pressure hydrocephalus (Fishman, 1978; Jennett and Teasdale, 1981; Zander and Foroglou, 1976). The symptoms that may accompany hydrocephalus are initially headache, vomiting, confusion, and lethargy, although it may be difficult to differentiate this from the effects of cerebral trauma. Figures 4.18–4.20 depict a combination of hydrocephalus ex vacuo and normal-pressure hydrocephalus in a patient posttrauma. Levin and his associates (1981) and Cullum and Bigler (1986) have demonstrated ventricular dilation in closed head injury suggestive of diffuse atrophic process. Such dilation was found to be associated with the presence of cognitive and memory deficits as well as length of coma.

Posttraumatic Epilepsy

In general, approximately 5 percent of patients with head injuries develop epilepsy; however, if only patients with hematoma or skull fracture are included then the percentage is much higher, somewhere around 30 percent (Becker et al., 1979; Jennett and Teasdale, 1981). The seizure pattern is usually one of the generalized type with underlying focal abnormality. Posttraumatic epilepsy following penetrating head injury also has a negative effect on life expectancy (Corkin, Sullivan, and Carr, 1984).

Cranial Nerve Damage

Although injury to cranial nerves is common when impact injury to the head occurs, the presence of cranial nerve defect does not necessarily correlate well with severity of cerebral damage (Becker et al., 1979; however, see Levin et al., 1979). Anosmia (see Levin, High, and Eisenberg, 1985) is common because the position of the olfactory nerve in the olfactory groove is most susceptible to shearing and tearing or compressive damage, again because of its position between the ventral anterior skull and the frontal brain regions. Doty and colleagues (see Doty, Shaman, and Dann, 1984) have developed a sensitive "scratch and sniff" test procedure for the detection of anosmia. Ocular motility is likewise frequently a cranial nerve injury sequelae, typically being manifested by third nerve palsy and, less common, fourth nerve palsy. Facial palsies may also be present, usually related to petrous bone fracture damaging the nerve. Hearing loss, tinnitus, vertigo, or ataxia may also occur as a result of eighth nerve involvement. Posttraumatic ocular nystagmus may also evolve into a permanent deficit.

Other Factors

As alluded to previously, trauma to the head initiates an extremely complex pathophysiologic process. Neuropathologists have long demonstrated that there may be little relationship between the nature and locale of initial impact or structural deformation of the skull and resultant damage throughout the brain. This combined with lack of animal models that can be adequately tested leaves much to speculation in the pathogenesis of brain trauma. There are several other factors that are known to contribute and these include acceleration and deceleration of the brain, the greater likelihood of damage occurring at the interface between tissues that have different physical properties (i.e., between white and gray matter, brain and blood vessels), and the tendency toward cortical damage rather than brain stem damage (Gurdjian, 1975; Jennett and Teasdale, 1981). Giulian and Lachman (1985) have demonstrated that the brain's own immune response following trauma may in fact stimulate astroglial proliferation. This may be a significant factor in the promotion of neural scar formation.

Forms of Trauma

Brain injury resulting from motor vehicular accident (MVA) is the most common form of cerebral trauma (Jennett and Teasdale, 1981). However, a significant number of traumatic injuries to the head are a result of (1) assault; (2) missile (e.g., bullet) or stab wound occurring from accident, assault, or suicide (see figs. 4.21 and 4.22); (3) sports accidents, in particular those related to boxing, soccer, and football; (4) occupational trauma, typically from an explosion or fall; and (5) home or recreational accidents, usually from a fall. Head injury resulting from assault or accidents connected with occupation, sports, home, or recreation typically are quite similar to vehicular impact injury in that the head is usually struck by or strikes a blunt object. However, with missile wounds a distinctly different clinical syndrome is present. Kirkpatrick and DiMaio (1978) have excellently summarized the effects of penetrating missile wounds on the brain (see figs. 4.21 and 4.22). In summary, their work indicates that, once the bullet penetrates the skull, a rather random pathway may be taken that is more dependent on the yaw of the bullet than the caliber of the firearm. Bone chips typically fragment into the brain producing additional damage. In a large percentage of the cases, the missile will be retained within the cranial vault and that ricochet of the missile from the inner surface of the cranial vault again provides for random trajectory and brain injury. Cerebral edema may develop and further add to the brain pathology. They also speculate that deformation of the brain toward the foramen magnum is likely the fatal mechanism in many gunshot wounds because of the compressive pressure effects on the brain stem.

Numerous studies, as well as common sense, have demonstrated significant injury effects in boxers, even in boxers who have never lost consciousness (Casson et al., 1984; Drew et al., 1986; Lampert and Hardman, 1984). The eventual neurologic damage in boxers tends to be generalized and nonspecific, with the end result being the syndrome of dementia pugilistica.

For want of another place to categorize cerebral involvement as a result of systemic burning, burn encephalopathy will be mentioned here. Severe burns to the body may result in a delayed reaction that will subsequently affect the brain (Mohnot, Snead, and Benton, 1982). Such so-called burn encephalopathies probably result from complex metabolic, hematologic, and hemodynamic abnormalities that may cause permanent damage. Such damaging effects are frequently of a generalized nature.

Neuropsychological Sequelae

Prognosis and classification of outcome following brain injury are made a difficult task by the intricate structural and functional systems of the brain. The most informative and proven guidelines in terms of classification of outcome are those specified by Jennett and Bond (1975; although see

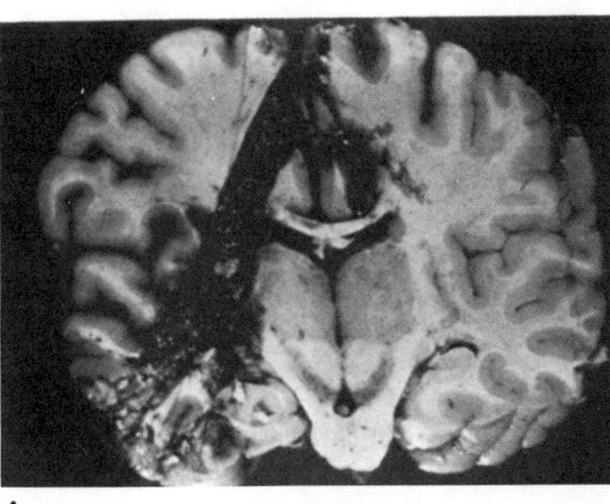

A

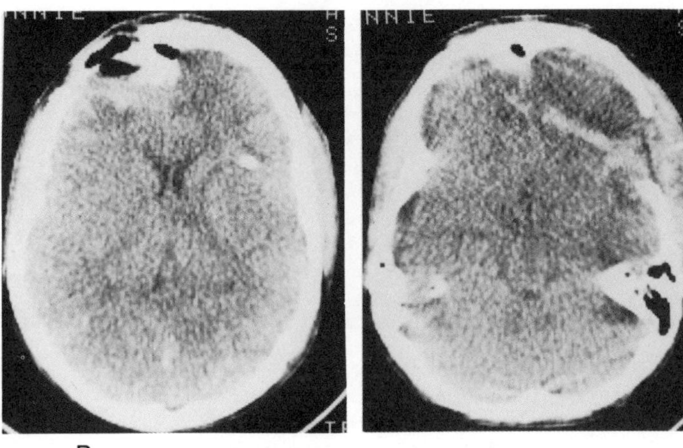

B

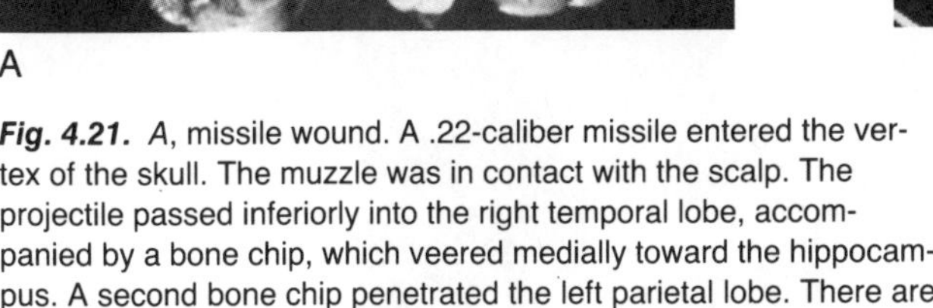

Fig. 4.21. *A*, missile wound. A .22-caliber missile entered the vertex of the skull. The muzzle was in contact with the scalp. The projectile passed inferiorly into the right temporal lobe, accompanied by a bone chip, which veered medially toward the hippocampus. A second bone chip penetrated the left parietal lobe. There are small contusions of the right temporal lobe inferiorly. Gases from the muzzle of the weapon do not appear to have enlarged the wound. From Kirkpatrick and DiMaio (1978). *B*, CAT scan depicting self-inflicted gunshot wound. A .22-caliber pistol was placed to the right temporal area, and the CAT scan depicts the trajectory of the bullet across the frontal lobe. The patient never lost consciousness. He developed a marked frontal lobe syndrome in terms of marked distractibility, heightened impulsivity, lack of goal-specific behaviors and perseveration, and intellectual impairment.

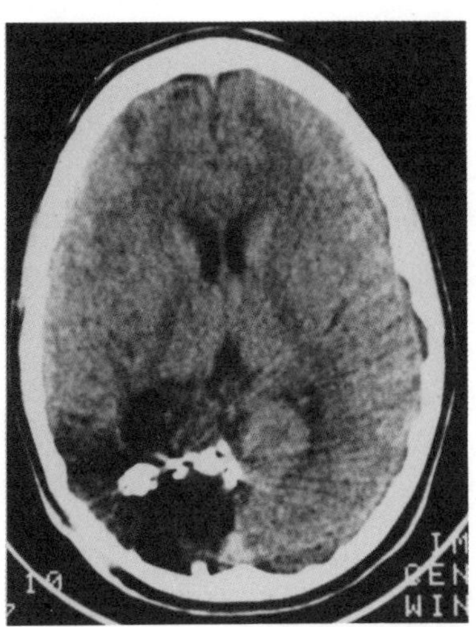

Fig. 4.22. Gunshot wound. The CAT scan demonstrates marked structural changes in the posterior left cerebral hemisphere of this 13-year-old male. This was a result of a shotgun blast to the back of the head. There are still bullet as well as bone fragments present. Clinically, the patient developed a right hemianopia and dyslexia. Interestingly, writing/spelling was quite preserved, and no specific intellectual deficits were present. The patient was able to return to school and, with special education assistance, has been making good progress academically.

suggestions for expansion by Smith et al., 1979). This system (the Glasgow Outcome Scale) distinguishes between five levels: (1) death, (2) vegetative state, (3) severe disability (conscious but disabled), (4) moderate disability (disabled but independent), and (5) good recovery. Naturally, the patient in persistent vegetative state is not amenable to much in the way of neuropsychological examination. This may also be true with certain patients with severe disability, but typically patients with severe disability can be fully examined from a neuropsychological standpoint, with such studies providing crucial diagnostic and prognostic information.

Cognitive dysfunction is commonplace when structural brain damage secondary to trauma is present (Bigler, Steinman, and Newton, 1981; Boll, 1982). The type and degree of cognitive disturbance are related to the site of focal damage and presence or absence of more generalized effects (however, see fig. 4.23). There is also some correspondence between whether structural damage owing to trauma is in the left or right hemisphere. Left hemisphere damage tends to result in more generalized cognitive dysfunction, whereas right hemisphere damage tends to be more specific to visuospatial, visuopraxic, and manipulospatial defects (Bigler, Steinman, and Newton, 1981). Results supporting these tendencies are presented in tables 4.1 and 4.2. See also figure 4.24.

Diffuse impact damage also produces a general reduction in most cognitive functions and measures (see table 4.3), although the deficits are not as great as those seen with degenerative disease (Bigler, Steinman, and Newton, 1981). The generalized deficits accompanying diffuse

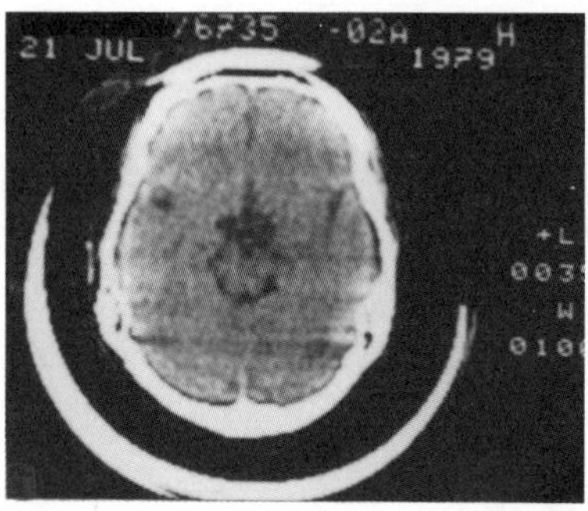

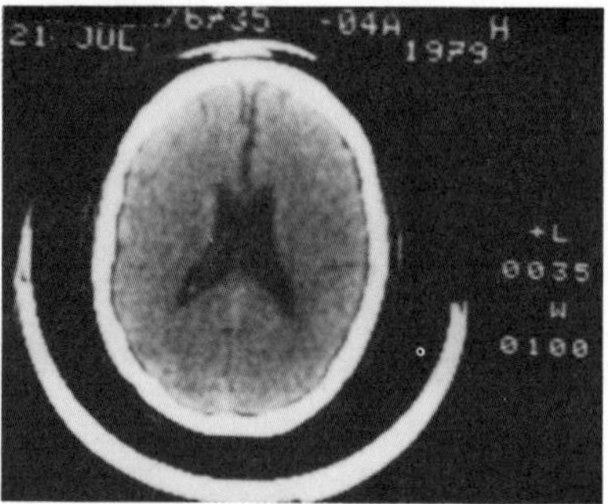

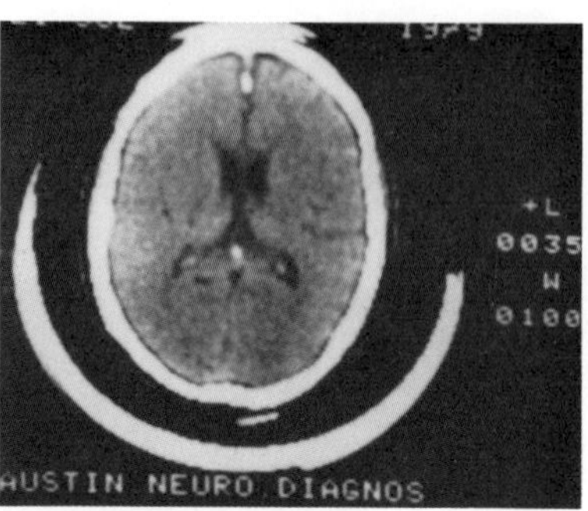

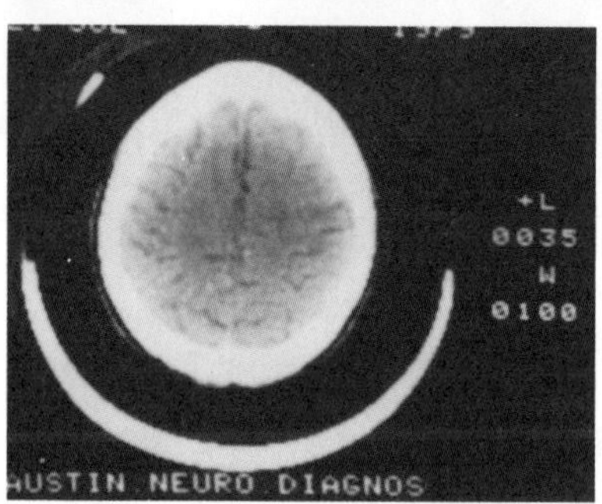

Fig. 4.23. Residual impairment. This 36-year-old man sustained traumatic closed head injury in a motor vehicle accident two and one-half years before examination. He was a college professor. CAT scan results show some enlargement of the ventricular system along with some greater prominence of the interhemispheric fissure and cortical sulci than would be normally seen in a man his age. There are no other abnormalities, however. Neuropsychological examination results clearly demonstrate residual impairment in higher cortical functioning. While well-learned intellectual functions were preserved (i.e., verbal IQ = 143), the patient performed quite poorly on the category test (84 errors) and the tactual performance test (total time of 32.6 minutes). When IQ is intact but other measures are significantly impaired, the condition is almost always related to organic dysfunction and indicative of deficits in new memory and learning. This case is a good illustration of the importance of comprehensive examination of the posttraumatic patient even though CAT scan results may not be very remarkable and "intellectual" functions appear intact (see table 2.2).

Table 4.1. ***Sample Size, Age, and Sex Distribution for Groups in Comparison***

Group	Sample Size	Male	Female
Diffuse damage (Age range: 16–50)	21	19	2
Lateralized damage—Left (Age range: 21–50)	14	12	2
Lateralized damage—Right (Age range: 19–40)	14	10	4
Control (Age range: 20–50)	36	17	19

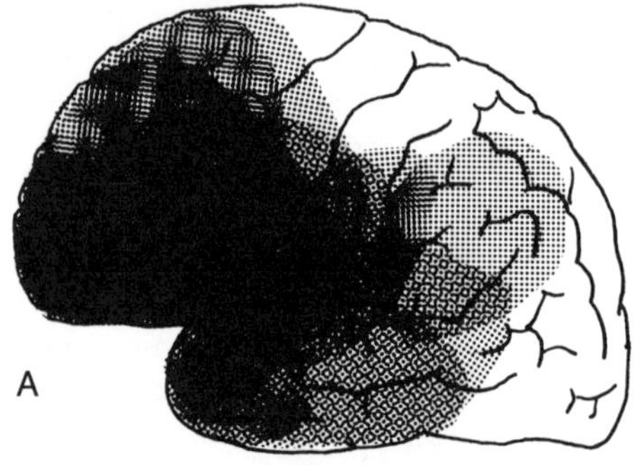

Fig. 4.24. Common hemispheric damage. *A* depicts the extent of residual left hemisphere structural damage as reconstructed from CAT scan results. The darker areas specify the areas of most common residual structural pathology. *B* is similar except that it represents right hemisphere residual damage. Note that the areas of greatest residual structural pathology lie within the frontotemporal regions in both the left and right hemispheres (see table 4.2). From Bigler, Steinman, and Newton (1981).

Table 4.2. *Group Comparisons by Hemisphere Damaged*

Variable	Left vs. Control Significance	Left Hemisphere Mean	Left Hemisphere *SD*	Left vs. Right Significance	Right Hemisphere Mean	Right Hemisphere *SD*	Right vs. Control Significance
Age	NS	34.1	10.5	NS	29.2	7.8	*
Education	NS	11.7	1.8	NS	13.2	2.8	NS
WAIS scores							
Verbal IQ	***	87.8	9.9	**	103.2	11.6	*
Performance IQ	***	90.4	11.9	NS	90.3	16.0	***
Full-Scale IQ	***	87.7	9.1	*	98.4	11.0	***
VIQ—raw score	***	47.8	10.5	**	63.6	11.3	*
PIQ—raw score	***	39.2	9.3	NS	41.6	12.2	**
FSIQ—raw score	**	87.3	17.3	*	106.8	18.3	*
Information	**	8.0	2.6	*	10.1	2.7	NS
Comprehension	***	8.4	2.1	**	11.4	2.8	*
Arithmetic	**	8.2	2.6	*	10.4	3.1	NS
Similarities	***	8.2	1.7	***	10.9	1.7	NS
Digit Span	**	6.5	3.7	*	8.9	2.5	NS
Vocabulary	***	8.2	2.9	**	11.4	2.1	NS
Digit Symbol	***	5.5	2.5	NS	6.8	3.1	***
Picture Completion	***	8.4	1.6	NS	8.8	1.7	***
Block Design	NS	9.2	3.3	NS	8.9	3.2	*
Picture Arrangement	NS	8.4	1.9	NS	9.1	2.9	NS
Object Assembly	*	8.2	2.8	NS	7.4	3.8	**
WMS scores							
I	NS	3.9	1.1	*	5.1	1.4	NS
II	***	4.4	0.8	NS	4.3	1.4	*
III	NS	5.9	1.7	***	8.1	0.8	NS
IV	NS	5.5	2.3	*	8.2	2.6	*
V	**	8.3	2.6	NS	10.1	2.0	NS
VI	**	7.4	2.9	NS	7.1	2.1	***
VII	**	7.8	3.5	***	12.5	4.0	**
Raw score	**	43.4	11.2	**	55.5	8.8	***
Memory quotient	**	75.1	15.0	**	90.8	12.2	***
Digits—Forward	NS	4.9	1.5	*	6.1	1.4	NS
Digits—Reverse	NS	3.4	1.3	NS	4.1	0.8	*
Category Test							
Total errors	***	78.8	36.6	NS	79.8	30.7	***
Trail-Making Test							
A (in seconds)	***	69.8	34.9	NS	51.1	16.5	***
B (in seconds)	*	188.4	88.2	*	99.7	45.7	***
B−A (in seconds)	*	118.7	76.4	*	50.9	31.8	NS
Errors A	NS	0.1	0.3	NS	0.2	0.4	NS
Errors B	NS	0.1	1.1	NS	0.5	0.5	NS
Aphasia Screening[a]							
Verbal	*	2.7	1.5	**	1.0	0.7	NS
Spatial	*	2.2	1.4	**	2.2	1.4	**
Sensory Perceptual Exam							
Errors Right	***	14.3	17.8	*	3.9	4.4	**
Errors Left	NS	3.9	4.1	*	15.6	20.1	***
Motor Exam							
Finger Oscillation							
Dominant	***	26.5	20.5	*	42.0	11.0	NS
Nondominant	NS	36.5	9.4	*	25.7	16.3	***
Strength/grip (kg)							
Dominant	***	31.3	15.7	NS	44.2	19.1	NS
Nondominant	NS	43.1	11.8	**	23.8	20.8	***

Source: From Bigler, Steinman, and Newton (1981).
Note: NS, not significant.
*p = 0.05–0.01.
**p = 0.01–0.001.
***p = 0.001 or greater.
[a]Based on the Russell, Neuringer, and Goldstein (1970) scoring method.

Table 4.3. *Comparisons with Patients with Diffuse Damage*

Variable	Control Mean	Control *SD*	Diffuse Damage Mean	Diffuse Damage *SD*	Significance
Age	36.4	12.2	34.9	13.9	NS
Education	13.7	2.8	12.5	3.6	NS
WAIS scores					
Verbal IQ	112.7	13.5	96.4	17.9	***
Performance IQ	109.9	11.2	87.7	16.1	***
Full-Scale IQ	112.0	11.9	92.2	17.1	***
VIQ—raw score	72.0	13.5	57.5	16.1	***
PIQ—raw score	53.6	9.4	39.4	10.9	***
FSIQ—raw score	123.8	26.6	93.8	25.7	***
Information	11.8	2.9	9.7	3.3	*
Comprehension	13.7	3.3	9.9	3.3	***
Arithmetic	11.7	3.5	8.2	3.5	***
Similarities	11.9	2.7	9.0	3.4	***
Digit Span	10.5	2.7	7.8	3.4	***
Vocabulary	12.5	2.6	10.3	3.3	***
Digit Symbol	10.4	2.6	5.8	2.8	***
Picture Completion	10.6	1.9	8.9	3.2	***
Block Design	11.1	2.9	7.4	3.0	***
Picture Arrangement	10.5	2.8	7.4	3.2	***
Object Assembly	11.0	2.9	6.9	2.6	***
WMS scores					
I	5.4	0.9	4.6	1.7	*
II	4.8	0.3	4.3	1.1	**
III	7.2	1.4	5.4	2.8	**
IV	10.2	2.9	9.2	13.8	NS
V	11.4	2.1	10.5	5.9	NS
VI	10.8	3.3			
VII	16.3	3.3	12.7	18.2	NS
Raw score	65.9	7.9	47.3	16.5	**
Memory quotient	112.0	16.1	79.6	18.1	**
Digits—Forward	6.5	1.3	5.7	1.2	NS
Digits—Reverse	4.9	1.2	3.4	1.8	**
Category Test					
Total errors	29.9	12.4	89.6	31.5	***
Trail-Making Test					
A (in seconds)	28.9	9.9	60.8	28.3	***
B (in seconds)	65.2	21.2	150.9	66.6	***
B–A (in seconds)	38.5	20.2	90.2	50.0	***
Errors A	0.0	0.2	0.3	0.7	NS
Errors B	0.4	0.9	1.3	1.3	NS
Aphasia Screening[a]					
Verbal	0.6	0.5	1.9	1.5	***
Spatial	1.0	0.8	2.3	1.5	***
Sensory Perceptual Exam					
Errors Right	1.4	2.0	5.5	5.6	***
Errors Left	1.3	1.9	5.9	6.9	***
Motor Exam					
Finger Oscillation					
Dominant	43.8	8.9	32.9	9.6	***
Nondominant	41.5	8.5	31.2	9.6	***
Strength/grip (kg)					
Dominant	38.9	12.2	39.5	8.6	NS
Nondominant	36.1	10.9	40.4	15.5	NS

Source: From Bigler, Steinman, and Newton (1981).
Note: NS, not significant.
*p = 0.05–0.01.
**p = 0.01–0.001.
***p = 0.001 or greater.

[a]Based on Russell, Neuringer, and Goldstein (1970) scoring method.

brain injury have long been known. Goldstein in 1942 indicated that patients with such damage commonly had deficits in sustained attention and speed of performance along with most other measures of cognitive functioning. Newcombe and Ratcliff (1979) provide a recent review of generalized decrement in performance present with diffuse cerebral damage. St. James–Roberts (1979) also provides an excellent review on neuropsychological sequelae following brain insult (see also Winogron, Knights, and Bawden, 1984).

Outcome and presence of neuropsychological deficit are also affected by age at the time of injury. In general, the younger the individual the better the outcome (Berger et al., 1985; Black, Shepard, and Walker, 1975; Boll and Barth, 1981; Brink et al., 1970; Heiskanen and Kaste, 1974; Levin and Eisenberg, 1979), and in preteen children this is somewhat independent of the severity of the coma or the length of posttraumatic amnesia (PTA) (Jennett and Teasdale, 1981). Such findings have long been known in animal studies, and this enhanced ability to recover has been related to greater plasticity in the immature central nervous system (Finger, 1978). This is not to say that children display full recovery, but rather that they tend to show more complete restoration of function than do adults. Relatedly, the recovery period is extended in children—up to five years posttrauma—(Klonoff, Law, and Clark, 1977), but with adults the upper limit is usually considered somewhat less (Jennett and Teasdale, 1981). With respect to earlier prognosis of ultimate outcome, studies have indicated that the patients' status be evaluated at six months posttrauma (or in cases in which severe posttrauma amnesia exists, it would be six months after restoration of more normal memory). Cerebral trauma past the fifth decade of life may result in much greater deficit because of interactive effects of trauma with normal aging degeneration (Bigler, Steinman, and Newton, 1981).

Children who have cerebral trauma are at high risk for there to be permanent intellectual deficits (Brink et al., 1970; Dennis, 1985 *a, b;* Dikmen, Matthews, and Harley, 1975; Heiskanen and Kaste, 1974), but greater potential for transfer of function and compensation (Finger, 1978). Adult patients may display less of an intellectual deficit, but a greater deficit in terms of adaptive and compensatory abilities (Jennett and Teasdale, 1981).

Numerous studies (Barth et al., 1983; Drudge et al. 1984; Rimel et al., 1981; Stuss et al., 1985; Van Zomeren and Van Den Burg, 1985) have demonstrated a variety of neuropsychological impairments, particularly in memory, following mild cerebral trauma. However, McLean et al. (1983) did not find significant neuropsychological sequelae one month following mild head injury, but did find endorsement of a variety of postconcussion symptoms in these patients.

An important variable in outcome is the length of posttrauma amnesia. PTA is defined as the time from trauma (after recovery from coma) to the time consistent and efficient memory function returns. The longer the PTA, the greater the propensity for lasting cognitive deficit (see also Levin et al., 1981). Another important variable is time of memory recovery after PTA clearing. Recovery of memory to a stable level of function has been shown to take place within six months (Jennett and Teasdale, 1981). If memory disturbance exists past this point, memory deficit may be permanent.

Features of anterograde and retrograde amnesia should always be evaluated in the patient who suffered head trauma. Historical and personal information on subtest 1 of the Wechsler Memory Scale (WMS) as well as the information subtest on the Wechsler Adult Intelligence Scale (WAIS) may provide an assessment basis for remote memory and orientation. Further questioning of family members and then subsequent questioning of the patient may also be helpful. For anterograde testing, use 15-, 30-, or 45-minute follow-up testing of the paragraph passages (subtest 4), visual memory (subtest 6), and paired-associate learning (subtest 7) of the WMS. Comparisons of WAIS IQ scores with WMS memory quotient scores may also be useful. Levin and co-workers (1979, 1981) have effectively used a selective reminding test of verbal memory to demonstrate anterograde memory deficits. Persistent general memory deficits frequently accompany residual trauma-induced structural deficits (Bigler, Steinman, and Newton, 1981), the deficits being present irrespective of whether the damage was to the left or right hemisphere. Also, this study demonstrated that greater verbal memory deficits were associated with left hemisphere structural damage, but that visual memory was more affected when right hemisphere pathology was present. Sunderland, Harris, and Gleave (1984) have demonstrated that memory failure for everyday life events is also the rule for the posttraumatic head injury patient who experienced severe head injury.

Levin et al. (1979) have recently studied patients with closed head injury in terms of quality of outcome. They found persistent intellectual deficits in most patients with severe head injury. This was believed to be primarily related to impaired capacity for storage and retrieval of information. Similarly, cognitive disturbance was manifested in various ways that appeared to have the same basis. In social situations, patients particularly had difficulty in filtering out extraneous material. Social withdrawal along with slowed speech and movement were common. Cognitive inefficiency was also frequent among these patients, usually taking the form of perturbed or slow thinking, diminished concentration, and impaired memory functioning. Increased aggressive behavior with low frustration tolerance was also common, as were features of depression and anxiety. In their study of severe brain injury, Levin et al. found that the presence of oculovestibular deficit was most predictive of persistent neuropsychologic dysfunction. This is certainly understandable, inasmuch as such a finding indicates both brain stem and cerebral involvement. Levin and his associates (1981) have also demonstrated the presence of posttraumatic enlargement of the ventricular system as another feature of outcome (see fig. 4.18).

Change in personality is likewise a part of the common sequelae to brain injury (Dikman and Reitan, 1974*a*, 1974*b*, 1977*a*, 1977*b*; Kwentus et al., 1985; Levin and Grossman, 1978). Jennett and Teasdale (1981) review data of 150 patients who had sustained severe brain injury but "recovered." Two-thirds of the patients had cognitive deficit similar to that just described by Levin and associates, along with two-thirds having change in personality. A most interesting finding was that a number of the patients with personality change had absence of specific findings on neurologic and neuropsychological studies. Oppositely, though, those without personality change rarely had residual cognitive deficit. Jennett and Teasdale summarize their results by suggesting three main emerging areas of personality change: (1) drive is typically diminished, the patient usually lacking initiative and having diminished motivation and interest; (2) affective changes are commonplace, hypomanic features and emotional liability being the most frequent; and (3) deficits in judgment and diminished social restraint, typically in the form of impulsivity, altered frustration tolerance, and an impaired sense of social propriety (see table 4.4). In older patients trauma may result in a behavioral picture very similar to that seen with disorders of dementia (see Wells, 1977). It should also be noted that there are major socioemotional and socioeconomic effects on the family when a family member sustains a severe brain injury (Livingston, Brooks, and Bond, 1985*a, b*).

Table 4.4. *Frontal Lobe Syndrome Features*

Personality or Behavioral Construct	Changes Caused by Head Injury
Capacity for social perceptiveness	Self-centered behavior Diminution or total loss of self-criticism Loss of ability to show empathy
Capacity for self-control	Random restlessness Impatience and impulsivity
Learned social behavior	Diminution in or loss of initiative; power to make judgments, plan, and organize Increased social dependency
Ability to learn	Mental slowness and rigidity of thought Reduced learning capacity
Emotion	Irritability, silliness, lability of mood, apathy, and increased or diminished sexual drive

Source: From Lezak (1978).

Note: These five areas summarize Lezak's conceptualization of the behavioral and personality changes that may accompany cerebral injury.

Postconcussion Syndrome

The most common symptoms and complaints following mild head injury are headache, dizziness, poor concentration, and poor memory, along with fatigue and increased irritability. These symptoms may appear very briefly and transiently but also may persist for several weeks. If these symptoms persisted, they were originally considered to be related to premorbid personality factors, traumatic neurosis, or litigation (Miller, 1961). Undisputably these variables are important, but more recent studies suggest that even with very mild injury to the head significant damage may result, thus implicating persistent mild CNS dysfunction of nonfocal origin to be present in these patients (Ewing et al., 1980; Fisher, 1982; Gronwall and Wrightson, 1974, 1975; Rutherford, Marrett, and McDonald, 1977). Because of the structural position of the hypothalamus and its relationship to the limbic system, it has long been hypothesized that with mild trauma the behavioral sequelae are related to disturbances of the hypothalamus and related structures (Newcombe and Ratcliff, 1979). Neuropsychological examination may be rather unremarkable, although frequent mild memory deficits are seen on formal testing. Similarly, clinical exam may reveal garrulousness, hypomania, or irritability again in a patient without demonstrable intellectual or other cognitive deficits. Jacobson (1969) states that these symptoms usually subside two months after injury. Careful attention must be directed to these patients' mental status before finally determining if they can return to work or school. Since litigation may be involved in a number of head injury cases (Bigler, 1986), the question of the validity of neuropsychological assessment measures frequently arises. Goebel (1983) has demonstrated that, for the experienced clinician, a comprehensive neuropsychological battery will typically separate out the individual who is attempting to falsify his or her disability. Repko and Cooper (1985) have further demonstrated the effectiveness of the MMPI in differentiating such cases.

Neuropsychological Assessment of the Posttrauma Patient

Diagnostic neuropsychological studies of the trauma patient will typically be designed to assess the extent of cerebral damage or dysfunction because etiology will already be known. Most trauma patients will have already had numerous neurodiagnostic studies (e.g., CAT scanning, EEG, skull X rays, etc.), and thus the extent of structural pathology is frequently already established by the time the patient is seen for neuropsychological evaluation. However, neuropsychological evaluation will provide critical information in terms of functional levels.

Because there is the likelihood of generalized involvement with any significant head injury, the initial evaluation of these patients should always be comprehensive. Once the comprehensive tests are completed, more specialized

A

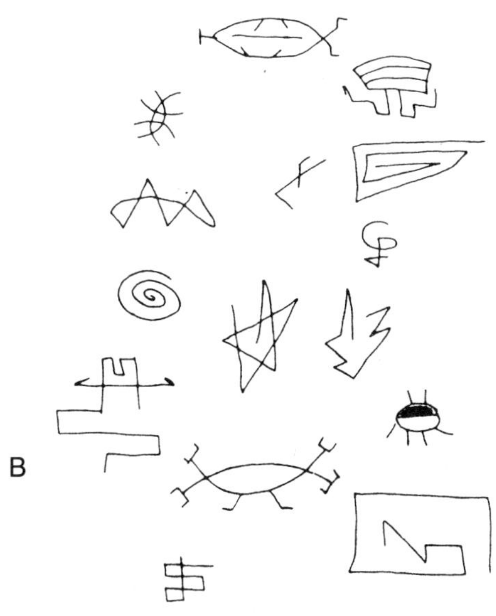

B

Fig. 4.25. Invention of novel designs by a patient when examined five years postinjury (*A*) and a control subject of similar age and education (*B*). Both samples were obtained under a free condition; that is, there was no stipulation of the number of lines that could be used in each drawing. Note the marked perserveration in the patient's designs despite explicit instructions to create novel drawings. In this test the patient is instructed to create as many novel designs as possible, within a specific time period. From Levin et al. (1985).

testing can focus on specific neuropsychological findings (e.g., aphasia) or be based on other neurodiagnostic studies indicating focal lesion. Specific neuropsychological studies might also examine a patient for a specific deficit (e.g., if a patient is shown to have right parietal-temporal lobe contusion, then extensive visuomotor, tactile-motor, and graphomotor tests should be done). Results presented in tables 4.2 and 4.3 may be used as guidelines in evaluating the brain-injured patient. Also, Levin and his colleagues have suggested the use of a novel designs test to assess perseveration in the patient with cerebral trauma (see fig. 4.25).

Cognitive Rehabilitation

During the last two decades, research and clinical experience has accumulated that indicates significant rehabilitation can take place in terms of recovery of cognitive function in traumatically brain damaged individuals (Goldstein and Oakley, 1985; Incagnoli and Newman, 1985; Prigatano, 1985; Rao and Bieliauskas, 1983; Sbordone, 1984). Neuropsychological test results are well suited to provide baseline information concerning a patient's deficits and then to guide the areas of concentration of the rehabilitation efforts. Undoubtedly, certain deficits, particularly when CAT results demonstrate significant structural abnormalities, will be permanent (Dikmen, Reitan, and Temkin, 1983). But, frequently, neuropsychological studies will demonstrate areas of strength or intact functioning that may be used as a basis from which to compensate for or adapt to the deficit (Prigatano, 1986; Sbordone, 1984).

CASE STUDIES

Case 1. At age 16 this patient was involved in a serious motor vehicle accident, sustaining closed head injury. Initial impact was in the left frontal region. The patient, however, sustained greater contrecoup injury in the posterior right hemisphere. Neuropsychological exam reveals left visual field defect associated with left-side neglect. CAT scan reveals the damage in posterior parietal-occipital regions (see fig. 4.26).

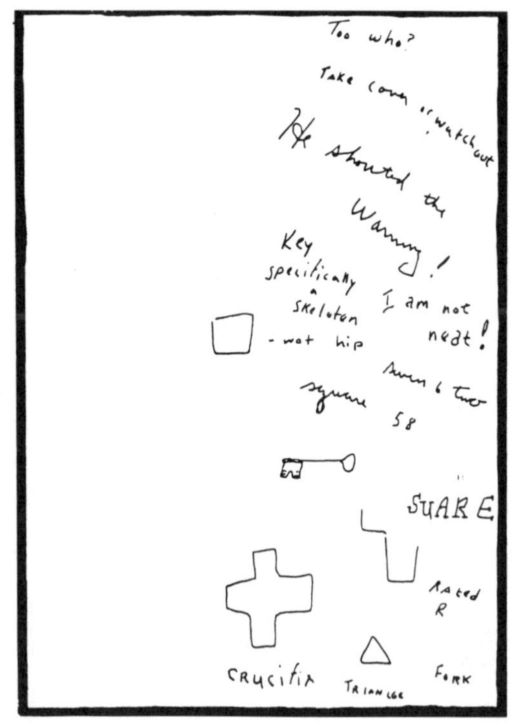

Age 20
Sex M
Education 8

Lateral Dominance Exam

	Eye	Hand	Foot
Right		X	X
Left			
Mixed	X		

Motor Examination

FOGD 36	SOGD 19	TPTD 8.7	TPT Both 5.1
FOGND 37	SOGND 20	TPTND 7.8	

Sensory Examination
Left homonymous hemianopsia, mild left side tactile extinction and dysgraphesthesia

Aphasia Examination
Central dysarthria, mild dysnomia otherwise WNL (Note the patient's left side neglect on drawings)

Memory Examination
WMS MQ = 87

LM 11	TPT-M 8
Digits 11	TPT-L 2
VM 5	
AL 15	

Intellectual/Cognitive Examination
WAIS Results: VIQ = 105, PIQ = 77, FSIQ = 93

I 8	DS 2	Category Test
C 13	PC 9	57 errors
A 12	BD 10	
S 10	PA 9	Trail Making
D 10	OA 2	(invalid)
V 12		

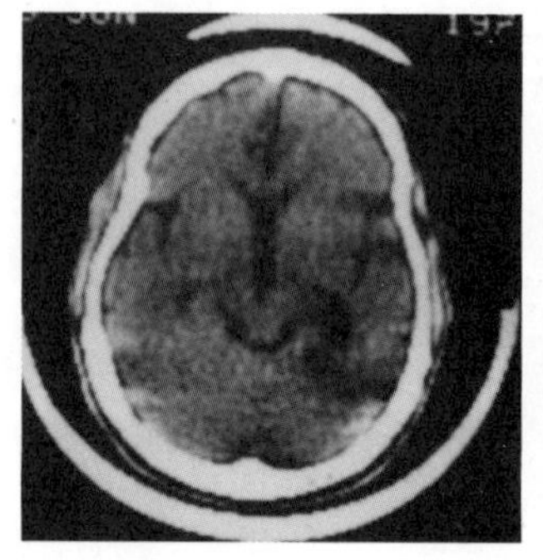
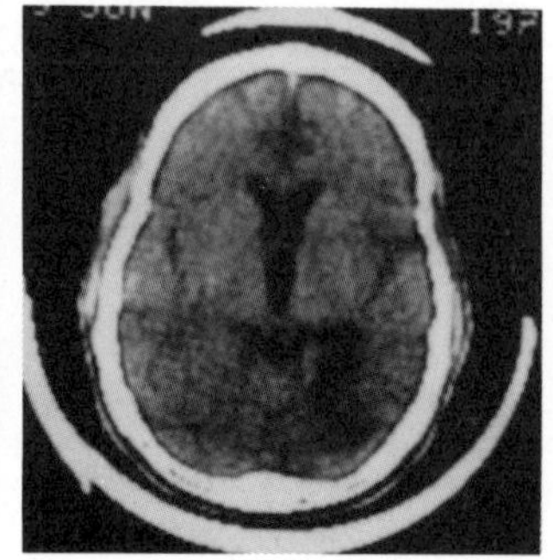
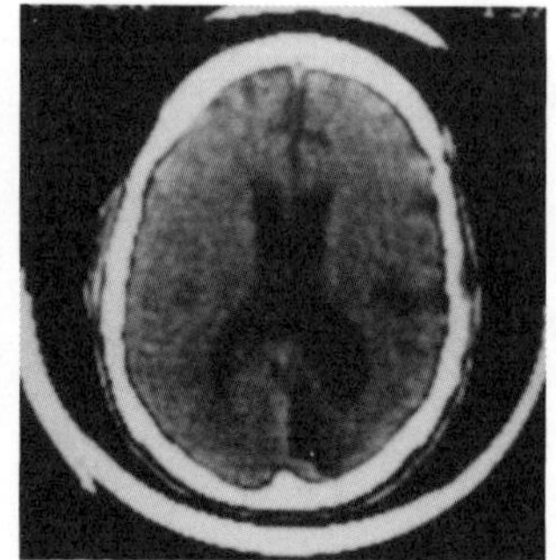
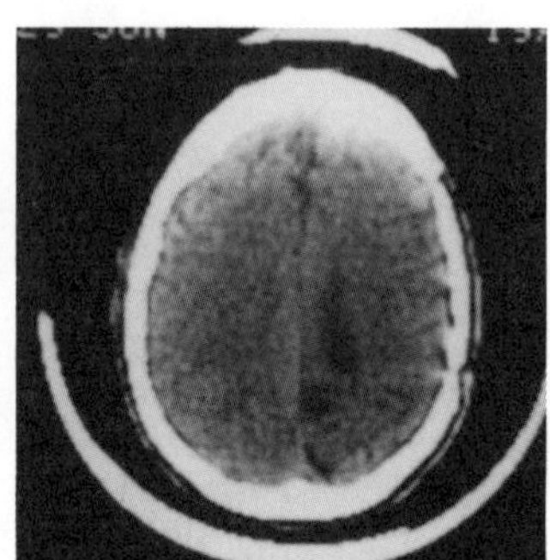

Fig. 4.26. Case 1.

Case 2. This 29-year-old man sustained a serious head injury in an auto-pedestrian accident. He had a large hematoma over the mid-left temporal region and a severe contusion to the temporal lobe in that region. The hematoma was neurosurgically removed. A partial temporal lobectomy was also performed to remove the severely contused brain tissue in that area likely subsequent to pressure and edema effects resulting in cerebral infarction. The patient has a dense right hemianopsia. However, in contrast to the patient in case 1, he does not display spatial neglect. Commonly, spatial neglect is more prevalent with right hemisphere lesions. Initially, the patient had a rather marked receptive dysphasia, but he has generally recovered with only mild dysphasic deficits remaining. (See fig. 4.27.)

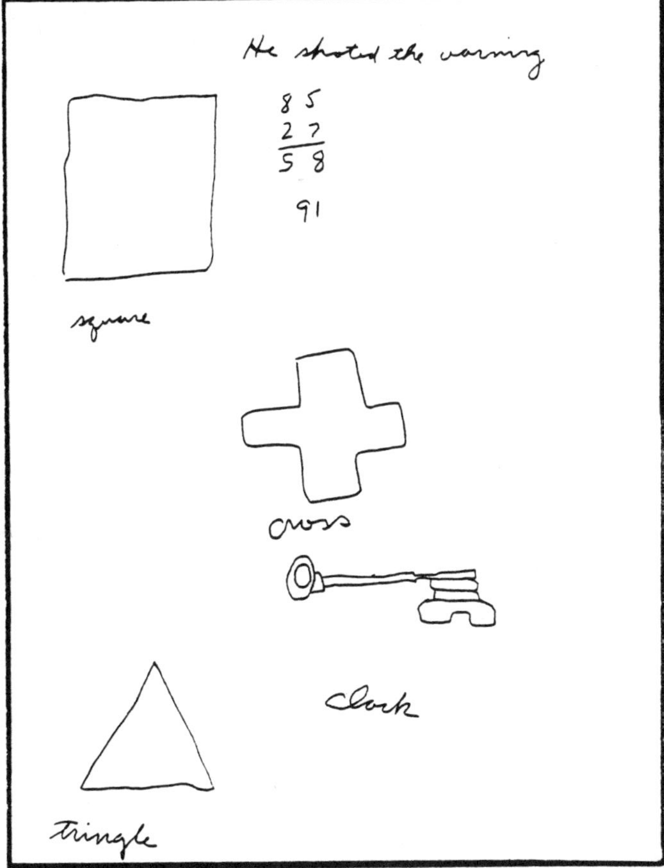

Age 29
Sex M
Education 12

Lateral Dominance Exam

	Eye	Hand	Foot
Right	X	X	X
Left			
Mixed			

Motor Examination
FOD 41 FOND 37
BOGD 52 SOGND 47
TPTD 7.9 TPTND 4.8 TPT Both 3.5

Sensory Examination
Right hemianopsia
Right tactile and auditory extinction
Mild bilateral finger dysgnosia and dysgraphesthesia

Language Examination
Conversational speech: intact
Comprehension: generally intact
Repetition of spoken language: intact
Confrontation naming: intact
Reading
Aloud: Mild dyslexia
Comprehension: Generally intact for what can be read
Writing: Mild spelling dyspraxia
Calculations: Mildly impaired

SSRT 8 errors
SSPT 8 errors

WRAT Scores
Reading 6.8
Spelling 7.2
Arithmetic 5.9

Memory Examination
WMS MQ = 64
LM 1.5, Digits 9, VM 8, AL 4
TPTM 6, TPTL 0

Intellectual/Cognitive Examination
Category Test 105 errors
Trail Making Test A 88 sec. B 154 sec.
FSIQ = 87 VIQ = 85 PIQ = 91

I 7 DS 5
C 7 PC 9
A 7 BD 11
S 8 PA 9
D 7 OA 9
V 9

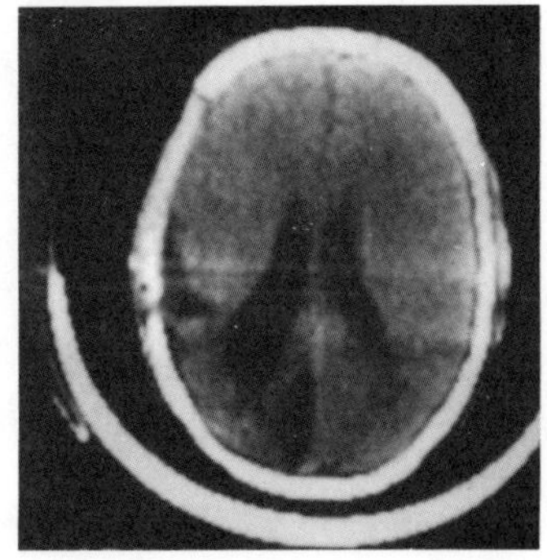
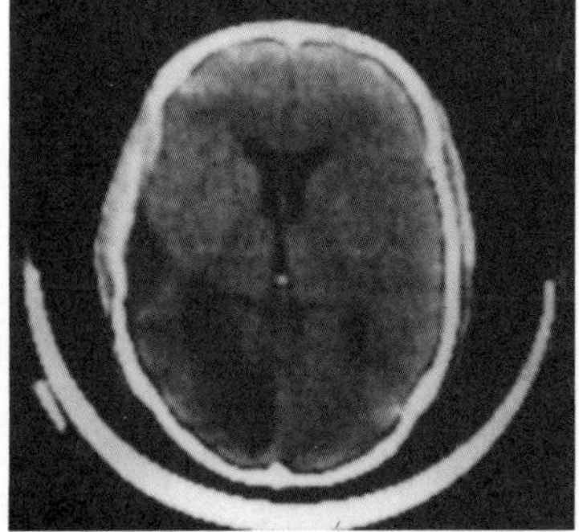

Fig. 4.27. Case 2.

Case 3. Twelve months prior to neuropsychological examination this man sustained serious traumatic injury to the face and skull when an exploding valve cover hit him at a high velocity. There was penetrating injury to the brain along with massive cerebral hemorrhaging. Neuropsychological studies reveal rather marked aphasic residual, but with preserved graphomotor abilities. Marked memory and verbal intellectual deficits are also present. CAT scan reveals rather diffuse encephalomalacia of the left hemisphere, along with the skull defect (fig. 4.28).

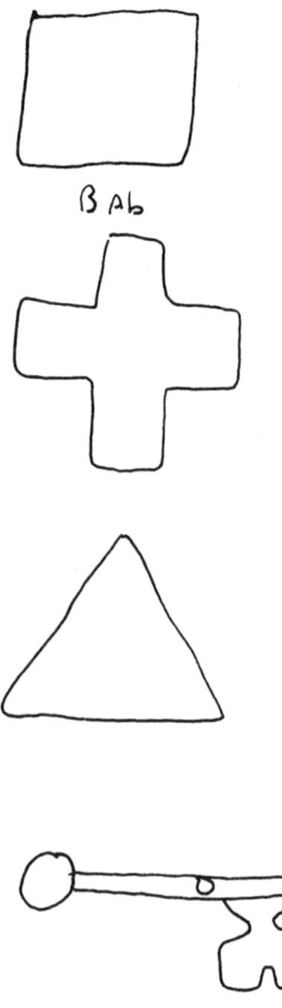

Age 32
Sex M
Education 4th

Lateral Dominance Exam

	Eye	Hand	Foot
Right		X	X
Left			
Both	X		

Motor Examination

FOD 36 SOGD 44 TPTD 13.1
FOND 29 SOGND 40 TPTND 11.5
TPT Both 4.5

Maladroit, awkward gait, poor integrative motor control.

Sensory examination

Right ear auditory extinction.
Bilateral finger dysgnosia

Aphasia Examination

Conversational Speech: Mild dysarthria, paraphasic, frequent echolalia
Comprehension: Impaired.
Repetition of Spoken Language: Impaired, melkibis, pikibus
Confrontation-Naming: Impaired-Triangle-tricue
Reading:
Aloud: Essential alexic
Comprehension: Impaired
Writing: Can copy letter and words but no spontaneous correct writing.
Calculations: Impaired

Memory Examination

Marked memory deficit is present, but contaminated by aphasic deficit
WMS MQ = 48
LM 0 TPTM 4
Digits 7 TPTL 1
VM 2
AL 3

Intellectual Examination

WAIS Results: FSIQ = 64
VIQ=58 DIQ = 77
I 2 D 2 DS 5 PA 4
C 4 V 4 PC 9 OA 8
A 3 BD 6
S 3

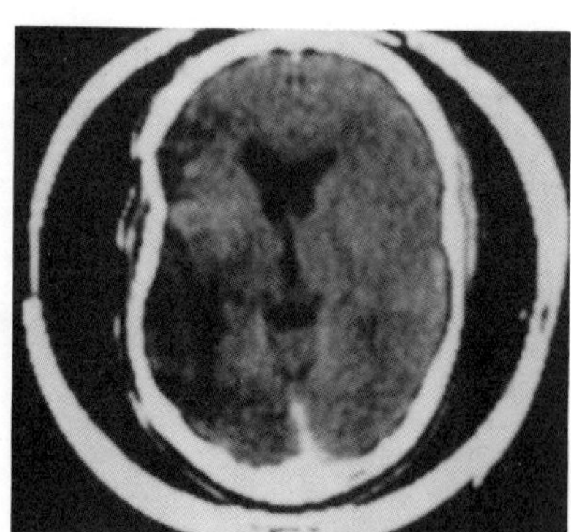

Fig. 4.28. Case 3.

Case 4. This patient sustained diffuse cerebral trauma in a motorcycle accident. CAT scan results reveal marked ventricular dilation along with greater destructive effects of an intracerebral and extracerebral hemorrhaging over the left frontal parietal region. Neuropsychological studies reveal marked deficit in all higher cerebral functions. The patient has a left hemianopsia with visuospatial neglect, well demonstrated by his drawings on aphasia screening. The marked graphomotor deficits are a result of a combination of spasticity and constructional dyspraxia (see fig. 4.29).

Age 19
Sex M
Education 12

Lateral Dominance Exam

	Eye	Hand	Foot
Right	X	X	X
Left			
Both			

Motor Examination
FOD 11 SOGD 10
FOND 3 SOGND 0
Spastic quadraplegia, greater on left side.

Sensory Examination
Left side tactile extinction.
Left side finger ognosia, agraphesthesia and osterognosis
Right side finger dysgnosia, dysgraphesthesia and dysstereogonosis
Visual agnosia

Language Examination
Conversational speech: Slow, dysarthric
Comprehension: Moderately impaired
Repetition of spoken language: Mildly impaired
Confrontation Naming: Dysnomic
Reading
Aloud:
Comprehension: Impaired
Writing: Impaired secondary to spasticity. Can verbally spell simple words
Calculations: Impaired

Memory Examination:
WMS MQ = 55
LM 2, Digits 8, VM 0, AL 5.5

Intellectual/Cognitive Examination
FSIQ = 58 VIQ = 70 PIQ = 49
I 3, C 3, A 4, S 5, D 4, V 5
DS 1, PC 2, BD 1, PA 1, OA 1
Category Test: 135 errors

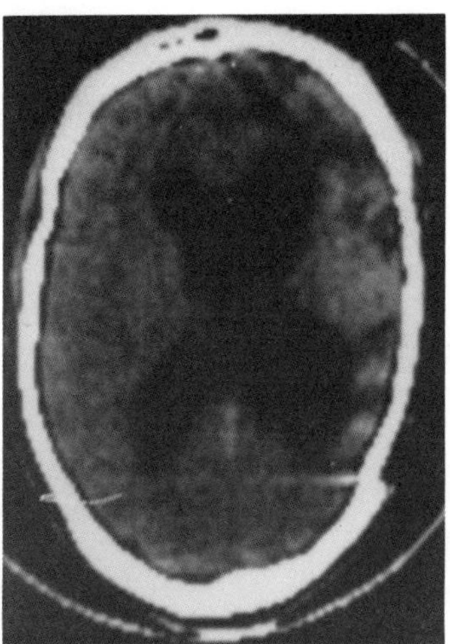

Fig. 4.29. Case 4.

Case 5. This 37-year-old schoolteacher sustained severe closed head injury in a motor vehicle accident. Behaviorally, her most marked deficit is in terms of immediate recall and short-term memory. She could not recall four words after a 30-second interval. Her memory quotient was 69. The marked memory deficit added to persistent orientation deficits. She also displayed emotional lability. CAT results reveal some generalized ventricular dilation, particularly of the temporal horns (fig. 4.30).

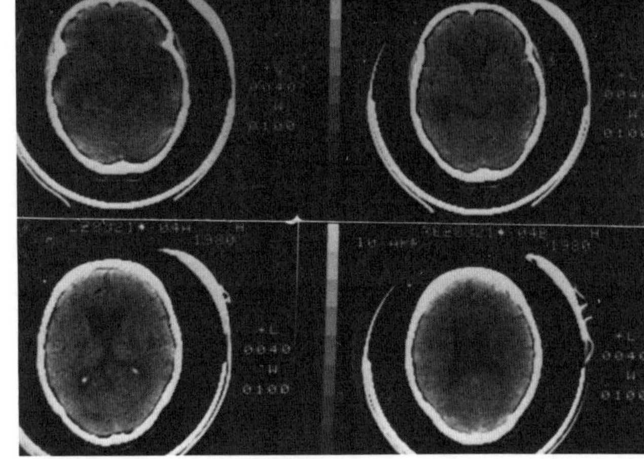

Fig. 4.30. Case 5.

Age 37
Sex F
Education 16

Lateral Dominance Exam

	Eye	Hand	Foot
Right	X	X	X
Left			
Mixed			

square cross triangle watch

He shouted the warning

85
- 27
62

Motor Examination:

FOD 42 SOGD 23 TPTD 5' DC (0 in) Positive Romberg
FOND 48 SOGND 19 TPTND 5' DC (2 in) Cerebellar ataxia (mild)
TPT Both 5' DC (1 in) Dyspraxic

Sensory Examination:

Right side tactile extinction, mild bilateral finger dysgraphesthesia and dysstereognosis

Aphasia Examination:

Conversational Speech: Generally intact
Comprehension: Mildly impaired.
Repetition of Spoken Language: Intact
Confrontation Naming: Mild dysnomia
Reading:
Aloud: Intact for simple words
Comprehension: Intact for simple, impaired for complex
Writing: Intact for simple, borderline impaired for more difficult/complex words
Calculations: Impaired

WRAT Scores:	SRT
Reading 8.4	8 errors
Spelling 5.2	SSPT
Arithmetic 4.3	34 errors

Memory Examination:

WMS MQ = 69 TPTM 3
LM 2, Digits 9, VM 6, AL 7 TPTL 0

Ingellectual/Cognitive Examination:

FSIQ = 69, VIQ = 65, PIQ = 77
I 2, C 2, A 3, S 3, D 6, V 4, DS 8, PC 2, BD 6, PA 5, OA 5

Category Test 83 errors Trail Making Test A 49 sec., B 166 sec.

Case 6. One year before the neuropsychological examination the patient sustained severe traumatic injury to the brain by self-inflicted gunshot wound. CAT results reveal the areas of brain injury following the bullet trajectory (fig. 4.31). The patient shot himself in the left temporal region, and the bullet destroyed much of the left temporal lobe. The bullet passed posteriorly in an oblique fashion and terminated in the right parietal-occipital area. Neuropsychological studies revealed visual field defects (right hemianopia, left quadrantanopia) consistent with bilateral damage to the visual projection system as well as marked residual dysphasia and memory disturbance. (Note CAT scan is in radiologic right-left, with the left side depicted on the right.)

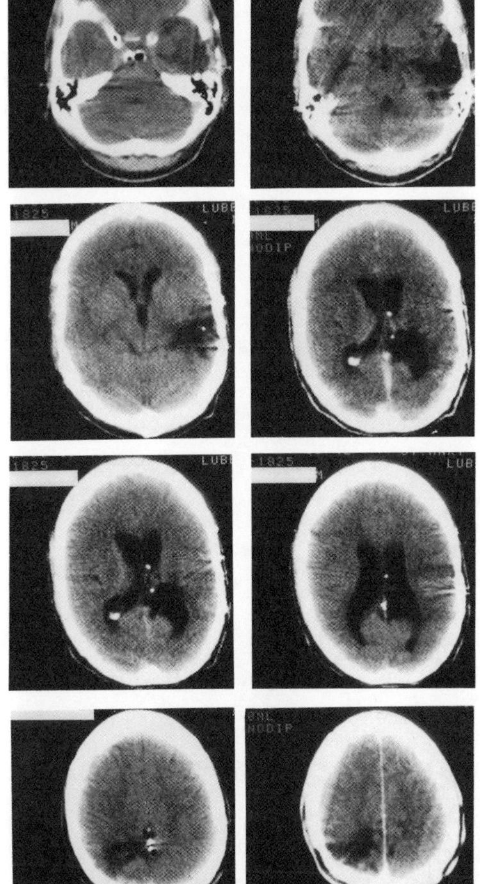

Fig. 4.31. Case 6.

Age 27
Sex M
Education 16

Lateral Dominance Exam

	Eye	Hand	Foot
Right	___	X	X
Left	X	___	___
Mixed	___	___	___

Motor Examination:
FOD 37 SOGD 43 TPTD 13.1 Mild ataxia
FOND 40 SOGND 50 TPTND 8.0
TPT Both 7.9

Sensory Examination:
Hemianopsia, quadrantanopsia, right side extinction, right side dysgraphesthesia and dysstereognosis

Aphasia Examination:
Conversational Speech: Mild dysarthria
Comprehension: Impaired
Repetition of Spoken Language: Mildly impaired
Confrontation - Naming: Dysnomic
Reading:
Aloud: Dyslexic
Comprehension: Impaired
Writing: Dysgraphic
Calculations: Impaired

SSRT 15 errors
SSPT 24 errors

Memory Examination:
Marked memory disturbance in all modalities
WMS MQ = <48, LM 2, Digits 8, VM 1, PA 1 / TPTM 4, TPTL 1

Intellectual/Cognitive Examination:
WAIS Results: VIQ = 66, PIQ = 52, FSIQ = 58
I 2, C 4, A 2, S 8, DS 6, V 4, DS 0, PC 5, BD 0, PA 6, OA 2

Category Test: 124 errors Trail Making Test: A DC B DC

Case 7. This 23-year-old man sustained closed head injury two years before the neuropsychological examination. He lost control of his sports car while traveling 60 mph and struck a large oak tree. Note the widespread structural damage indicated in CAT scan results (fig. 4.32)—focal infarction in the left frontal and occipital regions, generalized ventricular enlargement, signs of atrophy, and spotty areas of encephalomalacia. Neuropsychological exam reveals generalized impairment on essentially all measures, but with evidence of greater left hemisphere damage.

Age 23
Sex M
Education 14

Lateral Dominance Exam

	Eye	Hand	Foot
Right	X	X	X
Left			
Mixed			

Motor Examination:

FOD 39 SOGD 19
FOND 32 SOGND 17

TPTD 5.8 Moderate spastic paraplegia, bilateral
TPTND 11.9 Upper extremities spasticity associated with
TPT Both 6.2 marked deficit in integrative/alternating movements.

Sensory Examination:

Dense right hemianopsia, mild right side dysgraphesthesia

Aphasia Examination:

Conversational Speech: Dysarthric
Comprehension: Generally intact
Repetition of Spoken Language: Intact
Confrontation-Naming: Minor naming difficulties
Reading:
Aloud: Minor errors, possibly related to visual field defect
Comprehension: Minor errors of content present
Writing: Spasticity interferes but oral spellings is WNL
Calculations: Mildly impaired

Memory Examination:

Impaired memory in essentially all areas
WMS MQ = 59, LM 4, Digits 9, VM 6, AL 3/TPTM 4, TPTL 0

Intellectual/Cognitive Examination:

WAIS Results: VIQ = 93, PIQ = 90, FSIQ = 91
I 7, C 10, A 8, S 8, D 9, V 10, DS 10, PC 9, BD 9, PA 6, OA 9

Category Test 137 errors Trail Making Test: A 43 sec. B 183 sec.

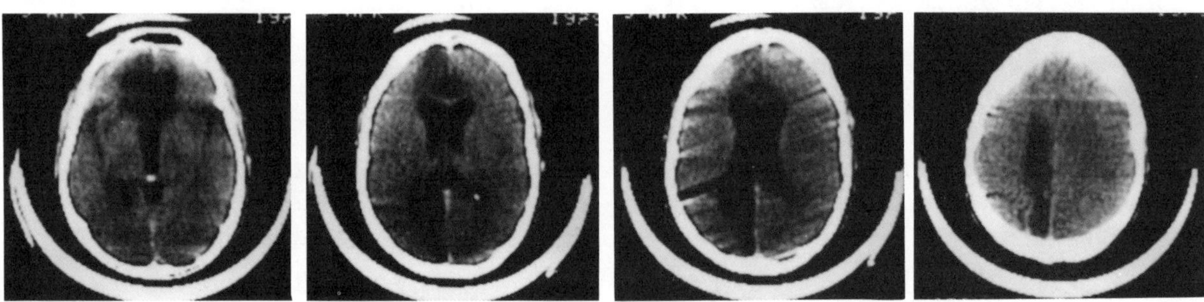

Fig. 4.32. Case 7.

Case 8. This 14-year-old girl sustained severe closed head injury in an auto-pedestrian accident. She was comatose for seven days. CAT scan originally showed small hemorrhage in the right internal capsular area, but this was resolved by six weeks. Neuropsychological testing demonstrates the importance of serial testing of patients with head trauma. When examined at six weeks posttrauma, the patient displayed left-side weakness and diminished coordination, left-side somatosensory processing deficit, constructional dyspraxia, and a variety of other cognitive deficits. However, by four months posttrauma, recovery is generally complete, although some residual signs of motor disturbance remain.

Age 14
Sex F
Education __

Lateral Dominance Exam

	Eye	Hand	Foot
Right	___	___	___
Left	___	___	___
Mixed	___	___	___

6 weeks post trauma

Motor Examination:

FOD	30	SOGD	8	TPT 5 min DC
FOND	12	SOGND	0	TPTND 5 min DC
				TPT Both 5 min DC

Sensory Examination:
Left side finger and palm dysgraphesthesia, left side dysstereognosis

Language Examination:
No dysphasia signs
Moderate constructional dyspraxia
WRAT Results
Reading 10.9
Spelling 9.9
Arithmetic 5.3
Speach Sounds Perception 1 error
Seashore rhythm 2 errors

Memory Examination:
WMS MQ = 94
LM 6, Digits 12, VM 11, AL 13.5

Intellectual/Cognitive Examination
WISC-R Results
VIQ = 97, PIQ = 65, FSIQ = 80
I 11, C 7, A 10, S 9, DS 11, V 11
Cod 5, PC 2, BD 6, PA 6, OA 4

Category Test 68 errors
Trail Making Test: A 28.3 B 77.9

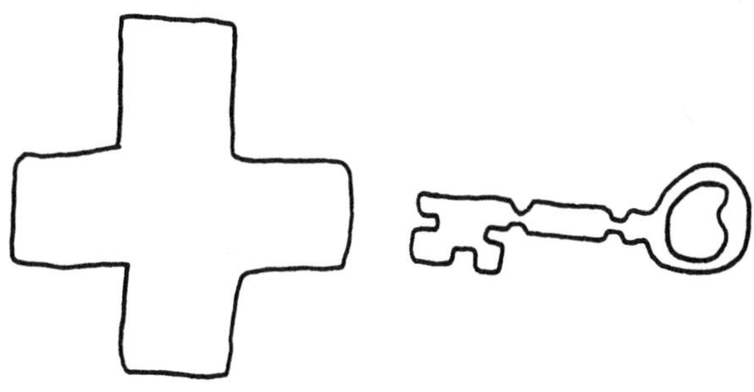

4 months post trauma

Motor examination (6 form board)

FOD 39	SOGD	23	TPTD	7.5
FOND 24	SOGND	21	TPTND	6.5
			TPT Both	2.3

Sensory Examination:
No errors.

Language Examination:
Normal
WRAT Results
Reading 10.4
Spelling 10.2
Arithmetic 7.2

Memory Examination
WMS MQ = 101

Intellectual/Cognitive Examination
VIQ = 112, PIQ = 101, FSIQ = 107
I 12, S 13, A 12, V 12, C 11, DS 11,
PC 11, PA 11, BD 12, OS 8, COD 9

Category Test: 12 errors
Trail Making Test: A 31 B 52

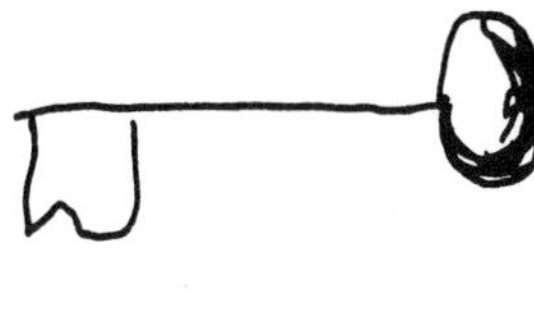

Case 9. This 12-year, 11-month-old girl sustained a severe closed head injury in a motor vehicle accident approximately one year prior to the evaluation. The CAT scan on top left (fig. 4.33) represents the CAT findings on admission to the hospital. Note that there is some reduction of the size and position of the right anterior horn. CAT scan 24 hours later shows significant cerebral edema with midline shift (top right CAT scan). The CAT scan on the bottom was taken 3 months postinjury and shows significant ventricular dilation, particularly in the right hemisphere. Premorbidly, the child was an above-average student. Neuropsychological test results indicate significant deficit in most areas of higher cognitive functioning with an overall reduction in level of ability. However, the child's achievement abilities in reading and spelling were preserved.

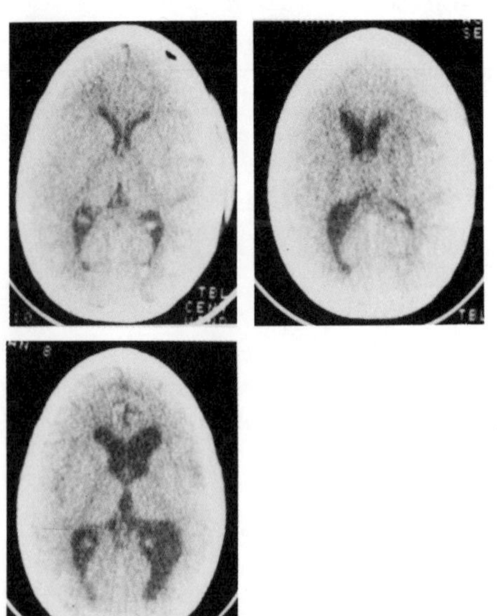

Fig. 4.33. Case 9.

Age 12 years 11 months
Sex F
Education 7th grade

Lateral Dominance Exam

	Eye	Hand	Foot
Right			
Left	X	X	X
Mixed			

Motor Examination

FOD	35	SOGD	19
FOND	29	SOGND	16

(6 form board)

TPTD	6.9
TPTND	5.4
TPT Both	4.9

Sensory Examination
Left side tactile and visual extinction.
Left side finger dysgraphesthesia.

Language Examination
Conversational speech: Dysprosodic, dysarthric
Comprehension: Generally intact
Repetition of spoken language: Generally intact
Confrontation - Naming: Dysnomia (inconsistent)
Reading: Intact
WRAT-R Results
Reading 6E 8.1
Spelling 6E 8.1
Boder: RQ = 108

Writing: WNL
Calculations: WRAT-R
Arithmetic 5.3

Memory Examination
WMS MQ = 89
LM 6, D 10, VM 10, AL 15.5

Intellectual Examination
WISC-R Results: VIQ = 91, PIQ = 86, FSIQ = 87
I 9, S 8, A 8, V 9, C 9, D (9), PC 7, PA 9, BD 10, OA 10, Cod 4

References

Adams, J. H., D. E. Mitchell, D. I. Graham, and D. Doyle. 1977. Diffuse brain damage of immediate impact type. *Brain* 100: 489–502.

Barclay, L., A. Zemcov, W. Richert, and J. P. Blass. 1985. Cerebral blood flow decrements in chronic head injury syndrome. *Biological Psychiatry* 20:146–157.

Barth, J. T., S. N. Macciocchi, B. Giordani, R. Rimel, J. A. Jane, and T. J. Boll. 1983. Neuropsychological sequelae of minor head injury. *Neurosurgery* 13:529–533.

Becker, D. P., R. G. Grossman, R. L. McLaurin, and W. F. Caveness. 1979. Head injuries. *Archives of Neurology* 36: 750–758.

Berger, M. S., L. H. Pitts, M. Lovely, M. S. B. Edwards and H. M. Bartkowski. 1985. Outcome from severe head injury in children and adolescents. *Journal of Neurosurgery* 62:194–199.

Bigler, E. D. 1986. Forensic neuropsychology. In *Handbook of clinical and behavioral neuropsychology,* ed. D. Wedding, A. M. Horton, and J. Webster. New York: Springer.

Bigler, E. D., D. S. Steinman, and J. S. Newton. 1981. Clinical assessment of cognitive deficit in neurologic disorder. II, Cerebral trauma. *Clinical Neuropsychology* 3:13–18.

Black, P., R. H. Shepard, and A. E. Walker. 1975. Outcome of head trauma: Age and post-traumatic seizures. In *Outcome of severe damage to the central nervous system,* ed. R. Porter and D. Fitzsimmons. Ciba Foundation Symposium, 34. Amsterdam: Elsevier, Excerpta Medica.

Boll, T. J. 1982. Behavioral sequelae of head injury. In *Head Injuries,* ed. P. R. Cooper. New York: Williams & Wilkins.

Boll, T. J., and J. T. Barth. 1981. Neuropsychology of brain damage in children. In *Handbook of clinical neuropsychology,* ed. S. B. Filskov and T. J. Boll. New York: John Wiley & Sons.

Brink, J. D., A. L. Garrett, W. R. Hale, J. Woo-Sam, and V. L. Nickel. 1970. Recovery of motor and intellectual function in children sustaining severe injuries. *Developmental Medicine & Child Neurology* 12:565–571.

Casson, I. R., O. Siegel, R. Sham, E. A. Campbell, M. Tarlau, and A. DiDomenico. 1984. Brain damage in modern boxers. *Journal of the American Medical Association* 251: 2663–2667.

Corkin, S., E. V. Sullivan, and F. A. Carr. 1984. Prognostic factors for life expectancy after penetrating head injury. *Archives of Neurology* 41:975–977.

Coxe, W. S., and R. L. Grubb. 1978. Central nervous system trauma: Cranial. In *Neurological pathophysiology*, ed. S. G. Eliasson, A. L. Prensky, and W. B. Hardin. 2d ed. New York: Oxford University Press.

Cullum, C. M., and E. D. Bigler. 1985. Late effects of hematoma on brain morphology and memory in closed head injury. *International Journal of Neuroscience* 28:279–283.

———. 1986. Ventricle size, cortical atrophy, and the relationship with neuropsychological status in closed head injury. *Journal of Clinical and Experimental Neuropsychology*. 8: 437–452.

Dennis, M. 1985*a*. Intelligence after early brain injury. I, Predicting IQ scores from medical variables. *Journal of Clinical and Experimental Neuropsychology* 7:526–554.

———. 1985*b*. Intelligence after early brain injury. II, IQ scores of subjects classified on the basis of medical history variables. *Journal of Clinical and Experimental Neuropsychology* 7: 555–576.

Dikmen, S., C. G. Matthews, and J. P. Harley. 1975. The effects of early versus late onset of major motor epilepsy upon cognitive-intellectual performances. *Epilepsia* 16:73–81.

Dikmen, S., and R. M. Reitan. 1974*a*. MMPI correlates of dysphasic language disturbances. *Journal of Abnormal Psychology* 83:675–679.

———. 1974*b*. MMPI correlates of localized structural cerebral lesions. *Perceptual & Motor Skills* 39:831–840.

———. 1977*a*. Emotional sequelae of head injury. *Annals of Neurology* 2:492–494.

———. 1977*b*. MMPI correlates of adaptive ability in patients with brain lesions. *Journal of Nervous & Mental Disease* 165:247–254.

Dikmen, S., R. M. Reitan, and N. R. Temkin. 1983. Neuropsychological recovery in head injury. *Archives of Neurology* 40:333–338.

Doty, R. L., P. Shaman, and M. Dann. 1984. Development of the University of Pennsylvania Smell Identification Test: A standardized microencapsulated test of olfactory function. *Physiology & Behavior* 32:489–502.

Drew, R. H., D. I. Templer, B. A. Schuyler, T. G. Newell, and G. Cannon. 1986. Neuropsychological deficits in active licensed professional boxers. *Journal of Clinical Psychology* 42:520–525.

Drudge, O. W., J. M. Williams, M. Kessler, and F. B. Gomes. 1984. Recovery from severe closed head injuries: Repeat testings with the Halsted-Reitan Neuropsychological Battery. *Journal of Clinical Psychology* 40:259–265.

Ewing, R., D. McCarthy, D. Gronwall, and P. Wrightson. 1980. Persisting effects of minor head injury observable during hypoxic stress. *Journal of Clinical Neuropsychology* 2: 667–668.

Finger, S., 1978. *Recovery from brain damage*. New York: Plenum Press.

Fisher, C. M. 1982. Whiplash amnesia. *Neurology* 32:667–668.

Fishman, M. A. 1978. Hydrocephalus. In *Neurology pathophysiology*, ed. S. G. Eliasson, A. L. Prensky, and W. B. Hardin. 2d ed. New York: Oxford University Press.

Giulian, D., and L. B. Lachman. 1985. Interleukin-1 stimulation of astroglial proliferation after brain injury. *Science* 228: 497–499.

Goebel, R. A. 1983. Detection of faking on the Halstead-Reitan Neuropsychological Test Battery. *Journal of Clinical Psychology* 39:731–742.

Goldstein, K. H. 1942. *After-effects of brain injuries in war.* New York: Grune & Stratton.

Goldstein, L. H., and D. A. Oakley. 1985. Expected and actual behavioural capacity after diffuse reduction in cerebral cortex: A review and suggestions for rehabilitative techniques with the mentally handicapped and head injured. *British Journal of Clinical Psychology* 24:13–24.

Gronwall, D., and P. Wrightson. 1974. Delayed recovery of intellectual function after minor head injury. *Lancet* 2:605–609.

———. 1975. Cumulative effects of concussion. *Lancet* 2: 995–997.

Gulbrandsen, G. B. 1984. Neuropsychological sequelae of light head injuries in older children 6 months after trauma. *Journal of Clinical Neuropsychology* 6:257–268.

Gurdjian, E. S. 1975. *Impact head injury.* Springfield, IL: Charles C. Thomas.

Heiskanen, O., and M. Kaste. 1974. Late prognosis of severe brain injury in children. *Developmental Medicine & Child Neurology* 16:11–14.

Incagnoli, T., and B. Newman. 1985. Cognitive and behavioral rehabilitation interventions. *International Journal of Clinical Neuropsychology* 7:173–182.

Jacobson, S. A. 1969. Mechanisms of the sequelae of minor craniocervical trauma. In *Late effects of head injury*, ed. A. E. Walker, W. F. Caveness, and M. Critchley. Springfield, IL: Charles C. Thomas.

Jennett, B., and M. Bond. 1975. Assessment of outcome after severe brain damage. *Lancet* 1:480–487.

Jennett, B., and G. Teasdale. 1981. *Management of head injuries.* Philadelphia: F. A. Davis.

Kirkpatrick, J. B., and V. DiMaio. 1978. Civilian gunshot wounds of the brain. *Journal of Neurosurgery* 49:185–198.

Klonoff, H., M. D. Law, and C. Clark. 1977. Head injuries in children: A prospective five year follow-up. *Journal of Neurology, Neurosurgery, and Psychiatry* 40:1211–1219.

Kwentus, J. A., R. P. Hart, E. T. Peck, and S. Kornstein. 1985. Psychiatric complications of closed head trauma. *Psychosomatics* 26:8–17.

Lampert, P. W., and J. M. Hardman. 1984. Morphological changes in brains of boxers. *Journal of the American Medical Association* 251:2676–2683.

Levin, H. S., A. L. Benton, and R. G. Grossman. 1982. *Neurobehavioral consequences of closed head injury*. New York: Oxford University Press.

Levin, H. S., and H. M. Eisenberg. 1979. Neuropsychological outcome of closed head injury in children and adolescents. *Child's Brain* 5:281–292.

Levin, H. S., and R. G. Grossman. 1978. Behavioral sequelae of closed head injury. *Archives of Neurology* 35:720–727.

Levin, H. S., R. G. Grossman, J. E. Rose, and G. Teasdale. 1979. Long-term neuropsychological outcome of closed head injury. *Journal of Neurosurgery* 50:412–422.

Levin, H. S., S. F. Handel, A. M. Goldman, H. M. Eisenberg, and F. C. Guinto, Jr. 1985. Magnetic resonance imaging after "diffuse" nonmissile head injury. *Archives of Neurology* 42: 963–968.

Levin, H. S., W. M. High, and H. M. Eisenberg. 1985. Impairment of olfactory recognition after closed head injury. *Brain* 105: 579–591.

Levin, H. S., Z. Kalisky, S. F. Handel, A. M. Goldman, H. M. Eisenberg, D. Morrison, and A. Von Laufen. 1985. Magnetic resonance imaging in relation to the sequelae and rehabilitation of diffuse closed head injury: Preliminary findings. *Seminars in Neurology* 5:221–232.

Levin, H. S., C. A. Meyers, R. G. Grossman, and M. Sarwar. 1981. Ventricular enlargement after closed head injury. *Archives of Neurology* 38:623–629.

Lewis, A. J. 1976. *Mechanisms of neurological disease*. Boston: Little, Brown & Co.

Lezak, M. D. 1978. Living with the characterologically altered brain-injured patient. *Journal of Clinical Psychiatry* 39: 592–600.

Livingston, M. G., D. N. Brooks, and M. R. Bond. 1985*a*. Three months after severe head injury: Psychiatric and social impact on relatives. *Journal of Neurology, Neurosurgery, and Psychiatry* 48:870–875.

———. 1985*b*. Patient outcome in the year following severe head injury and relatives' psychiatric and social functioning. *Journal of Neurology, Neurosurgery, and Psychiatry* 48: 876–881.

McClean, A., Jr., N. R. Temkin, S. Dikmen, and A. R. Wyler. 1983. The behavioral sequelae of head injury. *Journal of Clinical Neuropsychology* 5:361–376.

Miller, H. 1961. Accident neurosis. *British Medical Journal* 1:919–925.

Mohnot, D., C. Snead, and J. W. Benton. 1982. Burn encephalopathy in children. *Annals of Neurology* 12:42–47.

Newcombe, F., and G. Ratcliff. 1979. Long-term psychological consequences of cerebral lesions. In *Handbook of behavioral neurobiology. Vol. 2, Neuropsychology*, ed. M. S. Gazzaniga. New York: Plenum Press.

Payne, E. E. 1969. *An atlas of pathology of the brain*. East Hanover, NJ: Sandoz Pharmaceuticals.

Prigatano, G. P. 1986. *Neuropsychological rehabilitation after brain injury*. Baltimore: Johns Hopkins University Press.

Rao, S. M., and L. A. Bieliauskas. 1983. Cognitive rehabilitation two and one-half years post right temporal lobectomy. *Journal of Clinical Neuropsychology* 5:313–320.

Repko, G. R., and R. Cooper. 1985. A study of the average worker's compensation case. *Journal of Clinical Psychology* 41:867–881.

Rimel, R. W., B. Giordani, J. T. Barth, T. J. Boll, and J. A. Jane. 1981. Disability caused by minor head injury. *Neurosurgery* 9:221–228.

Russell, E. W., C. Neuringer, and G. Goldstein. 1970. *Assessment of brain damage*. New York: Wiley-Interscience.

Rutherford, W. H., J. D. Marrett, and J. R. McDonald. 1977. Sequelae of concussion caused by minor head injury. *Lancet* 1:1–4.

St. James-Roberts, I. 1979. Neurological plasticity, recovery from brain insult, and child development. In *Advances in child development*. Vol. 14. New York: Academic Press.

Sbordone, R. J. 1984. Rehabilitative neuropsychological approach for severe traumatic brain-injured patients. *Professional Psychology: Research and Practice* 15:165–175.

Siesjo, B. K. 1978. *Brain energy metabolism*. New York: John Wiley & Sons.

Smith, R. M., F. R. J. Fields, J. L. Lenox, H. O. Morris, and J. J. Nolan. 1979. A functional scale of recovery from severe head trauma. *Clinical Neuropsychology* 1:48–50.

Stuss, D. T., P. Ely, H. Hugenholtz, M. T. Richard, S. LaRochelle, C. A. Poirier, and I. Bell. 1985. Subtle neuropsychological deficits in patients with good recovery after closed head injury. *Neurosurgery* 17:41–47.

Sunderland, A., J. E. Harris, and J. Gleave. 1984. Memory failures in everyday life following severe head injury. *Journal of Clinical Neuropsychology* 6:127–142.

Van Zomeren, A. H., and W. Van Den Burg. 1985. Residual complaints of patients two years after severe head injury. *Journal of Neurology, Neurosurgery, and Psychiatry* 48:21–28.

Wells, C. E. 1977. *Dementia*. 2d ed. Philadelphia: F. A. Davis.

Winogron, H. W., R. M. Knights, and H. N. Bawden. 1984. Neuropsychological deficits following head injury in children. *Journal of Clinical Neuropsychology* 6:269–286.

Zander, E., and G. Foroglou. 1976. Post-traumatic hydrocephalus. In *Handbook of clinical neurology*, ed. P. J. Vinken and G. W. Bruyn. Vol. 24. Amsterdam: North Holland.

5. Degenerative Disorders Diffusely Affecting the Nervous System

Degenerative Diseases and Their Clinical Features

The term *degenerative disorder* denotes a progressive deterioration and loss of function in an individual who was previously functioning without deficit (Corkin et al., 1982; Hutton, 1986; Terry and Katzman, 1983). Degenerative disorders typically differ by the specificity of the loss of function, inasmuch as certain degenerative disorders only affect very specific brain nuclei, while others affect more diffusely the entire brain. Many of the degenerative disorders occur much more readily past the fifth decade of life (Joynt, 1981), and since the population of the elderly continues to expand, these disorders have become a more important facet of neuropsychological diagnosis. It is particularly important to be specific about the diagnosis of degenerative disorders. Patients with certain disorders, such as cerebrovascular or neoplastic disease, may present with symptoms similar to those of patients with degenerative disease. But whereas degenerative disorders are typically untreatable, cerebrovascular, neoplastic, and other related disorders may be treatable from the standpoint of halting progression. The following reviews the major degenerative disorders and the neuropsychological findings in such syndromes. Wells (1978) and Slaby and Wyatt (1974) treat the subject more comprehensively.

Alzheimer's Disease and Pick's Disease

Alzheimer's disease is a disorder that diffusely affects the cerebrum (Neary, Snowden, Mann, Bowen, et al., 1986), producing widespread atrophy as a by-product of cellular degeneration (see figs. 5.1–5.7). It is most commonly found in the fifth and sixth decades of life. Rocca, Amaducci, and Schoenberg (1986) place the annual incidence rate at 2.4 cases per 100,000 population between forty and sixty years of age and 127 cases per 100,000 after the age of sixty. The basic pathologic substrates are numerous plaques as well as neurofibrillary changes in the neuron (Cook, Ward, and Austin, 1979; Pro, Smith, and Sumi, 1980; Tomlinson, 1977). These are some of the same substrates seen with normal advanced aging (Haase, 1977), and therefore Alzheimer's has been thought of as a severe or speeded up form of aging. However, these changes have been interpreted by Adams and Victor (1977) as evidence that aging may simply render the individual more vulnerable to the process of Alzheimer's disease. The senile plaques contain a tightly knit core (amyloid) surrounded by products of degenerated nerve cells and nerve terminals, mainly dendritic, along with the neurofibrillary tangles, which are twisted cellular tubules (Buell and Coleman, 1979; Lewis, 1976). These neurofibrillary changes are also seen in dementia pugilistica (boxer's encephalopathy) and in patients with Down's syndrome, particularly those past the age of thirty (Lewis, 1978). The relationship between such neuropathologic findings in these disorders and Alzheimer's disease is not understood at this time. There is some evidence to suggest genetic transmissibility in the occurrence of certain Alzheimer's disease cases (Masters, Gajdusek, and Gibbs, 1981), but this genetic link only accounts for a small percentage of cases.

Recently, studies (Appel, 1981, 1982; DeKosky, Scheff, and Markesbery, 1985; Fishman et al., 1986; McGeer et al., 1984; Ulrich, 1985) have demonstrated that cholinergic input to the cerebral cortex is impaired in Alzheimer's disease. Specifically, there may be degenerative changes in the nucleus basalis of Meynert, a nucleus located just ventral to the globus pallidus. This is an important finding because the nucleus basalis of Meynert supplies cholinergic input to both the hippocampus and the cerebral cortex. Thus, the impaired cholinergic functioning may affect general cognitive operations of the cerebral cortex and specific memory operations of the hippocampus. Another recent study (Bondareff, Mountjoy, and Roth, 1982) has demonstrated in a variant of the senile dementia of Alzheimer's type a characteristic loss or degeneration of noradrenergic neurons of the brain stem nucleus locus ceruleus. Volicer et al. (1985) also have demonstrated serotonergic abnormalities in Alzheimer's disease. Brun and Englund (1986) have shown white matter degenerative changes in Alzheimer's disease that may be independent on the well-documented gray matter changes. This recent work appears promising in terms of delimiting possible neurotransmitter and neuronal system degeneration in Alzheimer's disease.

It should be noted that, even though there is clear evidence of cholinergic system deterioration in Alzheimer's disease, pharmacologic manipulation of the cholinergic system to increase acetylcholine levels has met with only equivocal effects in improving memory (Wettstein, 1983).

Pick's disease (lobular sclerosis) is pathologically distinct but not necessarily clinically distinct from Alzheimer's. Whereas Alzheimer's tends to be more diffuse in the distribution of atrophy, Pick's tends to more greatly affect the temporal or frontal lobes (see figs. 5.8 and 5.9) and also may more greatly affect one hemisphere (Lewis, 1978). The most salient histologic findings are loss of ganglion cells in cortex. The neurons that do remain in these areas of focal atrophy are commonly engorged, containing argentophilic (Pick) bodies within the cytoplasm. Astrocytic gliosis is also usually present. The senile plaques and

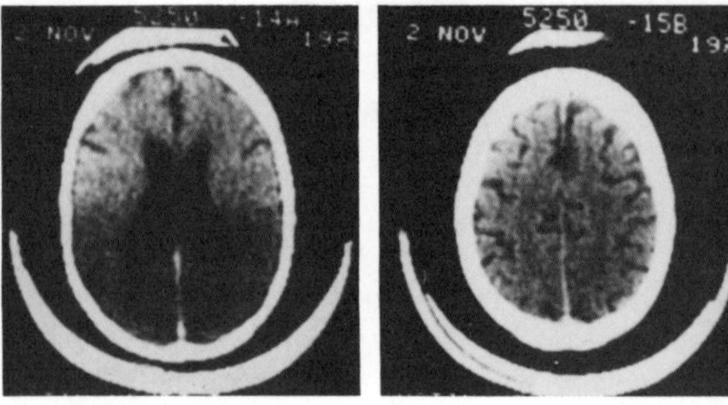

Fig 5.1. CAT scan of 59-year-old man with Alzheimer's disease. Note the ventricular enlargement and presence of generalized cortical atrophy.

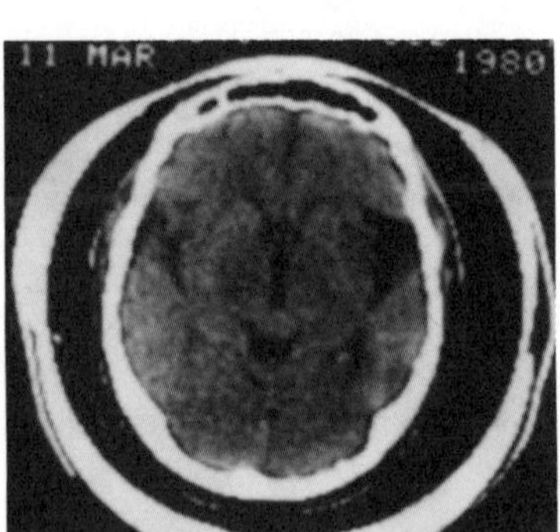

Fig. 5.2. CAT scan of 62-year-old man with Alzheimer's disease. Note the prominence of the sylvian fissures, particularly on the right. This connotes frontal-temporal atrophy.

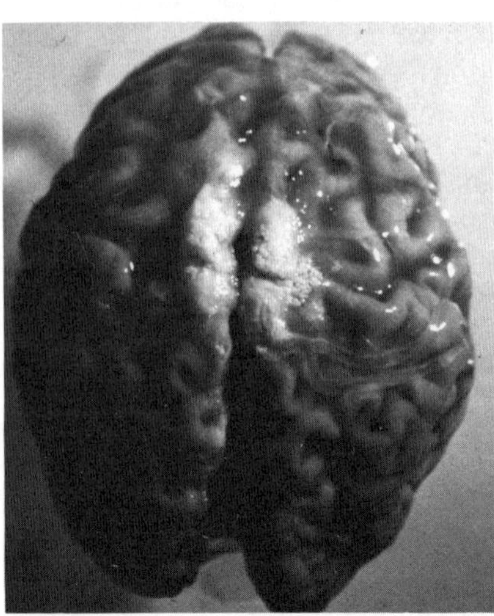

Fig. 5.3. Postmortem specimen from patient with Alzheimer's disease. Note the generalized atrophy.

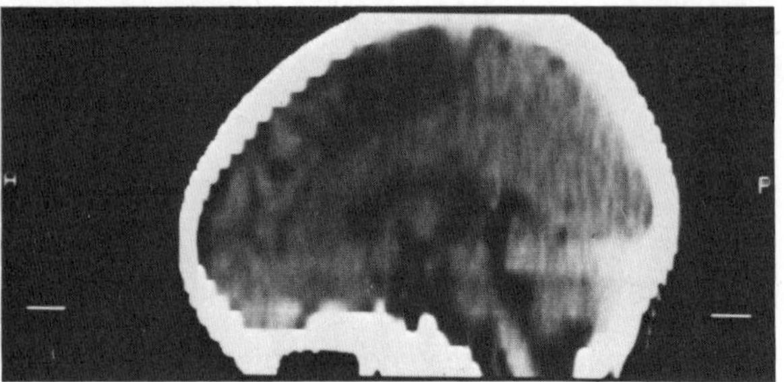

Fig. 5.4. Sagittal CAT scan of left hemisphere revealing deep cortical atrophy. The sagittal section is taken slightly left of midline as depicted by the dotted lines through the horizontal view in figure 5.5.

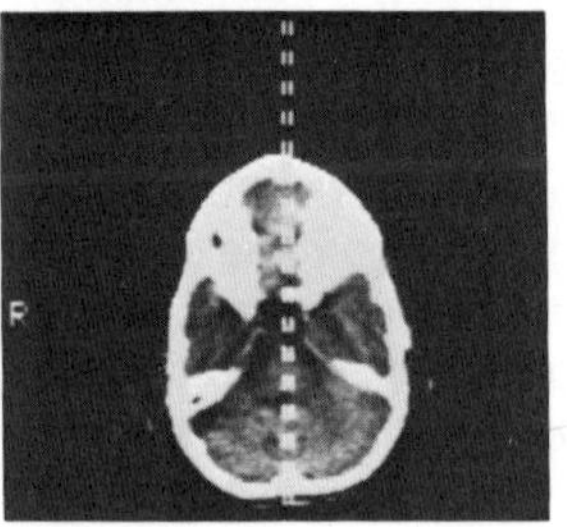

Fig. 5.5. Horizontal view of CAT scan in figure 5.4. Dotted lines indicate area of sagittal view (*left and right reversed*).

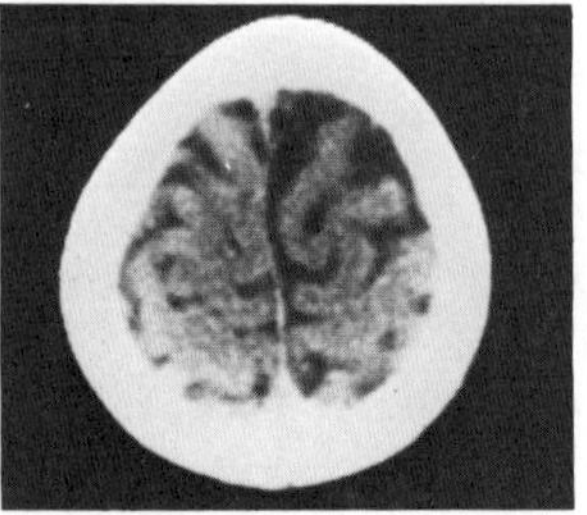

Fig. 5.6. Cortical atrophy. CAT film was taken near vertex and reveals marked cortical atrophy, greater in left hemisphere (*left and right reversed*). (Figs. 5.4–5.6 are scans of a three-year-old who suffered severe anoxia at birth and are presented to demonstrate the appearance of atrophy on CAT scanning.)

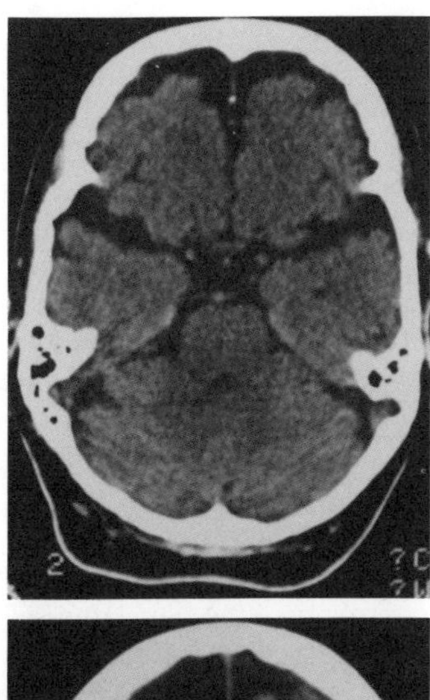

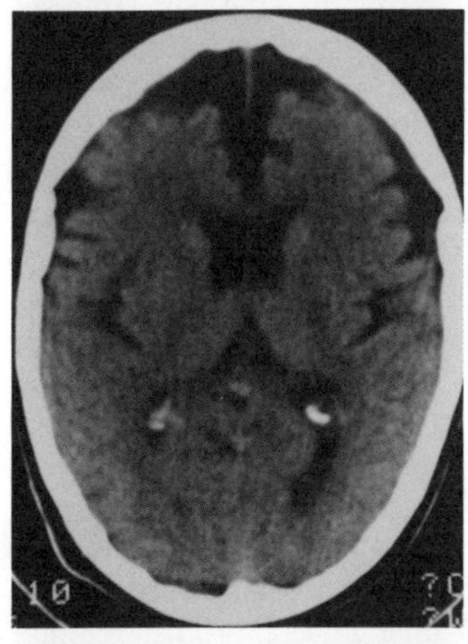

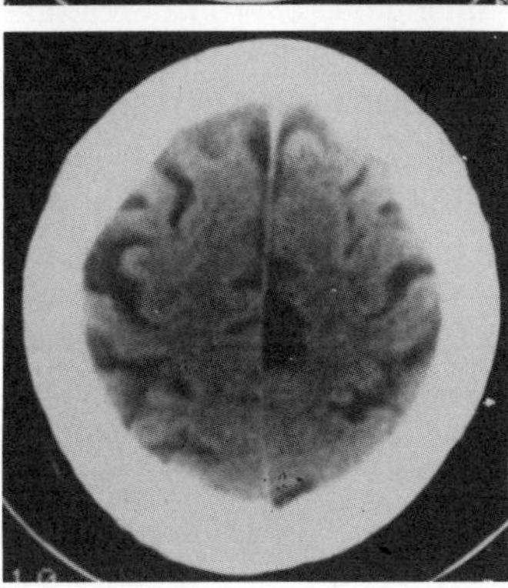

Fig. 5.7. Severe cortical atrophy in a patient with advanced Alzheimer's disease. Note the reduction in the size of the frontal and temporal regions.

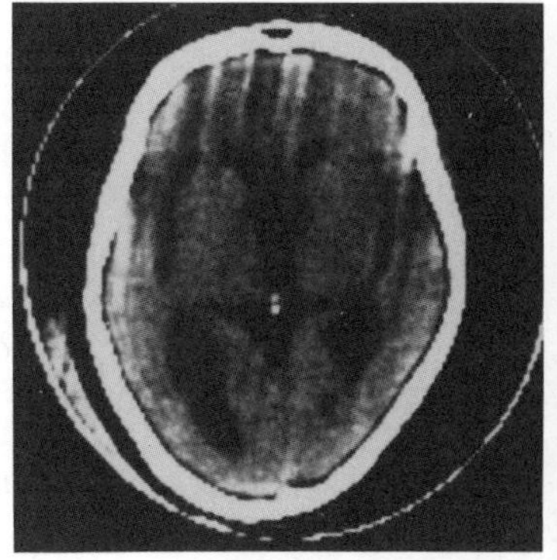

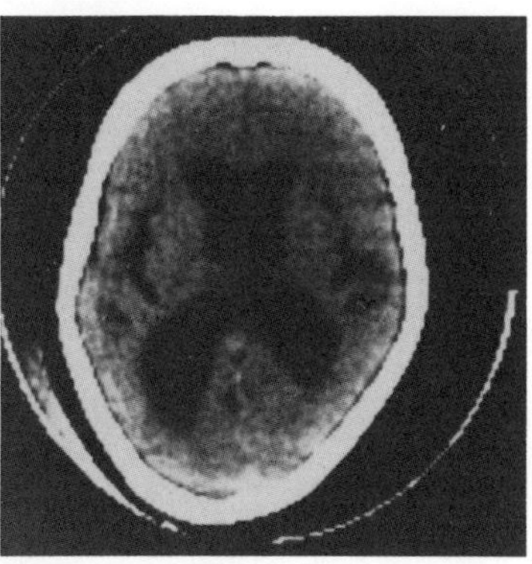

Fig. 5.8. Pick's disease. CAT scans of a 49-year-old woman with Pick's disease. Note the marked frontal and temporal lobe atrophy indicated by the severe widening of the sylvian fissure. There is also generalized ventricular enlargement.

neurofibrillary changes as seen in Alzheimer's disease may also be present, as well as cholinergic abnormalities (Uhl et al., 1983). Pick's disease is less common than Alzheimer's. (See figure 5.10 to compare atrophy related to neurosyphilis.)

Strub and Black (1981) outline at least four behavioral stages observed with Alzheimer's disease. The initial stage is typically characterized by failing abilities at work and increased forgetfulness. There may be changes in affect—depression, anxiety, restlessness, mild agitation. Deficits in judgment and comprehension of complex material are present. Neuropsychologic evaluation at this point will usually reflect borderline to mild decline in Wechsler Adult Intelligence IQ scores from presumed premorbid level of functioning, memory quotient may be particularly affected, and frequently the patient will display significant deficits in complex graphomotor tasks.

In the second stage, the cognitive deficits become more demonstrable and include pathognomonic signs of dysphasia and dyspraxia. The onset of corphologia (persistent hand movements mimicking picking movements, sometimes appearing as if patients were picking imaginary bits of lint off their clothing) may occur during this phase. Impaired mentation also occurs in the form of perseverative and tangential thinking.

The third stage displays further deterioration in essentially all higher levels of function. Aphasic speech may become prominent. Emery and Emery (1983) have demonstrated numerous language decrements in Alzheimer's disease patients, with increasing deficits directly related to the complexity of the language task. Likewise, Cummings and Benson (1983) contend that all Alzheimer's patients will display dysphasic symptoms. Similarly, apraxic disturbance increases, and the patient may develop severe visual agnosia, which compounds the apraxic disturbance (apractagnosia). Primitive reflexes become more prominent. Emotional features may be present, a result of the

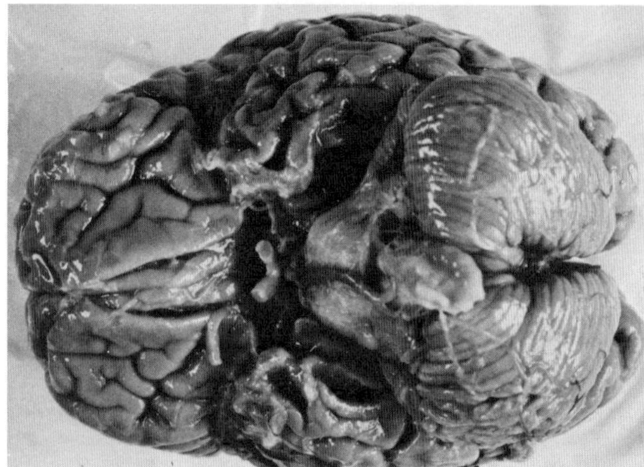

Fig. 5.9. Pick's lobular sclerosis. Note the prominent bilateral atrophy of the temporal lobes.

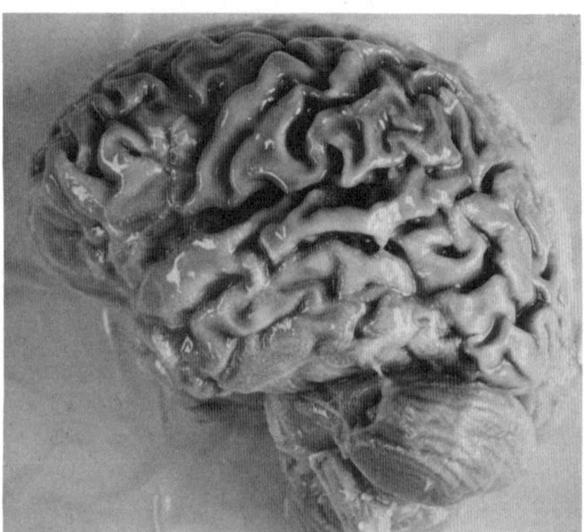

Fig. 5.10. General paresis. Note the dramatic generalized atrophy characteristic of neurosyphilis.

last vestiges of perception about their decline, loss of cortical control over emotional affect, development of pseudobulbar state, or any of these in combination. At this point an organic psychosis may evolve.

The fourth, or terminal phase, is associated with the final stages of the dementing process. There is essentially complete cessation of higher cognitive control and the aphasic, apraxic, and agnosic deficits become complete. In essence, the patient displays a state of decortication. Limb contractures ensue, and eventually whole-body contractures develop. The patient finally assumes a fetal position. At this point, death occurs secondary to pneumonia, aspiration, or other infection.

Pick's disease may follow a somewhat similar pattern, but frequently there are more noticeable changes in personality. Thus, the patient with Pick's disease may display distinct changes in social appropriateness, inappropriate jocularity, and diminished personal hygiene, grooming, and dress. The patient with Alzheimer's disease may display substantial deficits in cognitive abilities prior to the social decline and change in personal care.

Recent research has suggested that there may be some relationship between prior history of head injury and Alzheimer's disease (Rocca, Amaducci, and Schoenberg, 1986). It has long been known that in boxer's encephalopathy (i.e., dementia pugilistica) there are neuropathological changes similar to Alzheimer's disease (Terry and Katzman, 1983).

Huntington's Chorea

In Huntington's chorea the focus of atrophy may first result in wasting of the head of the caudate nucleus as well as other degenerative changes throughout the basal ganglia (see fig. 5.11). Cortical atrophy particularly in the frontal and temporal lobes also develops as the disease progresses (see figs. 5.11 and 5.12). (See fig. 5.13 for comparison of normal brain and one with "normal" atrophy.) Glial proliferation may also develop in the affected basal ganglia structures (Lewis, 1978).

Mann et al. (1981) have demonstrated selective aminergic neuronal changes in the basal ganglia of the brains of patients with Huntington's disease. Their research also implicates a relationship between aminergic (norepinephrine) alteration and the expression of the attending mental symptoms in Huntington's disease. Although Huntington's disease typically occurs after the third decade of life, it is sometimes found in juveniles (Goebel et al., 1978).

The hallmark features of Huntington's chorea are mental and intellectual deterioration in association with chorea. Emotionally, during early stages of the disease (and especially if mental symptoms predate the onset of definitive chorea), the patient may be diagnosed as having a major affective or thought disorder. Patients may also show many of the characteristic behavioral changes seen with Pick's disease, yet they do not display the dysphasic, dysgnostic, and dyspraxic deficits seen with advancing Pick's or Alzheimer's disease. They do display a rather uniform lowering of performance on most neuropsychological measures (Boll, Heaton, and Reitan, 1974; Norton, 1975) along with substantial deficits in memory (Weingartner, Caine, and Ebert, 1979). Although differentiation may be somewhat difficult in early phases of the disease (Klawans, Goetz, and Perlik, 1980), the characteristic chorea and mental deterioration develop in all cases. Josiassen, Curry, and Mancall (1983) demonstrated that the cognitive deficits in Huntington's chorea progress at an uneven rate. Deficits in cognitive flexibility occurred in later stages, while visuospatial and auditory memory deficits were the very earliest abnormal neuropsychological findings. Hayward, Zubrick, and Hall (1985) have also demonstrated sensory-perceptual deficits early in the course of Huntington's chorea.

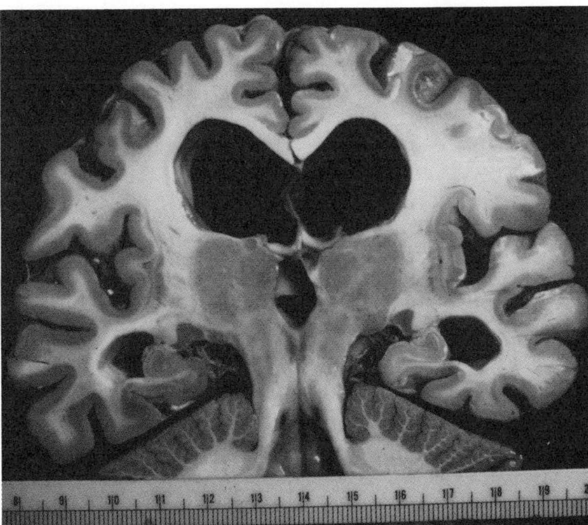

Fig. 5.11. Huntington's chorea. Thin coronal section of the cerebrum shows cortical atrophy and a large ventricular system. There is atrophy of the basal ganglia and especially of the caudate nuclei.

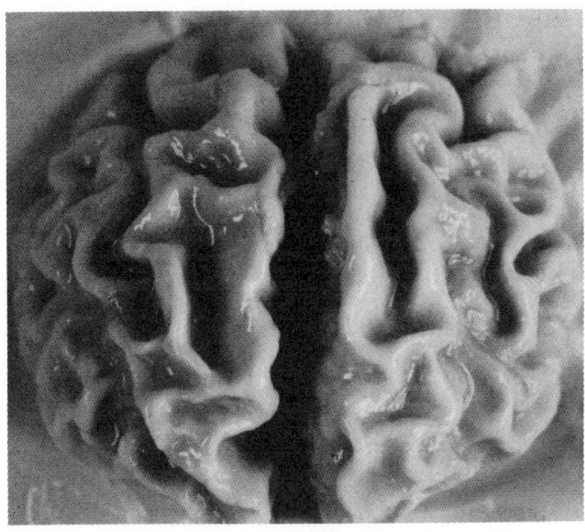

A

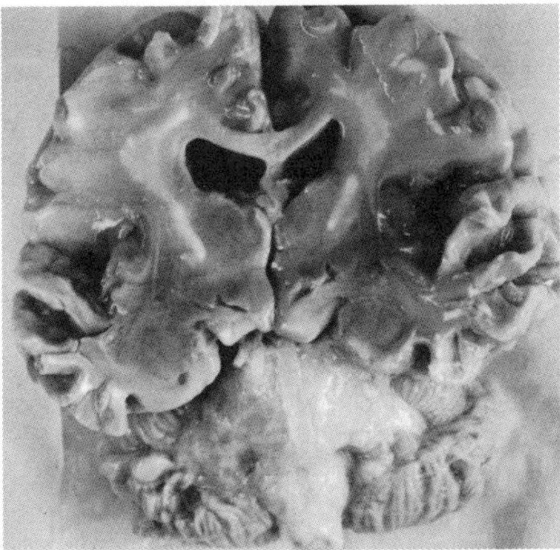

B

Fig. 5.12. Advanced Huntington's chorea. *A*, this picture depicts severe frontal pole atrophy. *B*, a coronal section demonstrating generalized atrophic changes.

Spinocerebellar Degenerations

Spinocerebellar degenerations are typically hereditary diseases that may result from either a dominant or recessive inheritance pattern (Collins et al., 1979; Haase, 1977). Friedreich's ataxia is a form of the recessive variety, typically involving corticospinal and spinocerebellar tracts. The dominant familial spinal cerebellar atrophies typically present with gradual progression first affecting balance and coordination and then speech and swallowing. There is potential for cerebral involvement. Early in the course of these disorders, cognitive deficits may be absent; however, as the disorder progresses, disturbances in higher cognitive functions may also occur.

Other Presenile Disorders

Several accounts of patients with various degenerative changes that do not appear to be caused by Alzheimer's, Pick's, or Huntington's disease but nonetheless fit the clinical pattern of deterioration have been reported (cited in Haase, 1977; see also Hudson, 1981; Kim et al., 1981). Falling into this category is the parkinsonism-dementia complex of Guam (Rodgers-Johnson et al., 1986), a disorder that has been found in an indigenous population of Guam. In this disorder, parkinsonism features are present, but clear features of dementia and frequently amyotrophic lateral sclerosis (ALS) are also present, incorporating a triad—parkinsonism, dementia, and ALS. Prominent frontal and temporal atrophy typically occurs.

Mesulam and colleagues (see Chawluk et al., 1986) have reported several cases of progressive aphasia without dementia. A distinction with these cases from Alzheimer's disease is that no other cognitive or higher cortical symptoms accompany the progression. The etiology of the disorder is unknown at this time. Bilateral medial temporal lobe ischemia may also produce a progressive dementia (Volpe and Petito, 1985).

Subcortical Dementia

Huntington's chorea, Parkinson's disease, and progressive supranuclear palsy represent dementing illnesses in which the locus of pathology is presumably subcortical rather than cortical, such as Alzheimer's disease. There is some evidence to suggest that these disorders can be differentiated from Alzheimer's disease and related cortical dementias by the absence of aphasic, amnesic, agnosic, and/or apraxic symptoms (Cummings and Benson, 1984; D'Antona et al., 1985; Huber and Paulson, 1985; Huber et al., 1986). However, Whitehouse (1986) argues that there is little clinical, neuropathological, or neurochemical support for such a distinction. With the ever increasing sophistication in brain imagery, this should help clarify this issue.

Clinical Features

Since these degenerative disorders will diffusely affect the nervous system, diverse effects on cognitive, sensory,

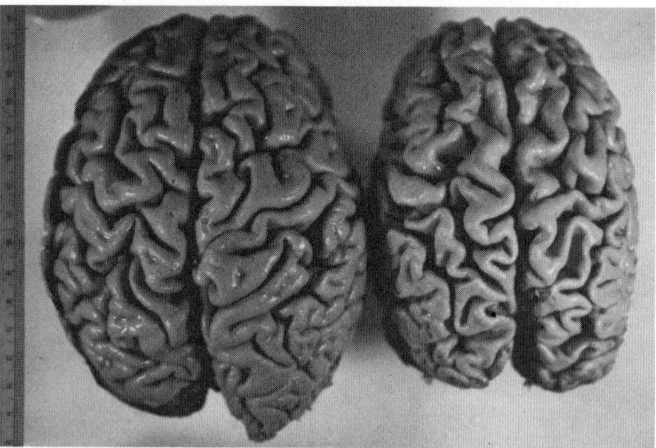

Fig. 5.13. Brain atrophy. The brain on the left is normal; the brain on the right shows atrophy with age. This is the "normal" atrophic process.

and motor function are commonplace. Thus, comprehensive neuropsychological evaluation is always recommended. Frequently, "crystallized" or well-established verbal functions (e.g., vocabulary) may be only minimally affected, but more "fluid" functions, such as recent memory or spatial-perceptual-motor functioning, may be severely impaired. Table 5.1 presents neuropsychologic test results of patients with degenerative disease and compares them with test scores of controls. As can be noted from inspecting this table, there is a rather uniform decline in most neuropsychologic functions without indication of focal or lateralized deficit. Such generalized decline in the absence of focal deficit is commonly the hallmark of degenerative disease (Caltagirone et al., 1979; Kaszniak et al., 1979). In addition to the generalized decline in neuropsychologic functioning, the patient with degenerative disease may display one or more of the various rudimentary or release reflexes (Gossman and Jacobs, 1980; Jacobs and Gossman, 1980; Liston, 1979*b*). Liston (1979*b*) has demonstrated that 59 percent of patients with degenerative disease will display one of the following primitive reflexes: snout, glabellar, palmomental, sucking, rooting, or grasp. The incidence of these reflexes in normal persons tends to range between 10 percent and 35 percent, steadily increasing with progression in age (Jacobs and Gossman, 1980). Thus, the combination of evidence of generalized impairment from most scores on neuropsychologic measures, presence of one or more of the primitive reflexes, and a clinical prodromal period of gradual decline suggests the presence of a degenerative disorder. It should be noted, however, that with Pick's disease, initial focal atrophy of the dominant hemisphere's frontal-temporal regions may produce what appears to be a focal aphasic disorder (Lewis, 1978). But, as the disease progresses, a rather uniform degenerative picture will eventually emerge (see Case 7).

Neuropsychological examination is particularly critical in the early detection and diagnosis of degenerative disorders, because such standardized tests as computerized axial tomography (CAT) brain scanning, electroencephalography, and regional cerebral blood flow measures may be insensitive or inaccurate (Bigler, Steinman, and Newton, 1981; Kaszniak et al., 1979; Liston, 1979*b*; O'Connor, Shaw, and Ongley, 1979; Wu et al., 1981; Yamaguchi et al., 1980). Neuropsychological studies of patients with verified degenerative disorders have demonstrated diagnosis accuracy rates in the 90 percent range (Caltagirone et al., 1979), but electroencephalography and CAT evaluations of patients with similar disorders may only accurately identify 50–70 percent (Liston, 1979*b*). Similarly, there may be little relationship between structural changes noted in CAT scan results and neuropsychological deficits (Bigler et al., 1985; Cutler et al., 1985; Turkheimer et al., 1984; Wu et al., 1981; also see fig. 5.14). Such comparisons underscore the importance of neuropsychological examination of patients who are suspected of having degenerative disorders. Table 5.2 reports data from a study of the effects of age on neuropsychological performance.

In terms of specific diagnosis of the degenerative disease process, Alzheimer's disease has the highest frequency (Wells, 1978). Table 5.3 summarizes the diagnoses in three reported series of 222 patients fully evaluated for dementia. If focal signs in addition to a degenerative picture emerge, it is likely that the patient has Pick's disease. (Although it should be fully determined that the focal signs are not secondary to a separate disease process, such as a cerebrovascular disease.) Choreiform movement disorder in association with generalized neuropsychologic impairment, particularly memory disturbance, is generally pathognomonic of Huntington's disease (Boll, Heaton, and Reitan, 1974; Butters et al., 1978; Caine, Ebert, and Weingartner, 1977). Parkinson's disorder may also take a degenerative course, in terms of generalized cognitive disturbance (Haase, 1977). Thus, the clinical picture of extrapyramidal involvement consistent with Parkinson's but with associated neuropsychologic impairment of generalized degree is suggestive of the subclass of Parkinson's disease with diffuse degeneration (Boller, 1980). Progressive idiopathic dementia presents like Alzheimer's disease (and, in fact, is probably in a subclass of it). Neuropsychological test results of patients with either disease are also similar (Weingartner et al., 1981). Although the absolute diagnosis of Alzheimer's disease, Pick's disease, and multi-infarct dementia is dependent upon postmortem confirmation, the study by Mölsä et al. (1985) has demonstrated good concordance between clinical diagnosis and clinicopathological findings.

With age, there may be some decline in a variety of neuropsychological processes (see table 5.2), but never to the degree seen with degenerative disease. For example, Jarvik, Ruth, and Matsuyama (1980) in a longitudinal investigation found that 84 percent of patients in their

Table 5.1. ***Effect of Disease on Neuropsychological Performance***

Variable	Degenerative Mean	Degenerative *SD*	Control Mean	Control *SD*	Significance
Age	66.2	9.0	59.6	7.1	*
Education	13.0	3.9	14.6	4.2	NS
WAIS scores					
Verbal IQ	92.1	20.9	123.5	10.3	***
Performance IQ	83.8	20.2	111.9	7.4	***
Full-Scale IQ	87.5	20.2	118.9	8.2	***
V—raw score	42.9	19.1	79.0	9.6	***
P—raw score	20.4	15.7	46.3	6.7	***
FS—raw score	62.8	31.3	124.7	13.2	***
Information	8.4	3.4	13.0	2.4	***
Comprehension	8.1	4.3	15.2	3.3	***
Arithmetic	6.4	3.7	13.3	2.6	***
Similarities	6.3	4.0	12.3	1.6	***
Digit Span	6.4	3.4	10.7	1.2	***
Vocabulary	8.4	3.9	14.7	2.8	***
Digit Symbol	2.8	3.2	7.7	1.7	***
Picture Completion	5.0	3.7	10.6	1.2	***
Block Design	4.3	4.2	9.6	1.5	***
Picture Arrangement	4.4	2.9	9.3	2.3	***
Object Assembly	4.5	3.2	9.4	1.5	***
WMS scores					
I	3.2	1.6	5.5	0.8	*
II	3.6	1.7	4.7	0.5	*
III	3.9	2.7	7.1	2.0	**
IV	4.2	3.5	10.3	3.3	***
V	8.3	2.4	11.3	1.3	*
VI	3.7	3.4	11.2	3.7	***
VII	7.2	5.3	14.3	4.7	***
Raw score	34.3	15.5	63.5	10.1	***
Memory quotient	79.1	20.2	121.9	16.9	***
Digits—Forward	5.3	1.5	6.5	0.9	*
Digits—Reverse	2.9	1.3	4.7	0.8	*
Confabulation	2.1	2.3	0.7	1.0	NS
Category Test					
Total errors	104.4	25.8	44.0	22.4	***
I	0.8	1.9	0.0	0.0	NS
II	4.9	5.2	6.0	0.5	NS
III	24.1	7.7	8.2	6.9	**
IV	27.8	9.6	11.6	6.8	**
V	21.3	7.9	12.2	7.4	NS
VI	19.5	9.4	8.2	6.4	*
VII	7.5	3.0	3.2	1.9	*
Preservation errors	11.1	5.9	2.5	1.7	*
Trail-Making Test					
A (in seconds)	84.2	49.5	43.5	11.9	***
B (in seconds)	258.6	153.8	93.0	26.6	***
B–A (in seconds)	176.8	112.4	49.5	22.8	***
Aphasia Screening					
Verbal	2.3	1.5	0.8	0.6	**
Spatial	3.1	1.4	1.2	0.9	***
Sensory Perceptual Exam					
Errors Right	5.6	5.8	1.0	2.8	*
Errors Left	4.7	4.6	1.4	2.1	*
Motor Exam					
Finger Oscillation					
Dominant	33.3	12.0	42.5	10.4	*
Nondominant	30.1	11.0	37.4	7.9	*
Strength/grip (kg)					
Dominant	35.0	11.7	34.2	9.8	NS
Nondominant	32.0	9.1	34.0	11.9	NS

Source: From Bigler, Steinman, and Newton (1981).
Note: NS, not significant.

*$p = 0.05–0.01$.
**$p = 0.01–0.001$.
***$p = 0.001$ or greater.

Table 5.2. *Effect of Age on Neuropsychological Performance*

Variable	50 and up Mean	50 and up *SD*	39–49 Mean	39–49 *SD*	21–35 Mean	21–35 *SD*	16–20 Mean	16–20 *SD*	Significance
Age	59.6	7.1	41.7	4.4	26.5	4.9	17.2	1.1	***
Education	14.6	3.3	14.4	3.3	13.9	2.1	11.1	0.9	*
WAIS scores									
Verbal IQ	123.5	10.3	108.7	10.7	113.9	16.5	114.6	9.1	*
Performance IQ	111.9	7.4	111.3	11.6	108.2	12.6	111.7	12.9	NS
Full-Scale IQ	118.9	8.2	110.3	10.1	112.2	14.6	113.2	11.6	NS
V—raw score	79.0	9.6	68.1	10.8	74.5	16.5	69.0	10.1	NS
P—raw score	46.3	6.7	52.9	9.7	56.0	10.1	57.7	9.8	*
FS—raw score	124.7	13.2	121.0	17.4	125.9	37.8	127.0	18.8	NS
Information	13.0	2.4	11.6	2.9	12.1	3.0	10.4	2.2	NS
Comprehension	15.2	3.3	13.2	3.1	13.9	3.2	13.2	3.8	NS
Arithmetic	13.3	2.6	10.1	2.7	12.2	4.1	11.3	2.9	NS
Similarities	12.3	1.6	11.5	2.2	12.6	3.4	12.0	2.1	NS
Digit Span	10.7	1.2	9.4	2.2	11.1	3.5	11.6	2.6	NS
Vocabulary	14.7	2.8	12.5	1.9	12.5	2.9	10.2	1.6	***
Digit Symbol	7.7	1.7	10.4	0.9	10.8	2.8	11.2	3.4	***
Picture Completion	10.6	1.2	10.5	2.1	10.9	2.1	10.9	2.8	NS
Block Design	9.6	1.5	10.7	3.1	11.7	3.2	12.5	2.9	NS
Picture Arrangement	9.3	2.3	10.0	3.0	11.3	2.5	10.7	2.6	NS
Object Assembly	9.4	1.5	11.4	3.3	11.3	3.2	12.7	2.8	NS
WMS scores									
I	5.5	0.8	5.4	0.9	5.4	0.8	5.1	0.8	NS
II	4.7	0.5	5.0	0.0	4.9	0.3	4.9	0.4	NS
III	7.1	2.0	7.3	1.0	6.9	1.6	7.6	1.5	NS
IV	10.3	3.3	10.0	2.8	10.6	3.2	12.4	2.7	NS
V	11.3	1.3	10.8	1.9	11.6	2.6	12.8	2.2	NS
VI	11.2	3.7	9.3	3.1	11.6	2.1	11.3	2.7	NS
VII	14.3	4.7	16.0	3.3	16.9	3.4	18.3	1.4	NS
Raw score	63.5	10.1	63.8	7.1	67.9	8.8	72.3	5.1	NS
Memory quotient	121.9	16.9	111.8	15.2	108.4	16.3	112.9	10.4	NS
Digits—Forward	6.5	0.9	6.2	1.3	6.6	1.5	7.0	0.9	NS
Digits—Reverse	4.7	0.8	4.4	0.9	5.1	1.4	5.8	1.3	NS
Confabulation	0.7	1.0	0.0	0.0	0.2	0.4	0.1	0.4	*
Category Test									
Total errors	44.0	22.4	24.8	8.1	26.3	8.8	26.9	10.1	*
I	0.0	0.0	0.1	0.4	0.2	0.4	0.0	0.0	NS
II	6.0	0.5	0.6	0.8	0.7	0.7	0.3	0.5	NS
III	8.2	6.9	6.0	6.0	6.0	4.6	4.8	5.1	NS
IV	11.6	6.8	5.4	5.5	3.4	3.3	5.1	6.9	NS
V	12.2	7.4	6.9	3.4	9.6	4.4	10.5	4.4	NS
VI	8.2	6.4	3.9	2.9	2.9	2.4	4.8	3.9	NS
VII	3.2	1.9	2.0	1.5	1.9	1.4	2.1	1.1	NS
Perseveration errors	2.5	1.7	2.4	2.3	2.3	0.9	1.4	1.8	NS
Trail-Making Test									
A (in seconds)	43.5	11.9	26.8	6.6	27.9	11.2	24.4	6.3	***
B (in seconds)	93.0	26.6	73.3	18.4	55.9	18.2	51.9	8.8	***
B–A (in seconds)	49.5	22.8	46.5	16.8	33.4	21.6	27.4	8.5	*
Aphasia Screening									
Verbal	0.8	0.6	0.5	0.5	0.7	0.6	0.2	0.4	NS
Spatial	1.2	0.9	1.5	0.8	0.7	0.9	0.8	0.6	NS
Sensory Perceptual Exam									
Errors Right	1.0	2.8	2.7	2.6	1.0	1.6	0.3	0.5	NS
Errors Left	1.4	2.1	1.8	1.7	1.0	1.9	0.3	0.7	NS
Motor Exam									
Finger Oscillation									
Dominant	42.5	10.4	45.7	6.6	45.3	10.8	48.3	5.7	NS
Nondominant	37.4	7.9	41.8	4.5	43.6	11.1	43.8	3.9	NS
Strength/grip (kg)									
Dominant	34.2	9.8	33.7	8.6	43.9	13.7	47.0	5.4	**
Nondominant	34.0	11.9	32.2	9.5	37.8	10.4	42.3	5.1	NS

Source: From Bigler, Steinman, and Newton (1981).
Note: NS, not significant.

*p = 0.05–0.01.
**p = 0.01–0.001.
***p = 0.001 or greater.

Table 5.3. ***Diagnoses of Patients Fully Evaluated for Dementia***

Disorder	*N*	(%)
Atrophy (probable Alzheimer's or Pick's)	113	51
Vascular disease	17	8
Normal pressure hydrocephalus	14	6
Alcoholism	13	6
Intracranial mass	12	5
Huntington's chorea	10	5
Depression	9	4
Drug toxicity	7	3
Dementia of unknown etiology	7	3
Other[a]	20	9

Source: Adapted from Wells (1978).

[a]Posttraumatic, thyroid-related, postencephalitic, psychiatric, neurosyphilitic, or having amyotrophic lateral sclerosis, postsubarachnoid hemorrhage, Parkinson's disease, pernicious anemia, hepatic encephalopathy, epilepsy, or Jakob-Creutzfeldt disease.

study who were older than eighty years were asymptomatic for organic brain disease. Similarly, Price, Fein, and Feinberg (1980) have demonstrated that the decline in cerebral function seen with degenerative disorders is quite apart from changes in neuropsychological status observed with senescence. Emotional disturbance may also mimic degenerative disease. Table 5.5 outlines features useful in distinguishing patients with truly degenerative or dementing processes from patients with functional depression. If results of neuropsychological studies are not found to be consistent with organic disease, then the diagnosis of pseudodementia should be considered (see Malletta and Pirozzolo, 1980). (See tables 5.4 and 5.5.)

Moss et al. (1986) demonstrated differential patterns of memory loss between Alzheimer's disease, Huntington's disease, and alcoholic Korsakoff's syndrome. Huntington's disease patients could perform within normal limits on a verbal recognition task whereas Alzheimer's and Korsakoff's patients were equally impaired. On immediate recall, the three groups were equally impaired across the various memory tasks; however, after a two-minute delay, the Huntington's disease patients demonstrated better retention than did Korsakoff's syndrome or Alzheimer's patients.

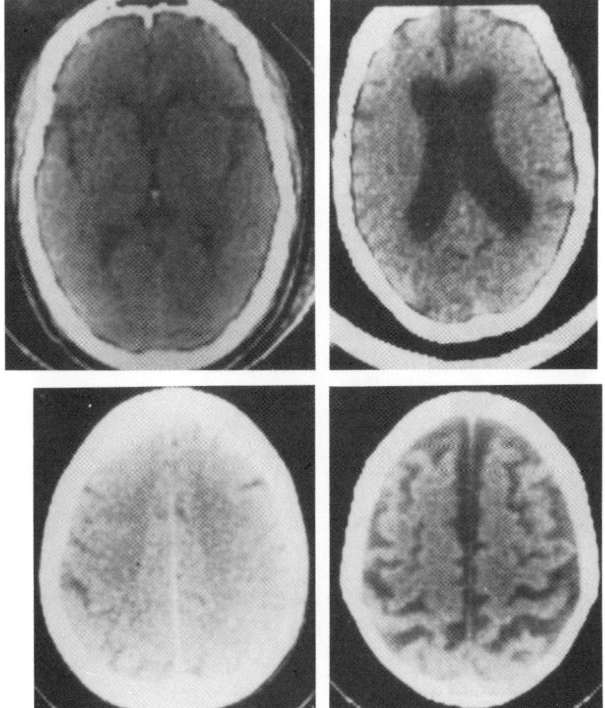

Fig. 5.14. The scans at left depict the range of ventricular enlargement and cortical atrophy present in the sample of forty-two patients. The two top CAT scans depict the patient with the least (*left*) and greatest (*right*) ventricular volume. The two bottom scans depict the patient with the least (*left*) and greatest (*right*) atrophy. The patient in the top left scan was a 53-year-old male who was a university professor (education, doctoral degree). WAIS results were as follows: VIQ = 105, PIQ = 91, FSIQ = 99. WMS results indicate an MQ of 70. Note that while the ventricular size is well within normal limits for age, the prominence of the sylvian fissures is indicative of frontal-temporal atrophy and the patient's measured atrophy indicates moderate cortical atrophy. The patient in the upper-right scan was a 74-year-old female who was a homemaker (education, high school). WAIS results were as follows: VIQ= 74, PIQ = 67, FSIQ = 69. WMS results indicate an MQ of 72. The top of the scan film was accidentally cropped in making the hard copy X-ray film. No frontal defect was present, however. The patient in the bottom-left scan was a 74-year-old female who was a homemaker (education, high school). WAIS results were as follows: VIQ = 93, PIQ = 82, FSIQ = 88. WMS results indicate an MQ of 68. The patient in the lower-right scan was a 78-year-old female who was a retired school teacher (education, college degree). WAIS results were as follows: VIQ = 97, PIQ = 73, FSIQ = 85. WMS results indicate an MQ of 87. From Bigler et al. (1985).

Foster et al. (1986) have been able to dissociate by positron emission tomography (PET) scanning the lateralization of apraxic features in Alzheimer's disease. Apraxia to imitation was associated with related visual-spatial deficits and impaired cortical metabolism in the right parietal area, whereas apraxia associated with command was associated in particular with left frontal metabolic deficits. Apraxia to command or imitation in the Alzheimer's disease patient may thus reflect neuronal dysfunction in distinctly different cerebral regions, depending on the type of apraxia. This study also demonstrates that in patients with presumed Alzheimer's disease there may be focal metabolic irregularities, and not necessarily an overall generalized metabolic disturbance.

Eslinger and Benton (1983) have examined visuoperceptual changes observed with aging and dementia. While there is a steady, moderate decline in visuoperceptual functioning seen with age, the changes in visuoperceptual abilities with dementing illnesses are typically severe. This distinction thereby permits easy clinical differentiation between "normal" age-related changes and pathologic changes associated with degenerative disorders. Eslinger et al. (1985) further demonstrated that 89 percent of their dementia patients in a study of normal aging and dementia could be identified by their impaired performance on the Benton Visual Retention Test, Controlled Oral Word Association Test, and Temporal Orientation Test (see also Eslinger et al., 1984). Berg et al. (1984) demonstrated a 95 percent correct classification of Alzheimer's patients using the digit symbol subtest of the WAIS and the dysphasic error scores on an aphasia screening test, when contrasted with age-matched controls. Similarly, Cummings et al. (1985) demonstrated significant dysphasic deficits in AD patients that enabled clinical differentiation from normal aging.

There is some evidence to suggest clinical subtypes in Alzheimer's disease as well (Chui et al., 1985; Mayeux, Stern, and Spanton, 1985). While it is clinically apparent that Alzheimer's patients will follow a different course of decline and, accordingly, this may form different groups of patients, these groups do not correspond to any specific type of cortical atrophy, and attempts to classify these groups via CAT findings have been unproductive (Massman et al., 1986; Naugle et al., 1985).

In terms of mental symptoms it is common for there to be a prodromal history of subtle losses in intellectual and memory function along with such "psychogenic" symptoms as anxiety, depression, and restlessness. Mild paranoia or ill-formed delusional states may also accompany the above. Liston (1979*b*) has indicated that in a series of fifty dementia cases the most frequent symptom was change in personality or behavior (78 percent) followed by disturbance in memory (50 percent). As dementia progresses, greater deficits in social and personal judgment typically become apparent. Frequently, professional and moral indiscretions may occur along with strikingly illogical and grandiose social or business blunders. Frank

Table 5.4. *Major Causes of Cognitive Dysfunction*

Major Causes of Dementia	Major Causes of Delirium

Alzheimer's disease
Multi-infarct dementia
Space-occupying lesions
  Chronic subdural hematoma
  Chronic abscess
  Frontal meningioma or metastatic lesion
Myxedema (hypothyroidism) or other endocrine causes
Pernicious anemia (vitamin B_{12} deficiency)
Bromide or other intoxications
Nutritional dementias
  Niacin deficiency (pellagra)
  Thiamine deficiency (Korsakoff's psychosis)
Alcoholic dementia
Chronic normal-pressure hydrocephalus
Dementia pugilistica
Neurosyphilis
Other infectious agents (viral, tuberculous, cryptococcal)
Specific neurologic syndromes (Wilson's, Parkinson's, Huntington's diseases; cerebellar degeneration; and multiple sclerosis)
	Drug toxicity (prescribed, street, over-the-counter)
	Alcohol abuse
	Trauma
	Subarachnoid hemorrhage
	Neurologic syndrome associated with metabolic or endocrine disorder
	Hepatic, uremic, or pulmonary dysfunction
	Hypoxia
	Hypoglycemia (also nonketotic hyperglycemia)
	Arsenic poisoning
	Lead in large doses
	Central nervous system or systemic infections (with or without fever)
	"Silent" pneumonia in the elderly
	Electrolyte disturbance
	Emboli
	Vasculitis
	Fecal impaction or bladder distention in the elderly
	"Silent" myocardial infarction in the elderly

Source: Adapted from Malletta and Pirozzolo (1980).

Table 5.5. *Symptoms and Profiles of Dementia and Depression*

Characteristic	Dementia	Depression
Onset	Unclear; others may be only vaguely aware until severity increases	Clear, perhaps after a major psychological event
Progression	Relatively steady decline	Uneven; often no progression
Symptom duration	Relatively long	Relatively short
Recognition by patient	Varies by stage, but patients nearly always unaware at moderate and severe stages	Patients nearly always very aware
Patient distress level	Low	High
Performance characteristics	Good cooperation and effort; "near-miss" responses; relatively stable achievement; little test anxiety; little "teachability"	Poor cooperation or effort; "don't know" responses; variable achievement; test-taking anxiety; some "teachability"
Affective behavior	Some ability	Marked disturbance
Everyday behavior vs. test behavior	Congruent	Incongruent[a]
Short-term memory	Always impaired	Sometimes impaired
Long-term memory	Unimpaired early in the disease	Often inexplicably impaired
Electroencephalography	Usually diffuse irregular slowing (SDAT)	Usually within normal limits
CAT Scan	Marked cerebral atrophy and ventricular dilatation	Usually within normal limits

Source: Adapted from Malletta and Pirozzolo (1980).
[a]Measure of affective behavior vs. test behavior.

confusional and disorientational states usually do not develop until later in the disease process.

Degree of Cortical Atrophy in Cognitive Impairment

There is some relationship between the degree of cortical atrophy and the level of cognitive impairment in Alzheimer's disease, but the relationship is far from linear (see fig. 5.14). Studies examining subtypes (see Chui et al., 1985) have also failed to demonstrate a specific relationship between the degree of cortical atrophy and neuropsychological impairment (see also Naugle et al., 1985). The best approach is to examine CAT findings over time (see case 2) where there begins to be a greater correlation between cognitive impairment and degree of cerebral atrophy (see also Bird, Levy, and Jacoby, 1986; Neary et al., 1986).

Vascular Disorders and Their Clinical Features

Multi-Infarct Dementia

Multiple sites of infarction within the cerebrum may produce dementia (Whisnant et al., 1979), and the infarction process may be progressive. This disorder is primarily related to the cerebral vasculature and is not of neural origin. Lacunar infarcts are the common substrates (Donnan, Tress, and Bladin, 1982; Haase, 1977). Rogers et al. (1986) have demonstrated in a prospective study that patients with multi-infarct dementia show decreased cerebral blood flow, whereas Alzheimer's patients do not until the dementia becomes quite prominent. The use of cerebral blood flow studies in conjunction with neuropsychological testing may prove to be diagnostic of Alzheimer's disease versus multi-infarct dementia (see also Cutler et al., 1985).

Cerebral Arteriosclerosis

Cerebral arteriosclerosis may have an insidious and progressive course and be associated with generalized neuropsychological impairment. Multiple infarction, as outlined above, may be a primary component in the degenerative process, but reduced blood flow or transient circulatory disturbance may also play a major role (Adams and Victor, 1977; Tomlinson, 1977; Whisnant et al., 1979).

Other Vascular Disorders

Other disorders of the vasculature, although rather rare in occurrence, may also produce a progressive decline in cerebral function. Disseminated lupus erythematosus and subcortical arteriosclerotic encephalopathy (Binswanger's dementia) fall into this category (Haase, 1977). Large arteriovenous malformations may "steal" blood away from the brain tissue and thereby produce atrophy. Likewise, progressive cognitive deterioration may result from carotid artery occlusive disease (see fig. 3.20).

Clinical Features

Although systemic arteriosclerosis does not generally predict cerebral arteriosclerosis, the presence of systemic arteriosclerosis may contribute to or indicate cerebral involvement (Haase, 1977). Essentially, neuropsychological examination of the patient suspected of having vascular disease is similar to that outlined for the patient with a degenerative disorder. Although CAT scanning provides no clear picture of disease in degenerative disorders, it is invaluable in diagnosing vascular disorders because areas of infarction may be easily identified (Lowry et al., 1977). Rogers et al. (1986) have demonstrated in a prospective study that patients with multi-infarct dementia demonstrate decreased cerebral blood flow, whereas Alzheimer patients do not show similar changes until the disorder is well advanced. Accordingly, the use of cerebral blood flow studies in conjunction with neuropsychological testing may aid in this differential diagnosis (see also Cutler et al., 1985).

Senile Dementia

The clinical and pathologic features of senile dementia are similar to those observed with Alzheimer's disease, although by definition senile dementia occurs only after the middle sixties. Haase (1977) suggests five types, in terms of clinical and behavioral findings, in addition to intellectual and cognitive deficits: (1) simple deterioration, (2) depression and agitation, (3) delirium and confusion, (4) hyperactivity with motor restlessness, and (5) paranoia. Neuropsychological studies of these patients reflect results almost identical to those seen in Alzheimer's disease.

There is some evidence accumulating, though, that suggests that onset in the presenium may take a more malignant course (Koss et al. 1985; Loring and Largen, 1985; Naugle et al., 1986; Neary et al. 1986; Seltzer and Sherwin, 1983). These studies suggest that the initial cognitive deterioration in patients with presenile onset may be greater than that seen with senile onset.

Extrapyramidal Disorders

Parkinson's Disease

Parkinson's disease is the most common of the extrapyramidal disorders and approximately 1 percent of the population over the age of fifty has it (Poser et al., 1979). There are typically a minimum of three essential symptoms for its diagnosis: (1) rigidity secondary to muscle tonus; (2) tremor (paralysis agitans), which is generally of two types—resting tremor (3–6 Hz) and action tremor (6–12 Hz), which is an exaggeration of the resting tremor—and (3) akinesia, hypokinesia, or bradykinesia (Ferrendelli and Landau, 1978; Poser et al., 1979). Although the motor deficits may be rather generalized and substantial, some well-preserved, fine motor control may be present because of the sparing of the pyramidal motor system. The presence of the first two features, as described above, results in the "cogwheel" sensation felt by the examiner when holding the biceps muscle and passively moving the limb of the parkinsonian patient. Zetusky, Jankovic, and Pirozzolo (1985) in a study of 334 patients with Parkinson's disease were able to separate these patients into two groups: postural instability / gait disturbance and parkinsonian tremor. The etiology of Parkinson's disease is multifaceted. The following represents the most common etiologic variables: postencephalitic, atherosclerotic, posttraumatic, or drug-induced (by reserpine, phenothiazines, or butyrophenones). Parkinsonian symptoms have also occurred as a consequence of carbon monoxide poisoning, intracranial tumor, and anoxia (Ferrendelli and Landau, 1978; Poser et al., 1979). Also, a good number of Parkinson cases have an idiopathic etiology.

The pathologic substrate producing the movement disorder in Parkinson's has been related to the basal ganglia, in particular the substantia nigra (see fig. 5.15). As such, treatment with dopamine-producing medications (levo-dihydroxyphenylalanine) has proved to be immensely beneficial. Severe parkinsonian motor involvement may be present in the absence of any other indication of cerebral dysfunction (see fig. 5.16), and thus specify the focus of pathology at the level of the basal ganglia. However, recent studies have revealed a variety of subtle cognitive deficits in certain patients with Parkinson's disease as well as the occurrence of frank dementia (Boller, 1980; Haase, 1977; Mayeux et al., 1981; Mortimer et al., 1982; Sroka et al., 1981). The cognitive deficits may, in part, be unrelated to the degree of basal ganglia involvement or the severity of parkinsonian motor symptoms present. Caution needs to be used when attempting to infer the degree of cognitive deficit present from the degree of motor involvement. Thus, in clinical examination it is important first to have a definitive diagnosis based on the presence of a parkinsonian movement disorder and then to determine if any cognitive changes are present.

Wilson's Disease

Wilson's disease, or hepatolenticular degeneration, is an inherited metabolic disease in which there is an enzyme deficiency in the binding of copper. It is an autosomal recessive disorder and results in hepatolenticular degeneration (Haase, 1977). The movement abnormalities, which result from abnormally elevated copper in the basal ganglia, may take the form of dystonia, chorea, or parkinsonian tremor and rigidity. The liver is also sensitive to the abnormally high copper levels. Treatment includes removing from the patient's diet all copper-containing foods as well as administering medications that reduce copper deposits in tissues. If treatment is not administered early or if it is absent, the patient will display a progressive worsening of the movement disorder along with dramatic changes in all cognitive functions. Characteristic abnormalities are usu-

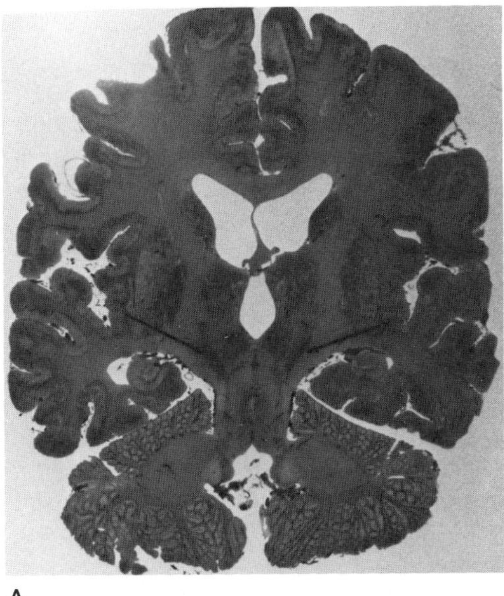

A

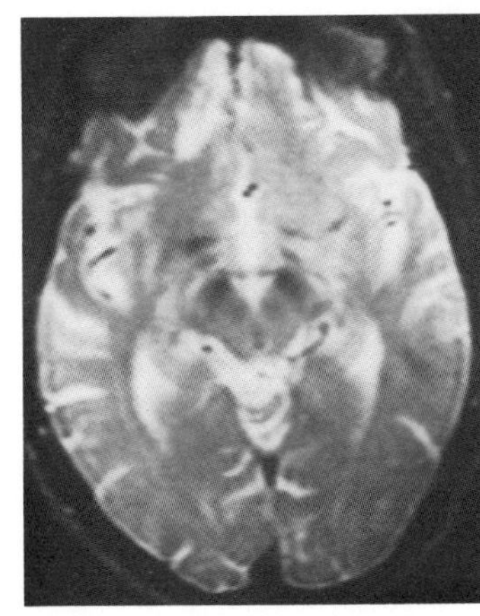

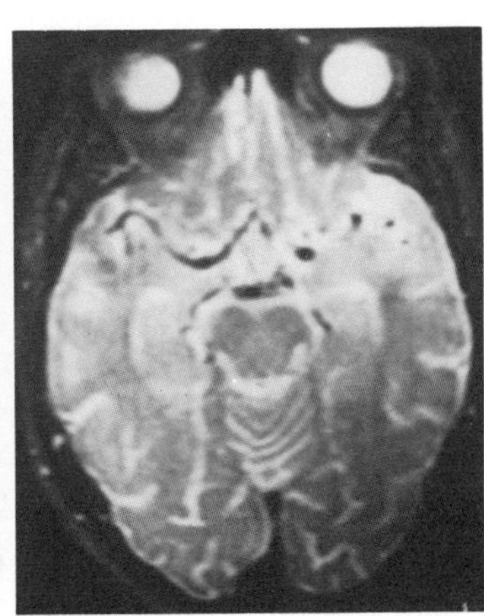

B

Fig. 5.15. *A*, Parkinson's disease. The oblique coronal section of the brain shows cerebral atrophy. The substantia nigra is paler than normal. (The normal dark color of the substantia nigra is due to the presence of melanin in the neurones.) From Payne (1969). *B*, the MRI scan on the left is from a patient with Parkinson's disease. Note the density change (*dark areas*) at the level of the midbrain representing degeneration of the substantia nigra. A comparison MRI scan in a normal patient (same age) presented at the right shows the normal density across the midbrain region.

Fig. 5.16. Aphasia screening drawings of a 66-year-old patient with Parkinson's disease. Patient has marked tremor. Note the impaired copying of the cross, but the deficit is related to the basal ganglia motor disturbance and not representative of a true constructional dyspraxia. Note also the deteriorated state of writing. The patient with Parkinson's disease can frequently initiate the first letter, but cannot sustain clear writing even for familiar words such as the patient's name (*written in the upper right corner*). This patient's cognitive abilities were found to be intact (verbal intellectual level measured 110). Thus, caution should be used in interpreting graphomotor results in patients with Parkinson's disease because the deficit may be specific to the basal ganglia involvement and not suggestive of cortical deficit.

ally found with computerized tomography (Williams and Walshe, 1981). The most common abnormalities observed include ventricular dilation, cortical atrophy, brain stem atrophy, and areas of hypodensity in the region of the basal ganglia. It should also be noted that the histologic features of acquired hepatocerebral degeneration are essentially identical to those of Wilson's disease (Finlayson and Superville, 1981).

Demyelination Disorders

Multiple sclerosis (MS) is the most common of the demyelinating diseases, affecting forty to sixty persons per 100,000 population who are most commonly twenty to forty years old (Berg, Chesanow, and Prensky, 1978). The disease is characterized by discrete, irregularly shaped lesions of demyelinated neural tissue (plaques). The most common presenting signs or symptoms are loss of visual acuity, diplopia, nystagmus, impaired extraocular movements, dysarthria, ataxia or incoordination, limb weakness, spasticity, hyperreflexia, paresthesias, and loss of proprioception (Appel, 1980). Demographic differences also exist, with there being a greater incidence in industrialized countries of northern Europe and the northeastern United States. MS is quite rare in equatorial countries. The pathogenesis of multiple sclerosis remains unknown, as does the reason for the demographic differences (Poskanzer et al., 1981).

Lesions may be widely disseminated throughout the central nervous system, but the most common areas are the optic nerves and chiasm; the brain stem, with particular preference for the medial longitudinal fasciculus; the cerebellar white matter; and the spinal cord, with particular preference for the corticospinal tracts, the posterior columns, and throughout the periventricular white matter. In the acute stage the lesion may be surrounded by inflammation or edema. However, with progression the chronic lesion typically houses a proliferation of astrocytic processes that eventually become glial scars or the so-called sclerotic plaques (Halliday and McDonald, 1977). Such lesion sites can now be readily identified with MRI scanning techniques (see figs. 5.17 and 5.18; also see Jacobs et al., 1986).

Neuropsychological studies of MS patients typically reveal sensory and motor deficits (see case 6) related to the underlying brain systems affected, but generally sparing cognitive functions not dependent on sensory input or motor control (Beatty and Gange, 1977; Cleeland, Matthews, and Hopper, 1970; Goldstein and Shelly, 1974; Ivnik, 1978; Matthews, Cleeland, and Hopper, 1970; Reitan, Reed, and Dyken, 1971). However, as the disorder progresses a picture of general cognitive disturbance may emerge (Haase, 1977). Peyser, Edwards, and Poser (1980) have demonstrated the relationship between severity of MS and presence of severe emotional factors that may be a part of the syndrome or in response to it. Thus, as a rule of thumb, the more chronic the MS disorder, the greater the likelihood of cognitive dysfunction.

Heaton et al. (1985) examined patients with either relapse-remitting or chronic-progressive MS and found that the latter group, as expected, demonstrated nonspecific deficits on all cognitive measures. Rao et al. (1984) have also demonstrated nonspecific memory deficits in MS patients, particularly in terms of spatial memory. These studies support the contention that patients with MS, particularly if it is of the chronic-progressive type, will develop cognitive symptoms in addition to the traditional sensory and motor deficits. Rubens et al. (1985) have demonstrated greater left ear suppression on verbal dichotic tests in patients with multiple sclerosis. They suggest that the basis for this finding is a disconnection of the auditory callosal pathway, a deep white matter structure that may be affected in MS patients. The clinical efficacy of this particular measure is still under debate.

Other myelinopathic diseases are not as common as MS and usually are related to some type of postinfectious inflammatory response. Thus, the patient with signs of retrobulbar neuritis in one eye, but without any other neurologic or neuropsychological deficits, may have a self-limiting inflammation. However, the patient with signs of retrobulbar neuritis in one eye only, who also has sensory and motor deficits and visual abnormalities in the "unaffected" eye, may in fact have MS.

Alcoholism

Cognitive decline progressing to frank dementia may occur with chronic alcoholism (Blusewicz et al., 1977; Idestrom, 1980; Kroll et al., 1980; Lishman, 1981; Parsons, 1980). The cerebral deficits likely arise from multiple causes including direct toxic effects of alcohol on the central nervous system (Mancillas, Siggens, and Bloom, 1986), vitamin deficiencies (particularly in the B complex vitamins [Reuler, Girard, and Cooney, 1985]), malnutrition, trauma (associated with falls while intoxicated), and secondary effects from multiple systemic disorders brought on by the alcoholism (Carlen et al., 1981; Lee et al., 1979). The generalized cerebral deficits that accompany chronic alcohol ingestion may occur in the absence of an earlier Wernicke's encephalopathy. When a Wernicke-Korsakoff syndrome is present, there is marked disturbance in recent memory along with frequent signs of confabulation, ataxia, and peripheral neuropathy (Poser et al., 1979). CAT scans of patients with chronic alcoholism frequently display diffuse atrophy (see fig. 5.19). It should be noted, however, that Parsons (1980) has demonstrated that measurable cognitive-perceptive deficits may be present in patients who just drink "socially."

Neuropsychological examination of the patient with chronic alcohol ingestion will typically show varying degrees of cerebral dysfunction with tasks requiring abstract reasoning and memory (e.g., the Category Test) as well as tasks involving higher level visual-spatial and manipulo-spatial abilities (i.e., performance IQ, Tactual Performance Test) being the most affected (Silberstein and Parsons, 1981). Various tactile sensory deficits may also be uncovered by the sensory-perceptual exam, but these likely are more related to the presence of peripheral neuropathy than to central disturbance, although both may be implicated. The degree of neuropsychological impairment appears to be related to the lifetime total amount of alcohol consumed (Svanum and Schladenhauffen, 1986). Advanced alcoholic dementia syndrome presents a neuropsychological picture essentially identical to primary degenerative disease. It should also be noted that even young adults with chronic alcohol abuse may show cortical atrophy on CAT scan along with neuropsychological impairment (Graff-Radford et al., 1982).

Infectious Disorders

Jakob-Creutzfeldt Disease

Jakob-Creutzfeldt disease is a devastating CNS disease, caused by a slow-acting virus, that leads quickly to death following a course of rapidly progressive dementia and motor disturbance (Masters, Gajdusek, and Gibbs, 1981). A variety of neural structures are involved, including the cortex, basal ganglia, pyramids, cerebellum, and frequently the anterior horn cells. Incapacitation takes place rather rapidly, and neuropsychological studies invariably indicate widespread and diffuse deficits.

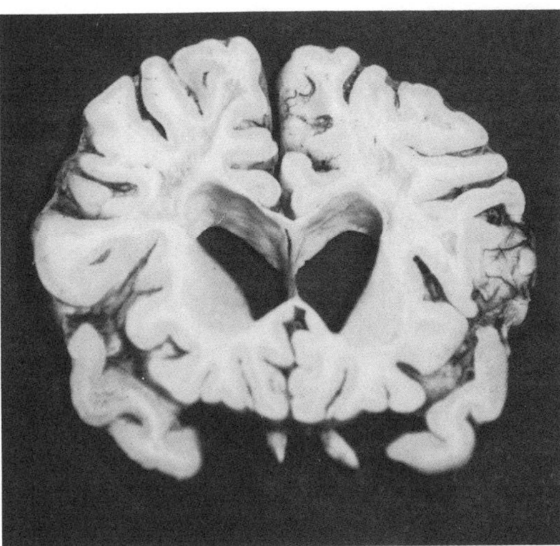

Fig. 5.17. Coronal section taken at postmortem examination of a patient with advanced multiple sclerosis. Note the ventricular dilation and also the wasting away of the central white matter. Notice that the ventricular dilation is disproportionate to the cortical sulcal pattern, suggesting that the ventricular dilation is due to white matter wasting rather than cortical atrophy.

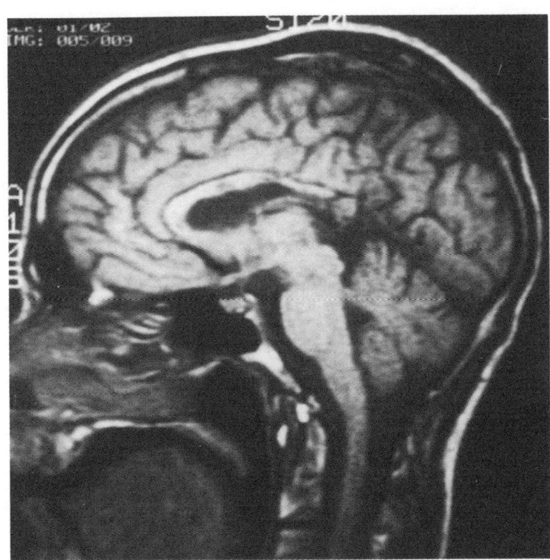

Fig. 5.18. Sagittal MRI scan of a 27-year-old patient with rapidly progressing multiple sclerosis. Note the dark areas in the corpus callosum, which represent focal areas of demyelination. At the time of the scan the patient was blind and demonstrated generalized motor weakness and spasticity as well as tactile sensory loss. Intellectually, his WAIS-R VIQ score was 104.

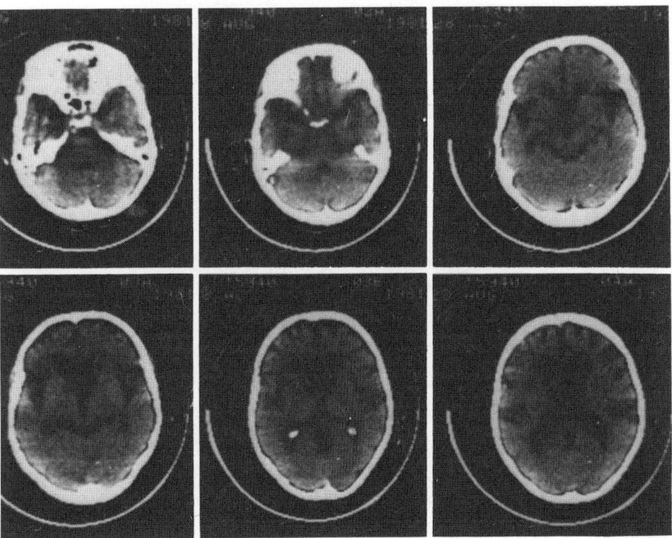

Fig. 5.19. CAT scan of a 64-year-old alcoholic woman. She had more than thirty years' history of alcohol use. She retired from teaching school at age 62, at which time she began to heavily abuse hard liquor. Note the presence of marked generalized cortical atrophy, particularly in frontal and temporal regions. Note the prominence of the sylvian fissure. Neuropsychological examination of this patient revealed dramatic deficits in all areas, particularly in short-term memory processing.

Other Infectious Disorders

Subacute sclerosing panencephalitis is a disorder related to the measles virus (Adams and Victor, 1977). Typically, the onset of symptoms is far removed in time from the onset of the original viral infection. The clinical picture is one of progressive neurologic decline. It usually affects children, but it has been reported in adults. Lues (dementia paralytica, general paresis, and syphilis encephalopathy), although now certainly not as common in occurrence as in prepenicillin days, still does occur, with patients usually displaying a slow course of neurologic decline and dementia. Two rare but still existent neuroviral diseases are Kuru and Behçet's syndrome. Kuru, a disease restricted to tribal people of New Guinea, produces a progressive neuromotor degeneration along with dementia. In Behçet's syndrome approximately 50 percent of the patients affected will display progressive neurologic decline that frequently affects visual and motor systems, progressing to blindness, paralysis, and dementia.

Neurosyphilis, although dramatically decreased in incidence since the advent of penicillin, still occurs with some regularity (Adams and Victor, 1977; Scheinberg, 1977). The neurosyphilitic infectious process typically is progressive with potential involvement of much of the CNS (see fig. 5.10). Neuropsychological studies typically reflect diffuse and generalized impairment.

Encephalitis, meningitis, or meningoencephalitis, as a result of a number of infectious agents, may also produce diffuse and widespread damage affecting a variety of cognitive functions. Infectious disorders will be discussed further in a subsequent chapter.

Other Disorders

Normal-Pressure Hydrocephalus

Normal-pressure hydrocephalus (NPH) usually is associated with the clinical triad of progressive mental deterioration, progressive gait disturbance, and urinary incontinence (Poser et al., 1979). The causal factor may be idiopathic, but NPH also may occur secondary to trauma, infection, or subarachnoid hemorrhage (Becker et al., 1979; Poser et al., 1979). It is commonly held that increased cerebrospinal fluid volume occurs secondary to intermittent or partial blockage of flow of cerebrospinal fluid uptake mechanisms (Fishman, 1978). CAT scan will show classic signs of hydrocephalus but without cortical atrophy (see fig. 5.20). Neurosurgical intervention in the form of shunting may have some beneficial effects, but the usual course of NPH is one of nonhalting, insidious progression. Neuropsychological examination will typically reflect the diffuse nature of cerebral disturbance. Serial follow-up neuropsychological evaluations may be the most sensitive indicators of the progressive deterioration associated with this disorder.

Muscular Dystrophy

Although the muscular dystrophies are characterized by progressive muscular weakness and wasting secondary to muscle degeneration, purportedly without central or peripheral nervous system involvement, intellectual deterioration or impairment has been reported (Karagan, 1979; Karagan and Sorensen, 1981; Whelan, 1987). Therefore, comprehensive neuropsychological evaluation of the muscular dystrophy patient is recommended to determine possible cerebral involvement.

Progressive Supranuclear Palsy

Progressive supranuclear palsy is a neurodegenerative disorder in which the initial presenting triad includes pseudobulbar palsy, dystonic extension of the neck, and supranuclear ophthalmoplegia (Kish et al., 1985). Dementia evolves in association with the progressive degeneration in this disorder, and frequently rigidity and bradykinesia may accompany the progressive elements of the dementia. The neuropathology of this disorder has been thoroughly discussed by Kish et al. (1985).

Alzheimer's Disease in Down's Syndrome

Individuals with Down's syndrome have a high predisposition toward Alzheimer's disease (Wisniewski, Wisniewski, and Wen, 1985), and such individuals may show a similar progressive deterioration (Heyman et al., 1983). Since the majority of Down's syndrome patients are at least mildly to moderately mentally retarded, the cognitive decline may be difficult to detect initially. Likewise, in terms of following these individuals clinically, it is important to establish a thorough baseline and then to repeat testing at nine- to twelve-month intervals.

Atypical Dementias

There are a variety of progressive dementias that do not fit any one diagnostic category. These include Alzheimer's disease-like disorders, but where there are prominent features of spastic paresis and ataxia that appear more prominent than the cognitive deficit (Aikawa et al., 1985), thalamic degeneration (Katz et al., 1984), and combination Alzheimer's disease features associated with progressive vascular disease (Levine, Grek, and Calvanio, 1985).

Metabolic Disorders

Wilson's disease is the primary degenerative disease of metabolic origin and has been previously discussed. A variety of metabolic disorders may eventually affect cerebral function, including myxedema, hypoparathyroidism, liver disease (chronic uremia and chronic dialysis), and remote effects of chronic systemic disease (Haase, 1977). Mention should also be made of metachromatic leukodystrophy, which is a disorder of myelin metabolism associated with progressive destruction of myelin. This disorder, although rare, produces progressive neurologic deterioration and global changes in all cognitive functions. Neuropsychological examination of such patients invariably occurs after the metabolic disorder has already been diagnosed. Thus, neuropsychological examination will be of utility in determining the extent of cerebral involvement.

Diabetes mellitus is one of the most common metabolic disorders and may be associated with a variety of neurologic sequelae (Lewis, 1978). Patients with adequate metabolic control may not display any specific neuropsychological deficits (Skenazy and Bigler, 1984, 1985), but Holmes (1986) has demonstrated some deficits in cognitive functioning in diabetic patients, this being associated with poor metabolic control. The most common neurologic sequelae associated with diabetes is in terms of peripheral neuropathy. Also, patients with chronic diabetes may run the risk of various general metabolic problems that may have untoward consequences in terms of neurologic function and, likewise, prolonged diabetic coma may result in cognitive sequelae. Multisystem failure as a result of diabetes may also result in subsequent anoxia. Diabetic patients tend to be hypertensive and, accordingly, hypertensive vascular disorder may also be a factor in certain diabetic patients.

Patients with chronic renal failure (Hart et al., 1983) or chronic obstructive pulmonary disease (COPD; Greenberg, Ryan, and Bourlier, 1985; Prigatano et al., 1983) may also produce significant decrements in neuropsychological functioning. Brief mention should also be made that older patients with nutritional deficiencies may perform poorly on complex memory tasks, due to metabolic factors (Goodwin, Goodwin, and Garry, 1983). Likewise, certain medications (e.g., steroids) may produce a transient iatrogenic-induced dementia (Varney, Alexander, and MacIndoe, 1984).

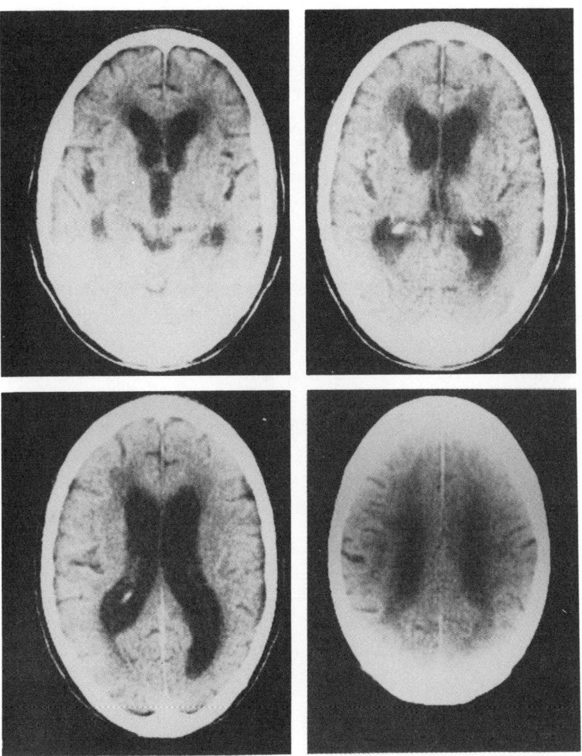

Fig. 5.20. Normal-pressure hydrocephalus. Classic configuration of marked ventricular enlargement in the absence of cortical atrophy seen with normal-pressure hydrocephalus as visualized by CAT scanning.

Relationship of Dementia to Degenerative Diseases

While all degenerative diseases that diffusely affect the cerebrum will eventually result in dementia, the presence of dementia does not necessarily connote degenerative disease. In the strictest sense, dementia refers to intellectual decline from a previous level of function. It implies no one substrate of pathology. The intellectual decline of dementia is commonly associated with deficits in memory, orientation, judgment, and affect (Wells, 1977, 1979). Thus, a host of disorders may produce dementia (see table 5.4), and all degenerative diseases that diffusely affect the cerebrum will produce dementia. Yet, one needs to keep in mind that the inverse is not always true—that is, dementia is not equated with degenerative disease. For example, dementia may be a result of trauma (see fig. 5.21) and the residual deficit may be static and nonprogressive. Similarly, psychological states, such as severe depression, may produce a pseudodementia and, of course, not be related to a degenerative syndrome at all.

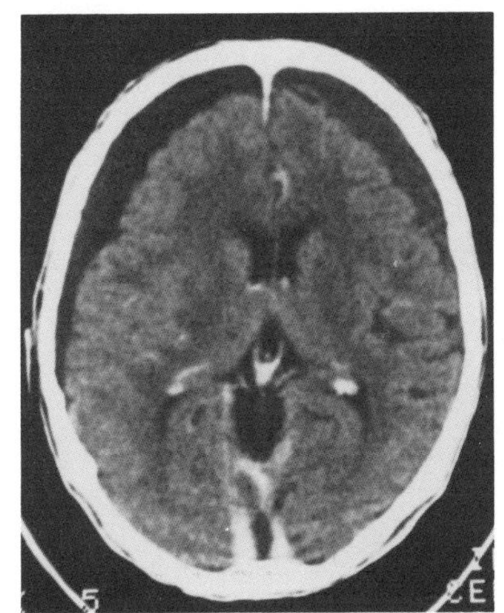

Fig. 5.21. This CAT is from an 83-year-old female patient who was brought in by her family because they believed she had "Alzheimer's disease." However, in reviewing the history, the family noted that the changes in her behavior coincided with a fall that she had taken while gardening. This CAT scan depicts bifrontal hygromas (*dark areas in frontal region*). Note that throughout the frontal region there are no signs of sulcal enlargement. Note also that there is no dilation of the anterior horns and that the anterior horns are displaced caudally. This is the classic configuration for bifrontal hygromas. Once the hygroma was drained, the patient had a complete restoration of cognitive functioning. This is an excellent case indicating the need for thorough neurologic and neuropsychologic evaluation in the detection of dementias, as this was a treatable, transient dementia.

CASE STUDIES

Case 1. The first three studies are of patients with Alzheimer's disease. This patient was a bank accountant who began displaying personality changes (careless about his dress, "forgetting" important engagements, withdrawing from family) as well as declining job performance. His CAT scan results are presented in figure 5.2. Neuropsychological examination reveals classic examination findings consistent with intellectual decline, particularly in the "fluid" performance-based tests; generalized cognitive impairment (i.e., markedly elevated Category Test scores and inability to perform the Trail-making test); and marked disturbance of memory. Patient also displays some dysphasic signs. No focal or sensory deficits are elicited, although he does make bilateral somatosensory processing errors.

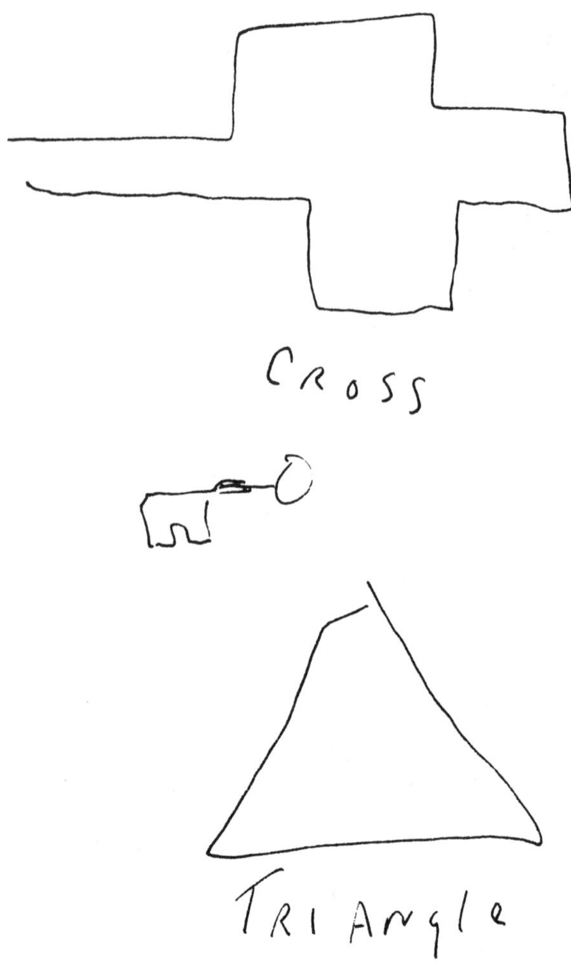

Age 61
Sex M
Education 14

Lateral Dominance Exam

	Eye	Hand	Foot
Right	X	X	X
Left			
Mixed			

Motor Examination

FOD 49 SOGD 45 TPTD 20.4
FOND 48 SOGND 36 TPTND 1 0 DC 5 in
TPT Both 15.0 DC 7 in
Alternating movements impaired
Frontal lobe grasp reflex present

Sensory Perceptual Examination:

Bilateral finger dysgnosia, dysgraphesthesia and dysstereognosis

Language Examination:

Conversational Speech: Generally intact but content is rather empty
Comprehension: Generally intact
Repetition of Spoken Language: Intact
Confrontation Naming: Mild dysnomia
Reading:
Aloud: Intact for simple words, impaired for complex words and complex sentences
Writing: Generally intact
Calculations: Impaired SRT 13 errors
SSPT 19 errors

Memory Examination:

WMS MQ = 70
LM 4, Digits 9, VM 3, AL 3
TPT Memory 1, TPT localization 0

Intellectual/Cognitive Examination:

FSIQ = 83, VIQ = 93, PIQ = 72
I 7, C 8, A 7, S 7, D 9, V 11
DS 0, PC 6, BD 0, PA 5, OA 5

Category Test: 128 errors
Trail Making Test: A 185 B 294 DC

Case 2. This patient was an engineer, retired for medical reasons, who has had a course of cognitive decline over the past six years consistent with Alzheimer's disease. Note that initially CAT scan results revealed only modest atrophy (mainly in Sylvian fissure) and that there was not much change from the 1977 scan to the 1978 scan (fig. 5.22). However, the 1982 scan demonstrated severe atrophic changes. Note also the progression of apraxic deficits in the patient's drawings from 1979 to 1982.

PROGRESSION OF ALZHEIMER'S DISEASE

Diagnosis first suspected in 1975. Patient has an engineering degree, and no history of related medical problems.

12-1-77 (55 y.o.)	9-3-78 (56 y.o.)
WAIS	WAIS
VIQ = 93	VIQ = 85
PIQ = 87	PIQ = 72
FSIQ = 90	FSIQ = 79
WMS	WMS
MQ = 63	MQ = 57

Sq

Scq

SQu

K

1979

Patient's attempt to trace

Sample guide drawn for patient

1982

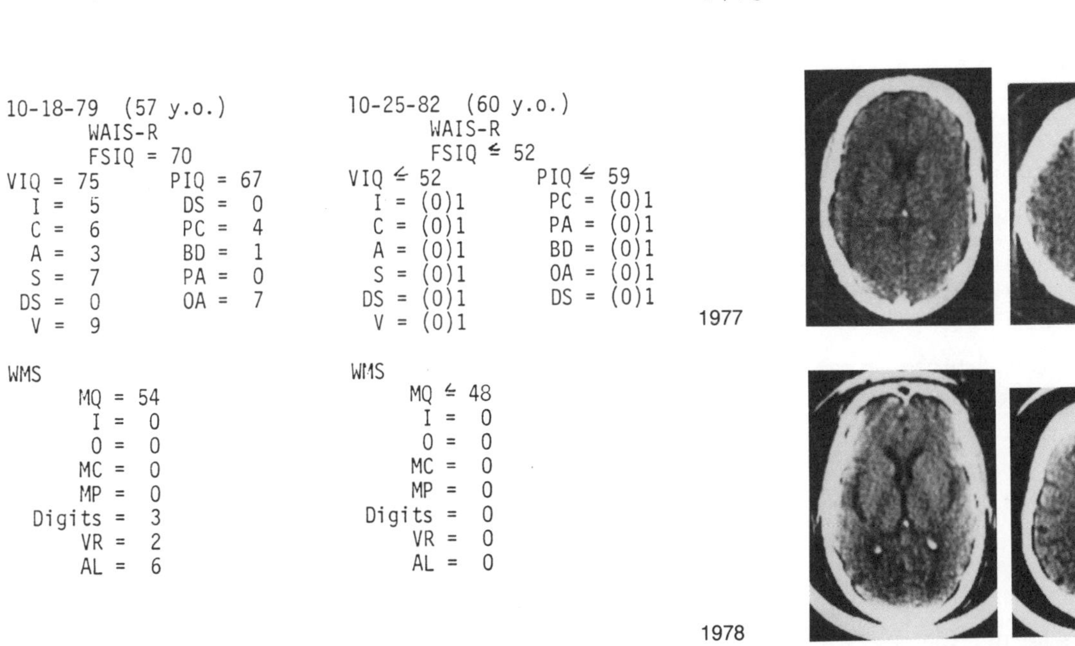

10-18-79 (57 y.o.)
WAIS-R
FSIQ = 70

VIQ = 75	PIQ = 67
I = 5	DS = 0
C = 6	PC = 4
A = 3	BD = 1
S = 7	PA = 0
DS = 0	OA = 7
V = 9	

WMS

MQ	54
I	0
O	0
MC	0
MP	0
Digits	3
VR	2
AL	6

10-25-82 (60 y.o.)
WAIS-R
FSIQ ≤ 52

VIQ ≤ 52	PIQ ≤ 59
I = (0)1	PC = (0)1
C = (0)1	PA = (0)1
A = (0)1	BD = (0)1
S = (0)1	OA = (0)1
DS = (0)1	DS = (0)1
V = (0)1	

WMS

MQ	≤ 48
I	0
O	0
MC	0
MP	0
Digits	0
VR	0
AL	0

1977

1978

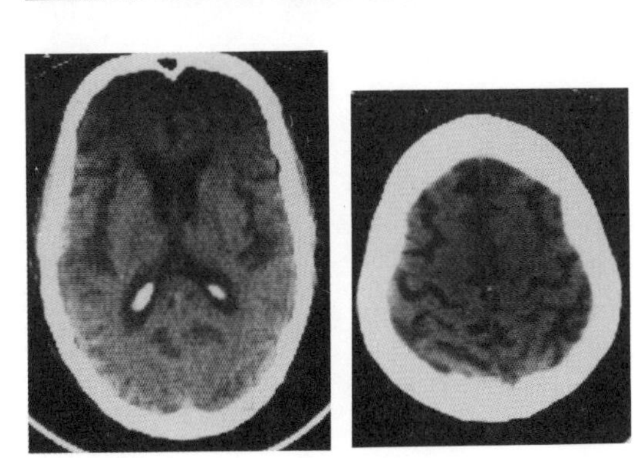

1982

Fig. 5.22. Case 2.

Case 3. This 59-year-old female schoolteacher was brought in by her family because of "personality change." She had been displaying erratic and out-of-character behavior for approximately one year, and it had deteriorated to such a degree that the school at which she was teaching suspended her, pending medical evaluation outcome. CAT scan results depict frontal pole atrophy but no other consistent findings. Neuropsychological examination revealed significant intellectual decline for a patient with a college degree who had been teaching school. Likewise, general cognitive functioning was significantly disturbed as evidenced by her elevated Category Test and Trail-making scores. Memory was also affected, but there were no consistent aphasic findings. Taken together these results are supportive of an early stage of Alzheimer's disease. See figure 5.23.

Age 59
Sex F
Education 16

Lateral Dominance Exam

	Eye	Hand	Foot
Right	X	X	X
Left			
Mixed			

Motor Examination:

FOD	41	SOGD	23	TPTD	5.2
FOND	38	SOGND	21	TPTND	7.5
				TPT Both	7.3

Alternating movements are slow, otherwise no additional motor deficit

Sensory Examination:
Sporodic tactile discrimination errors, bilaterally.
No focal sensory deficit found.

Aphasia Examination:
Essentially normal except for minor calculation errors and mild constructional dyspraxia.

Memory Examination:
WMS MQ = 90
LM 7 TPT M 5
Digits 10 TPT L 2
VM 5
AL 10

Intellectual/Cognitive Examination:
WAIS Results
FSIQ = 93
VIQ = 93 PIQ = 93
I 6 DS 9
C 4 PC 7
A 9 BD 6
S 12 PA 6
D 9 OA 4
V 9

Category Test
114 errors

Trail Making Test
A 49
B 178

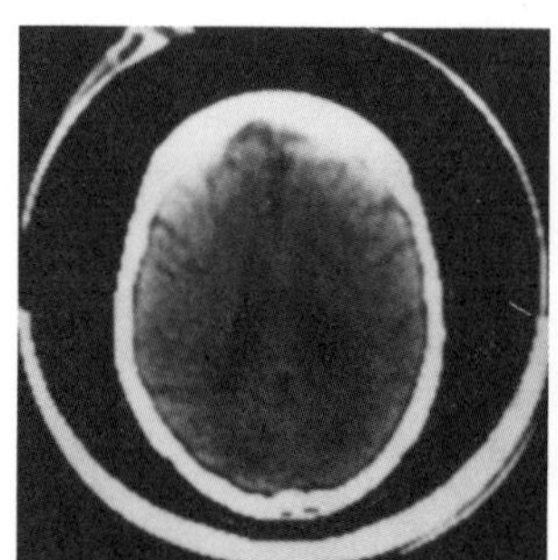
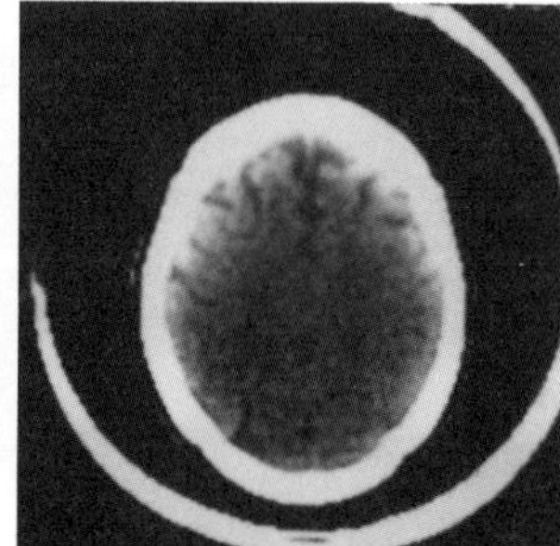

Fig. 5.23. Case 3. Note the focal frontal atrophy. The patient is a 59-year-old schoolteacher who, over the year before examination, displayed marked decline in teaching performance, erratic behavior, and disturbance of memory.

Case 4. This patient had a course of mental and neurological deterioration characteristic of Huntington's chorea. Onset of chroeiform movement disorder was approximately ten years earlier. CAT scan reveals distinct enlargement of the ventricular system with characteristic shape of the anterior areas when atrophy of the caudate nucleus is present. Neuropsychological examination revealed severe and profound generalized deficits. (See fig. 5.24).

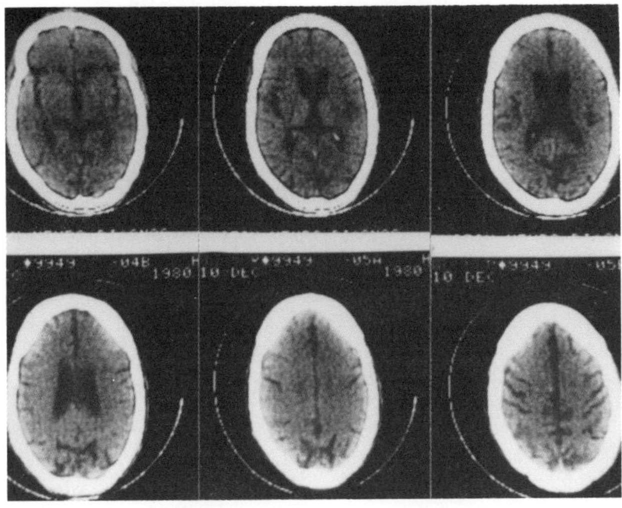

Fig. 5.24. Case 4. Mental and neurological deterioration characteristic of Huntington's chorea. CAT films reveal enlarged ventricular system, widening of the sylvian fissure (particularly on the left), as well as generalized atrophy.

Age 31
Sex M
Education 12

Lateral Dominance Exam

	Eye	Hand	Foot
Right		X	X
Left			
Mixed	X		

Motor Examination:
Advanced choreiform movements
FOD 12 FOND 12 SOGD 28 SOGND 20
Unable to perform any integrative/alternating movements

Sensory Examination:
Bilateral dysgraphesthesia, finger dysgnosia and astereognosis

Aphasia Examination:
Conversational Speech: Dysarthric
Comprehension: Impaired
Repetition of Spoken Language: Impaired
Confrontation-Naming: Dysnomic
Reading:
Aloud: Simple word recognition only
Comprehension: Impaired
Writing/Copying: Dysgraphic, apraxic
Calculations: Impaired

Memory Examination:
MQ = 52
LM 3, Digits 4, VM 0, AL 7

Intellectual/Cognitive Examination:
WAIS Results FSIQ = 52

VIQ = 56		PIQ = 54	
I	6	DS	2
C	2	PC	5
A	3	BD	0
S	0	PA	4
D	4	OA	3
V	1		

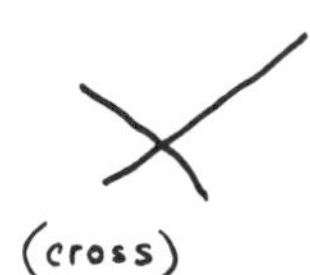

Case 5. This patient had a course of progressive deterioration over five years with the most prominent feature being severe ataxia. The condition was originally thought to be a type of spinocerebellar degeneration syndrome, but the patient was found to have abnormally high mercury values. It was then determined that the patient had been exposed to mercury and that her syndrome likely related to mercury poisoning. CAT scan results reflected marked cerebral and cerebellar atrophy. Correspondingly, neuropsychological examination revealed marked deficits in all higher cerebral functions. (See fig. 5.25.)

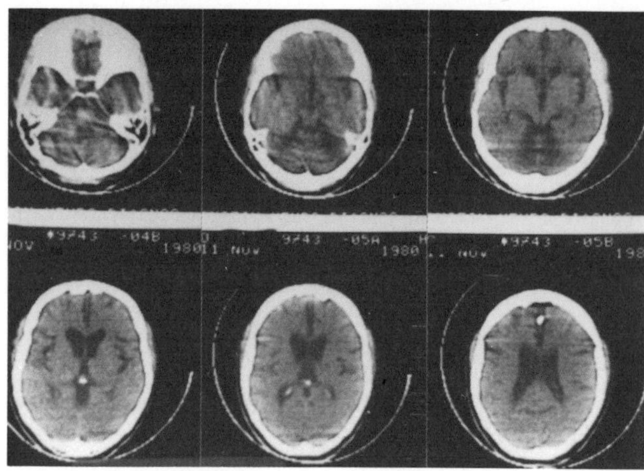

Fig. 5.25. Case 5. Atrophic disease. This patient had a course of deterioration over five years. What was originally thought to be a spinocerebellar degenerative syndrome was later determined to be related to mercury poisoning. The family had lived on an old, abandoned dump site.

Age 29
Sex F
Education 9

Lateral Dominance Exam

	Eye	Hand	Foot
Right	X	X	X
Left			
Mixed			

Motor Examination:
FOD 95 SOGD 20 Marked choreoathetosis
FOND 5 SOGND 15 Alternating movements impossible

Sensory Examination:
Bilateral finger dysgnosia, dysgraphesthesia and dystereognosis

Aphasia Examination:
Conversational Speech: Pseudobalbar speech pattern, content vacant, articulation poor.
Comprehension: Impaired
Repetition of Spoken Language: Impaired
Confrontation-Naming: Impaired
Reading:
Aloud: Alexic
Comprehension: Impaired
Writing/Copying: Dysgraphic, dyspraxic
Calculations: Impaired
SRT DC SSRT DC

Memory Examination:
WMS MA $<$ 50
LM 0 Marked memory deficit in all
Digits 4 areas. Immediate recall
VM 0 markedly defective.
AL 0

Intellectual/Cognitive Examination
WAIS Results FSIQ = 47
VIQ = 52 PIQ = 48
I 1 DS NA Category Test
C 2 PC 2 DC at subtest III
A 3 BD 0 after 50 errors
S 3 PA 4
D 1 OA 2 Trail Making
V 3 A DC
B DC

Case 6. This 31-year-old draftsman had been diagnosed as having multiple sclerosis about five years before neuropsychological examination. Since the onset of the disorder, he has had persistent ataxia as well as generalized sensory disturbance, particularly in sight and touch. During the height of an acute exacerbation, CAT scanning revealed several areas of diminished density and demyelination. This can be visualized in the CAT scan in figure 5.26. Neuropsychological examination is a classic picture of the patient with multiple sclerosis. The greatest deficits observed are those relating to sensory and motor functioning with intellectual and cognitive functions generally preserved, except when involving or requiring sensorimotor integration. As such, definitive sensory and motor findings are present that reflect a nonspecific etiology. Performance IQ is also depressed in this patient, which is very common because of the motor requirements necessary to perform most of the tasks. The delay in trailmaking times is related to the underlying motor deficit. Minnesota Multiphasic Personality Inventory results are also presented, and these results depict the common profile (3-1-2: hysteria-depression-hypochondriasis) found in multiple sclerosis patients. Such a profile implicates a mild to moderate depressive response associated with loss of function as well as significant underlying concern over somatic symptoms.

He shouted The WARNING

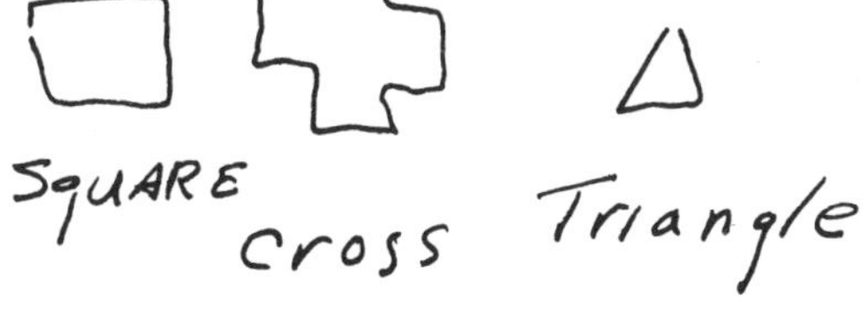

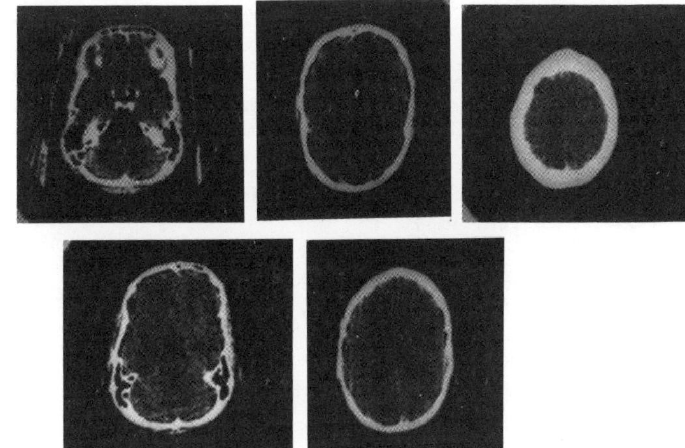

Fig. 5.26. Case 6. Multiple sclerosis. CAT scan reveals several areas of diminished density and demyelination.

Age 31
Sex M
Education 12

Lateral Dominance Exam

	Eye	Hand	Foot
Right	X	X	X
Left			
Mixed			

Motor Examination:

FOGD	45	SOGD	45	TPTD	10.2
FOGND	40	SOGND	42	TPTND	6.9
				TPT Both	4.2

Gait examination reveals moderate ataxia

Sensory Examination:
Mild bilateral dysstereognosis, finger dysgnosia and dysgraphesthesia

Aphasia Screening:
Dysarthric speech, otherwise WNL. Constructional praxis diminished.

Memory Examination:
WMS MQ = 87 LM 10.5, Digits 7, VM 6, AL 12

Intellectual/Cognitive
WAIS Results: VIQ = 92 PIQ = 81 FSIQ = 86
I 10, C 11, A 10, S 9, D 5, V 10; DS 5, PC 10, BD 6, PA 8, OA 7
CT error score 35 Trail Making Test A 70 B 142

MMPI Results
L 53, F 53, K 51, HS 70, D 68, Hy 74, Pd 69, Nf 51, Pa 56, Pt 62, Sc 63, Na 63, Si 56

Case 7. This patient presented with primary symptoms of change in personality about two years before the neuropsychological examination. He subsequently developed anomic aphasia and marked disturbance in memory. A diagnosis of Pick's disease has been made. Note the marked atrophy in frontal and temporal regions, particularly on the left (fig. 5.27). See also Wechsler (1977) for a detailed discussion of a similar case.

Age 73
Sex M
Education 16

Lateral Dominance Exam

	Eye	Hand	Foot
Right	X	X	X
Left			
Mixed			

Motor Examination:
FOD 28 SOGD 34
FOND 24 SOGND 31

Sensory Examination:
Mild bilateral finger dysgnosia and dysgraphesthesia

Language Examination:
Conversational Speech: Mildly paraphasic, halting
Comprehension: Impaired
Repetition of Spoken Language: Intact
Confrontation Naming: Dysnomic
Reading:
Aloud: Mildly impaired
Comprehension: Mildly impaired
Writing: Spelling dyspraxia
Calculations: Impaired

Memory Examination:
WMS MQ = 64
LM 1, Digits 7, VM 6, AL 2.5

Intellectual/Cognitive Examination:
FSIQ = 77 VIQ = 76 PIQ = 81
I 9, C 4, A 3, S 2, D 4, V 1
DS 2, PC 4, BD 2, PA 5, OA 3

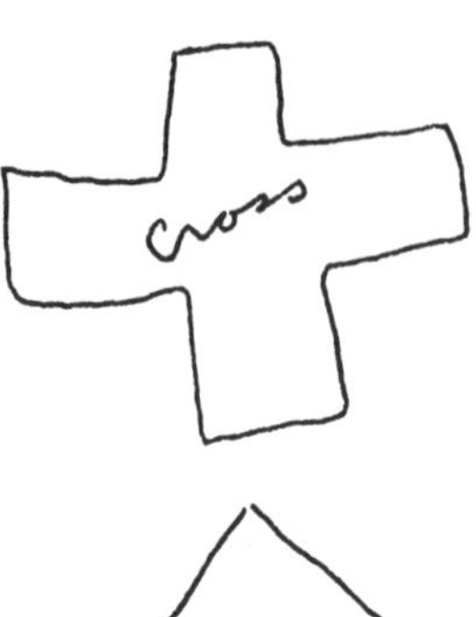

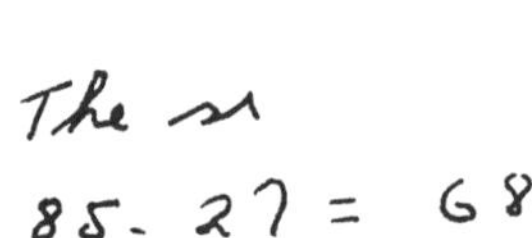

85- 27 = 68

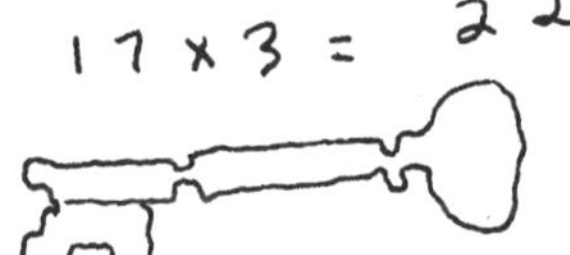

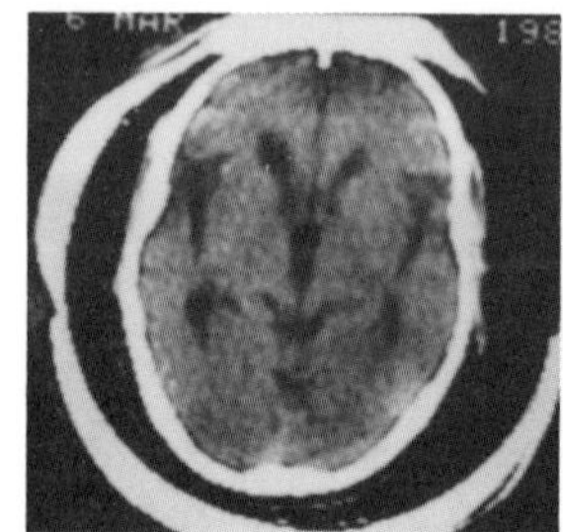
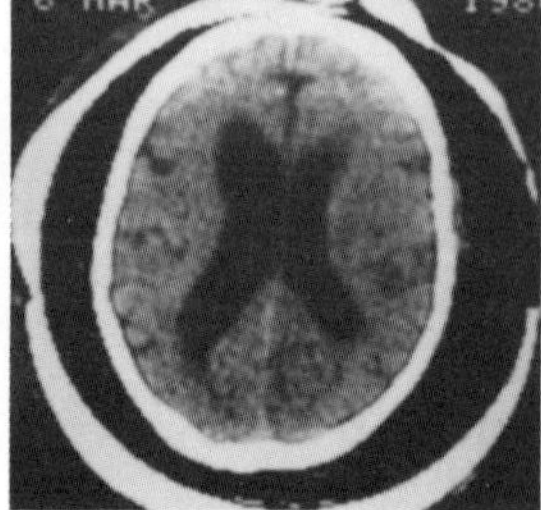
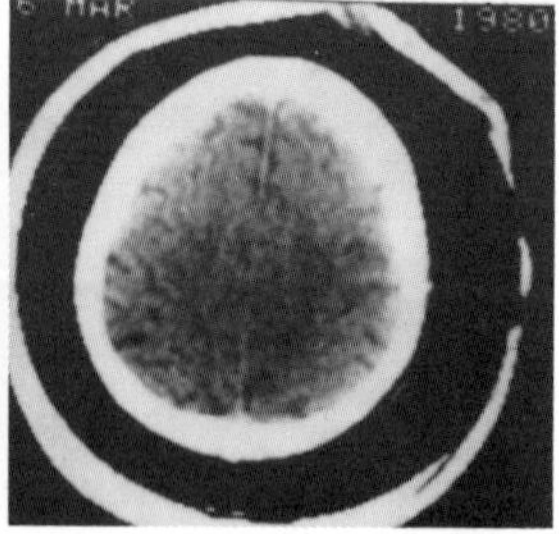

Fig. 5.27. Case 7. Patient diagnosed as having Pick's disease. Note the dramatic atrophy in frontal and temporal regions, particularly on the left.

References

Adams, R. D., and M. Victor. 1977. *Principles of neurology*. New York: McGraw-Hill.

Aikawa, H., K. Suzuki, Y. Iwasaki, and R. Iizuka. 1985. Atypical Alzheimer's disease with spastic paresis and ataxia. *Annals of Neurology* 17:297–300.

Appel, S. H. 1980. Multiple sclerosis. In *Neurology clinics*. Vol. 3. Ardsley, NY: Geigy Pharmaceuticals.

———. 1981. A unifying hypothesis for the cause of amyotrophic lateral sclerosis, parkinsonism, and Alzheimer's disease. *Annals of Neurology* 10:499–505.

———. 1982. Alzheimer's disease and dementia. In *Neurology clinics*. Vol. 4. Ardsley, NY: Geigy Pharmaceuticals.

Beatty, P. A., and J. J. Gange. 1977. Neuropsychological aspects of multiple sclerosis. *Journal of Nervous and Mental Disease* 164:42–50.

Becker, D. P., R. G. Grossman, R. L. McLaurin, and W. F. Caveness. 1979. Head injuries. *Archives of Neurology* 36: 750–758.

Benton, A. L., K. de S. Hamsher, N. R. Varney, and O. Spreen. 1983. *Contributions to neuropsychological assessment*. New York: Oxford University Press.

Berg, B. O., A. Chesanow, and A. L. Prensky. 1978. Demyelinating disorders. In *Neurological pathophysiology*, ed. S. G. Eliasson, A. L. Prensky, and W. B. Hardin. 2d ed. New York: Oxford University Press.

Berg, L., W. L. Danziger, M. Storandt, L. A. Coben, M. Gado, C. P. Hughes, J. W. Knesevich, and J. Botwinick. 1984. Predictive features in mild senile dementia of the Alzheimer type. *Neurology* 34:563–569.

Bigler, E. D., D. W. Hubler, C. M. Cullum, and E. Turkheimer. 1985. Intellectual and memory impairment in dementia. *Journal of Nervous and Mental Disease* 173:347–352.

Bigler, E. D., D. R. Steinman, and J. S. Newton. 1981. Clinical assessment of cognitive deficit in neurologic disorders. I, Effects of age and degenerative disease. *Clinical Neuropsychology* 3:5–13.

Bird, J. M., R. Levy, and R. J. Jacoby. 1986. Computed tomography in the elderly: Changes over time in a normal population. *British Journal of Psychiatry* 148:80–85.

Blusewicz, M. J., R. E. Dustman, T. Schenkenberg, and E. C. Beck. 1977. Neuropsychological correlates of chronic alcoholism and aging. *Journal of Nervous and Mental Disease* 165:348–355.

Boll, T. J., R. Heaton, and R. M. Reitan. 1974. Neuropsychological and emotional correlates of Huntington's chorea. *Journal of Nervous and Mental Disease* 158:61–69.

Boller, F. 1980. Mental status of patients with Parkinson's disease. *Journal of Clinical Neuropsychology* 2:157–172.

Bondareff, W., C. Q. Mountjoy, and M. Roth. 1982. Loss of neurons of origin of the adrenergic projection to cerebral cortex (nucleus locus ceruleus) in senile dementia. *Neurology* 32: 164–168.

Brun, A., and D. Englund. 1986. A white matter disorder in dementia of the Alzheimer type: A pathoanatomical study. *Annals of Neurology* 19:253–262.

Buell, S. J., and P. D. Coleman. 1979. Dendritic growth in the aged human brain and failure in senile dementia. *Science* 206:854–856.

Butters, N., D. Sax, K. Montgomery, and S. Tarlow. 1978. Comparison of the neuropsychological deficits associated with early and advanced Huntington's disease. *Archives of Neurology* 35:585–589.

Caine, E. D., M. H. Ebert, and H. Weingartner. 1977. An outline for the analysis of dementia. *Neurology* 27:1087–1092.

Caltagirone, C., G. Gainotti, C. Masullo, and G. Miceli. 1979. Validity of some neuropsychological tests in the assessment of mental deterioration. *Acta Psychiatrica Scandinavia* 60: 50–56.

Carlen, P. L., D. A. Wilkinson, G. Wortzman, R. Holgate, J. Cordingley, M. A. Lee, L. Huszar, G. Moddel, R. Singh, L. Kiraly, and J. G. Ramkin. 1981. Cerebral atrophy and functional deficits in alcoholics without clinically apparent liver disease. *Neurology* 31:377–385.

Chawluk, J. B., M-M. Mesulam, H. Hurtig, M. Kushner, S. Weintraub, A. Saykin, N. Rubin, A. Alavi, M. Reivich. 1986. Slowly progressive aphasia without generalized dementia: Studies with positron emission tomography. *Annals of Neurology* 19:68–74.

Chui, H. C., E. L. Teng, V. W. Henderson, and A. C. Moy. 1985. Clinical subtypes of dementia of the Alzheimer type. *Neurology* 35:1544–1550.

Cleeland, C. S., C. G. Matthews, and C. L. Hopper. 1970. MMPI profiles in exacerbation and remission of multiple sclerosis. *Psychological Reports* 27:373.

Collins, W. F., R. O. Burns, T. R. Johns, D. G. Kline, P. W. Myers, and G. R. Nugent. 1979. Common neuromuscular disorders and injuries to the peripheral and cranial nerves and spinal cord. *Archives of Neurology* 36:771–781.

Cook, R. H., B. E. Ward, and J. H. Austin. 1979. Studies in aging of the brain. IV, Familial Alzheimer's disease: Relation to transmissible dementia, aneuploidy, and microtubular defects. *Neurology* 29:1402–1412.

Corkin, S., K. L. Davis, J. H. Growdon, E. Usdin, and R. J. Wurtman. 1982. *Alzheimer's disease: A report of progress in research*. Aging, vol. 18. New York: Raven Press.

Cummings, J. L., and D. F. Benson. 1983. *Dementia: A clinical approach*. Boston: Butterworths.

———. 1984. Subcortical dementia. *Archives of Neurology* 41:874–879.

Cummings, J. L., D. F. Benson, M. A. Hill, and S. Read. 1985. Aphasia in dementia of the Alzheimer type. *Neurology* 35: 394–397.

Cutler, N. R., J. V. Haxby, R. Duara, C. L. Grady, A. M. Moore, J. E. Parisi, J. White, L. Heston, R. M. Margolin, S. I. Rapoport. 1985. Brain metabolism as measured with positron emission tomography: Serial assessment in a patient with familial Alzheimer's disease. *Neurology* 35:1556–1561.

D'Antona, R., J. C. Baron, Y. Samson, M. Serdaru, F. Viader, Y. Agid, and J. Cambier. 1985. Subcortical dementia. *Brain* 108:785–799.

DeKosky, S. T., S. W. Scheff, and W. R. Markesbery. 1985. Laminar organization of cholinergic circuits in human frontal cortex in Alzheimer's disease and aging. *Neurology* 35:1425–1431.

Donnan, G. A., B. M. Tress, and P. F. A. Bladin. 1982. A prospective study of lacunar infarction using computerized tomography. *Neurology* 32:49–56.

Emery, O. B., and P. E. Emery. 1983. Language in senile dementia of the Alzheimer type. *Psychiatric Journal of the University of Ottawa* 8:169–178.

Eslinger, P. J., and A. L. Benton. 1983. Visuoperceptual performances in aging and dementia: Clinical and theoretical implications. *Journal of Clinical Neuropsychology* 5:213–220.

Eslinger, P. J., A. R. Damasio, A. L. Benton, and M. Van Allen. 1985. Neuropsychologic detection of abnormal mental decline in older persons. *Journal of the American Medical Association* 253:670–681.

Eslinger, P. J., H. Damasio, N. Graff-Radford, and A. R. Damasio. 1984. Examining the relationship between computed tomography and neuropsychological measures in normal and demented elderly. *Journal of Neurology, Neurosurgery, and Psychiatry* 47:1319–1325.

Ferrendelli, J. A., and W. M. Landau. 1978. Movement disorders. In *Neurological pathophysiology*, ed. S. G. Eliasson, A. L. Prensky, and W. B. Hardin. New York: Oxford University Press.

Finlayson, M. H., and B. Superville. 1981. Distribution of cerebral lesions in acquired hepatocerebral degeneration. *Brain* 104: 79–95.

Fishman, E. B., G. C. Siek, R. D. MacCallum, E. D. Bird, L. Volicer, and J. K. Marquis. 1986. Distribution of the molecule forms of acetylcholinesterase in human brain: Alterations in dementia of the Alzheimer type. *Annals of Neurology* 19:246–252.

Fishman, M. A. 1978. Hydrocephalus. In *Neurological pathophysiology*, ed. S. G. Eliasson, A. L. Prensky, and W. B. Hardin. 2d ed. New York: Oxford University Press.

Foster, N. L., T. N. Chase, N. J. Patronas, M. M. Gillespie, and P. Fedio. 1986. Cerebral mapping of apraxia in Alzheimer's disease by positron emission tomography. *Annals of Neurology* 19:139–143.

Goebel, H. H., R. Heipertz, W. Scholz, K. Iqbal, and I. Tellez-Nagel. 1978. Juvenile Huntington's chorea: Clinical, ultrastructural, and biochemical studies. *Neurology* 28:23–31.

Goldstein, G., and C. H. Shelly. 1974. Neuropsychological diagnosis of multiple sclerosis in a neuropsychiatric setting. *Journal of Nervous and Mental Disease* 158:280–287.

Goodwin, J. S., J. M. Goodwin, and P. J. Garry. 1983. Association between nutritional status and cognitive functioning in a healthy elderly population. *Journal of the American Medical Association* 249:2917–2921.

Gossman, M. D., and L. J. Jacobs. 1980. Three primitive reflexes in parkinsonism patients. *Neurology* 30:189–192.

Graff-Radford, N. R., R. K. Heaton, M. P. Earnest, and J. C. Rudikoff. 1982. Brain atrophy and neuropsychological impairment in young alcoholics. *Journal of Studies in Alcohol* 43: 859–868.

Greenberg, G. D., J. J. Ryan, and P. F. Bourlier. 1985. Psychological and neuropsychological aspects of COPD. *Psychosomatics* 26:29–35.

Haase, G. R. 1977. Diseases presenting as dementia. In *Dementia*, ed. C. E. Wells. 2d ed. Philadelphia: F. A. Davis.

Halliday, A. M., and W. I. McDonald. 1977. Pathophysiology of demyelinating disease. *British Medical Bulletin* 33:21–27.

Hart, R. P. 1983. Chronic renal failure, dialysis, and neuropsychology 5:301–312.

Harvey, N. S. 1986. Psychiatric disorders in parkinsonism. I, Functional illnesses. *Psychosomatics* 27:91–98.

Hayward, L., S. R. Zubrick, and W. Hall. 1985. Early sensory-perceptual changes in Huntington's disease. *Australia/New Zealand Journal of Psychiatry* 19:384–389.

Heaton, R. K., L. M. Nelson, D. S. Thompson, J. S. Burks, and G. M. Franklin. 1985. Neuropsychological findings in relapsing-remitting and chronic-progressive multiple sclerosis. *Journal of Consulting and Clinical Psychology* 53:103–110.

Heyman, A., W. E. Wilkinson, B. J. Hurwitz, D. Schmechel, A. H. Sigmon, T. Weinberg, M. J. Helms, and M. Swift. 1983. Alzheimer's disease: Genetic aspects and associated clinical disorders. *Annals of Neurology* 14:507–515.

Holmes, C. S. 1986. Neuropsychological profiles in men with insulin-dependent diabetes. *Journal of Consulting and Clinical Psychology* 54:386–389.

Huber, S. J., and G. W. Paulson. 1985. The concept of subcortical dementia. *American Journal of Psychiatry* 142: 1312–1317.

Huber, S. J., E. C. Shuttleworth, G. W. Paulson, M. J. G. Bellchambers, and L. E. Clapp. 1986. Cortical vs. subcortical dementia. *Archives of Neurology* 43:392–394.

Hudson, A. J. 1981. Amyotrophic lateral sclerosis and its association with dementia, parkinsonism, and other neurological disorders: A review. *Brain* 104:217–247.

Huppert, F. A., and E. Tym. 1986. Clinical and neuropsychological assessment of dementia. *British Medical Bulletin* 42:11–18.

Hutton, J. T. (1986). Dementia. In *Neurologic clinics.* Vol. 4. Philadelphia: W. B. Saunders Co.

Idestrom, C. M. 1980. Alcohol and brain research. *Acta Psychiatrica Scandinavica* 62:1–209.

Ivnik, R. J. 1978. Neuropsychological stability in multiple sclerosis. *Journal of Consulting and Clinical Psychology* 46: 913–923.

Jacobs, L., and D. Gossman. 1980. Three primitive reflexes in normal adults. *Neurology* 30:184–188.

Jacobs, L., W. R. Kinkel, I. Polachini, and R. P. Kinkel. 1986. Correlations of nuclear magnetic resonance imaging, computerized tomography, and clinical profiles in multiple sclerosis. *Neurology* 36:27–34.

Jarvik, L. F., V. Ruth, and S. S. Matsuyama. 1980. Organic brain syndrome and aging: A six-year followup of surviving twins. *Archives of General Psychiatry* 37:280–286.

Jenkyn, L. R., A. G. Reeves, T. Warren, R. K. Whiting, R. J. Clayton, W. W. Moore, A. Rizzo, I. M. Tuzun, J. C. Bonnett, and B. W. Culpepper. 1985. Neurologic signs in senescence. *Archives of Neurology* 42:1154–1157.

Josiassen, R. C., L. M. Curry, and E. L. Mancall. 1983. Development of neuropsychological deficits in Huntington's disease. *Archives of Neurology* 40:791–796.

Joynt, R. J. 1981. Neurology of aging. *Seminars in Neurology* 1:1–59.

Karagan, N. J. 1979. Intellectual functioning in Duchenne muscular dystrophy: A review. *Psychological Bulletin* 86: 150–259.

Karagan, N. J., and J. P. Sorensen. 1981. Intellectual functioning in non-Duchenne muscular dystrophy. *Neurology* 31: 448–452.

Kaszniak, A. W., D. C. Garron, J. H. Fox, D. Bergen, and M. Huckman. 1979. Cerebral atrophy, EEG slowing, age, education, and cognitive functioning in suspected dementia. *Neurology* 29:1273–1279.

Katz, D. A., A. Naseem, D. S. Horoupian, A. D. Rothner, and P. Davies. 1984. Familial multisystem atrophy with possible thalamic dementia. *Neurology* 34:1213–1217.

Kim, R. C., G. H. Collins, J. E. Parisi, A. W. Wright, and Y. B. Chu. 1981. Familial dementia of adult onset with pathological findings of a "non-specific" nature. *Brain* 104:61–78.

Kish, S. J., L. J. Chang, L. Mirchandani, K. Shannak, and O. Hornykiewicz. 1985. Progressive supranuclear palsy: Relationship between extrapyramidal disturbances, dementia, and brain neurotransmitter markers. *Annals of Neurology* 18: 530–536.

Klawans, H. L., C. G. Goetz, and S. Perlik. 1980. Presymptomatic and early detection in Huntington's disease. *Annals of Neurology* 8:343–347.

Koss, E., R. P. Friedland, B. A. Ober, and W. J. Jagust. 1985. Differences in lateral hemispheric asymmetries of glucose utilization between early- and late-onset Alzheimer-type dementia. *American Journal of Psychiatry* 142:638–640.

Kroll, P., R. Seigel, B. O'Neill, and R. P. Edwards. 1980. Cerebral cortical atrophy in alcoholic men. *Journal of Clinical Psychiatry* 41:417–421.

Lee, K., L. Moller, F. Hardt, and E. Jensen. 1979. Alcohol-induced brain damage and liver damage in young males. *Lancet* 2:759–761.

Levine, D. N., A. Grek, and R. Calvanio. 1985. Dementia after surgery for cerebellar stroke: An unrecognized complication of acute hydrocephalus? *Neurology* 35:568–571.

Lewis, A. J. 1978. *Mechanism of neurological disease.* Boston: Little, Brown & Co.

Lishman, W. A. 1981. Cerebral disorder in alcoholisms: Syndromes of impairment. *Brain* 104:1–20.

Liston, E. H. 1979*a*. The clinical phenomenology of presenile dementia: A critical review of the literature. *Journal of Nervous and Mental Disease* 167:329–336.

——— 1979*b*. Clinical findings in presenile dementia: A report of 50 cases. *Journal of Nervous and Mental Disease* 167: 337–342.

Loring, D. W., and J. W. Largen. 1985. Neuropsychological patterns of presenile and senile dementia of the Alzheimer type. *Neuropsychologia* 23:351–357.

Lowry, J., A. C. Bahr, J. H. Allen, W. F. Meacham, and A. E.

James. 1977. Radiological techniques in the diagnostic evaluation of dementia. In *Dementia*, ed. C. E. Wells. Philadelphia: F. A. Davis.

McGeer, P. L., E. G. McGeer, J. Suzuki, C. E. Dolman, and T. Nagai. 1984. Aging, Alzheimer's disease, and the cholinergic system of the basal forebrain. *Neurology* 34: 741–745.

Malletta, G. J., and F. J. Pirozzolo. 1980. *The aging nervous system*. New York: Praeger.

Mancillas, J. R., G. R. Siggins, and F. E. Bloom. 1986. Systemic ethanol: Selective enhancement of responses to acetycholine and somatostatin in hippocampus. *Science* 231:161–163.

Mann, J. J., M. Stanley, S. Gershon, and M. Rossor. 1981. Mental symptoms in Huntington's disease and a possible primary aminergic neuron lesion. *Science* 210:1369–1371.

Massman, P. J., E. D. Bigler, C. M. Cullum, and R. I. Naugle. 1986. The relationship between cortical atrophy and ventricular volume. *International Journal of Neuroscience* 30: 87–99.

Masters, C. L., D. C. Gajdusek, and C. J. Gibbs. 1981. The familial occurrence of Creutzfeldt-Jakob disease and Alzheimer's disease. *Brain* 104:535–558.

Matthews, C. G., C. S. Cleeland, and C. L. Hopper. 1970. Neuropsychological patterns in multiple sclerosis. *Diseases of the Nervous System* 31:161–169.

Mayeux, R., Y. Stern, J. Rosen, and J. Leventhal. 1981. Depression, intellectual impairment, and Parkinson's disease. *Neurology* 31:645–650.

Mayeux, R., Y. Stern, and S. Spanton. 1985. Heterogeneity in dementia of the Alzheimer type: Evidence of subgroups. *Neurology* 35:453–461.

Mesulam, M-M. 1985. *Principles of behavioral neurology.* Philadelphia: F. A. Davis.

Mölsä, P. K., L. Paljärvi, J. O. Rinne, U. K. Rinne, and E. Sako. 1985. Validity of clinical diagnosis in dementia: A prospective clinicopathological study. *Journal of Neurology, Neurosurgery, and Psychiatry* 48:1085–1090.

Mortimer, J. A., F. J. Pirozzolo, E. C. Hansch, and D. D. Webster. 1982. Relationship of motor symptoms to intellectual deficits in Parkinson's disease. *Neurology* 32:133–137.

Moss, M. B., M. S. Albert, N. Butters, and M. Payne. 1986. Differential patterns of memory loss among patients with Alzheimer's disease, Huntington's disease, and alcoholic Korsakoff's syndrome. *Archives of Neurology* 43:239–246.

Naugle, R. I., C. M. Cullum, E. D. Bigler, and P. J. Massman. 1985. Neuropsychological and computerized axial tomography volume characteristics of empirically derived dementia subgroups. *Journal of Nervous and Mental Disease* 173: 596–604.

———. 1986. Neuropsychological and computerized axial tomography volume characteristics in senile and presenile dementia. *Archives of Clinical Neuropsychology* 1:219–230.

Neary, D., J. S. Snowden, D. M. Bowen, N. R. Sims, D. M. A. Mann, J. S. Benton, B. Northen, P. O. Yates, and A. N. Davison. 1986. Neuropsychological syndromes in presenile dementia due to cerebral atrophy. *Journal of Neurology, Neurosurgery, and Psychiatry* 49:163–174.

Neary, D., J. S. Snowden, D. M. Bowen, N. R. Sims, D. M. A. Mann, P. O. Yates, and A. N. Davison. 1986. Cerebral biopsy in the investigation of presenile dementia due to cerebral atrophy. *Journal of Neurology, Neurosurgery, and Psychiatry* 49:157–162.

Neary, D., J. S. Snowden, D. M. A. Mann, D. M. Bowen, N. R. Sims, B. Northern, P. O. Yates, and A. N. Davison. 1986. Alzheimer's disease: A correlative study. *Journal of Neurology, Neurosurgery, and Psychiatry* 49:229–237.

Norton, J. C. 1975. Patterns of neuropsychological test performance in Huntington's disease. *Journal of Nervous and Mental Disease* 161:276–279.

O'Connor, K. P., J. C. Shaw, and C. O. Ongly. 1979. The EEG and differential diagnosis in psychogeriatrics. *British Journal of Psychiatry* 135:156–162.

Parsons, O. A. 1980. Cognitive dysfunction in alcoholics and social drinkers. *Journal of Studies on Alcohol* 41:105–118.

Payne, E. E. 1969. *An atlas of pathology of the brain*. East Hanover, NJ: Sandoz Pharmaceuticals.

Peyser, J. M., K. R. Edwards, and C. M. Poser. 1980. Psychological profiles in patients with multiple sclerosis. *Archives of Neurology* 37:437–440.

Poser, C. M., M. Alter, R. D. Currier, and S. E. Hunter. 1979. Common demyelinating and degenerative diseases and extrapyramidal disorders. *Archives of Neurology* 36:759–770.

Poskanzer, D. G., A. M. Walker, L. B. Prenney, and J. L. Sheridan. 1981. The etiology of multiple sclerosis: Temporal-spatial clustering indicating two environmental exposures before onset. *Neurology* 31:708–713.

Price, L. J., G. Fein, and I. Feinberg. 1980. Neuropsychological assessment of cognitive function in the elderly. In *Aging in the 1980's*, ed. L. W. Poon. Washington: American Psychological Association.

Prigatano, G. P., O. Parsons, E. Wright, D. C. Levin, and G. Hawryluk. 1983. Neuropsychological test performance in mildly hypoxemic patients with chronic obstructive pulmonary disease. *Journal of Consulting and Clinical Psychology* 51: 108–116.

Pro, J. D., C. H. Smith, and S. M. Sumi. 1980. Presenile Alzheimer's disease: Amyloid plaques in the cerebellum. *Neurology* 30:820–825.

Rao, S. M., T. A. Hammeke, M. P. McQuillen, B. O. Khatri, and D. Lloyd. 1984. Memory disturbance in chronic progressive multiple sclerosis. *Archives of Neurology* 41:625–631.

Reitan, R. M., J. C. Reed, and M. L. Dyken. 1971. Cognitive, psychomotor, and motor correlates of multiple sclerosis. *Journal of Nervous and Mental Disease* 153:218–224.

Reuler, J. B., D. E. Girard, and T. G. Cooney. 1985. Medical intelligence. *New England Journal of Medicine* 312:1035–1038.

Rocca, W. A., L. A. Amaducci, and B. S. Schoenberg. 1986. Epidemiology of clinically diagnosed Alzheimer's disease. *Annals of Neurology* 19:415–424.

Rodgers-Johnson, P., R. M. Garruto, R. Yanagihara, K-M. Chen, D. C. Gajdusek, and C. J. Gibbs, Jr. 1986. Amyotrophic lateral sclerosis and parkinsonism-dementia on Guam: A 30-year evaluation of clinical and neuropathologic trends. *Neurology* 36:7–13.

Rogers, R. L., J. S. Meyer, K. F. Mortel, R. K. Mahurin, and B. W. Judd. 1986. Decreased cerebral blood flow precedes multi-infarct dementia, but follows senile dementia of Alzheimer type. *Neurology* 36:1–6.

Rubens, A. B., B. Froehling, G. Slater, and D. Anderson. 1985. Left ear suppression on verbal dichotic tests in patients with multiple sclerosis. *Annals of Neurology* 18:459–463.

Scheinberg, P. 1977. *Modern practical neurology*. New York: Raven Press.

Seltzer, B., and I. Sherwin. 1983. A comparison of clinical features in early- and late-onset primary degenerative dementia. *Archives of Neurology* 40:143–146.

Silberstein, J. A., and D. A. Parsons. 1981. Neuropsychological impairment in female alcoholics: Replication and extension. *Journal of Abnormal Psychology* 90:179–182.

Skenazy, J. A. and E. D. Bigler. 1984. Neuropsychological deficits in diabetes mellitus. *Journal of Clinical Psychology* 40: 246–258.

———. 1985. Psychological adjustment and neuropsychological performance in diabetics. *Journal of Clinical Psychology* 41:391–396.

Slaby, A. E., and R. J. Wyatt. 1974. *Dementia in the presenium*. Springfield, IL: Charles C. Thomas.

Sollee, N. D., E. E. Latham, D. J. Kindlon, and M. J. Bresnan.

1985. Neuropsychological impairment in Duchenne muscular dystrophy. *Journal of Clinical and Experimental Neuropsychology* 7:486–496.

Sroka, H., T. S. Elizan, M. D. Yahr, A. Burger, and M. R. Mendoza. 1981. Organic mental syndrome and confusional states in Parkinson's disease. *Archives of Neurology* 38:339–342.

Strub, R. L., and F. W. Black. 1981. *Organic brain syndromes: An introduction to neurobehavioral disorders*. Philadelphia: F. A. Davis.

Svanum, S., and J. Schladenhauffen. 1986. Lifetime and recent alcohol consumption among male alcoholics. *Journal of Nervous and Mental Disorder* 174:214–220.

Terry, R. D., and R. Katzman. 1983. Senile dementia of the Alzheimer type. *Annals of Neurology* 14:497–506.

Tomlinson, B. E. 1977. The pathology of dementia. In *Dementia*, ed. C. E. Wells. 2d ed. Philadelphia: F. A. Davis.

Turkheimer, E., C. M. Cullum, D. W. Hubler, S. W. Paver, R. A. Yeo, and E. D. Bigler. 1984. Quantifying cortical atrophy. *Journal of Neurology, Neurosurgery, and Psychiatry* 47: 1314–1318.

Uhl, G. R., D.C. Hilt, J. C. Hedreen, P. J. Whitehouse, and D. L. Price. 1983. Pick's disease (lobar sclerosis): Depletion of neurons in the nucleus basalis of Meynart. *Neurology* 33: 1470–1473.

Ulrich, J. 1985. Alzheimer changes in nondemented patients younger than sixty-five: Possible early stages of Alzheimer's disease and senile dementia of Alzheimer type. *Annals of Neurology* 17:273–277.

Varney, N. R., B. Alexander, and J. H. MacIndoe. 1984. Reversible steroid dementia in patients without steroid psychosis. *American Journal of Psychiatry* 141:369–372.

Volicer, L., P. J. Langlais, W. R. Matson, K. A. Mark, and P. H. Gamache. 1985. Serotoninergic system in dementia of the Alzheimer type. *Archives of Neurology* 42:1158–1161.

Volpe, B. T., and C. K. Petito. 1985. Dementia with bilateral medial temporal lobe ischemia. *Neurology* 35:1793–1797.

Wechsler, A. F. 1977. Presenile dementia presenting as aphasia. *Journal of Neurology, Neurosurgery, and Psychiatry* 40: 303–305.

Weingartner, H., E. D. Caine, and M. H. Ebert. 1979. Imagery, encoding, and retrieval of information from memory: Some specific encoding-retrieval changes in Huntington's disease. *Journal of Abnormal Psychology* 88:52–58.

Weingartner, H., W. Kaye, S. A. Smallberg, M. H. Ebert, J. C. Gillin, and N. Sitaram. 1981. Memory failures in progressive idiopathic dementia. *Journal of Abnormal Psychology* 90: 187–196.

Wells, C. E. 1977. *Dementia*. 2d ed. Philadelphia: F. A. Davis.

———. 1978. Chronic brain disease: An overview. *American Journal of Psychiatry* 135:1–12.

——— 1979. Pseudodementia. *American Journal of Psychiatry* 136:895–900.

Wettstein, A. 1983. No effect from double-bind trial of physostigmine and lecithin in Alzheimer's disease. *Annals of Neurology* 13:210–212.

Whelan, T. B. 1987. Neuropsychological performance of children with Duchenne muscular dystrophy and spinal muscle atrophy. *Developmental Medicine and Child Neurology* 29:212–220.

Whisnant, J. P., R. M. Crowell, R. H. Patterson, S. J. Peerless, J. T. Robertson, A. L. Sahs, and F. M. Yatsu. 1979. Cerebrovascular disease. *Archives of Neurology* 36:734–738.

Whitehouse, P. J. 1986. The concept of subcortical and cortical dementia: Another look. *Annals of Neurology* 19:1–6.

Williams, F. J., and J. M. Walshe. 1981. Wilson's disease. *Brain* 104:735–752.

Wisniewski, K. E., H. M. Wisniewski, and G. Y. Wen. 1985. Occurrence of neuropathological changes and dementia of Alzheimer's disease in Down's syndrome. *Annals of Neurology* 17:278–282.

Wu, S., T. Schenkenberg, S. D. Wing, and A. G. Osborn. 1981. Cognitive correlates of diffuse cerebral atrophy determined by computer tomography. *Neurology* 31:1180–1184.

Yamaguchi, F., J. S. Meyer, M. Yamamoto, F. Sakai, and T. Shaw. 1980. Noninvasive regional cerebral blood flow measurements in dementia. *Archives of Neurology* 37:410–418.

Zetusky, W. J., J. Jankovic, and F. J. Pirozzolo. 1985. The heterogeneity of Parkinson's disease: Clinical and prognostic implications. *Neurology* 35:522–526.

6. Neoplastic Disorders of the Nervous System

In general, intracranial tumors may be divided into two broad categories: (1) extracerebral tumors originating in the skull (osteomas, sarcomas, hemangiomas), meninges (meningiomas), cranial nerves (neuromas), or brain appendages (pituitary tumors) or from congenital cell rests (craniopharyngiomas, epidermoid cysts, teratomas, and colloid cysts), producing their neurologic and neuropsychological effects typically by mechanical compression of the cerebral structures; and (2) intracerebral tumors originating from glial cells (gliomas—astrocytomas, glioblastomas, oligodendrogliomas, and ependymomas) or metastasizing tumors (Coxe, 1978; Selikoff and Hammond, 1982; Vick, 1981). Keeping in mind the distinction between intracerebral and extracerebral tumors and examining the most commonly occurring tumors, there are five general types: gliomas, meningiomas, pituitary tumors, neurinomas, and metastases.

Commonly Occurring Tumors

Gliomas

Basically, gliomas result from neoplastic proliferations of glial cells of the brain, typically astrocytes and less frequently oligodendroglia and ependymal cells (cells lining the walls of the ventricles). Astrocytomas vary by degree of malignancy, ranging from extremely slow growing and relatively confined (grade I) to rapidly growing, invasive, and anaplastic (grades III or IV, commonly called, at this level of development, *glioblastoma multiforme*). All these tumors are similar in that they arise from the intraparenchymal brain cells and are therefore invasive. Figures 6.1–6.6 display typical configuration of gliomas.

The glioblastoma multiforme accounts for about 15 percent to 20 percent of all intracranial tumors, about 55 percent of all gliomas, and 90 percent of all cerebral gliomas (Adams and Victor, 1977). The glioblastoma is a highly malignant and very rapidly expanding neoplasm that may grow to an enormous size before discernible clinical signs develop (see fig. 6.5). In addition to abnormal glial cell proliferation, the glioblastoma multiforme develops its own vascular supply, and thus the entire structure (tumor plus vascular supply) produces a lesion of mass effect. Typically, focal and pathognomonic neurologic and neuropsychological findings are present that represent the locus of the tumor, but usually there are generalized signs also present that represent the mechanical distortion of the cerebral structures displaced by the size of the tumor and affected as a result of the mass effect described above. The glioblastoma may occur anywhere in the central nervous system (CNS). Less than 20 percent of the patients with glioblastoma live more than one year after diagnosis, and only 10 percent beyond that (Adams and Victor, 1977). Although recent advances have been made in treatment that may lengthen survival, unfortunately, even if life is prolonged, typically devastating incapacitation is present (Hochberg and Slotnick, 1980).

Astrocytomas are usually slower growing, but the ultimate clinical picture is quite similar to that of glioblastoma multiforme. There is a somewhat better prognosis with astrocytomas. Oligodendrogliomas are quite infrequent, occurring in only 5–7 percent of cerebral tumor cases. They are slow growing and similar to astrocytomas. The ependymomas arise from the ependymal cells that line the lateral ventricles. These tumors constitute less than 5 percent of cerebral tumors, and they are most common in infants and children.

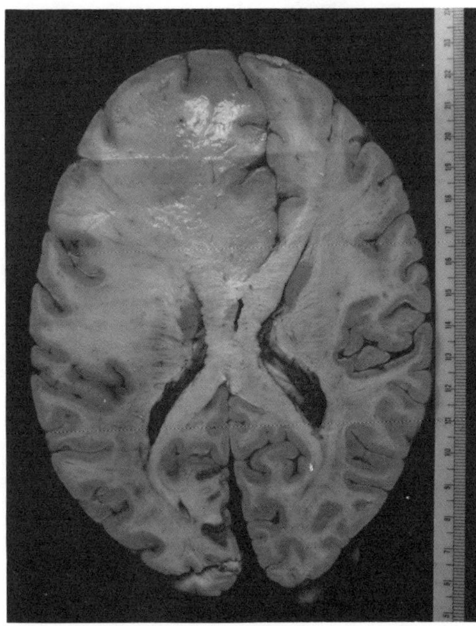

Fig. 6.1. Large low-grade astrocytoma of the left frontal lobe as depicted in this horizontal view. Note the marked displacement across the midline. Also note that the tumor locus is somewhat difficult to differentiate, as is frequently the case with low-grade tumors such as this. Contrast this with the tumor (glioblastoma multiforme) presented in fig. 6.31.

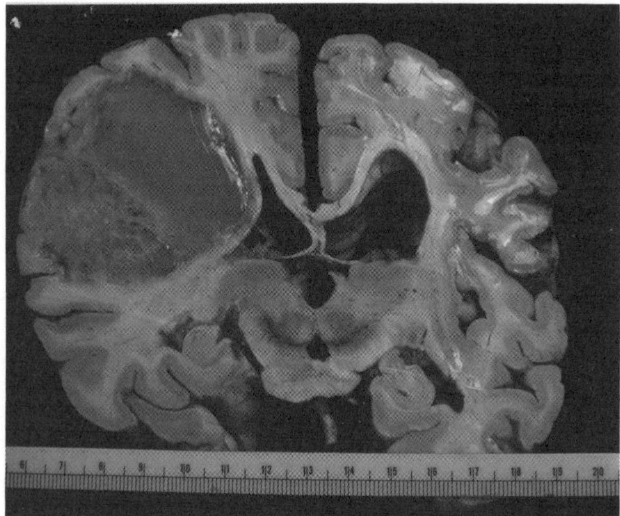

Fig. 6.2. A large metastasizing tumor is depicted in the right frontal-parietal area. Note the core of the tumor and surrounding edema and tissue softening. Also note the ventricular displacement and collapse. Note also the compression of the right temporal lobe and inferior ventricle, due to the expansion of the tumor.

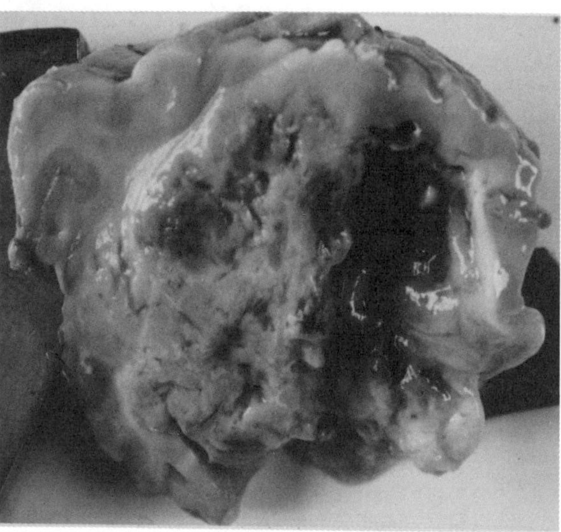

Fig. 6.3. Destructive glioblastoma multiforme. Brain section depicting the destructive effects of a glioblastoma multiforme. Note the extensive infiltration of the neoplastic process throughout the brain tissue.

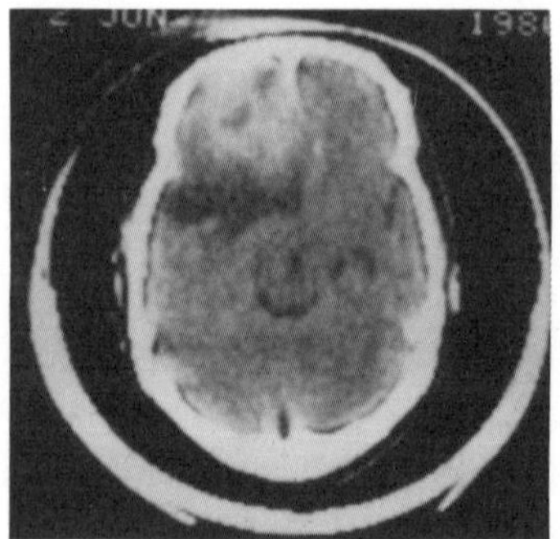

Fig. 6.4. Glioblastoma as identified by CAT scan.

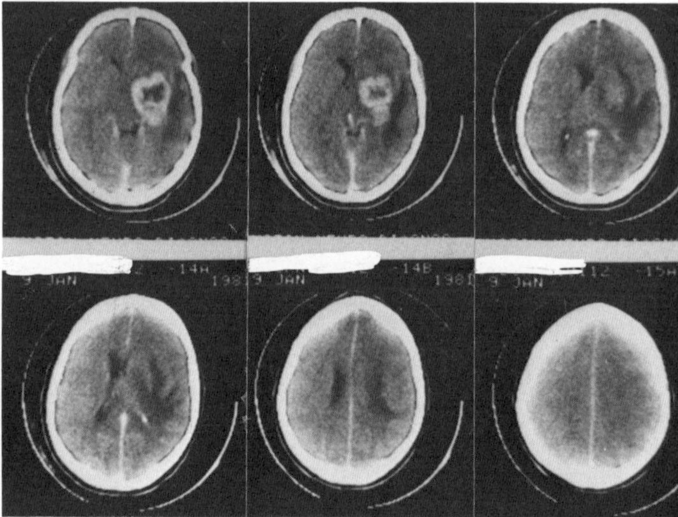

Fig. 6.5. Glioblastoma in central right hemisphere. Note the size and extent of the tumor and the ventricular distortion in this CAT scan of a 47-year-old woman. Surprisingly, the patient's presenting symptom (headache) and neurological and neuropsychological test results were negligible. Similarly, the patient's family reported no change in the patient's personality or behavior. With some neoplastic diseases, as in the case of this patient, the tumor may reach a substantial size before demonstrable behavioral or cognitive effects occur, particularly when the tumor is in the right hemisphere.

Meningiomas

Meningiomas arise in the dura mater or arachnoid space of the meninges. While they may occur at any age, the highest incidence is in the seventh decade of life (Victor and Adams, 1977). Because the tumor does not invade the brain tissue specifically (see figs. 6.7–6.9), it may reach a rather large size before producing symptoms (see case 3), particularly if the location is in an area of minor importance. The neurologic and neuropsychological signs, then, depend on the size and location of the tumor. Clearly, focal signs may not be evident with some meningiomas. Treatment outcome is good if the tumor is located in an accessible area; however, such tumors located inferior to the tentorium present considerable risks of morbidity. Inasmuch as the meningioma is typically benign (the exception being metastatic meningioma), surgical removal of the tumor may produce dramatic improvement and complete recovery.

Pituitary Tumors

The pituitary adenoma typically produces visual disturbance, endocrine disturbance, or both because of the nearness of the pituitary to the optic nerves, chiasm, and tracts, its role in hormonal regulation, and its proximity to and functional interrelationship with the hypothalamus. The expanding pituitary adenoma, as it extends upward out of the sella turcica, compresses the optic chiasm first and then may progress to the point of impinging on the temporal lobe or invading the third ventricle or posterior fossa (see fig. 6.10). Early detection results in the most favorable prognosis with new surgical techniques for treatment, removal, or both.

Although not truly a pituitary tumor, the craniopharyngioma produces a clinical picture quite similar to that of the pituitary adenomas. This tumor is thought to be a congenital tumor originating from the cell rests at the junction of the infundibulum and the pituitary (Lewis, 1976). The tumor usually develops above the sella turcica, depressing the optic chiasm and extending into the third ventricle (see figs. 6.11 and 6.12). This tumor is seen with greater frequency in children than adults.

Neurinoma

The most common neurinoma is that of the eighth cranial nerve and is typically referred to as an acoustic neuroma (also schwannoma or neurofibroma). These tumors usually originate on the vestibular division of the eighth cranial nerve just within the internal auditory canal. As they grow, they extend into the posterior fossa, thereby occupying the angle between the cerebellum and pons (i.e., the cerebellopontine angle). During their initial development, it is not uncommon for compression of the fifth, seventh, ninth, or tenth cranial nerve (fifth and seventh most commonly) to occur. With continued growth, they invariably displace and compress the pons and medulla, typically inducing cerebrospinal fluid obstruction. Hearing loss, headache, tinnitus, and ataxia have been reported as common clinical signs. Brainstem auditory-evoked response tests and CAT scanning are most effective (see fig. 6.13) in detecting an acoustic neuroma. Signs of cerebral involvement are usually not evident in the behavior of these patients. However, subsequent to surgery or when a lesion produces hydrocephalus, various cerebral or cognitive deficits may occur.

Metastases

Through hematogenous spread, carcinomas of the brain originate. The most common are a result of lung carcinoma, but metastasis of breast, gastrointestinal, and kidney carcinoma is also common and frequent (see figs. 6.14–6.17). The devastating aspect of metastases is that they are typically multifocal and many times diversely spread throughout the brain (see case 4). Generally, the clinical picture with carcinomatous brain implants differs little from that seen with glioblastoma multiforme. Prognosis is dismal.

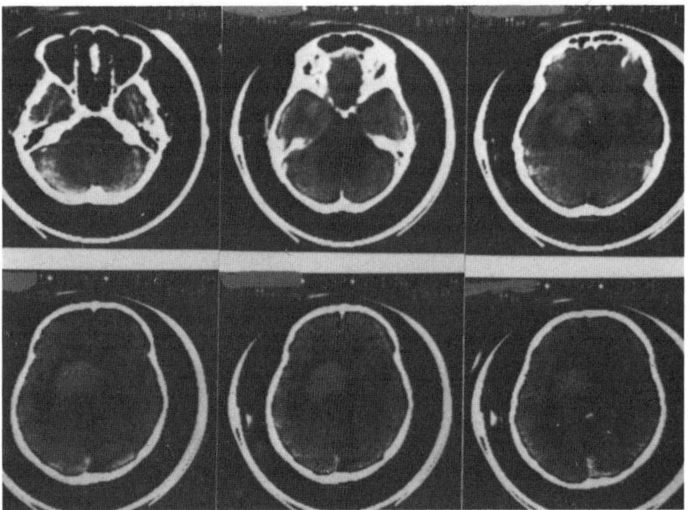

Fig. 6.6. Lesion in left thalamus. This 68-year-old woman presented with an evolving global aphasia, marked memory disturbance, right hemianopsia, and right-side hemisensory deficit in the absence of marked motor findings. The most parsimonious explanation of such findings would be a lesion located in the left thalamus. CAT scan confirms this explanation by outlining a large tumor involving the entire left thalamus, producing secondary effects throughout the left hemisphere, and including some direct invasion of the left temporal lobe.

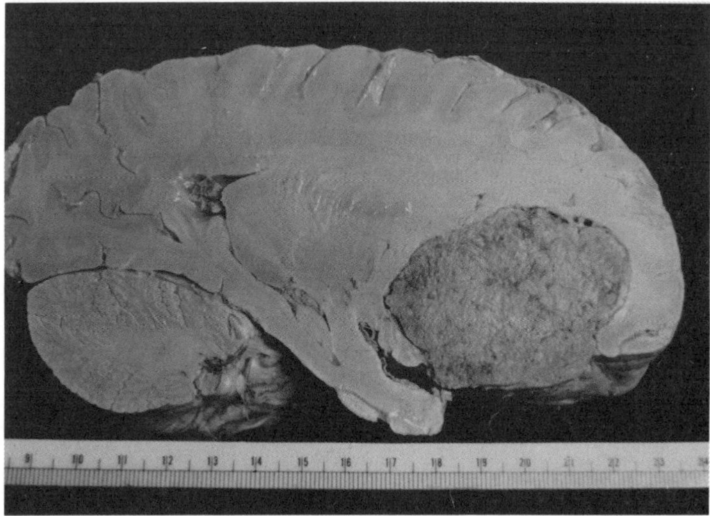

Fig. 6.7. Large meningioma emanating from the region of the olfactory groove as depicted in postmortem sagittal section. Note the size of the tumor and the displacement of the frontal and temporal lobes. Such tumors may grow to an enormous size before symptoms become clear. Fig. 6.8 depicts the presentation of such a tumor by CAT scanning.

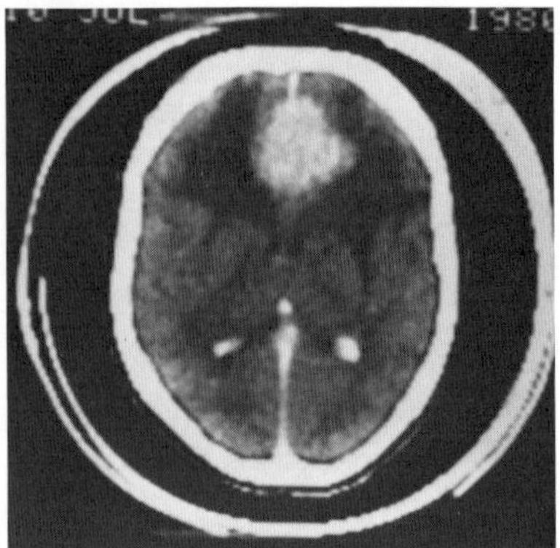

Fig. 6.8. Meningioma originating from the olfactory groove visualized by CAT scan. Note the edema and displacement of the brain, features commonly seen with meningiomas.

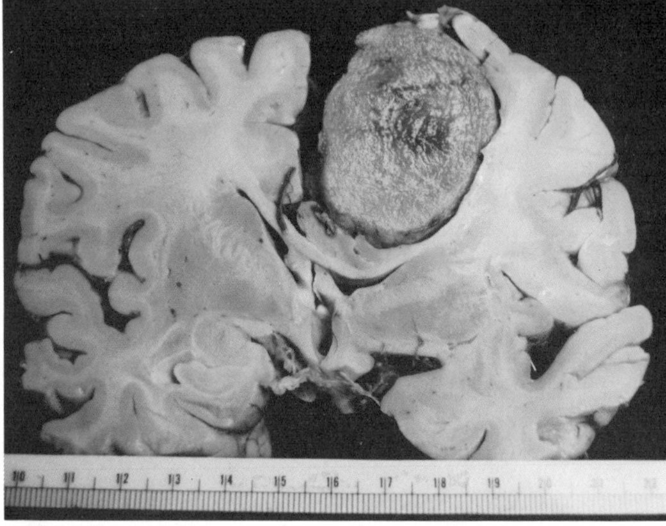

A

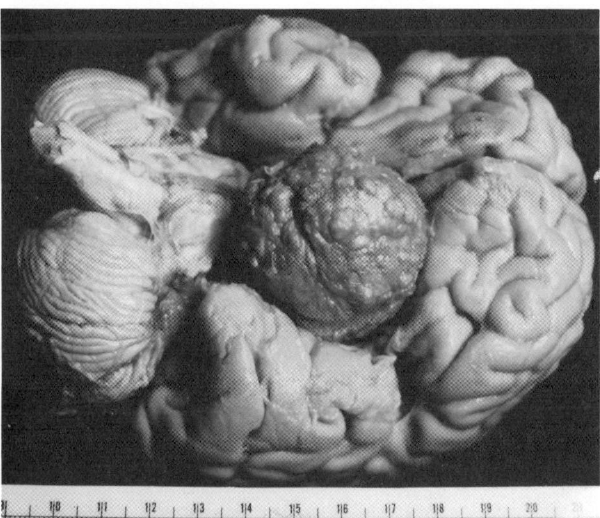

B

Fig. 6.9. *A*, large midline meningioma of the right frontal lobe. Note the size of the tumor, its circular appearance, the collapse of the corpus callosum, and ventricular displacement. *B*, large temporal lobe meningioma. Note how the tumor displaced the brain to accommodate its expansion.

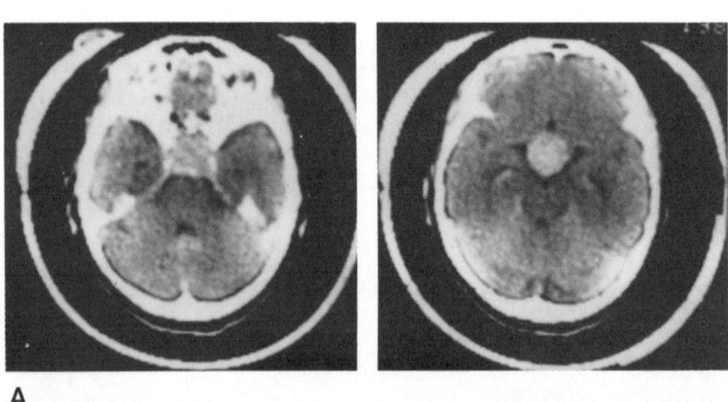

A

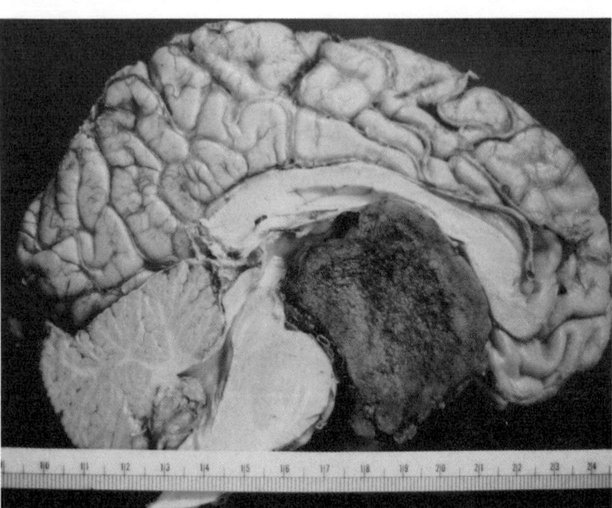

B

Fig. 6.10. *A*, pituitary adenoma expanding out of the sella turcica as depicted by CAT scanning. *B*, postmortem sagittal view depicting an enormous pituitary adenoma. Note the midbrain–brain-stem displacement and the upward expansion of the tumor.

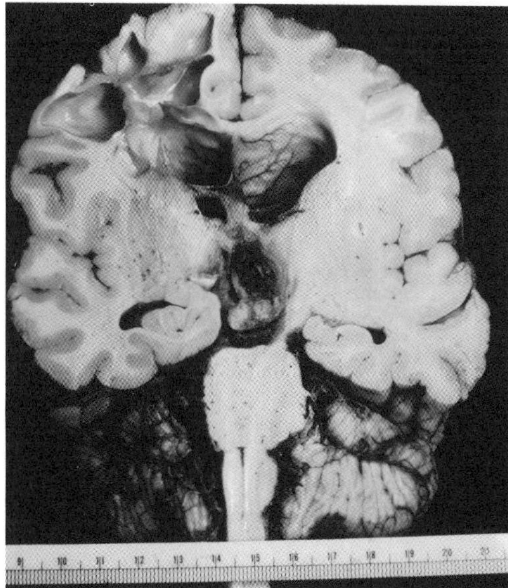

A

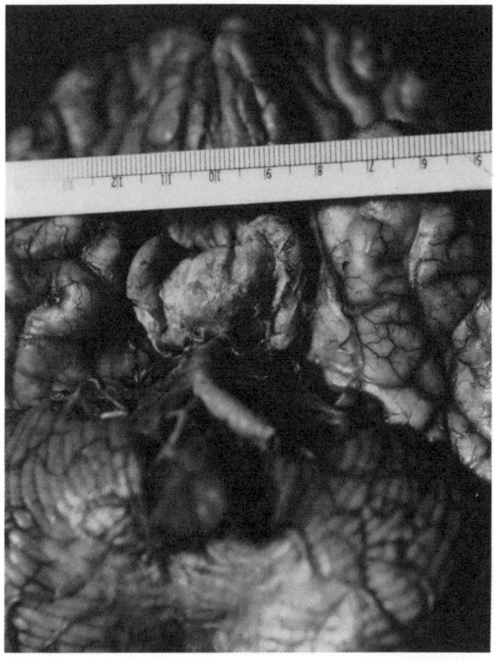

B

Fig. 6.11. *A*, coronal section depicting locus of craniopharyngioma. *B*, in situ depiction of craniopharyngioma, ventral view at autopsy.

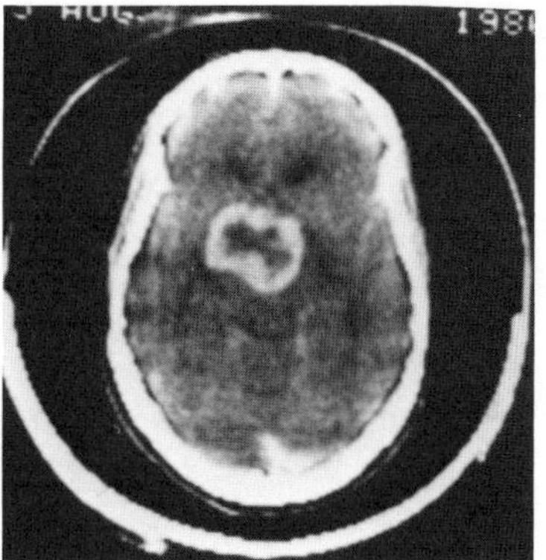

Fig. 6.12. CAT scan of craniopharyngioma.

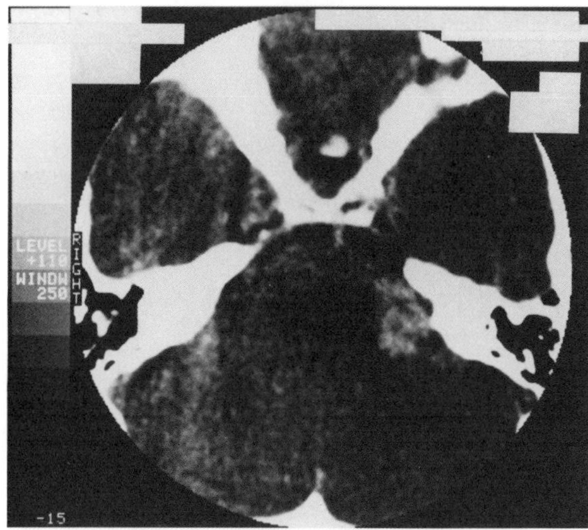

Fig. 6.13. Tumor of the eighth cranial nerve. This patient had neurofibromatosis (von Recklinghausen's disease), and tumors are not uncommonly seen with this disorder. The patient presented with progressive deafness, dizziness, and dysequilibrium.

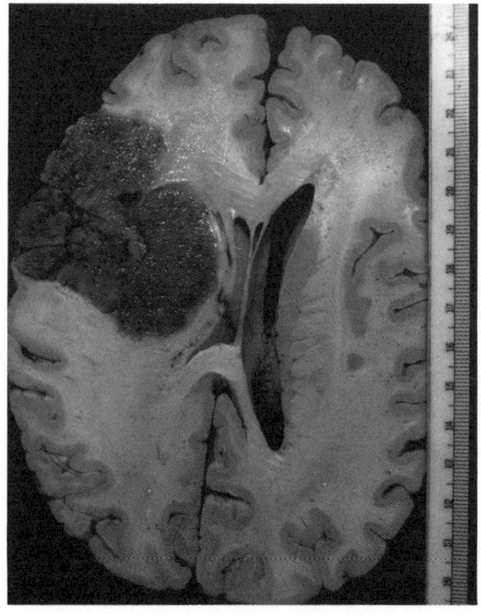

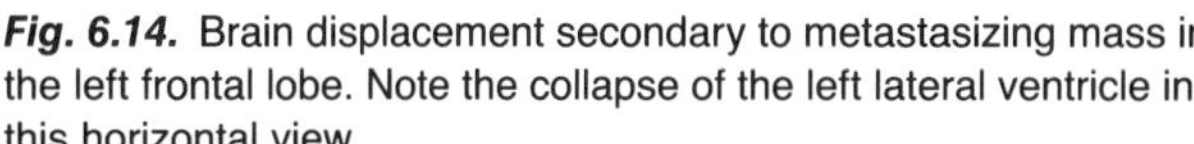

Fig. 6.14. Brain displacement secondary to metastasizing mass in the left frontal lobe. Note the collapse of the left lateral ventricle in this horizontal view.

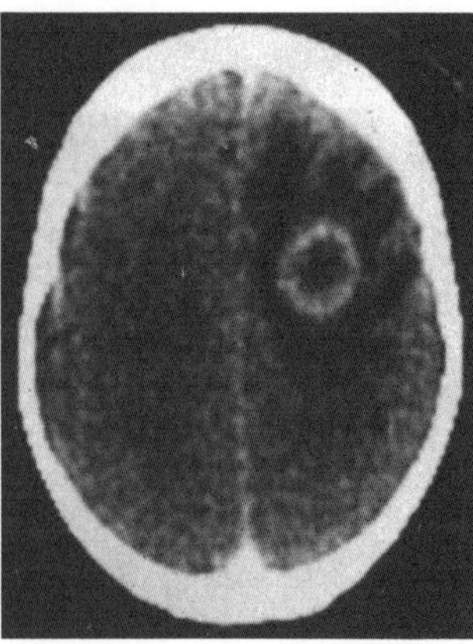

Fig. 6.15. Cerebral metastasis of systemic origin. Note in this CAT scan the ringlike appearance surrounding the tumor and the edema. This configuration is common with metastasizing tumors.

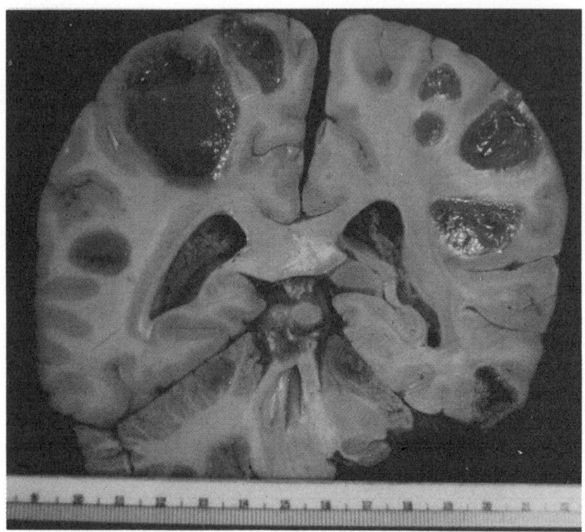

Fig. 6.16. Multiple metastasizing tumors secondary to prostate cancer. Note the multiple locations of tumor development.

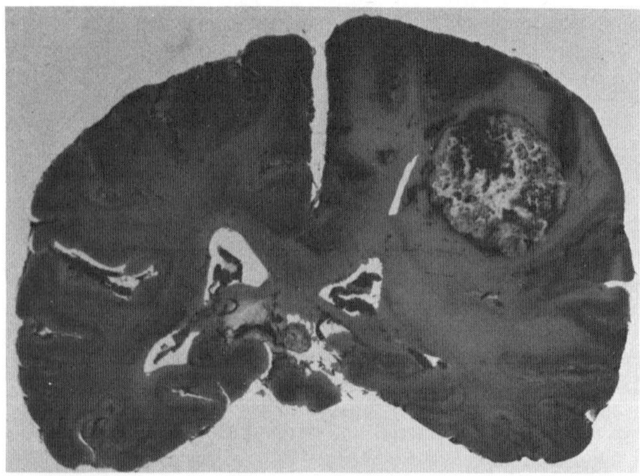

Fig. 6.17. Cerebral metastases from lung carcinoma. Large thin coronal section of the cerebrum shows a tumor in the right parietal lobe. The adjacent white matter is of a lighter color than normal, indicating edema. From Payne (1969).

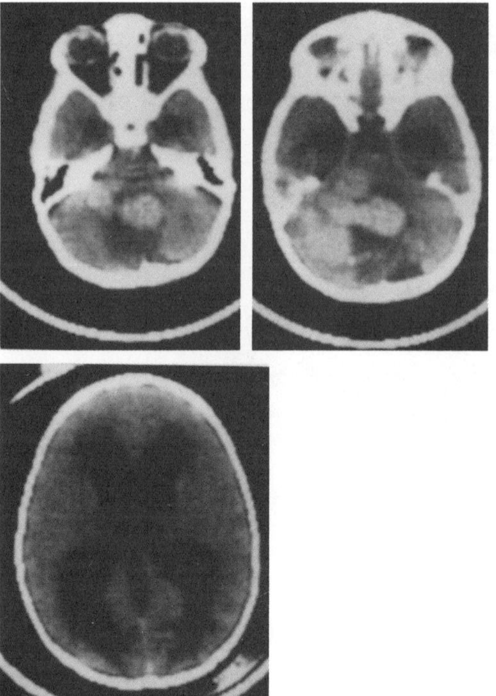

Fig. 6.19. Posterior fossa tumor in 3-year-old boy. The tumor originated in the medulla, but rapidly expanded to encompass much of the posterior fossa vault. The expansion of the tumor obstructed the fourth ventricle as well as the aqueduct, producing obstructive hydrocephalus.

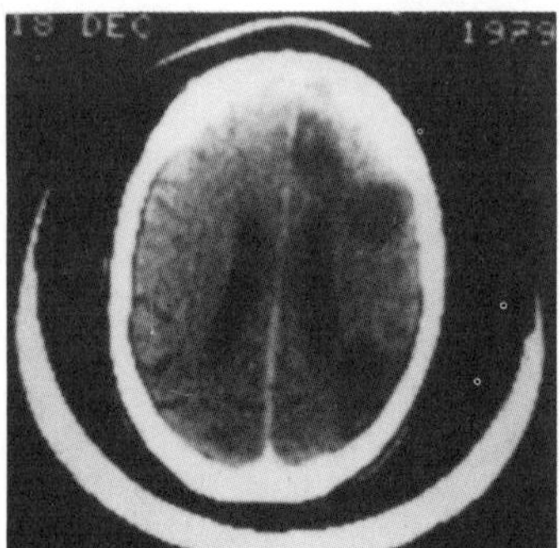

Fig. 6.18. Tuberculoma. This patient suffered from refractory tuberculosis and subsequent development of multiple tuberculoma of the brain.

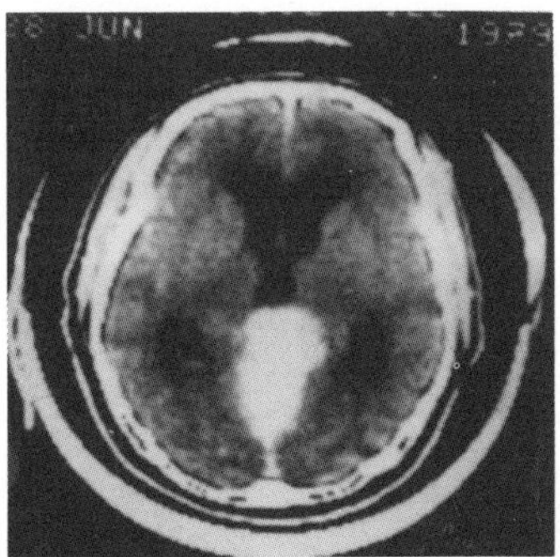

Fig. 6.20. Large arteriovenous malformation. This malformation of the basilar artery system produced obstructive hydrocephalus.

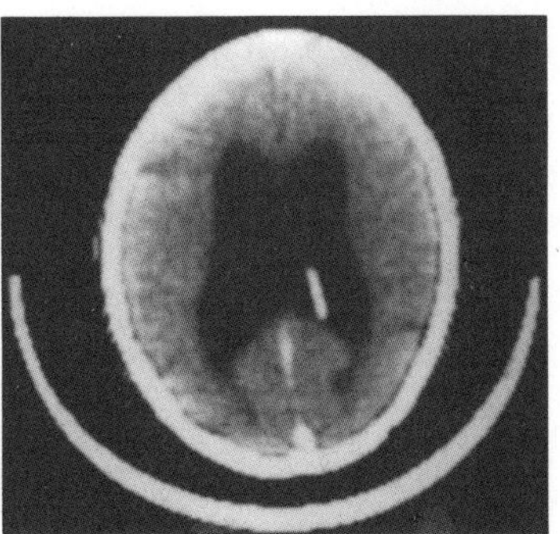

Fig. 6.21. Hydrocephalus after glioma removal. This patient had a large glioma removed from the midcerebellar region. Obstructive hydrocephalus developed, and although shunting (as visualized in the right ventricle) was performed, the hydrocephalus remained.

Other Tumors

Tuberculomas (and tuberculous meningitis) are truly uncommon but are still a complication of tuberculosis (DeAngelis, 1981). Tuberculomas are typically multifocal (see fig. 6.18). Parasitic cysts (i.e., toxoplasmosis) many times have neoplastic-like features (see fig. 7.5 in the next chapter). Pinealomas, tumors arising in the pineal gland, typically extend anteriorly into the third ventricle and may compress the hypothalamus. These tumors usually develop in childhood. Medulloblastomas are rapidly growing embryonic tumors that originate in the posterior aspect of the cerebellar vermis and the neuroepithelial region near the fourth ventricle. They, too, are more commonly seen in children than in adults (see fig. 6.19). Hemangiomas, or "vascular tumors," also occur, having an abnormal vascular origin and causing symptoms like those tumors cause (see fig. 6.20). (Figures 6.22–6.27 depict a variety of other tumors.) (See also chapter entitled "Vascular Disorders.")

Some form of brain edema invariably occurs with neoplastic growth and represents one of the major complicating factors. Also because of space-occupying expansion of the lesion, cerebrospinal fluid flow is usually compromised, producing alterations in intracerebral pressures. As a result of pressure, it is not uncommon to have brain herniations develop, the most common being subfalcial, temporal lobe—tentorial, or near the cerebellum—foramen magnum. Whether edema, intracranial pressure increase, or herniation occurs singularly or in combination, these factors are additive in terms of neurologic or neuropsychological deficits (see fig. 6.21). Hemorrhaging at the tumor site is also a common complication.

Central Nervous System Neoplasia in Children

Tumors of the posterior fossa (below the tentorium) (see fig. 6.19) are more common in children than adults (Bigler, 1980; Ford, 1976). Bray (1969) reviews data that suggest that two-thirds of the intracranial neoplasms in children are located subtentorially. With early detection of such tumors in children, there is relatively good outcome in terms of cerebral function, although motor deficits secondary to brain-stem cerebellar impairment are common (Knights and Hinton, 1973). Similar results have also been obtained with adults (see Norton and Matthews, 1972).

Clinical Signs

The prominent clinical sign of neoplasia is its progressive nature but relatively recent onset of cerebral involvement (see case studies). Various degrees of mental aberration may be the first signs. The changes may initially be nearly imperceptible, but over a period of time become prominent. In adults, the onset of seizures, in the absence of any other causal factor, has been associated with a higher incidence of tumor (about 35 percent of such patients have cerebral neoplasms) (Chou, Kramer, and Shapiro, 1979). The cognitive and emotional changes that may occur because of neoplasm are dependent upon the site and extent of tumor development. Frontal lobe tumors frequently result in personality changes, typically alterations in emotional tone and errors of judgment. Tumors in a variety of locales may produce or be associated with such generalized symptoms as lassitude, fatigue, or dizziness. Headache is also a common symptom, and the headache need not be of specific origin. Papilledema (bulging of the optic nerve head due to increased intracranial pressure) is also common, particularly for more anterior tumors. Hemorrhage into the tumor or adjacent cerebral tissue may occur. The patient may display signs of acute cerebrovascular disorder, but the examiner may find the primary cause related to neoplasm.

Clinical Outcome

Recovery from a neoplastic disorder is dependent on numerous factors, the most important frequently being the type, size, and location of the tumor (Hochberg and Slotnick, 1980). Meningiomas may be surgically removed, particularly if they are dorsally located, without serious neurologic sequelae. However, infiltrative tumors have considerable mortality, if not morbidity. Tumors of the di-

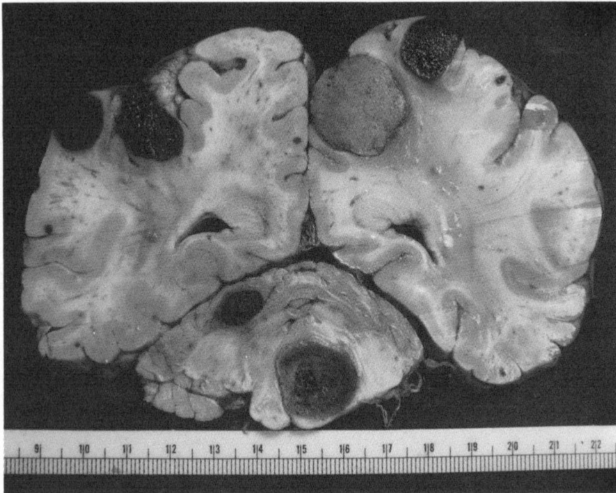

Fig. 6.22. Multiple malignant melanoma. Note the multiple loci of tumor development.

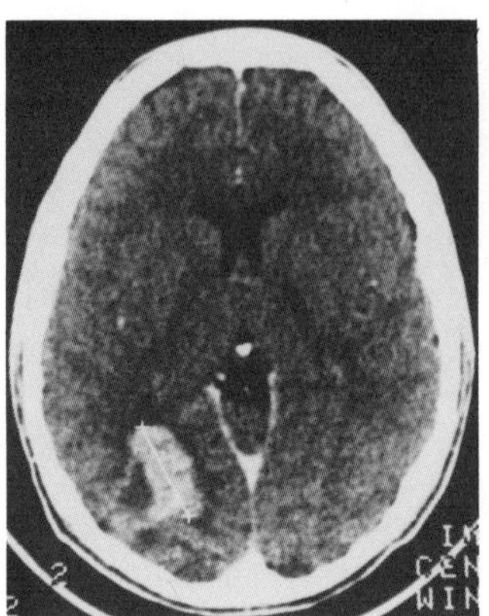

Fig. 6.23. CAT scan depiction of an ependymoma. Note the extension of the tumor from the lateral ventricle.

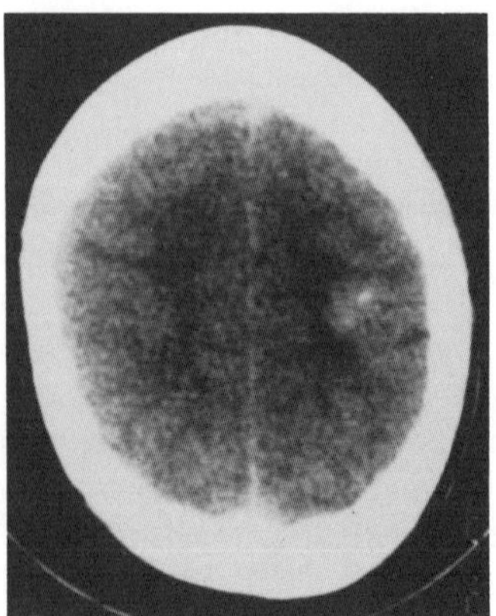

Fig. 6.24. CAT scan tumor appearance in right parietal region in a patient with neurofibromatosis.

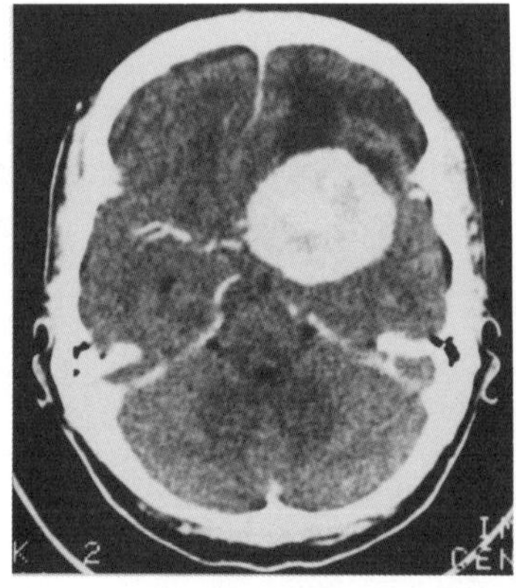

Fig. 6.25. CAT scan on the left demonstrates a large meningioma in the right frontal region. The patient presented with memory difficulties and impaired spatial abilities. Despite the enormous size of the tumor, she did not have any left-side weakness or deficit in basic intellectual functioning. Note the edema surrounding the tumor. The CAT scan on the right was taken three months post-surgical removal of the tumor. Although the tumor was enormous in size, only a small area of encephalomalacia developed in the base of the right frontal region. Following the operation, the patient had rather complete recovery and was able to return to teaching elementary school. (Compare this case with fig. 6.26.)

encephalon or brain stem may produce devastating deficits even though their size may be small (see fig. 6.28). Various iatrogenic effects secondary to radiation, chemotherapy, or both may also produce various specific neurologic deficits. Intracranial pressure effects produced by the expanding tumor, as well as edema, may also complicate outcome. (See figs. 6.29 and 6.30, which show secondary effects of tumor.) Frequently, tumors are detected too late to be effectively treated, and the patient will show a steady decline in cerebral function, eventually resulting in death, because of their relentless, progressive course. This occurs commonly with the gliomas because the primary tumor site may "seed" other regions of the brain producing multifocal neoplastic sites. Last, age complicates outcome. Older patients face less positive outcome.

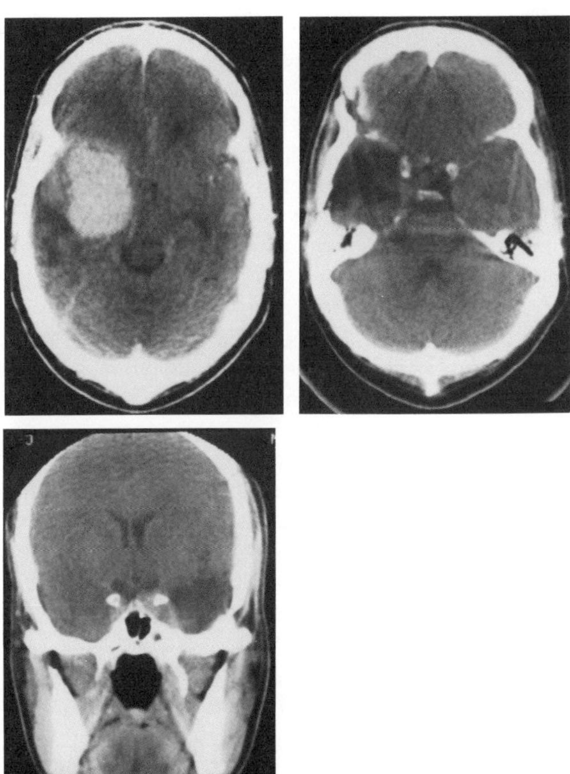

Fig. 6.26. CAT scan demonstrating a large meningioma in the left temporal lobe (depicted in the film at upper left). Note the displacement and collapse of the ventricular system. The CAT scans at upper right (horizontal view) and bottom left (coronal view) were taken three months postsurgical removal of the tumor. Note the extensive tissue loss due to compression of cerebral tissue and vascular supply by the expanding tumor. This patient had persistent personality, temperament, and memory changes secondary to this permanent temporal lobe damage.

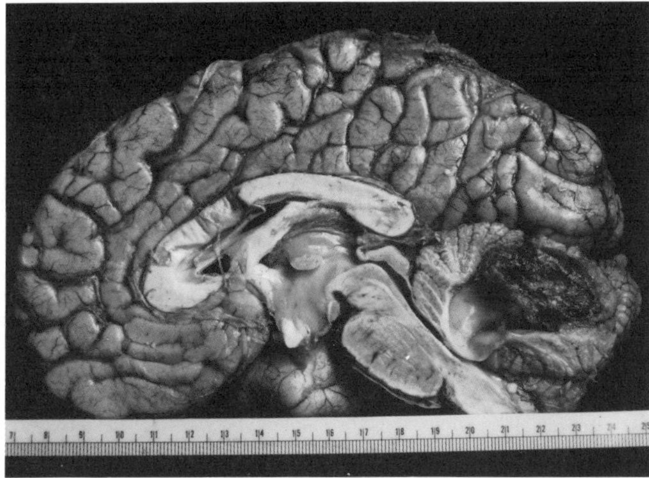

Fig. 6.28. Sagittal view of cerebellar tumor. Note the destructive effects at the level of the cerebellum and lower brain stem, but with preserved structural integrity of the cerebrum. Such tumors will produce focal motor deficits, sensory deficits, or both without cerebral signs, unless obstructive hydrocephalus or neoplastic spread occurs.

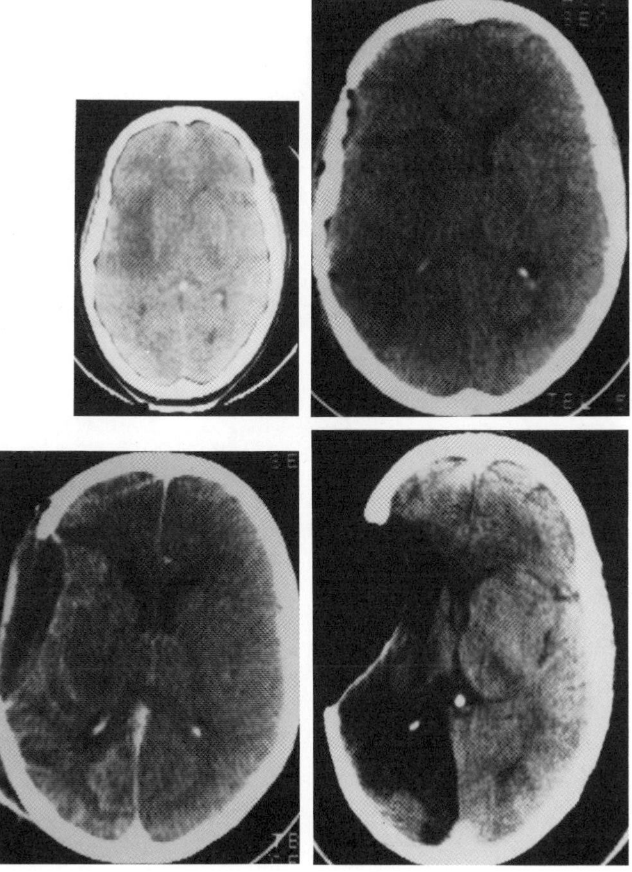

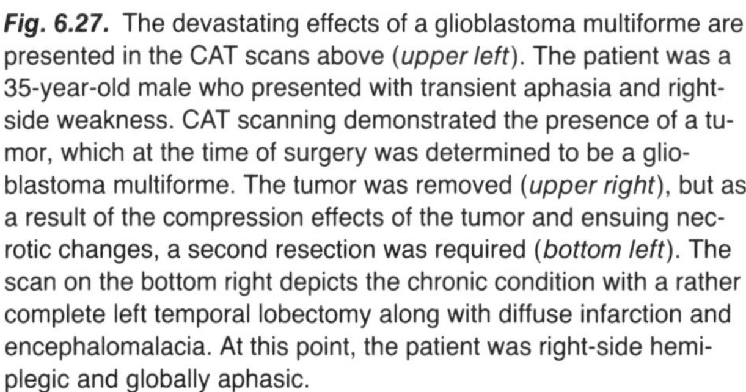

Fig. 6.27. The devastating effects of a glioblastoma multiforme are presented in the CAT scans above (*upper left*). The patient was a 35-year-old male who presented with transient aphasia and right-side weakness. CAT scanning demonstrated the presence of a tumor, which at the time of surgery was determined to be a glioblastoma multiforme. The tumor was removed (*upper right*), but as a result of the compression effects of the tumor and ensuing necrotic changes, a second resection was required (*bottom left*). The scan on the bottom right depicts the chronic condition with a rather complete left temporal lobectomy along with diffuse infarction and encephalomalacia. At this point, the patient was right-side hemiplegic and globally aphasic.

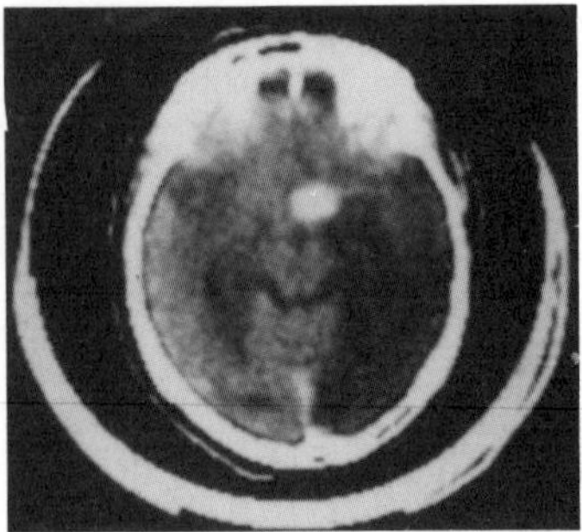

Fig. 6.29. Secondary effects of tumor. This patient's pituitary tumor expanded so much that it affected cerebral blood flow because of the effects of pressure on the circle of Willis. Note the marked infarction of the right hemisphere with the beginnings of infarction in the left.

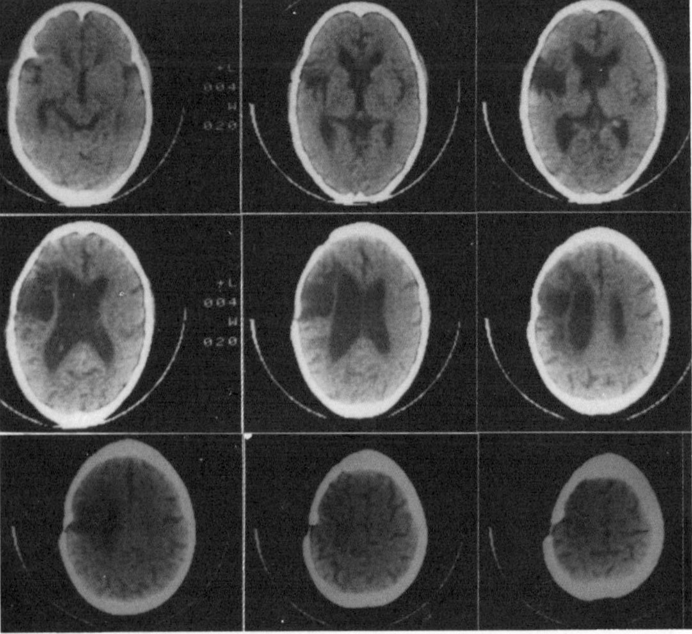

Fig. 6.30. Secondary effects of tumor. This 20-year-old man's family did not seek medical attention for him until he was comatose. CAT scan results reveal the postsurgical areas in the left hemisphere of focal destruction secondary to the neoplasm and surgical removal. The scan also indicates widespread and marked cerebral atrophy. The diffuse atrophic pattern may have resulted from chronic increased intracranial pressure as well as disturbances in cerebral blood flow.

Neuropsychological Findings

Detection of intracranial tumors has been revolutionized by the advent of computerized axial tomography (CAT) (Chou, Kramer, and Shapiro, 1979). Therefore, the neuropsychological evaluation will more than likely occur after the tumor has been detected. The utility of the neuropsychological examination is thereby related more to determining the extent of cerebral involvement. It also provides a baseline from which to follow the patient after surgery and postoperative rehabilitation. Similarly, in non-operable tumors, serial neuropsychological evaluations can chart the progression of the neoplastic process.

Neuropsychological results obtained from a tumor patient will, of course, be dependent upon the underlying regions of the brain being primarily and secondarily affected. As such, there is no "one" type of neuropsychological profile seen with neoplasia. Typically, the most focal, lateralized findings will be related to the site of pathology (i.e., core of the tumor) with the nonfocal, nonlateralized findings tending to be more related to the secondary diffuse effects.

Hom and Reitan (1984) have examined the relationship between rapidly and slow-growing cerebral neoplasms. As expected, the faster-growing tumors, such as in glioblastoma multiforme, produce greater deficits. Their research indicated that Halstead-Reitan was considerably more sensitive to the presence and degree of impairment as a result of tumor effects than was the Wechsler-Bellvue.

Behavioral Correlates of Cerebral Tumors

Tumors affecting the cerebrum may produce varied cognitive disturbances (Jamieson and Wells, 1979; Malmud, 1967; Williams, Bell, and Gye, 1974). There are no characteristic singular behavioral syndromes associated with neoplastic disease, but the type of symptoms may localize tumor site. For example, frontal lobe tumor may result in personality change. The following example represents such a case: T. J. was a 57-year-old tenured college professor (Ph.D. in history). He was married and had three grown children. He was quite conservative and very active in a local church. In retrospect the family first noticed that he started to lose interest in several of his home hobbies and his compulsive work habits. He would not prepare new lectures, would miss class, and would display little concern over these oversights. He then started to show change in speech content using vulgar and profane words that were clearly out of character for him. He also showed diminished concern over personal hygiene and dress. To the horror of the family, he was found to be carrying on an affair with one of his students. The family had assumed that "Dad was just going through a life adjustment crisis." They tolerated his behavior, feeling that once he "got it out of his system, he would come back to his senses." However, he subsequently had a major motor seizure at which time neurologic examination was sought. This examination indicated abnormalities, and CAT scan results suggested a large right frontal meningioma. This finding was confirmed at surgery. The patient recovered good function postoperatively, but never regained his overall premorbid level of ability.

This case demonstrates the significant changes in personality that may accompany frontal lobe tumors. Such slow-growing tumors bring on associated signs and symptoms in such a gradual fashion that typically neither the patient nor family members can specify onset. These slow-growing frontal tumors tend to be associated with change in personality and behavior, apathy, motor disturbance—particularly dyskinesia—and loss of spontaneity and initiative. More rapidly expanding frontal tumors result in confusional states with rather abrupt onset (Hecaen and Albert, 1978).

Tumors in parietal areas may produce lateralized somatosensory disturbance in the contralateral body side. Left parietal lobe tumors may result in language disturbance, whereas right parietal evolving tumors may induce spatial-perceptual-praxic deficits (see case 5). Visual disturbance or visual field defect may result with occipital lobe locus. Tumors arising in the parietal-occipital regions frequently show specific pathognomonic signs without serious disturbance in cognitive-emotional functioning, which is not the case with a frontal-temporal locus.

Tumors within the temporal lobe may produce a schizophreniform psychosis (Malmud, 1967). Depression and other emotional changes have also been reported. Some of these features may relate to tumor-induced seizure phenomena. In general, if psychiatric symptoms are present, the neoplastic disorder is within frontal, temporal, or both regions (see fig. 6.31).

The various behavioral as well as neurologic signs that may be induced by tumor development, as outlined above, may persist even after successful tumor removal. This is due to the neurosurgical intervention and the structural damage that the tumor causes, particularly if the tumor was of an infiltrative type.

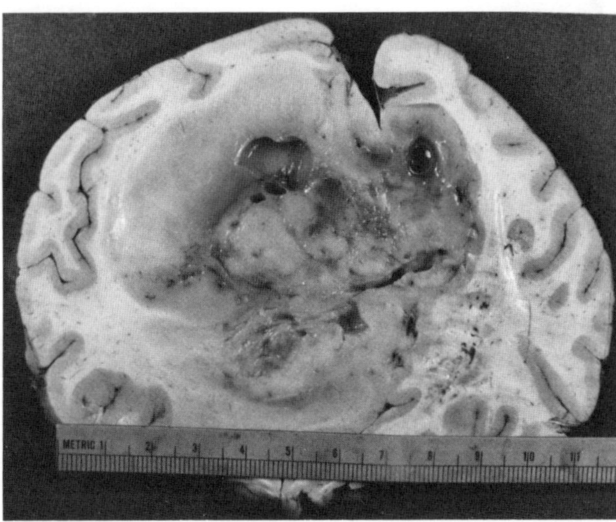

Fig. 6.31. Postmortem section of the frontal lobe depicting the position of a large astrocytoma (glioblastoma multiforme). The patient was initially diagnosed as schizophrenic with characteristic bizarre speech and behavior.

CASE STUDIES

Case 1. This patient was hospitalized on the request of her family because of inappropriate slurred speech, confusion, a persistent tendency to wander off, and an inability to handle her financial affairs. The family had postponed seeking medical attention because they felt that the mother was just gradually becoming senile.

The patient displayed right-side weakness, diminished finger oscillation speeds, and dysarthria, along with a variety of dysphasic deficits that suggested left-side deficit. The focal motor deficits, the less affected sensory exam results, and the dysphasic deficits indicating more anterior involvement all suggest left frontal lobe focal deficit.

CAT scan revealed a large neoplasm in left frontal region, which turned out to be a glioblastoma multiforme. The patient was operated on but with poor results. (See fig. 6.32.)

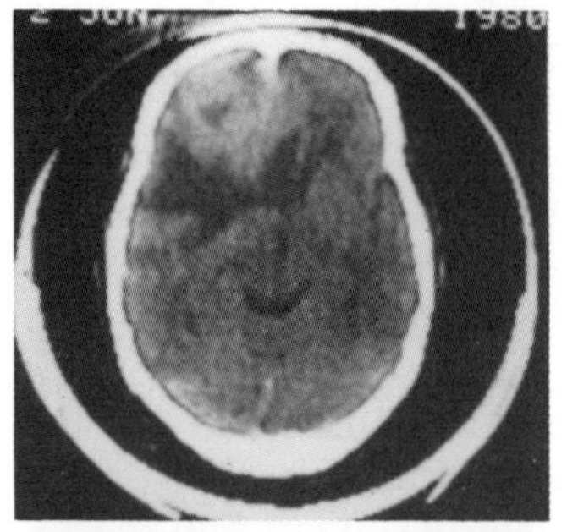

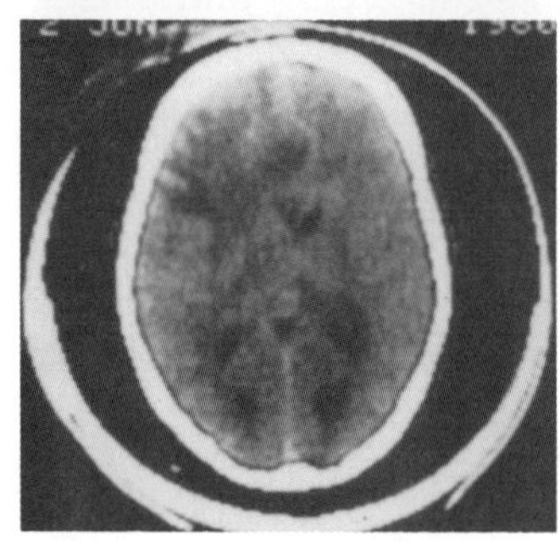

Fig. 6.32. Case 1. This 67-year-old woman was brought in by her family for examination after she took the family car and drove aimlessly about. She was able only to travel a familiar route and return home. The family felt that the mother was "just" showing signs of "senility" and thus was not alarmed by the emerging dysphasia that had been noticed for at least six months before the examination. CAT scan revealed a large glioma in the left frontal region that at surgery was found to be a glioblastoma.

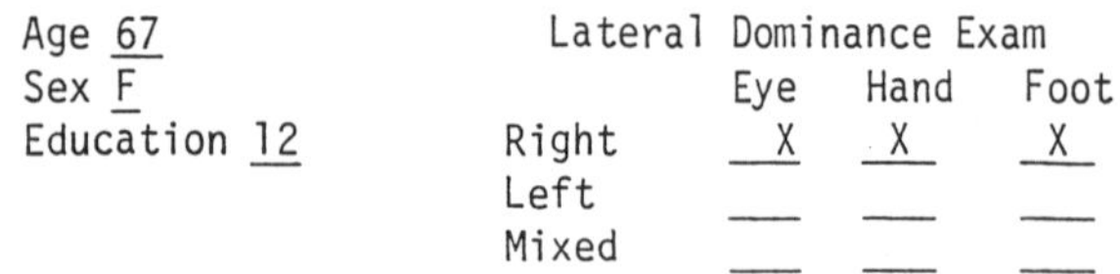

Age 67
Sex F
Education 12

Lateral Dominance Exam

	Eye	Hand	Foot
Right	X	X	X
Left			
Mixed			

Motor Examination:
FOD 17 SOGD 15
FOND 23 SOGND 18
Definitive right arm weakness present.
Alternating movements impossible.

Sensory Examination:
Aphasic deficit too pronounced to obtain reliable sensory exam. Simple touch was found to be intact.

Aphasia Examination:
Conversational Speech: Paraphasic
Comprehension: Impaired
Repetition of Spoken Language: Marginally intact.
Confrontation-Naming: Dysnomic
Reading:
Aloud: Dyslexic
Comprehension: Impaired
Writing: Impaired, dyspraxic
Calculations: Impaired

Memory Examination:
Impaired with aphasic overlay

Intellectual/Cognitive Examination:
Aphasic deficit too severe to permit intellectual assessment

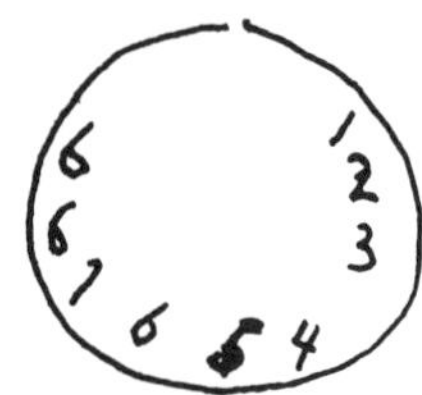

Case 2. This 27-year-old female presented with what initially appeared to be rather functional complaints—headache, chest pains, nervousness, tension. She was recently divorced, having financial problems, and under increasing stress at work (on an assembly line) but with declining performance. Her neurologic history was unremarkable as was her general medical history.

Exam results are definitive for focal right frontal deficit. This is related to the left-side weakness, performance-spatial deficits, and minimal left-side sensory deficit. CAT results revealed a large mass in the superior right frontal region, a mass that turned out to be a glioblastoma multiforme as verified by neurosurgical intervention. (See fig. 6.33.)

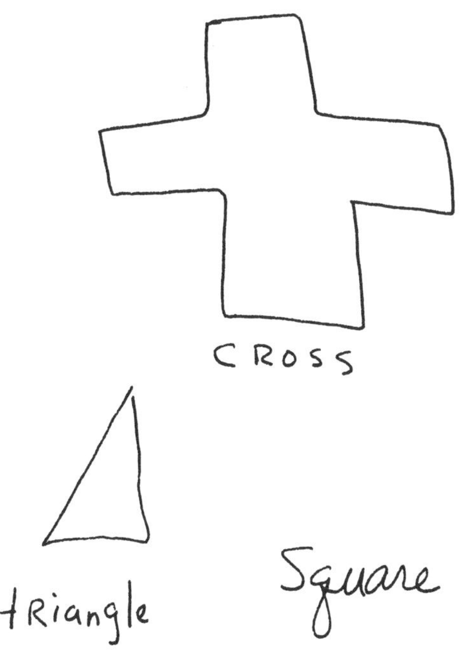

Age 27
Sex F
Education 12

Lateral Dominance Exam

	Eye	Hand	Foot
Right		X	X
Left	X		
Mixed			

Motor Examination:

FOD	32	SOGD	31	TPTD	7.9
FOND	27	SOGND	23	TPTND	10.2
				TPT Both	5.3

Sensory Examination:
WNL

Aphasia Examination:
WNL SRT 11 errors SSPT 3 errors

Memory Examination:
WMS MQ = 76
LM 3.5
Digits 10
VM 4
AL 12

TPT Memory 5
TPT Localization

Intellectual/Cognitive Examination:
WAIS Results
FSIQ = 79

VIQ = 87	PIQ = 71
I 6	DS 5
C 9	PC 7
A 8	BD 6
S 10	PA 4
D 9	OA 5
V 6	

Category Test 93 errors
Trail Making Test: B 120+ DC

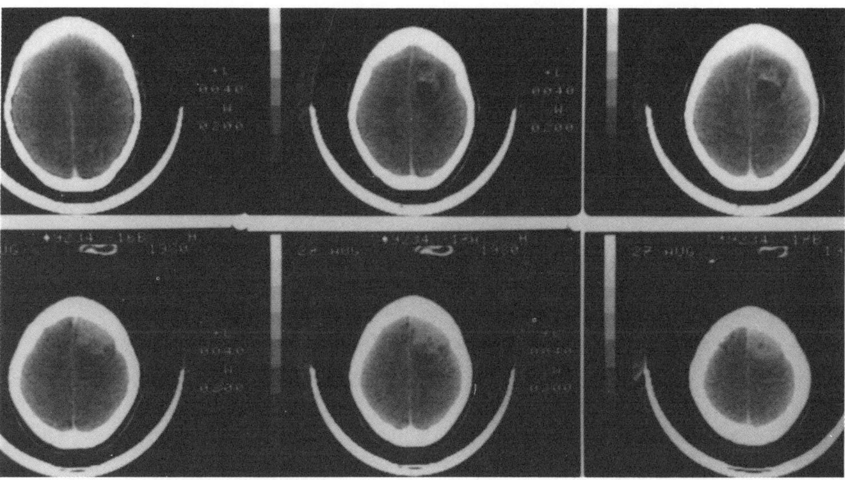

Fig. 6.33. Case 2.

Case 3. At the time of examination, this right-handed woman was 62 years of age. She was brought for examination by her daughter and husband who indicated that she had been displaying increasing changes in personality and confusion. They first noticed changes approximately a year before the examination, but the last three to six weeks she had become increasingly confused. While previously a fastidious housekeeper, she now refused to care for her home and her personal hygiene. She also displayed lack of initiative and motivation and could no longer manage her finances.

Tests revealed a rather obese, unkempt lady who insisted that she had no problem. She could not understand why we were doing these "silly" tests and did not realize that she was performing poorly. Actual test results as well as the clinical history suggested a degenerative disorder with marked dementia and memory disturbance. The patient also displayed a rather distinct bilateral anosmia. Although anosmia may develop in the degenerative process, it typically is late in the course of the disease. Thus, although the patient had the hallmarks of degenerative disease—dementia and memory disorder—the rather focal sign of bilateral anosmia indicated that the differential diagnosis would have to include a space-occupying lesion. It was suspected of being massive in size and situated anterior and ventral. CAT scanning resolved the diagnosis by demonstrating a large frontal tumor that was an olfactory groove meningioma. (See fig. 6.34.)

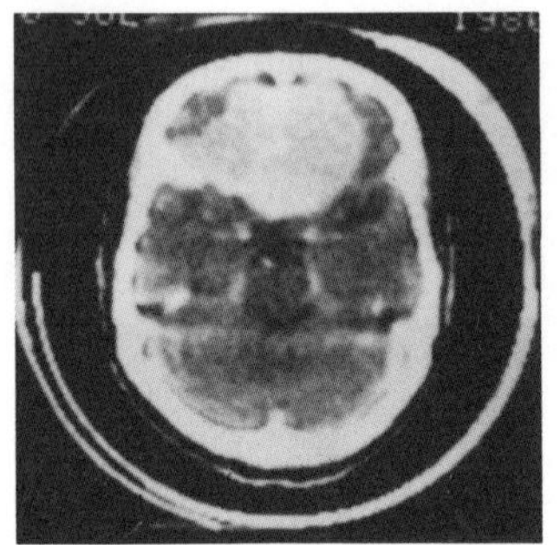

Fig. 6.34. Case 3.

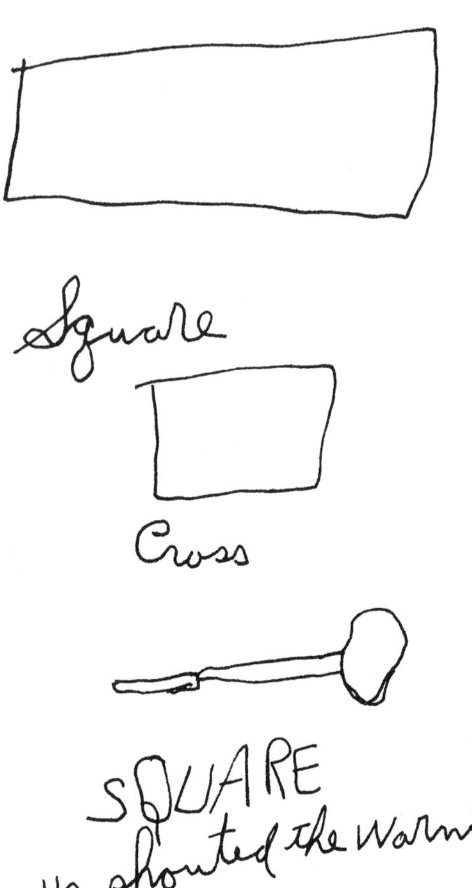

Age 62
Sex F
Education 12

Lateral Dominance Exam

	Eye	Hand	Foot
Right	X	X	X
Left			
Mixed			

Motor Examination:
FOD 18 SOGD 15 TPTD DC 0 in
FOND 10 SOGND 11 TPTND DC 0 in
TPT Both DC 0 in
Frontal grasp reflex present, alternating movements impaired.

Sensory Examination:
Bilateral anosmia, dysgraphesthesia, dysstereognosis, finger dysgnosia

Aphasia Examination:
Conversational Speech: Fluent but empty
Comprehension: Marginally intact
Repetition of Spoken Language: Intact
Confrontation-Naming: Dysnomic
Reading:
Aloud: Dyslexic
Comprehension: Impaired
Writing: Writing intact, graphomotor exam reveals constructional dyspraxia
Calculations: Impaired
SPT DC SRT DC

Memory Examination:
Marked memory deficit present
WMS = 69
LM 4 TPT M 0
Digits 7 TPT L 0
VM 3
AL 7

Intellectual/Cognitive Examination:
WAIS Results: FSIQ = 69, VIQ = 80, PIQ = 57
I 5, C 9, A 3, S 2, D 4, V 8, DS 0, PC 2, BD 0, PA 0, OA 2
Category Test: 117 errors
Trail Making Test: A 130 sec. B 180+ sec. DC

Case 4. This 61-year-old design engineer had presenting complaints of declining job performance, episodic confusion, and memory disturbance for three months before neuropsychological examination. CAT results reveal two circumscribed neoplasms (one located in the frontal region, the other in the temporal) with the "ring" appearance characteristic of metastasizing tumors (see fig. 6.35). The tumors were determined to be of pulmonary origin. Neuropsychological examination results are consistent with right hemisphere localization of dysfunction. The patient had definite left-side extinction along with drastically reduced performance IQ (particularly for an engineer). He similarly displayed substantial memory deficit. Graphomotor abilities were diminished. The observation that no focal weakness or motor deficit was present indicated the lesion to be anterior to the rolandic fissure. Taken together, the neuropsychological test results yield a profile consistent with rather nonspecific involvement of the right hemisphere. Behaviorally the patient displayed an aprosodic speech pattern with failure to appropriately imitate gestural tone. His perception of his loss in function was also impaired.

Age 61
Sex M
Education 16

Lateral Dominance Exam

	Eye	Hand	Foot
Right	X	X	X
Left			
Mixed			

Motor Examination:
FOD 52 SOGD 43
FOND 48 SOGND 38
Alternating movements poor, equivocal frontal grasp reflex, bradykinesia

Sensory Examination:
Left side tactile and auditory extinction otherwise normal exam

Aphasia Examination:
Essentially WNL except for calculation errors, given his educational and vocational (i.e. engineer) background. Poor construction praxis also present. Did not attend to the error of omission on drawing the cross (see left).

Memory Examination:
MQ = 81
LM 7
Digits 7
VM 6
AL 9
Periods of episodic confusion and amnesia

Intellectual/Cognitive Examination:
WAIS Results FSIQ = 86

VIQ = 96	PIQ = 75
I 11	DS 3
C 9	PC 5
A 7	BD 4
S 8	PA 4
D 4	OA 2
V 13	

Trail Making Test A 111
B 348

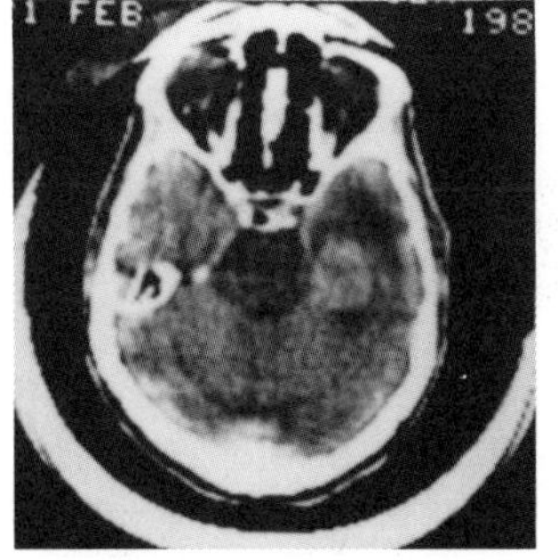

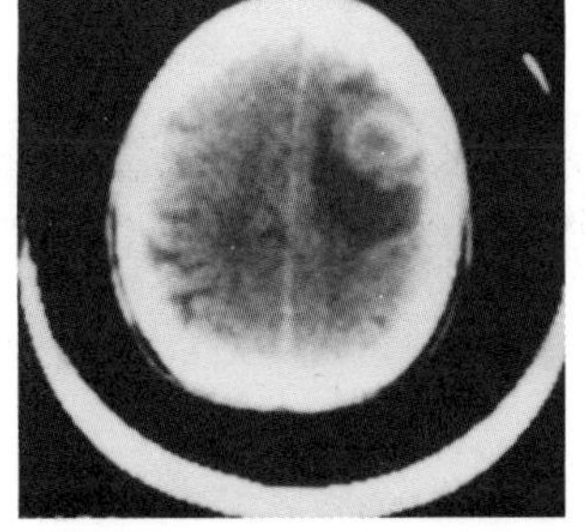

Fig. 6.35. Case 4. This 61-year-old design engineer had presenting complaints of declining job performance, episodic confusion, and memory disturbance of approximately three months' duration. CAT results reveal two circumscribed neoplasms (one located in frontal region, the other temporal) with the "ring" appearance characteristic of metastasizing tumors. The tumors were determined to be of pulmonary origin.

Case 5. This 21-year-old female had been operated on four years earlier for a right frontal astrocytoma. Unfortunately, the tumor could only be partially removed, and she had had several follow-up surgeries. CAT scan results show the destructive effects of the tumor in the right hemisphere as well as tumor expansion (see fig. 6.36). Neuropsychological examination indicates essentially total dysfunction of the right hemisphere. The patient displays all the features that one would observe in a patient with a hemispherectomy. Note the intactness of verbal function, demonstrating the functional separation of the two hemispheres.

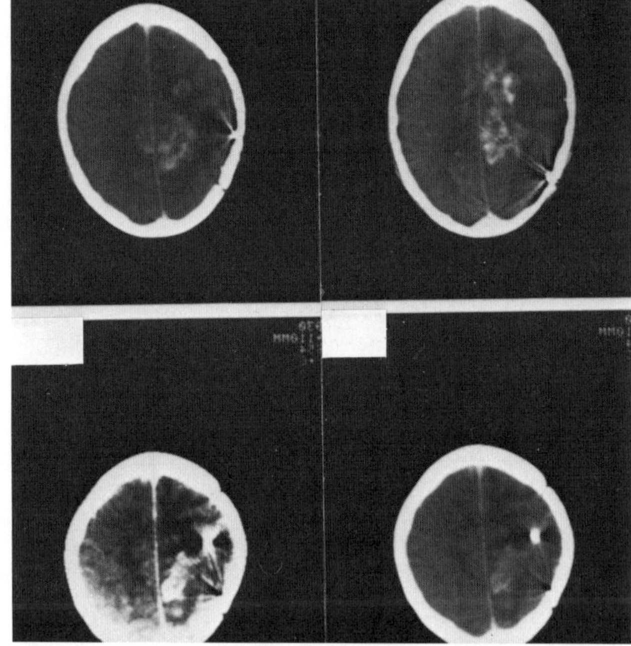

Fig. 6.36. Case 5. CAT scan (perspective with frontal lobe at bottom of frame) of patient with dysfunction of right hemisphere.

Age 21
Sex F
Education 13

Lateral Dominance Exam

	Eye	Hand	Foot
Right	X	X	X
Left			
Mixed			

Motor Examination:
FOD 17 SOGD 12 Left side hemiplegia
FOND 0 SOGND 0

SEnsory Examination:
Complete left side neglect
Left side astereognosis, agraphesthesia and finger agnosia
Left side hemianopsia

Language Examination:
Generally WNL

Memory Examination:
WMS MQ = 63
LM 2, DIgits 7, VM 6, AL 5

Intellectual/Cognitive Examination:
FSIQ = 74

VIQ = 91		PIQ = 56	
I	9	DS	3
C	11	PC	5
A	5	BD	3
S	11	PA	4
D	4	OA	2
V	10		

Category Test DC

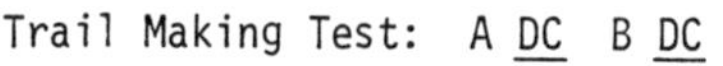
Trail Making Test: A DC B DC

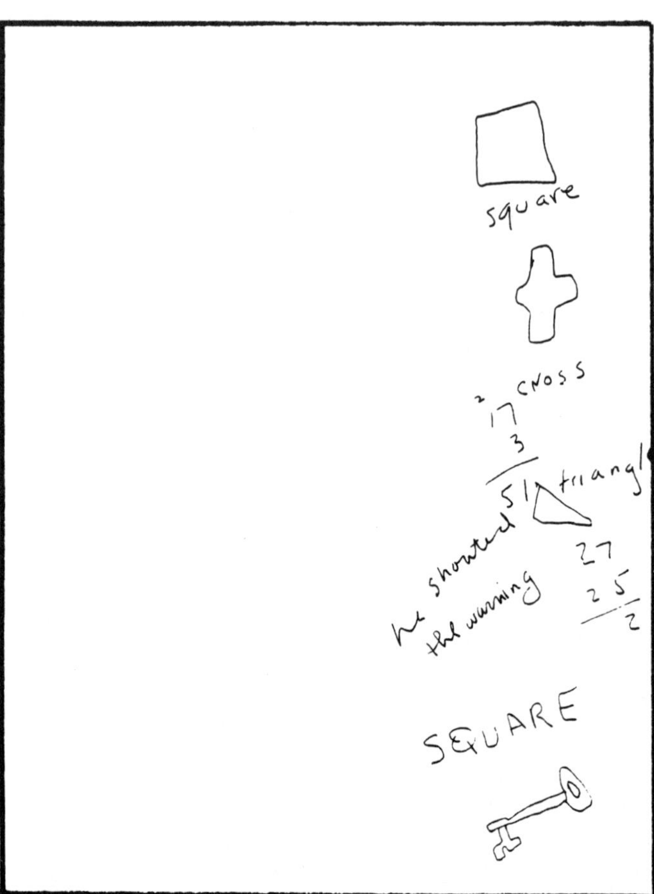

Case 6. At 40 years of age this physician presented with symptoms of headache and transient expressive dysphasia. CAT scanning (fig. 6.38, on the left) demonstrated a large mass in the left frontal region, which, at surgery, was determined to be a mixture of an oligodendroglioma and a grade III astrocytoma. This tumor mass was surgically removed, and he also received follow-up radiation treatment and chemotherapy. CAT scan results were also obtained one year postsurgery (fig. 6.37, on the right). Neuropsychologically, the patient's test data reflect overall reduction in cognitive abilities, but no specific deficits were present. At eighteen months postsurgery, the patient demonstrated deficits on the TPT, Category Test, and complex visual memory (Rey-Osterrieth CFD). The aphasia screening and Rey-Osterrieth (with three-minute recall) test results are displayed. Eslinger and Damasio (1985) describe a similar case.

Sex M
Education 20 (M.D.)

Lateral Dominance Exam

	Eye	Hand	Foot
Right	x		x
Left			
Mixed		x	

	Pre Surgery	Post Surgery (3 months)	Post Surgery (18 months)
Motor Examination	FOD 45 FOND 52	FOD 49 FOND 48	FOD 49 SOG 39 FOND 47 SOGND 44 TPT D 9.5 TPTND 7.5 TPT B 4.3 TPT-M 8 TPT-L 1
Sensory Examination	Completely intact in all modalities	Completely intact in all modalities	Completely intact in all modalities
Aphasia Examination	No dysphasic deficits WRAT Results Reading 12.5 Spelling 11.9 Math 10.0	No dysphasic deficits WRAT Results Reading 13.0 Spelling 11.9 Math 10.6	No dysphasic deficits WRAT-R Results Reading > 12 Spelling > 12 Math > 12
Memory Examination	WMS MQ = 101 LM 12 Digits 15 VM 4 AL 14	WMS MQ = 120 LM 12 Digits 15 VM 4 AL 14	WMS MQ = 129 LM 11 Digits 15 VM 8 AL 19

Intellectual/Cognitive Examination — WAIS-R RESULTS

Pre Surgery				Post Surgery (3 months)				Post Surgery (18 months)			
FSIQ = 100				FSIQ = 117				FSIQ = 120			
VIQ = 109		PIQ = 92		VIQ = 126		PIQ = 99		VIQ = 122		PIQ = 111	
I	13	PC	8	I	13	PC	10	I	13	PC	12
D.S.	14	PA	8	D.S.	19	PA	11	D.S.	17	PA	11
V	NA	BD	8	V	NA	BD	9	V	13	BD	9
A	12	OA	6	A	NA	OA	6	A	14	OA	11
C	9	DS	10	C	12	DS	10	C	11	DS	11
S	9			S	8			S	11		

	Pre Surgery	Post Surgery (3 months)	Post Surgery (18 months)
Category Test	NA	NA	66 errors
Raven's CPM	NA	NA	35/36
Trail Making Test Results	A 25 sec. 0 errors B 53 sec. errors	18 sec. 0 errors 36 sec. 0 errors	21 sec. 0 errors 42 sec. 0 errors

Case 6. *(continued)*

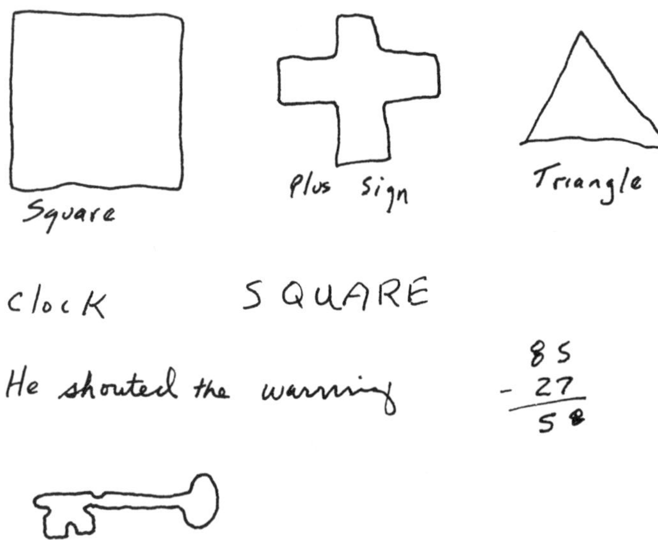

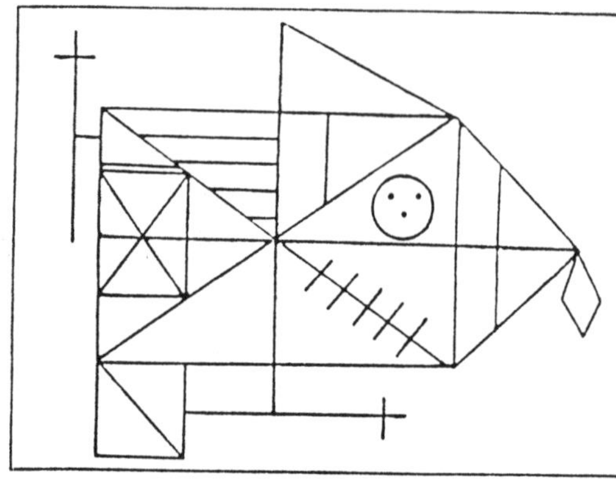

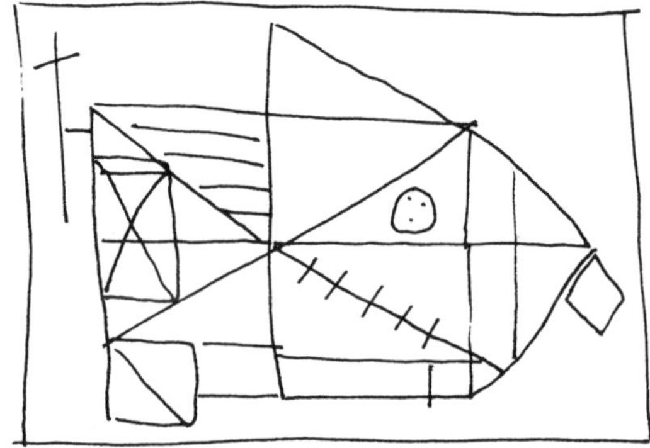

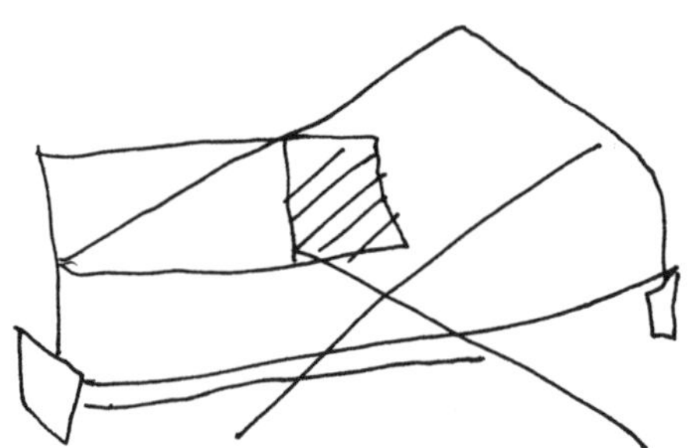

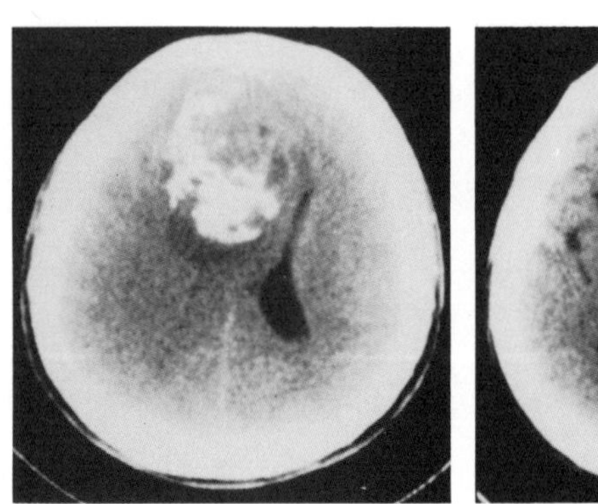

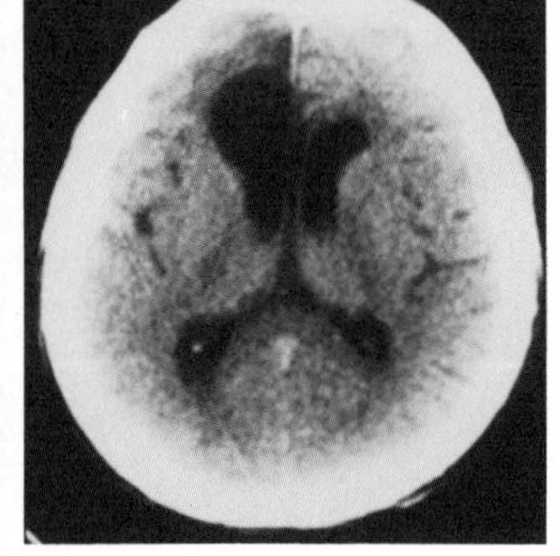

Fig. 6.37. Case 6.

References

Adams, R. D., and M. Victor. 1977. *Principles of neurology*. New York: McGraw-Hill.

Bigler, E. D. 1980. Child and adolescent neuropsychology. In *Emotional disturbance*, ed. J. E. Gilliam. Austin: University of Texas.

Bray, P. 1969. *Pediatric neurology*. Chicago: Year Book Medical Publishers.

Chou, S. N., R. S. Kramer, and W. R. Shapiro. 1979. Intracranial tumors. *Archives of Neurology* 36:739–749.

Coxe, W. S. 1978. Intracranial tumors. In *Neurological pathophysiology*, ed. S. G. Eliasson, A. L. Prensky, and W. B. Hardin. New York: Oxford University Press.

DeAngelis, L. M. 1981. Intracranial tuberculoma: Case report and review of the literature. *Neurology* 31:1133–1136.

Eslinger, P. J., and A. R. Damasio. 1985. Severe disturbance of higher cognition after bilateral frontal lobe ablation: Patient EVR. *Neurology* 35:1731–1741.

Ford, F. R. 1976. *Diseases of the nervous system in infancy, childhood, and adolesence*. 6th ed. Springfield, Ill.: Charles C. Thomas.

Hecaen, H., and M. L. Albert. 1978. *Human neuropsychology*. New York: John Wiley & Sons.

Hochberg, F. H., and B. Slotnick. 1980. Neuropsychologic impairment in astrocytoma survivors. *Neurology* 30:172–177.

Hom, J., and R. M. Reitan. 1984. Neuropsychological correlates of rapidly vs. slowly growing intrinsic cerebral neoplasms. *Journal of Clinical Neuropsychology* 6:309–324.

Jamieson, R. C., and C. E. Wells. 1979. Case studies in neuropsychiatry: Manic psychosis in patient with multiple metastatic brain tumors. *Journal of Clinical Psychiatry* 40:280–282.

Knights, R. M., and G. G. Hinton. 1973. *Neuropsychological test results in children with posterior fossa tumors*. Research Bulletin no. 7. Ottawa, Canada: Department of Psychology, Carleton University.

Lewis, A. J. 1976. *Mechanisms of neurological disease*. Boston: Little, Brown & Co.

Malmud, N. 1967. Psychiatric disorders with intracranial tumors of the limbic system. *Archives of Neurology* 17:113–118.

Norton, J. C., and C. G. Matthews. 1972. Psychological test performance in patients with subtentorial versus supratentorial CNS disease. *Diseases of the Nervous System* 33:312–317.

Payne, E. E. 1969. *An atlas of pathology of the brain*. East Hanover, N.J.: Sandoz Pharmaceuticals.

Selikoff, I. J., and E. C. Hammond. 1982. *Brain tumors in the chemical industry*. Vol. 381. New York: New York Academy of Sciences.

Vick, N. A. 1981. Brain tumors. *Seminars in Neurology* 1: 127–227.

Williams, S. E., D. S. Bell, and R. S. Gye. 1974. Neurosurgical disease encountered in a psychiatric service. *Journal of Neurology, Neurosurgery and Psychiatry* 37:112–117.

7. Infectious Disorders of the Nervous System

Infectious disorders of the central nervous system (CNS) may result in varied neuropsychological sequelae from permanent to only transient impairment (see table 7.1). Comprehensive reviews of the etiology and pathogenesis of infectious diseases have been provided by Adams and Victor (1977), Bell (1982), Ford (1976), and Lewis (1976). Further treatment of the subject from a clinical and neurologic standpoint has been amply provided by Baker (1981), Baker and Baker (1981), Ettinger (1981), Feigin and Dodge (1978), Sahs and Joynt (1981), Scheinberg (1977), and Smith (1981).

The brain and spinal cord tissue along with the cerebrospinal fluid (CSF) is normally sterile. Its main line of defense is its isolation through the blood-brain barrier and its isolation within the cranial vault. However, if this barrier is damaged or penetrated in some fashion, the CNS becomes highly vulnerable to the infectious process. Typically, infection occurs by one or a combination of the following routes: (1) hematogenous—infection through the vascular system, representing the most common route of infection; (2) direct access—usually associated with skull fracture or penetrating wound to the brain and dural tearing; (3) passage from infected cranial cavities—including the middle ear and mastoid region, frontal sinus and nasal regions, and the nasopharyngeal area; (4) intracytoplasmic spread—infectious spread by motor or sensory axons (appears to occur only with the rabies virus).

Infectious Disorders: An Overview

Infections of the CNS may be confined to the meninges (meningitis, sometimes referred to as leptomeningitis when the inflammation is restricted to the pia mater and arachnoid space) or to the CNS parenchyma (encephalitis, if only the brain is affected; myelitis, if only the spinal cord is involved; encephalomyelitis, if both brain and cord are involved; or meningoencephalitis, if both meninges and brain are involved). As will be discussed, certain CNS infectious disorders have a relatively good outcome, but others are frequently associated with permanent neuropsychological sequelae. Likewise, certain infectious processes may display a particular affinity for certain brain regions, whereas others may more diffusely affect the CNS. Table 7.2 outlines the various common agents of infection involving the CNS.

Meningitis

Meningitis may occur as a result of a wide range of infectious agents including viral, bacterial, fungal, and protozoal carriers (see fig. 7.1). Meningitis is commonly defined as an inflammation of the subarachnoid space and its bounding membranes. Such inflammation has its greatest effect on penetrating arteries and emerging veins of the brain as well as the potential for disrupting CSF flow. Thus, common cerebral consequences of meningitis are related to the inflammatory secondary effects on the cerebrovasculature and patency of the CSF system. Also, because the cranial and spinal nerves have to exit through small meningeal openings, they are very susceptible to damage secondary to compression by changes in intracranial pressure. Associated with these effects are the common symptoms of headache and stiff neck.

Possibly the most common meningitis is of viral origin, and it typically follows a relatively innocuous, self-limiting course, only infrequently resulting in permanent neuropsychological sequelae. Acute purulent meningitis, however, tends to be a more pathologic form of meningeal infection. With this type of infection there is some indication for greater incidence of thrombosis (Lewis, 1976). Tuberculous meningitis is a consequence of systemic tuberculosis (Adams and Victor, 1977). The cerebral pathology with tuberculous infection of the brain is usually associated with a thick exudate that affects the meninges, particularly in ventral regions of the brain, along with tubercles in the brain and ependymal surfaces. Additionally, severe arteritis may develop. All these factors interact to produce a rather severe neurological deficit in the patient with intracranial tuberculosis (see chapter 6, fig. 6.18). Syphilitic meningitis is usually associated with syphilitic encephalitis, and they combine to produce diffuse and generalized cerebral pathology.

Encephalitis

In general, encephalitis carries a poorer prognosis than meningitis in terms of neuropsychological outcome. The encephalitides can be generally divided into two groups: bacterial and fungal or viral and rickettsial (a common microorganism).

Bacterial and fungal encephalitic disorders are usually associated with direct invasion of the brain secondary to contamination of the cerebral tissue following an injury penetrating or opening the head (see fig. 7.2). Brain abscess occurs as a result of infection that penetrates the brain. Typically, the abscess is fairly confined to the site of entry. Thus, frontal sinus or sasopharyngeal infections that abscess affect primarily frontal brain regions. On the other hand, otitis media or mastoiditis infections that abscess are associated more with temporal involvement, cerebellar involvement, or both (see fig. 7.3). However, as pointed out by Adams and Victor (1977), infection may

Table 7.1. ***Neurologic and Neuropsychological Sequelae of Central Nervous System Infection***

Acute Effects Caused by Nervous System Infection	Intermediate and Chronic Neurologic Sequelae of Nervous System Infection
Abnormal electroencephalogram results	Aphasia
Aphasia	Arachnoiditis
Brain swelling, acute brain herniation	Brain abscess
Cerebral arteritis	Cranial nerve palsies
Cortical blindness	Hemiparesis or tetraparesis
Cranial nerve palsies	Hydrocephalus
Electrolyte disturbance	Intracranial calcifications
Hemiparesis, tetraparesis, ataxia	Mental defect
Memory disturbance	Microcephaly
Mental changes	Mycotic aneurysm
Seizures	Paraplegia
Venous sinus thrombosis	Peripheral nerve lesions
	Seizures
	Speech and language defects
	Subdural hematoma

Table 7.2. ***Central Nervous System Infections***

Nonviral

Bacterial diseases
- Bacillary dysentery
- Bubonic plague
- Cholera
- Leprosy (Hansen's disease)
- Pertussis
- Pneumonia encephalopathy
- Rheumatic fever
- Scarlet fever
- Typhoid fever
- Undulant fever (brucellosis)

Helminth infestations
- Ancylostomiasis (hookworm)
- Cysticercosis
- Trichinosis

Protozoan diseases
- Malaria
- Toxoplasmosis

Rickettsial diseases
- Epidemic and endemic typhus
- Rocky Mountain spotted fever

Spirochetal diseases
- Cerebral syphilis
- Rat-bite fever
- Relapsing fever

Yeast and mold infections
- Aspergillosis
- Coccidioidomycosis
- Histoplasmosis
- Miscellaneous fungal diseases

Viral

Adenoviruses

Arenavirus infections
- Lymphocytic choriomeningitis

Arthropod-borne (arbovirus) infections

Arthropod tick-borne encephalitis
- Colorado tick fever
- Kemerova virus disease
- Russian tick-borne complex of encephalitis

Group A
- Eastern equine encephalitis
- Western equine encephalitis

Group B—Flavivirus
- Dengue fever
- Japanese B encephalitis
- St. Louis encephalitis
- Yellow fever

Herpesvirus infections
- Chickenpox encephalitis
- Cytomegalic inclusion disease (salivary gland virus infection)
- Herpes simplex encephalitis
- Herpes zoster encephalitis
- Virus B (herpesvirus simiae) encephalitis

Infections suspected to be of viral etiology
- Behçet's disease
- Cat-scratch fever
- Epidemic encephalitis
- Infectious mononucleosis

Myxovirus infections
- Influenza encephalitis
- Measles encephalitis
- Mumps meningoencephalitis
- Newcastle disease
- Rubella (German measles)

Nonclassified virus infections
- Hemorrhagic encephalitis
- Infectious hepatitis encephalitis

Papovavirus infections
- Progressive multifocal leukoencephalitis (Jakob-Creutzfeldt virus)

Picornavirus (enterovirus) infections
- Coxsackievirus infections
- Echovirus meningoencephalitis
- Polioencephalitis

Poxvirus infections
- Smallpox encephalitis
- Vaccinia encephalitis

Rabdovirus infections
- Rabies

Slow latent viral infections
- Jakob-Creutzfeldt disease
- Kuru
- Progressive multifocal leukoencephalitis
- Progressive rubella panencephalitis
- Scrapie and visna
- Subacute sclerosing panencephalitis

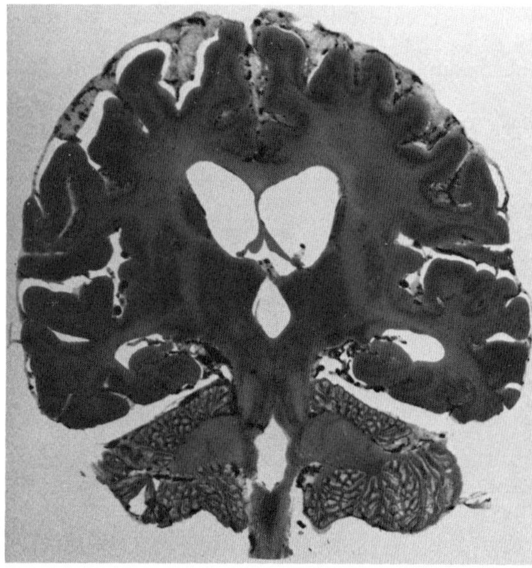

Fig. 7.1. Pneumococcal meningitis. Oblique coronal section of the brain. There is general cerebellar atrophy. The subarachnoid space over the vertex contains green exudate. The color of this exudate is characteristic of pneumococcal pus. From Payne (1969).

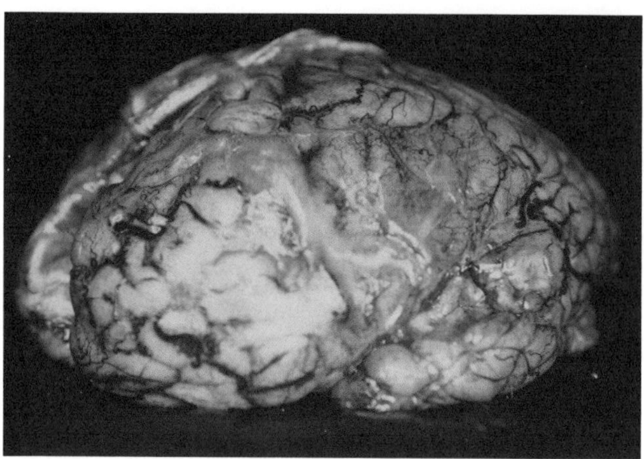

Fig. 7.2. Lateral view of cerebrum taken at autopsy. This patient suffered from a case of severe meningoencephalitis. Note the loss of definition across the surface of the brain and its swollen appearance.

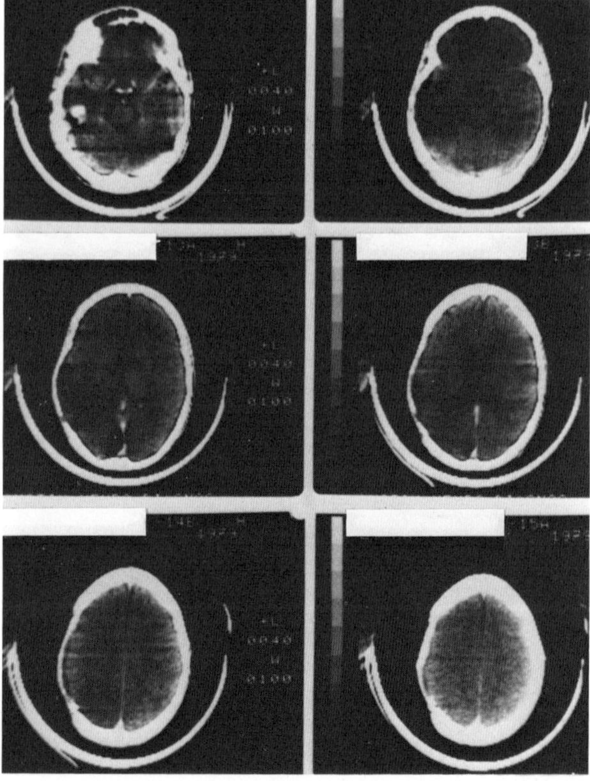

Fig. 7.3. Cerebral abscess. This CAT scan is of a 15-year-old boy whose cerebral abscess was secondary to otitis media.

spread throughout the brain, and focal deficits may develop quite remote from the point of entry. A brain abscess may develop from systemic septic foci, particularly from the lungs (see fig. 7.4). Neurosyphilitic bacterial infection may be widespread throughout the brain with the final result being general paresis (see fig. 5.10), tabes dorsalis (ataxia, lightening pains, and urinary incontinence secondary to spinal cord infection), or both.

Whereas there may be some tendency for bacterial or fungal infections to affect cerebral function more focally, the viral and rickettsial encephalitides frequently affect the parenchyma in a diffuse manner. Viral encephalitis may cause diffuse vascular dilation, serum exudation, perivascular hemorrhaging, acute arteritis, or any combination of these. Such effects may produce mild to moderate nonspecific degeneration of neurons, leaving myelin and glial cells relatively unaffected. Poliomyelitis results from the poliovirus affecting primarily the spinal cord, although cerebral involvement may also occur. The rabies virus travels from the site of the bite axoplasmically to the CNS (Lewis, 1976). The rabies virus has a destructive predilection for the spinal cord, brain stem, and hippocampus, but the neocortex remains relatively unaffected. Arbovirus (*ar*thropod-*bo*rne) infection occurs as a result of an insect bite—commonly a tick, mosquito, or mite. Encephalitis secondary to arbovirus infection commonly affects cerebral tissue in a diffuse manner. Herpes simplex infection may also produce encephalitis. In such encephalitic disorders the cerebral tissue may be diffusely affected with secondary effects of generalized edema. The presence of generalized edema may produce more focal damage in temporal regions because of the susceptibility of compressive damage to the inner table of the temporal bone in that region. There is also some indication the temporal lobes have a greater affinity for infection (Feigin and Dodge, 1978). Herpes zoster, which typically affects only the peripheral nervous system, may infrequently affect the cerebrum.

Intrauterine and Intranatal Infections

Some viral diseases may infect the placenta or cross from maternal to fetal circulation. In the last few days of pregnancy, poliovirus, western equine encephalitis, herpes virus, and coxsackie virus (causing infantile encephalomyocarditis) may cross the placental barrier. Such infections fortunately are rare. Genital herpes virus may also be transmitted to the neonate from maternal genital tract lesions during passage through the birth canal.

Rubella infection in the first trimester may cause severe congenital defects in the fetus, particularly involving the CNS, heart, eyes, and internal ears (Bray, 1969). A major effect of the rubella virus during this period is to interfere with CNS cellular division that may lead to microencephaly, polymicrogyria, cerebellar dysplasia, agenesis of the corpus callosum, or any combination of these effects. In addition to or instead of the cellular malformations, the rubella virus may produce an encephalopathy with associated focal, noninflammatory cystic degeneration, usually involving the white matter, but sometimes affecting the basal ganglia and thalamus (Lewis, 1976).

The parasite *Toxoplasma gondii* may be acquired by the mother and passed to the fetus. While the mother may remain asymptomatic, the parasite may invade the fetal brain producing severe destructive effects. The most common effect of such invasion is randomly distributed necrotic lesions with encapsulated and cystic remains of the parasite. This condition is termed cerebral toxoplasmosis (see fig. 7.5).

Delayed or Slow Viral Infectious Disorders

Subacute sclerosing panencephalitis (SSPE) is an infectious disease typically affecting children who have been exposed to measles or who have had a measles vaccination, but the extent of the relationship is not known (Lewis, 1976). This disorder typically follows a three- to twelve-month course ending in death, although the time from original infection or inoculation to death may be several years. The effects of SSPE are diffuse and thus produce generalized cerebral deficits during the progressive decline. In some rare instances, the progressive degeneration may be one to two decades past the original infection, this slow progression being most common with rubella (Townsend et al., 1982). Another slow virus is that associated with Jakob-Creutzfeldt disease (see chapter 5).

Specific Infectious Disorders

Herpes Simplex Encephalitis

As indicated previously, with herpes simplex encephalitis there is a tendency for the temporal lobes to be selectively affected, particularly the hippocampal area (Damasio et al., 1985; Hierons, Janota, and Corsellis, 1978). Having such a locus, this infection may produce a wide spectrum of behavioral abnormalities, but the unifying cognitive sequelae tend to be memory disturbances (Gianutsos, 1981). Because of the importance of the temporal lobes in the control and modulation of motivational and emotional aspects of behavior, as well as memory, any changes in personality or memory in the postencephalitic patient should be fully documented with psychometric and neuropsychometric measures. In such patients careful attention should be directed toward those tests that tend to tap temporal lobe processes. Lastly, it should be noted that the postinfection deficits may be partially ameliorated by cognitive retraining techniques (Gianutsos, 1981).

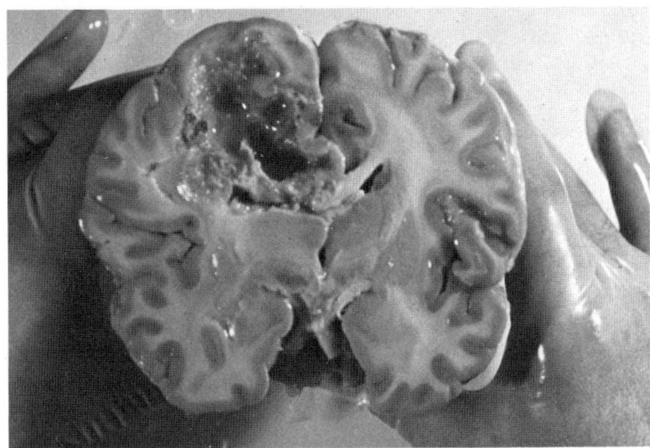

Fig. 7.4. Cerebral abscess. The coronal section illustrates the location of cerebral abscess secondary to systemic pulmonary infection.

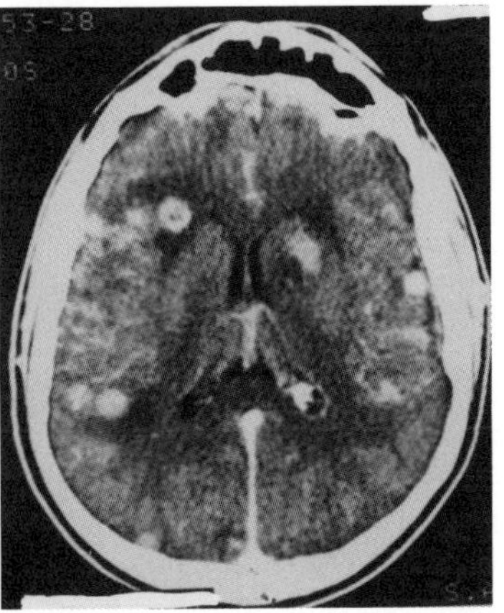

Fig. 7.5. Toxoplasmosis. CAT scan reveals several areas of encapsulated and cystic remains of the parasite.

Herpes Zoster

Herpes zoster (shingles) is a common viral infection, usually affecting peripheral nerves within a specific dermatomal distribution (Adams and Victor, 1977); however, in relatively rare instances, an encephalitis may develop (Horten, Price, and Jimenez, 1981). The encephalitic process, when it develops, may be recurrent (O'Donnell et al., 1981), and the infection may also involve the meninges (Reimer and Reller, 1981). There is no specific tissue group for which the herpes zoster infectious process has an affinity. Accordingly, the resultant damaging effects may be rather widespread, but focal destructive effects may also occur. Because of the diverse effects, neuropsychological studies of such patients should be comprehensive.

Progressive Multifocal Leukoencephalopathy

Progressive multifocal leukoencephalopathy (PMLE) is a degenerative disorder primarily affecting white matter and tends to occur in individuals with diminished immunologic protection (Lewis, 1976). Thus, it may develop in individuals who have chronic disorders, such as neoplasms of the reticuloendothelial system (Hodgkin's disease, leukemia, lymphosarcoma), sarcoidosis, severe cachexia (from whatever etiology), diffuse collagen disease, or as a consequence of corticosteroid therapy and the use of immunologic suppressants. After the onset of CNS symptoms, death may result within the first year, but reports have demonstrated extended survival for four to five years (Adams and Victor, 1977). It has been suggested by Lewis (1976) that this disorder be considered an opportunistic virus that develops its potent action in response to an impaired immune system. As its name implies, the degenerative effects are related to destructive changes in the white matter and supportive tissues. Since the infection results in rather generalized effects, neuropsychological studies of the patient with PMLE typically depict diffuse involvement.

Lupus Erythematosus

Systemic lupus erythematosus (SLE) may also affect the CNS (Carbotte, Denburg, and Denburg, 1986; Kaell et al., 1986). The resultant CNS involvement may occur through direct or indirect effects. Direct effects typically occur as a result of small vessel infarction which, in turn, results in widespread "micro" infarction throughout the cerebrum and brain stem. SLE may induce or be related to pathologic hypertension, and further cerebrovascular damage may ensue. Also, endocarditis may be associated with SLE, and cerebral embolic encephalopathy may develop. The numerous neurologic signs and symptoms of SLE include paralysis, cranial nerve involvement, aphasia, sensory disturbances, cognitive deficits, dementia, and derangements of hypothalamic functioning (Adams and Victor, 1977). What appears to be emotional disturbance in the SLE patient may in fact be the prodromal signs of a developing encephalopathy. From the neuropsychological standpoint, there is no single type of profile seen with SLE because the underlying cerebral pathology may be so variable. Thus, it is important to undertake comprehensive neuropsychological studies in the SLE patient in order to document the cerebral dysfunction present.

Acquired Immune Deficiency Syndrome (AIDS)

CNS complications in association with AIDS are commonplace. In some patients this is due to direct infection due to lowered immunity (see Navia, Jordan, and Price, 1986; Navia et al., 1986). Typically, these take the form of infections such as those seen with toxoplasmosis (Shaw et al., 1985). However, there appears to be a more specific process associated with AIDS in which a generalized encephalopathy develops. This AIDS encephalopathy typically begins with impaired concentration and progresses to the point disrupting all aspects of higher cognitive functioning. The course of this progression may take weeks to months to develop. Ho et al. (1985) have demonstrated that the human T-cell lymphotropic virus type III (HTLV-III), the etiologic agent of AIDS, is neurotropic, is capable of causing acute meningitis and dementia, and may also be the cause of spinal cord degeneration.

Toxic Shock Syndrome

Persistent neuropsychological sequelae may accompany Toxic Shock syndrome. Rosene et al. (1982) found a variety of cognitive deficits, including impaired memory and poorly sustained concentration. They speculate that the CNS involvement may occur as a direct effect of the staphlococcal toxin.

Neuropsychological Examination of the Patient with Infectious Disease

Neuropsychological examination of the patient with infectious disease will invariably occur sometime after the acute infectious stage and will generally be performed to determine the extent of cerebral involvement. Thus, the neuropsychological examination will not be used for differential diagnostic purposes, but rather to delimit the extent of the functional cerebral pathology present. As table 7.1 indicates, numerous neurologic deficits may attend CNS infection.

There is some tendency toward greater susceptibility of cerebral infection in those patients with chronic debilitating disorders. The most common have been listed as aging, malignancy, chronic malnutrition, alcoholism, diabetes, renal failure, and essentially any prolonged illness. Thus, the first step in neuropsychologically examining the patient should be to determine the circumstances surrounding the original infection. Neuropsychological dysfunction may be more a subset of the chronic disease process, and, if so, this needs to be differentiated from other causes.

There is a tendency for abscess disorders to produce

focal cerebral deficits that are related to the site of the original abscess. Because an abscess is more likely to develop in the frontal sinus, nasopharyngeal region, or mastoid cavities, it is common with abscess disorders to have frontal, temporal, or cerebellar focal involvement. Thus, neuropsychological examination of the patient with cerebral abscess should determine the extent of focal involvement and subsequently determine more generalized pathology.

With encephalitic disorders, there is tendency for more diffuse impairment, although herpes simplex may have a greater predilection for temporal lobes. Because of the potential for diverse cerebral dysfunction, the original neuropsychological examination should be thorough and fully comprehensive. Inasmuch as there may be recovery of function over time in patients recovering from encephalitis, follow-up neuropsychological examination is usually appropriate. Essentially similar procedures are appropriate for the patient recovering from meningitis who has shown neurologic residual.

Age at the time of CNS infection is likewise a crucial factor affecting the degree of residual deficit. Severe infectious disorders in infancy may produce lasting deficits and impair almost all response to treatment. For example, for three years we have performed follow-up exams of a little girl who had severe herpes simplex encephalitis at thirteen months. Prior to the infection she was a normal infant, meeting all developmental milestones well within normal limits. Testing was first undertaken eleven months after initial infection (at two years of age) with results from the Bayley Scales of Infant Development indicating a mental score of about thirteen months and a motor score of about fifteen months. At age three, the verbal scale remained the same, but motor scale had increased to seventeen months. By age four, she had displayed some further modest gains (verbal score equal to twenty-one months and motor score at approximately twenty-four months), but she remained approximately two to two and one-half years behind in development. She had mild residual right hemiparesis, was primarily echolalic in speech, and markedly hyperactive as well as having an extremely short attention span. The prognosis remains poor that this child will improve much. During the three years since diagnosis, she has been involved in a residential rehabilitation program, receiving intensive physical therapy, occupational therapy, cognitive retraining, and behavior modification training. Despite this intensive work, the gains are only modest. As with the devastating effects that may be associated with CNS infection during developmental years, CNS infection that occurs in senescence will typically result in marked residual deficit.

With meningitis, as long as no significant vascular complications occur and no distortion of the brain parenchyma occurs as a result of changes in intracranial pressure, recovery may be complete. In such meningitis patients, no detectable neuropsychological defects may be found on examination, even though the patients may have had rather profound neurologic signs and deficits during the peak of infection.

CASE STUDIES

Case 1. This 53-year-old man, who was a supervisor of a construction crew, developed a viral meningoencephalitis. Neuropsychological examination was conducted approximately five months postinfection. Behaviorally, the patient was hyperdistractable and hypersexual and had a short-term memory disturbance that led to some degree of ongoing confusion. He was disoriented about time and place. CAT scan revealed ventricular dilation, widening of the sylvian fissure, and bilateral encephalomalacia, which was more extensive on the right. Neuropsychological examination revealed a rather generalized cognitive deficit associated with dementia and memory disturbance. (See fig. 7.6.)

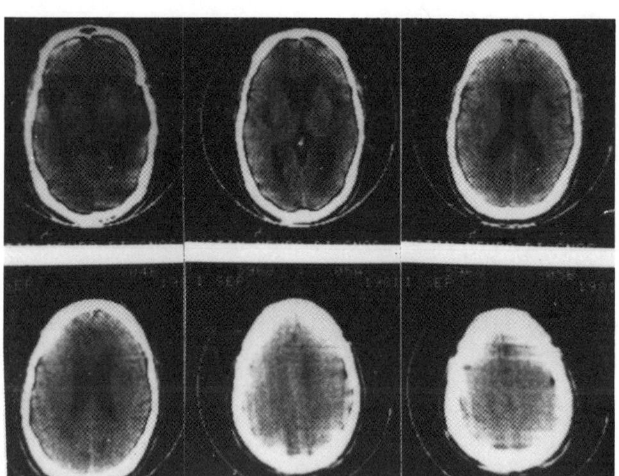

Fig. 7.6. Case 1. CAT scan shows ventricular dilation, widening of the sylvian fissure, and bilateral encephalomalacia, which is more extensive on the right.

Age 53
Sex M
Education 12

Lateral Dominance Exam

	Eye	Hand	Foot
Right	X	X	X
Left			
Mixed			

Motor Examination:
FOD 54 SOGD 44 TPTD 5 min DC 0 in
FOND 42 SOGND 43 TPTND 5 min DC 0 in
TPT Both 5 min DC 0 in

Sensory Examination:
MIld left sid dysstereognosis

Language Examination:
Some degree of constructional dyspraxia, otherwise WNL.

Memory Examiantion:
WMS MQ = 66
LM 0.5, Digits 10, VM 3, AL 4
TPT M 0, TPT L 0

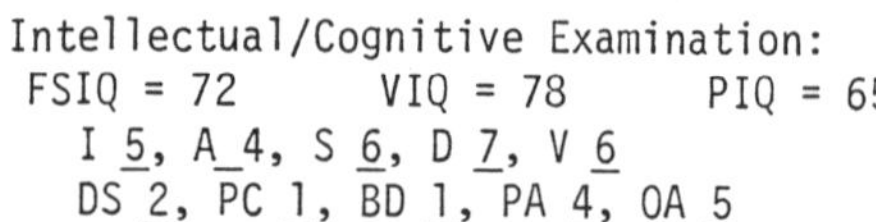

Intellectual/Cognitive Examination:
FSIQ = 72 VIQ = 78 PIQ = 65
I 5, A 4, S 6, D 7, V 6
DS 2, PC 1, BD 1, PA 4, OA 5

Category Test: 107

Trail Making Test:
A 71 sec. B 300+ DC

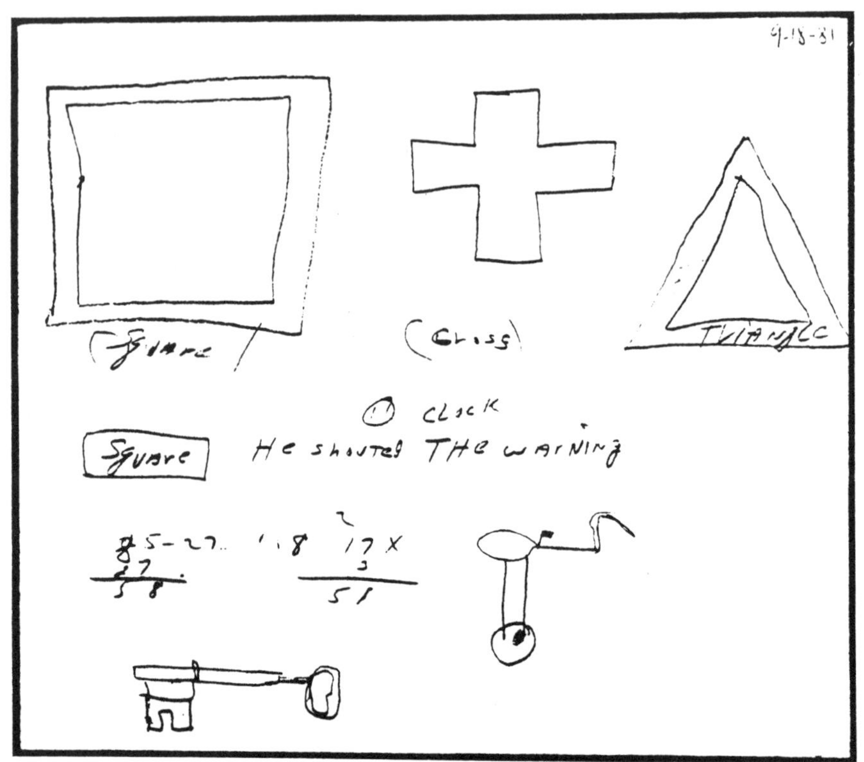

Case 2. This 69-year-old retired schoolteacher developed a cerebral abscess secondary to pulmonary infection. CAT scanning clearly demonstrated the focal position of the abscess in the posterior parieto-occipital region and the surrounding edema affecting much of the posterior right hemisphere (see fig. 7.7). Neuropsychological studies similarly indicated quite clearly posterior right hemisphere dysfunction in terms of the left side sensory findings (in the absence of lateralized motor deficits), constructional dyspraxia (in the absence of aphasic deficits), and significantly impaired performance IQ.

Age 69
Sex F
Education 16

Lateral Dominance Exam

	Eye	Hand	Foot
Right		X	X
Left	X		
Mixed			

Motor Examination:
FOD 25 SOGD 16
FOND 26 SOGND 13

Sensory Perceptual Examination:
Left side tactile, auditory and visual extinction. Left side finger dysgnosia, dysgraphesthesia and dysstereognosis.

Language Examination:
Constructional dyspraxia, L-R confusion

Memory Examination:
WMS MQ = 81
LM 7, Digits 8, VM 1, AL 15

Intellectual/Cognitive Examination:
FSIQ = 83, VIQ = 95, FSIQ = 83
I 8, C 1, A 7, S 8, D 6, V 12
DS 0, PC 2, BD 0, PA 6, OA 2

Category Test: 50+ DC
Trail Making Test: Trail A 240 B 306

Square

Cross

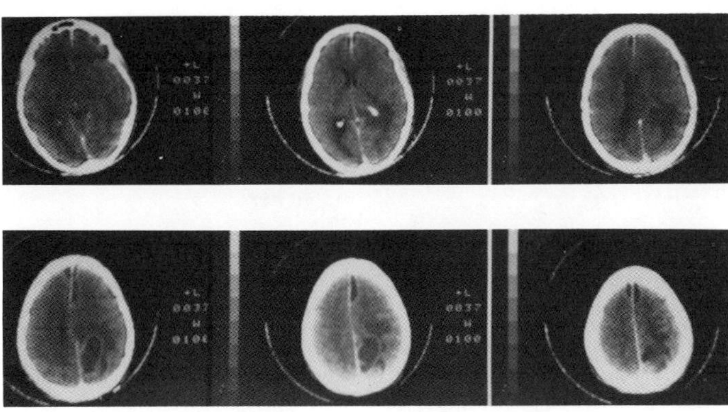

Fig. 7.7. Case 2. CAT scan demonstrates abscess in posterior parieto-occipital region and surrounding edema affecting the posterior right hemisphere.

triangle
He shouled a warning
clock
Seven
fork
Square
85−27=58

Case 3. This patient was a healthy, normal boy until nine years of age when he developed a viral meningoencephalitis. This resulted in prolonged coma for eleven days with residual general paralysis and spasticity and severe cognitive deficits. Seizures also developed as a consequence of the infection. The patient became a severe behavior problem, and he has been hospitalized in a residential psychiatric facility for the past five years. CAT scan, not shown here, demonstrated bilateral temporal lobe atrophy, diffuse cerebrocortical atrophy, and marked ventricular enlargement. Neuropsychological studies showed marked residual deficits in essentially all areas measured.

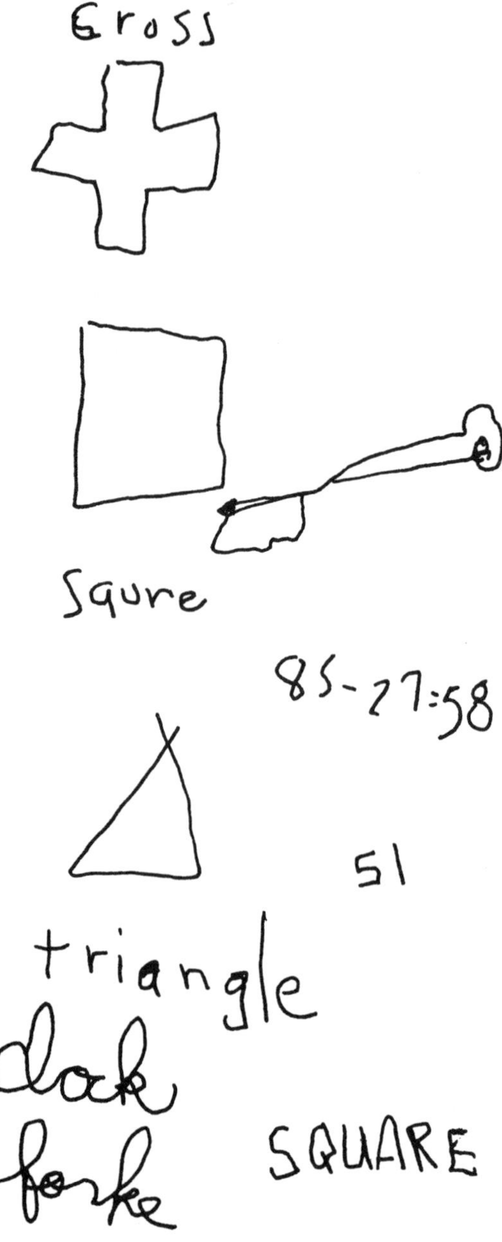

Age 21
Sex M
Education 12
(Special education)

Lateral Dominance Exam

	Eye	Hand	Foot
Right	X	X	X
Left			
Mixed			

Motor Examination:

FOD	20	SOGD	22	TPTD	10 min DC
FOND	18	SOGND	17	TPTND	10 min DC
				TPT Both	10 min DC

Sensory Perceptual Examination:
Bilateral findings of finger and palm dysgraphesthesia and dysstereognosis

Language Examination:
Dysfluent speech, constructional dyspraxia
spelling dyspraxia

WRAT Results
Reading 5.1
Spelling 4.7
Arithmetic 3.9

SSRT 13 errors
SSPT 13 errors

Memory Examination:
WMS MQ = 90
LM 7, Digits 9, VM 8, AL 16

Intellectual/Cognitive Functioning:
WAIS Results
VIQ = 76
I 4, C 5, A 5, S 4, digits 7, V 5
PIQ = 77
DS 4, PC 11, BD 7, PA 9, OA 2

Category Test 83 errors
Trail Making Test A 65 sec. B 279

Case 4. At age eleven this child developed a severe viral encephalitis, which progressed to the point of status epilepticus and prolonged coma. He ultimately survived but displayed pronounced postencephalitic encephalopathy. He was in the sixth grade when he came down with the infection, and up to that point he had no difficulty in school (was reported to be a "B student") and had no prior history of learning disability or any other related neurologic deficit. The scan on the left depicts initial CAT findings that were essentially within normal limits (fig. 7.8). The CAT scans on the right demonstrate rather marked atrophy and ventricular dilation. These scans were taken approximately three months postinfection. At the time of the follow-up CAT evaluation, the child's intellectual test results indicated a verbal IQ score of 62, performance IQ score of 71, and full-scale IQ score of 64. On the Kaufman Assessment Battery for Children, he had a sequential score of 58, simultaneous score of 70, and mental processing composite of 63. On the Wide Range Achievement Test, he had a spelling score of 4.5, arithmetic, 3.9, and reading, 5.4. His Beery Developmental Test of visual-motor integration was performed at the 10 percentile. His Raven's CPM was performed at the 25 percentile (26/36).

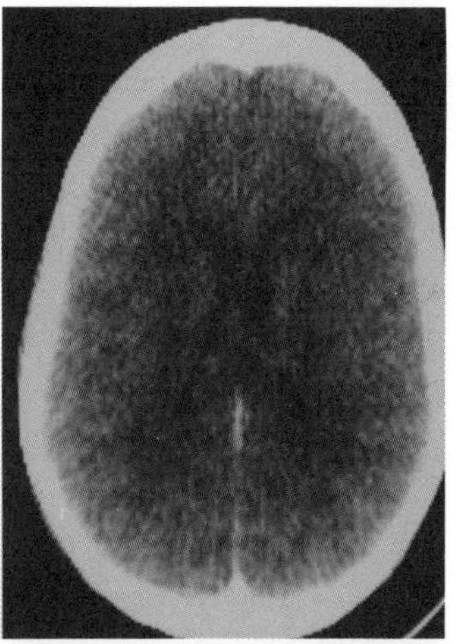

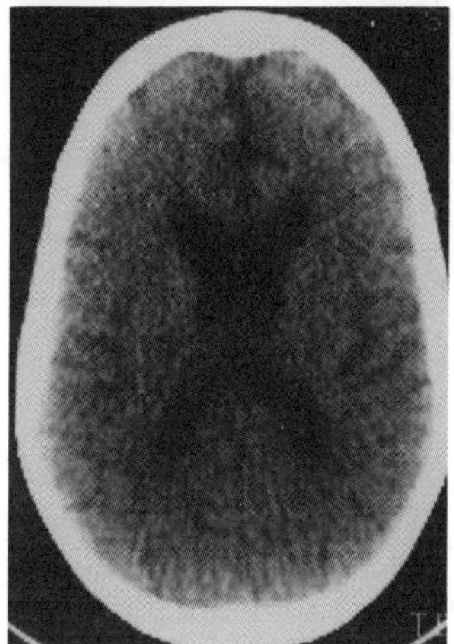

Fig. 7.8. Case 4. CAT scan on the top was taken one week after hospitalization for encephalitis. The child was in a coma at this time. Note the compression of the ventricular system, a sign of diffuse edema. CAT scan on the bottom was taken three months postcoma. Note the enlarged ventricular system and enlarged interhemispheric fissure and sylvian fissures, all signs of diffuse cerebral atrophy.

References

Adams, R. D., and M. Victor. 1977. *Principles of neurology*. New York: McGraw-Hill.

Baker, A. B. 1981. Viral encephalitis. In *Clinical neurology*, ed. A. B. Baker and L. H. Baker. Vol. 2. New York: Harper & Row.

Baker, L. H., and A. B. Baker. 1981. Nonviral forms of encephalitis. In *Clinical neurology*, ed. A. B. Baker and L. H. Baker. Vol. 2. New York: Harper & Row.

Bell, W. E. 1982. Central nervous system infections in childhood. *Seminars in Neurology* 2:87–191.

Bray, P. 1969. *Pediatric neurology*. Chicago: Year Book Medical Publishers.

Carbotte, R. M., S. D. Denburg, and J. A. Denburg. 1986. Prevalence of cognitive impairment in systemic lupus erythematosus. *Journal of Nervous and Mental Disease* 174:357–364.

Damasio, A. R., P. J. Eslinger, H. Damasio, G. W. Van Hoesen, and S. Cornell. 1985. Multimodal amnesic syndrome following bilateral temporal and basal forebrain damage. *Archives of Neurology* 42:252–259.

Ettinger, M. G. 1981. Brain abscess. In *Clinical neurology*, ed. A. B. Baker and L. H. Baker. Vol. 2. New York: Harper & Row.

Feigin, R., and P. Dodge. 1978. Central nervous system infections. In *Neurological pathophysiology*, ed. S. G. Eliasson, A. L. Prensky, and W. B. Hardin. 2d ed. New York: Oxford University Press.

Ford, F. R. (1976). *Diseases of the nervous system in infancy, childhood, and adolescence*. Springfield, IL: Charles C. Thomas.

Gianutsos, R. 1981. Training the short- and long-term verbal recall of a postencephalitic amnesic. *Journal of Clinical Neuropsychology* 3:143–153.

Hierons, R., I. Janota, and J. A. N. Corsellis. 1978. The late effects of necrotizing encephalitis of the temporal lobes and limbic areas: A clinicopathological study of ten cases. *Psychological Medicine* 8:21–42.

Ho, D. D., T. R. Rota, R. T. Schooley, J. C. Kaplan, J. D. Allan, J. E. Groopman, L. Resnick, D. Felenstein, C. A. Andrews, and M. S. Hirsch. 1985. Isolation of HTLV-III from cerebrospinal fluid and neural tissues of patients with neurologic syndromes related to the acquired immunodeficiency syndrome. *New England Journal of Medicine* 313:1493–1497.

Horten, B., R. Price, and D. Jimenez. 1981. Multifocal varicella-zoster virus leukoencephalitis temporally remote from herpes zoster. *Annals of Neurology* 9:251–266.

Kaell, A. T., M. Shetty, B. C. P. Lee, and M. D. Lockshin. 1986. The diversity of neurologic events in systemic lupus erythematosus. *Archives of Neurology* 43:273–276.

Lewis, A. J. 1976. *Mechanisms of neurological disease*. Boston: Little, Brown & Co.

Navia, B. A., B. D. Jordan, and R. W. Price. 1986. The AIDs dementia complex. I, Clinical features. *Annals of Neurology* 19:517–524.

Navia, B. A., E.-S. Cho, C. K. Petito, and R. W. Price. 1986. The AIDS dementia complex. II, Neuropathology. *Annals of Neurology* 19:525–535.

O'Donnell, P., T. Pula, M. Sellman, and D. Camenga. 1981. Recurrent herpes zoster encephalitis. *Archives of Neurology* 38:49–51.

Payne, E. E. 1969. *An atlas of pathology of the brain*. East Hanover, NJ: Sandoz Pharmaceuticals.

Reimer, L., and L. Reller. 1981. CSF in herpes zoster meningoencephalitis. *Archives of Neurology* 38:668.

Rosene, K. A., M. K. Copass, L. S. Kastner, C. M. Nolan, and D. A. Eschenbach. 1982. Persistent neuropsychological sequelae of toxic shock syndrome. *Annals of Internal Medicine* 96 (pt. 2):865:870.

Sahs, A. L., and R. J. Joynt. 1981. Bacterial meningitis. In *Clinical neurology*, ed. A. B. Baker and L. H. Baker. Vol. 2. New York: Harper & Row.

Scheinberg, P. 1977. *Modern practical neurology*. New York: Raven Press.

Shaw, G. M., M. E. Harper, B. H. Hahn, L. G. Epstein, D. C. Gajdusek, R. W. Price, B. A. Navia, C. K. Petito, C. J. O'Hara, J. E. Groopman, E.-S. Cho, J. M. Oleske, F. Wong-Staal, and R. C. Gallo. 1985. HTLV-III infection in brains of children and adults with AIDS encephalopathy. *Science* 227:177–181.

Smith, B. H. 1981. Infections of the dura and its venous sinuses. In *Clinical neurology*, ed. A. B. Baker and L. H. Baker. Vol. 2. New York: Harper & Row.

Townsend, J. J., W. G. Stroop, J. R. Baringer, J. S. Wolinsky, J. H. McKerrow, and B. O. Berg. 1982. Neuropathology of progressive rubella panencephalitis after childhood rubella. *Neurology* 32:185–190.

8. Convulsive Disorders

Epilepsy is one of the most common neurologic disorders, affecting about 1 percent of the world population (Martin, 1981). The actual seizure occurs when a group of neurons abnormally discharges, emitting the charge in such a synchronous fashion that it overrides normal physiologic functioning. The resultant effects on behavior depend upon the etiologic locus of the abnormality and whether it remains localized or spreads in a generalized fashion. Thus, seizure activity may only subtly, at times imperceptibly, affect cognitive functioning, or it may produce widespread effects, including loss of consciousness and tonic-clonic movement. Causes of epilepsy are as varied as its behavioral manifestations, with the more common being related to trauma, vascular disorder, or neurogenic disease process. Thus, any lesion in the brain from whatever cause may be potentially epileptogenic (Appel, 1980). It should be noted, however, that in approximately one-half of all seizure disorders, the etiology cannot be determined or related to any previous condition or causal factor.

There are numerous texts and review articles on the pathophysiology of convulsive disorders (Appel, 1980; Gastaut and Broughton, 1972; Hughes, 1982; Jasper, Ward, and Pope, 1969; O'Donohoe, 1979; and Prince, 1978). The intent of this chapter is to overview the subject and provide various guidelines for assessing patients with convulsive disorders.

Classification of Seizure Types

Once a group of neurons abnormally discharges, there are essentially three resultant effects that may occur: (1) the abnormality may remain localized and dissipate over time; (2) the discharge may spread, inducting surrounding neurons or neurons directly related by connecting pathways, but remain limited to these areas and not spread throughout the brain; or (3) the abnormal discharge may spread throughout the brain (Hardin, 1978). Following this scheme, seizures occurring in the first two categories are *partial* and those occurring in the third are *generalized*. In partial seizures, consciousness may be preserved as long as the abnormality remains in the cortex and restricted to one hemisphere. If there is some spread subcortically to limbic or thalamic areas, then consciousness may be lost. In generalized seizures consciousness is always affected. This loss occurs because the abnormality may spread generally across the brain, involving both cortical as well as subcortical structures. In certain generalized disorders (i.e., petit mal), the locus of pathology may reside subcortically with the centrencephalic projection of the pathophysiologic abnormality, thus resulting in generalized interruption of functioning.

The locus of pathophysiologic activity may correspond with the type of seizure experienced as well as with symptoms that may develop prior to (e.g., aura) or during the seizure. Thus, if the musculature is affected and contractions are produced, then frontal regions may be involved. Sensory disturbances may similarly implicate involvement of the particular sensory system being affected. Thus, visual symptoms may accompany a seizure whose focus is in the occipital region (see fig. 8.1). Peripheral nervous system discharge may involve hypothalamic regions. Loss of consciousness typically implies involvement of the upper brain stem and thalamus, thereby affecting their projection to and activation of cortical regions.

Table 8.1 reviews the classification scheme accepted by the International League against Epilepsy. Figures 8.1–8.6 depict various types of electroencephalographic (EEG) abnormalities seen with the epilepsies. Figure 8.7 demonstrates the type of results from Brain Electrical Activity Mapping (BEAM), a new computerized method for analyzing EEG data.

Partial Seizures

Partial seizures may be associated with either elementary or complex symptomatology. Focal motor (Jacksonian) seizures are an example of elementary partial seizures and usually originate focally and then gradually spread (see fig. 8.6). Thus, an "attack" may originate in the lateral precentral gyrus of the left hemisphere and produce initial twitching of the right thumb. As the abnormal discharge spreads, adjacent areas in the hand, arm, and face on that side only may become involved. The seizure then begins to dissipate with a gradual reduction in the clonic jerking. It does not spread to the other side.

Focal sensory seizures are similar, but originate in neural sensory systems. Thus, the patient may experience a sustained, involuntary sensory experience (either somesthetic, visual, vestibular, or olfactory). Partial sensory experience is perceived on the contralateral body side. Emotional experiences, memory experiences, or both may also occur with focal sensory seizures.

Autonomic seizures may be associated with a variety of autonomic functions including gastric motility, nausea, sweating, vomiting, incontinence, pallor, flushing, pupillary alterations, and tachycardia. Origin of the abnormal discharges associated with these seizures is typically in orbital frontal, mesial temporal, and insular cortical areas.

Psychomotor seizures are probably the best known of the partial seizures that have complex symptomatology. The origin is within the temporal lobes. Consciousness is

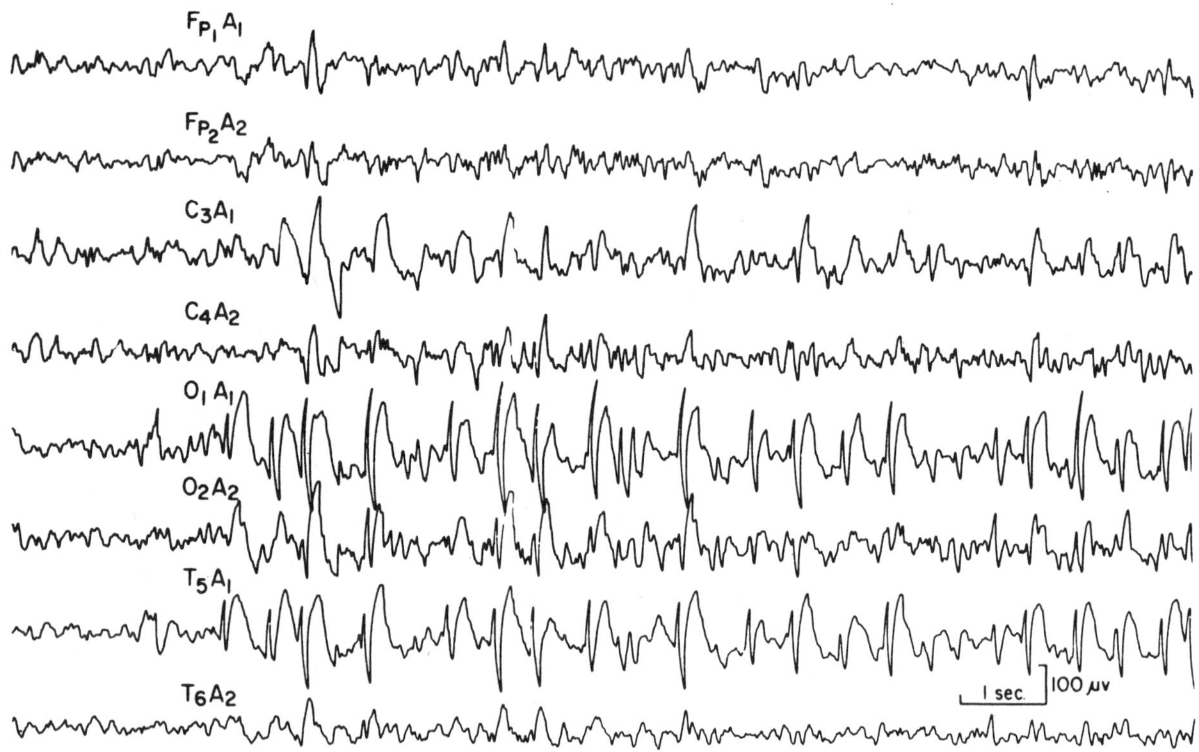

Fig. 8.1. Left occipital region (0_1) focus of high-voltage spike–and–slow wave discharge. Ten-year-old girl had simple partial seizures—versive, visual sensory, and psychic (deviation of the eyes and head to the right, sometimes followed by either a visual hallucination, unformed flashes of color or light, or blacking out of vision). Normal values from neurologic examination, and normal mental and motor development. No significant antecedent history. Normal pneumoencephalogram and arteriogram values. Seizures poorly controlled with phenytoin and primidone until they stopped at age three. Medication discontinued at age 15; no subsequent seizures for four years. The nature of the occipital lesion that was responsible for the seizures and was the source of the massive focal EEG discharge is not known. From Appel (1980). Courtesy of Geigy Pharmaceuticals.

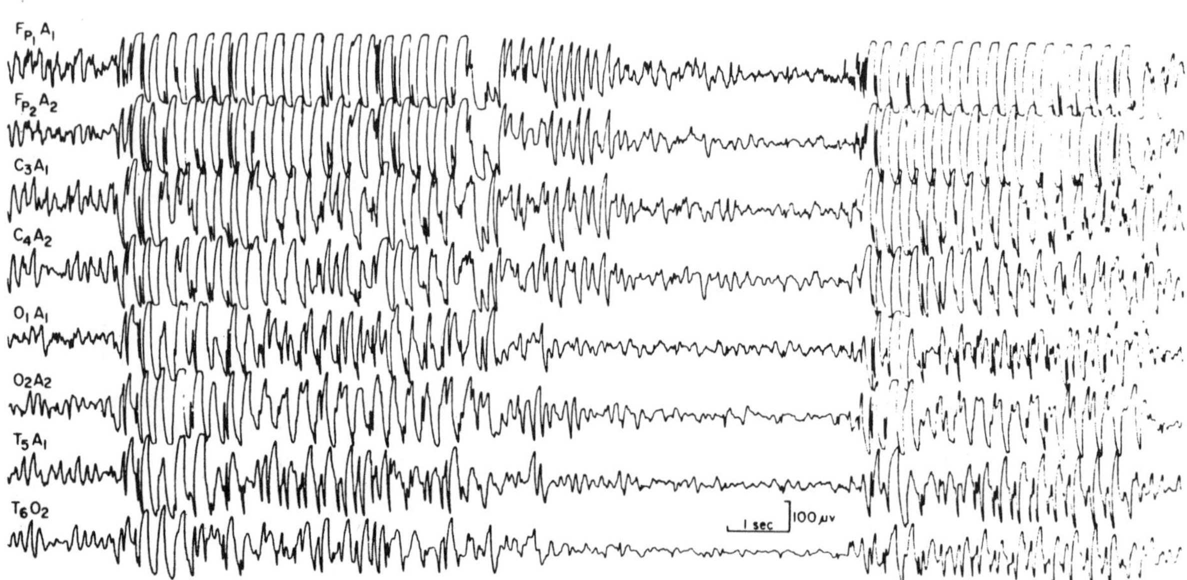

Fig. 8.2. Generalized seizures. Simple absence and absence with automatisms in boy age 11 years. Recent onset of brief lapses of responsiveness, sometimes associated with sniffing movements of the face and foot shuffling. Normal mental and motor development, and normal neurologic examination results. EEG sample shows a spike-and-wave burst (*left*), which was accompanied by sniffing, and a shorter burst (*right*), which was associated with unresponsiveness only. From Appel (1980). Courtesy of Geigy Pharmaceuticals.

Table 8.1. *International Classification of Epileptic Seizures*

- I. Partial seizures (seizures beginning locally)
  - A. Partial seizures with elementary symptomatology (generally without impairment of consciousness)
    - 1. With motor symptoms
      - a. Focal motor
      - b. Jacksonian
      - c. Versive (generally contraversive)
      - d. Postural
      - e. Somatic inhibitory (?)
      - f. Aphasic
      - g. Phonatory (vocalization and arrest of speech)
    - 2. With special sensory or somatosensory symptoms
      - a. Somatosensory
      - b. Visual
      - c. Auditory
      - d. Olfactory
      - e. Gustatory
      - f. Vertiginous
    - 3. With autonomic symptoms
    - 4. Compound forms
  - B. Partial seizures with complex symptomatology (generally with impairment of consciousness)
    - 1. With impaired consciousness only
    - 2. With cognitive symptomatology
      - a. With dysmnesic disturbances
      - b. With ideational disturbances
    - 3. With affective symptomatology
    - 4. With "psychosensory" symptomatology
      - a. Illusions
      - b. Hallucinations
    - 5. With "psychomotor" symptomatology (automatisms)
    - 6. Compound forms
  - C. Partial seizures secondarily generalized
- II. Generalized seizures (bilaterally symmetrical and without local onset)
  - A. Absences (petit mal)
    - 1. Simple absences, with impairment of consciousness only
    - 2. Complex absences with other associated phenomena
      - a. With mild clonic components (myoclonic)
      - b. With increase of postural tone (retropulsive)
      - c. With diminution or abolition of postural tone (atonic)
      - d. With automatisms
      - e. With automatic phenomena (e.g., enuresis)
      - f. Mixed forms
  - B. Bilateral massive epileptic myoclonus (myoclonic jerks)
  - C. Infantile spasms
  - D. Clonic seizures
  - E. Tonic seizures
  - F. Tonic-clonic seizures ("grand mal" seizures)
  - G. Atonic seizures
    - 1. Of very brief duration (drop attacks)
    - 2. Of longer duration (including atonic absences)
  - H. Akinetic seizures (loss of movement without atonia)
- III. Unilateral or predominantly unilateral seizures
- IV. Unclassified epileptic seizures (includes all seizures that cannot be classified because of inadequate or incomplete data)

typically impaired, but not lost. During the seizure there may be stereotyped, automatic, well-coordinated, but semipurposeful movements (see fig. 8.5). Behavior during these periods may remain rudimentary and rhythmic in the form of repetitive masticatory (lip-smacking) movements along with body rocking or hand movements of picking or patting all in association with an expressionless face. The patient does not interact with the environment in a meaningful manner. Some seizures may be more complex and prolonged. Patients may display erratic behavior that maintains an inappropriate and often bizarre emotional tone. Habitual but complex movements such as dressing or grooming may occur. Hallucinatory phenomena may occur along with fuguelike states.

The above features of complex partial seizures essentially can be broken down into six general types of symptomatology, which may be expressed singularly or in combination, as follows:

1. Impairment of consciousness only.
2. Cognitive symptomatology that is most commonly manifested as an alteration or distortion in time perception and disturbance in memory, but may also include *déjà vu* or *jamais vu* experiences, remoteness, detachment, depersonalization, or any combination of these. "Forced thinking" in terms of perseverative thoughts may occur.
3. Psychosensory disturbance in the form of perceptual distortion, hallucinations, or both, the most common being an alteration in size and object perception.
4. Affective symptomatology, typically in the form of negative emotion (excessive fear, anxiety, dread, etc.) that has a sudden onset and follows a stereotypic pattern, may occur.
5. Automatisms of a singular form (typically basic masticatory movements such as sucking, kissing, lip pursing) to more complex, but only semipurposeful movements (scratching head, brushing clothes, rubbing hands, etc.) to even more integrated movement (turning head in an orientation response) may develop in response to the aberrant electrophysiologic state.
6. Autonomic aspects such as pallor, flushing, sweating, abdominal distress, pupillary changes, and salivation may occur.

Since many of the symptoms with partial complex seizures involve this alteration in "mental" state or activity, there has been considerable speculation in the study of these disorders about their relationship with psychopathology (see Ervin, 1975, and Flor-Henry, 1969*a*, 1969*b*).

Generalized Seizures

Generalized seizures are those that result from bilateral brain involvement. If motor involvement is present, it is always manifested bilaterally. The following fall into the classification scheme of generalized seizures: generalized tonic-clonic seizures, absence seizures, tonic

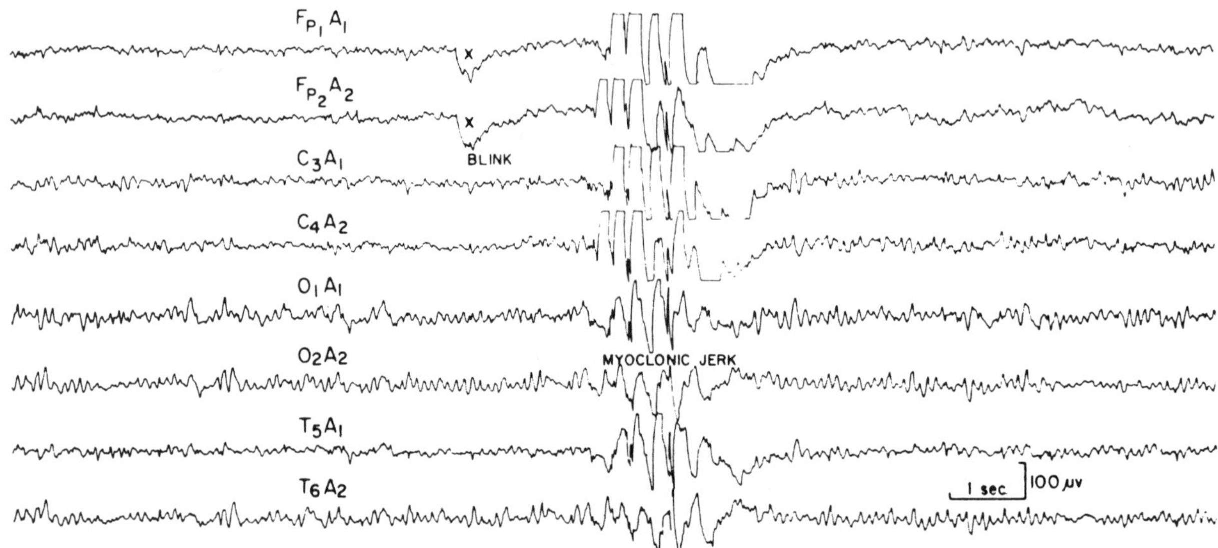

Fig. 8.3. Generalized seizures. Myoclonic and tonic-clonic seizures in woman age 24. At age 21, brief myoclonic jerks of the upper extremities developed without causing loss of consciousness; also occasional nocturnal generalized tonic-clonic seizures occurred. Normal intelligence; normal results from neurologic examination. EEG shows brief 3–4 Hz generalized spike-and-wave bursts and essentially normal background activity. From Appel (1980). Courtesy of Geigy Pharmaceuticals.

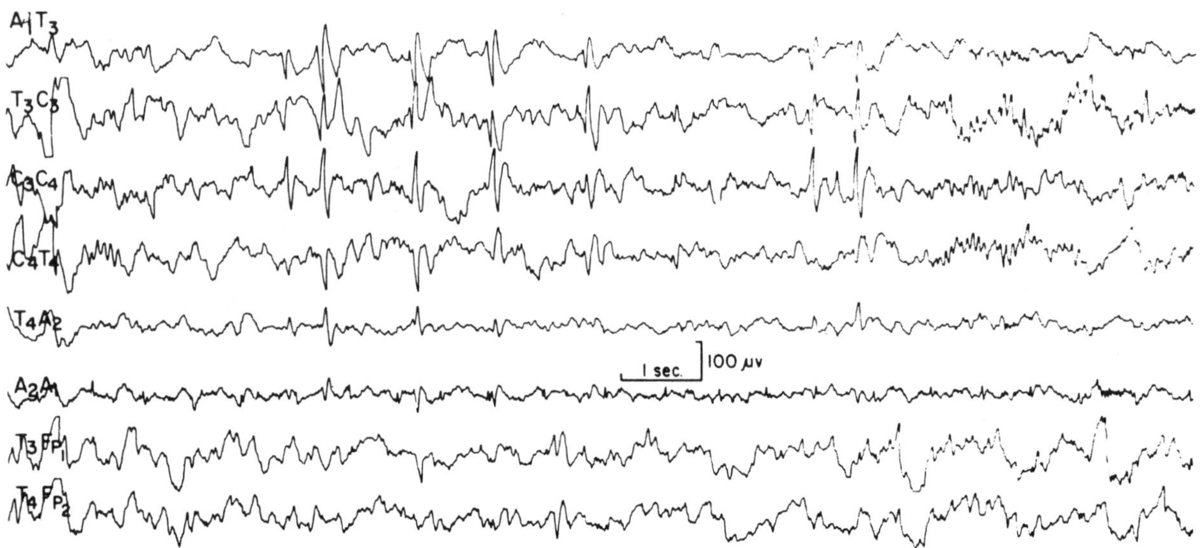

Fig. 8.4. Left central region (C_3) focus of spike–and–slow wave discharges. This region very active during sleep. EEG background activity is normal. Patient is boy age five. Four months before referral, onset of twitching of right side of mouth while asleep. A single generalized tonic-clonic seizure, beginning with twitching of the right face and arm, occurred on one occasion soon after falling asleep. Normal motor and mental development; no history of significant illness or injury. This is an example of the so-called benign centrotemporal epilepsy of children. Treated with 200 mg carbamazepine twice daily, with no recurrence of seizures. From Appel (1980). Courtesy of Geigy Pharmaceuticals.

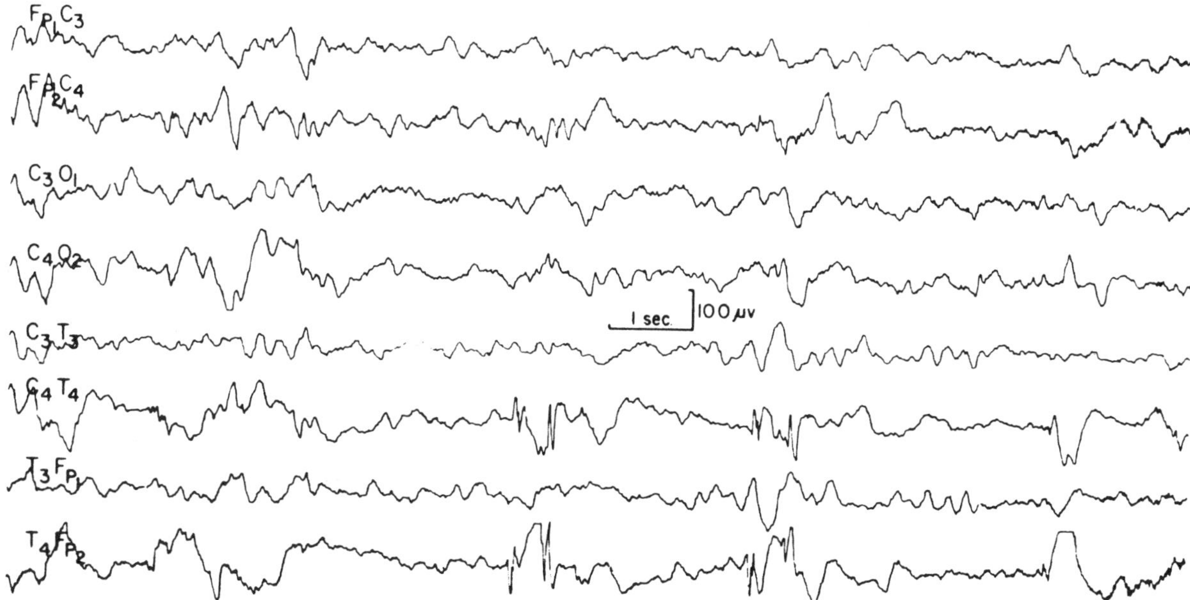

Fig. 8.5. Right temporal region (T_4) focus of spikes, polyspikes, and high-voltage slow transients. Complex partial seizures with automatisms. Girl age 15 years; first seizure at age four months, or possibly earlier. Attacks consisted of staring, with the head and eyes deviated to one side. Infant was treated with phenobarbital, and seizures stopped at age three years. Medication was discontinued at age five, and the child again had seizures. These were characterized by flushing of the face, staring, and aimless movements of the right arm; sometimes she experienced a "salty" taste. With onset of menses, the seizures changed, and two new types were experienced. One type began with the child saying, "Wait a minute"; then she had lip smacking, chewing, and swallowing movements of the mouth lasting about 50 seconds, after which she was responsive, complained of a "hot" feeling, yawned, and appeared groggy. In the other type of seizure, her right limbs became stiff, with the head turning to the right and the trunk bent to the right as if reaching for her right foot. Neurologic examination revealed some photophobia and "oscillating of the right eyeball" upon convergence, but was otherwise not remarkable. The fundi and fields were within normal limits. A CAT scan revealed the presence of a space-occupying lesion in the right temporal lobe. Surgical diagnosis: ganglioglioma, approximately 3.5 cm in diameter, in the right temporal lobe. From Appel (1980). Courtesy of Geigy Pharmaceuticals.

seizures, myoclonic seizures, atonic seizures, and infantile spasms.

Generalized Tonic-Clonic Seizures. The generalized tonic-clonic seizure, the so-called grand mal seizure, begins locally, but there is almost immediate spread (see fig. 8.3) because of the involvement of the diencephalon with its corticoreticular, thalamocortical, and corticothalamic interconnections. Consciousness is always lost. The tonic phase (generalized muscular contraction) is usually first, followed by the clonic phase (jerking). The seizure usually lasts thirty to forty seconds with termination of the seizure typically resulting in a state of unresponsiveness for three to ten minutes. When patients become arousable, they are typically confused and tired. Sleep then usually ensues. Although the seizure episode is complete at this time, electrocortical activity may remain abnormal. Confusion and impaired mental efficiency may last for several hours.

Absence Seizures. The absence or so-called petit mal attack is constituted by a sudden arrest of consciousness, lasting two to ten seconds. The patient typically stares vacantly into space, frequently with mouth agape and eyes slightly turned up. There may be no associated motor movement, but patients usually do not fall, even though they may be oblivious to environmental stimuli. Frequently, the child is thought to be daydreaming or inattending, but when these episodes continue to recur, it becomes obvious that this is not the case. Hyperventilation may precipitate the attack. The EEG typically reflects the classic three per second spike-and-wave activity (see fig. 8.2). There may be eye blinking at a similar frequency. The seizure may take a much more complex form, however, and include automatic, purposeless movements. There may also be changes in muscle tone.

Other Generalized Seizures. The other generalized seizure disorders are less common and will be briefly overviewed as follows: *Tonic seizures* are generalized seizures with sustained flexor and extensor tone, producing limb and trunk rigidity. The pathophysiology of this disorder is poorly understood. *Myoclonic seizures* are constituted of brief muscle contractions of individual or groups of muscles occurring unilaterally or bilaterally. There is no loss of consciousness. The onset of myoclonic epilepsy is typically associated with serious brain disease—such as in Jakob-Creutzfeldt disease. *Atonic seizures* have been previously characterized as "drop attacks," because the

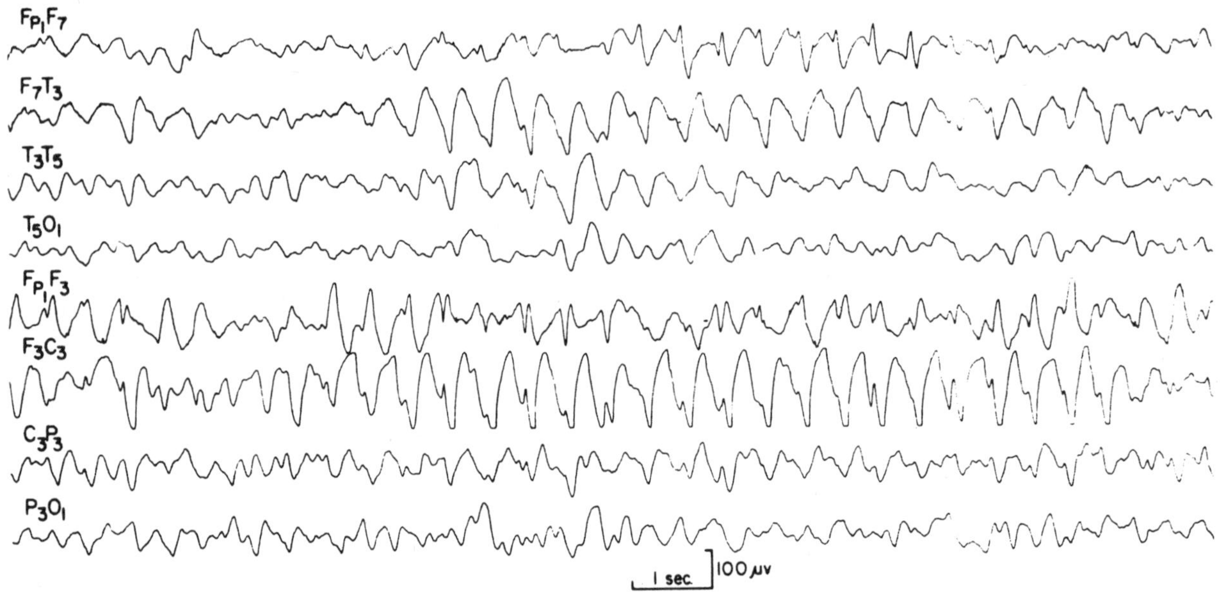

Fig. 8.6. Left frontal region (F_3) focus of continuous, rhythmic slow wave and spike–and–slow wave activity in boy eight years old. Simple partial seizures—versive, focal motor, and Jacksonian. Simple partial seizures evolving to generalized tonic-clonic seizures. Generalized tonic-clonic seizure at age eight months and another at nine months. In spite of treatment (phenobarbital and phenytoin), he continued to have prolonged generalized seizures. At age three years, attacks developed consisting of deviation of the head and eyes to the right, associated with unresponsiveness. These attacks have become increasingly frequent, and some seizures recently have progressed to include twitching of the right face, then of the right arm, and finally of the right leg. Normal development and intelligence, but some learning disability; no significant neurologic findings. CAT scan revealed hypodevelopment of the left hemisphere. From Appel (1980). Courtesy of Geigy Pharmaceuticals.

Fig. 8.7. Brain Electrical Activity Mapping (BEAM) results on a 26-year-old female who had experienced a serious anoxic cerebral injury but whose CAT, MRI, and routine EEG results were normal. The BEAM results clearly depict an abnormality in the right temporal region as demonstrated by the asymmetry present in the test results utilizing somatosensory stimulation. Other aspects of her BEAM studies (not depicted here) were likewise suggestive of temporal lobe dysfunction. BEAM studies have been shown to be useful in a variety of neurologic conditions, particularly where the deficits may be subtle. The clinical utility of the BEAM is fully discussed by Duffy and his colleagues (see Duffy, McAnulty, and Schachter, 1984). Oken and Chiappa (1986) discuss some of the limitations of this procedure. In studies relating cognitive dysfunction with BEAM results, the initial findings suggest good clinical correlation (see Duffy et al., 1984).

fundamental feature of the seizures is a loss of postural control. *Infantile spasms* are a disorder of infancy or childhood and typically consist of brief flexion or extension of the trunk, neck, or extremities or a flexion of the upper extremities and extension of the lower ones. There is a high incidence of these seizures in patients with mental and motor retardation. In those with definite infantile spasms, 50 percent have been shown to have underlying atrophic brain changes.

Behavioral Aberrations Associated with Epilepsy

Various alterations in behavior may be associated with the different aspects of the seizure itself. Additionally, the presence of underlying seizure disorder apparently places the patient at risk for various disturbances in emotion-personality integration (Bear and Fedio, 1977; Livingston, 1972; Pincus and Tucker, 1978; Pritchard, Lombroso, and McIntyre, 1980). In evaluating the patient with a seizure disorder, it is important to be able to differentiate those behaviors that may be directly related to the seizure process itself from those that may be more in the realm of personality alterations.

Preictal Phenomena. Preictal phenomena can generally be divided into a prodromal phase and an aural stage. The aura is usually associated with a delineated onset of abnormal electrophysiologic discharges that precede the epileptic discharge itself. Prodromal features, on the other hand, may not be associated with any specific detectable electrophysiologic changes, but a variety of emotional changes may be present. These emotional changes commonly occur in the form of increased lability, heightened anxiety, irritability, or depression (Pond, 1974). Frequently, it may be difficult, in the absence of direct EEG recording, to determine where a prodromal phase stops and the aura begins. Similarly, in partial complex seizures (the so-called temporal lobe or psychomotor seizure disorders) both prodromal and aural phenomena may be associated with varied alterations in mental functions, including hallucinations, forced thinking, illusionary ideation, alteration in personality, dissociative states, and alterations in motivational levels (Mesulam, 1981).

Ictal Phenomena. In the generalized epilepsies with clear motor manifestations, the ictal phase is unmistakable—loss of consciousness and tonic, clonic, or tonic-clonic stereotypic movements. However, seizure discharges that do not evolve into generalized epilepsy with loss of consciousness may result in varied alterations in cognitive abilities, including transient disturbance in level of consciousness, stupor, dysphasia, psychomotor activation or retardation, incontinence, amnesia, hallucinatory phenomena, and altered thought processes. Albeit infrequent, in certain seizure disorders aggressive rage reactions may occur during the ictal phase (Rodin, 1973; Stevens and Hermann, 1981). Severe, sustained, and well-organized aggressive outbursts are rare if not nonexistent (Delgado-Escueta et al., 1981).

Postictal Phenomena. Following the active phase of the seizure, the EEG may remain abnormal for a varied length of time, frequently in the form of disorganized background activity. Confusion during this period is probably the most common feature. As the EEG begins to return to normal, patients may be able to converse and move about, but they will usually have no recall of their behavior during this period. It has been speculated (Pincus and Tucker, 1978) that because of alterations in cortical control (i.e., inhibition) over emotion, basic emotions may be expressed during postictal periods that would not normally be displayed by the patient. Thus, if a patient with a well-documented seizure disorder shows various uncharacteristic behaviors following the resolution of the actual seizure, they are probaby related to postictal phenomena.

Seizure Disorders and the Temporal Lobes

Behavioral correlates of patients whose EEG results indicate temporal lobe abnormalities as well as those with bona fide convulsive disorders of temporal lobe origin deserve special comment (Nielsen and Kristensen, 1981). Strub and Black (1981) review a plethora of studies in this area and summarize the most common behavioral features (not in order of frequency) as follows: (1) increased emotionality, (2) elation or euphoria, (3) depression, (4) anger and irritability, (5) hostility and aggressive behavior, (6) altered and compulsive behavior, (7) circumstantiality, (8) viscosity (i.e., stickiness in general mode of behavior), (9) hypergraphia, (10) hyperreligiosity, (11) overconcern with philosophy, (12) dependency and passivity, (13) lack of humor, and (14) paranoia. If the temporal lobe abnormality is lateralized to the left there is a greater tendency for the expression of the verbal aspects, such as the hypergraphia, philosophical interest, and hyperreligiosity; whereas, lateralized right temporal lobe abnormality tends to be associated more with nonverbal emotional changes (Bear, 1977; Bear and Fedio, 1977). The changes in sexuality that may accompany temporal lobe dysfunction tend to be in the direction of hyposexuality, although the opposite may be true (Blumer and Levin, 1977). The sexual disturbance is thought to be related to hypothalamic-limbic system involvement. In a small minority of epileptic patients whose seizures are related to abnormalities in the temporal lobes, a schizophreniform psychosis may develop that closely resembles paranoid schizophrenia (Taylor, 1977). However, the work by Ramani and Gumnit (1982*a*, 1982*b*) questions the validity of this association. Various dissociative states (see Schenk and Bear, 1981), including multiple personalities, have been observed in epileptic patients whose seizures had origins in the temporal lobe (Mesulam, 1981). Tucker et al. (1986) also suggest that some atypical psychotic episodes, particularly those associated with episodic affective and cognitive disturbance, may be seen in patients with complex partial seizures of a temporal lobe origin.

Hysterical Seizure Disorders. Hysterical or functional seizures occur with some regularity in various hysterical and somatoform disorders. Also, epileptic patients may display functional seizures, usually associated with an attempt for manipulation or secondary gain. The hysterical fit is frequently quite unlike the bona fide seizure. Peculiar, nonstereotypic movements are commonplace. Wild gyrations, arm flailing, rocking, squirming, and resistance to persons helping (and sometimes purposefully striking helpers) are all common. At times, application of noxious pressure stimulation brings about cessation. In severe cases, hospitalizing the patient and using video recording and EEG telemetry will confirm the diagnosis (Ramani and Gumnit, 1982*a*, 1982*b*; Ramani et al., 1980). In conjunction with this, confronting the patient with the video record and initiating systematic reeducative type of psychotherapy can be effective (Ramani et al., 1980).

Klüver-Bucy Syndrome. The Klüver-Bucy syndrome, although quite rare, may be seen as a result of bilateral temporal lobe damage, from whatever cause. The behavioral syndrome present includes visual agnosia, hyperorality, placidity, hypersexuality, alteration in dietary habits, and hypermetamorphosis (tendency to attend and react to all stimuli). The syndrome was first noted in monkeys by Klüver and Bucy (1937), hence the name. The syndrome has also been well documented in humans (Terzian and Ore, 1955). In Pick's disease, in which focal pathology of the temporal lobes may occur, features of the Klüver-Bucy syndrome may be seen (Cummings and Duchen, 1981). Klüver-Bucy syndrome has also been reported in Huntington's chorea (Janati, 1985). Incomplete damage to temporal regions may also result in incomplete expression of the syndrome. It is also apparent that certain features of Klüver-Bucy syndrome overlap with certain behavioral aberrations associated with temporal lobe epilepsy.

Neuropsychological Assessment in the Patient with a Temporal Lobe Disorder. Electrophysiologic abnormalities related to temporal lobe disturbance can be established by electroencephalography. Neuropsychological technique will in turn establish whether there are coexisting deficits in cognitive behaviors. Personality studies will establish whether there are concomitant personality factors. Finally, CAT scanning will establish whether gross structural abnormalities exist. Thus, the evaluation of the patient suspected of having temporal lobe disorder is multifaceted and covers several disciplines. With respect to the neuropsychological examination, careful attention should be directed toward lateralized temporal lobe functions (i.e., left temporal lobe language functions; right temporal lobe visuospatial, visuomotor, and sequential processing functions; lateralized extinction in double simultaneous auditory stimulation; an impaired picture arrangement score in relation to intact block design performance or other performance IQ measures in relation to impaired rhythm discrimination [Seashore Rhythm Test] in the absence of receptive language deficits implicating possible right temporal involvement; impaired verbal memory with left temporal lobe damage and impaired visual memory with right temporal lobe damage). Milberg et al. (1980) have demonstrated that the information, vocabulary, and similarities subtest scores on the Wechsler Adult Intelligence Scale were selectively affected when patients with temporal lobe seizure disorders were tested. Furthermore, these researchers developed a discriminant function based on these findings that was able to differentiate between 75 percent and 80 percent of the patients whose epilepsy was caused by temporal lobe damage. The discriminant function was Vocabulary + Information/2 − Similarities. A cut-off score of zero was utilized, with a score below zero suggesting classification in the group whose epilepsy had temporal lobe origins. Glowinski (1973) has also demonstrated that epileptic patients whose disease sprang from temporal lobe damage performed poorly on the logical memory subtest on the Wechsler Memory Scale. These relationships may be important clinical findings in evaluating such patients. Attention should also be directed toward integrative and whole-brain function and toward establishing the presence or absence of the various behavioral manifestations that have been outlined above.

Neuropsychological Correlates of Epilepsy

The most comprehensive studies of the effects of epilepsy on cognitive performance are those of Dodrill (1978, 1981). He utilized the Halstead-Reitan Neuropsychological Test Battery, the Stroop Color-Word Test, and the Wechsler Memory Scale. Table 8.2 summarizes the findings of these studies. As can be seen from this table, the epileptic patient tends to display nonspecific deficits in terms of neuropsychological performance. This table should serve as a guideline in the neuropsychological assessment of the patient with seizure disorder.

Seizure Type. As the generalized seizures with tonic-clonic motor involvement and partial seizures with complex symptomatology tend to involve greater areas of the brain, it is not surprising that these disorders are usually associated with greater neuropsychological deficits (see Dodrill, 1981). However, it should be noted that the results in table 8.2 were derived from a diverse group of patients with seizure disorders. Thus, regardless of seizure type, there is a greater chance for cognitive deficit for this group than for nonaffected persons.

Seizure Frequency. Dikmen, Matthews, and Harley (1975, 1977) demonstrated that the greater frequency of major motor seizures is correlated with reduced performance on cognitive-intellectual measures. Similarly, poorly controlled or repetitively occurring seizures may be associated with deterioration in level of function (see also Dodrill, 1981; Klonoff and Low, 1974). Although this remains debatable, repetitive seizures over a prolonged period or poorly controlled seizures of chronic duration may be associated with progressive deficits in neuropsychological functioning (O'Donohoe, 1979).

Emotional Factors. Poggio, Walker, and Andy (1956) have described four main pathways by which seizure discharges may influence behavior as a result of repetitively main-

Table 8.2. *Guidelines for Cognitive Test Performance of Epileptic Patients*

Test	Cutoff (Inside/Outside)	Percentage Controls	Correctly Classified Epileptic Patients
Category	53/54 errors	76	49
Tactual Performance Test, total time	16.2/16.3 minutes	79	69
Tactual Performance Test, memory	8/7 blocks remembered	76	57
Tactual Performance Test, localization	4/3 blocks localized	77	52
Seashore Rhythm Test	26/25 correct	73	59
Tapping, total (males)	101/100 taps (average)	80	88
Tapping, total (females)	92/91 taps (average)	76	85
Trail-Making Test, Part B	81/82 seconds	79	64
Aphasia Screening	2/3 errors	79	53
Constructional dyspraxia	questionable/mild	80	49
Perceptual examination	6/7 errors	79	51
Name writing, total	.85/.84 letters/second	72	72
Seashore tonal memory	22/21 correct	73	60
Stroop, Part I	93/94 seconds	75	61
Stroop, Part II–Part I	150/151 seconds	77	63
Memory scale, logical memory	19/18 total memories	76	59
Memory scale, visual reproduction	11/10 total points	77	78
Summary: Total tests	6/7 outside normal limits	83	79

Source: Adapted from Dodrill (1978).

tained oscillatory potentials. These four pathways are (1) frontal granular cortex–caudatenucleus–dorsomedial thalamus, (2) peri-Rolandic cortex–putamen–lateral thalamic nuclei, (3) temporal cortex–amygdala–hippocampus–septum, and (4) visual striate cortex–pulvinar–lateral geniculate nucleus of the thalamus. While it is generally assumed that the transient features of paralysis, aphasia, and apraxia are associated with abnormal discharges within one or a combination of these circuits, it is also likely that these systems are associated with some of the emotional symptoms displayed. Whether the involvement of these systems continues after complete cessation of abnormal discharges is under debate (see Flor-Henry, 1969*a*, 1969*b*). However, some of the emotional symptoms observed with the seizure may also be related to some abnormal behaviors not occurring during postictal periods.

History of Seizures. A patient with a history of seizure disorder may become seizure free, typically after being on anticonvulsant medication for some time. While a history of seizure disorder certainly implicates the prior presence of abnormal brain function, the seizure-free patient may not display any signs of neurologic or neuropsychological deficit during such periods of remission (Thurston et al., 1981). Thus, a history of seizures may not result in adverse or impaired neuropsychological performance, particularly in children without a history of previously poorly controlled seizures, focal cerebral deficit, or a history of various seizure type combinations (Thurston et al., 1981).

Outcome Factors. Hermann (1982), utilizing the Luria-Nebraska Neuropsychological Test Battery, demonstrated that epileptic children with intact neuropsychological functioning were less aggressive, manifested fewer behavioral problems, and overall were more socially competent than those with poor functioning. Similarly, Dodrill and Clemmons (1984) demonstrated the effectiveness of neuropsychological testing in predicting school and life functioning success in young adults with epilepsy. The relationship between epilepsy and psychopathology remains unclear, however (Bear, 1985; Rodin and Schmaltz, 1984; Whitman et al., 1984).

Medication Effects. Since most patients with convulsive disorder will be on some type of anticonvulsant medication, there is the potential for medication effects to interact with neuropsychological test performance. Dodrill (1981) has fully reviewed literature on this topic. Determining the effects of medication on neuropsychological functioning is complicated by the fact that it reduces adverse physiologic irregularities, and the anticonvulsant effect on aberrant neuronal functioning may improve cognitive functioning. The most common anticonvulsant, phenytoin (Dilantin) may produce some decrement in tasks requiring motor performance without affecting cognitive functioning. Phenobarbital may initially produce sedation, or paradoxically in some children it may induce hyperactivity, attentional deficits, and disturbed behavior (O'Donohoe, 1979). Such effects will deleteriously affect neuropsychological performance. For children with adverse behavioral reactions to phenobarbital, the drug is usually discontinued and replaced by another anticonvulsant. Children who initially show only sedation effects from taking the drug usually adjust to such effects within two to three months, and deficits in neuropsychological performance at such times may be quite minimal (however, see Hartlage, 1981). Carbamazepine (Tegretol) is another frequently used anticonvulsant that may not produce significant deleterious effects on neuropsychological performance.

Dodrill's work may serve as a useful guideline in evaluating the patient with seizure disorder. It should also be noted that in evaluating the seizure patient with generalized epilepsy of the grand mal type that electrocortical activity may remain abnormal for up to forty-eight hours following the cessation of the seizure. Thus, neuropsychologic evaluation during that period will typically reflect greater impairment than that seen several days after cessation of the seizure.

Andrews et al. (1986) have compared phenytoin and carbamazepine on a variety of cognitive tasks in patients first diagnosed as having epilepsy. In this study, patients receiving phenytoin performed consistently less well on memory tasks than did those untreated or receiving carbamazepine. It was also noted that carbamazepine was associated with lowered levels of depression, anxiety, and fatigue. These results supported the purported psychotropic effects of carbamazepine.

CASE STUDIES

Case 1. This patient has a generalized seizure disorder of long standing. Onset of seizures was in the first year of life. His most recent EEG indicated focal spiking over the left temporal lobe with a spreading effect involving the entire hemisphere. CAT scan showed no abnormalities. Despite being on therapeutic dosages of phenytoin, carbamazepine, and valproic acid, he continues to have one or two seizures per month. Neuropsychological studies revealed a general lowering of performance across most measures but an absence of any focal abnormalities. This is the common configuration seen in patients with such convulsive disorders.

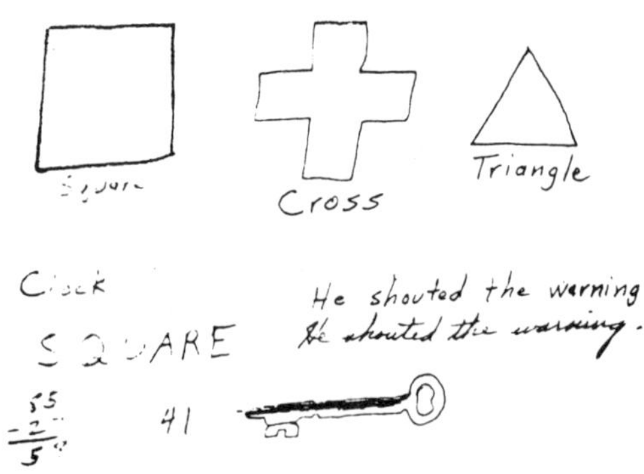

Age 24
Sex M
Education 12
(Special Ed.)

Lateral Dominance Exam

	Eye	Hand	Foot
Right	X	X	X
Left			
Mixed			

Motor Examination:

FOD	40	SOGD	41	TPTD	12.4
FOND	37	SOGND	43	TPTND	8.2
				TPT Both	6.5

Sensory Perceptual Examination:
Sporadic bilateral errors on finger recognition and graphesthesia otherwise WNL.

Aphasia Examination:
WNL except for calculation errors
Achievement Functioning:
WRAT Results
Reading grade level 9.1
Spelling grade level 11.2
Arithmetic grade level 6.1

Memory Examination:
MQ = 92
LM 5, Digits 10, VM 11, AL 15.5
TPT M 5, TPT L 1

Intellectual/Cognitive Functioning:
WAIS Results FSIQ = 87
VIQ = 89 I 8, C 7, A 7, S 8, D 9, V 8
PIQ = 86 DS 7, PC 8, BD 11, PA 6, OA 8

Category Test: 32 errors

Trail Making Test: A 62 B 117

Personality Functioning:
MMPI Results:
L 45, F 87, K 35
Hs 65, D 60, Hy 52, Pd 54, Mf 86
Pa 88, PT 74, SC 95, Ma 75, O 68

Case 2. This nine-year-old boy had an active seizure disorder that developed secondary to severe cat-scratch encephalitis. The neuropsychological examination was undertaken six months following recovery. The patient developed a fulminating encephalitis approximately ten days following a severe cat scratch. He had previously been ill with cat-scratch fever when rather suddenly he became stuporous and began convulsing. He was immediately hospitalized and at this point became fully comatose. He remained comatose for approximately two days, then began to recover. Over the next forty-eight hours he became fully alert and oriented. He remained in the hospital a total of nine days, was discharged, and returned to school in approximately three weeks. Premorbidly this child was apparently quite bright and had maintained an A average. Upon returning to school his average dropped to a C level, and he was noted to be hyperirritable, emotionally labile, and nonattentive. These features essentially completely abated over the next six months. However, he has developed a postinfectious seizure disorder, and his most recent EEG demonstrates a rather large spike focus over the right parietotemporal region. His seizures were of the major motor, generalized type. At the time of assessment he was being treated with Dilantin. Neuropsychological test results were, somewhat surprisingly, relatively within normal limits. There were two significant results: left-side dysgraphesthesia and the impaired arithmetic score. Such findings can be seen with right parietal lobe involvement, but in this patient that is somewhat complicated because of his left handedness. The dysgraphesthesia was consistently observed and likely relates to the lateralized seizure focus, with the implication being that a residual structural defect from the encephalitis remains in that region. This case is a clear demonstration of the absence of severe neuropsychological deficit in an individual with prominent seizure disorder.

Age 9
Sex M
Education 4th

Lateral Dominance Exam

	Eye	Hand	Foot
Right			
Left	X	X	X
Mixed			

Motor Examination:
FOD 41 SOGD 15 TPTD 70 sec.
FOND 37 SOGND 15 TPTND 30 sec.
TPT Both 20 sec.

Sensory Perceptual Examination:
Slight left side dysgraphesthesia, otherwise WNL

Language Examination:
WNL SSPT 3 errors SSRT 1 error

Memory Examination:
LM 11, Digits 12, VM 11, AL 16

Intellectual/Cognitive Functioning:
WISC-R Results FSIQ = 141
VIQ = 140 I 17, S 18, A 15, V 16, C 15, D 16
PIQ = 132 PC 13, PA 13, BD 17, OA 14, C 16

Category Test:
Error Score 24

Trail Making Test:
A 10 B 71

Academic Functioning:
WRAT Results:
Reading 7.4
Spelling 6.5
Arithmetic 4.3

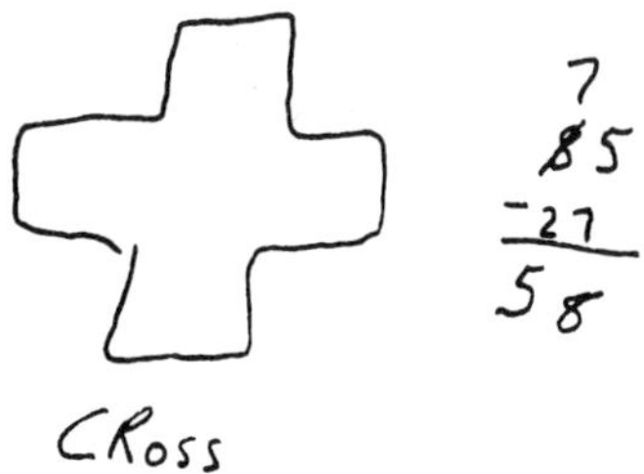

He shouted the warning

Case 3. This 39-year-old man was found to have bilateral temporal lobe spiking on his EEG. He had never had a major motor seizure but did experience, from time to time, the *déjà vu* phenomenon. The reason for neurologic consultation was persistent headache. Behaviorally, this man displayed many features common to patients with temporal lobe electroencephalographic abnormalities. He tended to exhibit emotional lability with swings from elation and euphoria to depression. He was extremely hypergraphic and would take notes whenever attending any type of community meeting or conference. He would daily outline the newspaper and had an elaborate file system to record data. It took him five years to write his master's thesis because he had to continually rewrite and update it. He was very compulsive and followed a rather strict routine. He was extremely passive. He was in a Ph.D. program in economics, but was dropped from the program because of his failure to meet scheduled deadlines. His reason for his dismissal was that he would constantly rewrite term papers, attempting perfection but never succeeding and thereby feeling that he could not hand in an "unfinished" project. He worked as a janitor in a church and had held this position for the past fourteen years. Despite his superior intellectual abilities he was unable to apply himself beyond this employment level. He was excessively religious but not in terms of a formal or orthodox religion. He felt his religious ideas were unique and personal, not part of a universal religion to be shared with others. He was also very philosophical, but again he primarily kept his ideas to himself. He actively became involved in various left-wing and radical collegiate movements, and during the late 1960s and early 1970s he was repeatedly arrested for his (nonviolent) involvement. Lastly, he was hyposexual, but his hyposexuality was not upsetting to him.

Neuropsychologically, his exam results are generally within a broad range of normal in terms of actual test scores. (On the personality exam, only scores above 70 are considered in the abnormal range.) However, it is interesting to note that he has a lowered MQ in relation to the superior level of functioning on intellectual measures. Additionally, he performs in the impaired range on the Seashore Rhythm Test and the Speech Sounds Perception Test, tests traditionally thought to be related to auditory/language/rhythmic processing of the temporal lobes. Note on his aphasia screening exam his obsessiveness in completing the task (i.e., "I could do better if I had more time").

SQUARE

He shouted the warning,

85
−27
58

Age 39
Sex M
Education 18

Lateral Dominance Exam

	Eye	Hand	Foot
Right		X	X
Left			
Mixed	X		

Motor Examination:
FOD 51 SOGD 42
FOND 46 SOGND 39

Sensory Perceptual Exam:
WNL

Language Exam:
Aphasia screening WNL
SSRT 8 errors SSPT 9 errors

Memory Exam:
MQ = 110
LM 13, Digits 13, VM 10, AL 16

Intellectual/Cognitive Functioning:
WAIS Results FSIQ = 127
VIQ = 129 I 15, C 15, A 13, S 15, D 14, V 18
PIQ = 121 DS 8, PC 12, BD 14, PA 15, OA 12

Category Test 37 errors
Trail Making Test: A 53 B 77

Personality Examination:
MMPI Results
L 45, F 50, K 70, Hs 61, DS 1
Hy 61, Pd 69, Mf 72, PA 65,
Pt 53, SC 54, Ma 55, Si 45

References

Andrews, D. G., J. G. Bullen, L. Tomlinson, R. D. C. Elwes, and E. H. Reynolds. 1986. A comparative study of the cognitive effects of phenytoin and carbamazepine in new referrals with epilepsy. *Epilepsia* 27(2):128–134.

Appel, S. H. 1980. Epilepsy. In *Neurology clinics*. Vol. 2. Ardsly, NY: Geigy Pharmaceuticals.

Bear, D. 1977. The significance of behavior change in temporal lobe epilepsy. *McLean Hospital Journal* Special issue: 9–21.

———. 1985. Temporal lobe epilepsy and the Bear-Fedio personality inventory. *Neurology* 35:284–290.

Bear, D., and P. Fedio. 1977. Quantitative analysis of interictal behavior in temporal lobe epilepsy. *Archives of Neurology* 34:454–467.

Benson, D. F., B. L. Miller, and S. F. Signer. 1986. Dual personality associated with epilepsy. *Archives of Neurology* 43: 471–474.

Blumer, D., and K. Levin. 1977. Psychiatric complications in the epilepsies: Current research and treatment. *McLean Hospital Journal* Special issue 4–103.

Cummings, J. L., and L. W. Duchen. 1981. The Klüver-Bucy syndrome in Pick's disease. *Neurology* 31:82.

Delgado-Escueta, A. V., R. H. Mattson, L. King, E. S. Goldensohn, H. Spiegel, J. Madsen, P. Crandall, F. Dreifuss, and R. J. Porter. 1981. The nature of aggression during epileptic seizures. *New England Journal of Medicine* 305: 711–716.

Devinsky, O., and D. Bear. 1984. Varieties of aggressive behavior in temporal lobe epilepsy. *American Journal of Psychiatry* 141:651–656.

Dikmen, S., C. G. Matthews, and J. P. Harley. 1975. The effects of early versus late onset of major motor epilepsy upon cognitive-intellectual performance. *Epilepsia* 16:73–81.

———. 1977. The effects of early versus late onset of major motor epilepsy on cognitive-intellectual performance: Further considerations. *Epilepsia* 18:31–36.

Dodrill, C. B. 1978. A neuropsychological battery for epilepsy. *Epilepsia* 19:611–623.

———. 1981. Neuropsychology of epilepsy. In *Handbook of clinical neuropsychology*, ed. S. B. Filskov and T. J. Boll. New York: John Wiley & Sons.

Dodrill, C. B., and D. Clemmons. 1984. Use of neuropsychological tests to identify high school students with epilepsy who later demonstrate inadequate performances in school. *Journal of Consulting and Clinical Psychology* 52:520–527.

Duffy, F. H., G. B. McAnulty, and S. C. Schachter. 1984. Brain electrical activity mapping. In *Cerebral dominance*, ed. N. Geschwind and A. M. Galaburda. Cambridge, MA: Harvard University Press.

Ervin, F. R. 1975. Organic brain syndromes associated with epilepsy. In *Comprehensive textbook of psychiatry*, ed. A. M. Freedman, H. I. Kaplan, and B. J. Sadock. 2d ed. Baltimore: Williams & Wilkins.

Flor-Henry, P. 1969*a*. Psychosis and temporal lobe epilepsy: A control investigation. *Epilepsia* 10:363–395.

———. 1969*b*. Schizophrenia-like reactions and affective psychoses associated with temporal lobe epilepsy: Etiological factors. *American Journal of Psychiatry* 126:343–344.

Gastaut, H., and R. Broughton. 1972. *Epileptic seizures*. Springfield, IL: Charles C. Thomas.

Glowinski, H. 1973. Cognitive deficits in temporal lobe epilepsy. *Journal of Nervous and Mental Disease* 151:129–137.

Hardin, W. B. 1978. Pathophysiology of clinical epilepsy. In *Neurological pathophysiology*, ed. S. G. Eliasson, A. L. Prensky, and W. B. Hardin. New York: Oxford University Press.

Hartlage, L. C. 1981. Neuropsychological assessment of anticonvulsant drug toxicity. *Clinical Neuropsychology* 3:20–22.

Hermann, B. P. 1982. Neuropsychological functioning and psychopathology in children with epilepsy. *Epilepsia* 23: 545–554.

Hermann, B. P., and M. Melyn. 1985. Identification of neuropsychological deficits in epilepsy using the Luria-Nebraska Neuropsychological Battery: A replication attempt. *Journal of Clinical and Experimental Neuropsychology* 7:305–313.

Hughes, J. R. 1982. *EEG in clinical practice*. London: Butterworth Publishers.

Janati, A. 1985. Klüver-Bucy Syndrome in Huntington's chorea. *Journal of Nervous and Mental Disease* 173:632–635.

Jasper, H. H., A. H. Ward, and A. Pope. 1969. *Basic mechanisms of the epilepsies*. Boston: Little, Brown & Co.

Klonoff, H., and M. Low. 1974. Disordered brain function in young children and early adolescents: Neuropsychological and electroencephalographic correlates. In *Clinical neuropsychology: Current status and applications*, ed. R. M. Reitan and L. A. Davison. New York: Halsted Press.

Klüver, H., and P. C. Bucy. 1937. "Psychic blindness" and other symptoms following bilateral temporal lobectomy in rhesus monkeys. *American Journal of Physiology* 119:352–353.

Lewis, D. O., M. Feldman, M. Greene, and Y. Martinez-Mustardo. 1984. Psychomotor epileptic symptoms in six patients with bipolar mood disorders. *American Journal of Psychiatry* 141: 1583–1586.

Livingston, S. 1972. *Comprehensive management of epilepsy in infancy, childhood, and adolescence*. Springfield, IL: Charles C. Thomas.

Martin, J. H. 1981. Cortical neurons: The EEG and the mechanisms of epilepsy. In *Principles of neural science*, ed. E. R. Kandel and J. H. Schwartz. New York: Elsevier-North Holland.

Mesulam, M.-M. 1981. Dissociative states with abnormal temporal lobe EEG. *Archives of Neurology* 38:176–181.

Milberg, W., M. Grieffenstein, R. Lewis, and D. Rourke. 1980. Differentiation of temporal lobe and generalized seizure patients with the WAIS. *Journal of Consulting and Clinical Psychology* 48:39–42.

Nielsen, H., and O. Kristensen. 1981. Personality correlates of sphenoidal-foci in temporal lobe epilepsy. *Acta Neurologica Scandinavia* 64:289–300.

O'Donohoe, N. V. 1979. *Epilepsies of childhood*. London: Butterworth Publishers.

Oken, B. S., and K. H. Chiappa. 1986. Statistical issues concerning computerized analysis of brainwave topography. *Annals of Neurology* 19:493–494.

Pincus, J. H., and G. J. Tucker. 1978. *Behavioral neurology*. New York: Oxford University Press.

Poggio, G. F., A. E. Walker, and O. J. Andy. 1956. The propagation of cortical after-discharge through subcortical structures. *Archives of Neurology and Psychiatry* 75:350–361.

Pond, D. A. 1974. Epilepsy and personality disorders. In *The epilepsies. Handbook of clinical neurology*, ed. P. J. Vinken and G. W. Bruyn. Vol. 15. New York: Elsevier-North Holland.

Prince, D. A. 1978. Neurophysiology of epilepsy. *Annual Review of Neuroscience* 1:395–415.

Pritchard, P. B., C. T. Lombroso, and M. McIntyre. 1980. Psychological complications of temporal lobe epilepsy. *Neurology* 30:227–232.

Ramani, S. V., and R. J. Gumnit. 1982*a*. Intensive monitoring of interictal psychosis in epilepsy. *Annals of Neurology* 11: 613–622.

———. 1982*b*. Management of hysterical seizures in epileptic patients. *Archives of Neurology* 39:78–81.

Ramani, S. V., L. F. Quesney, D. Olson, and R. J. Gumnit. 1980. Diagnosis of hysterical seizures in epileptic patients. *American Journal of Psychiatry* 137:705–709.

Rausch, R., and G. O. Walsh. 1984. Right-hemisphere language dominance in right-handed epileptic patients. *Archives of Neurology* 41:1077–1080.

Rodin, E. A. 1968. *The prognosis of patients with epilepsy*.

Springfield, IL: Charles C. Thomas.

———. 1973. Psychomotor epilepsy and aggressive behavior. *Archives of General Psychiatry* 28:210–213.

Rodin, E. and S. Schmaltz. 1984. The Bear-Fedio personality inventory and temporal lobe epilepsy. *Neurology* 34: 591–596.

Salazar, A. M., B. Jabbari, S. C. Vance, J. Grafman, D. Amin, and J. D. Dillon. 1985. Epilepsy after penetrating head injury. I, Clinical correlates: A report of the Vietnam Head Injury Study. *Neurology* 35:1406–1414.

Schenk, L., and D. Bear. 1981. Multiple personality and related dissociative phenomena in patients with temporal lobe epilepsy. *American Journal of Psychiatry* 138:1311–1316.

Schiffer, R. B., and H. M. Babigian. 1984. Behavior disorders in multiple sclerosis, temporal lobe epilepsy, and amyotrophic lateral sclerosis. *Archives of Neurology* 41:1067–1069.

Stevens, J. R., and B. P. Hermann. 1981. Temporal lobe epilepsy, psychopathology, and violence: The state of the evidence. *Neurology* 31:1127–1132.

Strub, R. L., and F. W. Black. 1981. *Organic brain syndromes: An introduction to neurobehavioral disorders*. Philadelphia: F. A. Davis.

Taylor, D. C. 1977. Epileptic experience, schizophrenia, and the temporal lobe. *McLean Hospital Journal* Special issue: 22–39.

Terzian, H., and G. D. Ore. 1955. Syndrome of Klüver and Bucy: Reproduced in man by bilateral removal of the temporal lobes. *Neurology* 5:373–380.

Thurston, J. H., D. L. Thurston, B. B. Hixon, and A. J. Keller. 1981. Prognosis in childhood epilepsy. *New England Journal of Medicine* 306:831–836.

Tucker, G. J., T. R. P. Price, V. B. Johnson, and T. McAllister. 1986. Phenomenology of temporal lobe dysfunction: A link to atypical psychosis-A series of cases. *Journal of Nervous and Mental Disease* 174:348–357.

Whitman, S., T. E. Coleman, C. Patmon, B. T Desai, R. Cohen, and L. N. King. 1984. Epilepsy in prison: Elevated prevalence and no relationship to violence. *Neurology* 34:775–782.

9. Neurological Disorders of Infancy, Childhood, and Adolescence

During infancy, childhood, and adolescence the nervous system progresses through the various stages of maturation, which concludes with final changes during late adolescence and early adult life. This process of maturation complicates the assessment of neurologic disorders in this age group, particularly in infancy and early childhood, because of the range within which certain functions may be acquired. Thus, what appears to be a deficit may be a lag in development (Satz and Fletcher, 1981). Such developmental issues must always be considered when evaluating a child, and therefore some further discussion of this area is warranted, prior to reviewing the various neurologic disorders that may affect the developing brain.

Developmental Issues

The effects of damage to the central nervous system (CNS) during various stages of development depend upon the age at which it occurs; the extent, location, and type of damage; and the function being measured (Bigler, 1987; Chelune and Edwards, 1981). For example, intrauterine effects on neural embryogenesis may not only produce a specific neural deficit but also produce subsequent maldevelopment of neural structures and systems. In such cases later development may be arrested or progress in an abnormal fashion. Since these effects may result from a myriad of factors and occur at equally variable times in development, it is frequently impossible to be definitive about their beginning.

During fetal and infant brain development, there is some equipotentiality of each hemisphere (reviewed by Chelune and Edwards, 1981; Boll and Barth, 1981). Thus, damage at such an early age that is restricted to one hemisphere may result in minimal deficits in certain cases (Kohn and Dennis, 1974). Similarly, Alajovanine and Lhermitte (1965) have demonstrated that damage restricted to either hemisphere could produce language deficits, thereby demonstrating some equipotentiality of the hemispheres for languages. This equipotentiality, however, progressively diminishes with age, so that by five years rather specific specialization and lateralization of brain function have taken place (cf. Boll and Barth, 1981). By puberty neural specialization is quite like that seen in adults. It is interesting to note that there is some degree of functional equipotentiality of the hemispheres while structurally the brain shows innately determined hemispheric asymmetries (Geschwind, 1979).

As mentioned previously, damage that occurs during fetal development may affect subsequent cellular differentiation, thereby producing more extensive dysfunction. When the damage or dysfunction is bilateral or diffuse, there is generally diminished capacity for other systems to compensate for the loss of function (Chelune and Edwards, 1981). Thus, the concept of recovery owing to equipotentiality applies mainly to a unilateral or singular focal area of damage or dysfunction. This variability is also seen in the case of cerebral lesions occurring in childhood: damage restricted to one hemisphere may produce less of a residual permanent deficit than that occurring from lesions that are bilateral (Dreifuss, 1975; Kinsbourne, 1974; Kohn and Dennis, 1974).

From a developmental and prognostic standpoint, it would be efficacious clinically to be able to predict functional outcome once a cerebral deficit was diagnosed. However, studies examining the predictive outcome in children with history of birth complication, anoxia, or trauma have been relatively disappointing (McCall, 1981). This has also been found to be the case, although not to the degree seen with the infant, with the cerebral deficit acquired in childhood (Chelune and Edwards, 1981).

The limited behavioral repertoire of the neonate further complicates the picture in terms of clinical outcome measures. For example, the newborn is considered neurologically normal if weight, appearance, breathing, crying, and sucking are normal for gestational age and the normal rudimentary reflexes of Moro, rooting, and walking are present (Buda, 1981; Dargassies, 1981). Since all of these functions are quite primitive and basic in nature, it is not surprising that abnormalities in such functions correlate poorly with eventual outcome measures of higher cerebral processes (Lubchenco, 1981; McCall, 1981). Nonetheless, the presence of risk factors implicating potential underlying neurologic deficits remains an important historical variable in evaluating the child suspected of having a neurologic abnormality.

Neurologic Syndromes

Genetic and Congenital Malformations of the Brain and Skull

A host of variables may be involved in the pathogenesis of brain or skull abnormalities. It is commonly assumed that the etiology of brain or skull deficits at birth lies within a complex interaction between genetic predisposition, genetic aberration, and intrauterine environmental effects (teratology). The potential number of genetic or congenital malformations is great and beyond the scope of this text. The classic texts of Bray (1969) and Ford (1976) fully cover these topics, though. What follows will thus be restricted to an overview of the more common anomalies. Related physical stigmata that may be associated with CNS disorder are listed in table 9.1.

Head Size. The child born with an abnormally small head can usually be considered to have a similar deficit in brain development. When head size is within normal limits at birth but fails to maintain development with the remainder of the body, this condition is called *microcephaly*. Associated with microcephaly typically is dysplasia of cellular growth, particularly in cortical regions, which may lead to an absence of normal sulci development (see fig. 9.1). On the other hand, head enlargement, *macrocephaly*, may be due to excessive brain growth (glial cells), hydrocephalus owing to ventricular enlargement, or hydranencephaly (hydrocephalus plus cortical destruction) (see figs. 9.2–9.5). Premature suture closing or craniostenosis may also alter skull size and similarly affect brain development (see fig. 9.6). Bradycephaly produces a skull defect by premature closing of the coronal sutures, producing a wide and short head. Scaphocephaly results from sagittal suture defect elongating the head. Regardless of the etiology of the head size deficit, there is typically some effect on brain development and subsequent neuropsychological functioning. Most commonly, there is a reduction in intellectual functioning as well as associated general impairment in higher cortical functions of diffuse origin. Focal deficits are uncommon. Hydrocephalus, regardless of etiology, usually is associated with some significant compromise in intellectual functioning, although the extent of the compromise is quite variable (Dennis et al., 1981).

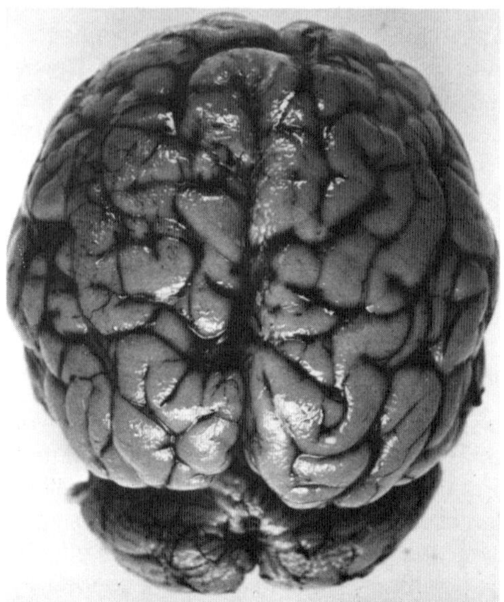

Fig. 9.1. Microcephaly. Note the incomplete frontal lobe development, the atypical gyral patterns, and the general size of the brain.

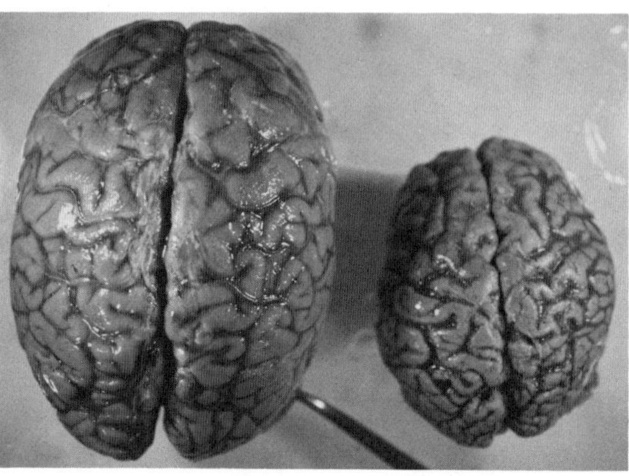

Fig. 9.2. Macrocephaly. The brain on the right is of normal size; the one on the left, macrocephalic.

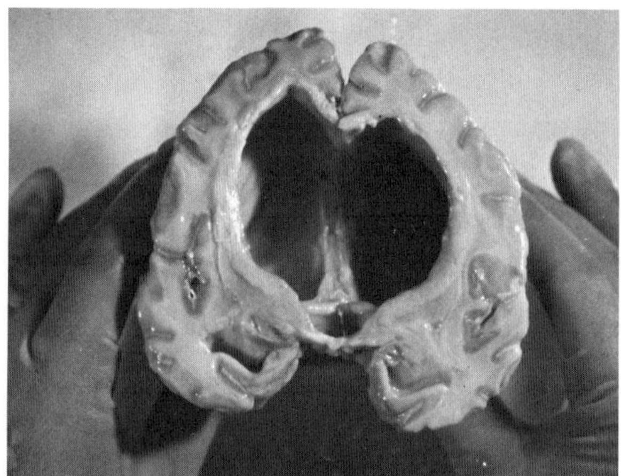

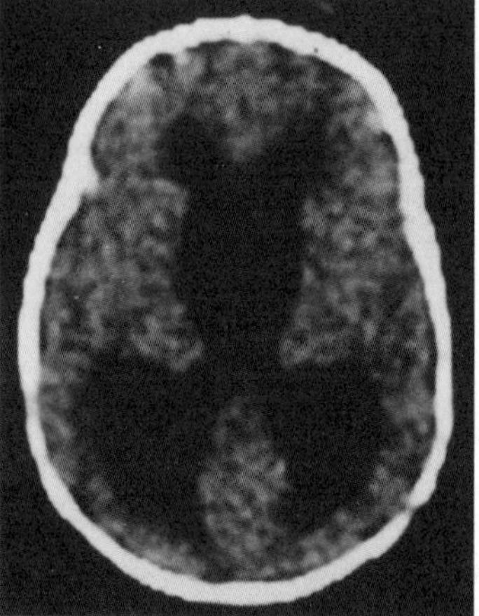

Fig. 9.3. *Top*, congenital hydrocephalus. Note the marked enlargement of the lateral ventricles with direct communication with the third ventricle. Note also the compression of the outer cortical tissue. *Bottom*, CAT scan of patient with marked hydrocephalus similar to that seen at left.

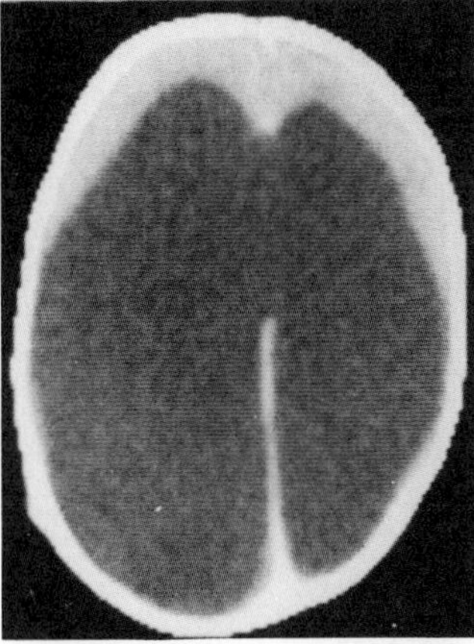

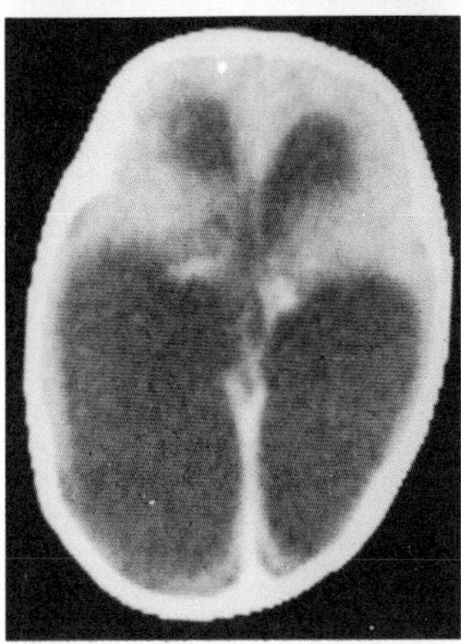

Fig. 9.4. Marked hydrocephaly. Note the nearly complete loss of cortical tissue. Courtesy of D. Karnik.

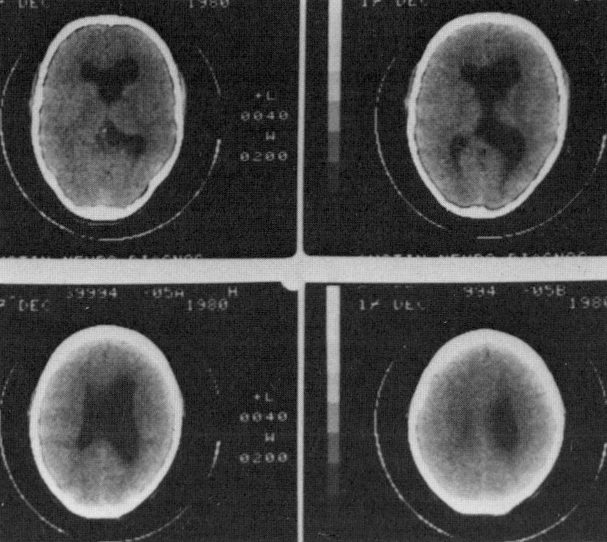

Fig. 9.5. Congenital hemiatrophy of the right hemisphere associated with hydrocephalus ex vacuo.

Table 9.1. *Stigmata Associated with Central Nervous System Anomalies*

Hair	Frontal bossing
	Whorls
	Electric wire
	Coarse, brittle
Eyes	Abnormal palpebral fissure
	Hypertelorism
	Strabismus
	Ptosis
	Epicanthus (absent, partial, or deep)
Ears	Malformed
	Asymmetric
	Pits or tags
	Set low (below 0.5-cm line through nose bridge and eye)
Nose	Antiverted nostrils
	Hypoplastic tip
	Hypoplastic philtrum
Mouth	Steeple palate
	History of cleft palate
	Small teeth
	Abnormal tongue shape or movements
Jaw	Prominent maxilla
	Micrognathia
	Prognathia
Torso	Vertebral defects
	Webbed neck
	Pectus excavatum
	Pectus carinatum
	Widely spaced nipples
	History of heart murmur
Skin	Dry, coarse, rough
	Café au lait spots
	Hemangiomata
	Nails—hypoplastic or dysplastic
Hands	Palm—transverse crease
	Abnormally small, broad hands given body size
	Thin, tapering hands
	Joint limitation
	Clinodactyly
	Broad thumb
Feet	Toe gaps
	Syndactyly
	Abnormally long second, third, or both second and third toes
	Broad first toe

Source: Adapted from Shaywitz (1982).

Cranial and Spinal Malformations. Incomplete closure of the skull or spinal column may take several different forms. In meningoencephalocele, the brain and usually an aspect of the ventricular system herniate through the skull and are held in place by a sac formed by the meninges. A meningomyelocele is a protrusion of the dura through a bony defect in the spinal column; a meningocele is similar, but does not involve the skull. In spina bifida there is incomplete closure of the spinal column; whereas, cranium bifidum, its counterpart, only affects the skull. All of these conditions may produce various cerebral, spinal, or cerebrospinal deficits. Hydrocephalus is common. With cranium bifidum microgyria, cellular dysplasia and dysplasia of the corpus callosum may be present. Invariably, if the spinal cord is involved paralysis is present. Mental retardation is also commonplace. Neuropsychological deficits are usually generalized.

Cerebral Anomalies. A variety of cerebral anomalies may occur independent of or as a consequence of cranial and spinal defects. Severe fetal aberrations of brain development typically are incompatible with life (see figs. 9.7 and 9.8). Similarly, early maldevelopment of the cerebrum will almost always be associated with some degree of mental retardation and generalized neuropsychological deficit.

Cerebral Vascular Disorders. Vascular disorders may affect children, although less commonly than adults, in a manner basically similar to that outlined in chapter 3. There is a greater chance of vascular accident occurring during premature birth or traumatic birth (see fig. 9.9). This is also true in terms of the anoxic effects (Lacey, 1985) on the brain (see fig. 9.10).

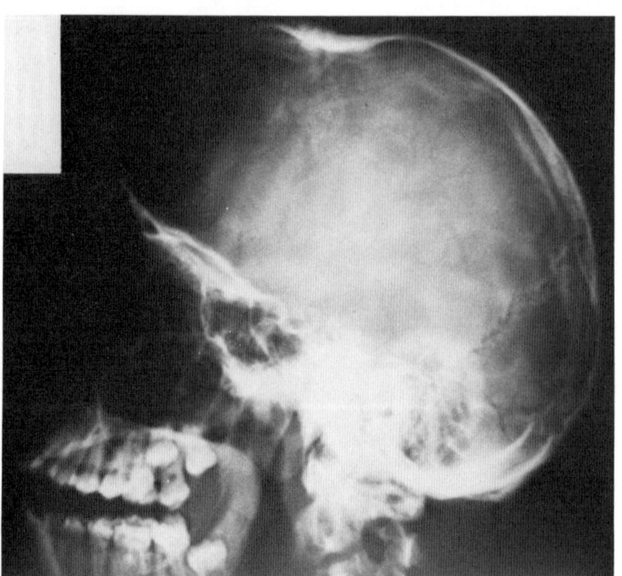

Fig. 9.6. Craniostenosis. Notice the indentation at the skull's vertex.

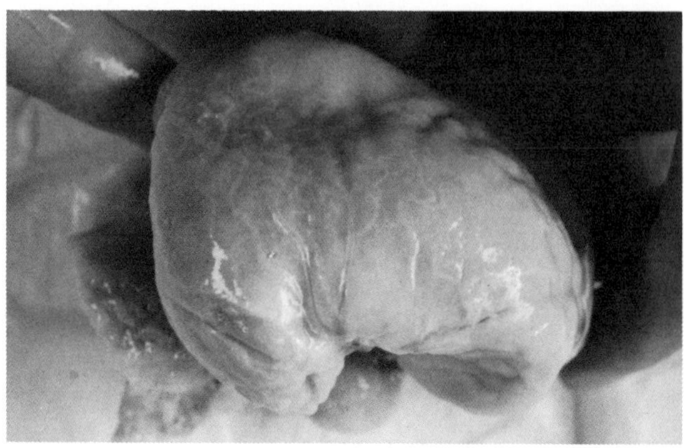

Fig. 9.7. Severe brain malformation with agyria.

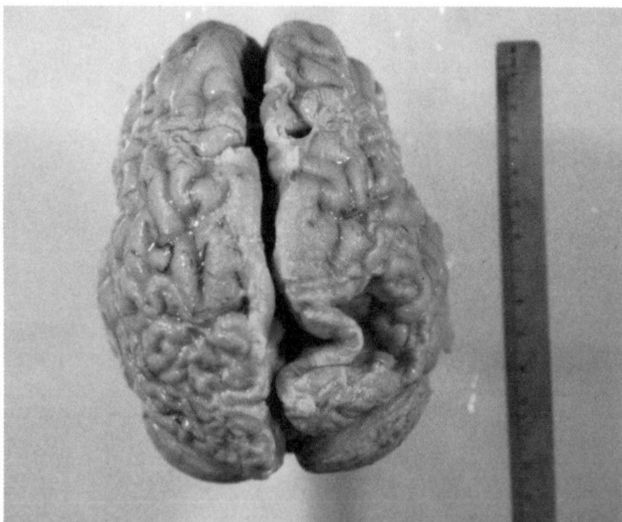

A

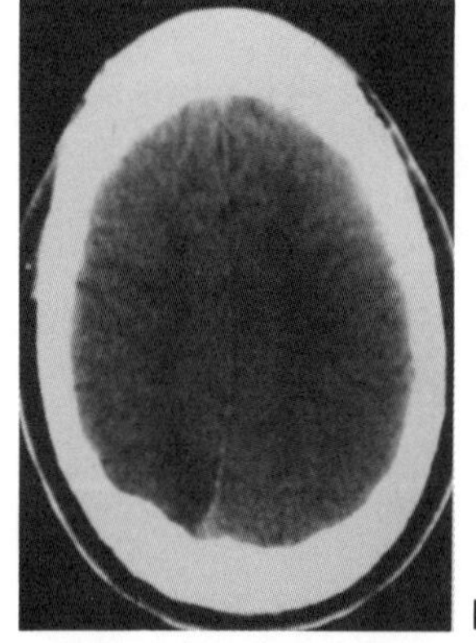

B

Fig. 9.8. *A*, malformed brain with anomalous gyral patterns and dysplasia. *B*, cerebral dysplasia of the posterior left cerebral hemisphere. This is in a 19-year-old male patient who is left-handed and severely dyslexic. Note that the posterior extent of the left cerebral hemisphere has a low density appearance on the CAT scan; this is common of dysplasic neuronal development. Also notice the asymmetry between the two cerebral hemispheres and the shift of the interhemispheric fissure.

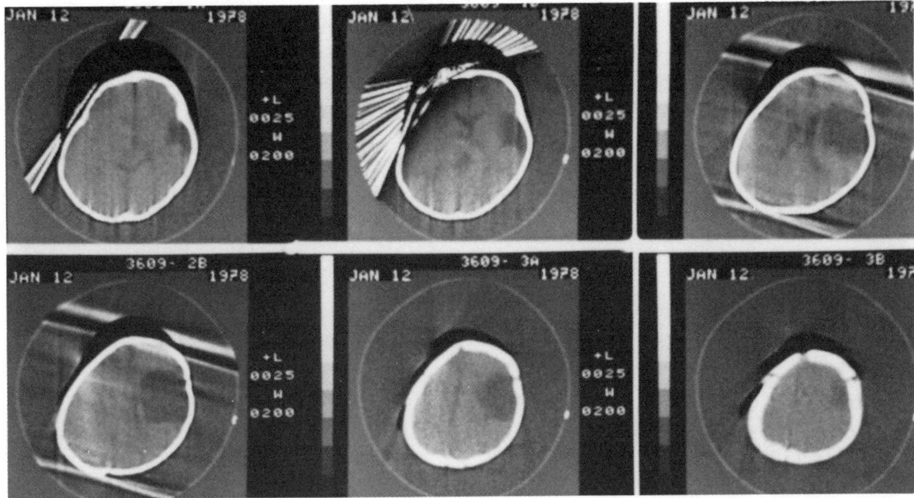

Fig. 9.9. Congenital skull malformation along with bilateral areas of hemorrhagic infarction. This child displayed significant delay in language acquisition.

Children with various cerebrovascular insufficiency syndromes may show marked improvement following surgical treatment that results in increased cerebral blood flow (Ishii et al., 1984). In such cases pre- and post-surgical neuropsychological studies are extremely useful.

Syndactyly and Craniocerebral Defects

Extra digits, digit rudiments, or the fusion of fingers may be associated with brain defect, because of the embryogenic relationship between certain neural and skeletal systems developing simultaneously. When skull defect is present with syndactyly the chance of related cerebral involvement is increased. There are also certain syndromes in which syndactyly is present, such as the Laurence-Moon-Biedl syndrome (obesity, retinitis pigmentosa, and syndactyly). Neuropsychological studies of the patient with syndactyly will typically indicate only nonspecific deficits; focal lesions are uncommon. Normal results from neuropsychological studies of the person with syndactyly generally imply that the skeletal anomaly took place independent of any cerebral effects. The varieties of syndactylism associated with cerebral impairment are reviewed by Adams and Victor (1977) and Ford (1976).

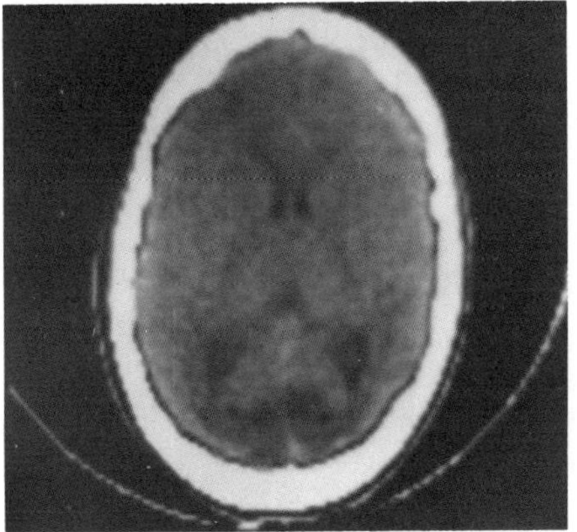

Fig. 9.10. Cortical blindness. This 10-year-old girl had a lengthy history of pervasive developmental delay and failure to progress academically. She had not had previous neurologic or neuropsychological evaluation, but had been diagnosed as mentally retarded. CAT scan reveals bilateral infarction in the occipital regions. Behaviorally the patient displayed distinct visual agnosia of common objects, although she could name them from touch. The patient has, of course, cortical blindness, and much of her delay was because of this unrecognized condition. The nature of the disorder was likely some congenital anomaly or unnoticed birth injury as the child was reported to be hypoxic.

Neurocutaneous Disorders

As with skeletal anomalies, there may be embryologic connections between certain neural and dermatologic disorders. The three major neurocutaneous disorders are tuberous sclerosis, neurofibromatosis, and cutaneous angiomatosis with CNS abnormalities (Miller and Bigler, 1982). In tuberous sclerosis, tumorlike growths affect the CNS, particularly in surrounding ventricular regions (see figs. 9.11–9.12). This condition occurs simultaneously with cutaneous lesions mainly over the nasal region. Neurofibromatosis of von Recklinghausen is a disorder affecting the skin (producing *café au lait* spots [fig. 9.13]), the

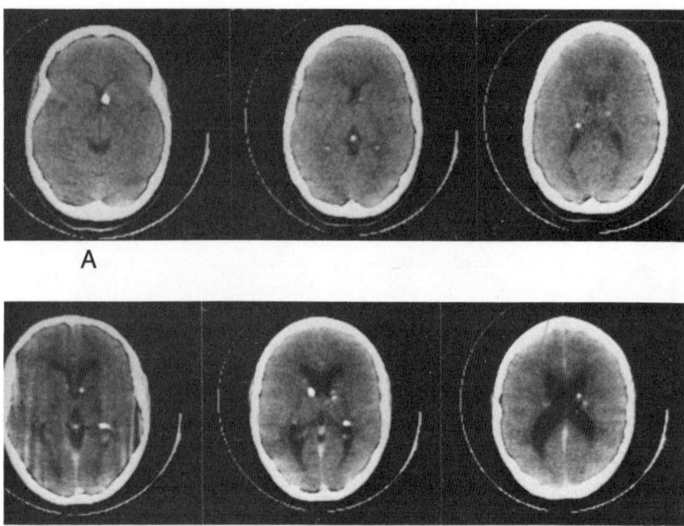

Fig. 9.11. *A*, tuberous sclerosis. Note the presence of areas of hyperdense lesion sites surrounding the ventricular system. This patient had a seizure disorder of a generalized type. The patient had only borderline deficits in intellectual and neuropsychological functioning. *B*, tuberous sclerosis. As in *A*, note the hyperdense lesion sites around the ventricular system. Both patients had seizure disorders that were generalized; however, this patient displayed more generalized and significant disorder. The degree of intellectual and neuropsychological impairment somewhat corresponds to the degree of structural aberration present, as evident in CAT findings.

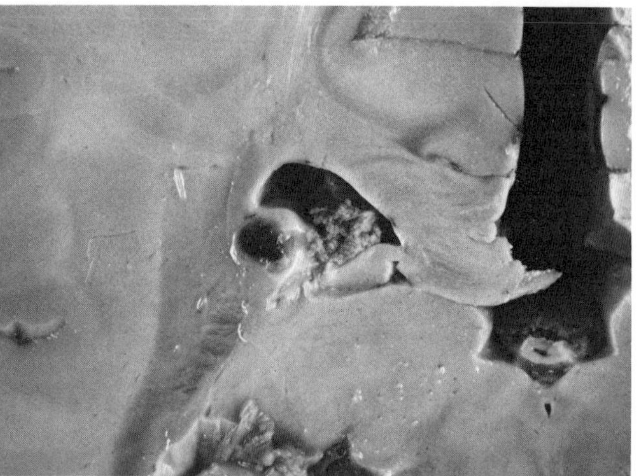

Fig. 9.12. Tuberous growth in postmortem examination slide.

CNS, and the skeletal and endocrine systems, taking the form of benign tumor growths. Cranial and spinal neurofibromas, gliomas, and meningiomas may develop, however. The Sturge-Weber syndrome best characterizes the cutaneous angiomatosis disorders with CNS effects. In this syndrome a large vascular nevus is present at birth, typically following the distribution of the ophthalmic division of the trigeminal nerve, but it may cover the entire side of the face. The nevus is deep red (port wine stain). Ipsilateral to the facial nevus is intracortical calcification, which may be extensive. Such patients typically have unilateral sensory and motor deficits, mental retardation, and some degree of generalized neuropsychological deficit. With tuberous sclerosis and neurofibromatosis the neuropsychological deficits may be quite variable. Mental retardation of borderline to mild proportions is common as well as some degree of nonspecific neuropsychological deficits. Focal deficits may occur when a tumorlike growth is of such a position and size to produce focal damage or disruption of some system.

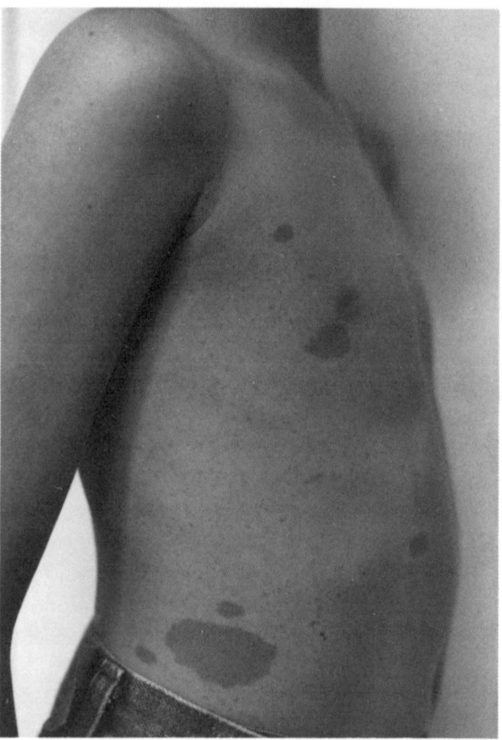

Fig. 9.13. Classic appearance of *café au lait* spots about the lateral surface of the chest and abdomen in this 11-year-old male child with von Recklinghausen's neurofibromatosis.

Arnold-Chiari Malformation

The Arnold-Chiari Malformation (ACM) of the brain is a congenital anomaly of the base of the brain. There are several types of ACMs, but the common denominator is cerebellomedullary malformation (Ford, 1976). A result of this malformation is frequently hydrocephalus. Developmental aberrations of the cerebral cortex, particularly polymicrogyria, may coexist.

Chromosomal Abnormalities (Chromosomal Dysgenesis)

Down's syndrome is the most common disorder associated with chromosomal dysgenesis. It is associated with various cerebral anomalies, including small size, simple convolutional pattern, small frontal lobes with thin superior temporal gyri, delayed myelination, and various forms of cellular dysplasias. Incomplete expression of the syndrome (mosaic variation) may be associated with various aspects of the above pathology. Down's syndrome and mosaics have various neuropsychological deficits, usually reflective of generalized and diffuse involvement (Buda, 1981). Two other fairly common syndromes are Klinefelter's and Turner's. Klinefelter's syndrome occurs only in men and is associated with an XXY chromosomal anomalous arrangement. The patient is usually tall with eunuchoid proportions, defective testicular development, and lowered intellectual level. Turner's syndrome occurs only in women and is associated with an XO anomalous chromosomal arrangement. Morphologically, the patients appear with webbed necks, delayed sexual development, triangular faces, and small chins. Mental retardation is usually present, and the neuropsychological pattern is typically indicative of nonspecific cerebral dysfunction.

Intrauterine and Neonatal Infections

Intrauterine and neonatal infections constitute a significant proportion of the causes of acquired cerebral deficits (Buda, 1981). The effects of such infections have already been discussed in chapter 7. Such infections may produce either focal cerebral deficits, generalized cerebral deficits, or both. One of the tragic factors associated with acquired immune deficiency syndrome (AIDS) is that it may be passed on to the fetus (Belman et al., 1985). Such infants may develop a variety of neurologic deficits and in some this may be progressive. Thus, a comprehensive neuropsychological examination is always in order for the child with a history of infection that may have affected the brain.

Fetal Alcohol and Drug Syndromes

Unfortunately, maternal care during pregnancy may be quite negligent, and alcohol abuse during pregnancy may result in a rather specific syndrome—the fetal alcohol syndrome. In this syndrome some degree of mental retardation is commonly present in association with a narrow forehead, short palpebral fissures, small nose, small midface, long upper lip, and deficient philtrum (see fig. 9.14; Sulik, Johnston, and Webb, 1981). Specific aberrations in various neuronal systems, possibly with specific alterations in hippocampal neuronal circuitry, have been demonstrated (West, Hodges, and Black, 1981). The fact that the syndrome develops with characteristic features suggests a critical exposure time during embryogenesis when neural tube and musculoskeletal differentiation is occurring. The incidence of fetal alcohol syndrome is alarming, 1980 incidence reports indicating one case in every 750 live births. The potential teratogenic effects of a wide spectrum of drugs (both prescribed and illicit) on cerebral development are not known at this time, but it is obvious that the infant born of a mother abusing drugs is at substantial teratogenic risk. Data are accumulating that cocaine may also affect cognitive development in the offspring of cocaine-abusing mothers (Chasnoff et al., 1985).

Epilepsy

Epilepsy, in terms of neurologic disorders of childhood, is one of the most common and may or may not be associated with significant neuropsychological sequelae. The effects of convulsive disorder on cognitive functioning are fully reviewed in chapter 8.

Degenerative Disorders of Childhood

Many of the progressive CNS disorders of childhood are of a heredodegenerative nature (Bray, 1969; Holmes and Logan, 1980; Menkes, 1974). Most of these disorders have varied effects on cortical functioning, and neuropsychological studies may be useful in monitoring their progression. Some of the more common disorders include variants of Huntington's chorea and Alzheimer's disease, dystonia musculorum deformans, Friedreich's ataxia (spinocerebellar ataxia), Charcot-Marie-Tooth disease, and hereditary optic atrophy (Leber's disease). There are several childhood degenerative disorders that affect primarily white matter, the most common ones being sudanophilic cerebral sclerosis, Pelizaeus-Merzbacher disease, and the leukodystrophies (see fig. 9.15). The neuropsychological findings and assessment techniques presented in chapter 4 apply to childhood degenerative disorders, although age and developmental issues must be considered.

Callosal Agenesis

Callosal syndromes were reviewed in chapter 1. In certain congenital disorders, dysgenesis or agenesis of the corpus callosum may occur (Lynn et al., 1980). Interestingly enough, with congenital absence or dysgenesis of the corpus callosum, the various callosal syndromes previously described may not be present (Pirozzolo, Pirozzolo, and Ziman, 1979). Because of the early onset of these disorders, there is significant compensation that occurs within ipsilateral control systems, subcortical interconnections, and—in those with some callosal fibers remaining intact—the remaining interhemispheric connections (Dennis, 1981; Lassonde et al., 1981). (See fig. 9.16.)

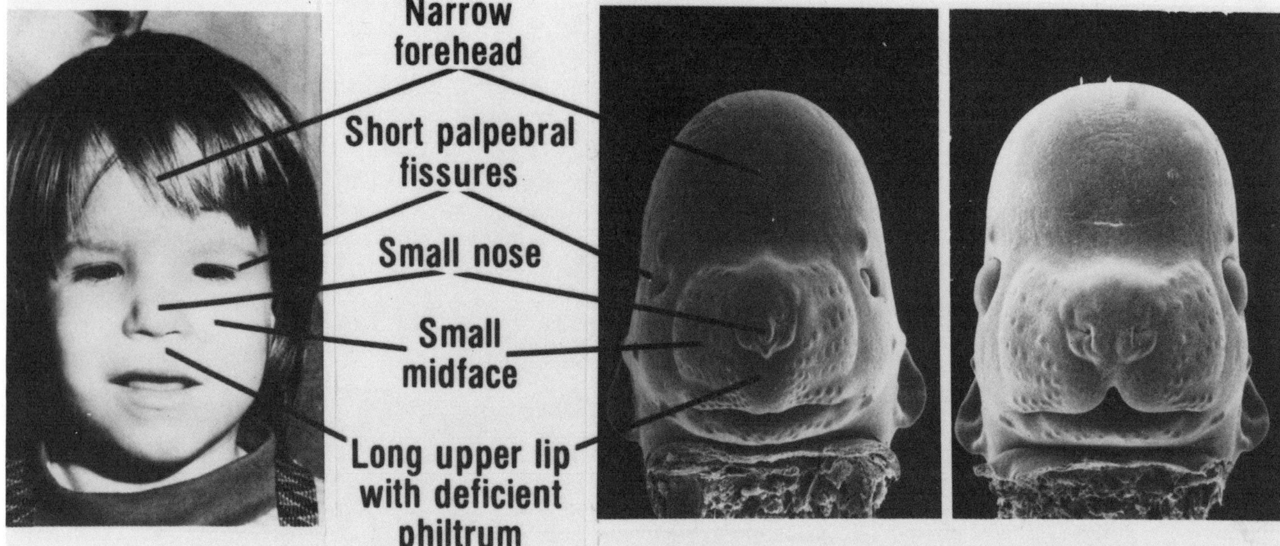

Fig. 9.14. Characteristic facial changes seen in children with fetal alcohol syndrome. From Sulik, Johnston, and Webb (1981). Copyright © 1981 by the American Association for the Advancement of Science.

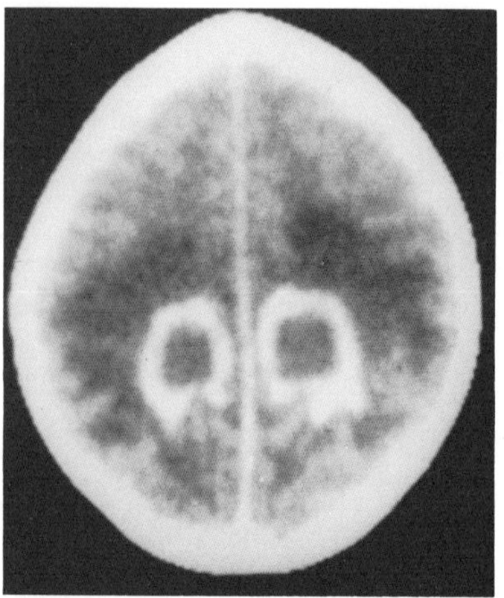

Fig. 9.15. Leukodystrophy. This CAT scan is of a nine-year-old boy with advanced leukodystrophy. The two high-density areas are seen postenhancement and represent focal areas of white matter degeneration. The patient first appeared for examination several years previously with "learning problems." At the time of CAT scanning, the patient displayed marked dementia and generalized deficits in all higher cortical functions. Courtesy of D. Karnik.

Traumatic Disorders

Traumatic injury has been thought to produce a less severe deficit in children than adults because of children's cerebral plasticity (Heiskanen and Kaste, 1974), but this thinking appears to be an oversimplification (see Chadwick et al., 1981; Chelune and Edwards, 1981; Klonoff, 1971). Traumatic disorders of the brain have been discussed in chapter 4, and the basic principles outlined in that chapter apply to traumatic disorders of childhood, with the exception that developmental and maturational features have to be taken into consideration.

Diabetes Mellitus

Insulin-dependent diabetes affects approximately 100,000 children in the United States. Over time, depending on the severity of the disorder, insulin-dependent diabetics, including children, may develop chronic degenerative complications in terms of retinopathy, nephropathy, peripheral neuropathies, and encephalopathies. Ryan et al. (1984) found that children with controlled insulin diabetic disorder did not demonstrate any specific neuropsychological deficits, although they did demonstrate some minor visuomotor irregularities. These results tend to parallel those seen in adults (Skenazy and Bigler, 1984, 1985). However, Holmes (1986) has demonstrated some neuropsychological deficits in diabetic patients, depending upon metabolic aberrations associated with the diabetes. Thus, for the well-controlled diabetic child, no specific neuropsychological syndrome may be present. However, there are children who may develop anoxia following severe insulin reactions or other complications, such as a diabetic coma, as well as a secondary metabolic encephalopathy. Such secondary factors associated with diabetes mellitus will obviously produce significant neural behavioral changes.

Aphasia in Childhood

Children who have developmental language disorders do not have an aphasic disturbance, per se, since they did not have normal language to begin with and then lose it. Benson (1979) suggests that the preferential classification for these disorders is in the form of language retardation and that childhood aphasia should be reserved for children who have developed language normally but after brain damage show language abnormalities. VanDongen, Loonen, and VanDongen (1985) have demonstrated a relatively close association between lesion localization in childhood aphasia and that seen in adults. Vargha-Khadem, O'Gorman, and Watters (1985) have demonstrated that with left hemisphere injury, particularly in the prenatal and early postnatal period, strong sinistrality develops. Also, children with cerebral injury prior to age five showed more complete recovery in terms of language function than those after that age.

Cerebral Plasticity in Childhood

The literature is replete with single case studies demonstrating amazing cerebral plasticity in some children (see figs. 9.16–9.17). Bigler and Naugle (1985) reviewed seven cases of such cerebral plasticity. The common theme with these is that the disorder or injury took place early, typically in utero. This permits a different type of brain reorganization in neural development, in contrast to the recovery of function that may be seen following an injury. For the greatest degree of plasticity to occur, it appears that the lesion needs to be lateralized and occur preferentially in utero or at least within the first year of life (see fig. 9.17).

CAT Scanning in Childhood Disorders

Although significant CAT abnormalities are associated with a variety of childhood neurologic disorders (Bigler, 1987), routine CAT scanning in children presenting with such problems as learning disorder has proven to be relatively unproductive. Denckla, LeMay, and Chapman (1984), Harcherik et al. (1985), and Shaywitz et al. (1983) have shown few CAT abnormalities in children presenting with learning disability, attention deficit disorder, Tourette's, infantile autism, and developmental language disorder. Behar et al. (1984) have demonstrated enlarged ventricles in adolescents with obsessive-compulsive disorder, though. The clinical significance of this latter finding is not fully understood at this point.

Language Disorders

Classification of language disorders in children from the neuropsychological perspective is lacking because of no uniformly accepted scheme. Ludlow (1980) has reviewed these limitations. Accordingly, deficits should be fully explained and outlined in terms of the functional deficit present. The glossary of terms by Ludlow (1980), presented in the appendix at the end of this chapter, provides

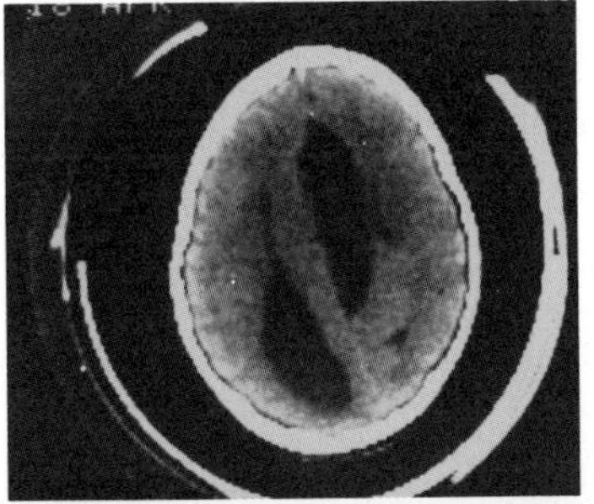

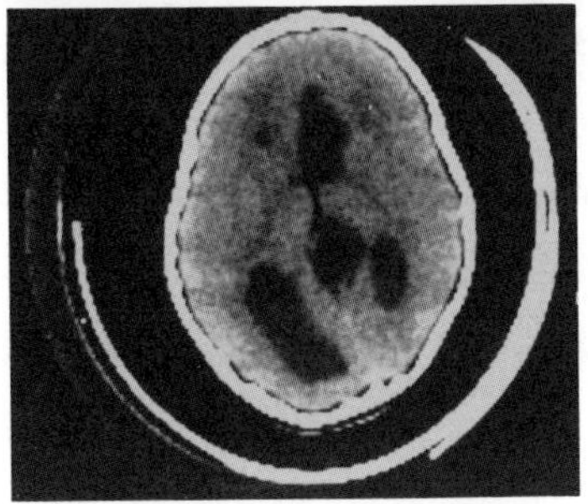

A

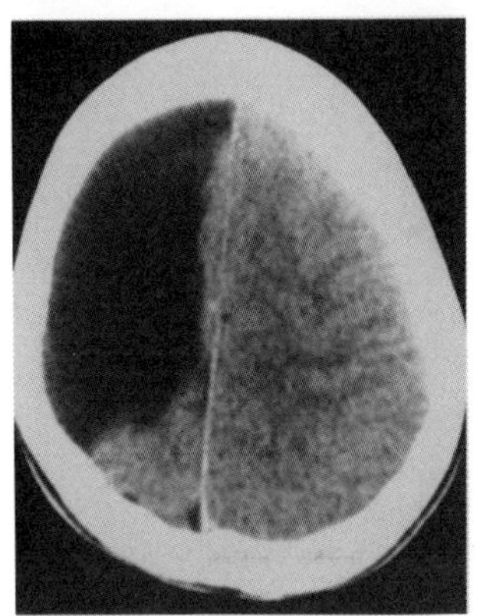

B

Fig. 9.16. *A*, agenesis of the corpus callosum. CAT scan of a ten-year-old girl showed agenesis of the corpus callosum as well as a variety of ventricular and cerebral anomalies. The child did not have a callosal syndrome. Intellectual studies indicated a verbal IQ of 59, a performance IQ of 55, and a full-scale IQ of 53. Neuropsychological studies revealed generalized cognitive deficits. Note that the deficits are bilateral involving both cerebral hemispheres and that there is generalized dysplasic involvement. Such cases typically do not show cerebral plasticity. This is to be contrasted with the CAT scan presented in *B*. The child in *B* suffered infarction of the left cerebral hemisphere involving all of the left frontal lobe and most of the left temporal and parietal, sparing only the left occipital. This infarction took place at five months gestation secondary to the mother taking an anticoagulant medication during pregnancy, which resulted in a hemorrhagic infarction. This child has only a moderate right side spastic hemiparesis and has normal language development. Intellectual studies have been in the average range throughout her childhood development. She has no deficit in reading, spelling, or mathematical computation. This case has been more completely discussed in the article by Bigler and Naugle (1985).

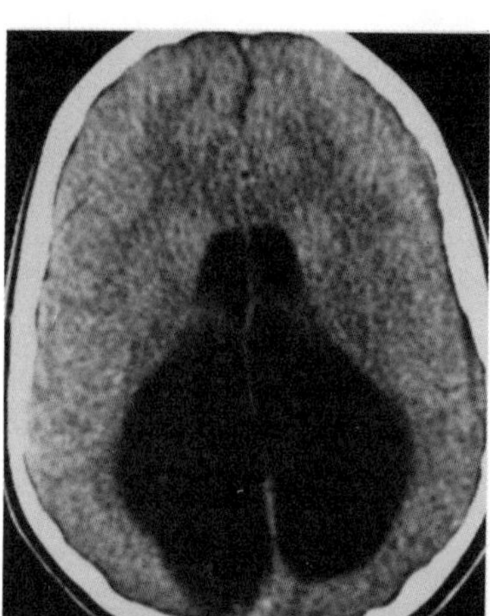

Fig. 9.17. This child had a large occipital meningoencephalocele removed at four days of age. Throughout infancy and childhood, she displayed amazingly normal development, despite the marked porencephaly as depicted in the CAT scan. The only major developmental delays came in visuoperceptual and visuomotor areas. Although there is essentially complete loss of the occipital lobe on the left and considerable involvement on the right, this child has developed normal verbal language abilities, including normal verbal intellectual functions (VIQ = 119).

a means by which aspects of language disorder can be discussed.

In terms of actual developmental language disorders, classification schemes by Myklebust (1954) and Ingram (1969) have been suggested. Myklebust outlines developmental aphasic syndromes similar to syndromes observed in adult disorders—thus predominantly expressive, predominantly receptive, mixed receptive and expressive, and central types with asymbolia. Ingram's classification scheme tends to blend severity with type and is presented as follows: (1) mild speech disorder with normal syntax and normal linguistic development; (2) moderate speech disorder (developmental expressive dysphasia) with retarded linguistic development but normal comprehension; (3) severe speech disorder and retardation of spoken language development, including impaired comprehension of speech; and (4) very severe speech disorder with gross failure of speech development, impaired comprehension of language (developmental receptive dysphasia), and severe generalized auditory processing deficit. This scheme frequently does not apply to acquired aphasic disturbance in children, because left hemisphere lesions tend to result in nonfluent expressive dysfunction, regardless of where the lesion may reside (Woods and Teubor, 1978).

In assessing childhood language disorders, additional neuropsychometric measures may be needed than those routinely given for neuropsychological evaluation. The Illinois Test of Psycholinguistic Abilities may be useful (Zaidel, 1979). Similarly, the Durrell Analysis of Reading Difficulty (Durrell and Catterson, 1980), the Boder Reading-Spelling Pattern Test (Boder and Jarrico, 1982), and the Key-Math Test (Connolly, Nachtman, and Pritchett, 1976) are all appropriate tests to further examine certain academic abilities in children suspected of having a learning disorder. Woods and Carey (1979) have demonstrated the effectiveness of utilizing a brief picture-naming task, a spelling task, rhyme completion, sentence completion (from the Boston Diagnostic Aphasia Examination), a relations task, a "that" clause syntax task, an ask-tell distinction task, and the token test in delineating childhood aphasic disturbances. From an experimental standpoint, dichotic listening tasks (Springer and Eisenson, 1977) may also differentiate such children, but the individual clinical efficacy and practicality of such tests remain to be proven. Table 9.2 provides a gross index of language development from four to twelve years of age (Weinberg and McLean, 1986).

Neurologic Bases of Learning Disorders

Geschwind's (1979) work, as well as the work of numerous others, has clearly demonstrated the anatomic and functional localization of various language functions in the dominant hemisphere, which is typically the left. Correspondingly, an enormous body of literature has demonstrated the damaging effects on language functions of lesions of the dominant hemisphere (see chapters 1 and 3, see also Albert et al., 1981; Benson, 1979; Brown, 1974). While the concept of "learning" implies a variety of complex neurobehavioral functions, the focus of human learning has been primarily directed to the functioning of language centers of the dominant hemisphere. Thus, much of the learning disability research has dealt with potentially dysfunctional systems of such language and related areas (Gaddes, 1980; Hynd and Obrzut, 1981; Knights and Bakker, 1976; Rourke, 1981). Although there has been some controversy in the past over the relationship between brain function and the presence or absence of learning deficit (see Satz and Fletcher, 1981, for review), the neurologic and neuropsychological studies of recent years provide unequivocal evidence for underlying cerebral dysfunction in certain disorders of learning. This point will be discussed first; discussion of the neuropsychological examination of the learning dysfunctional child will follow.

Neurologic Factors

Galaburda and Kemper (1979) and Galaburda et al. (1985) reported their important findings of a postmortem examination of a young man with dyslexia. Gross anatomic findings were relatively insignificant except for a region of polymicrogyria in the left temporal speech regions. The more distinct pathology, however, resided at the cellular level with findings suggestive of cellular dysplasias in limbic as well as primary and association areas of the

Table 9.2. ***A Summary of Symbol Language Battery Items***

Symbol Skill	Age of Emergence (Years)	Symbol Skill	Age of Emergence (Years)
Reading		A whole pie is divided into four pieces.	
Gilmore Oral Reading Test*		One piece of pie equals what fraction of the pie?	10–11.6
C-1, C-2: Monosyllabic words	6–8	Three pieces equal what fraction of the pie?	10.6–12
C-3: Simple compound polysyllabic words	8–9.6	What is one-fourth as a decimal?	10–11.6
C-4: Phonetically nonspecific polysyllabic words	9–11	What is three-fourths as a decimal?	10–11.6
C-5, C-12: Quantitative efficiency	10+	What is one-fourth as a percent?	10.6–12
Word labeling (from memory, given orally without visual input)		What is three-fourths as a percent?	10.6–12
dog-god	6–7	Nominal recall	
was-saw	7–8	Birthday	
tip-pit	7.6–8.6	Month and day	6–7
not-ton	9–11	Month, day, and year	8–9
live-evil	9–11	Name recall	
dial-laid	9–11	Monosyllabic (Dill, Brill, Dietz)	6–8
Spelling		Bisyllabic (Hertzberg, Rutman)	8–10
Monosyllabic (it, is, the, stop, spot, look)	6–7	Trisyllabic (Hertzenberg, Ravenstein)	10–12
Monosyllabic (hit, hot, hat, hut)	7–8	Four-syllable name (Hertzenberger, Schwartzenheimer)	12+
Monosyllabic (work, talk, girl, went)	7–8	Sequential order	
Monosyllabic, others (phone, should, could)	8–9.6	Counting from 0 to 10	
Polysyllabic (monkey, elephant, friendly, receive)	9–10.6	Forward (0–10)	4–5
Polysyllabic (purchase, ethics, delicious, delicate)	10–11.6	Backward (10–0)	5–6
Arithmetic		Letters of the alphabet	5.6–6.6
How many pennies is a nickel?	5–6	Days of the week	
If you had six apples and two friends, how many apples could you give each friend?	6–7	Forward	6–7
If you had nine apples and three friends, how many apples could you give each friend?	6.6–7.6	Backward	7–8
How many quarters in two dollars?	7–8	Months of the year	
How many half-dollars in five whole dollars?	8–9	Forward	8–9
If you had to walk 100 miles, and you could walk 10 miles an hour, how many hours would it take you to walk 100 miles?	9–10	Backward	9.6–11
Multiplication facts: 4×4, 6×7, 8×9	9–10.6	Reiteration	
		$2 + 2 + 1 - 2$	6–8
		$2 \times 3 + 2 - 1$	8–10
		$4 \times 4 + 4 - 3$ (or $5 \times 5 + 5 - 4$)	10–11.6
		Spatial orientation and graphic design	
		Draw a person	5+
		Print numbers (3, 5, 6, 7, 9)	5–6
		Print lower-case letters (b, d, p, q, w, z, m, n)	5.6–6.6
		Draw a clock	
		Appropriate size and placement	7–8
		Correct time	7.6–8.6
		Print or write three to seven lines telling me what you did last night	7.6+

Source: From Weinberg and McLean (1986).
*C- refers to form.

left hemisphere. These irregularities have been demonstrated in three other dyslexic individuals (see Galaburda et al., 1985). Several radiographic studies (Hier et al., 1978; Leisman and Ashkenazi, 1980; however, see Caparulo et al., 1981) have demonstrated similar abnormalities implicating left hemisphere involvement by the presence of atypical cerebral asymmetries in CAT scans of children with dyslexia. These asymmetries were distinctly different from what is normally seen in the nonimpaired child (cf. Devel and Moran, 1980). While such abnormalities may have their genesis in congenital damage (see Towbin, 1978), it may be more likely that genetic or cellular differentiation factors during fetal brain development may be the more common and critical factors (Galaburda and Kemper, 1979).

In addition to the anatomical data, recent electrophysiological studies of children with dyslexia using a topographic mapping technique have demonstrated aberrant electrocortical patterns, having lateralization to the dominant hemisphere but not being restricted to it (Duffy, Denckla, Bartels, and Sandini, 1980; Duffy, Denckla, Bartels, Sandini, and Kiessling, 1980; see also Symann-Lovett et al., 1977). The dysfunctional areas outlined by Duffy and his associates are consistent with cerebral areas that are necessary for various language functions, in particular reading. Similarly, clinical studies of children with left hemisphere brain lesions support the correlation between verbal learning deficits and left hemispheric involvement, particularly those involving posterior regions (Ludlow, 1980; Woods and Carey, 1979).

Neuropsychological Examination

The implications of the above research are that, in certain learning disabled children, there may be lateralized hemispheric dysfunction. Most commonly dysfunction will be in the left hemisphere, producing verbal-language or associated deficits. However, nondominant hemispheric deficits, typically affecting the spatial-gestalt aspects of information processing, may also interfere with learning. Thus, the first step in examining the learning disabled child is to determine if any focal or lateralizing signs are present. If motor, sensory, and language system integrity is present then careful examination of secondary association areas should be undertaken. It will also be important to rule out emotional factors that may be hampering learning ability.

As indicated previously, various morphologic stigmata may be associated with aberrant neurologic development (Shaywitz, 1982). Common stigmata were presented in table 9.1. Children with learning disabilities should be examined for the presence of such stigmata, and if stigmata are present, such findings further support the probability of underlying cerebral dysfunction.

Ehrfurth (1981) recently examined an adolescent learning disabled population. The most significant findings (see table 9.3) were in terms of bilateral finger dysgnosia and dysgraphesthesia along with dysphasic indicators in the absence of specific motor or primary sensory deficit.

Table 9.3. *Significant Neuropsychological Findings in Learning Disabled Adolescents*

Test	Learning Disabled Mean Score	Learning Disabled *SD*	Normal Mean Score	Normal *SD*
Finger Oscillation				
Dominant hand	45.68	5.02	49.63	7.00
Nondominant hand	40.86	6.64	44.59	5.74
Sensory-Perceptual				
Dominant hand	5.77	3.77	1.15	2.01
Nondominant hand	4.59	4.69	2.05	1.55
Aphasia screening	13.18	4.61	2.30	2.15

Note: All test scores were derived from the scheme of Russell, Neuringer, and Goldstein (1970).

Similarly, Lindgren (1978) and Rourke (1981) have demonstrated the significance of finger dysgnostic signs and the presence of reading disability (see also Johnston et al., 1981). Such clinical findings should provide guidelines in evaluating the learning disabled child.

Disorders of calculation have not been well studied. Schwartz, Kaplan, and Schwartz (1981) demonstrated the presence of Gerstmann's syndrome (finger agnosia, right-left disorientation, dysgraphia, and dyscalculia) in children that were dyscalculic but normal readers. These findings implicate dominant parietal involvement. However, it is well-known that certain calculation deficits are consequences of spatial processing deficits related to right hemisphere involvement (Rourke, 1981).

Some differentiation between hyperactivity and learning disability should be made at this point. Hyperactivity is a multifactorial behavior with potentially many underlying variables (Barkley, 1981; Buda, 1981; Levine and Oberklaid, 1980). Hyperactivity is not synonymous with learning disability. In the past, hyperactivity, minimal brain dysfunction, and learning disability were considered to be manifestations of a similar neurologic disorder (Rie and Rie, 1980). The concept of minimal brain dysfunction has been criticized by numerous investigators (Saunders, 1979; Taylor, 1983; Schuckit, Petrich, and Chiles, 1978) mainly because the term is vague and without specific diagnostic criteria. Currently, it is best to approach this area in terms of overlap of such clinical features of hyperactivity, attention deficit, and learning disability without employing the term "minimal brain dysfunction." If neurologic or neuropsychological findings of significance are reported, they should be specified and outlined, not simply put under the heading of minimal brain dysfunction. If the child is hyperactive, has an attention deficit, or is characterized by both, it needs to be ruled out first that these factors are not the primary variables affecting learning. It should also be noted that children with learning disability, hyperactivity, attention deficit, or any combination of these may be adversely affected in terms of their psychosocial development (Cantwell and Baker, 1977; Murray, 1979; Tramontana, Sherrets, and Golden, 1980). Such effects may, thus, influence and maintain certain behavioral abnormalities. Learning disorders that are neurologically based will typically persist into adulthood (O'Donnell, Kurtz, and Ramanaiah, 1983).

In summary, an examiner of the child who is significantly disabled in learning should rule out primary emotional disturbance. And once emotional disturbance is ruled out, if neuropsychological examination of such a child does not reveal posterior left hemisphere dysfunction (thereby implying the learning deficit to be associated with primary receptive language and associated areas), then careful examination should be made of motor systems and nondominant spatial-perceptual functioning. The observation of motor deficits in the learning disabled child may have implications for greater frontal lobe involvement, such deficits possibly affecting integrative learning-memory processes. Such deficits may be differentiated from the language-based deficits more frequently associated with posterior dominant hemisphere involvement. Findings of right hemisphere dysfunction may be related to a variety of secondary verbal functions that may be disrupted by deficits in spatial processing (Levin and Mohr, 1979; Searleman, 1977) as well as prosody (Ross et al., 1981; Ross and Rush, 1981).

Neurologic "Soft" Signs

Neurologic "soft" signs, such as mirror movements, synkinetic movements, and dysdiadochokinesia, as opposed to "hard" (i.e., hemiplegia, aphasia) neurologic signs occur in greater regularity in children with learning and developmental disorders (Bigler, 1987; Cummings, Flynn, and Preus, 1982; Nass, 1985; Shaffer et al., 1985). Such signs are normal and commonplace in young children, but by age ten they should be absent (Nass, 1985). This parallels neuronal maturation (Chugani and Phelps, 1986), particularly of the frontal lobe and corpus callosum. The presence of such findings may be the first clue as to an underlying neurodevelopmental disorder, although the exact relationship between such findings and neuropsychological outcome remains ambiguous (Taylor, 1983). Pugh and Bigler (1986) did find that adolescent schizophrenic patients who had pre-existing neurologic soft signs, or so-called MBD syndrome, had impaired neuropsychological performance when contrasted with adolescent schizophrenic patients who did not have such a prior history.

Pathologic Left-Handedness

Orsini and Satz (1986) have reviewed the literature in this area as well as conducted much of the primary research dealing with pathologic left-handedness. They suggest that the syndrome of pathologic left-handedness may include the following features: atypical or right-sided hemispheric speech representation, hypoplasia of the right foot, hypoplasia of the right hand, motor impairment of the nondominant (i.e., hand), impaired visual-spatial functions relative to preserved verbal cognitive functions (e.g., PIQ < VIQ), and low probability of familial sinistrality. In such individuals, there is a higher incidence of various learning and neurodevelopmental problems.

Neurobehavioral Syndromes in Childhood Disorders

A growing interest in behavioral and emotional factors that may accompany childhood brain disorders has recently taken place (see Rourke, Fisk, and Strang, 1986). The previously discussed research examining left cerebral dysfunction and depression may apply to children as well (Denckla, 1983). Weintraub and Mesulam (1983) have demonstrated a potential relationship between right hemisphere dysfunction and various emotional/adjustment problems, including the disturbance of interpersonal skills in addition to poor visual-spatial ability. Nussbaum and Bigler (1986), in a cluster analysis study of over 250 children presenting with learning disability, were able to identify 75 children that clustered into three different groups, according to their neuropsychological profiles. In the group with the greatest verbal linguistic deficits, this was found to be associated with greater depressive symptomatology, as endorsed by the child's parents on the Child Behavior Checklist (see table 9.5). Nussbaum, Bigler, and Koch (1986) also demonstrated that learning disabled children, regardless of the type of learning deficit or neuropsychological impairment, demonstrated problems in social interaction and with various intra- and interpersonal relationships. Also, Nussbaum (1986) has examined the relationship between anterior and posterior dysfunction, irrespective of hemispheric locus, and found greater impulsivity and attentional deficits in children with presumed frontal lobe dysfunction.

Childhood Autism and Schizophrenia

Childhood autism and schizophrenia fall under the category of pervasive developmental disorders. Originally these disorders were thought to represent the most severe forms of functional psychopathology (see Gregory and Smeltzer, 1977). However, at this point the clinical data clearly implicate an organic etiology in a majority of these disorders (Damasio and Maurer, 1978). For example, brain-stem and cerebellar abnormalities have also been demonstrated in addition to cerebral irregularities (Ornitz et al., 1985; Ritvo et al., 1986). Autism is typically diagnosed early in the preschool years. Behaviorally, the main features are self-stimulating behavior (twirling, spinning, rocking, repetitive hand movements, etc.); failure in language and effective communication; inappropriate relationship with inanimate objects, including fascination and preoccupation; and failure to develop appropriate social relations. Dissimilarly, childhood schizophrenia typically is diagnosed somewhat later but usually by the age of seven or eight and characterized by disturbance in

Table 9.4. *Examples of Dyslexic Patterns according to Boder*

Type I: Dysphonetic Reading/Spelling Pattern	Type II: Dyseidetic Reading/Spelling Pattern	Nonspecific Reading Disability
Age: 10 Grade: 4	Age: 7 Grade: 1	Age: 8 Grade: 2
Reading level: 1	Reading level: 1	Reading level: below preprimer
Reading quotient: 60	Reading quotient: 86	Reading quotient: 52
Correctly spelled 40% of words in sight reading vocabulary	Correctly spelled 40% of words in sight reading vocabulary	Correctly spelled 50% of words in sight reading vocabulary
SAP step	frget forget	Fat fast
FATsrr faster	iSS eyes	com came
ShAA shoe	Tadul table	Dllo blue
SAriciɾ store	nife knife	musn mother
tAEBa table	duy buy	sed said
(57) VIQ < (90) PIQ	(90) PIQ (103) PIQ	(87) PIQ ≅ (86) VIQ
Poor articulation, poor sequential processing	Visuomotor deficits (Beery Age Equivalent 5; 10), poor visual memory (BVRT), constructional dyspraxia (aphasia screening), seizure disorder (right posterior quadrant)	Generalized developmental delay (poor visuomotor, verbal, spatial abilities)
(69) (SEQ < (81) SIM)		

thought and affect, hallucinatory behavior, and bizarre speech, actions, or both.

Neurologic Factors

Damasio and Maurer in 1978 proposed a neurologic model for childhood autism. In this model they implicated bilateral involvement of the mesolimbic cortex, neostriatum, and anterior and medial thalamic regions. Another study by Damasio et al. in 1980, however, indicated that the morphologic abnormalities of the brain, as evidenced by CAT scan results, tended to be more extensive than proposed. Nonetheless, CAT scanning clearly demonstrated frank anatomic abnormalities, including hydrocephalus, in many autistic children. Similar findings also have been noted in CAT scan results of schizophrenics (Golden et al., 1981; Luchins, Weinberger, and Wyatt, 1979; Tanaka et al., 1981; Weinberger et al., 1979) as well as abnormalities on other neurologic measures (Bellak and Charles, 1979; Torrey, 1980), although such abnormalities are not diagnostic of childhood schizophrenia or autism.

Thus, it appears that an organic basis to childhood schizophrenia and autism is present. Neuropsychologically, these patients tend to show nonspecific deficits but also some indication for greater left hemispheric dysfunction, particularly in more anterior regions (Piran and Bigler, 1981). There also appears to be a greater incidence of mixed dominance and left-handedness in these disorders (Piran, Bigler, and Cohen, 1982; Shimizu et al., 1985; Tsai, 1983). Genetic factors in the expression of schizophrenia are also important. Marcus et al. (1985) have demonstrated a subgroup of offspring of schizophrenics who displayed various sensory-perceptual and motor deficits, not observed in matched controls. DeLisi et al. (1986) have also demonstrated ventricular enlargement in nonaffected immediate family members of schizophrenic patients.

Schizophrenic and autistic patients may show various motor deficits in alternating movements, mirror movements, fine motor control, general coordination, and gait. Although some of these features may be related to neuroleptic medication use, Vilensky, Damasio, and Maurer (1981) have plausibly demonstrated that dysfunction of the basal ganglia may be responsible for at least the gait disturbance commonly involved. Thus, the observation of distinct gait disturbance in either the schizophrenic or autistic patient should also alert the clinician to possible underlying cerebral dysfunction in these disorders. These findings are more fully discussed in chapter 10. The CAT scans in figures 9.18 and 9.19 are of a child diagnosed with autism and an adolescent diagnosed as schizophrenic. Both figures show definite structural abnormalities of the brain. The prior presence of MBD features in schizophrenics also appears to have a negative influence on outcome (Pugh and Bigler, 1986).

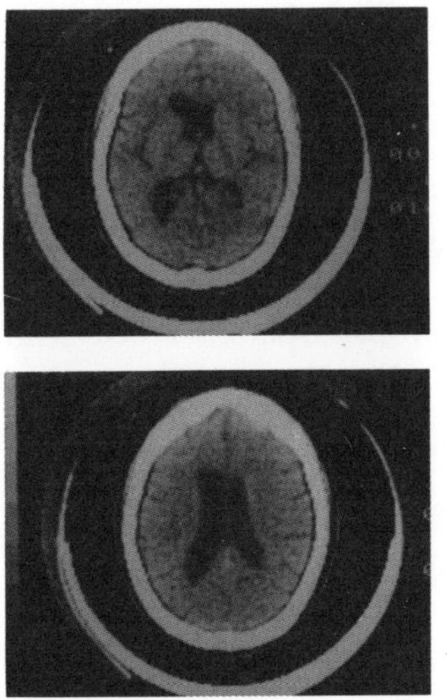

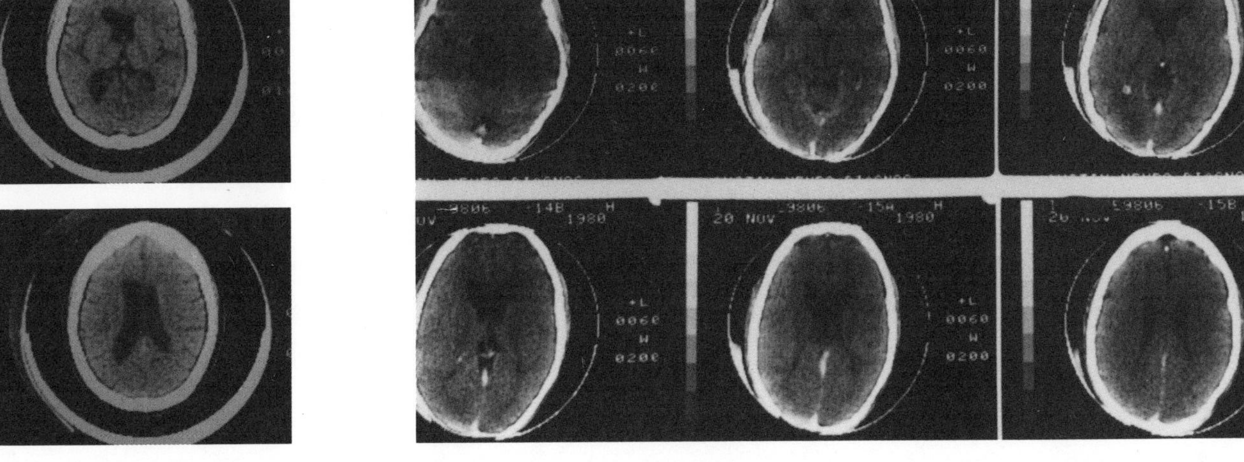

Fig. 9.18. CAT scan of patient once diagnosed as autistic. Note the distinct ventricular asymmetry. The left side enlargement indicates some degree of left hemisphere structural dysfunction. Such abnormalities may account for the "autistic" features of language disturbance.

Fig. 9.19. CAT scan of 21-year-old patient with diagnosis of schizophrenia. Note the abnormally large anterior horns of the lateral ventricles.

Classification of Higher Cortical Dysfunction in Children

There has been no consensus in terms of a classification scheme for higher cortical dysfunction in children. The outline written by the Child Neurology Society (see David et al., 1981), however, provides the best guidelines to date and is summarized below. It should be noted that this outline has not been empirically or clinically verified and is given only as an outline at this time.

Disorders of Motor Execution (Dyspraxias and Related Syndromes)

As previously defined, dyspraxia occurs as a failure to learn or execute voluntary motor activities even though no paralysis, sensory, motivational or attentional factors are present. Most childhood disorders of motor execution are developmental in nature, although acquired dyspraxias do occur. There are basically four distinctions that can be made in terms of dyspraxic disorders of childhood: motor dyspraxia, developmental maladroitness, constructional disorders, and tremorhypotonia. In motor dyspraxia there is a deficit in complex sequential motor execution. These children may have problems with pantomime, imitation, or actual use of objects. In developmental maladroitness the motor deficits tend to be more generalized, with particular slowing of all motor manipulative skills. Constructional dyspraxia is manifested in terms of pronounced graphomotor or constructional deficit in the absence of motor dyspraxia or developmental maladroitness. In the tremor-hypotonia syndrome, there is often a tremor (three to four per second) that becomes accentuated by action or stress along with gross and fine motor abilities typically being below chronologic age.

Disorders of Attention and Activity

Disorders of attention and activity have previously been ascribed as subsets of such diagnostic labels as minimal brain dysfunction, minimal brain injury, or hyperactive child syndrome. These labels are, however, no longer in vogue, nor are they descriptive (Taylor, 1983; Weiss, 1985*a*). The current terminology in use classifies such problems under the heading of Attention Deficit Disorder (ADD) and has variables about whether the attentional deficit is associated with hyperactivity or not. ADD with hyperactivity typically includes attentional problems, impulsivity, and hyperactivity. ADD without hyperactivity includes the attentional problems and impulsivity, but does not include motor hyperactivity. Onset is usually before seven years of age. Frequently, disorders of conduct and the presence of learning disability may be seen in a number of these children. Guidelines provided by the *Diagnostic and Statistical Manual (DSM-III)* of the American Psychiatric Association suggest that at least three of the following need to be observed to determine the presence of inattention: (1) often fails to finish things he or she starts, (2) often doesn't seem to listen, (3) is easily distracted, (4) has difficulty concentrating on schoolwork or other tasks requiring sustained attention, and (5) has difficulty sticking to play activity. *DSM-III* guidelines for classification of impulsivity indicate that to classify a child as impulsive at least three of the following need to be present: (1) often acts before thinking, (2) shifts excessively from one activity to another, (3) has difficulty organizing work (this is not owing to cognitive impairment), (4) needs a lot of supervision, (5) frequently calls out in class, and (6) has difficulty awaiting turn in games or group situations. The *DSM-III* classification for the presence of hyperactivity indicates at least two of the following need to be present: (1) runs about or climbs on things excessively, (2) has difficulty sitting still or fidgets excessively, (3) has difficulty staying seated, (4) moves about excessively during sleep, and (5) is always "on the go" or acts as if "driven by a motor."

When the ADD syndrome is present, the treatment of choice is stimulant medication (Abikoff and Gittelman, 1985; Weiss, 1985*a*) along with behavioral management. Recent longitudinal studies have demonstrated that ADD syndrome in childhood may represent a significant factor in adult psychopathology (Gittelman et al., 1985; Weiss et al., 1985). In such individuals some of the ADD symptoms may persist into adulthood.

Disorders of Memory

Disorders of memory may occur in childhood. There are essentially four basic types of memory disorders: (1) failure of registration (paramnesia), (2) material-specific memory disorder, (3) modality-specific memory disorder, and (4) generalized or global amnesia. If memory registration is specifically affected, then short-term memory and recall cannot take place. Such children will appear to have a disorder of memory, but, in fact, their disorder is one of registration. If care can be taken to ensure that the memory trace is in fact registered, the child will not display memory deficit. In examining these children, caution needs to be taken in ruling out any type of attentional deficit disorder that may account for the failure in registration. Modality-specific memory deficits occur in children that have recall problems specific to one modality (i.e., a child may recall a figure but not a verbal description of a figure). Material-specific memory disorders apply to disorders of memory integration. For example, a child with a material-specific memory disorder may fail to retain visual-verbal items but recall visual information alone. This child may have no significant auditory deficits when auditory ability is tested in isolation. Global memory disorders, as the name implies, are typically associated with some generalized disturbance in most or all memory processes. Such global disorders are usually associated with some type of definable neurologic disorder, trauma and acute encephalopathies of diverse etiology being the most frequent.

Generalized Disorders of Cognition (Mental Retardation)

A host of developmental disorders may be associated with mental retardation, but the required features are the presence of subnormal intellectual ability that is nonprogressive and language development that is consistent with mental age. There are also associated deficits in adaptive and social behaviors, and the deficits, both in IQ as well as social and adaptive behaviors, are displayed during preschool or early school years. The following outlines the *DSM-III* guidelines for the levels of mental retardation classification:

Subtypes of Mental Retardation	IQ Level
Borderline	71–85
Mild	50–70
Moderate	35–49
Severe	20–34
Profound	Below 20

CAT scan results may demonstrate some irregularities (see fig. 9.20) with various mental retardation syndromes, but it is also not uncommon to have a normal scan.

Care needs to be taken when diagnosing mental retardation because there are several complicating factors. For example, a child with a low average level of intellectual functioning who has a severe learning disability may appear to have features of a mental retardation syndrome. Likewise, level of intellectual performance on objective psychometric testing may be markedly affected by the presence of an attentional deficit disorder and/or emotional disturbance.

Developmental Disorders of Language and Speech

A child who does not use single words communicatively by eighteen months and simple short sentences by twenty-four months is considered to be at risk for a developmental language disorder. Language and speech functions are dependent on a variety of interrelated processes, including phonology, syntax, semantics, and pragmatics (language use). From a neurologic standpoint, five syndromes have been identified. Stuttering will also be discussed because it is frequently encountered in neuropsychologic practice.

1. Verbal Auditory Agnosia—Word deafness. Word deafness is a processing disorder associated with deficits in phonologic decoding in which the hearer has a severe comprehension deficit for auditorily presented language. Speech is nonfluent. Communication occurs by gesturing. Comprehension may be intact for nonverbally presented information.

2. Semantic-Pragmatic Syndrome. Children with semantic-pragmatic syndrome have particular deficits in comprehending language discourse, particularly *Wh*—questions. Comprehension and response to simple commands may be normal. Phonology and syntax are within normal limits. Expressive language is usually superior to

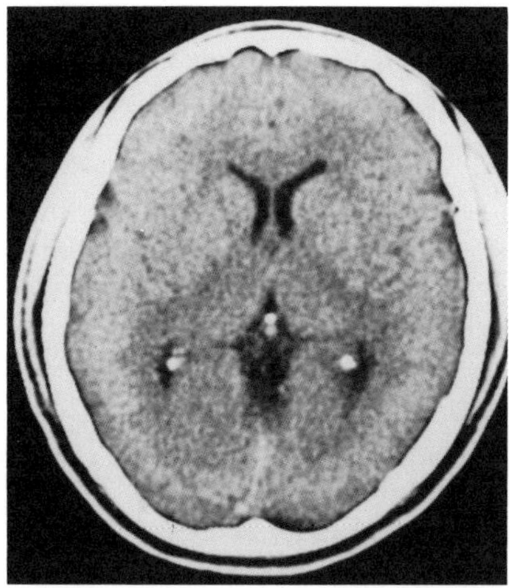

Fig. 9.20. The classic CAT configuration in a patient with Down's syndrome. Notice the shortness of the temporal and frontal region. The remainder of the CAT scan appears essentially normal. This patient's level of mental retardation was in the mild range (VIQ = 55, PIQ = 54, and FSIQ = 54). This patient was impaired on all measures of cognitive functioning on the neuropsychological examination, as would be expected given his level of mental retardation.

comprehension. Spontaneous speech is superior to elicited speech. Pragmatic content of speech is impaired.

3. Phonologic Syntactic Deficit Syndrome. The phonologic syntactic deficit syndrome is the most commonly seen of the developmental language disorders. The basic features are in terms of a dysfluent expression with aberrant phonology and simplified or abnormal syntax. Level of comprehension is typically better than expressive abilities, although comprehension may not be at an age-appropriate level. Children with this syndrome are also frequently found to have a variety of associated learning disability problems. The severity of the syndrome varies widely.

4. Speech Programming Deficit (Verbal Apraxia) Syndrome. In verbal apraxia, expressive deficit is quite severe but comprehension is usually adequate. The dysfluency may approach mutism. Speech is frequently unintelligible.

5. Phonologic Production Deficit (Developmental Articulation Disorder) Syndrome. In the phonologic production deficit syndrome the disturbance is primarily one of articulation. The articulation deficit persists beyond what would be ascribed to simple maturational factors. Comprehension is normal.

6. Stuttering. While stuttering is not considered to be a language disorder in and of itself, it is discussed here because of the frequency with which stuttering is seen in practice. Most stuttering disorders are related to non-neurogenic factors and are typically responsive to either maturation alone or adjunctive speech therapy. However, a variety of acquired neurologic disorders may be associated with the development of stuttering. This is particularly true in cases including damage in more medial left hemisphere regions. Also, involvement of the basal ganglia may be accompanied by onset of stuttering. In some children who have problems in terms of laterality and cerebral specialization, there may be interhemispheric competition for speech output that produces the stuttering.

Reading Disability Syndromes (Dyslexias)

The salient feature of the dyslexias is the deficit in reading ability that cannot be attributed to chronologic age, mental age, or inadequate schooling. Four syndromes have been suggested. In all of these syndromes, it is presupposed that the primary deficit is of reading, but the basis for the reading deficit is what differentiates the syndrome.

1. Language Disorder Syndrome. Dysnomia is a primary feature of language disorder syndrome. Secondary features are possible impaired language comprehension, possible impaired speech repetition, possible impairment of speech sound discrimination, or all of these. Visuomotor, visuoperceptual, and graphomotor skills are typically within normal limits.

2. Articulatory-Graphomotor Dyscoordination Syndrome. Children with this discoordination syndrome typically have features of a buccolingual dyspraxia in association with significant graphomotor disturbance. Although auditory discrimination and receptive language abilities are intact, these children typically have deficits in sound blending abilities.

3. Sequencing Disorder Syndrome. Children with a sequencing disorder syndrome are deficient in short-term verbal memory processing (i.e., that ability measured by the Digit Span Test) as well as visual memory. Naming and articulation are typically within normal limits.

4. Visual-Perceptual Disorder Syndrome. As the label implies, measures of visuoperceptual functioning in children with visual-perceptual disorder syndrome are impaired, and their deficit in reading is likely of a visuoperceptual nature. However, they typically function in normal range in terms of other visual-perceptual abilities. However, Benton's (1984) review of the research in this area suggests that this syndrome may not exist as a separate clinical entity.

5. Mixed Reading Disorders. A combination of the above syndromes may be present that results in mixed features.

Boder (see Boder and Jarrico, 1982) has suggested a somewhat different scheme that appears to have good classificatory power (Rosenthal, Boder, and Callaway, 1982). In her scheme the dyslexic child is categorized into one of three classifications in terms of whether the child's primary deficits are with phonetic processing (dysphonetic dyslexic), sight-say (visual-spatial-gestalt) features of reading (dyseidetic dyslexic), or a mixture of the two (dysphonetic-dyseidetic dyslexic). See case 6 for an example of this. Table 9.4 depicts the three types of dyslexia according to Boder.

Another similar disorder is the hyperlexia syndrome. The children with hyperlexia syndrome have a superior ability for reading; however, the material that is read is poorly comprehended. The accelerated reading ability appears to be mainly of a specific word recognition skill that does not generalize to any other type of superior language function. These children may show autistic features. Frequently they also show features of developmental maladroitness.

Disorders of Writing (Dysgraphias)

The dysgraphias are characterized by a deficit in one or more of the following areas of written language: fluency, legibility, spelling, and written grammar. In the majority of these children, the written language disturbance is associated with reading disturbance; thus, the syndrome is typically referred to as a dysgraphic/dyslexic syndrome. While handwriting is always affected, geometric form copying may not be as affected, but will typically be below average for age. The Coding or Digit Symbol subtests on the Wechsler Intelligence Scale for Children or Wechsler Adult Intelligence Scale will typically be distinctly below other performance test items.

Drug Abuse

Drug abuse will be more completely described in chapter 10. Suffice it to say that children with drug and/or alcohol abuse are at risk for the subsequent development of a variety of neurocognitive deficits. Also, it should be mentioned that prior history of "minimal brain dysfunction" or family history of alcoholism (see Tarter et al., 1984) may be particularly negative factors mediating the neuropsychological effects of alcohol abuse.

Child Neuropsychological Assessment Outline

Table 9.5 presents an outline of the comprehensive neuropsychological test battery that has been utilized at the Austin Neurological Clinic (Bigler and Nussbaum, 1988). Because of the multiplicity of potential problems in children presenting with learning or neurological disorders, a thorough and comprehensive battery is typically in order. Reitan and Herring (1985) have demonstrated a shortened form of the Halstead-Reitan Battery that is effective in screening children with cerebral dysfunction, but when recommendations for therapeutic intervention are necessary, it is recommended that a complete, comprehensive battery, such as that presented in table 9.5, be utilized. Table 9.6 outlines an effective organization of the test data in report form as depicted in table 9.7, and the case on pages 76–78 presents an actual case study in report form.

Table 9.5. ***The Comprehensive Austin Neuropsychological Assessment Battery for Children (Recommended Tests)***

Physical Measures	General Physical Features	Physical Anomalies
Height	Lateral Dominance	Facial features
Weight	Hand	Epidermal features
Visual acuity	Foot	(e.g., *café au lait* spots)
Head circumference	Eye	Hands
		Other anomalies
		(e.g., steepled palate)

Halstead Neuropsychological Test Battery for Children and
Reitan-Indiana Neuropsychological Test Battery for Children (Reitan and Davison, 1974)
(selected subtests)

Motor
1. Strength of Grip
2. Finger Oscillation
   - Electric—5 to 8 year olds
   - Manual—9 and older

Tactual Performance Test
1. 6 form/horizontal—5 to 8 year olds
2. 6 form/vertical—9 to 14 year olds
3. 10 form/vertical—14 to adult
4. Seguin/Goddard (Anastasi, 1969)—poor cooperation, or under age 5

Sensory-Perceptual Exam
1. Tactile
   - Single, Double Simultaneous Ipsilateral and Contralateral
2. Auditory
   - Single, Double Simultaneous

Table 9.5. *(continued)*

3. Visual
   Upper, Middle, Lower Visual Fields
   Single, Double Simultaneous
   Visual Fields
4. Finger Recognition
5. Finger Graphesthesia
   5 to 8 year olds, symbols X's and O's
   9 to adult, numbers
6. Form Recognition
   Included if the child scores one standard deviation below the mean on Tactile, Finger Recognition, and/or Finger Graphesthesia

Reitan-Aphasia Screening Battery (Reitan and Wolfson, 1985)
1. 5 to 8 year old form
2. 9 and older form

Wide-Range Achievement Test (Jasktak and Jasktak, 1965)
1. Reading (primarily a test of reading recognition)
2. Spelling (provides quantitative spelling level)
3. Arithmetic
4. Preacademic tasks as indicated

Boder Test of Reading and Spelling Patterns (Boder and Jarrico, 1982)
1. Provides qualitative information on spelling/reading

Durrell Analysis of Reading Difficulty (selected subtests) (Durrell and Catterson, 1980)
1. Silent Reading
   (measure of reading comprehension)
2. Oral Reading
   (measure of visual/auditory processing and reading comprehension)
3. Listening Comprehension
   (measure of auditory/verbal comprehension)

Beery Test of Visual Motor Integration (Beery, 1982)
1. Measure of perceptual motor ability

Raven's Coloured Progressive Matrices (Raven, Court, and Raven, 1979)
1. Measure of nonverbal abstract reasoning

Wechsler Intelligence Scale for Children—Revised (WISC-R) (Wechsler, 1974)
1. Verbal IQ subscales (Information, Vocabulary, Similarities, Arithmetic, Comprehension)
2. Performance IQ subscales (Picture Completion, Block Design, Object Assembly, Picture Arrangement, Coding)
3. Digit Span

Family History Questionnaire
1. Background Information
2. Pregnancy History
3. Birth History
4. Developmental History
5. Medical History
6. School History

Child Behavior Checklist—Revised (Achenbach and Edelbrock, 1983)
1. Provides an easily reviewed list of possible behavior problems
2. Provides quantitative scores on such personality scales as Depression, Aggression, etc.

Personality Inventory for Children—Revised (Wirt et al., 1982)
1. Provides quantitative scores on such personality scales as Depression, Aggression, etc.

Projective Drawings
1. House/Tree/Person (DiLeo, 1983)
   Kinetic Family Drawings (DiLeo, 1983)
   Provide qualitative information on self-concept, family dynamics, etc.

Behavioral Observation Inventory
1. Provides a short informal assessment of behaviors observed during the evaluation

Additional Measures Included as Needed

Benton Visual Retention Test (Benton, 1974)
Included if: 1. Questionable ADD problems
2. Deficient visuomotor performance (Beery) leads to questions about deficits in visual perception/memory versus visuomotor coordination

Kaufman Assessment Battery for Children (K-ABC) (Kaufman and Kaufman, 1983)
Included if: 1. Marginal or questionable LD

Table 9.5. *(continued)*

2. More in-depth information is needed concerning child's nonverbal intellectual abilities
3. Particularly useful subscales:
   Hand Movements (useful attentional measure)
   Gestalt Closure (useful visual processing measure)
   Matrix Analysis (useful nonverbal reasoning measure)
   Spatial Memory (useful visual memory measurement without a motor confound)

Other
Halstead Neuropsychological Test Battery for Children subtests administered to 9 to 14 year olds as indicated
1. Trails A
   (measure of sequential visual processing, attention)
2. Trails B
   (measure of sequential visual processing, attention, cognitive flexibility)
3. Seashore Rhythm Test
   (measure of sequential auditory processing, attention, auditory memory)
4. Speech Sounds Perception Test
   (measure of auditory processing, attention, sight/sound matching)

Note: Measures are scored according to individual norm tables provided with each specific test or according to normative information provided by Spreen and Gaddes (1969) or Knights and Norwood (1980).

Table 9.6. ***The Organization of Neuropsychological Test Results***

Motor (fine and gross)
- Strength of Grip
- Finger Oscillation
- Tactual Performance Test
- Beery Test of Visual Motor Integration
- WISC-R (Block Design, Object Assembly, Coding)

Visual/Spatial Processing
- Visual Acuity
- Sensory-Perceptual Exam (Visual exam)
- Beery Test of Visual Motor Integration
- Benton Visual Retention Test
- Trails A & B
- Tactual Performance Test
- Reitan-Aphasia Screening Battery (Visual Constructional tasks)
- K-ABC (Hand Movements, Gestalt Closure)
- WISC-R (Performance IQ Subscales)

Body Awareness
- Sensory-Perceptual Exam (Tactile, Finger Recognition, Finger Graphesthesia, Form Recognition)
- Tactual Performance Test

Auditory Verbal Processing
- Sensory-Perceptual Exam (Auditory)
- Seashore Rhythm Test
- Speech Sounds Perception Test
- Durrell (Listening Comprehension)
- WISC-R (Verbal IQ subscales)

Sequential Processing
- Digit Span
- WISC-R (Picture Arrangement)
- K-ABC (Hand Movements)
- Trails A & B
- Seashore Rhythm Test

Memory
- WISC-R (Digit Span)
- Benton Visual Retention Test
- K-ABC (Spatial Memory, Hand Movements)
- Durrell (Silent Reading—unstructured story recall, Listening Comprehension—structured story recall)
- Tactual Performance Test (memory for objects and location)
- Seashore Rhythm Test

Cognitive Development (knowledge, reasoning)
- Raven's Coloured Progressive Matrices
- WISC-R (Information, Vocabulary, Similarities, Arithmetic, Comprehension, Picture Arrangement)
- K-ABC (Matrix Analysis)

Attention
- Sensory-Perceptual Exam (Tactile, Auditory, Visual, Finger Recognition, Finger Graphesthesia)
- Benton Visual Retention Test
- Trails A & B
- Seashore Rhythm Test
- Speech Sounds Perception Test
- Durrell (Listening Comprehension)
- WISC-R (Arithmetic, Picture Completion, Coding, Digit Span)
- K-ABC (Hand Movements)
- Child Behavior Checklist
- Behavioral Observation Inventory

Academic Skills
- Reitan-Aphasia Screening Battery (Reading, Spelling, Arithmetic tasks)
- Wide-Range Achievement Test (Reading, Spelling, Arithmetic, Preacademic tasks)
- Boder Test of Reading and Spelling Patterns
- Durrell (Silent Reading, Oral Reading, Listening Comprehension)
- WISC-R (Arithmetic)

Personality/Behavioral
- Child Behavior Checklist
- Personality Inventory for Children—Revised
- Projective Drawings
- Behavioral Observation Inventory

Psychosocial Factors
- Parent Interview
- Family History Questionnaire
- Child Behavior Checklist

Table 9.7. *Format of the Neuropsychological Report*

Presenting Problem
- Referral Question (e.g., presenting seizures)

Background History
- Genetic (e.g., Down's syndrome, epilepsy)
- Pregnancy (e.g., complications—alcohol use, etc.)
- Birth and delivery complications—forceps, etc.)
- Neonatal (e.g., birth weight)
- Medical (e.g., significant head injuries)
- Family (e.g., parents' education, LD in the family)

Tests Administered

Assessment Results
- Intellectual/Cognitive Functioning
  - I.Q. scores
  - Subtest scores
  - Clinical description/interpretation
- Academic Functioning
  - Achievement scores
  - Clinical description/interpretation
- Neuropsychological Test Findings
  - Physical stigmata/physical measurements
  - Hand, eye, and foot dominance
  - Motor functioning
    - Fine motor
    - Gross motor
    - Praxic ability
    - Visuomotor copying
  - Sensory perceptual functioning
    - Vision (acuity/fields)
    - Hearing
    - Tactile (double simultaneous)
    - Graphesthesia
    - Stereognosis
    - Finger Gnosis
  - Language
    - Articulation
    - Receptive
    - Expressive
    - Naming
    - Spelling
    - Reading
    - Calculations
  - Memory
    - Verbal
    - Visual/spatial
  - General cognitive
- Personality/Emotional Functioning
  - Behavioral observations—subjective findings
  - Projective test results
    - Projective drawings
    - Thematic testing
    - Rorschach (1942)
  - Objective personality scores/patterns
  - Clinical summary
- Clinical Impression
  - Summary and integration of assessment results
  - DSM III format followed when appropriate
- Recommendations
  1. To referring doctor, including therapists the child may be seeing
  2. To school
  3. To parents
  4. When to followup
  5. Miscellaneous

CASE STUDIES

Case 1. At age two months this patient had spontaneous hemorrhage over the left parietal area. As a young child he displayed features of an attention deficit disorder with hyperactivity. By school age he additionally displayed deficits in academic achievement. Neuropsychological examination is consistent with what is commonly seen with residual dominant hemisphere parietal dysfunction—impaired tactile sensory processing, academic deficits, and impaired visual-verbal discrimination (Speech Sounds Perception test error score). Note also the presence of mixed laterality and lowered verbal IQ.

Age 11
Sex M
Education 5th

Lateral Dominance Exam

	Eye	Hand	Foot
Right		X	
Left	X		
Mixed			X

Motor Examination:
FOD 37 SOGD 21 TPTD 1.7 (6 form board)
FOND 33 SOGND 20 TPTND 1.5
TPT Both 2.9

Sensory Perceptual Examination:
Bilateral finger dysgnosia and dysgraphesthesia

Aphasia Examination:
Conversational Speech: Normal.
Comprehension: Verbally processed intact, Reading comprehension poor
Repetition of Spoken Language: Normal
Confrontation Naming: Normal
Reading:
WRAT Score 5.9 SSRT 11 errors
Spelling SSPT 20 errors
WRAT Score 4.5
Arithmetic
WRAT Score 2.9

Intellectual/Cognitive Examination:
WISC-R Results VIQ = 84, PIQ = 90, FSIQ = 85
I 8, C 11, A 4, S 7, D 8, V 7
DS 9, PC 9, BD 9, PA 10, OA 6

Category Test: 40 errors
Trail Making Test: A 18 B 36

Case 2. This nine-year-old girl had a history of long-standing learning deficit, particularly in reading. Medical history was completely negative. Neuropsychological examination results suggested left hemisphere dysfunction (compare results of this patient's tests with those in case 1, whose subject had verified parietal lobe damage). Electroencephalogram and CAT scan results were within normal limits. Note the mild right-side motor findings, presence of bilateral finger dysgnosia and dysgraphesthesia, as well as the dysphasic signs on aphasia examination. Note also that the verbal IQ is lower than the performance IQ. When such a profile is obtained of a child with significant history of learning disturbance, it is likely that the deficits in learning have an organic basis.

Kc'oce

Sauare

He seven the wonen,

Age 9
Sex F
Education 3

Lateral Dominance Exam

	Eye	Hand	Foot
Right		X	X
Left			
Mixed	X		

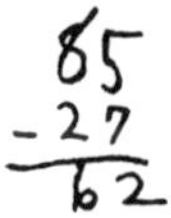

Motor Examination:
FOD 29 SOGD 15 TPTD 6.0 DC 3 in (6 form board)
FOND 30 SOGND 17 TPTND 2.8
TPT Both 0.7

Sensory Perceptual Examination:
Bilateral finger dysgnosia and dysgraphresthesia, greater on the right.

Aphasia Examination:
Features of dyslexia, dyscalculia, spelling dyspraxia, R-L confusion
WRAT Results
Reading 2.0 SSPT 36 errors
Spelling 2.6 SRT 5 errors
Arithmetic 3.3

Memory Examination:
WMS LM 10, Digits 7, VM 8, AL 10.5

Intellectual/Cognitive Exam:
VIQ = 90, PIQ = 100, FSIQ = 93
I 5, C 10, A 8, S 7, O 4, V 12
DS 7, PC 13, BD 7, PA 13, OA 10

Category Test: 49 errors (children's form)
Trail Making Test: A 20
B 115 (children's form)

Case 3. This seven-year-old boy had neurofibromatosis. He had the characteristic *café au lait* spots, particularly noted over the abdomen. This child also had a seizure disorder, the last EEG indicating the presence of bicentral temporal paroxysmal discharges and slower-than-normal background electroencephalogram patterns. He was on phenobarbital and Mysoline at the time of the examination. His mother's pregnancy and his eventual birth were both normal, and there have been no other medical complications. Developmental milestones were described as being delayed: the child not sitting until 9 months, not walking until 18 months, and not speaking until about 3.5 years. Beginning in infancy and continuing to the present, this child has displayed persistent hyperactivity and significant deficits in attention. The neuropsychological profile is indicative of rather generalized and nonspecific underlying cerebral deficit. CAT scan results were normal.

Age 7
Sex M
Education 1

Lateral Dominance Exam

	Eye	Hand	Foot
Right			X
Left			
Mixed	X	X	

Motor Examination:
FOD 27 SOGD 6 TPT Unable to perform
FOND 28 SOGND 10
Gait and general motor control was maladroit and awkward. Mirror movements present

Sensory Examination:
Simple touch intact. Unable to test for stereognosis and graphesthesia

Aphasia Examination:
Conversational Speech: Simple speech pattern with misarticulations.
Comprehension: Mildly impaired.
Repetition of Spoken Language: Generally intact.
Confrontation-Naming: Mildly impaired for uncommon objects.
Reading: Unable to read, some recognition of a few letters.
Writing: Impaired copying constructional apraxia.
Calculations: Impaired for age.
Achievement Functioning:
WRAT Results
Reading 1.9
Spelling P.6
Arithmetic P.8

Intellectual/Cognitive Functioning:
WISC-R Results FSIQ = 65
VIQ = 74 I 9, S 3, A 6, V 6, C 5
PIQ = 60 PC 8, PA 3, BD 3, OA 1, Cod 3

Category Test: 46 errors
Stanford-Binet: CA = 6-9
MA = 5-2
IQ = 74

Case 4. This child precociously developed the ability to read at age three but displayed clear signs of motor delay and impaired spatial-perceptual functioning. He was first tested at age six and results clearly demonstrate accelerated reading and spelling ability far above his grade level. All other cognitive functions and particularly motor tasks were performed in a mild to moderately impaired range. He has left-side neglect as well as an inability to perform the tactual performance test with his left hand. A marked constructional dyspraxia is present. EEG evaluation revealed right parietal-occipital focus. CAT scan results were, however, within normal limits. This is a case of hyperlexia with associated right parietal disturbance. Other features of this syndrome may be echolalia, perseverative behaviors, and delayed social development. Such cases demonstrate that various learning deficits may accompany right hemisphere dysfunction. He was subsequently reexamined at age eight and showed clear improvement. He had been in a specialized educational program with emphasis on motor training. Despite improvements, he continues to demonstrate a variety of signs of right hemisphere dysfunction, even though his EEG results were found to be within normal limits. (See table 9.8.)

Table 9.8. ***Case 4: Neuropsychological Test Results***

Variable	Age: Six years, four months	Age: Eight years, eight months
Grade	Kindergarten	Second
Handedness	Ambidextrous with right hand preference	Right
WISC-R		
Verbal IQ	100	113
Performance IQ	77	92
Full-Scale IQ	87	103
Information	11	13
Similarities	11	13
Arithmetic	11	11
Vocabulary	9	14
Comprehension	8	10
Picture Completion	6	8
Picture Arrangement	7	8
Block Design	10	10
Object Assembly	0	5
Coding	10	14
WRAT (Grade Level)		
Reading	9.3	10.1
Spelling	5.5	10.3
Arithmetic	2.2	3.9
Reitan-Indiana		
Category (Errors)	20	19
Tactual Performance Test		
Dominant	10.7	8.5
Nondominant	DC at 10 min. (2 in)	DC at 15 min. (2 in)
Both	6.5	4.9
Total time	26.2+	28.4+
Memory	6	6
Localization	0	1
Finger Oscillation (electric)		
Right	44	49
Left	41	40
Trail Making		
A	33	16
B	44	20

Note: DC, discontinued.

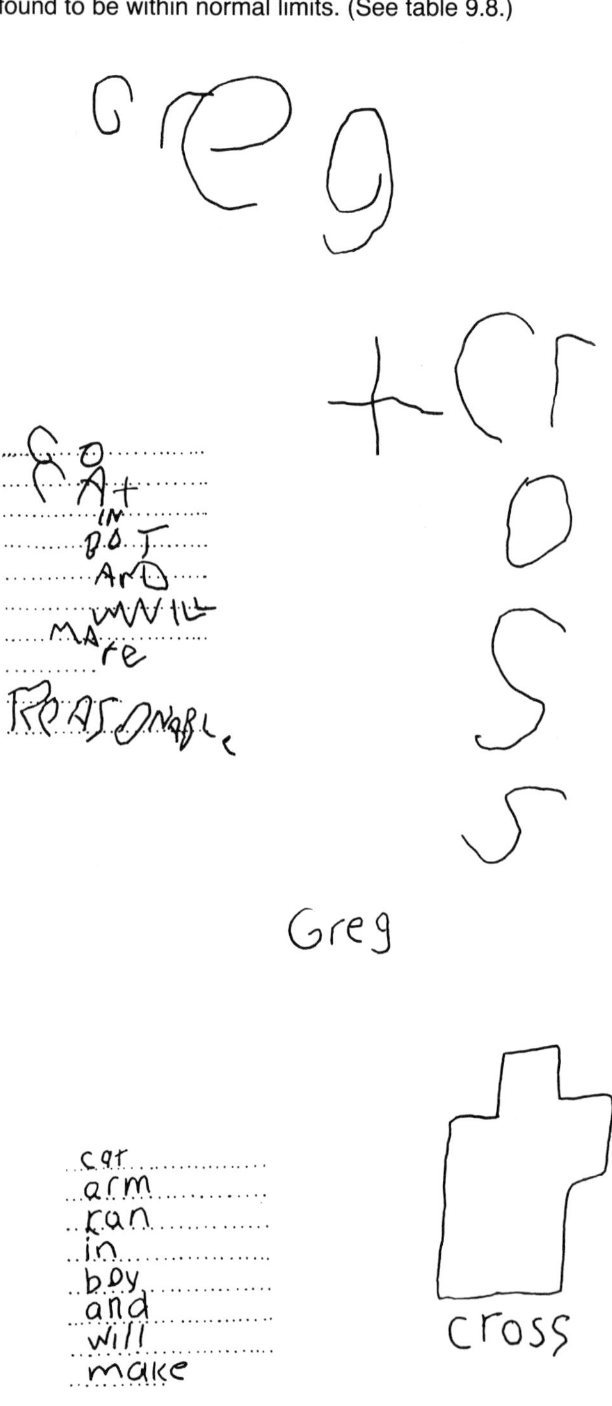

Case 5. When she was five years old, this child was diagnosed as having a grade 1 astrocytoma in the right temporal lobe. She had been having symptoms of seizure, headache, and dystaxia. Neuropsychological testing was undertaken at age seven when she entered kindergarten. Neuropsychological studies were somewhat difficult to do because of the patient's lack of cooperation, diminished attention span, and behavioral disturbance. Undoubtedly, the underlying cerebral dysfunction is a major factor in the expression of all these symptoms. The neuropsychological studies that were completed clearly indicate lateralized cerebral dysfunction in the right hemisphere, but also a general lowering of cognitive abilities. Clearly, the patient's verbal abilities are better than her spatial-perceptual-motor functioning. CAT scan results depicted the locus of focal pathology in the right temporal region, but there was also presence of prominent sylvian and interhemispheric fissures for a child this age, as well as density changes in frontal regions. These last findings are likely representative of the underlying structural defects responsible for the more generalized deficits noted on examination. Such structural changes are probably related to mechanical distortion and changes in intracranial pressure that may accompany tumor development. Note the significant deficit in arithmetic ability (on Wechsler Intelligence Scale for Children-Revised as well as achievement results). Such impairment is not uncommon with right hemisphere dysfunction and implicates a deficit in spatial processing and organization of arithmetic material.

Age 7 yrs. 4 mos.
Sex F
Education Kg.

Lateral Dominance Exam

	Eye	Hand	Foot
Right	X	X	X
Left			
Mixed			

Motor Examination:
Diminished motor coordination on left along with diminished strength. Cooperation could not be maintained to obtain accurate readings on FO and SOG tests.

Sensory Examination:
Left side neglect to tactile stimulation present. Would not cooperate in testing for stereognosis and graphesthesia.

Language Examination:
No specific dysphasic findings.
Achievement Scores
Word Recognition 1.1
Spelling 1.5
Arithmetic 0.1
Constructional deficits
Letter reversals in writing

Intellectual Functioning
WISC-R Results
FSIQ = 68

VIQ = 75	PIQ = 64
I 6	PC 5
S 7	PA 3
A 3	BD 2
V 8	OA 7
C 6	C 5
D 5	

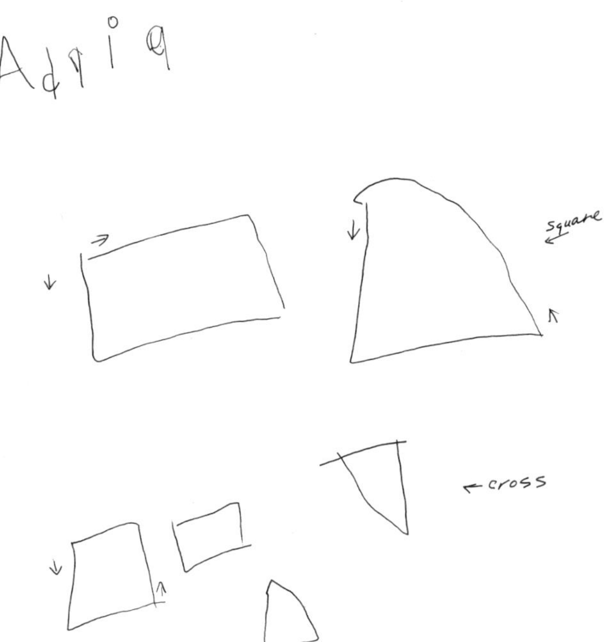

Fig. 9.21. Case 5.

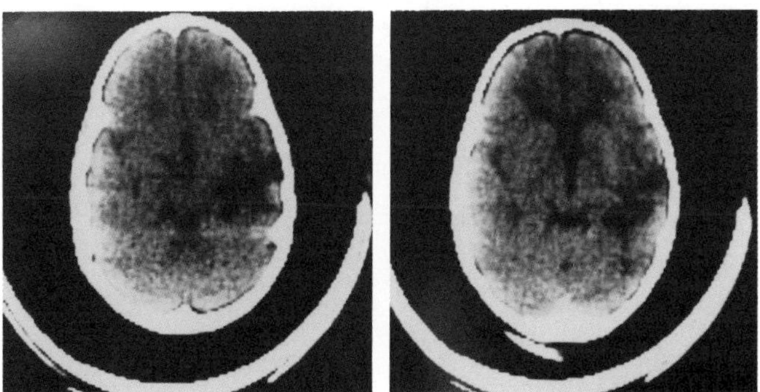

Fig. 9.22. Case 5.

Case 6. This ten-year-old fourth-grade male child was evaluated because of long-standing learning problems. He is right hand preferred for writing but shows mixed hand preference on other tasks. Motor developmental milestones were all within normal limits, but verbal milestones were slightly delayed as an infant. However, by school age the child was noticed to have severe impairment in terms of letter recognition abilities, had difficulty in learning letter sequences, and could not recite the alphabet. Motor skills continued to develop without any deficit, and by age ten he was an accomplished soccer player. Neuropsychological studies conducted at age ten reflect continued severe language-related deficits suggestive of posterior left hemispheric dysfunction. Note this child's poor performance on visual-verbal discrimination tasks (i.e., impaired Speech Sounds Perception Test) but not in auditory discrimination per se (i.e., normal Seashore Rhythm Test). This child also displays bilateral sensory-perceptual deficits on finger recognition, finger graphesthesia, and stereognosis testing. Note also the poor performance on logical memory subtest of the Wechsler Memory Scale but relatively intact ability to memorize word pairs (associate learning subtest). Such verbal sequential processing deficits in these children are commonplace. On aphasia screening, note the child's unusual spelling configurations. He can only either copy letters or words or write them from rote memory but has little ability to phonetically spell. Similarly, on the Durrell the child displays significant deficits in sight reading, word recognition, word analysis, and visual memory, but performs well within normal limits in terms of passive listening comprehension. No significant motor abnormalities were noted on neuropsychological testing. According to Boder's classification scheme, this child would be classified as a dysphonetic-dyseidetic dyslexic. EEG studies indicate left posterior temporal-parietal focus, consistent with the imputed locus of involvement as would be inferred from some of the neuropsychological studies. CAT scanning of the brain was normal.

Lateral Dominance Examination

	Eye	Hand	Foot
Right	X		
Left			X
Mixed		X	

Motor Examination:

FOD 33 SOGD 24 TPTD 4.3 (6 form board)
FOND 31 SOGND 23 TPTND 2.5
TPT Both 1.5

Sensory Perceptual Examination:

Bilateral errors on graphesthesia, finger gnosis and stereognosis

Language Evaluation:

Achievement Testing:

WRAT Results
- Reading 4.2
- Spelling 3.5
- Arithmetic 3.7

Durrell Analysis of Reading Difficulty Results
- Oral Reading 2M
- Silent Reading 2H
- Listening Comprehension 4M
- Listening Vocabulary 2H
- Word Recognition 3H
- Word Analysis 3H
- Visual Memory 2M

Speech Sounds Perception Test
34 errors

Seashore Rhythm Test
3 errors

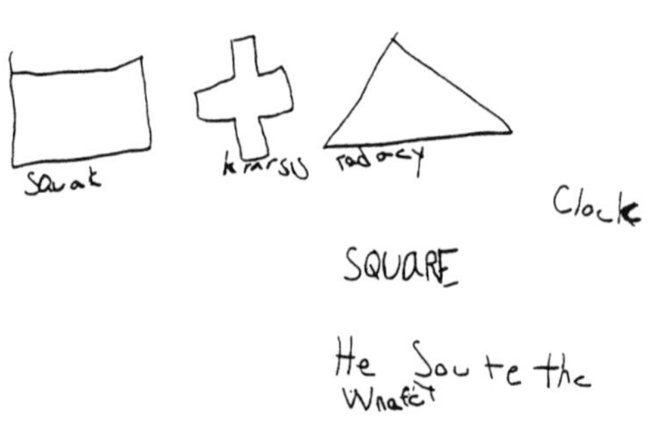

85
-27
58

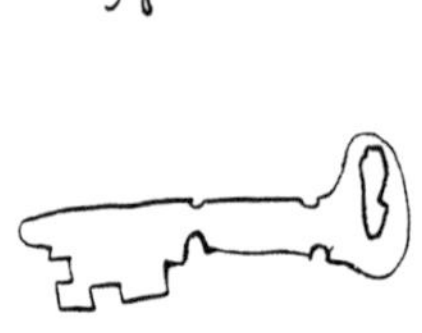

Memory Examination:

Wechsler Memory Scale Results
LM 4.5, Digits 7, VM 5, AL 12

Benton Visual Retention Test
10 correct, 3 errors

Cognitive/Intellectual Functioning:

WISC-R Results
VIQ = 91 FSIQ = 92
I 7 D 6, V 8, A 10, C 10, S 8
PIQ = 96
PC 10, PA 11, BD 10, OA 7, DS 10

Case 7. At age ten this male child was accidentally shot in the right frontal area with a .22-caliber pistol. The bullet entered the right frontal region transversing much of the right hemisphere and lodging in the right parietal bone area (see CAT scan films, note that the damage is essentially exclusive to the right hemisphere; what is visualized in the CAT scan is bone and metallic fragments as well as diffuse hemorrhage). Neuropsychological studies were conducted one month (in italics) following the accidental injury and at one year. Aphasia screening results are also presented for the initial examination (on the left) and the one-year followup on the right. The visual memory subtest of the Wechsler Memory Scale is also presented for the initial examination (on the left) and for the one-year followup. In the one-year followup visual memory test, the stimulus figure designs are presented in the lower right corner of each figure. On visual memory note the impoverished figures, not only during the initial exam, but on followup. This child has substantial visual memory deficits. Surprisingly, the constructional graphomotor deficits are not that prominent on the aphasia screening test despite rather generalized right hemispheric dysfunction. Results of neuropsychological testing display deficits primarily in all visuomotor, visuospatial, and visual memory categories, all deficits that would be expected given the child's generalized right hemispheric dysfunction. The child displays significant motor dysprosodic deficits. He is also unable to perform the TPT with the unaffected right side. Despite these rather marked impairments, note the intactness of the child's verbal/language abilities. Also note that the only achievement deficits seen with this child are in arithmetic tasks. It is not uncommon for children with right hemispheric dysfunction to display impaired arithmetic abilities, this being related to the role of right hemisphere gestalt factors in processing mathematical operations. Also contrast this case with case 6 in comparison of the difference between left and right hemisphere involvement as it may affect verbal language abilities. Although this child has received extensive occupational therapy, the neuropsychological test results at one year posttrauma are suggestive of rather substantial residual deficit that will likely be permanent.

Lateral Dominance Examination

	Eye	Hand	Foot
Right	X	X	X
Left			
Mixed			

Motor Examination:

FOD (39) 33 SOGD (3) 16 TPTD (DC unable to do)
FOND (0) 0 SOGND (0) 8 TPTD (DC unable to do)
Left side hemiparesis present, greater in upper extremity than lower

Sensory Perceptual Examination:

Visual field full
No visual extinction
Left side tactile extinction, left side astereognosis, agraphesthesia and finger agnosia that was unchanged over the 2 examinations.
Mild left ear auditory extinction

Language Evaluation:

No dysphasic deficits
Achievement Testing
WRAT Results
Reading(6.0) 6.5
Spelling (5.4) 6.4
Arithmetic (3.5) 4.1

Speech sounds perception test:
(DC) 7 errors

Seashore rhythm test:
(DC) 4 errors

Memory Examination:
Wechsler Memory Scale
LM (4.5) 4.5, Digits (10) 8, Visual Memory (1) 2, AL (6.5) 14

Benton visual retention test
Errors (DC) 10

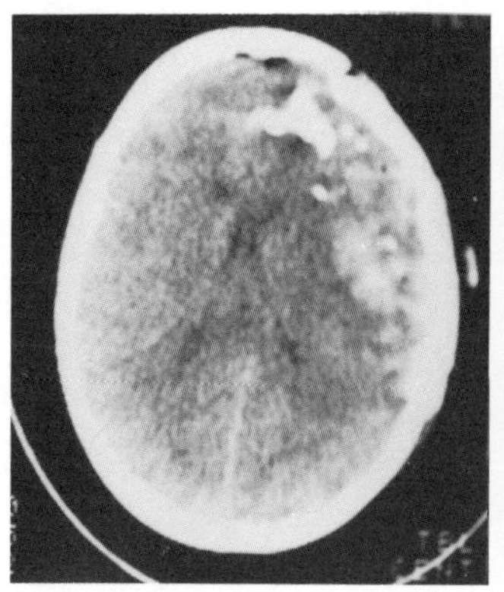

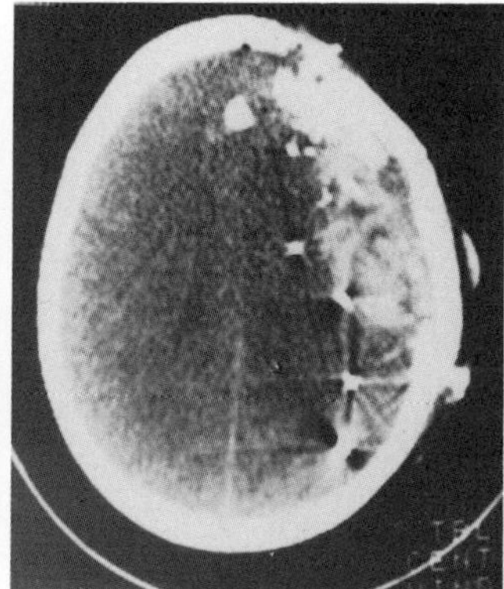

Fig. 9.23. Case 7.

Case 7. *(continued)*

Cognitive/Intellectual Functioning:
WISC-R Results
FSIQ = (73) 86

VIQ =(88) 96
I (7) 9, D (8)9, V (7) 8, A (8) 9, C (9) 8, S (10) 13

PIQ = (61) 78
PC (6) 8, PA (9) 11, BD (1) 6, OA (3) 4, C (1) 5

Trail Making Test:
A (75) 33 B (50) 248

Category Test
(DC) 79 errors

1 Month Post Injury

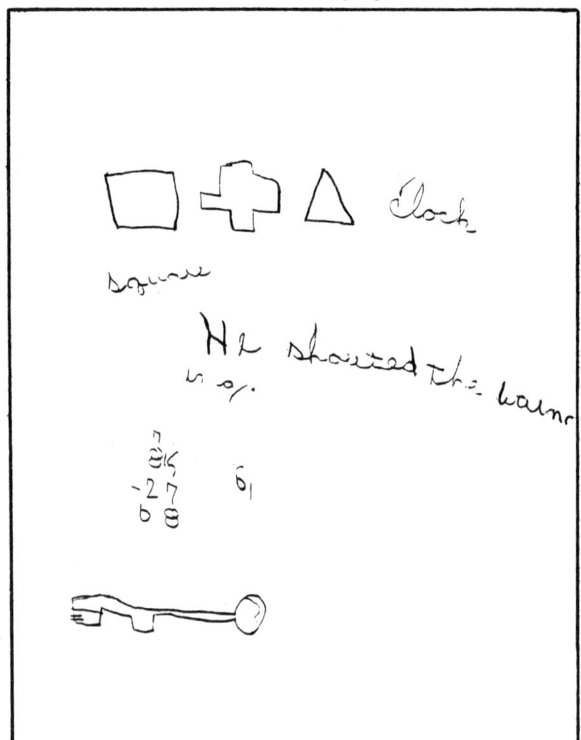

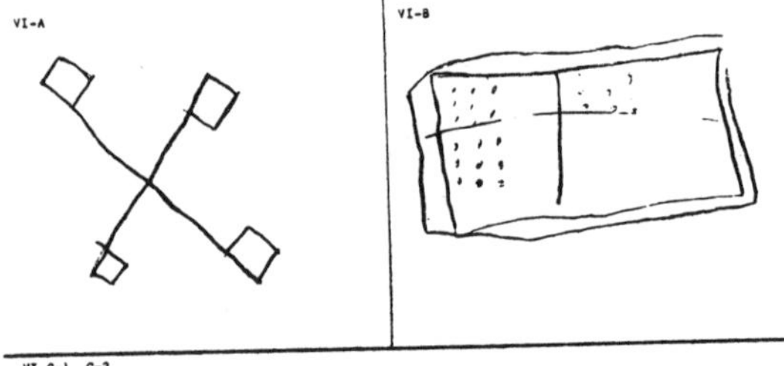

1 Year Post Injury

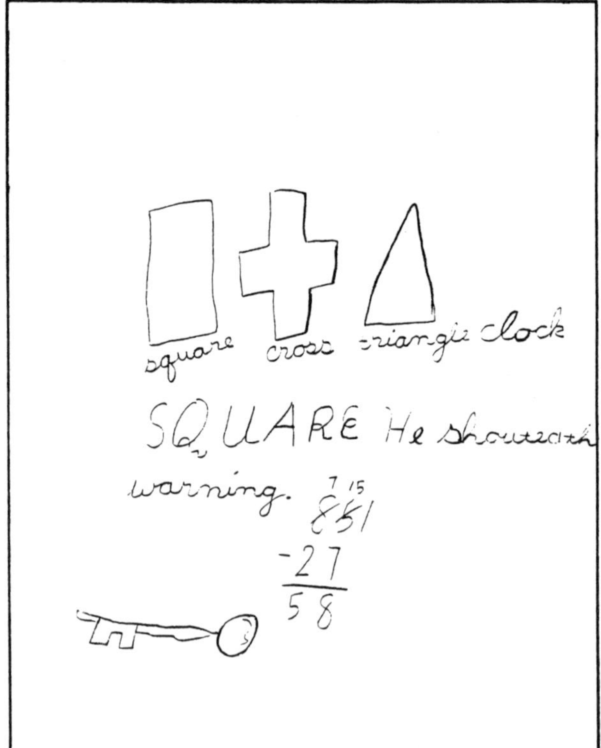

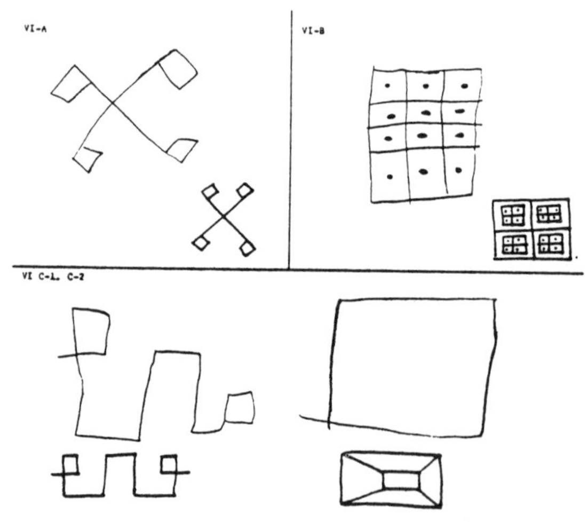

Case 8. This is a case of severe reading/spelling disorder that has been refractory to all remediation attempts. CAT scan demonstrates ventricular enlargement of the posterior horns of the lateral ventricles, bilaterally, suggesting possible surrounding dysplasic development in the posterior parietal-occipital region. The patient still had pronounced right-left confusion and was also inarticulate. At the time of the examination, he was 26 years of age. The patient was in special education all his life (until 20 years of age), and all forms of remediation have been attempted. He worked as a busboy in a restaurant. There would have been a more discrepant difference between his verbal and performance IQ had he not done so poorly on the digit symbol subtest, which is almost always affected in such patients. Note the normal performance on picture completion and object assembly; thus, when non-language and non–fine motor skill manipulation was required, the patient's basic perceptual processing abilities were intact. This case is one of bilateral posterior cerebral dysplasia associated with borderline IQ and pronounced learning disability, disproportionate to the lowered intellectual level. (The line with the cross hatches was this patient's attempt to do the math problem, 85 − 27 by counting it out by hand.) The patient's dyslexia is of a mixed dysphonetic-dyseidetic type, as determined by the Boder.

Age 26 years
Sex M
Education 12
(Special Ed.)

Lateral Dominance Exam

	Eye	Hand	Foot
Right	x	x	x
Left			
Mixed			

Motor Examination
FOD 47 SOGD 46
FOND 44 SOGND 44

Sensory Examination
Mild bilateral finger dysgraphesthesia.

Language Examination
Conversational speech: Inarticulate, halting speech
Comprehension: Concrete but normal comprehension for simple information
Repetition of spoken language: Normal
Confrontation - Naming: Normal
Reading: Alexic
WRAT-R Results
Reading grade level estimate < 3rd grade
Spelling grade level estimate < 3rd grade

Writing: Severe spelling dyspraxia
Calculations: Acalculic
WRAT-R
Arithmetic Results 3B

Memory Examination
WMS MQ = 74
LM 0, D 3, VM 2, AL 6

Intellectual/Cognitive Examination
FSIQ = 77, VIQ = 75, PIQ = 67
I 6, D 6, V 7, A 4, C 7, S 6, PC 10, PA 7, BD 7, OA 9, DS 4

Trails A 40 sec.
Trails B 121+ sec.

3 errors, patient quiet in frustration

85-27=

SQUARE

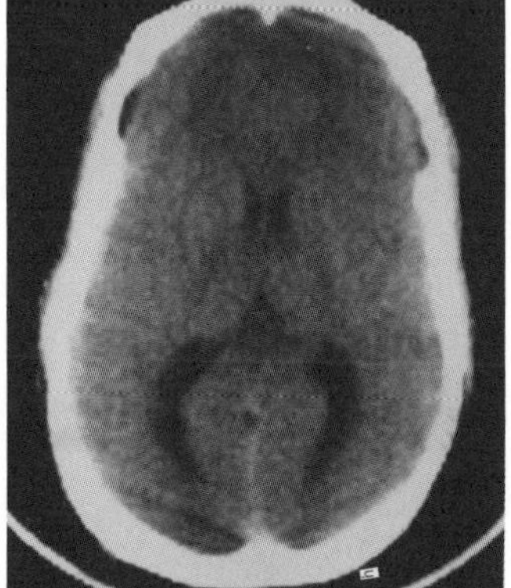

Fig. 9.24. Case 8.

Case 9. This 14-year-old male patient had a left frontal astrocytoma (grades I & II) removed from the left frontal region when 2 years of age. At age twelve, there was a recurrence of the tumor as well as a large cystic formation (films on left). The two CAT films on the right demonstrate the postsurgical changes in the left frontal region. Despite a dense right hemiplegia and hemisensory deficit and the extensive cerebral damage seen on the CAT results, this patient still had some isolated areas of intact functioning (e.g., grade appropriate reading). This case also demonstrates transfer of language function to the nondominant hemisphere when unilateral damage occurs in infancy to the dominant hemisphere.

Age 14 years 2 months
Sex M
Education 7th grade
(Special Ed.)

Lateral Dominance Exam

	Eye	Hand	Foot
Right			
Left	X	X	X
Mixed			

Motor Examination
Right side hemiplegia

FOD	35	SOGD	23.3
FOND	0	SOGND	0

Sensory Examination
Right side tactile sensory loss.
Hearing normal and no auditory extinctions to DSS.
Blind in left eye due to optic nerve compression.
Right hemianopia in the right eye due to left optic tract compression.

Language Examination
Conversational speech: Dysarthric
Comprehension: Intact
Repetition of Spoken Language: Intact
Confrontation - Naming: Intact
Reading WRAT Results
Reading grade level equivalent 7.6

Writing: Mild dysgraphia with distortion in size and form constructional dyspraxia

Calculations: Impaired
WRAT arithmetic results 3.6

Memory Examination
WMS MQ(estimate) = 57
LM 6, D 7, VM 3, AL 6.5
Benton 19 errors (8 left, 11 right)

Intellectual/Cognitive Examination
WISC-R Results: VIQ = 78, PIQ = 71
I 7, D 4, V 8, A 3, C 8, S 6, PC 1, PA 5, BD 2, OA 8, Cod (not done because of visual deficit)

Category Test: 93 errors
Raven's Test: 18/36

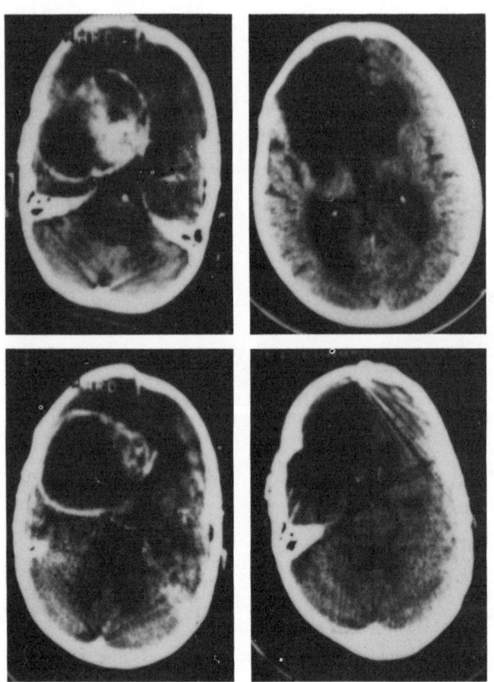

7 15
85
-27
58

Fig. 9.25. Case 9.

Appendix

Affricate: A consonant produced by first blocking airflow as for a stop and then slowly releasing the airflow, causing turbulence as in a fricative sound; for example, /ch/ as in cheese.

Grapheme: The sum of all written letters and letter combinations that represent one phoneme.

Lexicon: The words contained in a language and their semantic definitions.

Morpheme: The smallest meaningful unit of language, which occurs either as a word or within a word. For example, troubleshooting contains three morphemes, trouble-, -shoot-, and -ing. The acceptable use of words depends upon the morphemes they contain. Morphemes may be words or be appended to words; for example: verb endings, -ed, -ing; noun modifiers, -es, -s; adverb endings, -ly; and adjective modifiers, -er, -est.

Morphology: The morphemes contained in a language and the system of rules followed by speakers when combining morphemes in phrases.

Palatal fricative: A consonant made by partially blocking airflow between the palate and tongue, causing air turbulence and resulting in a sound; for example, /sh/ as in shoe.

Phoneme: A distinct sound unit recognized by speakers of a language. There are 46 phonemes in English: 9 vowels and 37 consonants.

Phonology: The speech sounds of a language and the rules followed by speakers when combining and pronouncing speech sounds.

Semantics: The meanings in words and phrases. For example, in English it would be unacceptable to say "bachelor's wife" since the two words are contradictory in meaning. Further, the sentence "The baseball bat hit the girl" is unacceptable since the baseball bat is not an animate object.

Syntactic structure: Descriptions of the structural relationships between words in a sentence—the representations of the grammatical pattern of a sentence; for example, "The man is going to the store" consists of Noun Phrase + Aux + Verb-ing + Prep + Noun Phrase.

Syntactic transformations: Rules that serve as definitions of the structures of different sentence types in a language. These rules describe the relationships between words, the overall form of sentences, and how simple sentences are changed from one type to another, such as questions, commands, passives, and embedded sentences. For example, transformations of the sentence "You are holding the boy up" are: question, "Are you holding the boy up?"; command, "Hold the boy up"; passive, "The boy is being held up by you"; and embedded sentence, "I can see that you are holding the boy up."

Unacceptable grammaticality: Syntactic structures or sentences that are recognized by native speakers of the language as not being well formed. Such sentences do not follow the rules for forming syntactic structures in a language.

Verb phrase: The part of a sentence that contains the verb (the predicate) as well as all words, clauses, and sentences modifying the verb. The verb phrase is [italicized] in each of the following sentences: "The man *won't go to the store today*"; "The girl *should see the man going to the store*"; and "They *had been dancing every dance when the club closed.*"

Voiceless bilabial (stop): A consonant made by occluding airflow completely at the lips, letting pressure build up, then releasing it in a sudden burst. The only voiceless bilabial stop in English is /p/.

References

Abikoff, H., and R. Gittelman. 1985. Hyperactive children treated with stimulants. *Archives of General Psychiatry* 42:953–961.

Achenbach, T., and A. Edelbrock. 1983. *The child behavior checklist-revised.* Burlington, VT: Queen City Printers.

Adams, R. D., and M. Victor. 1977. *Principles of neurology*. New York: McGraw-Hill.

Alajovanine, T., and F. Lhermitte. 1965. Acquired aphasia in children. *Brain* 88:653–662.

Albert, M. L., H. Goodglass, N. A. Helm, A. B. Rubens, and M. P. Alexander. 1981. *Clinical aspects of dysphasia*. Disorders of Human Communications vol. 2. New York: Springer-Verlag.

Anastasi, A. 1969. *Psychological testing*. 3d ed. London: Macmillan Co.

Barkley, R. A. 1981. *Hyperactive children*. New York: Guilford Press.

Beery, K. 1982. *Revised administration, scoring, and teaching manual for the developmental test of visual motor integration*. Cleveland, OH: Modern Curriculum Press.

Behar, D., J. L. Rapoport, C. J. Berg, M. B. Denckla, L. Mann, C. Cox, P. Fedio, T. Zahn, and M. G. Wolfman. 1984. Computerized tomography and neuropsychological test measures in adolescents with obsessive-compulsive disorder. *American Journal of Psychiatry* 141:363–369.

Bell, W. E. 1982. Central nervous system infections in childhood. *Seminars in Neurology* 2:1–123.

Bellak, L., and E. Charles. 1979. Schizophrenic syndrome related to minimal brain dysfunction: A possible neurologic subgroup. *Schizophrenia Bulletin* 5:480–489.

Belman, A. L., M. H. Ultmann, D. Horoupian, B. Novick, A. J. Spiro, A. Rubinstein, D. Kurtzberg, and B. Cone-Wesson. 1985. Neurological complications in infants and children with acquired immune deficiency syndrome. *Annals of Neurology* 18:560–566.

Benson, D. F. 1979. *Aphasia, alexia, and agraphia*. New York: Churchill Livingstone.

Benton, A. L. 1984. Dyslexia and spatial thinking. *Annals of Dyslexia* 34:69–84.

———. 1974. *The revised visual retention test*. 4th ed. New York: Psychological Corporation.

Bigler, E. D. 1980. Child and adolescent neuropsychology. In *Emotional disturbance*, ed. J. E. Gilliam. Austin: University of Texas.

———. 1987. The role of neuropsychological assessment in relation to other types of assessment with children. In *Assessment issues in child neuropsychology*, ed. M. G. Tramontana and S. R. Hooper. New York: Plenum Press.

Bigler, E. D., and R. I. Naugle. 1985. Case studies in cerebral plasticity. *International Journal of Clinical Neuropsychology* 7:12–23.

Bigler, E. D., and N. L. Nussbaum. 1988. Child neuropsychology in the private medical practice. In *Handbook of child clinical neuropsychology*, ed. C. R. Reynolds. New York: Plenum Press.

Boder, E., and S. Jarrico. 1982. *Boder reading-spelling pattern test: A diagnostic screening test for developmental dyslexia*. New York: Grune & Stratton.

Boll, T. J., and J. T. Barth. 1981. Neuropsychology of brain damage in children. In *Handbook of clinical neuropsychology*, ed. S. B. Filskov and T. J. Boll. New York: John Wiley & Sons.

Bray, P. 1969. *Pediatric neurology*. Chicago: Year Book Medical Publishers.

Brink, J. D., A. L. Garrett, W. R. Hale, J. Woo-Sam, and V. L. Nickel. 1970. Recovery of motor and intellectual function in children sustaining severe injuries. *Developmental Medicine & Child Neurology* 12:565–571.

Brown, C. C., and T. B. Brazelton. 1974. *Infants at risk: Assessment and intervention*. Piscataway, NJ: Johnson & Johnson.

Brown, J. W. 1974. *Aphasia, apraxia, and agnosia*. Springfield, IL: Charles C. Thomas.

Buda, F. B. 1981. *The neurology of developmental disabilities*. Springfield, IL: Charles C. Thomas.

Cantwell, D. P., and L. Baker. 1977. Psychiatric disorder in children with speech and language retardation. *Archives of General Psychiatry* 34:583–591.

Caparulo, B. K., D. J. Cohen, S. L. Rothman, J. G. Young, J. D. Katz, S. E. Shaywitz, and B. A. Shaywitz. 1981. Computed tomographic brain scanning in children with developmental neuropsychiatric disorders. *Journal of the American Academy of Child Psychiatry* 20:338–357.

Chadwick, O., M. Rutter, D. Shaffer, and P. E. Shrout. 1981. A prospective study of children with head injuries. IV, Specific cognitive deficits. *Journal of Clinical Neuropsychology* 3:101–120.

Chasnoff, I. J., W. J. Burns, S. H. Schnoll, and K. A. Burns. 1985. Cocaine use in pregnancy. *New England Journal of Medicine* 313:666–669.

Chelune, G. J., and P. Edwards. 1981. Early brain lesions: Ontogenetic-environmental considerations. *Journal of Consulting and Clinical Psychology* 49:777–790.

Chugani, H. T., and M. E. Phelps. 1986. Maturational changes in cerebral function in infants determined by FDG positron emission tomography. *Science* 231:840–843.

Connolly, A. J., W. Nachtman, and E. M. Pritchett. 1976. *Key math diagnostic arithmetic test*. Circle Pines, MN: American Guidance Service.

Cummings, C., D. Flynn, and M. Preus. 1982. Increased morphological variants in children with learning disabilities. *Journal of Autism and Developmental Disorders* 12:373–383.

Damasio, A. R., and R. G. Maurer, 1978. A neurological model for childhood autism. *Archives of Neurology* 35:777–786.

Damasio, H., R. G. Maurer, A. R. Damasio, and H. C. Chui. 1980. Computerized tomographic scan findings in patients with autistic behavior. *Archives of Neurology* 37:504–510.

Dargassies, S. S. 1981. Neurological examination of the neonate for silent abnormalities. In *Infants at risk: Assessment and intervention*, ed. C. C. Brown and T. B. Brazelton. Piscataway, NJ: Johnson & Johnson.

David, R., R. Devel, P. Ferry, G. Gascon, G. Golden, I. Rapin, P. Rosenberger, and B. Shaywitz. 1981. *Proposed nosology of disorders of higher cerebral function in children*. N.p.: Child Neurology Society.

DeLisi, L. E., L. R. Goldin, J. R. Hamovit, E. Maxwell, D. Kurtz, and E. S. Gershon. 1986. A family study of the association of increased ventricular size with schizophrenia. *Archives of General Psychiatry* 43:148–153.

Denckla. M. B. 1983. The neuropsychology of social-emotional learning disabilities. *Archives of Neurology* 40:461–463.

Denckla, M. B., M. LeMay, and C. A. Chapman. 1984. Few CT scan abnormalities found even in neurologically impaired learning disabled children. *Journal of Learning Disabilities* 18:132–135.

Dennis, M. 1981. Language in a congenitally acallosal brain. *Brain and Language* 12:33–53.

Dennis, M., C. R. Fitz, C. T. Netley, J. Sugar, D. C. F. Harwood-Nash, E. B. Hendrick, J. H. Hoffman, and R. P. Humphreys. 1981. The intelligence of hydropcephalic children. *Archives of Neurology* 38:607–615.

De Obaldia, R., and O. A. Parsons. 1984. Relationship of neuropsychological performance to primary alcoholism and self-reported symptoms of childhood minimal brain dysfunction. *Journal of Studies in Alcohol* 45:386–392.

Devel, R. K., and C. C. Moran. Cerebral dominance and cerebral asymmetries on computed tomogram in children. *Neurology* 9:934–938.

Diagnostic and statistical manual (DSM-III). 1980. Washington: American Psychiatric Association.

DiLeo, J. H. 1983. *Interpreting children's drawings*. New York: Brunner/Mazel.

Dreifuss, F. P. 1975. The pathology of central communicative disorders in children. In *The nervous system: Human communication and its disorders*, ed. D. B. Tower. Vol. 3. New York: Raven Press.

Duffy, F. H., M. B. Denckla, P. H. Bartels, and G. Sandini. 1980. Dyslexia: Regional differences in brain electrical activity by topographic mapping. *Annals of Neurology* 7:412–420.

Duffy, F. H., M. B. Denckla, P. H. Bartels, G. Sandini, and L. S. Kiessling. 1980. Dyslexia: Automated diagnosis by computerized classification of brain electrical activity. *Annals of Neurology* 7:421–428.

Durrell, D. D., and J. H. Catterson. 1980. *Durrell analysis of reading difficulty*. New York: Psychological Corporation.

Ehrfurth, J. W. 1981. Dominant hemisphere dysfunction in schizophrenia: A neuropsychological investigation. Doctoral dissertation. University of Texas at Austin.

Ford, F. R. 1976. *Diseases of the nervous system in infancy, childhood, and adolescence*. Springfield, IL: Charles C. Thomas.

Gaddes, W. H. 1980. *Learning disabilities and brain function: A neuropsychological approach*. New York: Springer-Verlag.

Galaburda, A. M., and T. L. Kemper. 1979. Cytoarchitectonic abnormalities in developmental dyslexia: A case study. *Annals of Neurology* 6:94–100.

Galaburda, A. M., G. F. Sherman, G. D. Rosen, F. Aboitiz, and N. Geschwind. 1985. Developmental dyslexia: Four consecutive patients with cortical anomalies. *Annals of Neurology* 18:222–233.

Geschwind, N. 1979. Anatomical foundations of language and dominance. In *The neurological bases of language disorders in children: Methods and directions for research*, ed. C. L. Ludlow and M. E. Doran-Quine. National Institute of Neurological and Communicative Disorders and Stroke Monograph, no. 22. Bethesda, MD.

———. 1984. The brain of a learning-disabled individual. *Annals of Dyslexia* 34:319–327.

Gittelman, R., S. Mannuzza, R. Shenker, and N. Bonagura. 1985. Hyperactive boys almost grown up. *Archives of General Psychiatry* 42:937–947.

Goldberg, T. E., and R. D. Rothermel, Jr. 1984. Hyperlexic children reading. *Brain* 107:759–785.

Golden, C. J., B. Graber, J. Coffman, R. A. Berg, D. B. Newlin, and S. Bloch. 1981. Structural brain deficits in schizophrenia. *Archives of General Psychiatry* 38:1014–1020.

Gregory, I., and D. J. Smeltzer. 1977. *Psychiatry*. Boston: Little, Brown & Co.

Harcherik, D. F., D. J. Cohen, S. Ort, R. Paul, B. A. Shaywitz, F. R. Volkmar, S. L. G. Rothman, and J. F. Leckman. 1985. Computed tomographic brain scanning in four neuropsychiatric disorders of childhood. *American Journal of Psychiatry* 142:731–734.

Heiskanen, O., and M. Kaste. 1974. Late prognosis of severe brain injury in children. *Developmental Medicine and Child Neurology* 16:11–14.

Hier, D. B., M. LeMay, P. B. Rosenberger, and V. P. Perlo. 1978. Developmental dyslexia: Evidence for a subgroup with a reversal of cerebral asymmetry. *Archives of Neurology* 35:90–92.

Holmes, C. S. 1986. Neuropsychological profiles in men with insulin dependent diabetes. *Journal of Consulting and Clinical Psychology* 54:386–389.

Holmes, G. L., and W. J. Logan. 1980. A syndrome of infantile CNS degeneration. *American Journal of Diseases of Childhood* 134:262–266.

Hynd, G. W., and J. E. Obrzut. 1981. *Neuropsychological assessment and the school-age child*. New York: Grune & Stratton.

Ingram, T. T. S. 1969. Developmental disorders in speech. In *Handbook of clinical neurology*, vol. 4, ed. P. J. Vinken and G. W. Bruyn. Amsterdam: North-Holland.

Ishii, R., S. Takeuchi, K. Ibayashi, and R. Tanaka. 1984. Intelligence in children with moyamoya disease: Evaluation after surgical treatments with special reference to changes in cerebral blood flow. *Stroke* 15:873–879.

Jasktak, J., and S. Jasktak. 1965. *The wide range achievement test manual*. Wilmington, DE: Guidance Associates.

Johnston, R. B., R. E. Stark, E. D. Mellits, and P. Tallal. 1981. Neurological status of language-impaired and normal children. *Annals of Neurology* 10:159–163.

Kaufman, A., and N. Kaufman. 1983. *Kaufman assessment battery for children: Administration and interpretive manual*. Circle Pines, MN: American Guidance Service.

Kinsbourne, M. 1974. Mechanisms of hemispheric interaction in man. In *Hemispheric disconnection and cerebral function*, ed. M. Kinsbourne and W. L. Smith. Springfield, IL: Charles C. Thomas.

Klonoff, H. 1971. Head injuries in children: Predisposing factors, accident conditions, accident proneness, and sequelae. *American Journal of Public Health* 61:2405–2417.

Knights, R. M., and D. J. Bakker. 1976. *The neuropsychology of learning disorders: Theoretical approaches*. Baltimore: University Park Press.

Knights, R., and J. Norwood. 1980. *Revised smoothed normative data on the neuropsychological test battery for children*. Ottawa: R. M. Knights Psychological Consultants.

Kohn, B., and M. Dennis. 1974. Patterns of hemispheric specialization after hemidecortication for infantile hemiplegia. In *Hemispheric disconnection and cerebral function*, ed. M. Kinsbourne and W. L. Smith. Springfield, IL: Charles C. Thomas.

Kovnar, E. H., W. S. Coxe, and J. J. Volpe. 1984. Normal neurologic development and marked reconstitution of cerebral mantle after postnatal treatment of intrauterine hydrocephalus. *Neurology* 34:840–846.

Lacey, D. J. 1985. Inability to verify parasagittal cerebral injury as a neuropathologic entity in the asphyxiated term neonate. *Pediatric Neurology* 1:100–103.

Lassonde, M. C., J. Lortie, M. Ptito, and G. Geoffrey. 1981. Hemispheric asymmetry in callosal agenesis as revealed by dichotic listening performance. *Neuropsychologia* 19:455–458.

Leisman, G., and M. Ashkenazi. 1980. Aetiological factors in dyslexia. IV, Cerebral hemispheres are functionally equivalent. *International Journal of Neuroscience* 11:157–164.

Levin, M. D., and F. Oberklaid. 1980. Hyperactivity. *American Journal of Diseases of Childhood*. 134:409–413.

Levine, D. N., and J. P. Mohr. 1979. Language after bilateral cerebral infarctions: Role of the minor hemisphere in speech. *Neurology* 29:927–938.

Lewandowski, L. J., and P. J. De Rienzo. 1985. WISC-R and K-ABC performances of hemiplegic children. *Journal of Psychoeducational Assessment* 3:215–221.

Lindgren, S. D. 1978. Finger localization and the prediction of reading disability. *Cortex* 15:87–101.

Lou, H. C., L. Henriksen, and P. Bruhn. 1984. Focal cerebral hypoperfusion in children with dysphasia and/or attention deficit disorder. *Archives of Neurology* 41:825–829.

Lubchenco, L. O. 1981. Gestational age, birth weight, and the high-risk infant. In *Infants at risk: Assessment and intervention*, ed. C. C. Brown and T. B. Brazelton. Piscataway, NJ: Johnson & Johnson.

Luchins, D. J., D. R. Weinberger, and R. J. Wyatt. 1979. Schizophrenia: Evidence of a subgroup with reversed cerebral asymmetry. *Archives of General Psychiatry* 36:1309–1311.

Ludlow, C. L. 1980. Children's language disorders: Recent research advances. *Annals of Neurology* 7:487–507.

Lynn, R. B., D. C. Buchanan, G. M. Fenichel, and R. R. Freemon. 1980. Agenesis of the corpus callosum. *Archives of Neurology* 37:444–445.

McCall, R. B. 1981. Predicting developmental outcome: Resume and redirection. In *Infants at risk: Assessment and intervention*, ed. C. C. Brown and T. B. Brazelton. Piscataway, NJ: Johnson & Johnson.

Marcus, J., S. L. Hans, S. A. Mednick, F. Schulsinger, and N. Michelsen. 1985. Neurological dysfunctioning in offspring of schizophrenics in Israel and Denmark. *Archives of General Psychiatry* 42:753–761.

Menkes, J. H. 1974. *Textbook of child neurology*. Philadelphia: Lea & Febiger.

Miller, V., and E. D. Bigler. 1982. Neuropsychological findings in tuberous sclerosis. *Clinical Neuropsychology* 4:26–34.

Morris, J. M., and E. D. Bigler. 1987. Hemispheric functioning and the K-ABC: Results in neurologically impaired children.

Murray, M. E. 1979. Minimal brain dysfunction and borderline personality adjustment. *American Journal of Psychotherapy* 33:391–403.

Myklebust, H. R. 1954. *Auditory disorders in children: A manual for differential diagnosis*. New York: Grune & Stratton.

Nass, R. 1985. Mirror movement asymmetries in congenital hemiparesis: The inhibition hypothesis revisited. *Neurology* 35:1059–1062.

Nussbaum, N. L. 1986. Personality/behavioral characteristics of children with various patterns of functional cerebral asymmetry. Doctoral dissertation. University of Texas at Austin.

Nussbaum, N. L., and E. D. Bigler. 1986. Neuropsychological and behavioral profiles of empirically derived subgroups of learning disabled children. *International Journal of Clinical Neuropsychology* 8:82–89.

Nussbaum, N. L., E. D. Bigler, and W. Koch. 1986. Neuropsychologically derived subgroups of learning disabled children: Personality/behavioral dimensions. *Journal of Research and Development in Education* 19:57–66.

O'Donnell, J. P., J. Kurtz, and N. V. Ramanaiah. 1983. Neuropsychological test findings for normal, learning-disabled, and brain-damaged young adults. *Journal of Consulting and Clinical Psychology* 51:726–729.

Ornitz, E. M., C. W. Atwell, A. R. Kaplan, and J. R. Westlake. 1985. Brain-stem dysfunction in autism. *Archives of General Psychiatry* 42:1018–1025.

Orsini, D. L., and P. Satz. 1986. A syndrome of pathological left-handedness. *Archives of Neurology* 43:333–337.

Piran, N., and E. D. Bigler. 1981. A neuropsychological investigation of the theory of schizophrenia. Paper presented at the Annual Meeting of the American Psychological Association, Los Angeles, CA.

Piran, N., E. D. Bigler, and D. Cohen. 1982. Ocular dominance and motor laterality in schizophrenia suggests a unique cerebral asymmetry. *Archives of General Psychiatry* 39:1006–1010.

Pirozzolo, F. J., P. H. Pirozzolo, and R. B. Ziman. 1979. Neuropsychological assessment of callosal agenesis: Report of a case with normal intelligence and absence of the disconnection syndrome. *Clinical Neuropsychology* 1:13–16.

Pugh, M., and E. D. Bigler. 1986. Schizophrenia and prior history of "MBD": Neuropsychological findings. *International Journal of Clinical Neuropsychology* 8:22–26.

Raven, J. G. 1965. *Guide to using the Coloured Progressive Matrices*. London: H. K. Lewis & Co.

Raven, J. G., J. H. Court, and J. Raven. 1976. *Manual for Raven's Progressive Matrices and Vocabulary scales*. London: H. K. Lewis Co.

Reitan, R. M., and L. A. Davison. 1974. *Clinical neuropsychology: Current status and application*. Washington: Winston.

Reitan, R. M., and S. Herring. 1985. A short screening device for identification of cerebral dysfunction in children. *Journal of Clinical Psychology* 41:643–650.

Reitan, R. M., and D. Wolfson. 1985. *The Halstead-Reitan neuropsychological test battery: Theory and clinical interpretation*. Tucson, AZ: Neuropsychology Press.

Rie, H. E., and E. D. Rie. 1980. *Handbook of minimal brain dysfunctions*. New York: John Wiley & Sons.

Ritvo, E. R., B. J. Freeman, A. B. Scheibel, T. Duong, H. Robinson, D. Guthrie, and A. Ritvo. 1986. Lower Purkinje cell counts in the cerebella of four autistic subjects: Initial findings of the UCLA-NSAC autopsy research report. *American Journal of Psychiatry* 143:862–866.

Rosenthal, J. H., E. Boder, and E. Callaway. 1982. Typology of developmental dyslexia: Evidence for its construct validity. In *Reading disorders*, ed. R. N. Malatesha and P. G. Aaron. New York: Academic Press.

Ross, E. D., J. H. Harney, C. deLacoste-Utamsing, and P. D. Purdy. 1981. How the brain integrates affective and propositional language into a unified behavioral function. *Archives of Neurology* 38:745–748.

Ross, E. D., and A. J. Rush, 1981. Diagnosis and neuroanatomical correlates of depression in brain damaged patients. *Archives of General Psychiatry*. 38:1344–1354.

Rourke, B. P. 1981. Neuropsychological assessment of children with learning disabilities. In *Handbook of clinical neuropsychology*, ed. S. B. Filskov and T. J. Boll. New York: John Wiley & Sons.

Rourke, B. P., J. L. Fisk, and J. D. Strang. 1986. *Neuropsychological assessment of children*. New York: Guilford Press.

Russell, E., C. Neuringer, and G. Goldstein. 1970. *Assessment of brain damage: A neuropsychological key approach*. New York: Wiley-Interscience.

Ryan, C., A. Vega, C. Longstreet, and A. Drash. 1984. Neuropsychological changes in adolescents with insulin-dependent diabetes. *Journal of Consulting and Clinical Psychology* 52:335–342.

Satz, P., and J. M. Fletcher. 1981. Emergent trends in neuropsychology: An overview. *Journal of Consulting and Clinical Psychology* 49:851–865.

Saunders, T. R. 1979. A critical analysis of the minimal brain dysfunction syndrome. *Professional Psychology* 293–306.

Schuckit, M. A., J. Petrich, and J. Chiles. 1978. Hyperactivity: Diagnostic confusion. *Journal of Nervous and Mental Diseases* 166:79–87.

Schwartz, J. E., E. Kaplan, and A. R. Schwartz. 1981. Childhood dyscalculia and Gerstmann's syndrome: A clinical and statistical analysis. *Neurology* 31:81.

Searleman, A. 1977. A review of right hemisphere linguistic capabilities. *Psychological Bulletin* 84:503–528.

Shaffer, D., I. Schonfeld, P. A. O'Connor, C. Stokman, P. Trautman, S. Shafer, and S. Ng. 1985. Neurological soft signs. *Archives of General Psychiatry* 42:342–351.

Shaywitz, B. A., S. E. Shaywitz, T. Byrne, D. J. Cohen, and S. Rothman. 1983. Attention deficit disorder: Quantitative analysis of CT. *Neurology* 33:1500–1503.

Shaywitz, S. E. 1982. The Yale neuropsychoeducational assessment scales. *Schizophrenia Bulletin* 8:360–424.

Shimizu, A., M. Endo, N. Yamaguchi, H. Torii, and K. Isaki. 1985. Hand preference in schizophrenics and handedness conversion in their childhood. *Acta Psychiatrica Scandinavia* 72:259–265.

Skenazy, J. A., and E. D. Bigler. 1984. Neuropsychological deficits in diabetes mellitus. *Journal of Clinical Psychology* 40:246–258.

———. 1985. Psychological adjustment and neuropsychological performance in diabetics. *Journal of Clinical Psychology* 41:391–396.

Spreen, O., and W. Gaddes. 1969. Developmental norms for fifteen neuropsychological tests for ages 6 to 15. *Cortex* 5:171–191.

Springer, S. P., and J. Eisenson, 1977. Hemispheric specialization for speech in language-disordered children. *Neuropsychologia* 15:287–293.

Sulik, K. K., M. C. Johnston, and M. A. Webb. 1981. Fetal alcohol syndrome: Embryogenesis in a mouse model. *Science* 214:936–938.

Symann-Lovett, N., G. G. Gascon, Y. Matsumaya, and L. T. Lombroso. 1977. Wave form difference in visual evoked responses between normal and reading disabled children. *Neurology* 27:156–159.

Tanaka, Y., H. Hazama, R. Kamahara, and K. Kobayashi. 1981. Computerized tomography of the brain in schizophrenic patients. *Acta Psychiatrica Scandinavia* 63:191–197.

Tartar, R. E., A. M. Hegedus, G. Goldstein, C. Shelly, and A. I. Alterman. 1984. Adolescent sons of alcoholics: Neuropsychological and personality characteristics. *Alcoholism* 8:216–222.

Taylor, H. G. 1983. MBD: Meanings and misconceptions. *Journal of Clinical Neuropsychology* 5:271–287.

Torrey, E. F. 1980. Neurologic abnormalities in schizophrenic patients. *Biological Psychiatry* 15:381–388.

Towbin, A. 1978. Cerebral dysfunctions related to perinatal organic damage: Clinical neuropathologic correlations. *Journal of Abnormal Psychology* 87:617–635.

Tramontana, M. G., S. D. Sherrets, and C. J. Golden. 1980. Brain dysfunction in youngsters with psychiatric disorders: Application of Selz-Reitan rules for neuropsychological diagnosis. *Clinical Neuropsychology* 3:118–123.

Tsai, L. Y. 1983. The relationship of handedness to the cognitive, language, and visuo-spatial skills of autistic patients. *British Journal of Psychiatry* 142:156–162.

VanDongen, H. R., C. B. Loonen, and K. F. VanDongen. 1985. Anatomical basis for acquired fluent aphasia in children. *Annals of Neurology* 17:306–309.

Vargha-Khadem, F., A. M. O'Gorman, and G. V. Watters. 1985. Aphasia and handedness in relation to hemispheric side, age at injury, and severity of cerebral lesion during childhood. *Brain* 108:677–696.

Vilensky, J. A., A. R. Damasio, and R. G. Maurer. 1981. Gait disturbance in patients with autistic behavior. *Archives of Neurology* 38:646–649.

Wechsler, D. 1974. *Wechsler Intelligence Scale for Children—Revised*. New York: Psychological Corporation.

Weinberg, W. A., and A. McLean. 1986. A diagnostic approach to developmental specific learning disorders. *Journal of Child Neurology* 1:158–172.

Weinberger, D. R., E. F. Torrey, A. N. Neophytides, R. J. Wyatt. 1979. Structural abnormalities in the cerebral cortex of chronic schizophrenic patients. *Archives of General Psychiatry* 36:935–939.

Weintraub, S., and M-M. Mesulam. 1983. Developmental learning disabilities of the right hemisphere. *Archives of Neurology* 40:463–468.

Weiss, G. 1985*a*. Hyperactivity. *Psychiatric Clinics of North America* 8:737–749.

———. 1985*b*. Pharmacotherapy for ADD-H adolescents workshop. *Psychopharmacology Bulletin* 21:169–177.

Weiss, G., L. Hechtman, T. Milroy, and T. Perlman. 1985. Psychiatric status of hyperactives as adults: A controlled prospective 15-year follow-up of 63 hyperactive children. *Journal of the American Academy of Child Psychiatry* 24:211–220.

West, J. R., C. A. Hodges, and A. C. Black. 1981. Prenatal exposure to ethanol alters the organization of hippocampal mossy fibers in rats. *Science* 211:957–958.

Whitehouse, D., and J. C. Harris. 1984. Hyperlexia in infantile autism. *Journal of Autism and Developmental Disorders* 14:281–289.

Wirt, R. D. Lachar, J. Klinedinst, and P. Seat. 1982. *The personality inventory for children, revised*. Los Angeles: Western Psychological Services.

Woods, B. T., and S. Carey. 1979. Language deficits after apparent clinical recovery from childhood aphasia. *Annals of Neurology* 6:405–409.

Woods, B. T., and H. L. Teubor. 1978. Changing patterns in childhood aphasia. *Annals of Neurology* 3:273–280.

Zaidel, E. 1979. The split and half brains as models of congenital language disability. In *The neurological bases of language disorders in children*, ed. C. L. Ludlow and M. E. Doran-Quine. National Institute of Neurological and Communicative Disorders and Stroke Monograph, no. 22. Bethesda, MD.

10. Neuropsychological Correlates of Abnormal Behavior

A thorough review of the biological bases of emotion is beyond the scope of this text. Nonetheless, a text dealing with neuropsychological diagnostics would be incomplete without providing guidelines for distinguishing between more specific organic disorders and those conditions considered to have more of a "functional" or nonorganic basis. At the outset, it may seem that it would be relatively easy to distinguish between organic and nonorganic disorders. However, many psychological disorders may mimic organic disorders (Heath, 1976). This is not surprising, since the brain mediates all emotion.

To some extent, much of the entire brain is involved in emotional control (see figs. 10.1 and 10.2). Valenstein and Heilman (1979*a, b*) have reviewed the psychophysiologic bases of emotion, and they point out the important tenet that to experience a certain emotional state the individual must have the appropriate cognitive set plus the appropriate level of arousal. Thus, cognition and arousal are intimately intertwined in the experience of emotion. The brain-stem reticular activating system, nonspecific thalamic nuclei, and certain regions of the neocortex are responsible for arousal (Magoun, 1963). The hypothalamus has input from ascending signals as well as direct controlling influence over visceral responses (endocrine and autonomic) in emotion. There is also significant input to hypothalamic functioning through the limbic system, which is similarly influenced by neocortical areas, particularly frontal areas. The perception of an emotional state as well as its expression is, thus, a complex result of interaction of these various neurologic systems. Therefore, emotional dysfunction may have as its basis an alteration within this complex neurologic network. The dysfunction may arise from structural, biochemical, or electrophysiologic aberrations.

Psychotic Disorders

Originally, schizophrenia, manic-depressive illness (now called major affective disorder), and autism were considered to be entirely functionally based (Gregory and Smeltzer, 1977). Over the last twenty years, however, incontrovertible data have been accumulating that clearly show the biologic role in the etiology and expression of these disorders.

Schizophrenia

The hallmark of the schizophrenic disorder, as outlined in the third edition of the *Diagnostic and Statistical Manual (DSM-III)* of the American Psychiatric Association, is in terms of the disturbance of thought in association with hallucinations, typically auditory and verbal. Secondary features of blunted affect, withdrawal and isolation, sleep disturbance, and positive genetic history may also be present. Thus, patients with a presenting history of such symptoms are candidates for the diagnosis of schizophrenia, provided that other causative factors can be fully ruled out. For example, certain seizure disorders, particularly those involving temporal regions, may manifest all of the above symptoms (Mesulam, 1981). Numerous electroencephalogram (EEG) studies have shown a higher incidence of EEG abnormalities in schizophrenia (Spohn and Patterson, 1979). Although there are no EEG patterns that appear to be pathognomonic of schizophrenia, several studies have suggested greater involvement of the left hemisphere in schizophrenia (Abrams and Taylor, 1979; Coger, Dymond, and Serafetinides, 1979; Guenther et al., 1986; Scarone et al., 1982; Shaw et al., 1979). Other studies have demonstrated bilateral temporal abnormalities (Fenton et al., 1980) and nondominant hemispheric dysfunction (Weller and Montague, 1979). Evoked response studies tend to side with those faulting left hemispheric dysfunction, particularly anterior regions (Shagass et al., 1979, 1980).

Computerized tomography studies (Jernigan, Zatz, Moses, and Berger, 1982; Jernigan, Zatz, Moses, and Cardellino, 1982; Nasrallah et al., 1982; Weinberger et al., 1982) of the brain of schizophrenic patients have similarly demonstrated abnormalities (however, see Tanaka et al., 1981). Several studies have demonstrated cerebral atrophy (Boronow et al., 1985; Donnelly et al., 1980; Golden et al., 1981; Heath, Franklin, and Shraberg, 1979), ventricular enlargement (Weinberger et al., 1980; Raz et al., 1985; Golden et al., 1980) (see figs. 9.17 and 9.18 of previous chapter), and density changes in left frontal regions (Coffman, Andreasen, and Nasrallah, 1984; Golden et al., 1981). These CAT findings suggest that there may be a variety of morphologic differences in cerebral structures between schizophrenics and normal persons. The exact relationship between CAT abnormalities and the expression of schizophrenic symptoms remains unknown (Luchins, 1982). Various studies have shown (see Golden et al., 1980) a positive correlation between the severity of CAT abnormalities and severity of deficit performance on neuropsychological measures in schizophrenic patients. Thus, if a schizophrenic patient has an abnormal CAT scan, the patient is also likely to perform poorly on neuropsychological tests (Golden et al., 1982). The reverse of this also tends to be true. Schizophrenic patients who demonstrate significant neuropsychological impairment tend to have abnormal CAT scans (Boucher et al., 1986).

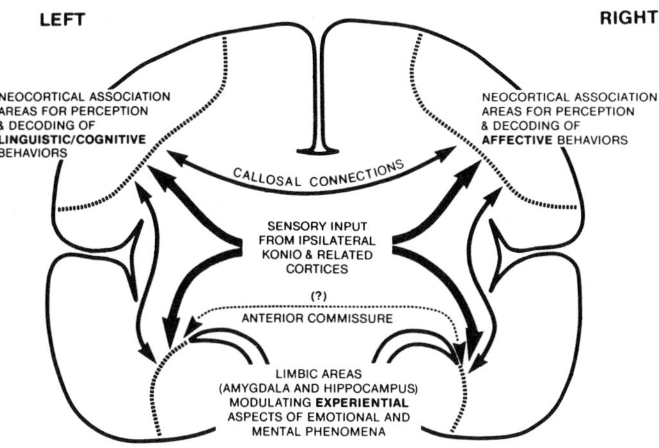

Fig. 10.1. Decoding by the forebrain of linguistic, cognitive, and affective behaviors. The essential neocortical areas for these various functions reside around the temporal-parietal-occipital confluence. The limbic areas modulate the experiential aspects of emotions and mental phenomena. Current evidence suggests that certain emotional experiences may be lateralized in the temporal limbic system. From Ross (1985).

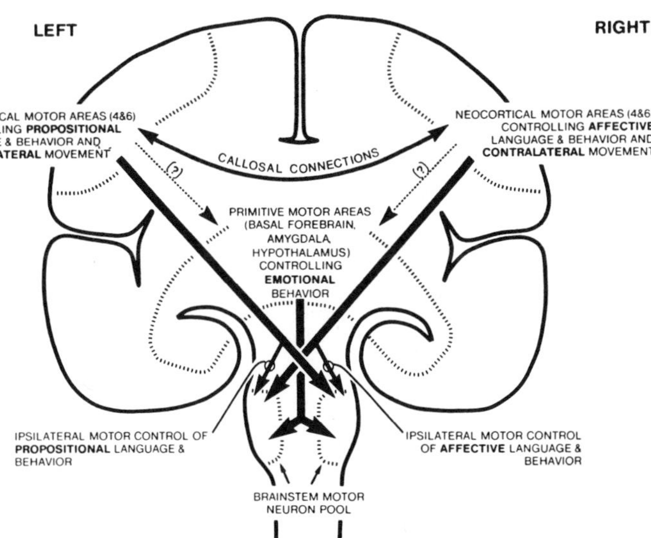

Fig. 10.2. Encoding by the forebrain of linguistic, cognitive, and affective behaviors. Extreme displays of emotions are probably organized through the basal forebrain, amygdala, and hypothalamus. The motor control of dominant cortical functions (such as propositional speech, gestures, and affective prosody) is both contralateral and ipsilateral, whereas volitional control of movement is predominantly contralateral. From Ross (1985).

The CAT abnormalities are static and nonprogressive, and thus do not change over time, at least in adulthood (Nasrallah et al., 1986). The presence of both CAT scan abnormalities and impaired neuropsychological performance suggests poor prognosis in responding to treatment and continued display of chronic symptoms.

Recent and comprehensive neuropsychological studies of schizophrenia are those of Piran (1981), Piran and Bigler (1981), and Ehrfurth (1981). These studies demonstrate an overall deficit in the schizophrenic's neuropsychological performance. These data are summarized in table 10.1. Special statistical analyses of these data implicate greater dysfunction in more anterior regions of the left hemisphere. Similarly, Piran, Bigler, and Cohen (1982; see also Magaro and Chamrad, 1983; Shimizu et al., 1985) have demonstrated a greater degree of mixed laterality in chronic schizophrenics, particularly a tendency toward left ocular dominance. These findings were interpreted as being consistent with greater left frontal abnormality, with the aberrant laterality pattern being related to a shift away from the dysfunctional left hemisphere.

Table 10.1 should be referred to as a guideline in the neuropsychological assessment of the schizophrenic. The schizophrenic patient with underlying cerebral dysfunction will typically display a neuropsychological profile suggestive of nonspecific deficit, frequently with some tendency toward greater left frontal or frontal-temporal findings (see Merrin, 1981). Accordingly, some schizophrenic patients may show a variety of language deficits (Faber and Reichstein, 1981). In terms of these more lateralized findings, it is not uncommon to observe a reduction in right-hand finger oscillation or strength of grip, greater number of right-side errors on the sensory-perceptual exam, and other findings of minor dyscalculia, dyslexia, dysgraphia, and spelling dyspraxia (see case 2). The severity of the neuropsychological deficit in the schizophrenic patient will typically not be of a magnitude to implicate active pathologic dysfunction as would be expected with neoplastic, cerebrovascular, or degenerative disorders. When clearly focal, lateralized pathognomonic findings are present, then more serious brain pathology not related to the schizophrenia must be suspected (see case 1). It should also be noted that certain seizure disorder states, particularly those involving temporolimbic areas, may produce a schizophreniform psychosis (MacCrimmon and Jones, 1986).

In Goetz and von Kammen's (1986) review of the literature of CAT abnormalities in schizophrenia, they conclude that CAT abnormalities are useful markers in delineating a group of chronic schizophrenics who demonstrate neuropsychological impairment, premorbid adjustment and global monoamine disturbance, poor treatment response to neuroleptics, a lack of positive symptoms, and a predominance of negative symptoms (see also Green & Walker, 1985). With advances in cerebral imaging techniques utilizing MRI along with microscopic neuropathic studies, additional insights into the neuropathology of

Table 10.1. *Neuropsychological Test Results of Patients with Schizophrenia and Controls*

	Psychiatric Group					
	Acute Schizophrenia		Chronic Schizophrenia		Controls	
Test Measure	Mean Score	*SD*	Mean Score	*SD*	Mean Score	*SD*
Full-Scale IQ	90.7	11.8	87.2	14.6	104.5	12.6
Verbal IQ	90.6	13.3	88.9	15.1	105.1	13.6
Performance IQ	92.7	12.9	86.9	15.3	102.2	10.7
Category Test	68.1	25.7	79.5	28.9	43.7	24.6
Seashore Rhythm Test	5.1	3.7	6.5	3.4	4.4	3.3
Speech Sounds Perception Test	9.2	5.3	11.0	6.8	7.4	5.8
Finger Oscillation Test						
Right	46.13	9.40	42.21	8.99	47.80	7.49
Left	43.40	9.74	38.83	9.25	43.75	6.99
Sensory Perceptual Exam						
Right—Total errors	1.56	2.61	2.85	4.14	2.42	3.00
Left—Total errors	2.35	3.80	2.92	4.36	2.17	3.38
Trail-Making Test						
A	41.3	13.6	45.3	18.1	33.1	23.3
B	120.7	60.5	141.9	72.6	68.5	49.3
Aphasia Screening						
(Raw score)	10.3	6.60	8.0	6.51	3.94	4.40

Source: Adapted from Ehrfurth (1981) and Piran (1981) and based on the scoring scheme of Russell, Neuringer, and Goldstein (1970).

schizophrenia have been established. Several lines of neuroanatomical research have demonstrated various abnormalities in the size and development of a variety of fronto-temporo-limbic and other cortical structures. Bogerts, Meertz, and Schönfeldt-Bausch (1985) have demonstrated significant volume reductions (degenerative shrinkage?) of a variety of medial limbic structures of the temporal lobe, including the amygdala, hippocampal formation, and parahippocampal gyrus in chronic schizophrenic patients. Similar findings have also been demonstrated by Brown et al. (1986), who demonstrated that the postmortem schizophrenic brain was significantly lighter than matched nonschizophrenic brains, had lateral ventricles that were larger in the anterior (by 19 percent) and particularly in the temporal horn region (by 97 percent in comparison to controls), and had thinner parahippocampal cortices (by 11 percent). Benes, Davidson, and Bird (1986) also have demonstrated various cytoarchitectural abnormalities in cortical laminar organization, particularly in the prefrontal region. MRI studies also tend to support these frontal findings (Andreasen et al., 1986); however, negative results also have been reported (see Johnson et al., 1986; Mathew and Partain, 1985). MRI studies have also consistently demonstrated abnormalities at the level of the corpus callosum (Kono and Hirano, 1986; Mathew et al., 1985; Nasrallah et al., 1986). Although the clinical significance of this is not understood at this point, schizophrenic patients have long been known to function poorly on some tasks requiring callosal transfer of information (Craft, Willerman, and Bigler, 1987).

Regional cerebral bloodflow studies (r-CBF) and positron emission tomography (PET) have demonstrated a variety of metabolic abnormalities in schizophrenia, particularly in frontal regions (Berman, Zec, and Weinberger, 1986; Gur et al., 1985; Weinberger, Berman, and Zec, 1986). However, some recent research has failed to fully support these findings (Kling et al., 1986).

From the assessment standpoint, one cautionary note deserves mention. Recent studies have assessed the potential role of anticholinergic medication (a common medication given to schizophrenic patients to combat neuroleptic side effects) in terms of the memory deficits in schizophrenic patients (Frith, 1984; Perlick et al., 1986). The results are equivocal at this point, but patients receiving large doses of neuroleptics and anticholinergics may have dysfunctional memory due to medication side effects.

Major Affective Disorders

Flor-Henry (1979) has found a greater percentage of EEG abnormalities in right temporal areas in patients with major affective disorder. Lishman (1968) has also demonstrated in patients who had a penetrating injury that depression and irritability were associated with greater bifrontal or right hemisphere involvement. Similarly, Abrams and Taylor (1979) studied 132 patients with affective disorder and found 31 to have EEG abnormalities, with 21 of these showing lateralized abnormalities and 15 showing right hemisphere abnormalities. Marin and Tucker (1981) review current research in this area, coming to the same conclusion.

Most recently, Ross and his colleagues (Ross et al., 1981; Ross and Rush, 1981; Weintraub, Mesulam, and Kramer, 1981) have proposed a scheme of right hemisphere damage analogous to aphasic disorder of the left hemisphere. The scheme, based primarily on dysfunctional prosody, has been previously presented in chapter 3, figure 3.25.

Specific neuropsychological studies are lacking in this area. Flor-Henry and Yeudall (1973) have demonstrated significantly diminished performance IQ scores in depressed patients, implying greater right hemispheric dysfunction. Newlin and Golden (1981) have similarly reviewed the literature available and conclude that there is greater potential for right hemispheric dysfunction in major affective disorder (see also Bear, 1983; Forrest, 1982; Freeman et al., 1985). Table 10.2 displays summarized data on ten patients independently diagnosed with major affective disorder. Note there is some tendency for diminished performance on tests typically thought to be associated with right hemispheric functioning. Similarly note that in general there is much better performance on all neuropsychological measures by patients with affective disorders in comparison with patients with schizophrenia.

Usually the patient with major affective disorder will have a clinical history consistent with symptoms of affective disturbance. On such clinical grounds the diagnosis of major affective disorder will usually be made. The referral for neuropsychological evaluation is to assess the potential of cortical involvement and not for establishing the diagnosis of the disorder itself. Table 10.2 provides a good guide to evaluating the patient with an affective disorder. Accordingly, there may be evidence on neuropsychological exam of greater nondominant hemispheric involvement. As with the schizophrenic patient, truly focal, pathognomonic findings would tend to implicate a separate neurologic disorder that should be further explored. Unlike patients with schizophrenia, patients with an affective disorder do not typically display serious verbal-cognitive deficits.

Autism and Childhood Schizophrenia

The disorders of autism and childhood schizophrenia have been discussed in the chapter on childhood disorders. There is unequivocal evidence that both autism and schizophrenia have a specific organic basis (see Damasio and Maurer, 1978; Damasio et al., 1980). Studies by Dawson (1983) demonstrated significantly greater left hemisphere than right dysfunction in autistic individuals. Dawson's studies have indicated that most autistic patients assessed were able to perform nonlanguage tests, such as Block Design and Object Assembly on the WAIS, within normal limits; however, such patients were quite dysfunctional on all measures of left hemisphere functioning (see also Dawson, Warrenburg, and Fuller, 1982).

Table 10.2. *Neuropsychological Test Results of Patients with Affective Disorder*

Neuropsychological Measure	Mean Score	*SD*
WAIS results[a]		
Verbal IQ	111.8	13.8
Performance IQ	97.2	7.1
Full-Scale IQ	106.0	12.3
WMS results[b]		
Memory quotient	105.3	9.5
Category Test		
Error score	45.7	30.0
Tactual Performance Test		
Time	15.5	2.9
Memory	8.0	1.0
Localization	4.0	0.5
Speech Sounds Perception Test		
Errors	5.6	2.2
Seashore Rhythm Test		
Errors	2.0	0.9
Aphasia Screening		
Rating scale	0.7	0.4
Sensory Perceptual Exam		
Right—Total errors	3.6	0.5
Left—Total errors	3.5	1.7
Finger Oscillation Test		
Right	52.0	6.0
Left	44.7	5.5
Strength-of-Grip Test		
Right	39.5	6.4
Left	38.7	7.1

Note: This table's data are derived from 10 patients, all independently diagnosed with major affective disorder, which was bipolar in type. All were on lithium maintenance at the time of examination. Mean age was 27.5 years (range 21 to 46 years), and mean educational level was 14.7 years (range 12 to 20 years).

[a]WAIS, Wechsler Adult Intelligence Scale.

[b]WMS, Wechsler Memory Scale.

Other Disorders

Headache

It would be inappropriate for neuropsychological studies to be initial diagnostic tests of a patient with headache. After thorough neurodiagnostic studies have been completed and no specific cause elucidated, psychological assessment is frequently important in headache cases to examine for the potential underlying functional causes. Since headache may be associated with a variety of neurologic disorders—in particular neoplastic, infectious, and cerebrovascular disorders—it is not uncommon to evaluate the patient who may have headache as a symptom. The evaluation of the patient, from a neuropsychological standpoint, in such situations is not to explore the headache, but rather to examine for the effects of the underlying cause of the headache. Traditional psychological assessment techniques should also be used to examine the patient for dynamic factors that may play a role because headache may be a symptom of masked depression (Blumer and Heilbronn, 1982).

Hypochondriasis and Conversion Reaction

The patient with hypochondriasis who converts emotional maladies to physical ailments continues with some perceived symptom in the absence of objective clinical findings (see fig. 10.3). These patients' symptoms correlate poorly with anatomical localization (see pp. 74–76). Thus, the patient may have paresis that does not follow the motor system distribution or sensory deficit that does not correspond to dermatomal organization. There is some tendency for conversion reaction to occur on the left body side (see review by Marin and Tucker, 1981). Hypochondriasis has been associated with the somatic equivalent to depression or anxiety (Brown and Vaillant, 1981), and accordingly such features should be the objective of more traditional psychological assessment. In a most interesting study, Flor-Henry et al. (1981) have demonstrated that, despite the preponderance of left-side hysteric motor and sensory symptoms, the hysteric patient tends to display left hemisphere neuropsychological dysfunction (see also Riley, 1984). Such findings may be related to hemispheric specialization of affective control. As has been implied in the previous sections of this text, left-side damage tends to result in more dysphoric mood reactions, frequently resulting in the "psychological" symptoms of despair, depression, and hopelessness and outward demonstrations of crying and anger. Oppositely, right-side cerebral damage may result in indifferent, euphoric reactions accompanied by degrees of anosognosia and dysprosody. This research has been reviewed by Sackeim et al. (1982). Thus, in the hysteric, the greater left hemisphere neuropsychological signs may not have a purely "functional" basis but may be related to hemispheric dyscontrol features in the regulation of affective behavior.

One should not forget that major medical illnesses may co-exist with psychiatric disorder and may in fact be a factor in the development of the psychiatric illness. The inverse may also be true, that psychiatric patients may not maintain good physical health practices due to their impaired mental health. Johnson and Ananth (1986) have found a variety of underlying medical problems in patients admitted to psychiatric hospitals that were otherwise undetected. On the other hand, there are patients who willfully and consciously either mimic or deliberately create symptoms (i.e., purposefully take a medication to create a symptom—e.g., atropine to produce dilation). This is the so-called Munchausen's syndrome. Some of these patients may present with neurologic symptoms (Batshaw et al., 1985) that turn out to be factitious.

Habit Spasm

Certain habit spasms, such as facial tics and grimacing, may have psychogenic origin (Weingarten, 1968). The psychogenic habit spasms have to be differentiated from organic disorders, particularly Gilles de la Tourette's syndrome (TS). In TS, motor and verbal tics are persistently present and not under volitional control. In about 50 percent of these patients the tic movement is associated with coprolalia. Neuropsychological assessment results of the patient with TS are generally normal except for deficits in nonconstructional visuopractic abilities (Incagnoli and Kane, 1981). This is not surprising, because the locus of abnormality in TS is thought to reside within aberrant brain-stem–basal ganglia–dopaminergic systems (Devinsky, 1983).

Chronic Illness

Certain chronic illnesses, such as diabetes, chronic renal disease, cardiovascular disorder, and pulmonary failure syndrome, also place the individual at risk for neurologic involvement (Brancaccio et al., 1981; Foley et al., 1981; Skenazy, 1982). Diabetic and renal disorders frequently affect cerebral functioning by altering basic metabolic processes. Much of the disturbance is transient, and cerebral functioning returns to normal after the metabolic disturbance (e.g., diabetic acidosis) returns to normal. However, repeated disturbance, such as uremic encephalopathy in chronic renal disease, may have permanent damaging effects, which may be progressive. Diabetes may have a significant effect on the cardiovascular system, producing hypertension. Chronic hypertension may then place the patient at risk for cerebrovascular disease.

Another factor that needs to be taken into consideration is the effect of chronic illness on performance of neuropsychometric measures. For example, Skenazy and Bigler (1984, 1985) demonstrated that chronic diabetics and a group of patients with various chronic illnesses performed significantly poorer on the Category Test compared with controls, even though there was no indication of cerebral dysfunction in either group. It is assumed that chronic illness likely affects various emotional factors that in turn influence cognitive abilities. Chronic heart conditions may also have profound effects upon cerebral functioning (Juolasmaa et al., 1981) either as a direct result of diminished vascular supply or embolic encephalopathy or secondary to chronic hypertension and ensuing hypertensive encephalopathy.

Substance Abuse

Chronic drug abuse may lead to organic cerebral dysfunction (Strub and Black, 1981). Table 10.3 depicts neuropsychological test results of a group of chronic inhalant abusers. These results reflect primarily a reduction in general cognitive functioning. This is a common pattern seen in patients with inhalant abuse practices as well as in those who abuse other types of drugs, including narcotics, stimulants, sedatives, hallucinogens, and any combination of these (see Bigler, 1979). The neuropathological effects of stimulants, hallucinogens, and alcohol have been discussed at length by Laposata and Lange (1985) and Ricaurte et al. (1985).

```
Weakness

     Greatest weakness on left side
     Some weakness all over
     Legs just give out
     Knees buckle
     Never know when it will strike
     Hands weak

TIC DOULOUREAUX

     Average 7 attacks a day (Do better if I lie still on bed
                               and don't move)
     Flashes of pain over face approximately every hour

Trouble sleeping
     Nervousness
     Tic douloureaux
     Cold sweats

Memory off
     Disorientation
     Disorganization

Almost constant nausea  (vomit often.  Quite suddenly)

Almost constant constipation

Have peculiar feeling that I am dying
Drool almost constantly

Lack of control over bladder
Either cannot urinate, or void all the time, one or the other

Exterior lower abdomen pain from hysterectomy scar tissue
Just feel wretched almost constantly
Pain in face
Pain in bladder
Pain in abdomen
Numbness in limbs
Pain in eyes
Trouble controlling urine
Trouble controlling feces
Trouble sleeping

Sudden and intermittent loss of balance
Feel terribly bilious most of the time
Dizziness

Terrible reactions to Tegretol
Controls pain to where I can live with it, but does make me sick
Makes me as if I am in a dream-like state

I often have some sort of "spell" where I don't know anything
Often happens after tic douloureaux attack

Am not really an employable person
```

Fig. 10.3. Actual symptom complaints in a patient with Briquet's hysteria. This patient had extensive medical and neurologic studies, all of which were negative. There was no underlying disorder elucidated in this patient, despite multiple evaluations, multiple physicians' examinations, and multiple diagnostic procedures. Despite this, the patient persisted with these various problems for years. Note the numerous symptoms. The patient brought this sheet of paper in with all of her symptoms typed so that she could "keep track of them all."

Table 10.3. *Neuropsychological Test Results of Chronic Inhalant Abusers*

Test Measure	Inhalant Abusers (*N* = 10) Mean Score	*SD*	Psychiatric Controls (*N* = 10) Mean Score	*SD*
Verbal IQ	86.1	5.9	103.0	12.6
Performance IQ	95.2	14.6	100.7	8.2
Full-Scale IQ	89.6	7.7	102.1	11.2
Category Test	80.3	27.4	44.5	19.4
Tactual Performance Test				
Total time	16.2	7.5	14.4	4.0
Memory	6.4	1.7	7.6	1.9
Localization	2.9	1.3	4.8	3.1
(ranked score)	7.4	3.0	3.3	2.8
Speech Sounds Perception Test	8.3	4.2	5.3	1.8
Finger Oscillation Test				
Dominant	43.0	6.0	47.5	5.0
Nondominant	40.1	4.8	42.7	7.4
Trail-Making Test				
A	51.7	23.4	32.6	13.1
B	113.5	40.7	72.2	35.9

Characterological and Aggressive Behavior Disorders

Research continues to accumulate that suggests organic factors in characterological disorders such as juvenile delinquency, sociopathy, and aggressive, acting-out behaviors (Gaffney and Berlin, 1984; Gorenstein, 1982; MacMillan and Kofoed, 1984; Mikkelsen et al., 1982; Rogeness et al., 1982; Sturge, 1982; Woods and Eby, 1982). Goldwater (1980) demonstrated that juvenile delinquents who showed the greatest degree of cognitive impulsivity also had the highest degree of impairment on various neuropsychological measures. Furthermore, her work demonstrated the possibility of greater left hemisphere dysfunction in the recalcitrant delinquent. Thus, from the clinical standpoint, in assessing the characterologically disordered, tests may demonstrate various neuropsychological impairments, and such findings may indicate a negative prognosis (Goldwater, 1980). However, the exact relationship between potential neuropsychological deficit and unacceptable behavior in the delinquent remains to be elucidated (Spreen, 1981; Hare, 1984).

Lewis et al. (1986) have recently assessed neuropsychiatric history in fifteen consecutive patients on Death Row in a state prison. All fifteen of these patients were found to have a history of significant head injury, and five of the fifteen had specific neurologic disorders. These authors speculate that impaired neuropsychological functioning may be related to some of the aggressive behavior seen in the characterologically incarcerated patient.

Panic Disorder

Panic disorder was originally thought to be of purely psychogenic origin (Gregory and Smeltzer, 1977), but recent studies with PET scanning implicate a neurobiologic basis to this disorder. Reiman et al. (1986) have demonstrated bloodflow irregularities in the parahippocampal region as well as various other nonspecific cortical metabolic aberrations in patients with panic disorder. Katon (1984) in a study of fifty-five patients with panic disorder determined that 89 percent of these patients presented with somatic complaints. The three most common were cardiac symptoms (chest pain, tachycardia, irregular heart beat), gastrointestinal symptoms (especially epigastric distress), and neurologic symptoms (headache, dizziness/vertigo, syncope, or paresthesias). Eighty-one percent had a presenting pain complaint. In this group of fifty-five patients, hypertension and peptic ulcer were the most common medical diagnoses, whereas depression and alcoholism were the most frequent psychiatric diagnoses. Accordingly, patients with panic disorder may have multifaceted medical and psychiatric clinical pictures. Coyle and Sterman (1986) have demonstrated that some patients (approximately 5 percent) with panic disorder may demonstrate focal neurologic symptoms as a manifestation of their panic attack. During nonpanic states, these patients have normal neurologic exam, present with multiple system complaints, and have symptom reproduction with hyperventilation. No specific neuropsychological studies have been done with panic disorder to date, and, accordingly, no specific neuropsychological pattern has been identified at this point.

Multiple Personality

There may be an organic basis in multiple personality. Mathew, Jack, and West (1985) have demonstrated r-CBF changes (hyperfusion) in the right temporal lobe during personality change in a female patient with multiple personality. Neuropsychological relationships have not been established with this type of patient group.

Depression

Various clinical studies of stroke (Cullum & Bigler, 1987; Robinson, Lipsey & Price, 1985), traumatic brain injury (Cullum & Bigler, 1987), and neoplastic disease (Cullum and Bigler, 1987) have demonstrated a greater tendency for depressive symptoms with patients with left hemisphere damage, particularly left frontal (see also Robinson et al., 1985). In such cases, there is clear evidence for an "organic" basis to the depression (see Dietch and Zetin, 1983). It should be kept in mind that this does not mean significant organic depression cannot be present with damage in other brain regions (see Freeman et al., 1985; Gass & Russell, 1986), but that it is just more likely to see depressive symptomatology associated with left frontal damage. The corpus callosum also appears to play an important role in the regulation of emotion and emotional expression. TenHouten et al. (1986) have demonstrated prominent "alexithymia" (lack of ability to express feelings verbally, impoverished fantasy life, difficulty verbalizing symbols) in commissurotomy patients. Borod et al. (1985) have demonstrated that right hemisphere damage patients, in comparison to left, have difficulty with oral expression of feelings and that they are less appropriate, more propositional than prosodic, and more descriptive than affective. These various lines of research point toward multiple factors in the emotional changes that may accompany brain injury. Accordingly, in terms of neuropsychological assessment, one should look for signs of lateralized cerebral involvement that may correspond with the occurrence of these depressive elements.

Fogel and Sparadeo (1985) have demonstrated that significant depression may accentuate focal cognitive deficits. They demonstrated this in a patient who had sustained a postoperative posterior right hemispheric lesion with subsequent evolution of a major depressive episode. When tested during this period of time, he had pronounced deficits in visual-spatial functioning. After pharmacologic and supportive therapy, he improved neuropsychologically. These authors caution that patients who have significant depressive disorder may have associated neurocognitive deficits that are accentuated by the depression, and, therefore, caution should be made in offering clinical inference concerning the test results in such patients.

Drug Effects

Many patients with a psychological or psychiatric disorder will be on medication, typically being one or a combination of either a minor tranquilizer or a muscle relaxant (e.g., Valium), a major tranquilizer (e.g., Thorazine), or an antidepressant (e.g., Tofranil, Pamelor, or Elavil). The taking of such medications may alter neuropsychological performance, and most research demonstrates motor functions and timed tests are those most significantly affected (for review see Heaton and Crowley, 1981). Tucker, Bigler, and Chelune (1981) have indirectly studied the effects of neuroleptic medication on neuropsychologic performance in psychotic patients. Results of that study suggest that while medication may significantly alter performance on various measures, if a neuropsychologic deficit exists, the *pattern* of deficit performance will be present regardless of the effects of medication and its disruption of psychotic symptoms. Therefore, medication effects certainly have to be taken into consideration in neuropsychological studies of patients on psychoactive medications, but such effects need not hamper interpretation of underlying neuropsychological deficit (see also Perlick et al., 1986).

Electroconvulsive Therapy

Electroconvulsive therapy (ECT) results in at least transient electrocortical disturbance, the most prominent associated post-ECT symptom being impaired short-term memory. Accordingly, clinical neuropsychological studies should not be undertaken during a treatment regimen with ECT, because the results could be invalid owing to the transient disruption of cerebral functioning (Malloy et al., 1982). If neuropsychological studies are needed, they should be deferred for three to four weeks following the last ECT treatment, and even at this point residual ECT effects may be present. Squire (1986) reviewed the literature on the effects of ECT on memory and derived the following conclusions. Patients who receive ECT may have transient memory disturbance for sometime following the last ECT, but by six months after treatment such patients perform as well on new learning tests and on remote memory tests as they did pretreatment and as well as patient controls. Bilateral ECT application appears to disrupt memory the most, whereas right hemisphere unilateral ECT results in the least disruption. Information during treatment will not be retained effectively and there may also be some degree of retrograde amnesia for events that preceded the first ECT treatment.

CAT Abnormalities in Neuropsychiatric Disorders

In addition to the CAT abnormalities in schizophrenia, as previously discussed, there appear to be ventricular size irregularities in severe endogenous depression (Beresford et al., 1986; Shima et al., 1984; Standish-Barry et al., 1986; Kolbeinsson et al., 1986), manic disorders (Nasrallah, McCalley-Whitters, and Jacoby, 1982), anorexia nervosa (Datlof et al., 1986), and obsessive-compulsive disorder (Behar et al., 1984). The clinical significance of these findings remains to be determined, and no studies to date have closely examined neuropsychological findings in such patients in relationship to the abnormal CAT findings.

CASE STUDIES

Case 1. This 50-year-old woman had a long-standing history of repeated hospitalizations for chronic schizophrenia. However, on her last admission her speech was markedly paraphasic and her memory was clearly disturbed. She was referred to the neuropsychology service for evaluation. The resultant profile clearly implicated more focal posterior left hemisphere involvement because of the right visual field neglect and presence of receptive aphasia. CAT studies confirmed this level of pathology. When such focal deficits are seen, even in psychotic patients, they almost invariably connote independent pathology not related directly to the psychiatric disturbance. Thus, it should always be remembered that the schizophrenic patient has the same probability of developing neoplasia, cerebrovascular disease, degenerative disease, or other disease as does the person who is not psychiatrically disturbed. (See fig. 10.4.)

Age 50
Sex F
Education 8

Lateral Dominance Exam

	Eye	Hand	Foot
Right	X		
Left			X
Mixed		X*	

*writes with right hand

Motor Examination:
FOD 23 SOGD 24 Unable to do TPT with
FOND 19 SOGND 21 either hand

Sensory Perceptual Examination:
Full visual fields but complete right visual field extinction to double sinultaneous stimulation. Mild right side tactile extinction. Bilateral finger dysgnosia, dysgraphesthesia and dysstereognosis, greater deficit on right.

Aphasia Examination:
Conversational Speech: Fluent but paraphasic
Comprehension: Impaired
Repetition of Spoken Language: Impaired
Confrontation-Naming: Anomic
Reading: Alexic
Writing: Agraphic, constructional dyspraxic
Calculations: Acalculic

Memory Examination:
WMS MQ 58
LM 0.5, Digits 5, VM 0, AL 6

Intellectual/Cognitive Examination:
WAIS Results VIQ = 57, PIQ 48, FSIQ 49
I 2, C 1, A 2, S 2, D 1, V 5
DS 0, PC 0, BD 0, PA 0, OA 0

Category Test: 49 errors/70 then DC
Trail Making Test: A 206 B DC

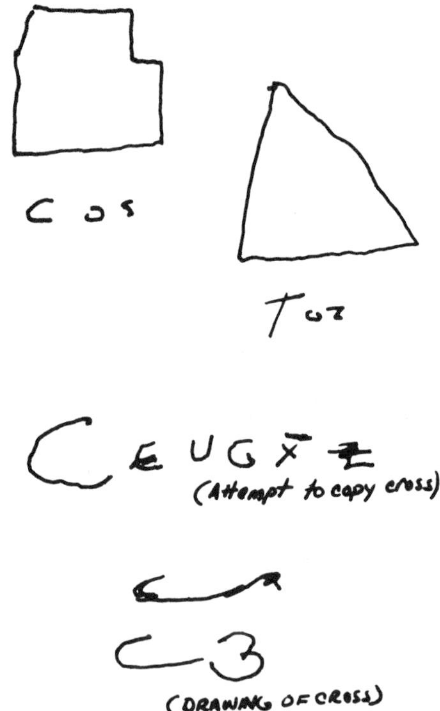

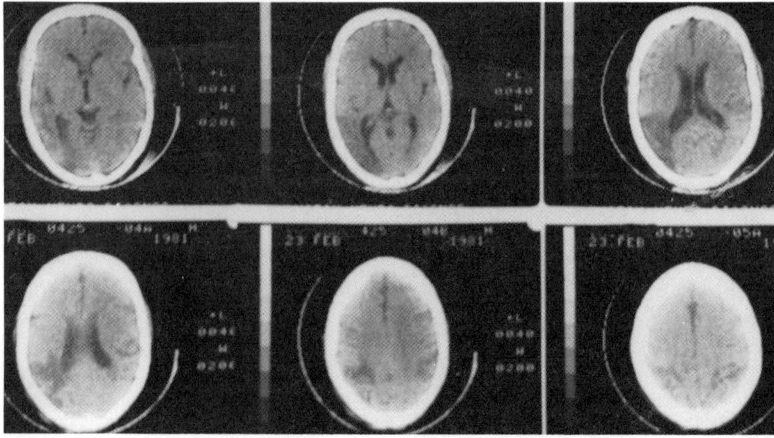

Fig. 10.4. Case 1. CAT scan of schizophrenic patient shows posterior left hemisphere pathology.

Case 2. This 20-year-old schizophrenic man had been ill for about three years when he underwent neuropsychological examination. Note the generalized disturbance in his level of performance on most measures. Such deficits are characteristically seen in the patient with chronic schizophrenia. Note the patient's lateral dominance exam and presence of right-side motor deficit in relation to the left. See also the various language-related deficits depicted in the aphasia screening test results.

Age 20
Sex M
Education 12
(Spec. Educ.)

Lateral Dominance Exam

	Eye	Hand	Foot
Right		X	X
Left	X		
Mixed			

Motor Examination:

FOD 42 SOGD 33 TPTD 8.3
FOND 49 SOGND 40 TPTND 7.9
TPT Both 6.4

Sensory Examination:

Mild bilateral finger dysgnosia and dysgraphesthesia
SSPT 16 errors
SSRT 11 errors

Language Examination:

Spelling dyspraxia, constructional dyspraxia, otherwise WNL

Memory Examination:

WMS MQ = 94 TPT M 5 TPT L 4
LM 9, Digits 10, VM 6, AL 18.5

Intellectual/Cognitive Examination:

FSIQ = 87

VIQ = 97	PIQ = 76
I 11	DS 6
C 6	PC 9
A 8	BD 5
S 13	PA 8
D 9	OA 5
V 9	

Category Test: 96 errors
Trail Making Test: A 35 B 70

Case 3. This patient developed a manic psychosis and upon hospitalization was found to have a large aneurysm involving the temporal branch of the middle cerebral artery. Neuropsychological studies demonstrate left ear extinction, impaired visual memory, and impaired performance on the Seashore Rhythm Test (in association with normal Speech Sounds Performance Test results and no dysphasic indicators). Similarly, in the absence of any signs suggestive of focal somatosensory or motor involvement, results are consistent with focal pathology restricted to the right temporal lobe (fig. 10.5).

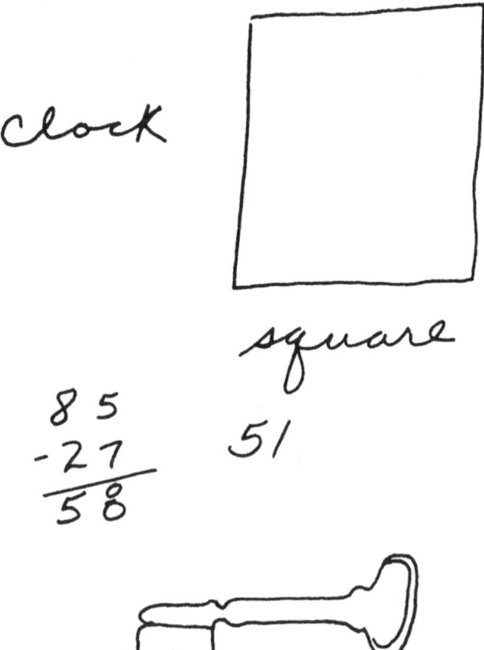

Age 49
Sex F
Education 12

Lateral Dominance Exam

	Eye	Hand	Foot
Right		X	X
Left	X		
Mixed			

Motor Examination:

FOD 59 SOGD 39 TPTD 7.9
FOND 47 SOGND 37 TPTND 8.3
TPT Both 5.1

Sensory Perceptual Examination:

Left ear auditory extinction, otherwise WNL

Language Examination:

No dysphasic findings
SSPT 7 errors/60 SSRT 10 errors

Memory Examination:

WMS = 110
LM 10, D 14, VM 7, AC 16
TPT M 7 TPT L 3

Intellectual/Cognitive Examination:

WAIS Results VIQ = 92, PIQ = 88, FSIQ = 90
I 8, C 8, A 8, S 7, D 12, V 7
DS 5, PC 7, BD 7, PA 6, OA 9

Category Test: 47 errors
Trail Making Test: A 58 B 130

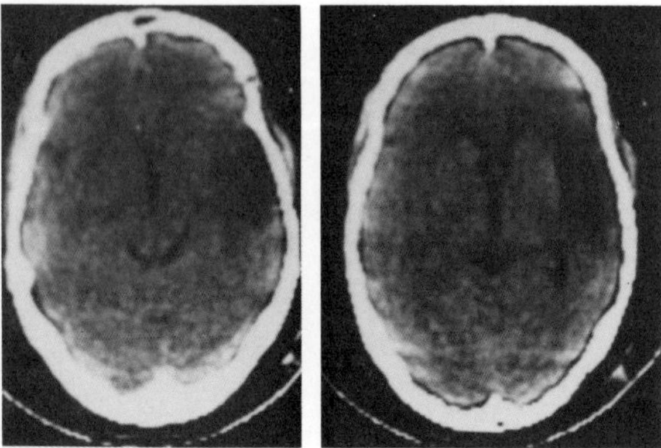

Fig. 10.5. Case 3.

References

Abrams, R., and M. A. Taylor. 1979. Differential EEG patterns in affective disorders and schizophrenia. *Archives of General Psychiatry* 36:1355–1358.

Andreasen, N., H. A. Nasrallah, V. Dunn, S. C. Olson, W. M. Grove, J. C. Ehrhardt, J. A. Coffman, and J. H. Crossett. 1986. Structural abnormalities in the frontal system in schizophrenia. *Archives of General Psychiatry* 43:136–144.

Batshaw, M. L., R. C. Wachtel, A. W. Deckel, P. J. Whitehouse, H. Moses III, L. J. Fochtman, and R. Eldridge. 1985. Munchausen's syndrome simulating torsion dystonia. *New England Journal of Medicine* 312:1437–1439.

Bear, D. M. 1983. Hemisphere specialization and the neurology of emotion. *Archives of Neurology* 40:195–202.

Behar, D., J. L. Rapoport, C. J. Berg, M. B. Denckla, L. Mann, C. Cox, P. Fedio, T. Zahn, and M. G. Wolfman. 1984. Computerized tomography and neuropsychological test measures in adolescents with obsessive-compulsive disorder. *American Journal of Psychiatry* 141:363–369.

Benes, F. M., J. Davidson, and E. D. Bird. 1986. Quantitative cytoarchitectural studies of the cerebral cortex of schizophrenics. *Archives of General Psychiatry* 43:31–35.

Beresford, T. P., F. C. Blow, R. C. W. Hall, L. O. Nichols, and J. W. Langston. 1986. CT scanning in psychiatric inpatients: Clinical yield. *Psychosomatics* 27:105–112.

Berman, K. R., R. F. Zec, and D. R. Weinberger. 1986. Physiologic dysfunction of dorsolateral prefrontal cortex in schizophrenia. *Archives of General Psychiatry* 43:126–135.

Bigler, E. D. 1979. Neuropsychological evaluation of adolescent patients hospitalized with chronic inhalant abuse. *Clinical Neuropsychology* 1:8–12.

Blumer, D., and M. Heilbronn. 1982. Chronic pain as a variant of depressive disease: The pain-prone disorder. *Journal of Nervous and Mental Disease* 170:381–406.

Bogerts, B., E. Meertz, and R. Schönfeldt-Bausch. 1985. Basal ganglia and limbic system pathology in schizophrenia. *Archives of General Psychiatry* 42:784–791.

Borod, J. C., E. Koff, M. Perlman Lorch, and M. Nicholas. 1985. Channels of emotional expression in patients with unilateral brain damage. *Archives of Neurology* 42:345–348.

Boronow, J., D. Pickar, P. T. Ninan, A. Roy, D. Hommer, M. Linnoila, and S. M. Paul. 1985. Atrophy limited to the third ventricle in chronic schizophrenic patients. *Archives of General Psychiatry* 42:266–271.

Boucher, M. L., M. J. Dewan, M. P. Donnelly, A. K. Pandurangi, K. Bartell, T. Diamond, and L. F. Major. 1986. Relative utility of three indices of neuropsychological impairment in a young, chronic schizophrenic population. *Journal of Nervous and Mental Disease* 174:44–46.

Brancaccio, D., R. Damasso, H. Spinnler, R. Sterzi, and G. Vallar. 1981. Does chronic kidney failure lead to mental failure? *Archives of Neurology* 38:757–758.

Brown, H. N., and G. E. Vaillant. 1981. Hypochondriasis. *Archives of Internal Medicine* 141:723–726.

Brown, R., N. Colter, N. Corselis, T. J. Crow, C. D. Frith, R. Jagoe, E. C. Johnstone, and L. Marsh. 1986. Postmortem evidence of structural brain changes in schizophrenia. *Archives of General Psychiatry* 43:36–42.

Coffman, J. A., N. C. Andreasen, and H. A. Nasrallah. 1984. Left hemispheric density deficits in chronic schizophrenia. *Biological Psychiatry* 19:1237–1242.

Coger, R. W., A. M. Dymond, and E. A. Serafetinides. 1979. Electroencephalographic similarities between chronic alcoholics and chronic, nonparanoid schizophrenics. *Archives of General Psychiatry* 36:91–94.

Coyle, P. K., and A. B. Sterman. 1986. Focal neurologic symptoms in panic attacks. *American Journal of Psychiatry* 143:648–649.

Craft, S., L. Willerman, and E. D. Bigler. 1987. Callosal dysfunction in schizophrenia and schizoaffective disorder. *Journal of Abnormal Psychology.*

Cullum, C. M., and E. D. Bigler. 1987. Lateralized cerebral dysfunction and MMPI revisited. Paper presented at the annual meeting of the International Neuropsychological Society. Washington, D.C.

Damasio, A. R., and R. G. Maurer. 1978. A neurological model for childhood autism. *Archives of Neurology* 35:777–786.

Damasio, H., R. G. Maurer, A. R. Damasio, and H. C. Chui. 1980. Computerized tomographic scan findings in patients with autistic behavior. *Archives of Neurology* 37:504–510.

Datlof, S., P. D. Coleman, G. B. Forbes, and R. E. Kreipe. 1986. Ventricular dilation on CAT scans of patients with anorexia nervosa. *American Journal of Psychiatry* 143:96–98.

Dawson, G. 1983. Lateralized brain dysfunction in autism: Evidence from the Halstead-Reitan neuropsychological battery. *Journal of Autism and Developmental Disorders* 13:269–286.

Dawson, G., S. Warrenburg, and P. Fuller. 1982. Cerebral lateralization in individuals diagnosed as autistic in early childhood. *Brain and Language* 15:353–368.

Devinsky, 0. 1983. Neuroanatomy of Gilles de la Tourette's syndrome. *Archives of Neurology* 40:508–514.

Dietch, J. T., and M. Zetin. 1983. Diagnosis of organic depressive disorders. *Psychosomatics* 24:971–978.

Donnelly, E. F., D. R. Weinberger, I. N. Waldman, and R. J. Wyatt. 1980. Cognitive impairment associated with morphological brain abnormalities on computed tomography in chronic schizophrenic patients. *Journal of Nervous and Mental Disease* 168:305–308.

Ehrfurth, J. W. 1981. Dominant hemisphere dysfunction in schizophrenia: A neuropsychological investigation. Doctoral dissertation. University of Texas at Austin.

Faber, R., and M. B. Reichstein. 1981. Language dysfunction in schizophrenia. *British Journal of Psychiatry* 139:519–522.

Fenton, G. W., P. B. C. Fenwick, J. Dollimore, T. L. Dunn, and S. R. Hirsh. 1980. EEG spectral analysis in schizophrenia. *British Journal of Psychiatry* 136:445–455.

Flor-Henry, P. 1979. On certain aspects of the localization of the cerebral systems regulating and determining emotion. *Biological Psychiatry* 14:677–698.

Flor-Henry, P., D. Fromm-Auch, M. Taper, and D. Schopflocher. 1981. A neuropsychological study of the stable syndrome of hysteria. *Biological Psychiatry* 16:601–626.

Flor-Henry, P., and L. Yeudall. 1973. Lateralized cerebral dysfunction in depression and in aggressive criminal psychopathology: Further observations. *IRCS Medical Science* 31–32.

Fogel, B. S., and F. R. Sparadeo. 1985. Focal cognitive deficits accentuated by depression. *Journal of Nervous and Mental Disease* 173:120–129.

Foley, C. N., M. S. Polinsky, A. B. Gruskin, H. J. Baluarte, and W. D. Grover. 1981. Encephalopathy in infants and children with chronic renal disease. *Archives of Neurology* 38:656–658.

Forrest, D. V. 1982. Bipolar illness after right hemispherectomy. *Archives of General Psychiatry* 39:817–819.

Freeman, R. L., A. M. Galaburda, R. D. Cabal, and N. Geschwind. 1985. The neurology of depression. *Archives of Neurology* 42:289–291.

Frith, C. D. 1984. Schizophrenia, memory, and anticholingeric drugs. *Journal of Abnormal Psychology* 93:339–341.

Gaffney, G. R., and F. S. Berlin. 1984. Is there hypothalamic-pituitary-gonadal dysfunction in paedophilia? *British Journal of Psychiatry* 145:657–660.

Gass, C. S., and E. W. Russell. 1986. Minnesota Multiphasic Personality Inventory correlates of lateralized cerebral lesions and aphasic deficits. *Journal of Consulting and Clinical Psychology* 54:359–363.

Goetz, K. L., and D. P. Van Kammen. 1986. Computerized axial tomography scans and subtypes of schizophrenia. *Journal of Nervous and Mental Disease* 174:21–35.

Golden, C. J., B. Graber, J. Coffman, R. A. Berg, D. B. Newlin, and S. Bloch. 1981. Structural brain deficits in schizophrenia. *Archives of General Psychiatry* 38:1014–1020.

Golden, C. J., W. D. MacInnes, R. N. Ariel, S. Ruedrich, C. C. Chu, J. A. Coffman, B. Graber, and S. Bloch. 1982. Cross validation of the ability of the Luria-Nebraska Neuropsychological Battery to differentiate chronic schizophrenics with and without ventricular enlargement. *Journal of Consulting and Clinical Psychology* 50:87–95.

Golden, C. J., J. A. Moses, R. Zelagowski, B. Graber, L. M. Zatz, T. B. Howarth, and P. A. Berger. 1980. Cerebral ventricular size and neuropsychological impairment in young chronic schizophrenics: Measurement by the standardized Luria-Nebraska Neuropsychological Battery. *Archives of General Psychiatry* 37:619–623.

Goldwater, D. L. 1980. Cognitive impulsivity and neurological impairment in juvenile delinquents. Doctoral dissertation. University of Texas at Austin.

Gorenstein, E. E. 1982. Frontal lobe functions in psychopaths. *Journal of Abnormal Psychology* 91:368–379.

Green, M., and E. Walker. 1985. Neuropsychological performance and positive and negative symptoms in schizophrenia. *Journal of Abnormal Psychology* 94:460–469.

Gregory, I., and D. J. Smeltzer. 1977. *Psychiatry*. Boston: Little, Brown & Co.

Guenther, W., D. Breitling, J-P. Banquet, P. Marcie, and P. Rondot. 1986. EEG mapping of left hemisphere dysfunction during motor performance in schizophrenia. *Biological Psychiatry* 21:249–262.

Gur, R. E., R. C. Gur, B. E. Skolnick, S. Caroff, W. D. Obrist, S. Resnick, and M. Reivich. 1985. Brain function in psychiatric disorders. III, Regional cerebral blood flow in unmedicated schizophrenics. *Archives of General Psychiatry* 42:329–334.

Hare, R. D. 1984. Performance of psychopaths on cognitive tasks related to frontal lobe function. *Journal of Abnormal Psychology* 93:133–140.

Hare, R. D., and A. E. Forth. 1985. Psychopathy and lateral preference. *Journal of Abnormal Psychology* 94:541–546.

Hare, R. D., and L. M. McPherson. 1984. Psychopathy and perceptual asymmetry during verbal dichotic listening. *Journal of Abnormal Psychology* 93:141–149.

Heath, R. G. 1976. Correlation of brain function with emotional behavior. *Biological Psychiatry* 11:463–480.

Heath, R. G., D. E. Franklin, and D. Shraberg. 1979. Gross pathology of the cerebellum in patients diagnosed and treated as functional psychiatric disorders. *Journal of Nervous and Mental Disease* 167:535–592.

Heaton, R. K., and T. J. Crowley. 1981. Effects of psychiatric disorders and their somatic treatments on neuropsychological test results. In *Handbook of clinical neuropsychology*, ed. S. B. Filskov and T. J. Boll. New York: Wiley.

Incagnoli, T., and R. Kane. 1981. Neuropsychological functioning in Gilles de la Tourette's syndrome. *Journal of Clinical Neuropsychology* 3:165–169.

Jernigan, T. L., L. M. Zatz, J. A. Moses, and P. A. Berger. 1982. Computed tomography in schizophrenics and normal volunteers. I, Fluid volume. *Archives of General Psychiatry* 39:765–770.

Jernigan, T. L., L. M. Zatz, J. A. Moses, and J. P. Cardellino. 1982. Computed tomography in schizophrenics and normal volunteers. II, Cranial asymmetry. *Archives of General Psychiatry* 39:771–773.

Johnson, R., and J. Ananth. 1986. Physically ill and mentally ill. *Canadian Journal of Psychiatry* 31:197–202.

Johnstone, E. C., T. J. Crow, J. F. Macmillan, D. G. C. Owens, G. M. Bydder, and R. E. Steiner. 1986. A magnetic resonance study of early schizophrenia. *Journal of Neurology, Neurosurgery, and Psychiatry* 49:136–139.

Juolasmaa, A., J. Outakoski, R. Hirvenoja, P. Tienari, K. Sotaniemi, and J. Takkunen. 1981. Effects of open heart surgery on intellectual performance. *Journal of Clinical Neuropsychology* 3:181–197.

Katon, W. 1984. Panic disorder and somatization. *American Journal of Medicine* 77:101–107.

Kling, A. S., E. J. Metter, W. H. Riege, and D. E. Kuhl. 1986. Comparison of PET measurement of local brain glucose metabolism and CAT measurement of brain atrophy in chronic schizophrenia and depression. *American Journal of Psychiatry* 143:175–180.

Kolbeinsson, H., O. S. Arnaldsson, H. Pétursson, and S. Skúlason. 1986. Computed tomographic scans in ECT-patients. *Acta Psychiatrica Scandinavia* 73:28–32.

Kono, E., and M. Hirano. 1986. Density values of the corpus callosum in schizophrenic brains. *Acta Psychiatrica Scandinavia* 73:33–38.

Laposata, E. A., and L. G. Lange. 1985. Presence of nonoxidative ethanol metabolism in human organs commonly damaged by ethanol abuse. *Science* 231:497–499.

Lewis, D. O., J. H. Pincus, M. Feldman, L. Jackson, and B. Bard. 1986. Psychiatric, neurological, and psychoeducational characteristics of 15 death row inmates in the United States. *American Journal of Psychiatry* 143:838–845.

Lishman, W. A. 1968. Brain damage in relation to psychiatric disability after head injury. *British Journal of Psychiatry* 114:373–410.

Luchins, D. J. 1982. Computed tomography in schizophrenia. *Archives of General Psychiatry* 39:859–860.

MacCrimmon, D. J., and G. B. Jones. 1986. Limbic system dysfunction as a factor in some schizophreniform psychoses: Case report and overview. *Canadian Journal of Psychiatry* 31:344–351.

MacMillan, J., and L. Kofoed. 1984. Sociobiology and antisocial personality. *Journal of Nervous and Mental Disease* 172:701–709.

Magaro, P. A., and D. L. Chamrad. 1983. Hemispheric preference of paranoid and nonparanoid schizophrenics. *Biological Psychiatry* 18:1269–1285.

Magoun, H. W. 1963. *The waking brain.* Springfield, IL: Charles C. Thomas.

Malloy, F. W., I. F. Small, M. J. Miller, V. Milstein, and J. R. Stout. 1982. Changes in neuropsychological test performance after electroconvlsive therapy. *Biological Psychiatry* 17:61–67.

Marin, R. S., and G. J. Tucker. 1981. Psychopathology and hemispheric dysfunction: A review. *Journal of Nervous and Mental Disease* 169:546–557.

Mathew, R. J., R. A. Jack, and W. West. 1985. Regional cerebral blood flow in a patient with multiple personality. *American Journal of Psychiatry* 142:504–505.

Mathew, R. J., and C. L. Partain. 1985. Midsagittal sections of the cerebellar vermis and fourth ventricle obtained with magnetic resonance imaging of schizophrenic patients. *American Journal of Psychiatry* 142:970–971.

Mathew, R. J., C. L. Partain, R. Prakash, M. V. Kulkami, T. P. Logan, and W. H. Wilson. 1985. A study of the septum pellucidum and corpus callosum in schizophrenia with MR imaging. *Acta Psychiatrica Scandinavia* 72:414–421.

Merrin, E. L. 1981. Schizophrenia and brain asymmetry: An evaluation of evidence for dominant lobe dysfunction. *Journal of Nervous and Mental Disease* 169:405–416.

Mesulam, M.-M. 1981. Dissociative states with abnormal temporal lobe EEG. *Archives of Neurology* 38:176–181.

Mikkelsen, E. J., G. L. Brown, M. D. Minichiello, F. K. Millican, and J. L. Rapoport. 1982. Neurologic status in hyperactive, enuretic, encopretic, and normal boys. *Journal of the American Academy of Psychiatry* 721:75–81.

Nasrallah, H. A., N. C. Andreasen, J. A. Coffman, S. C. Olson, V. D. Dunn, J. C. Ehrhardt, and S. M. Chapman. 1986. A controlled magnetic resonance imaging study of corpus callosum thickness in schizophrenia. *Biological Psychiatry* 21: 274–282.

Nasrallah, H. A., C. G. Jacoby, M. McCalley-Whitters, and S. Kuperman. 1982. Cerebral ventricular enlargement in subtypes of chronic schizophrenia. *Archives of General Psychiatry* 39:774–777.

Nasrallah, H. A., M. McCalley-Whitters, and C. G. Jacoby. 1982. Cerebral ventricular enlargement in young manic males: A controlled CT study. *Journal of Affective Disorders* 4(1): 15–19.

Nasrallah, H. A., S. C. Olson, M. McCalley-Whitters, S. Chapman, and C. G. Jacoby. 1986. Cerebral ventricular enlargement in schizophrenia. *Archives of General Psychiatry* 43:157–159.

Newlin, D. B., and C. J. Golden. 1981. Hemispheric asymmetries in manic-depressive patients: Relationship to hemispheric processing of affect. *Clinical Neuropsychology* 4:163–169.

Perlick, D., P. Stastny, I. Katz, M. Mayer, and S. Mattis. 1986. Memory deficits and anticholinergic levels in chronic schizophrenia. *American Journal of Psychiatry* 143:230–232.

Piran, N. 1981. A neuropsychological contribution to the theory of schizophrenia. Doctoral dissertation. University of Texas at Austin.

Piran, N., and E. D. Bigler. 1981. A neuropsychological investigation of the theory of schizophrenia. Paper presented at the Annual Meeting of the American Psychological Association, Los Angeles, CA.

Piran, N., E. D. Bigler, and D. Cohen. 1982. Ocular dominance and motoric laterality in schizophrenia suggests a unique cerebral asymmetry. *Archives of General Psychiatry* 39: 1006–1010.

Pugh, M., and E. D. Bigler. 1986. Schizophrenia and prior history of "MBD": Neuropsychological findings. *International Journal of Clinical Neuropsychology* 8:22–26.

Raz, S., N. Raz, E. D. Bigler, and E. T. Turkheimer. 1985. Volumetric assessment of CT abnormalities in schizophrenia. *Journal of Clinical and Experimental Neuropsychology* 7:630 (abstract).

Reiman, E. M., M. E. Raichle, E. Robins, F. K. Butler, P. Herscovitch, P. Fox, and J. Perlmutter. 1986. The application of positron emission tomography to the study of panic disorder. *American Journal of Psychiatry* 143:469–477.

Ricaurte, G., G. Bryan, L. Strauss, L. Seiden, and C. Schuster. 1985. Hallucinogenic amphetamine selectively destroys brain serotonin nerve terminals. *Science* 229:986–988.

Riley, K. C. 1984. Unraveling hysteria: A neuropsychological investigation of Briquet syndrome. Doctoral dissertation. University of Texas at Austin.

Robinson, R. G., J. R. Lipsey, K. Bolla-Wilson, P. L. Bolduc, G. Pearlson, K. Rao, and T. R. Price. 1985. Mood disorders in left-handed patients. *American Journal of Psychiatry* 142: 1424–1429.

Robinson, R. G., J. R. Lipsey, and T. R. Price. 1985. Diagnosis and clinical management of post-stroke depression. *Psychosomatics* 26:769–777.

Rogeness, G. A., J. M. Hernandez, C. A. Macedo, and E. L. Mitchell. 1982. Biochemical differences in children with conduct disorder socialized and undersocialized. *American Journal of Psychiatry* 139:307–311.

Ross, E. D. 1985. Modulation of affect and nonverbal communication by the right hemisphere. In *Principles of behavioral neurology*, ed. M.-M. Mesulam. Philadelphia: F. A. Davis.

Ross, E. D., J. H. Harney, C. deLacoste-Utamsing, and P. D. Purdy. 1981. How the brain integrates affective and propositional language into a unified behavioral function. *Archives of Neurology* 38:745–748.

Ross, E. D., and A. J. Rush. 1981. Diagnosis and neuroanatomical correlates of depression in brain-damaged patients. *Archives of General Psychiatry* 38:1344–1354.

Russell, E., C. Neuringer, and G. Goldstein. 1970. *Assessment of brain damage: A neuropsychological key approach*. New York: Wiley-Interscience.

Sackeim, H. A., M. S. Greenberg, A. L. Weinman, R. C. Gur, J. P. Hungerbuhler, and N. Geschwind. 1982. Hemispheric asymmetry in the expression of positive and negative emotions. *Archives of Neurology* 39:210–218.

Scarone, S., E. Pieri, O. Gambini, R. Massironi, and C. L. Cazzullo. 1982. The asymmetric lateralization of tactile extinction in schizophrenia: The possible role of limbic and frontal regions. *British Journal of Psychiatry* 141:350–353.

Shagass, C., R. A. Roemer, J. H. Straumanis, and M. Amadeo. 1979. Evoked potential evidence of lateralized hemispheric dysfunction in the psychoses. In *Hemisphere asymmetries of function in psychopathology*, ed. J. Gruzelier and P. Flor-Henry. New York: Elsevier/North Holland Biomedical Press.

Shagass, C., R. A. Roemer, J. H. Straumanis, and M. Amadeo. 1980. Topography of sensory evoked potentials in depressive disorders. *Biological Psychiatry* 15:183–207.

Shaw, J. C., S. Brooks, N. Colter, and K. P. O'Connor. 1979. A comparison of schizophrenic and neurotic patients using EEG power and coherence spectra. In *Hemisphere asymmetries of function in psychopathology*, ed. J. Gruzelier and P. Flor-Henry. New York: Elsevier/North Holland Biomedical Press.

Shima, S., T. Shikano, T. Kitamura, Y. Masuda, T. Tsukumo, S. Kanba, and M. Asai. 1984. Depression and ventricular enlargement. *Acta Psychiatrica Scandinavia* 70:275–277.

Shimizu, A., M. Endo, N. Yamaguchi, H. Torii, and K. Isaki. 1985. Hand preference in schizophrenics and handedness conversion in their childhood. *Acta Psychiatrica Scandinavia* 72: 259–265.

Skenazy, J. A. 1982. Neuropsychological and psychological effects in diabetes mellitus. Doctoral dissertation. University of Texas at Austin.

Skenazy, J. A., and E. D. Bigler. 1984. Neuropsychological deficits in diabetes mellitus. *Journal of Clinical Psychology* 40: 246–258.

———. 1985. Psychological adjustment and neuropsychological performance in diabetics. *Journal of Clinical Psychology* 41:391–396.

Spohn, H. E., and T. Patterson. 1979. Recent studies of psychophysiology in schizophrenia. *Schizophrenia Bulletin* 5(4): 581–611.

Spreen, O. 1981. The relationship between learning disability, neurological impairment, and delinquency. *Journal of Nervous and Mental Disease* 169:791–799.

Squire, L. R. 1986. Memory functions as affected by electroconvulsive therapy. *Annals of the New York Academy of Sciences* 462:307–314.

Standish-Barry, H. M. A. S., N. Bouras, A. S. Hale, K. Bridges, and J. R. Bartlett. 1986. Ventricular size and CSF transmitter metabolite concentrations in severe endogenous depression. *British Journal of Psychiatry* 148:386–392.

Strub, R. L., and F. W. Black. 1981. *Organic brain syndromes: An introduction to neurobehavioral disorders*. Philadelphia: F. A. Davis.

Sturge, C. 1982. Reading retardation and antisocial behavior. *Journal of Child Psychology and Psychiatry* 23:21–31.

Tanaka, Y., H. Hazama, R. Kawahara, and K. Kobayashi. 1981. Computerized tomography of the brain in schizophrenic patients. *Acta Psychiatrica Scandinavia* 63:191–197.

TenHouten, W. D., K. D. Hoppe, J. E. Bogen, and D. O. Walter. 1986. Alexithymia: An experimental study of cerebral commissurotomy patients and normal control subjects. *American Journal of Psychiatry* 143:312–316.

Tucker, D. M., E. D. Bigler, and G. H. Chelune. 1981. Reliability of the Halstead-Reitan Battery in individuals displaying acutely psychotic behavior. *Journal of Behavioral Assessment* 3: 311–319.

Valenstein, E., and K. Heilman. 1979*a*. Emotional disorders resulting from lesions of the central nervous system. In *Human clinical neuropsychology*, ed. E. Valenstein and K. Heilman. New York: Oxford University Press.

———. 1979*b*. *Human clinical neuropsychology*. New York: Oxford University Press.

Weinberger, D. R. Computed tomography (CT) findings in schizophrenia: Speculation on the meaning of it all. *Journal of Psychiatric Research* 18:477–490.

Weinberger, D. R., K. F. Berman, and R. F. Zec. 1986. Physiologic dysfunction of dorsolateral prefrontal cortex in schizophrenia. *Archives of General Psychiatry* 43:114–124.

Weinberger, D. R., L. B. Bigelow, J. E. Kleinman, S. T. Klein, J. E. Rosenblatt, and R. J. Wyatt. 1980. Cerebral ventricular enlargement in chronic schizophrenia: An association with poor response to treatment. *Archives of General Psychiatry* 37: 11–13.

Weinberger, D. R., L. E. DeLisi, G. P. Perman, S. Targum, and R. J. Wyatt. 1982. Computed tomography in schizophreniform disorder and other acute psychiatric disorders. *Archives of General Psychiatry* 39:778–783.

Weingarten, K. 1968. Tics. In *Diseases of the basal ganglia*, ed. P. J. Vinken and G. W. Bruyn. Handbook of clinical neurology, vol. 6. New York: Elsevier/North Holland Biomedical Press.

Weintraub, S., M.-M. Mesulam, and L. Kramer. 1981. Disturbances in prosody. *Archives of Neurology* 38:742–744.

Weller, M., and J. D. Montague. 1979. Electroencephalographic coherence in schizophrenia: A preliminary study. In *Hemisphere asymmetries of function in psychopathology*, ed. J. Gruzelier and P. Flor-Henry. New York: Elsevier/North Holland Biomedical Press.

Woods, B. T., and M. D. Eby. 1982. Excessive mirror movements and aggression. *Biological Psychiatry* 17:23–32.

Subject Index

Author Index

Numbers in italics indicate pages on which full references appear.